BARRELHOUSE KINGS

BARRELHOUSE KINGS

A Memoir

BARRY CALLAGHAN

McARTHUR & COMPANY

ACKNOWLEDGMENTS

"Ain't Nobody's Business" written by Grange-Robbins. Copyright MCA records/ASCAP. "All Around the World" written by Titus Turner, recorded by Little Willie John 1955. Copyright Rhino Records 1993. "Beale St. Blues" written W.C. Handy 1916, from *Louis Armstrong Plays W.C. Handy*. Copyright Sony Music. "Body and Soul" written by Edward Ideyman, Robert Soor, Frank Eyton, Johnny Green. Copyright BMG Music. "The Congo (a Study of the Negro Race)". D. Appelton-Century Company 1914. Copyright Nicholas C. Lindsay 1957. "Highway 61 Revisited" written by Bob Dylan. Copyright Warner Brothers Music. "Morley Callaghan's Eightieth Birthday" by Gary Ross from *Saturday Night* , May 1983. "Political Meeting" from *The Collected Poems of A.M. Klein* , McGraw-Hill Ryerson. "So this is Paris" by e.e. Cummings, Harcourt Brace & Company. Copyright Horace Liveright 1926. "The System of Dante's Hell" from *LeRoi Jones: Selected Poems* , Grove Press Inc. 1965. Copyright LeRoi Jones 1965. "Time for Judas: Book Review" by Margaret Atwood, from *Saturday Night* October 1983. Extract from *Watt* by Samuel Beckett. Copyright Grove Press Inc. Extract from *Waiting for Godot* by Samuel Beckett. Copyright Grove Press Inc. "When the Organ Played at Twilight" written by Raymond Wallace, Jimmy Campbell, Ray Connelly. Copyright Santly Brothers Music Incorporated, 1916.

Every reasonable effort has been made to find ownership of copyrighted material. Any information enabling the Publisher to rectify any right or credit in future printings will be welcomed.

CANADIAN CATALOGUING IN PUBLICATION DATA

Callaghan, Barry, 1937 –   PS8505.A43Z59 1998   C813'52   C98-931711-0
Barrelhouse kings: a memoir   PR9199.3.C27Z57 1998

1. Callaghan, Morley, 1903 – 1990.
2. Novelists, Canadian – 20th century – Biography. I. Title

Design and Composition *by* MICHAEL P. CALLAGHAN
Cover Design *by* TANIA CRAAN
Typeset *at* MOONS OF JUPITER, Toronto
Printed and Bound in Canada *by* TRANSCONTINENTAL

McArthur & Company   ISBN 1-55278-00-7
322 King Street West, Suite 402
Toronto, Ontario, Canada, M5V 1J2

10 9 8 7 6 5 4 3 2 1

For all my Barrelhouse Kings and Queens, *especially* Sevens.

Author's Note

This is a memoir, this is the back life of my father and my family in my mind's eye. There may be a mote in my eye but I've tried to make the story right, believing a man can be wrong-headed and still be right.

And I've tried to be fair. To be fair I have changed the names and combined the characters of some folks, mostly old neighbors. They did not ask to be remembered.

From time to time I have telescoped time for narrative reasons: Wilson died after I went to Amman, not before, and Bill Ronald died after Morley, not before. How else could he have been one of Morley's pall bearers (though I've been told that there was a "sighting" of Bill by a Cape Cod café owner who did not know he had died, two months after he'd been buried)?

Close friends will, I hope, recognize themselves and their voices, not only because I have a good memory, and have often taken notes, but until recently my work as a journalist led me to side-pocket a tape recorder and I wasn't shy with it. Sometimes the situation was suddenly comic, as when Bill Ronald and I found we were recording each other.

On occasion, when the politics were ripe — Yehuda Amichai, S. Agnon, and everyone else in Israel; Bassam in Amman and Kanafani in Beirut — I've thanked God for tape recorders and cameras.

When the politics turned rotten, I've thanked God and my lucky stars for archives, film and transcripts.

I've had a lucky tendency, too, to always keep special telegrams and wires and such, much as my father did, in a more chaste way, with his utility bills.

As for Morley, as for all the talks with my father! Well, we talked on the phone or in his living room almost every night of my adult life. He rehearsed what he wanted to say, he said what he said, he said it again, he sometimes wrote it down and said it again on the radio.

I tried to give back as much good talk as I got.

I cannot describe the silence in the night in my life without that voice, without that talk since he died.

Which way do I go now that I'm gone?

WAYLON JENNINGS

Nothing can be sole or whole
that has not been rent

W.B. YEATS

If you see a fork in the road,
take it.

YOGI BERRA

Book One

1

*I*t was a big house of amber-colored brick covered with ivy and wisteria. The rooms had heavy drapes at the windows, high ceilings and oak paneling painted white, with stained glass on the staircase landing, and in the late afternoon the central hall with its black marble fireplace was streaked and petalled with light from those windows.

"There's a real stillness here," my father said, standing in the stained light. "You can hear yourself think." He liked to stand in that light, lost in thought. He was a man who stood alone, yet was quietly content on our street of massive clumsy houses, an island enclave of sometimes shabbily kept mansions in the center of the sprawling city. And it was an island, silent in the center of the noisy town, silent except for a kilted piper on a Sunday morning piping the Mulls, Aylesworths, Lawsons, Woods, and Spencer-Clarks into church service, an island surrounded not by water but by deep wild ravines dense with scrub willow and sugar maple trees, the ravines of Rosedale, which had once been a dale of wild dog roses on the outskirts of the city.

"It's kind of like water standing too long in a jar, living around here," my father said. "You've got to see what's going on at the bottom of the glass." He had made up a little game that we played while sitting in the bay window of our living room. We played it between 4:30 and 6:30 in the afternoon. It was called Homburg Hats. My father had a notion that during those years all successful men, especially businessmen who thought of themselves as decisive and bold, as part of the backbone of the post-war nation, wore Homburg hats to work. Churchill wore such a hat.

My father believed that these men as they walked home, the evening newspapers folded and tucked under their arms, looking stern and impassive, actually had wild stories about themselves going on in their heads. He believed that their greatest dream would be to have their portraits taken by Karsh, a photographer famous for his Portraits of Greatness. But, under their heavy black Homburg hats, they all looked alike. We couldn't tell them apart. We were never close enough to them to know if the smell of panic or failure was on them. We could only call out, as if we had made a submarine sighting, "Homburg on the port side!" We did not live on a lively residential street but of an evening there were always at least two Homburgs. "Imagine," my father would say, "a Churchill, or maybe two on our street . . . who'd have thought it?" After all, Rosedale was a place of great stillness, of long silences between hats.

Edwina Wishall kept a silence. Her husband, the Reverend Canon Wishall, had worn a Homburg hat. "But he probably wears a snap-brim fedora now," Morley said, knowing that Canon Wishall had abandoned his wife and that she sat up into the early hours waiting for him, sleeping most of the day. Sometimes, she came out on to her front porch in the late afternoon and dusted the air with a feather duster. One day, a drunken drifter who had come up out of the ravine lay asleep on her lawn, having wrapped himself in a clear plastic sheeting against the damp and the wind. She came down the stairs and dusted the air over him. A tall man with spindly legs far too long for his body, a landscape architect and the owner of a well-known seedling and shrub shop, J. Dunnington-Grubb, cheerfully called "hello" as if nothing were the matter. She said "hello" and walked down the lawn under the shade of the big old elms, banked by honeysuckles, and talked to him earnestly about pigeons staining bricks under eaves and postal rates and local politics. She let the drunk go on sleeping. She thought of herself as practical and prudent, and wore heavy-soled shoes.

"That's right, sensible people wear sensible shoes," Ralph Little, a former city solicitor who owned several dry-cleaning shops, said as I was talking to a pasty-faced priest in front of the Jesuit mother house that stood on a knoll at the head of the Old Glen Road Bridge, a black steel footbridge that crossed the ravine. "Sensible shoes." Then Little added, "We're in the same business, you and me, Father. It all comes out in the wash, whether it's the cleaners or confession." They smiled wryly. They were both alcoholics.

J. Gordon Clery, a portly bachelor, lived across the road in a big stuccoed house. He always wore a Homburg hat. He wore it well. He had been a captain in the Hitler war and was a friend of the First War fighter pilot, Billy Bishop. He sometimes pinned one of Bishop's medals — given to him as a gift — on his lapel. His closest friend was Mr. Justice L.M. "Spence" Dabney. He, too, wore a Homburg. Together, they spent several evenings a week making old-fashioned scale-model airplanes out of balsa wood, testing their motors in Dabney's garage. They liked to talk about the War. "It happens to a lot of soldiers," my father told me. "They come home feeling alive but then something dies in them. Nothing can replace the excitement of the war, the excitement of nearly dying. They talk about it. They hold onto it for dear life."

Dabney was troubled by his son, Terrence, a lean eighteen-year-old who bleached his hair and played the French horn. Late at night, he would open his bedroom window and play "Taps" on the horn. "That way," he told me, "my father knows that I wish he was dead." I often saw Dabney and Clery, both of them pink-faced and stout, in the small stone-walled park on the edge of the eastern ravine, flying their planes, and I often saw Dunnington-Grubb at the same hour in the late afternoon as he strode home from his office. Bareheaded, beamish, he always nodded to my father but never spoke to him. My father waved and said to me, bemused, "There's no substitute for not having anything to say."

At night, I kept an eye on Clery's upstairs bay window, the pearl-gray drapes closed but the light left on until dawn. What went on behind those drapes, in that all-night lamplight? All that Telford the chauffeur could tell me was that Clery had a cigar and a pot of tea alone in the room at midnight. He had bought the china teapot on a cruise he had taken with Lady Kemper Oates on the Queen Elizabeth, sailing from Southampton to New York. Whenever he talked to Telford about that cruise he took his hat off and smoothed the nap with his forearm. But Telford didn't know why the light was left on. "What kind of guy sleeps with a light on all night in an empty room?" I asked my father. "Who's he waiting for?" My father smiled. "Maybe there's no one to wait for, or maybe he's waiting for Mrs. Wishall, or maybe there's something in him that just doesn't sleep."

I began to be drawn to lighted windows in the night, rooms suspended in the dark, pockets of amber light, night-lights in the secret lives of stolid men and women like Lady Oates, a widow who lived only a few blocks away in a great stone house that had a pipe organ in the central hall. She arrived almost every evening at Clery's gate in her old limousine with the hooded spare tire mounted on the front fender, getting out and hurrying along the flagstone walk under cover of a high brown fence and overgrown mock orange bushes. Telford said that she had refused to marry Clery when he had proposed to her on the Queen Elizabeth cruise. She had refused because she would have had to give up her title. "If you don't have to call her a Lady, you don't have to call her nothing," Telford said. The chauffeurs laughed cynically. They chatted and smoked for an hour-and-a-half beside the gatepost until it was time for her to go home, but every Sunday afternoon, Lady Oates and Clery — who wore a Royal Canadian Yacht Club blue blazer — went for a drive down to the lake in his limousine. Telford said there were silver sconces set in the plush beside the seats in the limousine and Clery always had freshly cut yellow roses in the sconces for Lady Oates. Telford laughed and said, "But they don't go nowhere. They don't go sailing. I drive them down to the lake and we purr along the lakeshore drive for a long time and sometimes they roll down the window and talk about the water and the lagoons and what a great long-distance runner Tom Longboat, the Onondaga Indian, was when they were young, but they never get out and then we come back home."

"Well, it must make them happy," my father said, "driving around town along the lakeshore like that, looking at the lake."

"Yeah, well, look at it this way," Telford said, "that lake's no river and this ain't no healing town."

Though this enclave enclosed by ravines had been disrupted during the Hitler war, with old family mansions turned into shabby rooming houses, the eavestroughs rotted and the rockeries overrun with lily of the valley and crab-grass, it was — when I was a boy — quietly resettling itself. "Some of these folks are musky as moles the way they keep their own counsel," my father said, "but you've got to remember that that's because so many of them are counselors." He laughed. He liked his own jokes. He liked these people because they were not curt or furtive, or skulkers. On the contrary, with the exception of Clery, they were unabashedly friendly, straightforward and cheerful as they passed each other on the street, as if they knew that amiability and the air of success were the most deceptive of all masks. They showed, in fact, a village chumminess, espe-cially toward their few elegant eccentrics — like Stratford "Strutty" Summers, the son of Brigadier General Arthur Summers, who wore lipstick and mascara, and sometimes wore a woman's blouse when he walked out at noon to the bank by Bloor and Sherbourne Streets. Often the manager came out of his corner office and shook hands with him. At night, when Strutty haunted the old footbridge, flirting with passing boys, or took to resting in a chair on the Jesuit veranda after the priests had gone to bed, he wore a pink dress. Whenever he heard young Terrence Dabney playing "Taps" on his horn, he would say, "Yes, Terrence, I hear you," and he would walk up toward the Dabney house, slipping the string to a little silver metallic evening bag around his wrist. One night I told him I thought he should wear a Homburg hat, and he said, "Oh, aren't we just too camp for words."

Even then — a decade after that War — Toronto was a city of spires and spite and aspiration, a city where King Billy — keeper of the spite — rode a white horse through the streets once a year at the head of the Orange Lodge parade — streets where sensible men lived in three-story narrow red-brick houses, a shop on the first floor, a flat on the second, and a tenant in the attic. A peaceable city, except for the odd riot or killing, where people still went for a Sunday drive through the Sabbath stillness in their cars, the drive being a way for family and friends, apt to forget to remember, to keep close.

Jack Kent Cooke, who owned the Toronto Triple-A baseball team, the Maple Leafs, sometimes parked his long fire-engine red Cadillac convertible with pleated chrome fin-guards by the yellow fire hydrant in front of our house so that he could talk to Morley about books, about Salinger and Fitzgerald, and song writing . . . he wanted to write songs . . . and for a while he thought he wanted to have a home in Rosedale (he tried to buy a house across the road from our house, but the man who had refurbished it so that he could pick and choose his next-door neighbor dismissed Cooke. "Yes, he's your friend, but he's too noisy, too vulgar, too American." Morley nodded, "Yes, he's my friend," but the house was sold to a portly, orderly man, Ralph Day, who had become a success in the embalming business). Cooke said, "Nuts," that his real dream was to own the Chrysler building in New York, "the most beautiful building in the world," a skyscraper he'd seen when he was only a door-to-door salesman. "Every day should be spring time," he said (he was a natural-born hustler), and every spring, at the beginning of base-ball season, he held a huge barbecue for "the sporting fraternity" on the front lawn of his Forest Hill home, featuring Joe King and his Zaniacs, the house band at a Yonge Street sleaze joint, the Zanzibar, and Cooke — after the speeches and a few drinks — would suddenly stand among the tall ballplayers with his hands in the air, as if he were about to take hold of the sky, smiling, like there was no end to what he could grab hold of. (Years later, when he was living in Washington, he sent Morley a lavishly printed booklet with the Chrysler building on the cover: "Well," he wrote, "I just thought you'd like to know: I bought it.")

Calvin Jackson, the plump, black, jazz pianist, who had a trio at the Plaza Room supper club in the Park Plaza Hotel, also drove through our streets of a Saturday or Sunday afternoon. He had a white Rolls-Royce and he drove slowly, letting himself and his beautiful blond wife be seen. He stopped sometimes by the curb at the laburnum tree to talk to my mother and father about other towns, other times. Jackson had known Gene Kelly and Morley had known Kelly, too. And Saroyan, and Lena Horne. And they talked about Art Tatum and Earl Fatha Hines. "I know a painter in Harlem," Jackson said, "who says he learned all about space in painting, negative space, by listening to Fatha Hines in the nightclubs. The silence between notes."

"Oh, I miss the nightclubs," my mother said, "I miss Chicago. I used to paint the town red there."

"My little house painter," my father said and put his arm around her.

My mother, Loretto, was an art student when she met my father. She went often to Chicago to visit the Ryans, a coffin boat family who had come out of Cork during the Great Hunger — but she particularly went to Chicago to be with her older cousin, Viola, a beautiful young Detroit woman who, like herself, had been educated in a convent school. Viola was one of Dion O'Banion's girlfriends. O'Banion, the owner of a flower shop, was also known as Legs, a gangster, a killer as ruthless as the Irish boss Charlie Lonergine or Al Capone. He often drove the two young women around Chicago in his bulletproof car, stopping to buy phonograph records for them, and his mother. "I bring my mother records every week," he told a newspaperman piously.

He also took the two young women to speakeasies, or to the Napoli Cafe and Big Jim Colosimo's restaurant, or Sherman's, where Fats Waller was the house pianist. They met gangsters and musicians and a priest who heard gangsters' confessions at Holy Name Cathedral, where O'Banion had been a choirboy. His flower shop was in the shadow of the church. My mother brought those phonograph records home from Chicago. No one in her family had ever heard of the players: Mezz Mezzrow, James P. Johnson, Sidney Bechet, Pops Foster, Pee Wee Russell. She loved listening to Jimmy Blanton bow his bass and to Pee Wee Russell play on what she called his "licorice stick." A few years later, after Capone had ordered O'Banion killed, after O'Banion had been shot dead among the lilies in his flower shop — with Legs never getting a chance to reach for the two automatics he had holstered in specially sewn suitcoat pockets — Capone said, "Like everyone else, his head got away from his hat. . . . It was his funeral."

The body "lay in state" for three days and there were twenty-six truckloads of flowers delivered to the church. Loretto, who loved flowers, kept a yellowed newspaper clipping about the funeral in the bottom drawer of her dressing table: "Silver angels stood at the head and feet with their heads bowed in the light of the ten candles that burned in the hands of the solid gold candlesticks . . . Beneath the casket on the marble slab that supports its glory, is the inscription, 'Suffer little children to come unto Me.' And over it all the perfume of flowers . . . Vying with the perfume was that of beautifully dressed women of ganglords, wrapped in costly furs and supported slowly down the aisles by excellently tailored gentlemen with steel-blue jaws and a furtive glance ever-active."

Only two weeks before his death, O'Banion had been given a diamond-and-ruby-set watch at a dinner held in his honor, and among those at the festive board applauding the gangster were the Chief of Detectives of the Chicago Police Department and more than twenty of his highest officials and about ten city executives. O'Banion's newly-wed wife was there, and Viola, too. After the funeral, the Chief — when questioned about the supper and the gift — said he "thought the party was given for someone else," and cousin Viola, telling the police that she thought she had been invited to a Sodality of the Blessed Virgin social, left town and came to Toronto by train, staying for several weeks with Loretto and her three sisters and two bachelor brothers on Roxton Road.

The gay and cheerful sisters, whose satinwood dressing table drawers were cluttered with silk scarfs, white lace gloves, little bags of lavender scent, were very devout. They treasured their glass vials of holy water from St. Joseph's Oratory in Québec (the Oratory still houses the heart of blessed Brother André: it was once stolen from its case in the Oratory and then returned: the odor of sanctity — the sisters liked to joke because they had great humor — was probably too much for the thief). Viola felt at ease with the sisters. They were like her own family, except that she wore silk dresses not just to supper but to lunch in the house, and she hung her silk stockings to dry from the shower nozzle. She kept her company entirely to the women. They went boating in the lagoons in the bay and watched a white horse dive from a tower into the Hanlan's Point water. "She was kind of homey, a proper looking kind of girl," my father said. "You didn't see O'Banion and his world in her eyes at all." She had asked only that no one bring cut flowers in to the Roxton Road house while she stayed there. She did not want to be reminded of the flower shop in the shadow of the church. When she went home to her family, my father rode with her on the train as far as the Long Branch station, a little outpost on the skirts of Toronto, to assure her that she was not being shadowed by "ever-active" gentlemen with "steel-blue jaws."

When I was seven or eight, my mother held me in her arms and spun with me in a dance on our living room rug, teaching me Chicago songs:

Wrap your chops
Round this stick o' tea
Come along, get high with me
I'm twenty-one, I've just begun
I'm viper mad

I learned that "tea" and "viper" were words for marijuana, they were the magic words for shouters and side-men, and I used to chant their names — Meade Lux Lewis, Zutty Singleton, Cootie Williams, Illinois Jacquet, Benny Moten, Earl Fatha Hines, Jack Teagarden, Avery Parish . . . and sometimes, playing on the front lawn of our house, down among the ant hills and dust mounds, I would reach out with my arms to my mother as she sat in the second floor window and sing in a sweet soprano, like Cootie Williams: *Squeeze me mama, till my face turns cherry red, chee-ery red.* The stern white-haired scientist who lived downstairs in the duplex, Dr. George Wright, said I was a strange child, said I looked like a child but didn't sing like a child, but my mother told the good doctor that he was one of the inventors of new bombs for the war and because of that he lived in an even stranger world of *boomlay, boomlay, BOOM.* Reading to me from a book of poems while we ate lunch — Campbell's Tomato Soup, meatloaf and dateloaf bread — my mother chanted:

> *Barrelhouse kings, with feet unstable,*
> *Sagged and reeled and pounded on the table,*
> *Pounded on the table,*
> *Beat an empty barrel with the handle of a broom,*
> *Hard as they were able*
> *boom, boom, BOOM,*
> *With a silk umbrella and the handle of a broom,*
> *Boomlay, boomlay, boomlay, BOOM.*

One day, my mother, instead of making lunch, took me across town to a west-side narrow, red-brick corner house on Delaware Avenue. I remember the street name because my father was telling me tales every night to put me to sleep and they were tales about the Delaware Indians.

My mother took me there for a girl's birthday party . . . a girl I didn't know. And there was a tall woman in charge of the party who had three names . . . Mary Lowrey Ross . . . a woman whose stride was loose and easy, whose voice was deep, whose laughter crackled lustily out of her throat from too much smoking of Players Navy Cut. She led me into the living room, a clutter of easy chairs, sofas, papers, books, cigarette ash. There were girls everywhere and I insisted I wanted to speak to the father of the house. A girl named Nancy marched me to the hall. She pointed up the stairs. "My father's up there, in the attic. He's up there all the time in the attic." The only attic I had ever seen was at the house of my three aunts: empty picture frames and old death cards and wire dressmaker's mannequins and broken oil lamps, steamer trunks with rusted hinges, the dust floating in shafts of light from a small oval window.

I didn't know why a man — my mother said he was one of my father's closest friends — would want to work in an airless attic room, so I remember agreeing to hold hands with the girls and we paraded around the dining room table wearing paper pirate hats. Then, suddenly, there was a man standing over us, square-jawed, skin like ash. He spoke to the tall woman and she smiled a little, and then without speaking to us he went back upstairs.

Through the years, on Saturday nights, this man — Eustace Ross — arrived at our house with his wife Mary, for a night of talk and laughter with our two other family friends, J.K. and Hallie Thomas, and anyone else who dropped in. He fascinated me. I almost never heard his footsteps. He would come up the veranda stairs, enter, his fedora plunked on his head, and grin at no one in particular, and then drift sideways into the room, making no noise. He always sat near the fireplace, in an antique chair. It was a butler's chair, thin-boned legs and ribbing, the arms too high for comfort, but he liked to sit in it, stolid, incongruous, his elbows jutting out over the arms, slumped in a chair that allowed no slumping.

He would sit in silence, and depending on his mood, his depressions, he would take almost no part in the early, quick bantering talk of the evening or he would defiantly break in, blurting out something sharp, even hurtful (one night, the philosopher Jacques Maritain was explaining how important it was to understand that what was missing between images in dreams, what was missing from the dream that had its own logic, was the conjunctions — and

Eustace, exasperated, suddenly hissed, "Listen for God's sake, he's explaining Freud to us, he's explaining Freud . . . ").

Those Saturdays were nights of strong, friendly, acerbic talk. It was conversation *pour le sport*. Ideas were bandied or booted about and throttled. Unsuspecting guests fell into silence at the fierceness of the arguments, at the sound of such raucous laughter and slanging. Sometimes guests missed the point. No one was trying to prove anything. It was give-and-take, tentative thrusts, end-runs, all informal and playful and intimate in the moment's sincerity.

There might be a painter there, William Ronald, wearing snakeskin boots and a paisley suit, or a fastidious account executive, Bill Graham (whose wife, Eleanor, was one of the founders of *Canadian Forum*), or Gordon Sheppard — an intense young film maker who was living with Heather Stratton, the Playmate of the Year (later murdered on the west coast) — or, Marshall McLuhan, who one night tilted his head and closed his eyes and wondered aloud — "Why is it that people in our city, unlike the rest of the world, go out of their houses to be with friends and go into their homes to be alone?" Eustace had pawed the carpet with his heavy shoes. "What bunk," he'd said, "what utter bunk."

I always tried to be near Eustace as he sat mumbling a terse aside. A dour, taciturn man who worked all day scanning meteorological maps, the incoming Highs and Lows, he was a sniper. He went in for ambush, witty and cutting, his mouth squared by the lines of his jaw. He would laugh, a wide and silent laugh. Some heard his jokes, no one heard his laugh. And almost no one read his poetry, though he was the first modern poet in the country, a good poet, admired by Morley and praised by Marianne Moore. "I'm not neglected," he said to me one night. "To be neglected you've first got to be known."

My father loved Eustace's pranks. When there were great public debates going on in the city newspapers he would adopt the role of the colonial reactionary he and Morley abhorred. He wrote preposterous letters to the newspapers, curmudgeonly letters, bigoted, always extolling the British or Ulster Orange cause, letters ripe with diatribe, the usual ignorance. He signed them "Old Flag," knowing the Old Flag editors at the newspapers would eagerly print such nonsense. No one, except his Saturday night friends, knew who "Old Flag" was. No one really knew who Eustace was. Morley knew a little about him. He confided in Morley from time to time, and Morley told me that Eustace had fought in the First World War, and had been gassed in the trenches, that he had suffered shell-shock. Only Morley, my mother, and his wife, Mary, knew that he was a mesmerist who believed that during the Second World War he had received messages from spirits, messages that he took so seriously he wrote to the Prime Minister and to the U.S. War Department warning them that there was going to be an invasion of western Ireland.

The War Department had written back and told him to leave them alone but he had studied the Department note with his philatelist's glass and decided that several type-keys had been filed down, and after analyzing the flawed letters, he had de-coded another secret message, this one telling him to disregard the obvious order, it was a deliberate deception, and to carry on! He did — with time out for a period of shock treatments for acute depression — writing poetry and receiving messages, not only from his spirits but from Prime Minister Mackenzie King, who always wore a Homburg hat. "What a world," my father said years later — after we knew more about the Prime Minister, — "King was getting messages from his dead mother and talking to his dead dog and at the same time he had the mesmerist Eustace yakking at him on the other end of the line."

Nothing seemed more important to us on those Saturday evenings than conversation. We talked about the whole wacky, murderous world as if it were all taking place on just the other side of the backyard fence. The more excited we got, the angrier we got, the more we sang. I remember once, at one-thirty in the morning when my brother was singing — *If Beale Street could talk, married men would take their beds and walk* — Tom Hedley, a young pal and my first editor who had gone down to New York to take a job at Esquire, yelled into the back porch darkness, at the darkened windows of our neighbors, "Orwell and Auden are bankrupt, bankrupt." I was sure the neighbors, Clery and Dunnington-Grubb and Dabney, lying in the dark, kept awake by our carousing, wondered what brokerage or accounting firm Orwell & Auden could be. But neighbors in Rosedale never complained about carousing, and certainly never called the police. They were discreet. They kept their own peace, their silence. They were nearly always in bed, all lights out (except for Clery) before the eleven o'clock night news. They never went to sleep on bad news. Silence was their grace note. It was in that silence that my father sat late at night at his desk in the library after everyone had gone home, a desk over a radiator, facing into a window at the front of the house. He sat every night in that amber box of window light, shaping the silence between his hands in which he heard voices, whispers:

> *Be in me as the eternal moods*
> *of the bleak wind, and not*
> *As transient things are —*
> *gaiety of flowers.*

Morley taught me to croon the songs of eastern seaboard college men who wore blazers and pork-pie hats:

> *We're poor little lambs who have lost our way,*
> *Baa, baa, baa.*
> *Gentlemen songsters off on a spree,*
> *Doomed from here to eternity,*
> *God have mercy on such as we,*
> *Baa, baa, baa.*

My mother grew wistful when she listened to me sing that song: I was her little lamb, a doomed gentleman songster. It was she — and not my father — who took me on my fifteenth birthday to the Colonial Tavern to hear old Pops Foster play the bass and — after she had sent him a note — bow the bass just for her on "Black and Blue" and "Body and Soul." *What did I do to be so black and blue?* she sang as we walked home, as cheerful as a woman could be on a stroll with her son in the indigo hours.

When I was a little older, I took my own time strolling in a long narrow dance hall at 345 College Street — the "Porters' Hall" — a pool hall on the first floor and dance floor on the second, the stairwell air dry with the sinus-clotting dust of unshelled peanuts (big burlap bags filled with peanuts were warehoused on one of the upper floors), and the disc jockey in this rhythm and blues joint was Kenny Holdip, a moon-faced and gap-toothed black man who told me, "You dream what you be dreaming, ofay, but all I want outa my own life in my lifetime is a little pink bootie, my 'skey, and my slave." He worked at his "slave" every day as a garage-hand, spray-painting bunged up cars in the Dundas Body & Wrecking Shoppe behind a Methodist church, but at night on Tuesdays and Saturdays he hunkered down over his turntable by the front window, drinking Alberta Premium whiskey while two older women with bulging necks and thick ankles sat at the door taking money, loose change and the odd folding bill that they put into a pink and gold Churchill cigar box as couples in the shadow light of the floor "slow-danced" belly to belly, "grinding coffee" to Elmore James ("Dust My Broom"), Amos Milbourne ("One Scotch, One Bourbon, One Beer"), Ray Charles ("I Live on a Lonely Avenue"), Gatemouth Moore ("Going Down Slow"), Bo Diddley ("Somebody's Crying"), Little Willie John ("All Around the World"), Johnny Otis ("Bad Luck Shadow"), Earl Bostic ("Flamingo"), Dinah Washington ("Time Out for Tears") . . .

Nearly every Saturday night, a pudgy white man with soft fey manners and startled blue eyes sat between the two older women with a small pile of scuffed paperback books on his lap, strung out on reefers, wagging his finger as he licked his lips, trying to softly and very precisely explain to the two patient women that Plato was "only a ofay just like me in a BOOM town, Ath-eens, this guy from Ath-eens with his gonads for the good sweet boys . . . and you know what he say? — he say that there be no time for tears, that there be no time a-tall, 'that to be patient under suffering is best, and that we should not give way to im-patience, and because no human thing is of serious im-por-tance, grief stands in the way of that which is most required.' Pow," he said, as if he were blowing a dandelion seedball off the end of his finger. "Ooo-popa-Pow!"

"What is most required, child," one of the two old women said, "is 50 cents in the box and peace in your heart." This woman, who warned me one night — "Boy, you being white being with too many black girls going to get your white behind skinned to the bone," — always kept a protective eye open for a guileless sweet lost man-child, Little Eddie Till, who used to strut up and down the flights of stairs jive-talking:

> Cool as the breeze
> on Lake Louise,
> I ain't no square
> from Delaware,
> I got lard in my hair.

And I would reply:

> There I be, man,
> walking the beach
> looking for ash trays
> in their wild state. . .

Then he would lay his hand out in the air, palm open, doing a pimp-walking shuffle-step in the doorway, saying, "Give me five on one 'cause the other four are sore," touching his thumb to my thumb. "We is cool on the skin circuits, man." He died young of heroin and drink, bung-holed in the brain, stumbling like a little old derelict man around the steel newspaper coin boxes on the street corners, hand-clapping a song to himself, *pitty-pat pitty-pat, slip 'n' slap*, side-stepping his own shadow, oblivious to the dudes warped on bingo wine, dudes flashing a knife, oblivious to the sometime switch-blade brawls in the Porters' Hall, trying to remember . . . "I jess can't remember, I jess can't remember yo' name, no, I got it, Cal-hoon, you one bad-ass white boy, Cal-hoon . . . "

When Little Eddie Till died, for a while grief stood in my way. I had the mournful feeling that he would quickly be forgotten, that he was born to be forgotten, because he was someone with no one to tell his story, and I wanted to tell his story but I had no idea what his story really was, and then, in that same week, my favorite aunt died.

Aunt Alice was a *frapturous* woman who baked chocolate and maple walnut cakes and gave them to friends and relations who couldn't eat all of her cakes and threw them away. She was a woman who seemed so chirpingly happy that my father shied away from her as if she were the carrier of some disease of the brain — a gaiety that was almost gaudy — and as we drove in a procession of black limousines up by Highway 7 to a new graveyard on the northwestern outskirts of the city, as the casket was carried by pall bearers in morning coats across a barren flat land, I realized it was just that: a flat farmer's field that was now a boneyard, barren, with no upright grave stones, no dates, no stories chiseled in stone monuments, no wit, no pious celebration, no revenge, no completion.

There were only tiny, bald, pecunious markers — dates and a name — sunk in the grass so that the big lawn mowers could mow freely, nudging aside the plastic wreaths of flowers, ugly day-glo wreaths. Grief, grief, how could there be grief when there were no stories to be remembered?

Years later, talking to my mother about grief while listening to Schubert's *Quartet in D Minor, Death and the Maiden* (in which the four movements are in the minor, *all* four movements), I got a little loose-tongued on bourbon and told her that one night her poor little lamb had lost his way and been off on a gentleman's spree in Mexico City, sporting with someone whose music she had danced to in Chicago. "There was licorice in the air," I said. And this man had told me, looking me straight in the eye with his watery eye, that he was going to die, *I'm going to die . . . I'm going to die and be dead and gone . . .* It was his heart, he said. His heart, he said, "felt like it was choking on weeds," but he "sure as shit didn't give a shit for grieving" — and he told me also, once we got to story-telling over a bottle of tequila, that O'Banion, the Chicago

O'Banion, our Viola's O'Banion, when he was buried in Mount Carmel cemetery after Capone had killed him, had been refused holy earth, consecrated
ground . . . but he himself had known the priest who was O'Banion's friend
back then, and confessor — a Father Patrick Malloy — and Malloy had said a
prayer over O'Banion anyway, refusal or no, quietly goading the "goody-two-
shoes" archbishop — and my mother said, "Who's that who told you that?"
and I said, "Pee Wee Russell."

"He's old enough to be *my* father," she said. "What're you doing with
him? What're you doing in a whorehouse? What were you doing in Mexico
City?"

"It happens," I said, "it happens, so we got looped anyway, me and a
good old newspaper guy from Detroit, Doc Green, and Bud Freeman, too." It
was incredible, I said. I had met them all because after checking in I'd left my
hotel and gone for a walk, and I had come across a man reading *Patriotic Gore*
in Alameda park. I had seen the name — Edmund Wilson— on his book and
had introduced myself, saying, "I sure as hell didn't expect to find anyone
reading my old friend Edmund Wilson's book in this park," and he had said,
"I'm Bud Freeman," to my disbelief — because the great tenor saxophonist
was spiffed up and dressed like a British gent.

He sat like a banker, trim and alert — and so we talked and he told me
that he "much admired" Wilson's portrait of Justice Oliver Wendell Holmes
— saying "much admired" just like Wilson — and then he told me that he and
Pee Wee were playing in town with Brubeck and Thelonius Monk and though
he admired Monk he didn't "much like him" — not as a man. "His self-indulgences are abrasive. Of course, when he plays it sounds like something else
altogether, his self-indulgences sound fearless." We went to the Mexico City
race track to get to know each other, which we did, liking each other. Later
that night we ended up in a fancy whorehouse and Pee Wee played his clarinet while Bud and I sat staring at the young faces of girls as old as the Maya.
There was one girl who seemed purely Mayan with her charcoal-smoke eyes
and a brown blade nose and long straight sleek black hair (coming in her —

and I did *not* tell my mother this — was like hollering into the grave, the way Kazantzakis says in his memoirs that his father had taken him to his grand-father's grave and they had knelt down and scooped a small hole into the earth and yelled down at the old man so that the dead and the living would know each other).

The woman came with me for two days and we went to the pyramids of the Moon and the Sun at Teotihuacan and prayed on top of the Moon, not for an escape from death but for a re-birth after death, and sat cross-legged in the long grass. Her toenails were blue. The serpents in her eyes were blue. In sunlight, her black hair was blue. She liked rubbing my neck and the pads of flesh on my fingers. "There are tiny fish in your fingertips," she said. "You will have to feed them."

"How?"

"There is no cruelty in your tenderness. Fish have teeth."

So I told that to my mother.

I told her I had a weakness: there was no cruelty in my tenderness. I had fish to feed.

2

Late at night, in my early twenties, I would finish reading in a room close to the Pontifical Institute of Medieval Studies where I was working on my MA thesis — Edgar Allen Poe's *The Narrative of Arthur Gordon Pym* — a novel about a Nantucket sailor boy who had survived the terror of internment in the dark hold of a ship and a mutiny and the breaking apart of that ship as it crossed the equator, and he had drifted through uncharted waters, driven by currents farther south than anyone had ever gone, discovering a map that was true only in his own mind, until, in the Antarctic, pursued by black men who spoke no known tongue, he disappeared in a skiff into the silence of a great white womb of ice.

He'd gone mapmaking, disappeared, and somehow he had come back to tell this tale.

I liked that.

It seemed to me that life at its best was when men and women came back to tell tales, some taller than others, but the truth was always in the telling.

Of a ride here. There.

I took a Diamond Taxi ride every second or third night down to the old Barclay Hotel on the corner of Simcoe and Front streets. It was the only night-club hotel in town, housing twenty-five or thirty "permanent" guests: one was a rich "fag-hag" (her great grandfather had been a Father of Confederation) who kept a papier-mâché head of a bull in her room and she used to order martinis and sit on her bed with her homosexual friends and bet on who could loop more fancy garters over the horns of the bull.

Sometimes she sat in on a big poker game that was held every Thursday night in the hotel, a game run by Maxie Bluestein, who was also known as Maxie Baker. He was a hard-nosed bookmaker who had managed to control the big time gambling in the city and, in 1961, to keep the Magaddino Mafia family from Buffalo and their local henchman, Johnny Pops Pappalia, out of the Toronto betting rackets. The vicious Pops — wielding a baseball bat — and a lug named Frank Marchildon, had tried to beat Bluestein to a pulp in front of the hat check room of the Town Tavern on Queen Street — a supper club and bar where Billie Holiday, Jimmie Rushing, Stan Getz, Earl Fatha Hines had played — but Bluestein had come up out of a crouch and had nearly killed them with a knife.

One night someone from Bluestein's poker game had gone down the hotel hall with a knife to where flamboyant Little Jackie Shane lived alone and had tried to kill him . . . but the sleek beautiful black transvestite with almond-shaped eyes, who wore satin capes and Yves St. Laurent raw silk pant suits and sang the blues like Little Willie John, had punctured the man's neck with the high heel of his shoe.

Shane had fronted a band, Frank Motley and His Motley Crew, featuring Frank and His Dual Trumpets. Frank was famous in the local dives for playing two trumpets at once. (He was on stage the night that Art Cuccia threatened to stick me cross-wise in the heart with a knife in the upstairs lounge of the Holiday Tavern, and Clarkie Ader — whose sister I had slept with — said to me, "If he's white I'll kill the fucker for you." When I said, "Jesus, man, I'm white," he smiled and said, "On the moment, man, I just forgot. You almost more nigger than any nigger I know." The Tavern's bouncers tumbled me down the stairs. Their logic before giving me the heave: "If you ain't here then Cuccia don't give us no trouble." Three years later the police shot Cuccia dead between the eyes during a "break-and-enter"into a house.) It was true that such people — such "permanent guests" — lived in the hotel and used the hotel and gave it a certain character, but the Barclay's main business was the nightclub on the second floor.

I had discovered the nightclub because I'd met a young woman who was writing her thesis on John Donne's *Divine Poems*.

She was double-jointed and she could — by crossing her legs behind her head — turn into a ball and roll around on the floor, singing songs. And I used to chant at her:

> *On a round ball*
> *A workman that hath copies by, can lay*
> *An Europe, Afrique, and an Asia,*
> *And quickly make that, which was nothing, all . . .*

She thought she wanted to get into show business and one afternoon I went with her to the Barclay. She showed her act to a short-arm-fatty talent agent named Joey Postum who gaped as she rolled around the stage, singing "Oklahoma" and "I Love Paris in the Springtime," dressed in her home-made sequined suit. Postum fell to his knees, laughing. He thought it was the "most off-the-wall" act he had ever seen, but he didn't hire her.

That same day, I met Goffredo, the maître d'.

Goffredo had worked his way from bus boy at the King Edward Hotel to greeter at the One-Two on Adelaide Street. He'd gone to Le Cabaret on St. Clair, and then he'd been hired to run the Barclay nightclub for Al Seigal, a sour-faced heavy-set man who had started out selling ice cream in the streets of Detroit, and then had become a jukebox distributing millionaire and the owner of the Elmwood Casino in Windsor and the Barclay in Toronto. Once, after I had been at his table for an hour, not saying a word, Seigal got up to go and said, "Nice talking to you, kid." When I looked at him, mystified, he said, "You know how to keep your mouth shut. Smartest conversation I've had in a year."

Goffredo used to arrive in mid-afternoon in a funereal Cadillac, a limousine. One of his customers, a used-car hustler who had billed himself on the Golden Mile as The Mayor of Motor City, had gone bankrupt. He and Goffredo had cut a cash deal before the man got out of town. "I was lucky," Goffredo said, "to get a luxury car at my price. It's out of my league." His clientele were easy spenders, men who wore soft leather shoes even in the winter slush, who seemed to have endless casual cash — but Goffredo had been brought up in Milano in the after-grime of the war and, as one of the house gamblers said, he had been taught "to nurse his nickels." Married to a pretty country woman, he was gentle and quick — if a little star struck — and he wanted flair in his life. Shrewd about the surface of things, he knew how to handle the headliners . . . Liberace, Jackie Mason, Redd Foxx, Ford and Hines . . .

He wore silk suits with hand stitching on the lapels, real buttonholes, and two inches of French cuff at the wrist, jet and gold cuff links. Every afternoon at five o'clock, he brushed lacquer on his nails. "My diners expect a little shine," he said. He knew his clientele, how to handle them because he knew what gestures gave them a good feeling about themselves. He used to lean against a lectern just inside the door, an old gooseneck lamp shedding yellow light on the reservations book. I listened to him as he poured me tumblers of cognac and told me how he felt about his steadiest customers — the low-ball flesh-peddlers and garment dealers from Spadina Avenue who, he said, always wore white-on-white shirts with long Hollywood collars because the shiny thread in the cloth looked like tinsel in the stage lights . . . their shirts were "just like their lives, cheap thrills." He had a huge crush on a blond woman in the chorus line. I was, at his request, to bring him little books of poems. He had never read poetry. Neither had she. Among the books I brought him, he liked the poets in the little Peter Pauper Press series of translations, and after he lacquered his nails he would sit with her while she had a pot of tea (she was English) and he would read Baudelaire or Verlaine to her.

She had a stern Anglo-Saxon pertness, her gestures chiseled and brittle. He talked to me about the mysterious darkness in her. His love for her puzzled and pained his friends. Goffredo had had a succession of beautiful women . . . the stars of various shows, women who were commanding and sensual. At that time, I had a friend, Joan, who was part of a baton twirling act, The Lounsbury Sisters, good honest women whose mother's front room in a small house in a small town west of Toronto was stacked with baton-twirling trophies from all over North America. They had performed several times on the Ed Sullivan show, hurling twirling fiery batons at each other — wheels within wheels rolling — singeing their pale bodies. One night, a local hood — one of Johnny Pops' pals with connections to Stefano Magaddino — spoke to me in the toilet. "I don't get it," he said.

"What?"

"You're a young guy, a kid, and you're with a star, I seen her on Sullivan."

"So?"

"So what's Fredo doing with this thin-lipped broad who got a mouth like a razor from the chorus line who don't even dance so good, who's upsetting his wife, too?"

I went back to my table, sat down and said mischievously to Joan, "I don't know, I don't think I'm up to this, you and me. After all, you're a star."

She looked at me blankly. She didn't know what I was talking about. Neither did I, really. Then she said, "I dunno, my mother likes you."

I began to laugh. "That settles it," I said.

"What?"

As the hood came out of the toilet, wiping his hands, I gave him a tight little conspiratorial wave. He gave me the thumbs-up. I gave him the thumbs-down. He shook his head, he didn't know what was going on, so he came over and sat at the table.

"There's something you want to tell me?" he said, looking concerned.

"The person I really get along with," I said, "is her mother."

Joan thought I was making fun of her.

I was trying to make fun of myself. And the hood.

But he didn't laugh.

And she got up and left. I never saw her again.

"You let her go so easy like that," the hood said, "a star," and he shook his head.

The hoods were always there, grim and sullen. They drove in from Guelph or Cooksville — where they ran a small illegal gambling casino in an old farmhouse set far back from the road, and also extortion and loan sharking operations, preying on Sicilian and Calabrian shop owners in Toronto and Hamilton. There was talk of a taxi company out of Hamilton that was becoming a front for moving drugs on behalf of the Magaddino family who were still trying to muscle in on the rackets in Toronto. All of them dressed in black suits like seminarians and some of them wore Homburg hats and in the winter they wore Bennies or long double-breasted overcoats almost to the ankles.

Elio Pontiggia, a friend of mine, also dressed in black. In the graduate school with me, he had been known affectionately as Eli the Fanatic because he not only dressed in black but sometimes wore a black hat and told people he was a Jewish scholar studying the Kabala. He had read many of the mystics but his only successful ascent had been as a champion collegiate pole vaulter. After graduate school he went back to Utica, his hometown, and went into the haberdashery business, specializing in clothing for priests, black suits. Elio asked me to be Best Man at his wedding.

His uncle Anselmo, who lived in an unpretentious frame house, was my host and Anselmo was troubled on the night I arrived, the night before the wedding. He was troubled because not only someone "from outside" the family — but someone who wasn't even an American — had been "trusted enough so he's gonna stand up beside our boy at the altar." He asked me whether we could talk at his kitchen table. Wearing a sweater and slacks, Anselmo was small and slightly balding. He had a stutter. He said, "I hear you're a writer, a reporter, you know what's what."

"I've been told I know when to keep my mouth shut," I said.

"Silence is good. This is a religious family," Anselmo said. He reached across the table and patted my hand.

He said he knew I was from Toronto and he knew the city. He didn't know it like he knew Montreal — where he had business with Carmine Galante, he said — but he knew it nonetheless. He always stayed in "a clean little dump on the Lakeshore, the Dutch Sisters. You know that place?" I said I knew it. He wanted to know if I had ever heard of Alberto Cucci. I said that I had. He said, "What you know?" I knew, I said, that he'd been a drug-runner, who'd used a bakery shop in Toronto as a front.

"He was baking it," I said. "Big time."

"Right," Anselmo said. "This is absolutely right, so what happens?"

"Where?"

"To him?"

"Last I heard he got arrested in Cleveland, got out on bail — which Magaddino had refused to pay, twenty thousand — and he said he was going to Buffalo to kill Magaddino."

"That's the last?"

"Yeah."

"The last."

"Yeah."

"This is also right. But you don't hear nothing about him now."

"No."

"Not likely."

"No."

"We got him, tied him up with baling wire."

I told him I wanted to have a word with Eli.

"Ah, Elio," he said with a warmth that was almost wistful. "Elio, he's like an angel, Elio wants to be an angel, he tries so hard . . . "

"Yeah," I said.

I spoke to Eli in the hall. I told him I knew what was going on, that I was being taken into the family, told secrets I didn't want to know. I didn't want to have Anselmo in my life, Anselmo always knowing that I knew.

"My uncle, he means well," Eli said, and went into the kitchen. A little flushed, he came out with Anselmo, who said, "Let's talk a little more, a little respectable. We can be respectable. There's a judge I'm gonna meet tonight, so we'll meet him. At one of our clubs. We'll all meet him. We'll have a good time," and as we went out to the car he said, "The real trouble we got in Canada is we can't get to who we gotta get to, your judges, you don't elect your judges, what kinda democracy don't elect its judges?"

The next morning, during the wedding mass, at the consecration — the tinkling of the bells — at the transubstantiation when the bread and wine *are* the Body and Blood — I stayed seated in my pew. Parishioners got into line and went up to the rail to take communion. I hadn't been to confession in several years. I was a serious lapsed Catholic. I sat alone. Soon I realized that the whole church was going to communion, including all the boys in black. Anselmo, standing in the aisle, saw that I was not going up to the rail. He looked at me, perplexed, and then turned and said in a loud throaty whisper, a whisper full of exasperation as he opened his hand to me and the congregation, "What's he done that's so bad he can't go to communion?"

I told this story to Goffredo. He laughed. I told it to him on the night one of his more ostentatious spenders came into the night club, the tall, brash, bright-eyed newspaper owner John Bassett, and his friend, the Commissioner of Football, Jake Gaudaur. (Little did I know that Bassett would be my first publisher, a high-style and strut kind of guy, astute about most things, dumb about others: running for a seat in the federal parliament, he had told his chauffeur to drive him to the working class corner of Spadina and Dundas and there he had stood at the streetcar stop, towering over tiny Portuguese laborers, beaming, looking splendid in his cashmere top coat, and he had seemed surprised when he lost the election.) Bassett and Gaudaur were late for the last show and were sitting alone in the empty room. They spoke to Goffredo. He spoke to the chorus line. Money changed hands. The line agreed to dance again while the two men ate and talked alone at ringside. The waiters hung about in the demi-gloom, half-asleep. "Some men need a performance," Goffredo said, "just to eat."

A Chicago Black Hawk left-winger, who regularly wandered into the club after hours when the team was playing in town, stood watching them while squeezing an orange tennis ball. "Good for the grip," he said, drunk, pouring himself whiskey from an alligator-skin-covered hip flask, forgetting that he was in a bar, muttering incoherently, full of menace, to his constant friend, a guy who had a string of fat girls, "Blimpos" he called them, who performed at stag parties. "We're talking flesh, man, when we're talking tits here we're talking serious tits. Those two guys want a chorus line, I'll rent 'em a chorus line."

Goffredo's favorite customers — those who amused him most, and tipped him best — were the garment hustlers, who came in on Tuesday or Wednesday nights with their "clothes-horse broads," laughing and mincing, trying to tease the hostess who stood at the top of the stairs. She had come third in a national beauty contest because she had a baby face, a sensuous lower lip and gargantuan breasts. She would give the women red carnations, a special touch, at least that's how Goffredo thought of it.

He had that peculiar maître d's disdain for his customers, deploring their deportment while catering to their demands, feeling demeaned as he took a perverse pleasure in so easily ingratiating himself with vulgar men. He was most popular among those he loathed, men who came through the doors with their hands out, men who liked to be touched, embraced and taken arm-in-arm to ringside, even if the room was completely empty. He knew a gentleman never expected to be touched, let alone embraced by a maître d', so he had a routine for these men: it was called the Fuck-'Em-In-The-Armpit-Caress-'Em-On-The-Ass routine. He'd slip his arm around the man's waist and move his

hand up into the man's armpit, a generous, consoling, and obsequious gesture, and as they walked together to the front-and-center table at ringside
he'd give the man little jerking lifts in the armpit, while his guests were left
behind to envy such warmth and to find their own way. Then, as the man sat
down, Goffredo's hand, in a quarter-moon sweep, would drop down lightly
and curve under the man's rump, caressing him across the cheeks of his ass
just before it hit the chair, and the garment hustler, beaming, would tuck
money into Goffredo's hand; it was a ritual, complete.

Goffredo could accommodate anyone. In the manhunt that followed his
beating of Bluestein, Pappalia stayed in the hotel, quite openly eating supper
through the show, night after night. "He's waiting to see what happens,"
Goffredo said. The police never came. Finally, he went to them, surrendering
near the Rosedale subway station . . . he was given eighteen months for the
beating, then was handed over to Robert Kennedy's prosecutors in the U.S.,
where he was sentenced to ten years in Sing Sing for his part in the French
Connection heroin smuggling ring, the same ring for which Cucci had been a
runner. When Pappalia himself was finally murdered in Hamilton in 1997,
Johnny Pops, like O'Banion, was refused the blessing of the church. Goffredo
had accommodated Pappalia and dozens like him, but he used to say almost
wistfully that he wished he had someone he could look up to, someone he
could serve with admiration and pleasure.

Though there were many, many women in his life, he was a lonely man
who had very few friends. I think that's why he talked to me, gave me tumblers of cognac. He didn't want to hurt anyone. He didn't want to hurt his
wife. He loved her. But, as he said, she didn't know what he was talking about
when he talked to her. Whatever little lift of wonder he felt about life, it got
cut short when he was home with his wife. She thought his wanting to read
poetry aloud in the kitchen while she cooked, poetry that no one understood,
including himself, was ridiculous. He would drive me home in the early morning hours in his limousine, but not all the way home, not unless it was raining,
because I liked to get out of the car and walk alone across the footbridge in the

early morning hours, so he would leave me by the Bloor Street stairs that went down to the bridge that crossed the ravine.

When I stood alone at night on the footbridge over the ravine I felt that I was in the arms of the trees. I could feel the dew and hear the dong of the Old City Hall clock bell and muffled foghorns from the lake would remind me of what Telford the chauffeur had said, "That lake's no river and this ain't no healing town." As I turned up our street, heading home, the overhead street lights were like wind lamps hidden in the maple leaves. Everything was in shadows. If Mrs. Wishall was awake, she was sitting in the dark. All the houses and clumsy mansions were dark, except for Clery's upstairs window and my father's front window where he sat into the early hours, a writer working at his desk, the floor lamp shedding light over his shoulders, staring into the dark outside the window, an oblong of amber light.

I often stood out on the lawn at the edge of a flower bed, watching him, sometimes moving in so close I could reach out and touch the glass, yet he could not see me — lost as he was in the little confessions his characters were making — and since the glass was like a mirror, silvered by the night, I was standing on the other side of the mirror, watching as he mouthed a phrase, bringing a voice, a plea, secretly to life in the open view of anyone passing on the street.

One night, I was standing at the edge of the flower bed facing his box of light but it was empty — he was somewhere else in the house — and I stood for a long time waiting for him to appear, but then out of the dark I saw a policeman. He came close and said quietly, "What're you doing?"

"Just waiting."

"For who?"

"No one," I said. "Just waiting."

He circled to my other side. He could see the empty chair behind the window, too.

"What do you do?"

"I go to school."

"You go to school, eh?"

"Yeah," I said. I didn't like cops. "What's wrong with that?"

"Nothing. Nothing at all," and he came around so that he could look straight into my face, squinting so I'd be sure to see how patient and shrewd he thought he was. He stepped on a clump of marigolds.

"And what're you going to do when you're outa school?" he asked.

"I don't know. A writer, maybe," I said.

"What kind of writer?"

"One that tells stories," I said. As he turned again, the light from the window caught his face and I could see that he was gray at the temples.

"Oh yeah," he said, and he seemed amused.

"Yeah."

He asked me if I lived there, in the house, and if I knew about the prowlers and robberies and the perverts down in the ravine. "Have you ever seen the guy with the moustache who wears the pink dress?" And I said, "Sure, he's the Brigadier General's son," but he said, "No, he's no brigadier. He's never done a thing in his life, and neither's his son." Then, taking me by the elbow, he asked, "Are you a good swimmer?"

"No," I said, surprised. "Not at all."

"Neither was my little boy."

"Really," I said.

"Yeah. He ate too much and went swimming and got cramps and nearly drowned."

"He didn't drown?"

"No. I saved him, but his legs were all bent up to his chest, you know, and they never really straightened again, they never grew."

"I'm sorry," I said.

"Yeah, it's too bad, he never grew in the legs, and he's got a big head, too, like it's too big, you know, but it's full of stories, and one day he said to me, 'Maybe my head's too big because it's too full of stories.'"

The policeman took off his cap, looked inside it, and then put it back on his head. He stood for a moment in silence, and then said good-night and warned me to watch out for the man in the pink dress. "He's harmless, but you never know." He went down the slope into the shadows, off into the dark to wherever he had parked his car.

My father was back sitting in his box of amber light, his head cocked to the side, listening, with only the glass between us. I wanted to knock on the glass and tell him that I realized even the police have secret stories, little healing confessions they want to make while standing in the dark. I felt that I knew something a young man does not often know, and I knew it with the kind of innocence I could see in my father's eyes as he sat hearing his voices, staring into my eyes, unaware that I was there.

3

The other day, I had a Hires Root Beer. It was good. It was really good because I haven't had a Hires Root Beer since I was twelve or thirteen, playing baseball in Willowvale Park. It was not known as a park, it was known as Christie Pits because it had been an old sand quarry fronted by Christie Street — and the quarry had been filled in and grassed-over into a flatland. The shallow, slow-moving Garrison Creek that had once angled through the quarry — ripe with the stench of sewage — had been buried under it. When Father McMahon, the priest who was my coach, said, "There's a river under here, it's a healing grace," I didn't know what he was talking about. I couldn't imagine a river that had been buried like a dead body could ever heal anybody, and, as far as I knew, grace was a Jesus-child in the lap of Our Lady. Anyway, I didn't want water. I wanted a Hires Root Beer. After every game I went up the hill from the Pits to the corner confectionery store and drank three bottles of Hires.

I was the pitcher on the team, the St. Peter's Church Bantams, and I also batted clean-up. There were tall link-fences and wire screen dugouts around the ball diamond and the infield was always well raked, but hardly anyone came to watch us play. A thousand people could sit in the bleacher benches and on the hillside watching a baseball game. That's what they had done when my father was a boy. He had pitched in the Pits, too. He couldn't hit, though. His older brother could hit. His brother was Burke. He was one year older and one inch taller than Morley. He was Morley's catcher. They were called "a battery" but I have no idea why a pitcher and his catcher were called "a battery." Burke could catch and hit but he wanted to be a singer, an opera singer. He was a bass baritone and, though as a boy he had scissored photographs of his favorite ballplayers out of the Toronto and Buffalo newspapers and had pasted them into scrapbooks, he didn't have much interest in being a player. But Morley did. He took his baseball seriously. He thought for a while about being a pro baseball player. He paid attention to his pitching arm, his right arm. He rubbed it down with ice that he chipped from the saw-dust covered block in the kitchen ice-box. He tried to sleep on his left shoulder. He was five-foot-eight with dark brown, curly hair, blue eyes, and he had a good roundhouse curve and a fast ball.

When he was twenty and playing in the senior city sandlot leagues, his father told him that since he had worked the two summers before — traveling around the province's country roads selling magazines to the lonely wives of farmers — he should still be looking for summer work. His cousin got him a job in the Laidlaw lumberyard, "slugging" lumber alongside five "hunkies," unloading six-by-two scantling from boxcars. "At that time," Morley said, in his memoir, *That Summer in Paris*, "I was also reading wildly. I read Dostoevsky, Joseph Conrad, Sinclair Lewis, Flaubert; *The Dial, The Adelphi,* and the old *Smart Set*, edited by H.L. Mencken and George Jean Nathan; Katherine Mansfield, D.H. Lawrence — everything. Yet in the summer it was baseball that absorbed me . . . Our ball team, a very good one, one of the best in the city, had some rough tough players with a rich fine flow of language who were not concerned with my interest in Conrad and Dostoevsky or by my brother's beautiful voice — only my curve ball and my brother's batting average. After I had been working two weeks in the lumberyard my turn came to pitch a game." In the first inning

Morley noticed that his arm felt unusually light. Coming around out of his windup, the pitch felt weightless, and he had no speed on the ball. Boom. He got knocked out of the box. "To hell with that lumberyard," he said.

An old school friend, Art Kent, had got a job reporting on the morning paper. At night, Morley, lonely for company and living on the northeast outskirts of the city, on the far side of the Don Jail and the Don River valley flats, went into town and tagged along with Kent on assignments on the beat, and it wasn't long before he told himself that reporting would be much easier on his pitching arm than slugging lumber in the hot summer sun. He paid a visit to the afternoon paper, the *Toronto Daily Star.* An elderly gentleman at the reception desk, impressed by his earnestness, and believing he had a big story to report to the city editor, called a Mr. Harry Johnston.

"This stocky, plump, long-nosed man with hair graying at the temples and a deliberately alert manner came out to the desk and said brusquely, 'The city editor, Mr. Hindmarsh, is on his holidays. I'm Johnston. What is it, young fellow?'" Morley said he was from the university and was a very good reporter and wanted a job. Johnston said they weren't hiring anybody. Morley said, "Let me work around here for a week. If at the end of the week you think I'm no good, don't pay me anything." Johnston walked away.

At the same hour the next day, Johnston, in his shirt sleeves, came to the hall desk and this time Morley walked into the city room with him. "Look here," he insisted, "what I said yesterday . . . I'll work for nothing for a week. If I'm any good, keep me on and when the city editor comes back you have in me another pretty good reporter. What do you lose if it doesn't cost you anything?"

Morley's effrontery seemed to attract him. Smiling a little, he asked, "What's your name?" and he wrote it down. "You won't be on the salary list but come in at seven in the morning," and he walked away abruptly.

"I had never been in a newsroom," Morley said. "This one had a row of desks running the length of the room and a big round city desk at which there were four deskmen. At seven in the morning Mr. Johnston was one of them. He hardly spoke to me. I sat down nervously. In a little while one of the deskmen came hurrying to me with a small sheaf of clippings from the morning newspaper. 'Scalp these obituaries,' he said." For two hours, typing with two fingers, Morley rewrote the lives of the dead. It was a summer job. His right arm felt fine. He could get back to playing serious baseball. As it turned out, that was the last summer he played baseball. For the rest of his life, he typed with two fingers.

Morley, his elbows on his knees, was sitting in the wooden bleachers behind third base, watching me pitch. He had taught me how to pitch in the cinder parking lane at the back of our fourplex when we lived on Walmer Road in the shadow of Casa Loma, showing me a one-seam fastball and then a cross-seam slider and an overhand curve, throwing the ball back to me so hard that I got used to the pain of a ball smacking into my glove, and then, standing close behind me, he made me understand with the shadow-feel of his own body that in the windup, balance was everything . . . I rocked, *left foot right foot left foot right foot* . . . "It's the same with boxing," he said. "If you've got the weight equally distributed, then you've got the leverage to throw a real good hook and it's hard to get knocked down if you're balanced . . . " and he would crouch and we would begin to spar and sometimes he hit me hard, hoping I would understand that a punch never hurt as much as I feared it would . . . "That's Balzac, all great art. Contrast, the balance between things. Throw me your high hard one."

Sometimes I would try to cross him up, uncoiling from my windup and uncorking a submarine pitch. At the movie houses where I had seen Laurel and Hardy and The Three Stooges and Larry Parks pretending he was Al Jolson who had pretended he was black by wearing black-face, I had also seen, between features, a film-short on black baseball players, and I'd loved the old black pitcher Satchel Paige who had said, "Never look back — someone might be gaining on you" — and he had thrown a looping submarine ball that no one ever seemed to see to hit. Because I was cocksure (at twelve I had figured out how to stand with a hitch to my hip and my mouth open as if I had a chaw of tobacco tucked in my cheek), I'd throw a submarine pitch during a game and let out a *whoop* when the batter, a kid who'd never seen anything like it, swung and missed, and my coach didn't like my whooping and Morley told me to cut it out because I sounded like some kind of showboat, but pretty soon I was known on the city sandlots as Showboat.

Morley, wearing a tweed jacket of mulberry and brown, was the only father sitting on one of the plank benches in the stands at Christie Pits. I played with kids from immigrant families, like Pat Dunion, whose father slugged heavy coal bags, or Joe Sawchuk at second base, who decades later became the scorekeeper for the Toronto Blue Jays, or anxious and fractious boys — foster children who had lost their fathers early in the war. Father McMahon was gentle-spoken with quick soft hands, an infectious smile. When I wasn't pitching, he let me play center field. Behind me, in the middle of the great park, was the white-washed fieldhouse with dressing rooms for boys and store rooms for the groundskeepers, some of whom were homosexuals (we did not seem so unnerved by homosexuals back then: the Acme Farmers Dairy driver was one, and for a period, so was the Brown's Bread driver . . . far scarier to us were those nuns who seemed to like inflicting pain; those who made us wet our hands in the snow before giving us the strap so that the blows would really hurt). The fieldhouse had a toilet, the rows of heavy porcelain urinals taller than the boys, the running water always so cooling to the room that reeked of urine in the summer, and, hanging around the toilet outside the fieldhouse under an elm tree, there were always six or seven men, dishevelled, ruddy-faced, puffy, with broken shoes . . . brown-paper-bag drunks who liked to frolic and fall down in center field, pretending they were hook-sliding into home plate. One fellow had fish tattooed all over his body. He said he knew all about fish. He knew all their names. He said he had St. Peter's fish tattooed over his heart. I told him he should be swimming in Father McMahon's buried river. He sang, *Oh bury me not on the lone prairie . . .* These men took a liking to me because several of them had played sandlot baseball against Morley, playing for the Lizzies, the Broadview YMCA, the old Columbus Boys' Club.

"He was a fine pitcher, and his brother, too, could swing the bat."

"Looks like he's put on weight, and why not," said another.

"These have been long years."

"And your father's quite a man for the writing."

The inning ended.

"Are you coming to bat?"

"Whack one out here, Morley!"

"The kid's not Morley. That's Morley's kid."

The next week I pitched a no-hitter, striking out twelve. In the morning *Globe and Mail* there was the headline:

MORLEY CALLAGHAN
HEAVES NO HITTER

Morley Callaghan pitched a no-hit game as St. Peter's defeated Geco Boys' Club 23-0, in the TMBA Bantam tournament Saturday. Callaghan struck out 12, walked 2.

Morley asked me if I was upset. I said no, but before the next game I went up to the young reporter who covered sandlot baseball and I said, "My name's not Morley, my name's Barry."

"Oh yeah," he said, with a kind of measured smile. The next morning the *Globe and Mail* headline read:

BARRY CALLAGHAN
YIELDS ONE HIT

Barry Callaghan pitched a one-hitter as St. Peter's blanked St. Thomas 7-0 in a CYO bantam baseball play-off game. Callaghan fanned 12 in his winning mound display.

And the next week, when the headline read:

CALLAGHAN BLASTS
TWO HOME RUNS

I thought, Good, that settles that, and I had a Hires Root Beer. And another, and another.

4

The Callaghans were a southwest Cork family, Callaghans from King Ceallachán, who died in the shadow of Cashal Mount in AD 954. Ceallachán, a diminutive of *ceallach*, is a very old — pre-Christian — word meaning *bright-headed*, and it was a favored name among the *Eoghanacht*, the tribal groups who controlled the southwest, the kingship of Munster at Cork, before the rise of Brian Boru of the *Dál gCais*. The last king Ceallachán is remembered for having marched north to defeat the Danes at Dublin. He then turned southwest, into the midlands, marching to Clonmacnois, then the greatest library in Europe. He burned it. As my friend John Montague said to me once, after I'd needled him about being a late-comer Norman, "Your king was a fucking Irish Attila the Hun," a man born in the blood who lived in the blood. His grandson, Murchadh Ua Ceallacháin, was the first to pass the surname hereditarily. For more than four hundred years, the whole area around the Blackwater River and the castles at Clonmeen and Dromaneen was *Pobal ui Ceallacháin*, Callaghan country, controlled by chieftains whose cultural inheritance was the *creach*, the cattle raid.

The family was wrecked by the wars with the English of the seventeenth century, and in 1643, seventeen O'Callaghan "gentlemen" were declared outlaws by the newly installed English landowners, and in 1652 20,000 acres of the ruling chief, Donncha O'Callaghan, were confiscated and the extended family was broken up and transplanted, leading — as with so many other of the old Gaelic aristocracy — to emigration to the continent, particularly France and Spain. In 1944, Don Juan O'Callaghan of Tortosa, Spain, was recognized as the senior descendant in the male line of Donncha.

As for those who remained behind in the fragmented *Pobal ui Ceallacháin*, most stayed alive as stone masons, shoe makers, farmers, poachers and paupers, until the nineteenth century, when nothing could save the Callaghan families — or others from the Blackwater hills and farming patches around the town of Mallow — from the potato blight and Great Hunger. In the 1840s, many fled to Wales, to the coal mines, and that's where Tom — Morley's father — was born, and where some in the family wrote their name as "Calligan," though Tom's mother, Mary, who died in 1918 in the village of Leytonstone, was buried as "Callaghan."

While Tom was a child, his father became a soldier in the English army, and Tom was moved to London where he had no prospects, no expectations. At twelve, he and another boy, who was fourteen, sailed in steerage across the ocean to Montreal, and went on by rail to Toronto and a town to the northwest, Bradford. Tom reported to a doctor there as an indentured child servant. His pal went into the first bar that would have him, "and he never came out," Tom said. (As a consequence Tom never drank, not even at Morley's wedding, where he refused to drink the toast to the bride — which Loretto's oldest sister, Anna, refused to ever forgive, dismissing him as "a prideful teetotaler.") Tom, small-boned and delicate, worked diligently out of indenture. He paid his debt and went back to Toronto determined to put down roots in a new *Pobal ui Ceallacháin*.

As a man, with a broad moustache and a kindly mellifluous voice, he didn't talk about his childhood in Wales and London. He didn't talk about the doctor. And Morley didn't talk about those years either, a little ashamed that his father had been indentured, and suspicious of any sentimental attachment to lost aristocracies. He did talk about his father's hard scrabbling life alone in Toronto, supporting himself with odd jobs, going through high school as a good student. But in his last year Tom failed his mathematics exam. Then he failed a second time. He could only try it twice. His schooling was over. He had to have a job, so he found work for a while as a clerk in a law office and then as a clerk at Eaton's Department Store. He was fired because clerks were forbidden to read newspapers after 8:30 in the morning. He was found reading the news after the appointed hour. He then got work as a waybill clerk for the Canadian Railway Express. He was a generous man but not generous to himself; he never forgave himself for not going to university, for not realizing his dream — to be a lawyer. He saw his place as a belittlement of himself. (It is a word that runs through Morley's stories: *belittlement*, and Morley seems to have been very conscious of his father's *place*. While he was seventeen and in IV form, Morley filled out a Self-Analysis Blank For The Purposes of Vocational Guidance, answering dozens of questions, like his home reading habits; the number of birds he could identify [5] and wild flowers [10]; if he attended mass [52 times] or Sunday school [no]; how much money he'd earned during the year [$75]; possible occupations [author, representative to Parliament, lawyer]; the makers of Canada he admired [Laurier, W. Lyon Mackenzie, Lord Durham, Joseph Howe, George Brown]; and — whether he shared his father's work [NO]; and, as for his father's occupation . . . he identified his father only as T. and after that Morley scored the occupation space with a crude X). But Tom — clerk or not — was beautifully spoken and he loved poetry, wrote poetry, was deeply involved in Liberal politics, and he could deliver the speeches of Edmund Burke, and Laurier, too (his proudest moment as a member of the executive of the Mackenzie Liberal Club, 1902–3, was shaking Laurier's hand). Tom, however, was doomed to be a clerk because he was outspoken. He was a progressive liberal. He had attempted to organize a union in the CNR. He had opposed sending Canadian soldiers into "Butcher" Kitchener's English army to fight the Afrikaners in the Boer War. He had denounced the war in street corner debates. One night, a mob gathered to lynch him outside his boarding house. As Tom stood his ground, his landlady, a woman from England who supported the war, rushed out of the house. Wagging a broom, she held back the mob.

The girl he loved, and later married, Mary "Minn" Dewan, watched from her own room in the narrow red-brick row house on Shuter Street. She had come south to Toronto from the Blue Mountain boat-building town of Collingwood on Georgian Bay, taking work as a seamstress. She had been home-schooled in a crofter's stone cottage, but somehow she had poems of Tennyson by heart. And most of Poe. Whereas Tom knew Byron, Keats, Moore, Swinburne and Kipling. When they walked out together to lectures and union rallies, she wore flat shoes. She was taller than Tom, big-boned, with broad cheekbones, firm through the shoulders, pale blue eyes, not ponderous but slow-moving, measured. She had a sensual reserve, which Morley inherited.

Catholic at the font and very respectable, they were nonetheless not cowed by parish priests; their oldest boy was named Burke (1902) after the English statesman, Edmund Burke, and Morley — born in 1903 — was named for John Morley, chief secretary for Ireland in William Gladstone's government. As liberals, they were deeply opposed to the churlishness that separate religious schools bred, the narrowness of mind that made drolleries of dreams on streets like Wolfrey Avenue. (There was a curious inattention to the correct spelling of names in the Callaghan family: Minn often spelled her maiden name as Dwan, and she always spelled Loretto's name as Loretta — and most curious of all, for five years as Morley sent out his first stories to magazines, he wrote his return home address as Woolfrey Avenue.) They sent their boys to the public schools, Withrow and Riverdale, a defiant act in those days when the city was famous in its own mind for preachers, police, sectarian marching bands, and officers of the Grand Order of the Orange Lodge who liked to sing:

> *Titter totter, holy water,*
> *Slaughter the Catholics every one.*
> *If that won't do*
> *We'll cut them in two*
> *and make them live under the Orange and Blue.*

Tom loved opera and bought expensive records and played Caruso or John McCormack singing "Sweetly She Sleeps My Alice Fair" on their elegant

Victor Victrola console that had a hand-crank. Minn was not a singer. She had a stern streak, an unforgiving streak. She never quite forgave Tom for failing mathematics. She always said *failure* as if the word itself were an affront to her. On Sunday afternoons, when Tom wanted to relax in his garden and wrestle with his boys, she made him wear a hard collar, tight to the chin. He did not oppose her. Though she was tall and big-boned, she seemed always to be frail, suffering from "the vapors" and periods of lethargy. With his engaging smile, Tom was always devoted to her — shared everything with her — but to Morley he often seemed inexplicably irritable and distant, as if he were harboring a deep sadness, and in his sadness he would sing along with John McCormack, cranking the console handle until Burke joined him, his son's deep baritone shivering plates on the rack in the dining room, their words booming out into the backyard. Tom loved words. He had a relish for words. He would talk enthusiastically about words, the wonder of words (a gift my brother Michael inherited, a cherishing of words beautifully used and the need to explain that cherishing earnestly). Tom wrote poetry. Some of it was satirical verse, which he contributed to two local newspapers, the *Telegram* and the *Moon* (he read all the local newspapers every day, saying the newspapers "were the poor man's university"). As for his serious poems, he wrote out fair copies on the blank backs of CN cost sheets in a sinuous spider-like hand —

> You have your songs whose dear notes echo
>> Like chiming bells that are swung
> High in the dusk of a cloud-swathed steeple
>> But all my songs are sung.

> You have the dreams of your gossamer spinning,
>> Frail as the mists that spread
> Over the olive-green tent of the willows,
>> But all my dreams have fled.

In the evening, when the weather allowed, he weeded his backyard garden of cabbages, peas and rows of corn, strawberries and roses, and it was *his* backyard: though he never became more than a clerk, by 1916, while his boys were in high school, he paid off the mortgage on his house. And on Sundays — shunning church service but wearing his Sunday celluloid collar and his bowler hard hat — he and the two boys would walk to a local bandshell to hear a regimental band — some of the sidewalks were still wooden — or fly one of Morley's model airplanes (he had won a trophy, the Special Prize for Model Aeroplanes from the Long Branch Aviation School in 1916) or watch a lacrosse game on one of the lovely islands across the bay, the lagoons in the bay also being a natural setting for regattas. One afternoon Babe Ruth hit his first professional home run out of Hanlan's Point stadium. Minn, Tom and Morley later cheered in the same stadium, after Burke sang with the Canadian Opera Association in the role of the King in *Aida*. That night, Burke seemed to have a future as a bass baritone, and they all took the ferry back across the bay to the city docks, and then a radial car, walking home past the Don Jail and up Broadview Avenue, which overlooked the Don River and the broad valley. After picking fresh corn from the backyard on the way into the house, they cranked up the victrola, playing their big twelve-inch records . . . Moussorgsky's "Yeremouskka's Cradle Song," Jesse Crawford's organ solo, "La Paloma," Leon Rothier singing *Isis et Osiris* and *Don Carlos*. They chanted along like good soldiers as Taylor Holmes recited on record all of *Gunga Din*, ending in laughter as Six Jumping Jacks sang "I Faw Down An' Go Boom!" As Morley looked back, he saw that it was more than Minn and Tom might have expected . . . but Minn expected a lot: Burke had a future as a singer and she had decided that Morley had the fiber for politics. She had set poems and speeches for him as a boy to memorize. If he forgot his lines, she sent him down the rickety wooden stairs into the dimly lit cellar, chilling in the winter and stifling in the summer, always humid and rank with the smell of damp stone and bare earth, locking the door behind him until he had his lines by heart.

5

"Time to wake up, Mr. Prime Minister."

It was 1925.

Minn liked to call him The Prime Minister. It was her joke. She could joke about politics and the Prime Minister because she was serious. She wanted Morley — who was at the university — to be an orator, a great debater, an established lawyer (completing Tom's dream), and then a politician. She and Morley talked and talked, and early in his adolescence he had started calling her "his old chum" — he had become her confidant, listening to her complaints amidst her sudden bouts of listlessness. "One mistake," she warned Morley, "one failure, if you let it stand, can shape the whole of your life. Your father should not be a clerk. He should be a university man. And he isn't, all because of high school mathematics."

"Wake up!"

He rolled over, got out of bed, and had breakfast with his mother. Tom was gone early, always punctual at his job. Most often breakfast was a sliced grapefruit, toast with jam, and tea, and looking like a casually well-dressed college man (he was never stylish or dapper) he left the house on Wolfrey Avenue, a two-and-a-half-story, red-brick detached home among apple orchards and lace curtain neighbors.

After his summer of baseball and re-writing death notices at the *Star*, Morley had gone back to the university. He had begun writing short stories, some of them dryly comic (the first that he sent out to a magazine was about a man who wanted to run away from his family but he had flat feet and had lost his arch supports so he couldn't). He may have been trying to write stories, but he was on his family's political course: he was now going to engage in an international intercollegiate debate and public forum — The Proposition: *Resolved*, That Any Citizen Should Have The Right At Any Time To Advocate Whatever Economic Or Political Doctrine Or Policy He Chooses. His partner for the AFFIRMATIVE, who met him at Union Station — both of them carrying

Gladstone bags — was Paul Martin, a wall-eyed young man given to ornate and mellifluous rhetoric. Born in the shanty-town Le Breton flats section of Ottawa but brought up in the working-class border town of Windsor, Martin had come to the University of Toronto with a firm hold on his bootstraps: he intended to be someone. Now he and Morley were going to Pittsburgh. The year before, Pittsburgh had defeated Oxford, so they were not expected to do particularly well. They won. It was a surprising international victory for their University. Morley Callaghan and Paul Martin were feted at Hart House — the oak and stone refuge "for young gentlemen" on campus — when they arrived back home, and touted as young men with promising political careers in the Liberal Party. As it turned out, Morley completed law school — out of a sense of obligation to his parents — but he let politics pass.

At a college dance at Newman Hall (named after John Henry, the English Cardinal and intellectual), Morley met Loretto, an art student, the youngest daughter in a family of eight children. Her great-grandfather had come to the country as Corporal Dee from Limerick to fight in the war of 1812. Her clay-pipe-smoking grandmother, a Ryan, had come on a famine boat, the *Governor*, leaving Limerick in 1847 with 147 passengers, of whom 20 — including a Ryan daughter — had died at sea and 20 had been so ill on arrival at Toronto that they were taken directly to hospital. Ryans married into Hamlin immigrants, Hamlins married into Dees. Loretto was a Dee. Her father, a house painter (but also a regular attendant at all the trotting horse tracks), provided his large family with a three-story house of many spacious rooms. The Dees had taste and they had style. They were not shy. As teenagers, two of the girls — Toots and Loretto — had flown in bi-planes; Ambrose owned a motorcycle with a sidecar; and Joe — the youngest — kept a big English bull dog and knew almost every bootlegger in the city. (Joe had gone bald in his early twenties and my aunt Anna said that that was a punishment for having made a Protestant girl pregnant, married her out of necessity, and then divorced her, out of necessity, leaving a son, Phil, loose in the world, to grow up and eventually become a dealer at a black-jack table in Las Vegas.) There were Chinese carpets on the floors of the house, Japanese wall hangings, contemporary paintings (Kane) in gilded frames, and Royal Crown, Susie Cooper and Moorecroft in the china cabinets. Loretto dressed like a Gibson Girl. "She had brown eyes and black hair and a Renaissance profile," Morley said. She — unlike her sisters, who were staunch catechists — read well, could draw, and she wrote little stories for the newspapers. She had an independent playful spirit. Morley seems to have loved her at first meeting, but she came from a family of women who were finickity about men (her three older sisters were so critical that they remained spinsters all their lives). Her dance card for the MEDS Annual Dance and Ball — in the season that she met Morley — was not only full but Morley was not on it. Shortly after O'Banion's death, shortly after cousin Viola had gone from the big and elegant red-brick Dee house on Roxton Road to Detroit, Loretto went to Chicago, alone, prompting a letter from Morley:

> Dear Loretto,
>
> Did you get there? Are you there? Are you reading this and if you're not who is? You know that I oughtn't write to you until I hear from you. When sweethearts go away lovers always wait and hear from them before they write. That is the tradition. And in any event it is good policy because a lover might send a burning hot message to his well beloved, or at least to the address she gave him, only to discover later on that the address had burnt down before she got there.
>
> So in writing this letter I'm just feeling my way.
>
> Come on, be a sport, tell me if you got there. If you'll just tell me I'll write you a letter that will make the sun turn into an iceberg.
>
> There was a three hundred thousand dollar robbery at the Union Station the other day. Mail bags.
>
> Come on now. Write me do you hear?
>
> > Morley
>
> Your lover of inestimable value but alas sadly neglected by you these last few days. What does it avail a man if he have a sweetheart and she turns out to be a baloney?

Morley, having completed his college year, went back to work for a second summer at the *Star*, but he was no longer limited to obituaries, to scalping the dead. He was sent out to cover the hotel beat. Visitors to hotels, he thought, might turn out to be strange characters — characters he could not only use in interviews, but use in the little stories he was writing. He was already working on his own style, stories in which he was trying to get at a new language — a language that could be transparent, a language that would "see" the "thing" so directly that no one would be aware of his style. His style, he told his sparring partner at the university gym — the heavyweight boxer Joe Mahon — was going to be like glass: it would be a counterpuncher's style: he was a counter-puncher who suspected footwork and flash, fancy pugs who believed they should get points for "pressing the fight."

When Morley boxed, he laid back in the weeds of his own mind, trying to understand the other fighter's weakness. He would step into that weakness and hit hard. A clean sharp shot. That's what he wanted prose to be. He remembered one time at twilight sitting at the typewriter in the sunroom of his parents' home. He could smell the lilacs. A night bird cried. A woman's voice came from a neighbor's yard. He wanted to get that down so directly that no reader would ever think of it as literature. He remembered being with a girl one night, and on the way home, walking along, he felt the world had been brought close to him; there seemed to be magic in the sound of his own footsteps, even in the noises of the street cars, all mingled with the girl's kiss, the memory of the little run he had noticed in her stocking, the way she said good-bye to him. He didn't believe any of it had to be written up. There it was, beautiful in itself . . .

Then, one noontime, crossing the street to the Star building, he saw a tall broad-shouldered, brown-eyed man with a heavy black moustache coming out of the building. He was wearing a peak cap. He had a quick, eager, friendly smile. Morley knew he must be the new man from Europe, Ernest Hemingway. "We began to talk. . . . There was a real sweetness in his smile and wonderful availability, and he made me feel that he was eagerly and deeply involved in everything: he had a strange and delightful candor . . . Words came from him not in an eloquent flow but with a quiet, tense authority. 'James Joyce is the greatest writer in the world,' he said. *Huckleberry Finn* was a very great book. Had I read Stendhal? Had I read Flaubert? Always appearing to be sharing a secret; yet watching me intently. He had seemed pleased that I was so approving of the intention behind the great Stendhal style. And there was Melville; if I was interested in symbolism, *Moby Dick* was the great work. And what did I think of Stephen Crane? Did I agree that *The Red Badge of Courage* was a great war book?

"Suddenly he asked how old I was, and I told him, and he said he was seven years older. Then he said solemnly, 'You know, you are very intelligent.'

"'Well, thanks,' I said uncomfortably, for people I knew in Toronto didn't say such things to each other.

"'Do you write fiction?' he asked.

"'A little.'

"'Have you got a story around?'

"'Yes.'

"'When do you come down here again?'

"'On Friday.'

"'Bring the story along,' he said. 'I'll look for you,' and he got up and left . . .

"On Wednesday I was waiting in the library with my story, and within five minutes Hemingway appeared. He had some proofs in his hand. 'Did you bring the story?' he asked. I handed it to him. 'I brought these along,' he said, handing me proofs of the first edition of *In Our Time*, the little book done in Paris on special paper with hand-set type. 'I'll read your story,' he said, 'and you read these.'

"We sat across from each other at the table, reading and not a word was said. His work was just a series of long paragraphs, little vignettes. They were so polished they were like epigrams, each paragraph so vivid, clean and intense that the scene he was depicting seemed to dance before my eyes. Sitting there I knew I was getting a glimpse of the work of a great writer.

"When he saw that I had finished with his proofs he put down my story and said quietly, 'You're a real writer. You write big time stuff. All you have to do is keep on writing.'

"He spoke so casually, but with such tremendous authority, that I suddenly couldn't doubt him. 'Now what about my proofs?' he asked. Fumbling a little, and not sounding like a critic, I told him how impressed I was. 'What do your friends in Paris say about this work?' I asked.

"'Ezra Pound says it is the best prose he has read in forty years,' he said calmly."

6

At St. Peter's, I had been a choirboy, a soprano with a strong voice. I had sung the midnight mass solo at Christmas ("O Little Town of Bethlehem") and the "Regina Coelli" on Easter Sunday. On those days, Morley had come to mass. Otherwise, he slept late into the morning (as he did every day, because he wrote at night after everyone was asleep in bed), while my mother went to mass — but always a little late: the sermons bored her.

Our choirmaster was Harry O'Grady and one year he asked me to sing at the St. Patrick's evening held in the basement auditorium of the church. Father McMahon, my baseball coach, had insisted that my father come and sit at one of the long tables and eat pancakes and sausages for supper, and listen to me sing "Clancy Lowered the Boom" as Harry played the upright piano. My father could not hide his discomfort; Tin Pan Alley Irish tunes turned him queasy, the mere mention of "colleens" drove him to drink, which, of course, was what disquieted him about the Irish — the drink.

I stood up by the piano, lifted my head and, like a trouper, began to sing:

> O that Clancy, O that Clancy,
> Whenever they got his Irish up
> Clancy lowered the boom, boom, boom, boom . . .

I forgot the verse, so Harry (a showman, who played the organ at Shea's movie-house between features) took me back to the chorus:

> *O that Clancy, O that Clancy,*
> *Whenever they got his Irish up*
> *Clancy lowered the boom, boom, boom, boom. . .*

The crowd loved it, thought it was hilarious, and joined in: *boom, boom, boom, boom . . . boom, boom, boom, boom . . .*

My father hunkered down and shook his head. Father McMahon was mortified. He said, as we went home, "Sorry about the pancakes."

The next week, he phoned, saying he had three tickets for a performance of Beethoven, Chopin and Sousa.

"Sousa?" my father said to my mother.

"You must go," my mother said.

We drove in Morley's Chrysler Airflow on a Wednesday night to Jarvis Collegiate. Father McMahon was flushed, buoyant. I was wearing a shirt and tie, Morley had put on his Homburg hat. "We might meet the Prime Minister," he'd said wryly to my mother before leaving.

We sat in the auditorium. The lights went down, there was a lot of shuffling on the floor below us, the scraping of chairs and music stands. And then the lights came up and Morley and the priest gaped. There were twenty or twenty-two students seated in four arcing rows. Each was strapped into an accordion. The conductor lifted his baton, and before Father McMahon could say anything, the orchestra started in on Beethoven: *da-da-ta-DAH, da-da-ta-DAH . . .*

I thought it was wonderful. I had never heard twenty accordions. The band then tried a *polonaise* by Chopin, and at the end of the evening, the crowd stood in place and marched to Sousa, cheering wildly when it was over.

Morley drove Father McMahon home to the church. They said very little. When he got out of the car, the priest said wanly, with a sheepish smile, "Perhaps a penance . . ."

When we got home my mother, full of enthusiasm, said, "Well, how did it go?"

"How old am I?" Morley asked.

"Forty-one," she said.

"Forty-one . . . Sometimes I wonder what city I live in," he said, sending me to bed as he sat down to have a coffee, still wearing his Homburg hat.

Morley didn't talk to many reporters about writing while he was at the *Star*, but one man he did talk to was an older columnist, Greg Clarke. He was "a little guy with a wonderful strut, a lot of charm, and shrewd gray eyes." He often played the imp so that he could be blunt, and he had become a bantering friend of Hemingway's. After Hemingway had given him a signed copy of *Ten Stories & Three Poems*, he had said: "It stinks. You see, it's bumpy. What you gotta do in order to be a great feature writer on *The Star Weekly* is write nice and smooth, you see, and sort of flow your language on. Don't *hammer* it on, for God's sake."

Before leaving Toronto, Hemingway told Callaghan and Clarke that he wanted them to put together separate lists of the writers they thought should be read in their time. It was his way of making clear to Morley what Morley already knew — as a ballplayer and as a lover, he might feel at home in his hometown, but as a writer he was an alien. (Hemingway had told Ezra Pound in a letter that he thought Canada was a "fistulated asshole.") Morley mailed the lists to Hemingway, care of Guarantee Trust in Paris:

For Little Darlings:
    Clarke's Famous Cruises
    Fly Fishing by Sir Edward Grey
    The Little White Birdey by Sir James M. Barrie
    Chapt. 21 of Revelations
    All of Mr. Barrie's works
    Christmas Carol by Mr. Dickens

Great Expectations by Mr. Dickens
The Drama of the Forest by Arthur Heming
Mr. Parkman's entire works
Two Little Savages by Ernest Thompson Seton
All of Charles G.D. Roberts animal stories
The Catalog of Barlow's Ltd.
Jane Eyre
Kipling's Of All the Tribes of Tegumi

MORLEY'S MUDHENS
Anderson's Winesburg Ohio
Chekhov's Ward Six
George Moore
Madame Bovary
The Red and the Black: Stendhal
Spoon River Anthology
The Death of Ivan Ilytch &
Anna Karenina
The Red Badge of Courage
Conrad's Heart of Darkness
Keats' Ode to a Nightingale

With these lists, Morley mailed seven of his own short stories:

1925

Hem,

To get down to brass tacks . . . Are these stories good enough to be recommended by you to some publisher? That is a frank question rather than a prayer . . . I can't help thinking they are ready for publication. Would it be better to send them to every publisher on the continent, or, to lift them from the reach of Canadian clap-trap would I need a preface from a literary gent of the first water?

Morley Callaghan

He waited for a word. None came. He waited. He was sure he would hear from Hemingway. Then one night, after telling Loretto to meet him downtown, he hurried to where she stood under a street lamp. He had a letter from Paris, just a few lines written in a small cramped hand, but it was signed by Ford Madox Ford. Morley's longest story, the only one shown to Ford by Heming-way, was apparently too long for *The TransAtlantic Review*, which Ford was editing in Paris, but he wanted to know if Morley could send him something shorter? "I was full of joy and excitement. Taking Loretto's arm, I hurried her along the street, telling her Ford was a great man in English letters, the collaborator of Joseph Conrad. 'Didn't Hemingway say he would tell them about me in Paris?' I said. 'Well, he's telling them.' Crossing in front of the Catholic cathedral I stopped suddenly. 'I'll go to Paris. I'll take you with me,' I said. Laughing, not quite believing me, she asked how I could get to Paris if I studied law. But that night I knew in my heart that I had touched the world beyond my hometown. In Toronto, Paris indeed became my city of light."

He wrote Hemingway again.

Oct. 11, 1925

Dear Hem —

Here are three stories . . . I've quit the Star. I'm now a law student. Have a lot of time and could do a good deal of writing if I knew how I stood . . . I am not liable to get a swelled head from too much encouragement here. With one or two exceptions, anybody who reads a story of mine maintains a respectful silence. Do you think my stories are too bare?

October 22, 1925

Dear Cal —

The three stories came this morning. I've just finished reading them . . . 1st, "The Wedding Dress" story, which is a hell of a good story . . . Christ don't be an ass and say you could go on and write if you knew how you stood etc. God knows you're in the most depressing and discouraging surroundings — but that's what makes a writer. You have to catch hell . . . If you want encouragement and backing let me tell you right now and you can cut this out and paste it in the front of your prayer book that you have the stuff and will be a hell of a fine writer and probably the first writer that's ever come out of Canada.

Yours always,

Hem

Morley then heard from Robert McAlmon, a Paris editor and publisher. Hemingway had dedicated his first book of stories, *In Our Time,* to him and he had let McAlmon read Morley's stories.

Jan. 8, 1926

Dear Callaghan

Your stories have the odor and timbre of authenticity . . . Both these stories (especially "The Wedding Dress") — all your things for that matter — have a pulse. I published Gertrude Stein's *The Making of Americans* for its pulse . . . Miss Moorehead writes that she is getting out a new number of *This Quarter.* Her address is 22 Boulevard de France, Monte Carlo, Monaco . . . Eliot Paul and another man are publishing a magazine, *transition* by name, I believe, in France. I will give them these things . . . Ezra Pound also will get out a three times a year magazine.

Yours,

McAlmon

On a winter afternoon at twilight, Morley phoned home to ask if there was any mail. His mother told him a parcel had arrived from Paris, "and I asked her to open it. In a moment she said, 'It's a book or a magazine, and it's called *This Quarter.*' And then I heard her gasp, 'Son, your name is on the cover!' I hurried home. That orange-colored cover was the second number of *This Quarter* and it had the names of the contributors in bold black lettering: James Joyce, Ezra Pound, Gertrude Stein, Ernest Hemingway, Kay Boyle, Morley Callaghan . . . " Morley's hands were trembling as he opened the magazine; there was his story, "A Girl with Ambition." After eating dinner with his parents he hurried out to meet Loretto, surging with confidence as he crossed the Queen Street bridge over the Don River. He was twenty-two.

Morley told me about those days late one winter afternoon as we walked across the footbridge over the ravine. He was coming home from the Dominion Store where he had been shopping for groceries — hauling his two-wheeler wire shopping cart that was loaded with plastic bags, the bags bulging with "boil-in-bag meals" and chelsea buns and canned fruit salad — the food a man eats while he is living alone in a big house, his wife having died.

"I was twenty-two when I began to get this curious sense of life falling into place whether I wanted it to or not. I wanted it, of course, I wanted to be published but it was almost as if it was out of my hands, happening in some pattern that was true only to itself beyond my wildest dreams."

He was hunched forward, shrunken, as he pulled his cart across the bridge. His right shoulder (his pitching arm) was lower than his left. A vertebra in his neck had so deteriorated that he was always in pain, a pain he kept to himself. He wouldn't let me haul the cart.

"And it came to me then, at twenty-two, contemplating my world around me, that the artist is almost always instinctively an anarchist. Temperamentally he uses his own eyes, he trusts his own eyes. He doesn't let anyone come along and correct his vision. The fundamentalists who come along, Christian or whoever, they're always trying to correct your vision." The Jesuit house loomed up between the branches of the bare trees on the knoll at the end of the bridge. He paused, just for a step, and then kept on going, still talking.

"The writer who confirms in the reader what the reader already knows is curiously enough a kind of fundamentalist. He has to be, because the real artist always wants to force the reader to see it his way, or her way, and that's what was so extraordinary when I was twenty-two. I was seeing it all my own way but suddenly people who were abroad, people like Hemingway and Pound and William Carlos Williams and Fitzgerald, were eager to see it my way. And they did. Of course," he said, and he laughed, "you also have to realize that if you live long enough and write long enough — if you're a real artist you'll change the way you see things, but the people who were excited by your work, the people who were with you when you were young, they will end up resenting you. Because you'll be denying them their youth. Their youth will have become their conventional wisdom, and there you'll be, the anarchist all over again, all alone, telling them they could not keep up."

Pulling hard on his wire cart full of groceries, he had got at least one good step ahead of me as we came off the bridge and on to our home street. He was excited. One of the Jesuits, a brisk-looking young man standing on their veranda, waved to us as we passed. I wondered if he knew that in the old days a man with a moustache, wearing a pink dress, had often relaxed on that veranda late at night, waiting for the call of a horn or a sign from a passing fellow, a possible friend. We waved back.

August 12

Dear Hem,

I haven't done any writing for some months . . . I'd like to write better but don't want to try and do it self consciously. I used to be able to do it without thinking much about it. Now I am thinking how I am writing. I'd like to do it, have a decent natural style without being so damn conscious of having a style. F.M. Ford thinks of himself almost every sentence he writes. See. It's damn complicated I guess, but I suppose I'll live through it.

Callaghan

Then, Morley got a letter from Ethel Moorehead, the editor of *This Quarter*.

Dear Morley Callaghan

I have put in your story: "The Wedding Dress" tho' I preferred "Last Spring They Came Over" but Robert McAlmon tells me he sent it to Jolas who has taken it for *transition* . . . Keep your best for *This Quarter* for it is the best.

Enclosed please find our check for $19 in payment for your story in our 3rd number.

Yours sincerely,

Ethel Moorehead

"There was an afternoon years ago," Morley said, lathering butter on to a piece of rich chelsea bun, having his instant Maxwell House coffee at a table littered with envelopes and papers, the envelopes being bills for electricity and gas and the telephone . . . "it was an afternoon when I was sitting in the reading room of a public library, reading a little book of Ezra Pound's, and at that time he was just a name to me. It was a book of prose, short notes on reading and writing. The direct, irreverent tone fascinated me. The words didn't seem to be coming from a literary gent. As a boy sitting in a library in Toronto in those days, Pound in Italy was a thousand miles away, yet I remember I felt sure I could talk to him about writing if I ever got the chance, and he'd know what I was talking about . . . "

He heard from Pound, who was in Rapallo, Italy.

23 Oct. 1927

Dear Mr. Callaghan:

If agreeable to you I shall probably use both your "Predicament," and "Ancient Lineage" in No. 3 (*Exile*). Putting them together seems to me to indicate your existence and whereabouts, i.e., state you as an author, better than giving 'em one at a time, as simply stories (plus ou moins anonymes).

> Yours in media
>
> P(ound)

"I was walking around in a trance," Morley said, "rejoicing that Ezra Pound admired my work. Then I heard that Max Perkins at Scribner's in New York, having read a story of mine called 'Amuck in the Bush' in the *American Caravan*, had got hold of the story that Ezra Pound had ('A Predicament') and he asked me for another one. I quickly sent 'A Regret for Youth' to him. Then Perkins asked if I could get Pound to release 'A Predicament' to them. I cabled Pound."

> Dec. 24, 1927

Dear Mr. Pound:

I hope you got my cable advising you not to use the story called "Predicament."

Here is the explanation. My agent in New York, Brandt and Brandt, had sent my stories to Scribner's who had asked to see them. "Predicament," of course, was one of the stories. I had heard that your magazine, *The Exile* was discontinuing because of trouble with the customs or something to that effect. I wrote Robert McAlmon but he said he had heard no word from you. When I got your letter Scribner's had my stories and had decided to take "Predicament" for the magazine, with some others. I had nothing else to send you because my stories were all down in New York, and though I wrote for them, I didn't get any back for some time. I explained to Brandt that you were using the story "Ancient Lineage" so they sent it back, and I'm sending you a story, a short one so you can use it with the other if you want to, called, "The Life of Sadie Hall," which is an experiment after reading "The

American Tragedy." McAlmon liked this story and I like it myself, though I can see that it's not suitable for commercial magazines. It's a contrast to "Ancient Lineage" though. If you don't like it I'll write something else for you. Maybe you'd rather use "Ancient Lineage" alone though.

Would you please let me know?

19 Jan '28

Dear Callaghan:

Exile No. 3. left here for press about a month ago. I got your cable, and omitted "A Predicament": the other has gone to Covici, and I suppose to the printer.

. . . *Exile* runs for those who can't be printed elsewhere, or for stuff no one will touch. Don't, therefore, for Xt' his sake, send anything you can get paid for elsewhere.

Perhaps you'd better ask Brandt's advice, as to whether continuing in *Exile* is advisable. "The Ancient Lineage" has, I suppose gone to press, at any rate it is too late to break up No. 3. and extract it on chance of its being vendible.

It may be that the first year of *Exile* (Nos. 1. – 3.) has done its work. If both *Dial* and *Scribner's* are opening up.

You might let me have your opinion, re/ whether you personally want the stand kept open, and if you think it ought to be kept on, you might say WHY, i.e, what authors there are needing a blow-hole.

yours
P(ound)

Scribner's appeared:

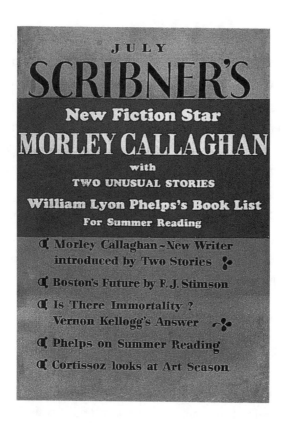

JULY
SCRIBNER'S
New Fiction Star
MORLEY CALLAGHAN
with
TWO UNUSUAL STORIES
William Lyon Phelps's Book List
For Summer Reading

❦ Morley Callaghan~New Writer
introduced by Two Stories ❦

❦ Boston's Future by F. J. Stimson

❦ Is There Immortality ?
Vernon Kellogg's Answer ❦

❦ Phelps on Summer Reading

❦ Cortissoz looks at Art Season

"For some years," Morley said, as he got up to boil water for another cup of instant coffee, buttering another chelsea bun, "Pound came to represent a troubling question among American intellectuals. Could a great artist be forgiven — because of his art — for his crimes against the state? How far can a man go in condemning his own country? Over the years the climate changes. I don't think Pound was ever crazy. Can you imagine what a young Pound would be saying today about America and what he would have said about the Vietnam War? Pound may have had no sense of patriotism — as a communist citizen understands the word — but I'll tell you what he did have. A passionate integrity in his thoughts about prose and poetry, the meaning of words, and the use of language, a basic necessity for civilization. It got down to this with me, and I'm sure with a thousand other writers too; from the beginning he helped make me feel the importance of the single word and its relationship with the next word. Not long before he died, I heard about Pound again. He had been released from the hospital for the insane and he was living in Italy. An English priest, a Jesuit who was traveling through Canada, had come to see me and we talked about Rome, and he said suddenly, 'Oh, I had a long talk with Ezra Pound.' 'Really,' I said, because I had heard that Pound wasn't talking to anyone but just fell into long silences. 'What did you talk about?' They had talked about many things, the priest said, and then Pound had said suddenly, 'What do you think of St. Anselm's proof of the existence of God?' I was charmed. As I remember it, St. Anselm's proof came from the idea of perfection. Perfection. God, as the artist? The perfect anarchist. Somehow, the question seemed right — coming as it did from Ezra in his old age, thinking about perfection as he got ready to die."

7

Morley was in New York following on the publication of his first novel, *Strange Fugitive*. He had a fine, warm meeting on a Friday with Perkins and the Scribner's sales force, and he had been fêted on Friday night by William Carlos Williams, who told him the novel was so troubling it had kept him awake all night, but on the weekend he was alone. Stranded. Loretto was in Chicago.

Strange Fugitive was a novel about a bootlegger, the first novel in America in which the hero was a gangster and a murderer. *The New York Times* said: "So fresh and vivid is Mr. Callaghan's style, so sharp and convincing his characterization, so sparkling his dialogue, that one has the urge to place the laurel crown on his brow without more ado . . . No one interested in what is really alive and vital in the writing of the younger generation of novelists can afford to be ignorant of Mr. Callaghan's work."

On a brisk Sunday afternoon, he stood on Fifth Avenue in front of Scribner's Bookstore and saw the window stacked with his novel. He was incredulous. He counted the copies: twenty-six. Like a step-pyramid. Pale green, pale purple, with an ink drawing of his head, sporting his new black moustache. He sent a thousand dollars home to his mother (who bought some penny stocks, and because they were penny stocks, she thought she was being prudent).

He walked up the Avenue in the sunlight as far as the park, then he crossed over to the little square and the fountain by the Plaza. No one was sitting on the benches. It was too cold. The park looked bleak in the sunlight. Entering the Plaza he thought of Scott Fitzgerald. Yes, Scott Fitzgerald. He walked slowly through the marble halls, past the Palm Court where a harpist was playing a Cole Porter tune, past the desk, and out through the 57th Street entrance, full of wonder at how everything was unfolding, especially for him . . . wondering at Fitzgerald, because on the Friday past Perkins had taken him totally by surprise by telling him that it was not Hemingway and certainly not Pound, but Scott Fitzgerald — a man he had never met — who had first urged Morley's stories on Scribner's.

Again, he thought it all seemed to have a pattern of its own making. He went back to his hotel. There he had a letter from Loretto who had returned home from Chicago.

Thursday morning,

Dear Boy Owizya: —

The evenings are years without you. Sunday night I got back to Toronto about 9:30 and my eyes were woozy from the motion of the train and I felt sleepy; thought all I would have to do was drop on the bed and sleep. I crawled into bed prepared for slumber, but the little devil eluded me. I ambled and rambled all over the bed, pulled the covers on and pulled them off, and after two hours tussle I went downstairs and had some bread and jam and tea . . . you see how I am just existing until you hold me in your arms again and kiss me. I'll never let you go away from me again, so you had better make the most of your time while you have the opportunity. When you come back I am going to put a chain around your waist and mine and you will never be able to move without me. I insist on being within reach of your arms.

After getting into bed Monday night, with an angelic smile on my face and hands folded under my head, I pictured myself in your arms, you holding me tight and kissing me. I surprised myself by letting out a contented little grunt and snuggling down farther into the bed. I miss you very much and when I see you I will run and throw my arms around you and smother you. I will hold you so tight I will be able to feel every rib in your body, even through the stomach. It may melt away in the heat . . .

Your own

Loretto

Morley took the first train home. He and Loretto went to supper in a stylish café in the King Edward Hotel in which Burke was singing. It was a glad night. He sang "You're the One I Care For" and "When the Organ Played at Twilight" for them:

> *That old fashioned song in the twilight,*
> *Will always bring memories of you,*
> *I think of your eyes and the shy light,*
> *I saw when you said, "I'll be true."*

Burke was about to go to Los Angeles with his singing coach. The next day Morley wrote to Perkins.

Nov. 14, 1928

Dear Perkins,

Here is something that I thought you might tell me about. Do you think *The New Yorker* would be a good magazine for my stories? They have never printed fiction before, but are going to start with that story of mine called "An Escapade."

Morley Callaghan

Nov. 26, 1928

Dear Callaghan:

As for *The New Yorker* I think it has a very excellent type of circulation from your standpoint and ours . . .

Maxwell E. Perkins

Morley's first collection of stories, *A Native Argosy,* appeared in the spring of 1929, a few weeks before he got married.

Dear Callaghan:

. . . Sinclair Lewis called me up yesterday to ask about you and to speak with tremendous enthusiasm about the book. He means to write about it somewhere. He wants to know you, and when you come down, we ought to manage it.

Maxwell E. Perkins

Morley did not go out carousing on the night before he married. He went boxing (he didn't look like a fighter — Ford Madox Ford said he could always see Morley coming, "perambulating his paunch before him"). His friend and sparring partner, Joe Mahon, was twenty pounds heavier, a man who had won the international intercollegiate heavyweight championship at West Point. Circling around big Mahon, Morley noticed a grim smile on his face. He realized Mahon was trying to blacken his eyes. "He kept jabbing at my eyes. It tickled his sense of humor to think of me showing up at my wedding with a black eye. Just before we quit, he, in his eagerness and frustration, swung so hard to my head that when he missed, for the first time in all our boxing, he fell flat on his face." Morley went home with a little strut to his stride.

They married in April of 1929 in her parish church of St. Francis. Loretto wore a gown of white satin with Chantilly lace medallions on the bodice and skirt, the skirt studded with pearls. Morley wore a single-button morning coat — the button riding on top of his little paunch — and pearl gray spats. Burke sang during the signing of the register. The evening newspaper, with a bold charm, said, "Mr. and Mrs. Callaghan will leave immediately for New York and Paris . . . Mrs. Callaghan will not only be Mr. Callaghan's inspiration in his writing, but also his friend and critic, as she has been since she met him."

Three days later, they sailed for Paris on a small liner, the *Oleander*. "On the way to Paris," Morley said, "we stopped over in New York and had lunch with Perkins . . . he began to grumble about Americans who went to Paris to become expatriated. It was all wrong, and he hoped we wouldn't stay too long in Paris. Just the same we were to be sure to look up Scott Fitzgerald . . . Nothing formal was needed. Just walk in on Scott and he would be delighted." And then Perkins said he had heard that Hemingway, in some French town, had been watching the middleweight champion of France in a bout with some hapless incompetent fighter and the champion, making a monkey out of him, had been punishing him badly. And after the bout had ended, Hemingway had jumped into the ring and knocked out the champion. "The story sounded incredible to me," Morley said, "but Perkins obviously believed it."

In Paris, Morley and Loretto rented a room in a hotel and then moved to a tiny flat above a grocery store at Square de Port Royale, rue de la Santé, Bâtiment No. 2 — in the shadow of the walls of the great Paris prison. Being near the prison seemed right to them because on the boat they had become friendly with a big lonely priest who over a period of ten years had walked out of Death Row to the execution chamber with sixteen men. The priest suffered from fevers. He had been persuaded to take a three-month leave of absence. "No prison," he told Morley, as they stood together on deck talking about Thomas Aquinas and the efficacy of love, "should be built that denies an inmate some wild hope of escape." The priest, the inmate of his own nightmares, had changed clothes three times a day on the ship, breaking out into sweats that left him soaking wet. The priest also had a thirst. He had run up the biggest bar bill on board. With a strained smile he had said as they parted, "Ah well, you'll forget all about me and life on Death Row."

They thought about him almost every morning because their hotel window looked directly down on the stone court of a local hospital's Hall of the Dead. Every morning, five or six funeral processions came out of the yard, moving along the cobblestoned street, bells tinkling, the line of mourners — mostly small women in shapeless black dresses — moving awkwardly behind the high hearse and its indifferent coachman wearing a tricornered hat. Loretto thought the funerals were quaint. "Don't be surprised if I start breaking out in sweats," Morley said. The silver tinkling of bells filled him with a foreboding.

Then, living on the rue de la Santé, they crossed under the gaze of the proprietor of their flat, a woman — her cheeks red and her teeth white — who wore the same black silk dress every day as she sat at her desk. Chez Madame Bochniak. Morley and Loretto always smiled at her, anxious to be friendly and anxious to appear at ease, though each day began under the eye of that woman in black in the shadow of the prison wall. Once out in the sunlight, however, they visited museums, went to the movie houses to learn French, sat at the cafés at the corner of Montparnasse and Raspail, expecting they might casually meet writers in the Quarter.

"On one corner was the Dôme," Morley wrote in his memoir. "It was like the crowded bleachers of an old ballpark, the chairs and the tables were set in rows extending as far as the next café, the Coupole. It had an even longer terrace. Opposite the Dôme, on the other corner, was the Rotonde . . . and by an intersecting side street was a small café, the Séléct, which was open all night. We sat at the Coupole . . . As it got darker, the whole corner seemed to brighten and take on its own exotic life . . . Paris was around us . . .

and Loretto amused herself, doing little pencil and ink sketches of men and women seated close by us on the terrace, little torn scraps of paper,

this was her Paris, and it offered to us what it had offered to men from other countries for hundreds of years; it was a lighted place where the imagination was free."

He had Hemingway's address in his pocket but he waited for a while before calling on him. He wanted to get his bearings, his balance, and he also wanted "to be with his girl" (it was one of the endearing things about their love that till she died in her eighties, Morley always referred to Loretto as "his girl"). Late at night they wandered over to the river and went along the quai. He did the thing he used to do back home, he whispered lines of Poe: "And thou were all to me, love, a fountain and a shrine . . ." And then as they stopped and stood watching the river, Loretto hummed "I Can't Give You Anything But Love, Baby." They were eager and confident, though the distant, faint ringing of bells in the night reminded Morley of the morning funerals.

Of a late afternoon, after coming home from walking the little streets and alleys of the Left Bank — "getting the lay of the land" — Loretto washed their socks and stockings and handkerchiefs in the sink while Morley worked on a new novel, sitting in his bare feet, bent over a tiny portable Remington type-writer (the novel — which would be called *It's Never Over* — opens with a man "outside the jail, gaping at the window of the death-cell high up on the wall"). It was summer and the late sun was hot. Loretto flattened the handkerchiefs on the window panes to dry, with a perfect press . . . sometimes two, or three . . . or after three days, four or five. One afternoon, about a week after they had impetuously dropped by the Scott Fitzgerald flat unannounced (and Fitzgerald, a little drunk, had stood on his head, trying to impress Morley), Scott came by their flat without warning, wondering if they didn't want to go over to the Ritz for drinks and get to know each other a little better. "Then," Morley said, "his eye caught the handkerchiefs smoothed out on the windowpanes . . . Childlike in his curiosity, he approached the window, touched one of the handkerchiefs and turned to Loretto. 'What is it? What are you doing with these handkerchiefs, Loretto?'

"'Just this,' she said. Tearing one of the stiffly dried handkerchiefs from the pane, she calmly folded it, and it looked starched and neat. Since she had no facilities for ironing, she said, this was the method employed. And Scott, musing, was simply delighted . . . Oh, he said, he would certainly use it in a story. Day by day, he said, he sought out fresh little details like this one for use in his stories . . . "

Then, about one week later, Robert McAlmon set up a supper for them with James Joyce. As they got dressed to meet Joyce in the Trianon, peeling handkerchiefs off the window panes, Madame came upstairs and informed them that they had been investigated by the police. A sharp-eyed prison guard, stationed in the yard across the street, had worried about the changing white patches on the window panes, had worried that they were signals to a prisoner and he had spoken to the police and the police had spoken to Madame, asking, "What are they doing with those white patches of cloth? What do they mean?"

Madame, heaving with laughter, assured Morley and Loretto that she had convinced the police that they were not criminals or criminal accomplices. "The man is only a young writer, harmless," she had said, "yes, harmless," sure that Morley would be pleased with her.

Cleared of any connection to convicts who might have been dreaming of escape, and happy to know that they were regarded as harmless, they went to the Falstaff to drink a toast to their freedom and then — full of anticipation — went on to the Trianon, a restaurant known for its fine food near Gare Montparnasse. They sat down to have supper with James Joyce and his wife, Nora.

"He was," Morley wrote, "small-boned, dark with fine features. He had thick glasses and was wearing a neat dark suit. His courtly manner made it easy for us to sit down, and his wife, large-bosomed with a good-natured face, offered us a massive motherly ease. They were both so unpretentious I couldn't say, 'Sir, you are the greatest writer of our time,' for Joyce immediately became too chatty, too full of little bits of conversation . . . his voice was soft and pleasant. His humor, to my surprise, depended on puns. Even in the little snips of conversation, he played with words lightly."

After supper, they were invited to the Joyce apartment, and Morley walked along the narrow, dark street beside Joyce. But, as he did all his life when he was excited, Morley began to talk and walk rapidly, thinking Joyce was beside him, absorbed in what he was saying. Then he heard the anxious pounding of a cane on the cobblestones, and turning he saw Joyce far behind him, groping his way along the sidewalk. He had forgotten that Joyce could hardly see.

When they got to the Joyce apartment, Morley found the living room was all in a middle-class pattern, with a brown-mottled wallpaper, a mantel, and a painting of Joyce's father hanging over the fireplace. Mrs. Joyce brought out a bottle of Scotch and put a record on their machine. Morley and Loretto looked at each other in astonishment. Aimée Semple McPherson, the pretty, seductive blond evangelist from California, who actually was a Canadian, was preaching a sermon. She had a warm, low, throaty and imploring voice. As they listened, Loretto and Morley exchanged glances, aware that the Joyces were watching them intently, while McPherson's voice rose and fell in a tone of ecstatic abandonment, taking on an ancient familiar rhythm, becoming like a woman's urgent love moan as she begged, "Come, come on to me. Come, come on to me. And I will give you rest . . . and I will give you rest. Come, come . . . " Morley and Loretto averted their eyes, afraid the Joyces would know what they were thinking, but Joyce had caught their glance and he chuckled, and Mrs. Joyce burst out laughing. Nothing had to be explained. Grinning mischievously, in enormous satisfaction with his small success, Joyce poured them another drink.

Before much more could be said, Joyce's daughter and son came in. It was time to leave. They shook hands, said good-bye. Out on the street, Morley, feeling an extraordinary elation, cried, "O tell me all about Anna Livia! I want to hear all about Anna Livia. Well, you know Anna Livia. Tell me all. Tell me now." They didn't want to go back to their apartment, to the prison wall and the tinkling of bells. They went to the Coupole, saluting the great statue of Balzac by Rodin as they passed into the ocher light of the almost empty dining hall. At the bar, after a glass of champagne, a friend asked Loretto if she could do the Charleston. She got up on a table and danced as if she were on stage at Big Jim Colosimo's. She danced, criss-crossing her knees, slapping her hands on her knees. A young, sandy-haired man, a Serbian count who had been sitting alone all night at the bar holding a single long-stemmed red rose in his hand, watched her. He ordered more champagne, but he was told by the bartender that the dancing girl was Morley's wife. "With a shy, yet gallant bow to me from a distance," Morley said, "he asked if he had permission to give Loretto the rose."

8

There was no doubt about it. Angels had perched on Morley's shoulders, that's what he'd written to his friend, Joe Mahon. "I walk around with these big happy birds with angel wings pleading my case to the world." He felt that there was an unreality about the way everything had fallen into place for him: Hemingway, *This Quarter,* Joyce, *transition,* Pound, Scribner's, Paris . . .

Morley and Loretto had stayed in Paris for five months, meeting everyone in the Quarter . . . he'd boxed regularly with Hemingway at the American Club and they'd gone to Chartres and Biarritz and then there had been the knockdown and the quarrel, with Hemingway spitting blood in Morley's face and Morley retreating into a silence about their fight that lasted some thirty years . . . a nursing of wounds, a mistake of mis-placed dignity. A refusal by either Hemingway or Morley to reach across silence.

Returning from Paris, Morley and Loretto lived for nearly a year in an old stone farmhouse in Pennsylvania. He had friends there, the writers Josephine Herbst, John Herrmann and William Carlos Williams, and Nathan Asch, son of the great Yiddish novelist, Sholem Asch. Morley was going to buy the farmhouse and become a permanent resident until he took a close look and discovered that all the foundations were worm-holed and rotten. They went home to Toronto for the birth of my brother, Michael, and then moved back to New York and settled into rooms in the Madison Hotel.

He had published *It's Never Over* (his "prison" novel — Fitzgerald called it his "deathhouse masterpiece") and then a novella, *No Man's Meat* — about lesbian lovers — and another novel, *A Broken Journey* in 1932. He felt entirely at ease in New York. "Ideas were alive on the street. You could hear their footsteps."

One weekend, feeling expansive and confident, he brought his mother and father down to Manhattan by train, expecting his mother, though she was crofter country by upbringing, to take to the city because she had a firm brashness about her, while he thought his father, so reluctant and often retiring, would be cowed by the city's pace and canyons.

Minn settled into the hotel as if she were at home. (My brother remembers that she brought him a splendid red toy train. He set it up on the floor by her feet where she could watch him play.) Morley went out walking with his father. It was a walk he wrote about: "My father was following me a few steps behind in a way that annoyed me. He was looking up the avenue at how the line of the buildings cut like a cavern into the horizon. Certain it was making him feel humble, I said lightly, 'Quite a city, eh? Makes you feel strange.' He seemed puzzled about something, but then he said quietly, 'No, it isn't that it seems strange. It doesn't seem half as strange as I thought it would.'"

Morley assumed that his father would be wide-eyed and wondering, not just at the city but at how easy his son was on the sidewalks of New York. He said tartly, "Well, I got a big kick out of it the first time I looked around."

"I mean, it reminds me of London," his father told him. "It's different, of course, but it gives me some of the same feeling, maybe it's just the big-city feeling London had."

Morley had let slide from his mind that his father had come across the Atlantic on a ship as a twelve-year-old child from London. Morley didn't know what to say. He suddenly wondered what his father had been like as a child.

"I'd love to see Wall Street. Could we go there?" his father asked.

They took the subway downtown. They walked through the narrow streets of the financial district, his father grabbing his arm, pointing at things. Once he asked Morley the name of a big new building, and when Morley couldn't tell him, he darted across the street, peered at the brass plate near the door, and then he bounded back through the traffic, with Morley standing on the sidewalk, sure that he'd be killed, feeling helpless.

"But it was when we were down at the waterfront," Morley wrote, "looking across the river at the tugboats and the sunlight on Brooklyn, that we really began to feel closer together. My father had been sniffing the air, smiling to himself and peering in the doors of seamen's taverns as we walked along. Suddenly, he took an extra sniff, his face wrinkled up in a wide grin, and he stood still, crying out, 'It smells like a fish market!' We were at Fulton Street Market and the smell of fish was very strong. On the road there were little bonfires of refuse. Grim, old, slow-moving seamen passed us on the sidewalk. 'Yes sir, it's a fish market.'

"'Sure it's a fish market, but what about it?'

"'I haven't smelled anything like it in years.'

"'Just a stench to me. Let's move along.'

"'Isn't it lovely? It reminds me of Billingsgate in London,' he said. 'When I was a boy I often used to go down to the market.' Turning, he got the smell of fish again, looked across the river, took a deep breath and was delighted.

"'Why didn't you ever mention being a kid in London before?'

"'I must have forgotten it. It seems such a long time ago.'"

Perplexed, Morley felt that he knew little or nothing about his father, that somehow he had lost sight of him, but as they kept on walking they began to share in the discovery of broken-down poolrooms in the Lower East Side, and they liked the swarm of Italian, Chinese and Jewish faces. "And it was not nearly as strange for my father, the man walking beside me in the good, freshly-pressed blue serge suit and the hat on the back of his head, as it was for me — foreign faces, bright colors, dirty streets, the odors of a seaport he had long ago forgotten, all had come alive for him down there by the waterfront. Again and again he said, 'When I was a boy,' and the softness and innocence of his voice left me full of wonder. Is this, I thought, what he was like when he was a kid? Maybe he'd always had an easy, curious way about him."

Feeling a little shaken, feeling that he had not looked closely enough into his father's face and that his father had kept something precious from him, something they could have shared and delighted in, Morley took him by the arm. "Let's go back to the hotel," he said, "and maybe Loretto and I should go back home, too," he added, a restless excitement growing in him, a great hunger to know what his father had dreamed of as a child . . .

In the mid-thirties, having moved back to Toronto, Morley wrote three extraordinary novels: *Such Is My Beloved, More Joy in Heaven* (a story based on the notorious bank robber, Red Ryan, who — Aunt Anna maintained — was a cousin through our coffin boat Chicago Ryans), and *They Shall Inherit the Earth*. In keeping his family alive through the Depression, he had sold some twenty short stories to *The New Yorker* alone. But in 1938, one year after I was born, acedia, a dropsy of the spirit, got to him and he panicked. The Spanish Civil War, Stalin and the show trials, and the rise of Hitler left him profoundly cynical. In his staggered thought he saw not grace, but thugs, liars and frauds abounding on all sides. His friend, Jacques Maritain, wrote that there was a "surging up of irrationalism as an elemental force getting rid of all doctrine, truth, and rational structure . . . (causing) intellectual conviction to dissolve and rot." Morley saw rot and loss of conviction all around him. Suddenly, he couldn't write stories. "I had either lost my talent or no longer had anything to say." He had no income. He tried to borrow money, using his car as security, his stylish Chrysler Airflow.

"I can remember," he wrote, "the summer night when I was out on the street at twilight, walking slowly up and down in front of my house, asking

myself what was going to happen to me. I was broke. I couldn't write anything anyone wanted to read. Was I a morning glory? After all the quick early
successes, was I all washed up? I felt an apprehensive chill, thinking of the
new life ahead, and then a moment of blind panic bewildered me and left me
in a sweat."

For weeks he was morose, scuffling about the house, incapable of doing
any work. He hated his apathy. He tried to "sit, sit, recover and be whole."
Joyce died. Poland fell. FDR said he would never enter the war. A friend in
Nova Scotia drowned in a river that everyone said flowed backwards. "Of
course, that was an optical illusion," he said, "but her death wasn't." He rummaged through his desk drawers. He turned up an old play that had aroused
some earlier interest in New York and he borrowed money on a life insurance
policy and went to work. Loretto's sister, Toots, payed the rent.

He got up late every morning, had breakfast, got dressed and walked up
to the corner to get the noon paper and came home, took off his blue serge suit
coat, slipped on a tweed sports jacket, put his small old portable Underwood
that had been with him on rue de la Santé in Paris on a table by the front window, and opened a pack of Players. He became a chain smoker, smoking each
weed down to his staining fingertips, lighting a fresh cigarette from each tiny
butt. He bought 5¢ newsprint scribblers in Woolworth's and tore the scribbler
pages in half (a habit he kept until he died), typing, rewriting, cramming the
margins with a tiny scrawl, the letters half-made (a "w" always a "u"). Arrows
tracked arrows. Loretto puzzled over the pages, typing clean copy at the dining
room table on a small old Remington portable.

Within the year, the Theater Guild in New York had taken an option on
the play. It was called *Going Home,* about a son hoping to take revenge on his
hated father. For a year and a half the Guild paid him advance royalties. He
gave Toots her money and paid the rent. He thought he had curbed his panic.
He wrote another play, sold it to two young producers, and drew more option
money, expecting to have two plays produced on Broadway in one season. He
still had no inclination to write stories but he felt buoyant, he was stiltwalking,

and it seemed ridiculous to him that he had once lain in bed and smelled failure in his bones.

"Those were exciting days," he said, remembering all the train trips to New York. He liked riding trains, sleeping in a lower berth. The soothing *clickety clickety clickety click,* the nighttime calming coolness of the window glass against his cheek, whispering with wry self-mocking amusement, *It is not without hope that we suffer and we mourn,* lines his mother had quoted at hard moments all her life. He liked coming into New York in the morning, stepping briskly into the big hall of the station. "I recall meeting Lawrence Langner, who, with Theresa Helburn, *was* the Theater Guild, under the clock at Grand Central Station so we could go to his home in Westport, Connecticut, and later look at an actress who might be right for my play. It was a little after the time of Dunkirk, and on the train, still being coldly objective about the war, I told Langner that the British, having been driven off the Continent, had lost the war, but they could still be on the winning side, if the U.S. entered the war. He was angry. We had a violent argument. Yet we looked at our actress that night and rejected her, and I could still believe all was going well."

After the bombing of Pearl Harbor, FDR took America into the war. Morley wasn't surprised. He believed FDR had always intended to get into the war. "It was all an act," he said. "Everyone was on stage. Even Generals had begun to talk of the Theater of War. North Africa became a Theater. For daring young men. The Eastern Front had become a Theater. There was even a theater at the Terezhin concentration camp.

"I was obsessed with the stage. All the daring young men on flying trapezes. I would meet my agent and try and figure out when my plays would open on Broadway. I often met William Saroyan at three in the afternoon and did not leave him until five in the morning. I sat around with Saroyan and the boys in Lindy's. That's where I met Betsy Blair. She was in the chorus of *Panama Hattie* and Gene Kelly was courting her, and so Bill Saroyan and I went with them to Ralph's, a joint that was popular with theater people, and she ended up in one of Saroyan's plays, playing *St. Agnes of the Mice.* Betsy and Gene got married, and over the years — when Gene was living in Hollywood — I'd hear from him, how he was still reading my books. I liked it, that he was reading my books. But back then, the movie star, whoever he was, who was supposed to be in my play, he suddenly quarreled with his studio and returned to the movies. The Guild dropped my play. I told myself I still had the other play. I had read in the New York papers that my two producers were now casting, a director had been signed, so I went home and waited to hear when rehearsals would begin."

The family went to my aunts' Lake Simcoe cottage. (It had been paid for by Aunt Toots, a cheerful, almost good-looking woman who warded off bitterness and disappointment by putting herself through bouts of prayer: after Loretto married, she went into a Carmelite nunnery, prepared to take a lifelong vow of cloistered silence; months later, she came out, a weary disconsolate wreck, and became the trusted private secretary to a very successful mining promoter: he was so devoted to her that he wrote discreet, but chaste, love notes, calling her Molly, and when he died — their relationship never sexually consummated — he left her a small fortune, which was challenged by his family. On the advice of her oldest brother Phil, an accountant and champion lawn bowler — married to the cake-baking Alice — she yielded her rights, being told by Phil that a fight would require not only "too much meanness" but would call into public question the propriety of her relationship with the promoter: it was the triumph of lace curtain Irish respectability.) I played croquet on the lawn with Toots and my other aunts, all fed by a Japanese cook who served the "girls" — and visiting priests — martinis or gin with lime rickey every afternoon at 5:30.

But Morley sat alone in the city in the summer heat and he waited. He wasn't writing. He was waiting. He realized one day that he had hidden all his ties in the bottom of a drawer. He had done this after seeing a newspaper cartoon of a haberdasher who had hanged himself. He thought this was funny as he hung his ties on the tie-rack again, but he had a nagging hunch that the panic was on him once more, that he was coming unhinged.

Wyndham Lewis had come to Toronto to get away from the war and he was living in room 11A in the drably respectable Tudor Hotel on Sherbourne Street, across the road from the Selby Hotel where Hemingway had housed for a while. He called Morley. Morley lunched with him, and though he found Lewis to be shaken, nervous, middle-aged and graying, a man in need of a little lift, Morley was wary and on edge. And antagonistic. For no good reason. He couldn't get Lewis in focus. He couldn't get his own feelings in focus. He took Lewis to Earl Birney's flat. Lewis turned up his nose at the poet's sparse furnishings. Morley took him to E.J. Pratt's fine big house. Pratt was a poet and a professor. "This is more like it," Lewis said, taking a drink of gin. Morley resented his tone bitterly. Gin is a charwoman's drink, he thought, remembering his mother had always told him that. Still, he didn't know why he was so bitter. Maybe because Lewis had told him the town was a "sanctimonious ice-box."

He met Lewis at supper parties — literary parties where the men wore "black tie" and the women wore gowns. He tried to be friendly. He couldn't. He was angry. Angry about Lewis snubbing Birney, though he didn't really care about Birney. Then Lewis wrote admiringly about Morley's short stories, saying, "These are tales very full of human sympathy — a blending of all the events of life into a pattern of tolerance and of mercy," and he asked Morley if he could paint his portrait. Morley declined. He knew it was ridiculous to decline. He was spiteful though he had nothing to be spiteful about. He admired Lewis' paintings.

He felt sure that he was in trouble. It was all around him. There were aphids on his mother's roses, his father's corn turned mealy. He woke up one morning and couldn't see. For an hour he thought he was in a waking dream. But he was blind. Stone cold. (In the early 1970s I went through the same thing — that curious dovetailing in our lives, father and son — losing my sight . . . being led by a friend out of an old trattoria on Yonge Street, Luigi's, almost glad after weeks of tension that I could not see, tired of seething in angry silence at so many betrayals.) Was it blind panic? Glimmers of light came back, but Morley was afraid. He heard hilarious lovers walking the streets and resented them. He brooded on his fear and tried to accept that he might be blind for the rest of his life. There was so much that he hadn't seen. He still didn't know anything about his father's childhood. He wondered what he knew about his own childhood, about his own children. He felt his way into bed and, to his surprise, slept. He awoke, his sight returned.

He got on a night train for New York. In the morning, when his two producers found him waiting, there was such embarrassed pain in their eyes that he felt he had acted unfairly by showing up without warning in their office. "But they were men of sensibility and gentleness, and they took me into their big, inner, broadloomed office and confessed that one of the principal backers, just before putting up the money, had got drunk and boarded a plane for the west coast, and his wife, who tracked him down, had had him committed to a sanitarium as an alcoholic, and, of course, she had cancelled his investment in the play."

Morley sat in the broadloomed office and considered the matter as if it were a normal occurrence. "It was very comfortable in that handsome office," he wrote, "and my young producers were men of delicate insight and consoling voices. They knew how I felt, I knew how they felt, and though we talked about finding another backer, I could tell they had shopped all around and the jig was up. They had taste, discernment and style, but it was known they hadn't made money in the theater.

"My mood bewildered me. I was so heavy hearted that I could hardly smile. I was filled with superstitious uneasiness, a kind of recognition of the fact that failure was following me. I had seen it coming two years ago on the street outside my house. It had caught up with me. For two years I had been on the run, kidding myself that my luck had changed. Now I had to go home to my family. I was right back where I had been, waiting for panic to possess me."

He had friends in New York, a professor and his young wife, living on 26th Street, and before going home on the train he called on them. He told them about the collapse of his plays. "I began to make ironic jokes about the two young producers, and then about the alcoholic angel. But finally my friend stood up, staring at me, white-faced, his mouth twisted. 'Cut it out,' he pleaded.

"'What's the matter?'

"'I don't know,' and he groped for words and then blurted out, 'This offends me. Something is wrong. You shock me.'

"'What can I do? What should I be doing?'

"'I would be more sympathetic if you were out somewhere dead drunk and lying in the gutter. Both plays! It's incredible. And you sit there turning it all into a farce.'

"Suddenly I felt relieved. Because my friend was disgusted, I knew he couldn't smell panic on me. I felt no panic at all. I became almost apologetic. I had to explain that I understood what had happened to me. I'd tried to change the direction of my work, and I had failed. My number hadn't come up. I was going to go on writing, but I didn't know which way I would turn, and I didn't know what I would say to Loretto when I went home. I understood, too, that out of pure sympathy my friends were trying to stir up rage and despair in me. Looking back on that night, a turning point in my life, I think I avoided the dreadful chill a man feels when he wonders if he is marked for failure by saying to myself, 'Well, here I am. If I'm demoralized, let's get it over with. It has happened before. It may happen again. I'm still here.'

"I accepted failure as a normal part of my life. I became aware that there might be other times — panic times — and they would be like little deaths, but as long as I didn't end up liking those deaths — that was the great trick; not to develop a secret love for those little deaths — then the spark in my spirit would flame again because I wanted to remain alive."

Morley phoned the cottage and told us to come down from the lake. We — my mother, brother and Uncle Ambrose — came home. I remember it was raining. There was a sour smell in the house, as if the windows hadn't been open for a long time. He said it wasn't the windows, it was the radio. He had gone out, leaving the radio on, and didn't come back for three days, and the transformer had overheated and blown up. There were stains all over the walls. Ambrose said he would paint the room. My mother never asked Morley where he had been for three days. He said he was feeling fine but he had a hunch he wasn't ready to start writing stories. He romped on the floor with me and my brother. I was six years old, and one day I wandered off and was found by a policeman several miles away in the Woolworth's store where Morley bought his scribblers. The policeman took me home. (I have resented the police all my life.)

I was warned that if I wanted to go for a long walk, I should walk around my own block. I was warned not to step off the curb unless I looked right, and then left. I was warned not to be friendly with men who were too friendly. I was warned not to feed nuts to squirrels, that they were near-sighted and would bite my fingers without intending to, and they carried diseases. I was warned not to think too much about girls. I hadn't thought about girls at all. What I thought was that big people — parents, uncles, aunts and policemen — were afraid. They had to be afraid, they were so full of warnings.

Morley got a call. He went down east to Halifax to work on a film with the Navy. He went out into the gray Atlantic on one of the sleek corvettes that shadowed destroyers, trying to protect them from Nazi submarines. My mother was lonely. Now she was like the other wives on the street: alone. Morley seldom phoned and he wasn't much of a letter writer. She began to dance with me in the living room, teaching me to sing, *I saw my baby there, stretched out on a long white table, oh so cold, so bare* . . . She told me she loved to listen to the trombone player Jack Teagarden sing that song, "Saint James Infirmary." I liked the song, too (and would sing it with my brother over Morley's body in the graveyard during his interment in 1990), and I wished I had a name like Teagarden. A man having tea in a garden all day long, playing the trombone at night.

My mother used to take me once a week to the Dee house for tea in the garden with my maiden aunts. Ambrose knew how to make the Japanese cook's dry martinis (to this day the smell of gin brings to me the chirring laughter of spinsters and the scent of powdered and perfumed silk). Ambrose liked to have a martini once a week before putting on a good suit and a snap-brim fedora and going to the evening trots at Dufferin Race Course.

Then Morley had an accident on the deck of a corvette while in port. He was knocked over the side and was left dangling from a rope. He nearly was crushed between two great steel hulls grinding together. It took a long time to get him into a sling and haul him back up on deck. He was surprised at his own calm. He had never been so close to death and he had kept his calm. After that, he said that death didn't frighten him, not the actual dying. It was the leaving behind of love, unfinished love, that was heartbreaking. Years later, he told my friend, the writer Seán Virgo, that death itself held no fear for him: it would just be gurgle, gargle, gasp.

In 1943, the Canadian Broadcasting Corporation asked him to become chairman of a travelling radio series of political and economic discussions, a weekly half-hour show called *Of Things to Come*. It quickly became a controversial show that impinged on political sensitivities. He crossed the country twice from hamlet to town during the last two years of the war, conducting townhall meetings, and since he was an ardent, skillful debater, still very much the child of Tom, with a passion for politics and a grasp of economics, he angered many men.

He became a celebrity. He got a reputation for being quick-witted, argumentative and feisty, for not being afraid of anybody in debate, of not currying favor. Like a large part of the country, his father and mother sat hunched by their radio, listening to him.

His old debating partner, Paul Martin — who was by then a Cabinet Minister in the federal government — warned him that several powerful men were trying to pull political weight to get him fired. And he had said, "Well, I know you'll protect me, Paul." After that, their relationship was never quite the same. "We kind of looked over our shoulders for each other and we were never there."

Morley became a columnist for *New World*, a glossy magazine modeled on *Life* and bank-rolled by the industrialist and horseman, E.P. Taylor, who would go on to breed Northern Dancer, the great runner and even greater stud. The magazine, which was to show less stamina and have a shorter run, was edited by John Kempster Thomas, a tall man Morley's age, who became a close family friend. Morley and Loretto called him John, but even as a child I felt free to call him J.K. — not to be flip or cheekily familiar, but because he was the kind of man who moved with all the placid aplomb of an adult while being openly available and accommodating to a child. Perhaps this was because, as a child in London, his family had been abandoned by the father and J.K. had been put out to fend among relatives.

He had made his way "through dint of hard work," as they used to say, coming, eventually, as a student to the University of Toronto. He received a scholarship then that sent him to Paris to study with Henri Bergson at the Sorbonne. He was articulate, affable without being overbearing; he read widely, and liked to fall from his height — with the full of his weight — into chairs, talking as he fell. I remember him starting an hour-long description of Jean-Paul Sartre's tome, *Saint Genet*, on just such a descent. He had married a very pretty Vassar girl, the daughter of the former Dean of New York University Law School. Hallie Tompkins, with intelligence and a gift for slightly loopy but acute observations — a generosity of spirit well tuned to J.K.'s expansive and sometimes eager cynicism — had been one of the editors of the *Vassarion*, along with Elizabeth Bishop, the great poet.

In 1935, going to the Sorbonne, she had stayed with Bishop in Paris in a seven-room apartment that had five fireplaces and a cook. She had met J.K. one evening when she and Bishop found themsleves in a crowded Russian café and the young philosophy student offered them his table. He was so charming that Bishop (who had not yet come out of the closet as a lesbian) invited him for tea the next day. One tea led to a tryst; Hallie went to Boston to work for Little Brown, the publisher, and J.K. also arrived in Boston to study with Alfred North Whitehead. Her family could not have been terrifically pleased but Hallie followed her heart and married J.K. close to her family home on Lake George, New York. They moved to Toronto where he taught philosophy at Trinity College, and then became editor of *New World*. Hallie was as articulate as J.K. and fiercely loyal. She and Loretto shared that. And style. They both had style. And courage . . . if their men operated on the edge of hopes and ambitions, then they never let on if they were afraid; they stood unblinking, capable of great grace, or great anger if anyone attempted to belittle their men, family or friends. So J.K. and Hallie were the other regular Saturday night couple, Morley and Loretto's friends for life.

9

On a Friday night at eleven o'clock, as General Patton nosed his tanks for Berlin, as Hoagy Carmichael sang "Stardust," Morley got off the train in Montreal and walked down the long platform to the ivory marble hall of Windsor Station. He went out to Peel Street and stood on the cobblestone hill to hail a cab. The taxi took him past the square where lovely and quaint *barouches* were usually lined up at the curb but the hour was late, the curb was clear. The taxi did not take him to his hotel, the Ritz-Carlton, but let him off, carrying his overnight Gladstone bag, in front of a bar on Dorchester Street.

The overhead sign outside said JACK & LOU'S BAR AND GRILL but it was known as Slitkin's and Slotkin's. Slitkin, the small gentle-spoken Lou Wyman, had come from Central Europe before the First War, and the big palooka with the cigar, Slotkin, was Jack Rogers, out of New Jersey. From the early twenties they had been partners, working the East coast, and whatever town or burg they had "stood in bed" in, they were strictly lower east side, working with wise guys and pugs in the walk-up gyms, first as coaches, and then as promoters, staging fights in Boston, Buffalo, Philly, Brooklyn and Montreal. They had the handle on the deals, the saw-offs, the stiffs . . . but as the Second War started, they gave up promoting and settled in Montreal and opened up their joint, in that wide-open city, a joint that had white tablecloths on the tables and plush gray carpeting on the grill room floor. They wanted the room to look like their private place. They thought of themselves as private guys who had a public. They didn't have a bartender. They were the bartenders. They didn't have a greeter at the door. They were the greeters. They poured the drinks, counted the cutlery, and kept some customers on the cuff. They wore Homburg hats, black tuxedos, and four-in-hand ties "to make sure the air of dignity is truly dignified."

In those days of Premier Duplessis (who took payoffs from gangsters and cardinals alike) and a hundred "protected" *barbottes* (gambling houses) and east end streets crowded with hookers, and Camillien Houde (Mister Five-by-Five, His Worship the 350-pound Mayor) and young soldiers and sailors on leave, and Lili St. Cyr at the Gaiety, their clientele was made up of reporters, racketeers, the boxing clan, hoofers, public relations men for the breweries, and stars in show business. The walls were cluttered with signed photographs: Two-Ton Tony Galento, Rocket Richard, Tommy Dorsey, Frankie Filchock, The Ink Spots, Frankie Sinatra, Sugar Ray Robinson and Jack Dempsey, Judy Garland and Lucille Ball, Jack Kearns and Gratien Gelinas, Jackie Robinson and Gypsy Rose Lee. They flocked in after midnight (though there were curfew liquor laws, the police never closed the grill room doors) and stayed until dawn, the bar always crowded with men bending an ear.

Whenever Morley went into the bar, his closest friend was usually there on his reserved stool, the sporting writer at the *Gazette*, "Whispering" Dink Carroll. His closeness with Dink went back to the early thirties, when, because of the Depression, Dink had left Montreal and gone to Toronto to work as a publicist for the Toronto Maple Leaf Triple-A baseball team, a job he hated. He and Morley met almost every afternoon at Bowles Lunch, and whenever Morley had a new story or part of a new novel he showed it to Dink. But as soon as the War started, Dink went back to Montreal and refused even to visit Toronto. So they met at Slitkin's and Slotkin's, and talked about Morley's writing again.

Morley thought he was at a turning point. He was ready to go to work on a novel, his imagination quickened by a woman he had come to know at Slitkin's and Slotkin's. There was something about her, a guilelessness that was dangerous — she refused to see that as she socialized openly with black men she not only aroused rage among white men but among black women, too; she — who would become Peggy in *The Loved and The Lost* — refused to see that her sense of unsullied aloofness might just as easily be a pig-headed self-indulgence, and night after night she sat as if she were quite safe in Slitkin's and Slotkin's, having a lamb chop.

Slitkin, as he explained once on radio, called the joint an Italian restaurant. They served steaks and lamb chops. Frankie Carbo, the New York mobster, liked the steaks. So did Camillien Houde. Lili St. Cyr and Jackie Robinson liked the lamb chops. The whole Montreal Alouettes football team ate there, calling the grill room their training table. Police ate there, and the "foxes" in the law courts, and reporters and some professors.

"We're not here to sell coffee," Slotkin said. "People want a steak and to wash it down with a bottle of beer. We're here to make a profit."

"To fill up the joint," Slitkin said.

"It's not a joint, not a joint. I told you that before, it's a dignified place."

"When you fill up the dignified place . . . "

"You don't fill up a dignified place," Slotkin insisted. "There aren't so many people to fill up a dignified place."

"There's not that much room to move them dignified around, we don't even have enough knives and forks."

"That's what makes the place interesting. You get these two-fisted egg beaters in here . . . "

"There was a guy hollering for a knife and fork," Slitkin said, laughing, "and he just picked up his steak and started eating it with his hands . . . "

"That's the wonder of our place," Slotkin said. "It's a good thing, to pick up a steak between your pinkies, the sweeter the meat the nearer to the bone . . . "

Slotkin was one of those hard guys who can make an insult sound like a compliment. No one ever seemed to be upset with him. If someone was, Slitkin was the conciliator, a softer guy who kept Slotkin out of trouble. Slitkin said he had been a fighter at 126 pounds but one newspaperman said, "If he threw a punch in a china shop, it's his hands that'd break." He was a soft touch for a free drink, a free meal, and he was a very good listener.

"There weren't many listeners there," Morley said. "They were nearly all talkers. Ear-benders. That's what I called it. The Ear-benders Club. Even the gangsters couldn't button their lips, they were talkers."

There was a little man known as "Derle" (Doyle) — who was a henchman for Frankie Carbo who managed Jake Lamotta. Carbo was in Slitkin's and Slotkin's all the time, and so was "Derle" — who was "officially" the trainer for the Montreal fighter, Johnny Greco. Actually, he was a guy with "muscle" who got things done. One night, Carbo and everyone else got up from the table and Morley was left alone with "Derle".

"Suddenly here was this guy looking at me, wanting to bend my ear but we had nothing in common so he began telling me how he would go about getting the vote out in certain districts for Carbo in New York, telling me about the very strong-arm tactics he used. The point is, in normal life, I would never hear anything like this, never come up against this. Carbo was a very big gangster who ran a large part of the fight mob, very dangerous and a very much feared man was Frankie Carbo. Yet there Carbo was, and "Derle." This was, shall we say, a mixed society. The newspaper guys, yes. But you'd see Jack Dempsey, Jackie Robinson, and also A.J.M. Smith the poet, and all the fight managers were there and you could talk boxing all night."

It was surprising in such a masculine sanctuary, with so many volatile men and so many local gangsters — like the hit-man Berkovitz, and Frank Petrillo — clustered around the bar, drinking heavily until the early hours, that there were so few arguments, and almost no fights. Not that there weren't provocations. Berkovitz, a sinister poker-faced thug, would sit at a table with a mouth full of B-B shot, and he could hit anyone in the room with the shot, which stung, but anybody who was hit — rather than get angry — would accept the "joke" and make a point of getting friendly with Berkovitz. It was common sense. But one dispute did set Morley to thinking.

One of Slotkin's ex-pugilist protégés, Maxie Berger, had hung up his gloves and gone into the clothing business. He tried to sell suits at Slitkin's and Slotkin's and he persuaded Peter McRitchie, who was the managing editor of the *Gazette*, to buy one of his suits. McRitchie got into a brawl at the bar one night and Slotkin, who had once billed himself as the heavyweight champion of Belgium but, as Morley said, "Probably couldn't lick a stamp," threw McRitchie out, ripping the lining of his new suitcoat.

After a period of penance, McRitchie returned to the bar, but every time he saw Maxie Berger, as a joke, he would open up his suitcoat and say, "See, Maxie, you make lousy suits." Berger was humiliated. He pleaded with McRitchie to let him make a new suit. McRitchie refused. He wore the suit everywhere. No one bought Berger's suits. Eventually Berger went belly-up, a broken man. Everyone at the bar thought the situation was amusing. Morley turned it into a tragic story, *The Many Colored Coat*, with McRitchie as Harry Lane and Berger as Mike Kon.

"But there's one other night I must remember" Morley said, "and it was on toward the end of the Houde regime — before the new mayor, Drapeau, closed everything down in the city. The place had been terrific for me. My imagination, without my trying, had come alive again, and I had finished my other novel about my time with the boys in Montreal, *The Loved and The Lost*. My publishers, John Gray and Frank Upjohn at Macmillan, decided they should have a party in Montreal to launch the book and have it at the Ritz. Now, people I knew were at this party — Madame Casgrande, and Camillien Houde, and Frank Scott, the Dean of the Law School, all the people I might have seen in the daytime were at this party. But I said to Upjohn, there are two guys you should really have, Slitkin and Slotkin. And they came.

"They were a little out of place at this gathering, but Slotkin had all the brassiness in the world, so — not quite sure why he was there — he said to Upjohn, 'What business are you in?'

"'Books,' Upjohn said.

"'The books, eh?'

"'Yes, that's right, I make books.'

"'Oh well,' Slotkin said, 'we should get along fine. I know lots of book-makers.'

"The party went along very well. And Slitkin, who was a gentle soul, he found it hard to find a role for himself among all these folks, so he did a perfectly natural thing, since I was meeting maybe a hundred people. Slitkin, standing five feet away, he would see when I was talking to someone and he'd see my eyes were wandering, so just as if he were in our hangout, in the saloon, he would move over calmly and take whoever it was by the arm and lead them away, saying, 'Well, now, Morley needs to have another word with someone else,' all done so absolutely gracefully, so naturally, no one minded.

"Then Slotkin said to Slitkin, 'What's this book of Morley's about?' And Slitkin said, 'Don't you understand, our place is in that book,' and Slitkin began to show him that their joint was in the book, so Slotkin went to the table where the books were and he said to Upjohn, 'Sell me one of those books,' but Upjohn said, 'I can't, they're not for sale,' so Slotkin looked to see how much the book was, took the money out of his pocket and pressed it very firmly into Upjohn's hand and said, 'Here, thanks for the book.'

"Then he looked around, trying to find the Mayor, Camillien Houde, and he saw Houde was surrounded by a lot of people, but he wanted the Mayor to sign his book so he went over and tapped the Mayor on the shoulder and the Mayor half-turned and said, 'Yes, just a minute,' and Slotkin waited a minute and tapped his shoulder again, and the Mayor half-grunted and Slotkin turned away, discomfited. He tapped the Mayor hard on the shoulder and he said, 'My partner is Johnny Davis.' And it was astonishing, you see, because Davis was what they called 'the edge man,' the guy that gets the licenses, the silent secret partner, the guy who got paid off in the halls at City Hall, the guy, by the way, that Berkovitz the hit-man eventually shot and killed — so the Mayor turned around, beaming, and cried, 'Yes, of course,' and signed the book. Slotkin always knew just like that how to handle himself. He knew where the action was."

After the party a group, including the Mayor, went from the Ritz-Carlton to Slitkin's and Slotkin's for drinks and supper. At about two in the morning, the jovial Mayor (who was married to an undertaker's daughter and who had once tried to make a living by gluing coal dust into balls and selling them, who had been interned during the War for advocating civil disobedience and who, for a decade of his life, had lived on milk and gin) suggested that Morley sign the City's Golden Book. He explained that Queen Elizabeth had signed his book and Morley should, too, so the Mayor called for his driver and limousine, and Dink Carroll, Robert Lapalme the cartoonist, John Gray, Frank Upjohn, and Morley and Loretto drove with the Mayor to the City Hall, passing the Mount Royal Hotel on the way (where there were two reserved suites: one, the Mount Royal Club, for the biggest card games in the city, attended by only the richest and most respected citizens in politics or on police commissions or in finance; the other was for the Mayor himself — "the mayor of the Little People, the Great Houde-ini" — who said he refused to bother the little desk clerk, and so never checked in and never checked out, and therefore was never "there," never receiving a bill). The City Hall was dark, not a light in the windows. The hugely rotund Mayor went from door to door. He did not have his keys. All the doors were locked. He ordered his driver to find a basement window that could be discreetly broken, break it, crawl in and come to the front door and let the Mayor and his party in to the Hall. Twenty minutes later, the driver, his cap under his arm, his face and coat smudged with dirt, happily opened the door.

The Mayor led everyone up the wide stairs to his Chambers and the Golden Book was opened on his desk. Amidst laughter and the handing around of a silver flask, Morley signed the book, and Loretto signed, too. The driver took photographs. With the book signed and closed, with Morley and the Queen keeping company, they all went downstairs and got into the limousine and went back to Slitkin's and Slotkin's.

"There was a schoolteacher, of all things, in there," Dink said, "and she found out Morley was there and she came over to him and says, 'Are you Morley Callaghan?' And he says, 'I confess,' and she says, 'Mr. Callaghan, I've got to ask you a question,' and he says, 'What is it?' and she says, 'When you get into this business of talking about collectivism, do you say — The group *is* or the group *are*?'

"He says, 'Lady, you aren't a teacher, you're a grammarian.'

"And Slotkin, who was sitting there listening to this, he says to Morley, 'What's a grammarian, I'm a Yiddel myself.'"

At four in the morning, Slotkin — an earnest gambler — was playing gin rummy with a man who had had a lot to drink. Slotkin dealt him his cards. The drunk picked up his cards, looked at them, put his head on the table and fell asleep. He slept for two or three minutes until Slotkin, impatient, yelled, "Hey drunk, wake up. Let's play the game." The drunk woke up, looked at his cards, laid them down and said, "Rummy."

Slotkin picked up the hand, saw that it was rummy, tore up the cards, tore up the deck, and paid the man. It was time to go, to pay the bills and spill out in the dawn light on to Dorchester Street, hooting and hailing a taxi.

Slitkin said, "Remember, this isn't a place where you come in and be strange, you feel like you're home, you just was not ever strange, not here."

Whenever Morley was in Montreal he felt guilty about Hugh MacLennan, well-known for his novel, *Two Solitudes*. He often wrote Morley little notes wondering why they never saw each other when Morley was in town. Morley decided he had to be courteous. He phoned MacLennan and they agreed to meet late the next afternoon at MacLennan's flat for a drink.

Morley knocked on the door. MacLennan was disgruntled and peeved and above all, tired. He'd had almost no sleep. The problem, he said, was a joint just around the corner, a dive full of loud low-life who caroused till dawn. He had complained to the police but as usual the police did nothing.

"Have you ever been in it?" Morley asked.

"No, never," MacLennan said sternly.

"Never been in the joint?"

"No. And last night was terrible," MacLennan said. "I got no sleep at all."

After a while, Morley finished his rye-and-water and said he must go, that Dink had tickets for the Canadiens hockey game.

"When I was out on the street," Morley told me, "I didn't know whether to laugh or cry. I hadn't had the heart to tell him I was one of the lowlifes, that that was Slitkin's and Slotkin's, and even worse, even more sad, he had just written to me, saying how much he admired *The Many Colored Coat*."

"Sounds apocryphal," I said wryly.

"Yeah, maybe, but it's true," he said.

Coming home from Montreal, Morley felt good. He took the streetcar down to Eaton's and bought a new pair of shoes. He didn't often buy shoes. He usually got his old shoes re-soled by Badali the Shoemaker on Bathurst Street (he was the bass soloist in the St. Peter's church choir when I was the soprano soloist).

Then, in 1946, his brother's life stopped.

Burke died with nowhere to turn. In a panic.

Older by a year, he had been a singer, but there was a silence about Burke in our family, about his death.

Snap-shots of him had been slipped into books that stood unopened on shelves in our house. Big posters announcing his recitals had been locked in an old steamer trunk in the coal cellar. Morley, a storyteller, had never told me a thing about his brother. I had grown up with no sense of him at all.

In the summer of 1925, in the month that Morley sent his stories to Paris, the *Toronto Star* compared Burke to the great Russian bass baritone, Chaliapin.

He was also paid as the lead soloist at the Metropolitan Methodist Church, and the magazine, *Musical Canada,* celebrated his "fine sense of dramatic force, his power of interpretation, the full resonant quality of his voice and his wide range" — two octaves and a third — saying, "Three years ago, Burke T. Callaghan, the young Toronto Baritone, had neither experience nor training. He became a pupil of Mr. T. Watkin-Mills, the famous English Basso. Now he has to his credit the winning of first prize for bass solo, operatic class, at the Ontario Music Festival, and also for bass solo at the Canadian National Exhibition Musical competitions."

By 1927, Burke had sung Sibelius, the *St. Matthew Passion,* the King in *Aida,* and had begun to sing at the King Edward Hotel, hosting supper concerts in the Studio Room, programs that were carried "live" over CNRT on all Canadian National trains crossing the country. He'd got quietly married, he looked dapper. He wore a snap-brim fedora at a jaunty angle.

In 1928 — against his mother's advice and Morley's, both believing he should go to New York — he followed his teacher to Los Angeles, where he gave recitals but found little paying work. He lived with the Watkin-Millses, and then alone in a room. His parents sent him one dollar every week out of Tom's salary. Soon, though he was taller than Morley, he weighed only 140 pounds. A weariness crept into his letters — written in an open vulnerable hand.

As the spunk went out of him, two shadows appeared briefly in his letters, a woman — Madeleine, his wife — and their baby girl. He wanted to know if his mother had written to Madeleine, though Madeleine lived close by the Callaghan house. Burke said he hadn't seen Madeleine or the baby for a long time and worried about how he was going to buy Madeleine a winter coat. He wondered, petulantly, why she couldn't get a part-time job, to help out. He seemed detached, strangely so. His mother was just as removed. She warned against sending all his "little bit of money" to his wife, who would just spend it. It is hard to know if this was a family tone, a family reticence, or animosity toward the woman on his mother's part, or an indifference on his.

But something was wrong from the beginning, some unspoken betrayal, some failure of love.

When Burke — without work — began to go to pieces, his mother wrote and said, "Dad, like me, did not want you to give in to come home until you had made good there." He came home anyway, telling his mother that he had been having chilling night dreams. He told her he also had a day dream. He was sure that he was going to come home and sing for Lady Eaton, and once she heard how wonderfully he sang she would send him to New York to study.

Morley, who was in Manhattan at the time, on his way to Paris with Loretto on their honeymoon, met a well-known voice coach and spoke to him about Burke. Morley sent Burke a letter of introduction to the coach and went on to Paris. Inexplicably, Burke waited a year, and then he took an overnight train to New York, walked to the address on Morley's envelope, saw that no one by the voice handler's name was on the bell plate, and got directly on a train and came home.

I know nothing of his subsequent singing career. It seems that as everything broke open for Morley, everything broke down for Burke. His failure must have come between them. There is one and only one postcard that Morley sent to Burke — a sepia photograph of the Café Dôme "that used to be so very famous," Morley wrote on the back, "but now it is full of tourists. But it does look a little different than the places in Toronto, don't you think?" The postcard was addressed to Wolfrey Avenue, as if Burke — a married man with a child — had no home of his own. I don't remember Burke ever being in our home, not by himself, not with his two children, not for Sunday suppers with Tom and Minn; but then I was young when he died, only nine, and I must be mistaken. He was Morley's only brother. He must have been in our house.

More than fifteen years after Burke's quick and futile trip to New York, he appeared in a *Globe and Mail* folio newsletter to its carrier boys. He looked confident. He was handsome, with soft eyes, a soft smile. He was wearing a dark topcoat, a white scarf, but not his fedora. He was wearing a Homburg hat. As the District Manager for C District, he had been appointed Supervisor of Toronto City Carrier-Salesmen. The door-to-door newsies. In an article titled: "Burke Callaghan's Review of City Routes," he wrote, "Boys, can you see the importance of your job? *You* are the *king-pins* of the *entire system . . .* "

It must have been awkward if not awful between Morley and Burke, the "battery" — Morley the celebrated writer, Burke the grown-up delivery boy.

Burke came down with a hacking cold, what he thought was a strep throat, and though he was still married to Madeleine and had two children, he went home to his mother and father. He seemed bewildered. They didn't ask why he had come to them. They didn't settle him down in his boyhood bed, but had him sleep — as if he were something of a stranger — on the living room sofa. They didn't call a doctor. At first, he seemed to be improving, but he worsened and could hardly breathe, and was rushed by ambulance north of Toronto, to the Gravenhurst Hospital for consumptives.

Two weeks later, Morley drove where he and his brother had walked, along Wolfrey Avenue. He felt such shortness of breath himself that he had to stop the car. He saw his father coming along the street, a solitary figure. Morley got out of the car and caught hold of him.

"Look," he said quietly, "I don't know what we'll say to mother," trying to ease the blow by showing concern for his mother. "It's terrible. He died."

"Dead. He's dead?" Tom, though he had great eloquence — though he was a spell-binding talker at the table or in a debating hall — always masked his deepest feelings and he stood there saying nothing, lonely and waiting. Morley, determined to control his emotions, and as if to give Tom assurance that Burke was not gone from them forever, said in a sensible tone, "Well, we have one of us in another world."

Morley was astonished when his father, who was not a religious man, nodded. He took his father's arm and asked, "What about mother? Will you tell her or will I?" His father, turning away, said, "I can't tell her," and they went into the home and into the kitchen where Minn was making a cup of tea. "Hello son," she said. "Were you at the hospital?"

She was seventy but she still had eager blue eyes. "Sit down, Mother," Morley said. "Come on now, sit down," and when she sat down, apprehensive because Tom had said nothing, Morley spoke in an even tone. "I might as well say it straight out. He died. Suddenly he died. Yeah."

Her head fell back and she said, "No. No," and then wailed, her hands over her face, "dear God, no."

"Mother," Morley said sternly, "don't go on like that." Tears were running down her cheeks. He put his arm around her but he scolded her. "What good does it do to go on like that?" He gave her a little shake which made her look up and she saw how stern he was so she said, "I won't, I won't. I'm all right." (Years later, Morley — troubled, as he talked about it — asked me how he could possibly have wanted to cheat her out of her tears and wondered why he had not found the grace to say, "Weep if you want to. Why shouldn't you weep?")

Finally, she said, "Who was with him? Who saw him?"

"Helen," Morley said.

"Not his wife? Helen?"

He knew she was thinking of this Helen, whom she had not met, or even heard of until two weeks before. Apparently, Burke had had a bickering brittle marriage. There had been many quarrels. Minn had told Morley that she was sorry for Burke because he had never known any real love from a woman, and then, when he had been rushed to the hospital, Helen, a lovely girl, had appeared at the hospital weeping and wanting to throw herself in his arms and cover him with kisses, and that was how they learned she had been his lover for five years.

His mother whispered, "Helen?" and she rocked back and forth, and he was sure she was thinking of her son's life, and then, Helen — suddenly Helen — the unexpected and just discovered bright spot in his life. Morley thought his mother had the look of a wondering child as she said, "It's like a story, isn't it?" seeing his death in that light, as a story, and she was consoled.

Morley told me that this moment had a profound effect on his writing. The dead son had taken on an *other* life as soon as his mother saw that he was a story. Morley — talking with his eyes closed, as he did at moments of greatest intensity — said that maybe no one is ever remembered unless he is a great story. People live their lives, doomed to be quickly forgotten — because they have no story. "People with no story tellers have no history," Morley said. "No one remembers facts, unless the facts get into a story." He was glad that his mother had found consolation and wonder as she mulled over the story of her son. It had become a story for Morley, too, so that one evening on the radio he began, "A writer told me this story. He had a brother in his middle forties who had had a heart attack, who after a week of intensive care seemed to be improving rapidly. Then, suddenly he died and the writer had to go to the family home and tell his father and mother that their son, his brother, was dead . . . "

In breaking the silence, Morley had kept Burke alive.

This moment in his family kitchen, this story, haunted Morley. He recounted it in detail in his 1987 novel, *Our Lady of the Snows,* and it seems that he was so ashamed of his hardness with his mother that he finally gave her her tears:

"Sit down, Mother," Gil said gently and she did, yet couldn't take her eyes off his face. Now there are just the three of us, he thought, just the three of us now. "Look, Mother, try and take it easy, please," he said quietly. "Philip's gone. He didn't make it."

"Oh, oh, oh," she wailed, and her cry was desolate as she rose in the chair. He said sternly, "Don't, don't, Mother, don't go on, it's bad enough for us. Crying will make it worse. You mustn't cry, do you hear? If you cry it'll be terrible. Now don't." Afraid of her tears, he sounded angry. "Sit down." Shaken, she nodded obediently. "I'm not crying. I understand, Gilbert. I won't make it worse. I won't, Gilbert," and when he sat down the three of them were silent, each afraid of the others' silence.

All the years of their lives were in this silence in that kitchen. His father's gray eyes hadn't changed their expression. His father had got what he wanted in his life: to own his own home, owe no money, have his family, and say what he wanted to say. He was a very articulate man and all he said now, breaking the silence, was, "Peg . . . "

"What, Joe?"

"Do you remember Philip's little yellow suit?"

"Yellow velvet. When he was four. I remember, Joe." Her eyes began to fill with tears, and then, remembering she had been told not to cry, she swallowed and sat back stiffly on the chair.

"Mother, Mother," Gil said, feeling stricken as he went to her and kissed her hand, "cry if you want to. Why shouldn't you cry now? It's a good thing, Mother," and he was ashamed that in protecting himself from the panic within him he had denied his mother her tears, ashamed, he knew, because it was something he might remember the rest of his life. "I'll be all right, Gilbert," she said. "When I'm alone, I'll cry," and he let her be.

Through Philip (Burke), Morley also wanted to say something about love: he wanted to say that even if love was illicit, even if Burke had betrayed his wife, if that love had hurt no one, if it was secret, private, and rooted in wonder, then life could be a wonder, life could be kept alive in the imagination, in stories.

"Now listen to me," he blurted out, startling them. "Philip looked after his wife and children. He never hurt Alice. He loved his children. Yes, Alice was a good woman, but she never wanted to share Philip's life or share his dreams. Good as she was, she could never make Philip feel she found joy and wonder in being with him. No ecstasy. She couldn't be his companion. Then he found this woman, this Lenore, and he found love and sacrifice in her, and yes, wonder in being together. Without it, it's a dead life for a man. He found life in Lenore. Yet it was a secret thing, they kept it a hidden thing so you two and Alice would not be hurt, and all that Lenore asked was to see him before he died. Oh, Mother, don't you see?"

"All in secret, a secret," she whispered, half dreaming.

"That was Philip," he said.

"I thought I knew my own son," his father said. "Didn't I know him at all? Peg . . . Peg . . ." he said, turning to her, for she was lost in her own thoughts.

"It's like a story," she said suddenly. "Yes, a story," and as she repeated it, the wonder in her eyes and in her changing face startled Gil. The hurt, lost look had gone.

The light of her wonder and dreams was all in her brightening blue eyes, as if her dead son was now taking on a new life in her imagination.

"You're right," Gil said. "It's quite a story . . . "

Driving carefully on the slippery street, he thought of his mother's changing face and the light coming into her eyes when she whispered, "It's like a story," as if she knew she could keep Philip alive in a story. It was the truth. He must have known this himself some years ago, Gil thought, known it when he left college and began his wandering, believing he would become a writer. And what a beginning he'd had; just two years after graduate school he'd had a poem and a story printed in the Paris Review . . . Without noticing, he drove through a red light, but no cop was on the corner and it was snowing harder.

Many of the bare bones of Morley's universe are in this kitchen story.

In the year his brother died, Morley began to write short stories again (I don't mean to imply that his death was any kind of specific release). He turned one of those stories into a novel, *Luke Baldwin's Vow*. It was for boys. It was set in the Blue Mountains of Collingwood where his mother and the Dewans had come from. I was ten. I asked my grandmother if she had read it. She said, "No." I did not read it either. That didn't matter to Morley. He was back in stride. It was now 1947 and he wrote *A Cap for Steve*, a beautiful story, which I read because it really wasn't about a baseball cap, it was about how we got our dog, Maize.

Then, after Christmas Day supper at our house, Tom suffered a gastric hemorrhage. Everyone went over to the Wolfrey house to be with him. I was left with a neighbor, told that I was too young to see someone die. The neighbor, a sports writer named King Whyte, explained that the naked woman in the photograph on the living room mantel was his wife — the band singer, Dorothy Alt — and he gave me a big pocket watch with a sweeping second-hand. I sat in bed and thought about her bare body and watched the hand. The second-hand put me to sleep (this particular evening became part of the opening of my first novel, *The Way the Angel Spreads Her Wings*). The next morning, everyone was happy. Tom had not died.

Tom was stubborn. Every day in the spring he went out to weed and hoe in his garden. Every day, Morley took my brother to see him and every day Morley got down on his knees, tapped at Tom's puffy ankles, prodding the swollen fluid-filled membranes, and gave his father "a good setting out" because the doctor had said that if Tom did not stop working the garden and if he didn't drink eight glasses of water a day, he would die.

He died.

My brother, Michael, had always felt an incredible bond with Tom. I'd had a feeling for my grandfather, too, but I had hardly known him. I remember crawling through his corn patch, listening to him read Keats, and his warning me not to eat the red berries on bushes. But Michael had a passion for him . . . and told stories about how Tom "used to caper for me with light dancing in his eyes as he hopped about whistling and making faces . . . because he had to see a child laugh, had to see what he wrote about in one of his verses for the local newspapers —

> Come children, be my books,
> With laughing love-lit eyes,
> Where clear as Holy Writ,
> Immortal wisdom lies . . .

"I looked hard at him," Michael said about the night before Tom died, "but he didn't look at me. His cheeks were sunken because his teeth were out on the table, and a white bristle was on his cheeks and jaw. His yellowish white hair had grown long. He was proud of his full head of hair, as was Minn because years before the hair had started to recede and Minn had massaged his scalp for half an hour each evening to bring it back but now it was matted on the pillow . . . I stood helplessly, staring for a sign. I could hear his voice in my mind, 'I'm busy,' he said, 'I'm just too busy now.' I knew he wanted to say something to make me laugh, but he was too busy . . . when there was a long pause between breaths, when that happened, I held mine so I could listen. Then, his breathing . . . it began to move, slowly like a freight car pushing past, click, click, click and by."

He died.

The bond was there, but why was it so deep? I've often thought it came from Michael's childhood. He had a habit as a child — a summer habit at Lake Simcoe, Aunt Toots's cottage. He would see the dock and toddle off onto it and keep on walking and walk off the end. I walked off to Woolworth's. He walked off the ends of docks. It was Tom who leapt into the water after him, fully clothed. It was Tom who caught his sinking body and brought him back safely to the surface.

Michael was a dockwalker.

Maybe we were all dockwalkers in the family.

Morley sold the family house on Wolfrey Avenue and Minn came to live with us. I was given my own baseball glove (instead of a hand-me-down from my brother) and I pitched a no-hitter and brought a black boy, Joe Lovell, to my room to play with my toys. After he went home, Minn said to me: "Black is black and white is white and the twain shall ne'er meet."

I told my father. He was furious. It was the only time I ever heard my father yell at his mother. She said she was sorry and gave me a dry kiss and money and told me to take Joe to the Midtown Theater to a movie. I took him to see *The Jolson Story*. After the movie, I didn't understand why he was hurt and angry. He didn't speak to me for two years, but I went to see Larry Parks sing in black face nine times. I joined the church choir and tried to sing the "Kyrie" as if it were "Mammy." The choir master suggested that I take up ping-pong.

I did, and won the school ping-pong championship. I brought home a silver trophy and Morley put it on a window sill beside his school trophy for model airplanes. He bought a ping-pong net and paddles, stippled green rubber on one side, green sandpaper on the other, and every night after supper we cleared the dining room table, put up the net, and played ping-pong.

Even Minn played. She had long arms and could whack the ball. She always wanted to play for a nickel or a dime, knowing she would lose. It was her way of giving me money. Morley hardly ever gave me money. He was tight-fisted and liked to tease us — even my mother — that he had no money. The teasing was enraging.

I knew he wasn't flush, but I knew he wasn't poor either, not the way some of my schoolmates' families were. All through my school years I was angry at him about money. Every year he bought me one jacket and two pairs of trousers, bringing them home from a sale at Eaton's, telling me I had to like the look of them because he had chosen them. My allowance was a pittance. (After-school jobs were out for me as I was always on the field — at his urging — or in the gym, playing and practicing.) He wondered sourly why I never went out with the daughters of those rich men who wore Homburg hats.

"I don't have the money," I cried. "You've got all the money."

"You refuse to understand," he would moan. "I got through the Depression, I got my family through those years writing short stories, serious stories for serious magazines. That's what I did. That was insane enough, but I have no pension, no unemployment insurance . . . "

That was true, but it did not alter the fact that the act of giving gave him no pleasure. He was good at accepting. Aunt Toots gave our family the Chrysler Airflow, sent me to De La Salle boys' summer camp, took Loretto on holidays to Mexico . . . He accepted these gifts with equanimity and ease. But he pinched his own pennies, though he knew how awful, how destructive such niggling over money is in families. It's in his stories — sons and fathers driven apart by money. He just couldn't help himself.

All my schoolboy life my mother helped me by secretly giving me money, loose change. Still, that was a kind of scrounging. I think this is why my brother and I have always spent what money we've had as fast as we got it. Or maybe we were profligate, by nature.

Minn died. He took me to the hospital to see her the night before she died. She lay in a little forest of hanging bottles and bags and was wired up with tubes, but she could speak and quoted some lines of poetry. She told me that she had left me a few hundred dollars in her will which I would get when I was twenty-one. (My father never gave it to me, though I asked.) She also took off her wedding ring and told Morley to give it to the grandson who married first. (Years later, Morley gave me the ring to give to Nina.)

I was going to miss playing ping-pong with Minn, a big-boned, old woman who sometimes seemed like a large, swooping bird at the other end of the table, and I was going to miss her lace. Minn always wore lace at her throat and lace at her cuffs, and though she was big and she was stern she always seemed delicate to me. Perhaps it was the paleness of her eyes. I was also sorry that I had snitched on her to my father about Joe Lovell. She didn't need to be yelled at by her son, turned in by her grandson.

The Loved and The Lost was published in New York and Toronto. Morley went to that Ritz launching party in Montreal, the party that led to the break-in at Houde's City Hall and the signing of the Golden Book. Then he came home and waited for the reviews of the novel. Many reviews were ridiculous, chastising Morley for daring to write a novel set in Montreal when he was an alien from Toronto, or for setting out to solve the Black and White race problem and failing — something he hadn't tried to do at all. It was the first time I watched him read reviews. He was hurt, enraged, humiliated. "Stupid," he kept saying. "How could they be so stupid? The book's not trying to solve the race question. For God's sake . . . " He walked in circles of gloom and fury for days. Maritain had written to say that Peggy, the heroine, had the mysterious qualities of a saint, but Maritain was in Paris. I understood that somehow Morley was helpless, that there was no way for him to hit back, no way to correct the stupidity. After all, this was a novel Edmund Wilson would later compare to the work of Chekhov and Turgenev.

Then he bought our house on the ravine in Rosedale. Morley got it at a very low price in a quick estate sale. It was a big, broken-down rooming house.

We all, with help and direction from Uncle Ambrose, fixed and painted the house. Our rich neighbors found this very amusing. I discovered gardening and built the long rockery that runs the length of the front of the house. Morley took up his chair by the library window that overlooks the rockery. He got down to work on a new novel. He was in a hurry. Burke was dead. Minn was dead. Tom was dead. He was halfway home to death himself.

Morley and Loretto hurried to Montreal. Death was too much on their minds. They needed a weekend at the Ritz, some nights out at the jazz clubs (where they heard young Leonard Cohen give his first public reading).

They were standing in the Mariner's Church, the antique church that the forlorn lover in *The Loved and The Lost* had tried to find in the snow-bound streets: *Soon the bells would ring in that little church nearby. He could get his bearing from the bells. Then he heard it, coming from the west and only a little way off, quick light chiming bells calling, softly calling, and he hurried in that direction; but the ringing faded away. He stopped and waited. Again he heard the light silver chiming. He followed where it beckoned, back to the east and now tantalizingly close; then it was gone . . . and he wandered around confused, not knowing which way to turn, tormented by the soft calling bells . . . But he went on with his tireless search. He wandered around . . . it was warm and brilliant. It melted the snow. But he couldn't find the little church.*

Morley was showing the little church to Loretto. The bells began to ring, a light silver chiming. She felt a drawing of all the nerves around her mouth. Then the pain. She howled, then let out another howl at a pain so intense it seemed to come up through the roots of her teeth, knocking her into a backward stutter-step. She howled with every breath, the pain so acute she didn't know she was howling.

It was her first attack of *tic douloureux*, a neuritis of the trigeminal nerve — the main sensory nerve of the face, a tic that has no specific cause, and no successful treatment, despite the fact that it has been known for centuries. The slightest or most trivial things bring on an attack — a knock at the door, a shake of the bed, a breeze, eating, or the chiming of bells. The pain comes with astonishing suddenness, little red-hot needle jack-hammers, and no pain killers work. It ceases abruptly, regresses spontaneously, sometimes for months, even a year.

They had had so many deaths close in on them. Now they were going to get pain, like they'd never dreamed of.

After that day, the *tic* always came back. She lay in her mahogany spindle bed, the bed her father had carpentered, his wedding bed, the bed she had been conceived in, and she howled. We hung about in the stairwell, in the petalled light, and listened for hours, helpless, hoping beyond hope for a spontaneous regression. Once, tormented by having to hear her howl, I grabbed a little brass dinner bell in the shape of a girl wearing a hoop skirt and I ran upstairs ringing the bell and to our astonishment the pain stopped. The next time, the bell made it worse.

Twice, the only relief was to go into hospital and into her brain with a knife. There was nothing else to do. Her teeth were taken out, her body shivered from the side effects of drugs — all taking a toll on her heart. In her brain, they severed the nerves to her face, her beautiful face, the chestnut candle-white skin. Now, there was always a terror behind her eyes, even when she laughed. Her face fell. Without nerves, without feeling, the muscles sagged and her cheeks fell, and finally, with no nerves around her lips, she drooled like an old crone and wore a bib, a child's bib stained with drool and food, but Morley — who tried to treat her as if she were not an invalid, as if her left hand had not bunched into a fist because of a stroke — would say to a visitor who stepped unawares into the living room, "And this is my wife, my girl, Loretto," unblinking, unabashed, and she, sitting in her nest of shawls, reading, chain-smoking, would smile gaily, somehow the ghost of a pleased young woman rising up in her eyes, and sometimes I saw the inward sensual pleasure of the woman who had danced with me in her arms in her loneliness, the woman who taught me how to dance. The dance was in her eyes, and the terror. "I never," she said sardonically, "want to hear the sound of church bells again."

10

Mother invited Edmund Wilson for supper for the first time when I was twenty-three. As a joke, I rang the little brass bell to bring them to the table — and shuddered at how thoughtlessly I might have brought on an attack — and we ate in the dining room, under the chandelier. Out came the good silver, wine (which was certainly not the everyday rule with Morley), a lace tablecloth. At the end of the evening, Wilson told Morley that he was astonished at the conversation.

"You treat your sons like equals. They talk to you as if they were fellow men in their house."

Michael quoted a little doggerel he had written in college:

Oh we'll talk and we'll expound
On what makes this world go round.
Yes we'll be talking of all the things,
All the things of which we know nothing . . .

There was always talk at our table. Very little silence, unless someone was sulking or sick. It could be elegant free-for-all talk (as when Wilson was there) or more like midget wrestling in the mud when we were alone and wound up. We never came to blows but we often left each other full of dents. We never agreed to disagree. We disagreed. The failure of minds to meet was not taken as a failure. We were expected by Morley to be alert, gutsy, able to absorb the odd, cheap shot, and to know the difference between lightning and the lightning bug. The conversation was whatever the moment demanded and whatever was demanded was allowed.

For guests, this could be mildly terrifying. Morley — so unassuming as he sat down at the head of the table — was no sooner down and flanked by his sons than the sparring began. You had to be on your toes. (Morley had a monthly public workout on the nationally popular television program "Fighting Words," moderated by the acerbic critic, Nathan Cohen, where the anti-Callaghan mail reached record proportions in the late fifties — centering on his "loquaciousness, his willingness to talk about everything, seeming to know everything.") He *was* well-informed. He read all the new books, and the three daily newspapers . So did we. It was quite clear: we were to be our own men in our own house, our private world. And guests were to be who they were, too, in that private world. There, we could be totally public with each other. Our Saturday night gatherings were the same. That's why they were so much fun. It was our private place and the rules of the place were — no matter who you were — that there were no rules.

Morley had his own presence. It was a peculiar presence, commonplace and yet compelling. The stamp of who he was was on him from the beginning. There's a description of him from 1936, by a man named Bernard Preston in the magazine, *Saturday Night*. It is written in the arch diction of the time, but it got hold of him very well: "And what does he talk about, this laxly intent artist, this indolently active thinker? The answer is: Everything! Everything, that is, that bears relation to life. He is passionately opposed to ignorance, he must have awareness, and so spends hours daily reading newspapers from all over the world. He loves the crowd at a prize-fight, at a football or a hockey game, at a boxing match. He is intensely interested in politics, in the wider sense of the word, and used to speaking in public . . . he will discuss ships and sealing wax with equal impartiality. He is so thoroughly detached mentally that he feels readily at home in any realm of thought or any part of the globe . . . Contact with alert minds is as the breath of his nostrils to him. He admits readily, with no sense of confession, that he likes New York better than any other place. He finds doubtless that there he can enjoy not only a freer interchange of ideas, but that ideas are much more rife and original than in most centers. The very air teems with stimulation . . . He reconciles a profound knowledge of the world and a mature youthfulness with an apparently artless ingenuousness and young wisdom, and exercises keen critical ability with seeming carelessness. In other words, he embodies equipoise, balance, sanity . . .

"In the course of a particularly eloquent exposition of the difficulties of the modern writer in keeping up, or keeping on, he will stop for a few good night words with his little son Michael, a lad with the eyes of a Raphael cherub, and eyelashes that would turn a Hollywood beauty green with envy. Comes the final embrace, the little feet patter off to bed, while the author resumes . . . "

That little boy, of course, became a big boy. A few years later, Mother had a Caesarean section. I was born. I trundled along behind the big boy, as the baby brother. He was six years older. He always sat on the right hand of Morley at the dining-room table. I always sat on the left. Six years. It is a long time. Too long. I never really knew what my brother was doing. He never knew what I was doing.

I remember looking out of our bedroom window and seeing that he had shinnied up a drainpipe on a house — a three-story house — clinging to the pipe, all alone against the wall, and he swung himself up onto the steep roof and walked around. I thought, WOW. I wondered why he did that. On that steep slope, going up and sitting on the peak. That seemed to be his world.

We didn't have a lot to talk about, not personally. Except that we were Morley's sons. Morley's fierce independence and his sense of security and the love he held in his heart for his children had led him, unafraid, to grant his children their own independence, their own fierce pleasure in being. We learned to love the sound of ourselves talking, yelling, laughing, slanging . . . and as Morley baited us, we went for him as if he were live bait.

Michael was the master of this. He loved words. He loved the sound of words. He loved to talk, to wrangle, to dispute. When Michael was a child, Morley had said of the old dockwalker, "He has already a metaphysical streak, a need to go to the beginnings of things, and a silence that is almost mystical." This was true. Going to the root of things was in his bones. He could see a situation with a clarity that was stunning. Of course, that clarity had the cast of his own character — which, for all his wildness of energy was deeply conservative. But that was not the issue. Conservatism was the coloring. Clarity was the issue.

I remember a visiting writer, after he had been with Michael for a couple of hours, came away astonished. He had thought that Michael had little interest in contemporary poetry. To an extent, that was true, but the writer said, "I've got to tell you this, I've seldom come across anyone who has such a sharp eye for what is right and what is fakery in poetry."

So there we were. Let loose upon each other. On Saturday nights this could be very funny because the three of us had the same habit: while talking, we paced. There were times in the living room — large as it was — that it seemed we were operating on radar . . . and thank God we were . . . we criss-crossed in the sea of our rhetoric, stopping to stomp a foot to make a point, sitting down to make a further point, standing up, faking to the left, going to the right. Sometimes this became insane: the big dog, Nikki the white standardbred poodle, would uncurl from the chesterfield beside Loretto and prance along with us or counter to us, as the whim struck him. To my mother, this was amusing, to an outsider, hilarious.

There was a problem. If we could be our own men in our own house in relation to our father, we believed we could be our own selves anywhere. Maybe, but Michael and I got into trouble outside our private world, outside the house. Morley was much cleverer about the outside world than we were. He could convey "an intransigent honesty" but it was nearly always in the context of a "corresponding humility . . . together with a ready friendliness toward the whole world." This friendliness was not, however, rooted in humility. He had long since decided that he, in his heart of hearts, "could be close to almost no one and therefore friendly to all." He thought it was either dishonest or a great act of self-deception to say . . . to believe . . . that you could actually love more than two or three people. "Only politicians, athletes and preachers are stupid enough or vain enough to say I love you to tens, hundreds, even thousands." This allowed him to be genuinely amiable with a vast host of people because he knew he couldn't with any honesty care about all of them.

When I became a reporter and sat down to supper with Pierre Trudeau for the first time in 1968, he was another guy running for office who might have been invited to one of our family suppers. When I sat down in 1970 with Golda Meir, she was, like most politicians, someone who had bullied her way into power and wanted her own way, without contradiction. If she had been at our supper table, questions would have been asked. So, when I met her, I asked them. And when she was sarcastic, I was sarcastic. This seemed to startle people, upset people. Arrogance was a word I heard over and over again. But I wasn't arrogant. Michael wasn't arrogant. We were asking questions, having a talk — as forthright as we could be, as forthright as grown people should be — as if we were in our own living room. (When I became a teacher, this was the way I tried to conduct my classes . . . as if we were in a living room in which anyone could interrupt at any time and there was no such thing as a stupid question, only stupid answers, and as the teacher I was in charge of the answers . . .) I was certainly naive. Being public in private was one thing. Being private — being who we were — in public, was another.

Michael couldn't hide what he thought, wouldn't hide how he felt. His forthright audacity, his clarity of mind . . . everything that we found so charming at home turned to dockwalking out in the world. He became a journalist, assistant to the president of the largest advertising company in the country, a documentary film producer, the owner of his own consulting company. Timid friends watched him take the walk, careful men hung back, spellbound but reluctant to go into the water with him. Life was not our dining room, not our living room.

So Michael kept grandfather Tom close to his heart, and later in his life he took Aunt Anna — the least of dockwalkers in our family — into his house so that she could die in private, comforted and with dignity, and not in some group home. She was the least loved of my mother's family, she was the one who had disapproved of Tom's refusal to drink the wedding toast . . . a spinster who seemed to have a spinsterish heart, but he let her know that she was loved, became her final confidant as she went down into the deepest of dark waters, and, as Tom would have done, he wrote a poem about her after she died —

AUNTY UP

Fastidious, meticulous, and sedulous,
My maiden aunt lived to be ninety-nine.
While these habits mattered, she was fine.
After twenty years of final decline
She moaned, "God's left me here behind,"
And was lonely and incredulous.

Book Two

1

So this is Paris . . .
Waiter a drink waiter two or three drinks
what's become of Maeterlinck
now that April's here?
(ask the man who owns one
ask Dad, He knows).

E.E. CUMMINGS

The first time I saw Paris, it was 1963, August rain in the morning and heavy, humid heat in the afternoon. I had married Nina, a woman Edmund Wilson described in his journals as "a big blond Ukrainian-Russian beauty," who worked in broadcasting and had a gift for whimsy —

There once lived a black widow spider,
Who spun a trap that would hide her.
From inside came wails
Of drunken young males —
Who were lured by her apple-fly cider.

We were on our honeymoon. We stayed around the corner from Deux Magots in the Hotel Lennox, 9 rue de l'Université, in a room with tall windows and an overstuffed bed, a high carved headboard. We liked that bed. We were night hawks and we liked that bed in the morning, a bed built like a big barge riding high off the floor, white lace-trimmed down-fitted duvets, six puffed-up white linen pillows, the kind of bed — in the pale morning light through the shutters — you could leave the world in with a kiss. To Madame, as tourists, we were a scandal: we not only refused to quit our room till around noon, we stayed out till three or four in the morning, which meant Monsieur — who slept beside the large, heavy oak doors with their nunnery-like clattering chains and locks — had to awake and get up from his cot to let us in.

"Un vrai scandale . . . "

Over a café au lait at the hotel, I learned from a professor, who stayed in the Lennox every summer, that Joyce had lived there for a while. The professor, a skewed eager look in his eye, whispered: *Once upon a time and a very good time it was there was a moocow coming down along the road and this moocow that was coming down along the road met a nicens little boy named baby tuckoo . . . His father told him that story . . . He danced:*

> *Tralala lala*
> *Tralala tralaladdy*
> *Tralala lala*
> *Tralala lala*

I said, "Tra la," and wished the professor well.

With a note from Morley's publisher whom we had met in London, the snaggle-toothed Timothy O'Keeffe, I went to call on John Montague, a young writer from Ulster who lived in Paris with his French wife, Madeleine. I had liked his *Poisoned Lands,* the tone of his mad priest —

> *Shapeless, shapeless man in black,*
> *What is that donkey's cross upon your back . . .*

I got out of a taxi on rue Daguerre, a market street of men with stubble-covered faces and lean bony wives perched on stools by the cash registers, and searched out a courtyard on the other side of a passage-way, stumbling over the cobbles.

I didn't know what to expect. After all, I hadn't published a book. I hadn't published anything. Montague was tall and lanky, he lived with his wife in a studio apartment at the end of the yard. He was charming, somewhat shy, with a nervous engaging smile, a little impish. He had a slight stutter and was intelligent and easy to talk to after a half bottle of Irish whiskey. We went out walking, Montague taking me past the American Club. He stopped and said, wagging his finger, "That's the place, in there, where your father bloodied Hemingway. Do you want to go in?" I said, "Not now, another day." He was taken aback, but I was having a fine time getting him to talk about his poetry. So we went to the Falstaff and then to the Dôme and had beers, and he said he sometimes met Beckett in the Falstaff, and we ended up talking about Joyce and the church and sex and how Saint Anselm had said the flesh was a dung hill, and Montague said, "The church is cruel, like all old sinners."

I went to see him again and once more we went striding along at a quick pace, on our way to the Coupole. This time we side-tracked through the ancient high-walled cemetery off Raspail, an enclosed chamber of rotting flowers and weathered sculpture, sheltering wings of stone and puppy dogs of stone, and as we walked we held close to the gray wall, hemmed in by archangels in full battle gear. Montague said somberly: "We'll go to the grave of Baudelaire," and then, after a few steps, we stood looking down at a carved stone body stretched out on a slab.

The monument was smothered by plants of a wine-dun color, coagulated blood, and the features on the stone face were in a state of decomposition. The feet were not carved in human shape. They were like clumps of clay torn out of the sodden earth.

"Is it much like Baudelaire, do you think?" Montague asked. I didn't say anything. Montague snickered, little crow's-feet at the corners of his eyes.

"It's not the real grave. Now we'll go to the real grave, now we'll go and see the real thing."

But we began talking and joking and drifted among the tombs and through the far gate into the street and the honking cars and as we passed the American Club, Montague asked again, "Do you want to go in? According to your father, it was quite a fight?"

"No, I know how he fights," I said.

"They were the contenders," he said.

At the Coupole, as we ceremoniously touched glasses of Chambertin, I remembered the grave and said, "Damn it, I didn't see the real grave." Montague chortled.

"You know," and he poured himself another glass and stretched his long legs into the aisle, ignoring the puffy-faced seedy headwaiter, "I had one on the academic business world just the other day." He began to smile at his own joke. "I was outside this very place at about three in the morning and Samuel Beckett came by with a woman, looking for a bed. So I offered him mine, which he accepted. The next morning, I wrote to the University of Buffalo, which collects his laundry lists and so forth and said: 'Sirs — I have the sheets between which Samuel Beckett had a woman. How much will you pay?' But I've yet to receive a reply."

We talked about a book I had given him, the only book I had with me from Canada, the journals of the poet Saint-Denys-Garneau. He wanted to know if I wished him ill, putting such a stricken and death-haunted soul in his hands, and I said, No, he'd just have to understand that I came from the land God had given to Cain, all stone and black water and a strange yearning for ice that gets into the soul, and we laughed and strolled back toward rue Daguerre, passing the cemetery. "Is there another Baudelaire's grave?" I asked.

"Ah, it's there, it's there, we'll find the real thing tomorrow," he said.

"Two graves! You're sure?" I said.

"I've heard my own father has two graves," he said, "but I don't know if that's true."

We did not go back.

Two days later, I wandered with Nina for hours among the tombs and searched for Baudelaire's other grave, then asked an attendant, who eyed me from beneath his cap, which had a hard shiny black visor, as if I were peculiar, if there was another grave for the body of Baudelaire. Another grave! Nina reminded me, in the intensity of my pursuit, that we had met in London the great old Irish poet, Patrick Kavanagh, and sitting in his favorite pub, The Plough, he had said, in his one-lunged wheezing growl, "I'm in love with the Beatles, I'm in love with the Beatles, they don't give a damn . . . "

"You're too intense about everything," Nina said.

I tried as hard as I could to be light-hearted.

Later that night, with Montague unaware that I had been prowling through the tombstones, we were talking about poetry and Montague said, "We carry the grave with us — when will poets stop writing about bad drunks and bad cops and get to the real thing . . . love and death. What one learns from women is that we can bring light to another's face . . . but by the very act of loving we put out the light."

"Put out the light," my mother used to call. "Don't forget to put out the light . . . "

That was back when grandfather Tom, standing by the low hedge around our lawn, told me, "Don't eat those red berries, you'll die," and I collected them in my pockets and crept between houses at night and threw a handful of berries at a bedroom window until a face appeared against the glass . . . and then the woman I knew was alone in the room, Miss Murphy, put out the light and came back to peer between the drawn curtains, looking . . . "And no one is ever there," I heard Miss Murphy say later to my mother, the two women standing in the dark, holding hands. "No one is ever there."

Several nights later, I threw more berries at her bedroom window. I hoped she would come naked to the window. She never came again. They took her away by ambulance. "Her blood exploded in her," my father said. I thought I understood what "a curse" meant: I had put the curse of the red berries on her.

Then my grandfather Tom died. I was sure he had eaten red berries.

"His head was full of blood," my mother said, "a hemorrhage."

And I said, "No, he was full of red berries."

In Paris, a few years later, two women turned down a dark side street. They were eating strawberries, two good-looking women eating plump red strawberries from a cardboard box. I wanted to warn them: It is dangerous to eat red berries with me around, and I turned east, going to the flat of Montague's friend, William Hayter, the engraver and painter who had taught Giacometti, Tanguy, Masson, Nevelson, Ernst, Picasso, Miro, and Calder . . . it seemed he had taught everyone at his Atelier 17, rue Didot — and he stood silhouetted in his courtyard doorway against a glow of light. My heart sank as I said hello. He was holding a box of strawberries.

"I thought I heard someone knocking," he said.

"And no one is ever there," I said.

"No," he said and laughed heartily, clapping me on the shoulder.

He was compact and agile, his flesh tight about the bone for a man of sixty-five. His brown hair dappled with gray hung over his ears. His jaw, cheekbones and nose were severe, chiselled. His eyes were almost pellucid: a crystal glint of light in them, and, under the eyes, the lace lines of age in his skin. He hopped stiff-legged across the room, looking for a moment like a spry boy pretending to be a hobbled man.

His young west country Irish woman (he had left his wife to be with her) was standing barefoot on the tile floor, wearing a mini-sack shift, and — twenty-seven — she swung sensually about the room, laughing and prodding Montague in the ribs with her finger, her full breasts and buttocks straining against the cloth. Bill watched her, her wide-set eyes, aquiline nose, full mouth; a smiling taut man, possessive. Her name was Désirée.

We sat at a long board table facing Bill's canvases: ribbons of sounding color, wavering lines yearning for spontaneity. Désirée was beautiful in the ocher light from the lamps and candles, reaching around our shoulders with wine and bowls of food, touching and caressing Bill, and we began to exchange limericks and songs. I quoted Nina:

> She was but one and twenty,
>> Preferred a Kinsey text.
> She scorned her suitors plenty
>> With shouts of "Oversexed!"
> Each move a young man made,
>> She solved with little panic,
> And mocked,"I'll be the ice berg,
>> And you can be 'Titanic.'

The talk turned to music, so I gave them:

> There was a young man from White Rock
> Who tied harpsichord strings to his cock;
> When he had an erection
> He played a selection
> From Johann Sebastian Bach

Désirée pattered about in her bare feet.

"Not exactly the conversation," Montague said, "that great men are supposed to have."

"And what would the world think of us, Montague?" Désirée asked.

"The world never thinks much," he said, "which is why they expect great men to exist in perpetual moments of concentration."

They were playing John Lee Hooker's music. *Boom boom boom boom, Gonna set you right down.* With her long hair swirling, Désirée pranced and kicked her legs and pulled her skirt high on her thighs. Montague was up dancing with her and she looked powerful beside his long lean frame, grabbing him at the waist, spinning him around. Bill, smiling, moved around them, clapping, urging them on, but stalking them, too.

Désirée fetched a granny dress and a granny cap. She held them out to me, ordering, "You referee." As she dressed me in granny clothes, turning me into an old crone, a *cailleach* from the watery Irish hills, I saw that Bill and Montague were slouching toward the center of the room, squaring off, pawing at each other. They circled warily, Bill intense, Montague a little bewildered, ham-fisted but reluctant. There were loud smacks: Bill was hitting Montague open-handed on the side of the jaw. He pursued the swaying, shying Montague. There was a crack and Montague's cheek was red and Désirée bolted between them but she locked her arms around me, blaming me for being all wrong as the old woman, blaming me for not understanding how to come between two men, blaming me for not knowing how to use the powers of an old crone. "People will die because of you and you won't know why."

Bill served us wine. We ate. Montague said a few lines:

One thing to do,
Describe a circle
Around, about me,
Over, against you . . .

2

Over the years, I came back again and again to Paris and to the Hayter house, a Bauhaus studio apartment with one two-story wall that was all windows on rue Cassini, near the Observatoire, around the corner from the Closerie de Lilas. By the early seventies, Montague had left his wife (as I'd separated from mine), had gone to Cork, and married another French woman. But I kept coming back. If I didn't have a hotel room, the Hayters gave me a key and a pallet bed under the stone stairs. The bed was always there for me. They made me feel I was one of theirs, a rambling man who was welcome when he showed up, so I always sang a blues that made Bill laugh:

All around the world
I'd rather be a fly,
Lying up on my baby
Till the day I die.

Got a toothpick in my hand,
Dig a ten-foot ditch,
Running through the jungle
Fighting lions with a switch . . .

Staying at the Hayter house or living, as I did in 1979, in a flat on rue de la Chaise, 22, close to Sèvres-Babylon (where I completed *The Black Queen Stories*), I often ambled over late at night to the Closerie de Lilas — only ten minutes away — where I had fallen into the habit of taking a before-bed drink — a double armagnac. The same trim and accomplished bartender was always there. No matter how much time had passed between visits, when the bartender saw me lurking on the fringe of the crowd, he set my armagnac in a small balloon glass by the cash register, allowing me to thread through the clustered bodies to my drink, giving me my ease. Then I always stood by the piano, beside the elderly pianist — his dyed black hair combed flat to his liverish pate — playing with all the trite flourishes of a good whorehouse style. He played the three o'clock in the morning songs that always made me feel a yearning for lost intimacies, though I knew that as long as I was standing in Paris no emotion was lost forever. The pain was a nostalgia for the future, because Paris — and this is its deepest mystery — always seems to be verging on a promise . . .

There was a night, however, when my feet did not take me to the Closerie. I had a hankering to go around the corner past Hayter's to the Observatoire and follow the length of the Santé wall to where Morley and Loretto had lived, to stare up at the first floor window panes my mother had filled with white handkerchiefs, patches, signals. Because it was a bright night, I thought the moon might fill those empty panes with a whiteness, eerie signs of the pale goddess, but it turned out to be a night of running clouds and absent-minded turns to the right when the left had been intended, and I found myself standing back-to-the-wall in the shadows of a badly lit corner, the Boulevard St. Jacques, facing an auto repair garage, looking to the upper floors of plastered walls pocked by black windows, a pewter gray plaster, knowing that up there was where Brassai lived, the great photographer of ordinary Paris life, and around the corner, Samuel Beckett . . . his *thoughts as rigorous as trees reduced by winter* . . . and maybe, I thought, sentimentally, if I stood long enough, I'd see him coming along the sidewalk, his handsome hawk head, eyes flaring . . . I stood across from his door, humming and singing to myself as if I might summon him up, chanting louder, and then louder *Boomlay boomlay boomlay boom*, my voice carrying into the small world of the Quarter.

"The Quarter, ah, the Quarter, it was like a small town." Morley was re-membering. "The terraces crowded with well-known drunken poets or painters, celebrated for their stupor rather than their art . . . A tourist bus would pass, the tourists gawking, and Flossie Martin, the ex-Follies girl, plump but still golden-haired and pink-and-white-complexioned, who refused to go home to the States, would stand up and yell an obscenity at the staring tourists in their bus . . . and cheerful little old women, selling newspapers, would cry out, '*Ami du peuple.*' Another vendor in a high falsetto voice, '*Chocolat, fruits glacés, cacahouettes, messieurs, dames.*'"

There was a night when Morley and Loretto were walking home at two in the morning and they passed a crowded dance hall, the Jockey, jazz blow-ing from the open door . . . and then, at the end of the block, they took a chair at the Closerie under chestnut trees, joining Scott Fitzgerald and Mary Blair, who happened to already be there. She was an actress who had been married to Edmund Wilson. And Scott was wearing the most elegant felt hat that Morley had seen in Paris. "In color," he said, "it was lighter than pearl-gray, almost white." Musicians appeared under the trees, playing violins, and then Morley and Scott began to laugh because the musicians were playing the American popular song "Ramona" and it made them all feel nostalgic. "Scott, one elbow on the table, had been looking gravely at Loretto, her deep dark eyes, her black hair, her self-possession, sitting in the glimmerlight. 'You know, Loretto,' he said impulsively, 'every time I look at you I see old castles behind you.'"

"Perhaps the musicians were making us think of home," Morley recalled in his memoir, "or maybe it was the presence of Mary Blair, for Scott started talking about Edmund Wilson. He had a reverence for Wilson, but now he was talking about an amusing evening and a little ditty of Wilson's. He had me say it with him, but all I remember now is, 'Come on pup, lift your paw up . . . ' When Mary and Scott were leaving I said, 'That's the grandest hat I've ever seen in Paris, Scott.' 'It was an Italian hat,' he said. Taking it off, he gave it to me."

Loretto told Morley to give the hat back, but Scott put it on Morley's head. Loretto made Morley give it back. It became known as the night they passed the hat because Scott became insistent. "Take it," he said, "I want you to have it." And Loretto made Morley give it back.

In 1979, long after the owners of the Closerie had cut down the chestnut trees, about nine years after I had l separated from Nina and my son, Michael, and about a year after my first book, *The Hogg Poems and Drawings*, had been published, I was standing by the piano in the Closerie (I can't help it, my mind leap-frogs back and forth through time, overlapping years, lives. No family can have a linear awareness of itself; the lives of families are layered). I was wearing a black broad-brimmed felt hat. I had had several drinks. Suddenly I was hailed by a voice I knew. It was Désirée. I left the Closerie arm in arm with her friends, Con Levanthal and his wife, Marion Leigh (Hayter, wanting to play tennis in the morning, had gone to bed). We passed the boarded-up Jockey Club. "There's no good jazz in Paris anymore," Con said. "There's very little of anything that's any good anymore. Old bones on the limp." He laughed as he hobbled along the sidewalk. He was, Désirée said, a Dublin Jew and Beckett's oldest friend in Paris — and he hobbled because of corns, bunions and ingrown toenails. I found him courtly, sensual, tough-minded yet full of easy laughter, a sly gaiety cocooned in melancholy, happily married to Marion, who was in her sixties with a surprisingly pert figure, erratic and talkative as he was meditative. Con led us into Le Scott Bar (no connection to Fitzgerald), a room of bordello-pink chairs and pink tables, and a blowsy Madame whose two "daughters" bowed to Con. "She runs wonderful whores upstairs," Con said. Madame nodded with blushing approval. We sat at a long table by the bar. Cognac and champagne were put on the table. "Are you able?" Con asked, as I poured myself three fingers of cognac, and I said, "Sure," trying to show no flicker of surprise as I felt Marion's hand ease down the back of my trousers, prodding under and forward till she had me full in the grip, smiling like a convent girl as Con said, "Heaney is exactly the verse the English expect is Irish . . . because it seems so English. You agree?"

Marion gave me a squeeze, taking me to the edge of breathless pain.

"Yes," I agreed.

"Désirée says you like the horses," Con said.

"I do."

"We must go together, the train to Deauville."

"Absolutely."

"Lunch on the lawn."

"Chantilly first," Marion said.

"We could," Con said.

"And what about Kinsella?" Désirée asked.

"Black — black, black, black. The best of them, maybe," Con said. "But then, maybe not. He's so black, so closed in."

"Next week," said Marion, easing her grip. "Chantilly."

"Désirée says you like limericks and the like?"

"Yes."

"Let's make one up."

"Now?"

"Sure. On something impossible."

"Like what?"

"I don't know. Marion, pick something."

"Thomas Aquinas," she said.

"Thomas Aquinas!"

"Yes."

We ordered another bottle of champagne. We wrote a line on a paper coaster, stroked out a phrase, wrote out another, called out rhymes, and finally set down a verse on a pink napkin —

> *Nothing was so fine as*
> *St. Thomas Aquinas:*
> *His six arguments for God*
> *Struck atheists as odd,*
> *Who thought man was a clod,*
> *A mere pea in a pod.*

We all agreed that the limerick was awful.

We drank more wine.

"Where're you staying?" Con asked.

"Hayter's," I said. "The bed under the stairs."

After settling our bill, we left Le Scott Bar to walk southeast on Montparnasse at four o'clock in the morning, to the Levanthal door beside a little flower shop. Outside his flat, Con said, "I sent Sam your book, and told him he should see you." I felt a tingling in the back of my neck. "When he reads the book, he'll call. We'll set it up," Con said.

"That'll be great," I said.

"Just remember the silences," he said.

"What?"

"He stops talking. Don't feel you have to say anything. Don't say any-thing. Let the silences be silent."

Beckett's call came. He was firm, courteous, setting aside the following morning at eleven sharp, at the Café Français in a traveling salesman's hotel across the road from where he lived. I remembered a story Bill Hayter had told me about Beckett opening his bathroom window to find a sweating eager-eyed academic clutching the drainpipe, whispering, "Beckett, a word." And Beckett had shaved as if the man weren't there, and had left him cling-ing to the outside wall. I was so pleased at being able to meet Beckett — because, I hoped, if he was going to take the time it meant he admired the Hogg poems — that I went to visit my friend, Robert Marteau, the poet, in his flat near the Seine. He was a lover of porcini mushrooms and fine Bordeaux wines, and he cooked me — and his woman, Neige — a meal and we ended up in the early hours chanting translations of his poetry over the roofs of rue de Beaune, over the Seine:

The source of breath

abides in the absent mouth . . .

nothing moves the unmoved mover.

I walked home through the empty streets, though it was more like traipsing full of pleasure, walking in the wake of a water truck past the stone towers of the Saint Germaine church, through Saint Sulpice square, along rue Ferou, and skirted the Luxembourg gardens and then around the corner of the Closerie to Hayter's. I fell headfirst into my pallet under the stairs — won-dering why Morley had never gone in for the drink, why he'd always been a counterpuncher, waiting for someone to make a mistake so that he could step in, his feet planted, and drive a perfect left hook home.

In the morning, Désirée gave me a kiss on the forehead. Bill, thirty years my elder, had been gone for an hour, out playing tennis, and she said: "You've got ten minutes."

I felt heavy on my feet trying to hurry to the corner where I had cried *Boomlay boomlay boom*, the Boulevard St. Jacques, the Hotel PLM, Café Français across the road . . . a hotel for Japanese and Korean software drummers and provincial avocats . . . the perfect place for Beckett to hole up in, safe from crazed American academics on the prowl. At eleven sharp, he appeared.

Lean, tall, willowy, a narrow head, circular smoked-black glasses, deep eye sockets, the sinister insularity of a bird; in the glare of morning light reflected in the plate glass, he seemed to be cast in negative. A firm modulated voice, "Mr. Callaghan," diction deliberate. He had a liquid, slow moving elegance, head cocked back, a slight sway to the narrow hips, a light, almost feminine drag at the ankles — more the lope of America than the stride of Paris; the walk of a man who sees a long straight flat road ahead, empty space . . . but well-tailored for the emptiness . . . cashmere sweater, black Cardin shirt open at the throat. Perhaps, I thought, only an elegant man at ease with his elegance can understand real filth . . . dust bins, decrepitude, Krapp.

He took off his glasses. His eyes were ice blue, the radiance that reflects off snow, small dark pupils like holes, big ears, long fingers, whitish skin, and a curious movement to his fingers . . . the long little finger moved in sections, segmented, like a water spider's leg coming down to the water surface; the long little finger lay across his cheek, tapping, touching the nostril, I got a sudden sense of crustacea . . .

He sat encapsulated in silence, calm . . . perhaps it was a momentary shyness, boredom, inertia, conservation of energy, or the extremity of ease . . . a silence, it seemed, that was his outer skin, to be penetrated, puzzled over, patiently appreciated; sitting as we were, side by side, our backs to the light, he offered me a small brown cigar and coffee and we sat like two burghers on a bench; I felt woozy, I realized I was batting my eyes, trying to focus . . . "Hello, hello," I said.

"Hello."

"Hello," I said again.

"I've brought your book, creature called Hogg," he said very quietly. He smiled. "Read it. Very fine," he said, as he looked at the opening epigraphs, riffled to the back, felt the page thickness, thumbed along the page edges until he found the drawings, paused over each, put the book down again, said, "Thank you," got up leaving the book in front of me, and sat on the other side of the table in silence. I wrote: "For Samuel Beckett, on a morning of sunlight, over a morning coffee." He picked up the book, read the inscription, smiled and said, "Thank you very much." Silence.

"Con," he said.

"Con," I said.

"Yes," he said.

"Con," I said, laughing lightly, "a fine man, and boy, we had a night the other night, a lovely man."

Suddenly, with soft-spoken affection, he said how he had met Con: a Jewish student in Dublin whose father had owned a shop in Mary Street specializing in rosaries and religious paraphernalia, who had held small regular literary soirées, and then he, Beckett, had left Dublin for France to study . . . and then had gone back to teach at Trinity, and disliking teaching, had set out for Germany, where he'd gone to brood, and from Germany — before he'd known he was to be a writer — he'd resigned Trinity, to stay abroad, where no one could reach him or interfere with him, and Con, his friend, had been given the same job, his job, which Con had kept all the years till he retired ten years previous to Paris . . .

"The night before, two nights ago, we were like two hoboes hobbled by drink," I said, "there we were in the dark, a tall man executing a jig, a shuffling small man on bad feet, Mutt and Jeff, just like you did Godot in Berlin."

He smiled.

"Except Con has ingrown toenails. No one in the play has such nails," he said.

"Maybe the good thief," I said.

I waited.

"What do you do," he said, "when you're not Hogg?"

I told him. I'd taught. Still did, at the university in Toronto. Been a war correspondent in the Middle East, southern Africa . . . I liked to gamble, the horses. Silence. I also reminded him of *Exile*, the magazine I'd begun to publish, and, "Yes," he said, "it comes out rather irregularly, and John Montague, he contributes poems there. A lot of his work." I reminded him that once I had written to him asking him for his own work, something, anything, expecting nothing, and he'd written back, a very courteous card. "Yes . . . explaining I had literally nothing to offer . . . " His exact words from five years earlier.

I said how peculiar it was to be there with him (he put on his dark glasses): a week earlier, coming in overnight to Paris on the train from Munich, I'd toyed with two images of myself: Watt, hurtling backwards with his arms outflung, babbling into a thorn bush (a muffled croak, Beckett's laughter), and also, that moment when Krapp is in his boat, the gentle rocking with the woman in the bottom of the punt, when he's at one with the woman, at one with the water . . . "In the boat, yes," he said, "yes," touched by some recollection. "Yes, the water, the rocking . . . "

He asked about Hayter, how was his health? They had worked together on a portfolio, a short text about his farm in the Marne. I said I'd seen the text, and the engravings. "He has genius," Beckett said. I said the young artists surrounding him in the atelier seemed poky and plodding in comparison, plenty of get-up and *do do do* in the morning, but little daring.

"Done," he said.

"Who?"

He took off his dark glasses.

"Done."

Silence.

I told him how Hayter had told me to come and work with him for a while in the atelier.

"As Hogg or as Hayter?"

"Right," I laughed, "anyone who works with Hayter ends up imitating Hayter."

"It's not his fault," Beckett said. "And how long have you known Montague?"

"Back to '63 . . . I came to Paris on my honeymoon. I thought if I could ever get him to stand on one leg he'd be like an Irish crane looking for water."

Silence.

He opened the tin of cigars and then closed the tin.

"Does Montague go to Canada?"

"Yes."

A smile.

"You'll never go to Canada," I said.

"No."

He ordered more coffee, thimble cups of espresso, and lit another small brown cigar.

"And your place in the country?" I asked.

"It is a very unromantic landscape, in the Marne, a house on a hill, there are workers and tractors in the fields, but a great expanse of sky, an expanse of sky . . . "

Silence.

"It's very interesting, you can watch the complete movement of the sun through the sky, you can watch it come up in the northeast and go down in the northwest, and move over you, so you get all the seasons."

Silence.

"Do you travel to Ireland?"

I told him about driving up into the Healey Pass, in the southwest. "The rock face, the barren jaw-bone of stone, the road, serpentine, and getting out of the car, the whole great valley lay before us, me and Claire — the woman I live with — the wind on us, so that we lay down in the crotch of the stone only to look up, in coitus, into the window of a family car slowly putting by, a family of four agape, disappearing in as much roar of exhaust as a little Ford could muster, leaving us laughing."

He smiled.

"Laughter's hard on the sex," he said.

"There we were, caught in the bottom of Krapp's boat."

He slipped the cigar box into his coat pocket. "The landscape that touched me most," he said, "was the hills south of Dublin, the Wicklow hills. The light."

I told him about stopping at a farm in those hills, asking for water from an old woman, blind, who had a prize pet guinea cock on a string, a silvery ugly bird. And before I could say it, Beckett said, "She ran everything," as if it had been his own mother, or a favorite aunt. And then, shaking his head, he said, "No. I don't know the place, or the woman." He tucked his pink plastic disposable lighter into his pocket. Slowly, politely, he was closing down the conversation. And then he startled me, asking, "What's the line you like most from your Hogg?"

"'The most abrasive lie,'" I said, not hesitating, "'was the perturbed loving look in his eye.'" He smiled. A wry smile or a polite smile? I couldn't tell.

"Well, I must be going," he said. "You'll come back to Paris, of course you will if you're coming to work with Bill, you'll be back. We'll talk again." He stood, surprisingly tall, his movements measured to the required courtesies. In the street, we shook hands, a bony hand clasp, and then his looping turn away, his long legs, the sashay of his narrow hips, the drag and turn of his ankles, elegant, a loose walk, peculiar for a man whose characters are so often up to their necks in barrels and earth . . .

As I walked in the early afternoon light toward the Hayters', along the street toward the iron gate on rue Cassini, I was spent, I wanted to lie down, to sleep, but I also felt a huge rush of energy: I had been lucky in my life, meeting great older men . . . and having a great old man for a father, men of integrity who had a rigor and an energetic staying power to go with their talent (Ezra Pound was probably right: genius was ten percent talent and ninety percent character) . . . I had come to know Edmund Wilson, Brownie McGhee and Sonny Terry, Eustace Ross, Bill Hayter, Yehuda Amichai, James T. Farrell, Robert Marteau, and now Sam Beckett . . . *boomlay boomlay boomlay boom*, my barrelhouse kings . . . it was a surge, an exultant flood of faith that I felt, like a gambler gets when the dice keep coming as called. I hurried along to the

Cassini gate, hurried to lie down and catch some sleep under the stairs, knowing I would awake later in the afternoon to who knows what or whom. Someone was always dropping in at Bill Hayter's for a late afternoon cocktail, a small supper . . . a wild mix of people from all over the world came to see Hayter, and though I still hadn't seen Baudelaire's real grave, and though I didn't for a moment believe that Paris — as Paris — was a place of great French writers and painters anymore, I felt that I was at the center of the last remnant of the Quarter that had so beguiled Morley.

As I lay down in the silence of Hayter's great studio house with the two-story-tall windows and the faint scent of simmering garlic on the stove mingling with oil and turpentine in the air, I thought, Morley, Morley . . . come on over, meet the gang, we'll tell tales, you show me your Paris, I'll show you mine . . .

3

Before telling of the time in 1986 when Morley and I did meet and amble through each other's memories in Paris, I have to tilt back to the fifties when I was a teen-age boy, when Morley and I did not get along. We didn't get along at all.

The rift between us was so severe that when I went to college in 1957, taking a noon train to Windsor, he wouldn't come to the door to talk to me, to say good-bye. As I went out the door, scowling, glad to be leaving my home, my mother handed me one of his novels (I had read almost none of his work), *Such Is My Beloved,* and said, "Read this on the train, maybe you'll find out something about your father you don't know." I shrugged. He thought my life at nineteen was a wreck. He blamed the priests. "They taught you nothing," he said bitterly. He should have blamed Bisi and Fat Saul, though the priests had played their part.

In the summer of 1956, as I turned nineteen, the city decided to reassess all residential taxes in Toronto. Assessors were sent out, fanning through the avenues and alleys. Their reports came back to a large second-floor office on Victoria Street in downtown Toronto. There were ninety men and women in the office. I was responsible for stoops. For every stoop listed in the assessor's report, I entered a charge of six dollars. A man with one arm from Barbados was in charge of three-piece bathrooms, a man from Budapest was in charge of outbuildings and electronic garage doors, a couple from England who dressed in medieval velvets, with little tinkling bells on their sleeves, were responsible for porticos, walls, semi-walls, barriers and fences. They held weekend parties for their fellow workers featuring foods that encouraged flatulence — great cast iron pots of baked beans and split-pea soup — and they received weekend visitors while lying "abed" speaking of "musicality" and the "tincture of scent": they actually put up a hand-lettered poster in the office, promising that a visiting friend from Carlisle could fart the opening bars of "Rule Britannia." One day they asked Bernie Busbaum, the office manager, "What exactly is a fence? How do you define it? We think we know what a wall is but what is a fence?" The kid sitting beside me said, "You steal my watch and sell it to a guy for a price, he's the fence." Bernie stared out the window. He had the heart of a snitch. He kept track of who was late in the morning, who took too long for lunch, and who tried to leave early. He kept a black book and let everyone know that he intended to use it. As a result, workers were on time but they had no idea what they were doing or why.

Among them was Dieter, about twenty-six, who always came to work immaculately groomed — gray suits with vests, a white shirt and dark tie, hair closely cropped, who took me to lunch one day and told me in a measured hushed voice that I mustn't make the mistake of thinking that Hitler had been wrong about everything . . . that he, Dieter, had been in the Hitler youth, and anyone could see that it was an ignoble accident of life that he had to take orders from someone like Bernie Busbaum, a man obviously incapable of ordering anything. I wondered how such a young man, a Nazi, had got into the country, and when I told all this to two Jewish workers who were planning to go into pre-meds, they laughed cynically and told me I didn't know anything about my own town, that there was a club on Sherbourne Street brimming with young Nazis, that there was still a quota system in place for Jews at the University of Toronto Medical School. Harvey Specter said his real problem was not bewildered young Nazis but how to deal with the fact that — since he intended to be a surgeon — the cutting up of bodies didn't bother him at all but a naked girl, touching a naked woman, so upset him he sometimes got sick to his stomach. "I mean what the hell's the matter with me?" he asked, on the verge of tears.

Though the touching of naked girls had become one of my obsessions (Bernie Busbaum had warned me to keep my hands off a beautiful Jewish girl who was in charge of fake brick siding: "You goyim got your own," he had said, and promised to blacklist me), my real fascination in that room was with a Coke dispensing machine, where every twenty minutes someone would drop in a coin and a heavy glass bottle would clunk down through the innards and come to rest behind a little plastic door.

A sturdy black man, a very black man who had a wide almost volup-tuous smile, sat hunkered beside that machine. He seemed to do no assess-ment work at all. He waited for Coke customers. He was threatening, and with a crazed kind of glee he insisted that anyone who bought a Coke had to give him the bottle. I didn't like Coke but once I saw what was going on, I fed the machine and handed him my bottle. He said, "Hi, man, my name's Bisi." He opened his mouth, still somehow smiling as he angled the bottle cap between his molars, fixed me with muddy brown eyes, and bit the cap off the bottle. My stupefaction was his satisfaction. Twenty times a day, he bit open Coke bottles. He was obviously a showboating bully, perhaps dangerous, per-haps a goof. It was hard to tell. One day, he had a word behind his big hand with Bernie and Bernie — white-faced — agreed that he should certainly be able to leave the office ten minutes early every day (toward the end of sum-mer, Bernie whispered to me, "That guy threatened to bite off my little fin-ger!"), so that when the rest of us walked out of the front doors of the office building we found him parked by the curb in a yellow convertible with a hooker he had hired to come into the car beside him — a hard-faced, tarted-up blonde who sat beaming at the boys. I decided I had to get to know him. When someone called him the Nigger King, Bisi laughed and said in his clipped missionary school accent that Yes, his father was a king, all his ancestors were kings, so I yelled back, "So were mine, the kings of Cork." Bisi looked puzzled. He thought I meant the kings of Coke.

His name was Olabisi Ajala and he was from Nigeria. He said he was twenty-eight, but being born in the jungle, he couldn't know for sure. Burly through the shoulders, educated by nuns, he exuded a guileless charm that was a cover for cunning. "When I smile," he said, glowering playfully, "I may be getting ready to bite you." He also said he was a movie star. He said this with utter conviction. "I am a star, man." And he was. He had played in a film that I had actually seen; he had played Robert Mitchum's guide and Susan Hayward's protector in a successful jungle pot boiler, *White Witch Doctor.*

In the film, Bisi had died a heroic death. In life, after the directors had completed all their film work in the jungle, he had whinged and wheedled his way on to a studio plane to Hollywood. There, full of strut and babble, he had hobnobbed over lunch with Elizabeth Taylor, Mitchum, Doris Day . . . he carried a little leather case that looked like a large shaving kit: it contained black-and-white glossies, his proof; and he had married a beautiful black woman, a tall model who, he said, had been on the cover of EBONY magazine. So far as I could find out, he had done no work in Hollywood. Then, very late one night, he had received his draft notice. He and his wife had immediately got into a rented car (his driving papers were false, so he never paid for the car; he never, he said, paid for anything), and then drove to Canada, settling in Toronto, taking the summer tax job, assessing the unsuspecting citizens of the city.

I was earning an adult salary. I had dollars in my pocket. My father had never given me much spending money, being — as I've said before —tight-fisted, open to gifts but not much for giving. But I was flush so I decided to buy a suit. A real suit. Not the kind of suit my mother and father would have bought me, because they always shopped at Eaton's — a dry goods department store, a sensible store, a money-back, guarantee-free-delivery store with men's ties, hats and underwear on the first floor, along with clocks and ladies' purses, and a small perfume counter. Inside the main door to the store, there was a bronze of a seated Timothy, the founder, and my mother and father, when they went shopping and banking downtown, met by the big toe of that statue. It was the custom to rub Timothy's toe for good luck. After all, he was a good man, he had his own elegant stone church on St. Clair Avenue, Timothy Eaton Memorial, a church he had built to himself, a fine grace note for a man expert in dry goods. But I didn't want one of his suits "off-the-rack." I wanted a suit "made-to-measure." I liked the sound: made-to-measure. I wanted a suit that would be who I was. I went shopping along Yonge Street.

Yonge Street had a raunchy, tawdry ripeness. The first cocktail lounge in Toronto, The Silver Rail, was on Yonge Street and it was where I had my first drink in a bar, a Tom Collins, four years under age, and my first Crooks cigar soaked in rum. And then, in a men's furnishing store only a block from the bar, beside the Imperial Theater — an old movie house with swollen pendulous chandeliers in a long lobby — I bought my first suit, a single-breasted one-button-roll flannel suit with hand-stitching on the lapels. That's how I met Fat Saul Ellison, a man I came to love, a man who said he would steal a hot stove and go back for the smoke.

It was a store divided. Little Artie Bateman owned the haberdashery — the shirts, ties, socks, the chrome and silver cuff-links and tie clips. His secret dream was to own a nightclub. Being small and wiry, Artie had won a limbo competition on a cruise ship. He thought a calypso club would be a success, if only he could find a backer, someone with big seed money. Joe Sokoloff owned the furnishings, the slacks, suits, the sports jackets and top coats. The most stylish top coat, a heavy midnight blue wool, was called a Bennie; it was nipped at the waist. Trousers had a slight taper to the cuff. Joe had a slight limp to the left, and what he called a "weakness for the till." Because of his "weakness" he was a successful businessman, expert in going south — going bankrupt — with twenty thousand in his wife's name. Saul worked for Joe. At nine o'clock in the morning, every morning, Saul had a coffee and a Danish and warmed up for the day's action by playing three card monte with Joe. Joe could never catch the black queen. He always got stuck for the price of a coffee and Danish. Joe didn't mind. He liked to keep Saul happy and loose. When he was loose, Saul "could sell a suit to a seal." He sold me my suit.

It was a fine suit, spring weight and soft flannel, with natural shoulders, the sleeves cut to show one inch of cuff. The shirts that most men and boys wore were Brooks Brother button-downs, fine-lined squares on squares, variations on graph paper, with their ties clipped to the shirts, and their hair cropped. But my hair was long and I didn't own a tie clip. I bought several Egyptian cotton shirts, the collars free, one of them a dust rose. I thought it looked fine with my gray suit. As I walked out of our house and down our street one Saturday night, a neighbor — with a broad smile that was both wondering admiration and disapproval — said, "That looks like a shirt only a nigger would wear."

"No nigger I know," I said.

Bisi was waiting at the other side of the footbridge, on Bloor Street by the stairs, in his yellow convertible. He was wearing a tweed suit jacket, a gray button-down shirt with a gray tie, and he was smoking a pipe. He beamed, flashing all his teeth. "You one fine looking white boy," he said. "Fine," and then, switching to his missionary accent, he said, "and now, to the evening's events."

We went to a bar. He told me why he had wanted to go out with me on that Saturday night. He was going to take me to a dance hall on College Street, the Porters' Hall, because he wanted me to meet a beautiful woman, one of his wife's closest friends since coming to Toronto. He was going to introduce me to her so that I could dance with her, and then, "You trim her." He was sure I would. And I could do it twice, or maybe three times — he had to trust my judgment and friendship — and then I was to tell her that he, Bisi, secretly loved her, and wanted her, and she should give him some trim, too. He looked sublimely happy, a great conspirator. I thought he had broken his brain opening Coke bottles.

We sped through the summer night in his yellow convertible to a dance hall on College Street, a dirty, red-brick building with a pool hall on the first floor. There were four or five black men shooting snooker on 8-ball size tables. Bisi, in his tweeds and smoking his pipe — looking like a college don — stood in the center of the room and bawled out, "Ten goodly dollars, no one of you gentlemen can beat my man here." He was pointing at me. I couldn't believe him. Sullen black men holding cues were staring at me. I tried not to panic. Bisi had no idea whether I could shoot pool or not. And if I could, if I was a "shooter" — it was an invitation to get my hands broken. But no one in the room had ten dollars, so Bisi — taking me triumphantly by the arm — moved me out and up the narrow stairs. I could hear music from above, feel the thudding beat in the walls. I came up against two black men on the staircase landing, and one growled, "What you doing here, motherfucker?"

"With me, with me, the gentleman is with me," Bisi cried. Incredulous, they let us pass, and we paid the two portly women at the door fifty cents each, and stepped into the hall, a dimly lit narrow room with chairs lining each long wall, couples crowded on to the dance floor, black bodies in a sepia light, in sly step behind the beat, about to strut, preening and sliding into a loose snap of the hips as Bisi lunged around the room, on the prowl. Left alone, I didn't know if I was scared or not.

I knew I was alone, the lone white man in the room, a ghost in a pink shirt.

I stood with a hitch to my hip and put my hands in my pockets, trying to be casual.

Bisi was talking to a tall woman. Even in the shadow-light I could see that she was beautiful and had what my father liked to call "carriage," a self-confident bearing because she knew she was beautiful. Bisi waved. I tried to step lightly past a seated row of women with glistening hairdos I'd never seen before, rolls of sheen and pomade. The tall woman was listening to Bisi and watching me. Then I felt a hand on my arm, a woman rising up against me, pressing close. "Why's a sweet child like you on the loose?" We danced, a little awkwardly. I was used to convent girls who, even as they nestled and danced close, managed a modesty. This was a woman with hips. This was sensuality, the reek of sex, lightened by her mocking but not malicious laughter when she said at the end of the tune — "One Mint Julep" — "You dance pretty fine, child. Not fine as wine but pretty fine. For a white boy."

"You'll have to teach me," I said, looking for Bisi, who was suddenly up beside me, saying, "She's gone. You let her get away." He was angry and hurried me out of the hall, muttering, "We'll find her, we'll find her. "

Two weeks later, at two in the morning, I was in a cramped apartment over a cake shop on Harbord Street. There was a lamp with a pleated pink plastic shade beside the bed. The music over the radio was Randy's Blues, the all-night program from Nashville. Randy did commercials for Royal Crown Hairdressing in pig-latin, *Rayesoil Crayesown Hayesair Drayesessing* . . . or *Start Your Own Chicken Farm: Buy One Hundred Baby Chicks By Mail.* Randy was spinning Fats Domino's "Please Don't Leave Me," and we were standing flat-footed in the pink shadow-light, swaying, stripped down naked, black and white on the beat — or, not black . . . but a body of burnt and copper-tinged umber and sienna. She was the most stately woman I had ever seen, the first black woman I had known naked, full-breasted, slender yet solid through the hips, long-legged yet light on her feet, and Sharon was her name.

"Rose of Sharon," I said.

"Don't you Rose of Sharon me. My father was a preacher."

"What'd he preach?"

"He made me promise him I would never go with a white man, an' look at me."

"What's he hold against white men?"

"That's too dumb for a smart white boy."

"I'm not hurting you."

"Just don't come on by with that Bisi."

"I thought he was your friend."

"You are pretty, and pretty is all you need to know."

"You *shtuppin* her?" Saul said.

"Yeah."

"Holy shit. No kidding."

"So what?"

"Nobody goes out with niggers."

"A black woman."

Saul was sitting in his chair between swatches of cloth, reading the racing form. He paused, musing. He liked to think things over. I thought this was fine, and funny, too. He didn't mind if I laughed quietly while he was thinking. He thought people looked funny while they were thinking. "You ever see six guys all in a row reading a racing form? Like six dead birds on a wire. That's the good thing about Jews when they pray. They move their bodies. Too bad I don't pray."

I put my arm around his shoulder. For a man whose game was deception, three card monte, he was always absolutely guileless with me, straight, and I didn't know why, but I loved him for it, loved him for letting me into his world.

"What does she do?" he asked.

"She's twenty-eight, a legal secretary."

"She's half-way home to being your mother."

He went back to reading the racing form, saying, "You need a place to get laid, you can use mine." He was intent on the races.

"She's got her own place," I said.

"No shit," he said. "It saves me clean sheets. *Mazel tov.*"

There was a betting shop upstairs, over the haberdashery front end of the store. It was run by Billie (he was the only bookmaker and pimp in town who had listed himself in the phonebook, as Billie's Enterprises), a small man with round black eyes and a sloping forehead, who sweated all the time, a low-class hustler, pusherman, fence for junk and a bootlegger who handed out business cards to strangers on the streetcars and handled a phone in the afternoons for a bigger bookie named Poodles John. The phone was in the front room on the second floor and Billie would open at about noon. There was a radio and a phone, decks of cards and cigarettes, and blinds on the two windows.

Downstairs, Saul, stroking the Hollywood collar of his shirt, looked up and said, "What's doing, let's get lucky." He was never lucky. He was divorced, living alone in a top-floor Queen Street room, a hot plate in one corner, the bathroom down the hall — a $2 horse player, frenetic, fast-talking, laughing, no real gripe against anyone, always a little scared, but eagerly hustling overpriced cheap suits off-the-rack all day.

"I like the 2 horse in the first, who do you like?"

"Me? What do I know?"

"Never mind. You got the touch, I can tell. Pick a horse."

In the evenings, he would take me to the Mercury Club behind the Imperial Theater and the clothing store, on Victoria Street. The club was owned by the great quarterback, Joe Kroll, and the boxer, Sammy Luftspring. There were blowsy single women in their late thirties in the place. "Ripe pickings," Saul said, "lovely ripe pickings." He was always courtly, almost avuncular with women. "Sweet, sweet, even the worst women are sweet. I do whatever to make a woman feel good. A good-feeling woman is a gift to your life." He liked to talk about the women he had had and all the women he had nearly had, and all the horses that had hit the wire fading in the stretch to be second. Over fifty, not quite as fat as his nickname, but with a bad heart, he played his life like it was so many small thefts: "Steal me some time." "Steal some living." "Steal some luck." (Years later, about once a year I would get a phone call from a harried Saul. The bookies were after him, threatening to knee-cap him. Sometimes it was two hundred dollars, sometimes three. Too much for him. I would give him the money over a quick lunch at Bassell's or the Tops, and he always wrote out a little note, an IOU. "From you I would never steal," he said, "not from you, ever," pressing the note into my hand.)

Saul bet every day with Billie upstairs. He was Billie's steadiest "small shooter," his steadiest loser. But Billie was in trouble with Poodles John, a big, heavy-set Greek who drove a white Cadillac and kept two white poodles in the front seat beside him. Poodles thought Billie was either stealing from him or not working hard enough, not getting enough action off the street. He warned Billie, "You're in the phonebook, Enterprises, yet you turn shit — you turn loose change and that don't even pay the rent on this phone."

Poodles, sitting down, took a lady's lipstick mirror from his vest pocket and clipped his moustache with small scissors. Then he said, "You think eh, Billie, you think what to do."

Billie set up an afternoon poker game. The players complained about the phone and complained about Billie answering the phone and sticking betting slips to his sweating arm or neck while dealing. Sometimes, when the phone rang, he lost track, dealt the cards wrong; the players told him to pay attention. Poodles phoned and asked for the day's count and told him to raise some more action or he was out. That evening Billie sat for half an hour running the window blind up and down, thinking. Saul said, "I bet you Poodles don't do nothing," and Billie said, "You bet. Now I know I got trouble."

Billie had a string of hookers who worked the Warwick and Wilton Court hotels — $10 turkeys he called them. The next day, he arrived with Carrie; she was bemused, bored, had a loose mouth and wide, flat feet. Billie had figured out a package deal for the local clerks and shopkeepers. He'd spread the word himself along the street: "Five flat on a horse, two bucks for the broad." The poker players came along and took a chair and paid no attention to Carrie; at thirty minutes to post time she settled into a half-lotus squat in front of the chesterfield, waiting.

By the end of the week, at about one o'clock, men in button-down shirts and Brooks Brothers suits, with horn-rimmed glasses, crew cuts and clean nails, were standing in an awkward line up the stairs, three or four stairs apart, discreet, not talking, sometimes snickering quietly to themselves. They bet on any horse, usually the Best Bet from the *Globe and Mail*, sat for six or seven minutes in front of Carrie and her Kleenex box, and then went back to keeping their shops — shoe and jewelry and ladies' lingerie stores. The card players paid no attention.

I told Bisi and Bernie Busbaum about Carrie and Bernie smiled indulgently, disdainfully, as if he were disapproving, but by the end of July he was nearly always late coming back from lunch because he'd had to stand too long in the line up the stairs to Billie's room. He said nothing to me.

One late afternoon a young kid gave Billie the number of a horse and seven bucks and asked to get laid. Carrie lifted her dress and got on her back, saying, "I don't get much call for this."

Business was good for Billie. A lot of the owners and salesmen, all neat and quiet, got tired of the girl but became hooked on the horses. Poodles John was pleased. He shifted his heavy bettors to Billie's phone. He began parking his Cadillac by the curb at six o'clock every evening, waiting for Billie, petting the two "toy" dogs, complaining that "the slut" was going to cause them grief. Poodles was the boss and Billie — after a talk with Poodles — called off Carrie, who went back to sleeping through the afternoon.

"You think you know something about me," Bernie said after Carrie was closed down, "I know something about you. I told you to stay away from that girl."

"What girl?"

"Don't fuck with me," he said angrily. "Jewish is Jewish."

Bisi was angry, too. He refused to bite open my Coke bottles. He knew I was going to the Porters' Hall every Tuesday and Saturday night, seeing Sharon.

One week after I ended my assessment job, I was sitting with Saul in the store and decided to walk two blocks to the City Hall to see if I would be able to get a job the next summer. As suspected, Bernie had blacklisted me, and the woman clerk, looking up from my file, said, "We certainly don't want someone like you working for the city again."

"Oh yeah," I said. "Can I see that?"

"No."

"I'd love to read it."

"I bet you would."

I went back to the clothing store. "He probably wrote what he wrote while he was sitting with Carrie between his legs," Saul said.

"I can see him," I said, "sitting there in his black ankle socks, and his black loafers with the little leather tassels. I hate guys who wear shoes with little leather tassels."

A man hurried through the front door, tan hair a little mussed, clear plastic rims on his glasses, scuffed shoes.

"A teacher, ten-to-one a teacher — they and musicians always got scuffed shoes," Saul said, going warmly, expansively to the man, taking him by the elbow to the rack of charcoal-gray suits.

"The chalk, the dirt on this color, is very appreciated by teachers," Saul said confidentially. "Nobody notices, five, six months, then you get it cleaned. Two pair of pants," he said, lowering his voice to a whisper, "you steal the year cheap."

The high school teacher held out his arms and slipped on the suit coat. Saul moved him up into the triple mirrors, so close that he could not see himself, tapped the man on the *tuchis,* smoothed his thighs, tucked him under the armpits, and then Saul rested his belly in the small of the man's back.

"Touch, touch, till they're on their toes, terrify them," he had told me, "then let them down into $49.50, let on like you believe in education, good grooming, a little edge for the teachers, the hope for the future, then $45 flat, wear it home, put what you got on in a box . . . "

As the man, flushed and embarrassed, walked out of the store into the afternoon light wearing his new suit, Saul eased back in his chrome chair, satisfied, and said, "First fuckin' rain that suit'll go up like a window blind."

Then, he stood up and buttoned his suit coat, and with a fine propri-
etary air, walked slowly to the front of the store, singing quietly, *School days,*
school days, good old golden rule days . . .

4

And then there were the priests.

In 1950, my father sent me to St. Michael's College School. I was thirteen, no sign of strife or mournfulness in my eyes. I was a good athlete but I
wasn't big. I had seen that certain boys my size — because they had a stride,
a bearing — weren't jostled, weren't shoved. I adopted a stride, as if I were
coming down off the pitching mound, a chaw of tobacco in my cheek, into the
classroom. Boys almost twice my size let me be. One big fellow let me be with
a kind of affectionate amusement. He used to clamp his hands on my shoulders and lift me straight up in the air, a gesture of warmth. He was George
Chuvalo. When he let me down I would slug him as hard as I could. He
wouldn't flinch. We were friends. One day he made a loud noise in Latin
class. I was sitting in front of him. The priest turned from the chalkboard,
came down the aisle, and back-handed me in the mouth. My mouth was full
of blood. Chuvalo said, "I made the noise, Father." The priest looked at me,
he looked at Chuvalo, and said, "Let that be for all your sins, of omission and
commission, Callaghan." Chuvalo asked me to help him with his Latin. I
found that he had an ear for poetry. Catullus wasn't on the course but he was
very good with Catullus. The priest didn't like Catullus at all. He wasn't too
quick. Several priests weren't too quick. Father Lally, a tall, prematurely balding young man, told me indignantly to leave his "religious knowledge" class
because I had asked him questions about free will and Luther and predesti-
nation. "You're too young to debate these matters," he said (unfortunately,
Morley at our supper table had tried to explain to me in some detail the
integrity of Luther's spiritual and intellectual dilemma), and Father Mullins,

my feisty French teacher, thinking I was sulky and a smart-ass, announced to the class — after he threw a small chair at me — that I was "born for the rope." I took to signing my class tests in French with a noose.

The school had been founded by the Basilian Fathers in 1852 at a grassy site on Bay Street called Clover Hill, priests who ministered to the embattled Irish Catholics of Toronto, only ten to fifteen percent of the population at the time. In that town, sometimes called Little Belfast, Catholics were on their toes or on their uppers. For decades, the students of St. Michael's had long since sung about themselves as the Fighting Irish. You could be Polish, but if you went to St. Michael's and played for one of their football or hockey teams, you were Fighting Irish, bound in prayer to show how tough you could be. At pep rallies before games, a thousand male students, following the big brass band on the gym stage, would sing:

> *Oh my name is MacNamara*
> *I'm the leader of the band,*
> *Although we're few in number,*
> *We're the finest in the land . . .*

The same order of priests was in charge of the Catholic college in the University of Toronto and PIMS, the Pontifical Institute of Medieval Studies attached to that college. Because they were a liberal teaching order drawn to neo-Thomism, the great contemporary Catholic philosophers of France — Etienne Gilson and Jacques Maritain — became part of every seminarian's experience. So, I entered as a child into the world of enthusiastic jock-Catholicism, where a priest who had gone through PIMS might speak to me (à la Maritain) of the nature of poetry and beauty and how poetry "approached metaphysics" — and then he might lustily sing along with me our banal school song:

> *There's a red light on the track*
> *For Boozer Brown, Boozer Brown,*
> *There's a red light on the track,*
> *For Boozer Brown . . .*

There's a red light on the track,
It'll be there when we get back,
There's a red light on the track,
For Boozer Brown . . .

As we go marching
And the band begins to P-L-A-Y,
Hear the people shouting
Old SMC will surely win today.

I had no idea who the Boozer was, but we had a Father Brown; he was an affable man who patrolled the lunchtime cafeteria with a sawed-off broomhandle that he would sometimes crash across the shoulders of rough-house boys, and there was Father Marshall who gave boys whisker rubs on their bare bellies after gym class, and Father Mulcahey who made students who had been late for class try to cut the lawn — single blade of grass by single blade — with the scissors kindergarten kids used to cut construction paper, and Father Whelan — with his pert coterie of visiting convent girls — who drank. Boozing, a touch of sadism, whimsy, longing, and the metaphysics of beauty, were in the marrow of a culture that bred raw violence and a clumsy benevolence.

One fall day in my first year, the legendary Athletic Director, Father Ted Flanagan, a gentle-spoken, good-looking man, walked me to the field where the senior A football team was practicing. He had been watching me play quarterback in House League football. He said I had "a natural throwing arm," and he could see me playing quarterback some day for the Seniors. He wanted to take me to a practice so that I would get a feel for the spirit of SMC athletes who sheltered under the wing of Michael, the warrior archangel.

As we stood on the chalked sidelines — a small boy palming a football beside a priest with his hands in the belt to the skirt of his black soutane — he asked, "Who's your favorite player on our team?" and I said, "Mike Lisko," a lineman who wore a moustache. Father Flanagan smiled. "Ah, Lisko," he said. "Last week, when we were playing the East York Goliaths, their defensive guard went right over Mike and tackled our quarterback for a loss. On the very next play, Mike bit him on the leg. That fellow didn't try to come over Mike again." Father Flanagan smiled. "The will to win, and prayer," he said, "It's almost . . ." He didn't finish his thought.

I knew I had heard something totally crazy. I loved the craziness. It was the craziness of our hockey team, the "Majors" — the farm team for the Toronto Maple Leafs whose motto was — If You Can't Beat Them In The Alley You Can't Beat Them On The Ice. The hockey players — many from northern mining towns like Copper Cliff and Porcupine and Sudbury — were not ordinary schoolboys: squeezing tennis balls to improve their grip while sitting in class, some were semi-literate and all were semi-pros . . . and a few, like Dick Duff and Dave Keon and Frank Mahovlich, were destined to be poets on the ice, fighting jock-Catholics who became legendary figures in the national psyche, entering into metaphysics, hockey being the first principle of our national life.

(Some years after Morley died, when I was in Venice giving readings from my short stories, I was asked if I wouldn't like to go to Rome and read there, too. "We know how you love Rome," they said, but I said No, I was going home, I had to be home for supper on Friday night. "Must be a special supper," they said.

It was. I wouldn't have missed it for the world. I was only sorry that Morley had to miss it. Two thousand people, most of them men, sat down, eight to a table, to eat supper on the floor of St. Michael's High School Hockey Arena. It was a supper to celebrate the Athlete of the Year for the past fifty years.

It was as if no time had passed. The keynote speaker, a fighting jock-Catholic, gave a dislocated talk about old priests, pucks, school cheers, education, sweat, the bonding that comes with winning, and sat down. A prayer was said before the introductions.

I was the Athlete of the Year for 1954. The names were called and we went up on stage. Dick Duff held open his arms. We embraced. He was 1955.

Frank Mahovlich said, "When I saw your name I thought you'd be speaking and we'd be here all night." He was 1953.

We stood on stage together, and I thought Morley would have seen, with a slightly wry eye, that standing there between Mahovlich and Duff I was approaching metaphysics. He certainly would have liked that. But in the fifties, who could have known. I had become a basketball player almost by default.)

In my second year, after being smashed face-first into the pipes of a hockey net at a six-in-the-morning practice (I was not very good), and then — after classes — finding myself on a November football field lying with my face in ice water and mud stuffed up my nose, I decided to give up hockey and football and become a basketball player. The gym was warm in the winter. That's how it happened.

My father, who had always come to watch me play football, as he had come to baseball games, asked me only one thing about basketball: "Does everyone wear white running shoes like that?" I think he was worried that white shoes — as opposed to the black he had worn as a boy — were somehow not manly enough. Anyway, in all my career — and for six years in high school and college I spent two to three hours every day in a gym — he only came to watch me play once. It didn't matter. I was happy to be left alone. I played and played. My grades in school had begun to slide, but the headline in the *Globe* read

BARRY CALLAGHAN, 15
ST. MICHAEL'S IRON MAN

for on a Friday night, I had played in a midget game and been high scorer; played in the junior game and been high scorer; played in the senior game and been high scorer. My coach, Father Crowley, had put his arm around me after the final game. "That was quite a night, Sweetwater," he'd said. I liked that. I liked Iron Man but I liked Sweetwater better. Sweetwater Clifton played for the Harlem Globetrotters. I told people I was going to play for the Globetrotters, I'd be the first white man ever . . . It was a good story, and I liked the story so much that one night I went to see the Globetrotters play at Maple Leaf Gardens and at half time I stood in the passageway to the dressing rooms and as Sweetwater Clifton came close I stepped toward him and said, "They call me Sweetwater, after you." His eyes narrowed and he sneered, "You crazy, kid," leaving me angry and flushed with humiliation. I still liked being called Sweetwater, but now I intended to play for Boston, the Celtics.

I was reading Plato's dialogues, reading Egyptian and Medieval History and the journals of Stanley as he trekked through Africa in search of Livingstone. I wasn't studying. I was mightily bored by class. I was failing everything except a particular tradition in our family — public speaking. My brother, who had gone through the school for five years before me, had won the Cadwallader Trophy for public speaking every year, and every year I won the trophy, too. My father did not send me down into a cellar until I had my lines by heart as his mother had. He made me stand on the staircase landing, with all that stained glass behind me, delivering the speech over and over again as he stood in the well below, listening, until he nodded approval.

As I entered fourth year, Father Crowley took me aside and said, "Callaghan, you're trying to do four things when you can only do three. You're drinking (it was known that I kept a bottle of whiskey in my locker), you're playing basketball, you sleep with girls, and you're trying to be a student. You've got to drop something." I took his advice to heart. When the year was over, I was a better basketball player (I had special coaching on some Saturdays . . . under Fred Thomas, a great black player from Assumption College in Windsor, a man who had led his college team to victory against the Globetrotters and then had gone on to play for the Globetrotters, and who is now in the Afro-American Hall of Fame in the United States), I had a "white book" with the names — for that year — of thirty-six girls in it, I could drink a bottle of whiskey but seldom got drunk, and I had failed three of seven courses.

Father Crowley had a mournful conversation with me, and for the first time in my life there was a mournful look in my eyes. We were going to see the principal. Father Crowley, because I was naturally bright, believed the school had a degree of responsibility for my scholastic failure. He wanted me to know that whatever happened in my fifth and final year, I would have an athletic scholarship to Assumption College in Windsor. We sat down with Father Regan, the principal, and my failing grades were adjusted so that I could enter fifth year and go on strutting my stuff on the court.

That summer I met Saul and Bisi and stepped into their world of window blinds and witch doctors.

That summer I hung out at the Porters' Hall and slept in Rose of Sharon's bed.

By September, I was back in school and full of scholastic intentions. I astonished my history teacher by blurting out, "There are strange things done 'neath the midnight sun" and then declaiming *The Cremation of Sam McGee*, talking about the mystical relationship between fire and ice, and how each little village, each town was an incubator of fire in the countryside with a Sam McGee sitting in it, grinning, crying, "Close the door, close the door." The teacher thought he saw an intellectual fire in my eye and left me alone in my chair at the back of class. I didn't tell him I had dreamed of my grandfather chanting *Sam McGee* after I'd spent an evening studying the mystical glacier paintings of Lawren Harris. It wasn't until early in the winter that he discovered I hadn't read one page of my history textbook. He was too disappointed to be enraged, and by December, I was bleary-eyed in the mornings and bored, and a great swollen silence had come up between me and my father, broken only by my eruptions of rage that were almost hysterical. His weary air of sorrow and understanding exasperated me even more: "I am not one of your stupid stories," I screamed, though I had not read his stories.

I have to try and explain something here about Morley and me, as father and son: Morley had given me, as a boy and as a young man, an enormous amount of freedom; he did not hover over me, hound me, hector me, and certainly he never gave me a hiding; perhaps he was aloof or lazy, perhaps he was wrapped up in his own world. But though he did not pay a lot of attention to what I was doing from day to day, he had somehow made me understand what he expected of me, and he had persuaded me that I should expect the same from myself. I knew that I was responsible for the freedom I had been given. If I failed that freedom, if I did less than my best for my self, then I was what he called "a slob." Though knowing seldom stopped me from acting like "a slob," I knew when I was belittling myself. As I turned my freedom to license, as I behaved irresponsibly, I accepted the responsibility (not in any way to be confused with guilt) and when my failures flared into the open, I responded with rage — a rage at myself but a rage I dumped on Morley.

I had one confidante, the last priest to hear my confession, Father David Bauer, a thoughtful young man, a former hockey player, who had stopped me in the hall one noon hour: "I'd like to ask your father something, it's for a kid I'm talking to. How does someone become a writer?" And I said I knew the answer: "You read, and you write. The rest is just talk. That's what he always says." He asked if I would come around and talk to him after practice and I said I would. After practice, he said, "So talk," and I did.

He was unflaggingly honest, at ease with ambiguities. We talked about sex and about God (Morley and I had had a fierce confrontation in our kitchen, as I had insisted that he tell me whether he believed in God, whether he had a relationship with God . . . and he had tried to slip the question the way a club fighter slips a punch, and then he had said, "Look, if there is a God, and if I am in the image of that God, then the best thing I can do is be true to myself, to my best sense of myself, and if I'm true to myself then I'm true to God, and I expect that's good enough for God and if it's not, what can I do . . . ?" And I, standing across from him in the kitchen, had yelled, "That means there's no God greater than you . . . " And he said, "No, I'm just a writer, I work with words, and I'm a father doing the best I can"), and Father Bauer had said, when I told him this story, "Maybe you're right in a way you don't know you're right, because we know God works with words, His words are what we've got, and He is our Father, maybe He's doing the best He can . . . "

This sounded vaguely heretical to me. But I liked it, so I told him that when I was fifteen I had gone to midnight Christmas Mass with a girl and we had taken communion and then had walked all the way home, a long way in the silence and whiteness of snowbound streets, and in the deep silence of her sleeping house, suffused with a sense of being blessed, we took off our clothes and lay naked, nestling and kissing, at peace, and I had felt this light, a light lifting itself up in my chest . . . and that was the best, I thought, that I could ever be, and every time I made a love to a girl or a woman, even when I was drunk, I was after that peace, that light . . .

"Do you still go to communion?" he said.

"No."

"Well, there's your problem."

"I don't go to confession. I don't know how to confess what I just told you."

"You just did."

"Not really."

"You want to make it real?"

"Sure."

He made the sign of the Cross.

"Bless me Father," I said, "for I have sinned."

"Are you sorry for your sins?"

"Yes."

"For penance, say five Our Father's and promise to try to think well of your father at least once a day."

We laughed and were shyly embarrassed for a moment, but then I said, "It's hard to think well of him, he thinks he knows what I'm thinking about before I'm thinking it, and this lets him stay totally tied up in himself, stuck in his penny-pinching little world that he thinks is so big because he's making it up . . . "

Father Bauer shook his head.

"Do you think you actually hate your father?"

"No. He enrages me."

"Why?"

"Because he thinks he knows what I'm thinking, who I am, and my brother is the same way. No matter what I say or do, they know, but I am not what they know, not at all . . . "

"What are you?"

"I'm at school. I'm a complete screw-up at school. I'm just shadow-boxing the whole time."

"You're in your father's shadow?"

"No. I never think about it because I'm not."

"Not what?"

"In his shadow."

"He's a great writer."

"He's my dad and I don't like the way he's my dad."

"It's a big world . . . "

"I've got my own world. He's got his world and I've got mine and I never think about him in it." I laughed, happily. I didn't want to be anyone other than who I was. "I got a whole private world, which even you don't know about, and I love it. When I'm playing basketball, when I'm out with people who know me, they don't know him. He's on radio, or somewhere else. But where I play . . . wherever I play, I'm a star."

Father Bauer put his arm around my shoulder. "Don't get me wrong," he said. "I worry about you, that's all. I'm afraid it's going to be too long before you feel that light inside you again. I'm afraid you're going to fail . . . this school was probably the worst school in the world for you . . . "

"No it's not."

"Why not?"

"Where else would I have got to talk to you?"

He believed the school had been corrupted, spiritually and intellectually, by the contractual link with the Maple Leaf professional hockey team . . . the hard-nosed Conn Smythes of the world cozying up to priests and the priests loving it. That was Father Bauer's earnest concern. So many of the best priests loved it, basked in it, believed in it — the corruption. He was intent on rooting out that corruption, cancelling the contract, getting rid of the Maple Leafs, but who, he wondered, would ever believe him if he were to say that Foster Hewitt — the Leaf broadcaster — was the voice of corruption in the land?

The astonishing thing is, within a few years, the Maple Leafs were out of the high school and Father David Bauer — not very popular among some fellow priests, having returned the school to amateurism — went on to build the National Olympic Hockey program, becoming a national icon, blending educational concern and spiritual care into the will to win. He died young.

All through the months that I talked to Father Bauer after basketball practice, I was going to the Porters' Hall at night, which meant I didn't get out of bed until noon on Wednesdays and often did not come home on Saturday nights; I also hung out with Fat Saul at evening card games in a second-floor joint on Queen Street run by Herschel the Dipper (he was known as a quick-fingered dealer who "dipped" into the pot once he got his immigrant players drunk — the whiskey always free at his table); I shot pool all day Saturday at Long John's, a flat over a furniture store on King Street rented by a Louisiana black man who was six-foot-six, a flat he ran as a booze can with a pool table, or I shot pool at the Hub, the only black barbershop for men in town that had a small poolroom behind it: the floors sloped and the tables were warped, which gave warp-heads an advantage, and there were plenty of those because the poolroom was beside a government liquor store where I learned that if you grazed the neck of a bottle of whiskey with a glass cutter just below the government's seal and then snapped the bottle, you could drink the whiskey and get another bottle free because the seal was intact; I contracted a virulent strain of gonorrhea, was rushed to St. Michael's Hospital in the night and nearly died — I was given the last rites — and in the midst of my fever was told: a) by a stern doctor that I would be sterile ; b) by the nun in charge that

I would "sizzle" in hell for my sins; c) and later by a social worker, who had
— by law — to be told who my partner was, that such was the punishment of
the Lord for mixing the races. My father asked me why I was so drawn to this
world of black dance halls, and I said, "It's like moonshine . . . "

"It's slumming," he said. "It's *nostalgie de la boue*."

"It's dancing, good times . . . "

"It's showboating. That's all. I've written about this. You're showboating."

When I left the hospital I was warned I would not be able to play basketball for at least three or four months, if ever. Two weeks later, I scored 31
points. I was also told by my father that he had been assured by the nuns in
charge of the hospital that such illnesses were held in the strictest confidence,
that I should not let anyone in the high school know why I had been away for
more than three weeks. The morning that I reported to the Director of Studies,
Father Timmins, his bald dome gleaming under a fluorescent light, he looked
up and said, "Well, got yourself a case of the clap, eh!"

"Strep throat," I said.

Through the following months, I passed the after-hours in the House of
Hambourg on Cumberland Street. Clement Hambourg, from a family of
Viennese classical musicians, had come to Toronto in the late thirties. By the
late fifties, hip to what he called the goof butts, Clem started a cellar jazz club
featuring very young but great talents: Moe Koffman, Archie Alleyne, Norm
Amadio and Ed Bickert. There were reefers, and there was laughter about the
weed: "To get this stuff, man, you got to go all the way down to Florida, check
into a beach front hotel, open up the windows and wait for the hurricanes to
blow the seeds in from Cuba," and there were stronger drugs as well, but I
never had a taste for drugs. I don't like taking aspirin, but I could drink a bottle of Alberta Premium rye whiskey straight up and then move on to cognac
as an early morning chaser. At four in the morning, we ate hot slabs of prime
rib roast beef that Clem's wife cooked in ovens upstairs, and then I eased on
home to my girlfriend's house on Bleeker Street as she strutted her stuff in her
high heel sneakers in the dawn light. She was in her mid-twenties and shared

the house with her mother who had her own lover, a sullen Swede. Never once did her mother intrude and for that matter, strange as it seems, I have no recollection of my father ever demanding to know where I was . . .

When the year ended, I had passed one exam out of nine — English Composition, and that barely: I had written a short story about meeting a panhandler on Yonge Street, a story my father liked, but he was angry, humiliated, and fearful for my future. I was unconcerned. I was sure that I had my athletic scholarship to Assumption College — my "fixed" fourth year marks would allow me entry into their program for American students — and so I packed my bag (actually, Morley's old Gladstone bag that he had taken as a student debater to Pittsburgh) and rode the train to Windsor to meet the Athletic Director. That was the day Morley, sitting in his dressing gown, having a late breakfast, refused to come to the door to say good-bye. And when I called out, "See you later on Lake Louise, cool as the breeze," he threw his poached egg on the floor. My mother gave me a book to read, *Such Is My Beloved,* and she also said: "There's an old proverb . . . 'He who takes his revenge within thirty years has acted in haste.' If you really want to hurt your father, wait thirty years."

She smiled, as if she knew something I did not know, and she did. I hugged her good-bye, thankful for her love and loyalty, thankful for how often she had tried to forgive me and see things my way without betraying her husband's trust. She knew how long thirty years is. She knew how things change in thirty years.

I got off the train in Windsor, full of confidence, and took a taxi to the College, to the office of the Athletic Director. I sat down in Father Hussey's office, a big, fleshy bluff man. I asked him what the conditions of my coming to play basketball were. He looked at me as if I were demented. He said that he had heard about me, heard that I was a good ballplayer, but also he had heard that I was a lot of trouble . . . but that was beside the point . . . he said there was no scholarship, there had never been talk of a scholarship. I was welcome to try out for the team like anyone else if I could find a way to get to the College, find a way to pay the housing and tuition fees. The priests, my coaches, had lied to me.

Geezus fucking Christ, I thought. Holy shit!

It was a long train ride home. I saw my face in the train window. I was for a fact looking mournful. To distract myself, I read *Such Is My Beloved*. That sent me into a real slump. The novel was startlingly good.

Morley, shaking his head as if he had known all along that I would get suckered by my coaches, said that what really bothered him was the notion that he had thrown his poached egg on the floor. It was not true, he said. "Your mother made that up," and then he said he would give me the cost of the tuition and six dollars a week to spend. My residence rent would be my problem.

Saul, commiserating, said he would send me ten dollars a week, any clothes he could steal from the store, and anything he won over a hundred dollars at Herschel's card games.

My mother asked me how I had liked *Such Is My Beloved*. I said, "Fine," and then I added that I felt like one of the hookers. "Fucked."

"Don't talk to your mother like that."

A few months later I was walking alone in Windsor on a warm September night, walking under campus trees, a fresh breeze off the Detroit River, thinking, I'm alone, at last I'm alone on my own, and I began to sing my brother's favorite song out loud, *If Beale Street could talk, if Beale Street could talk, married men would take their beds and walk* . . . when a man stopped me. "I heard you singing," he said. "I could trust a man who sings in the night, in the dark." I thought that was a pretty good way of saying hello, and replied, "How do you do?" And he said, "Fine, I'm Father Fehr. Call me Bob."

As it turned out, I was lucky. The Basilians, with several schools on the continent, had decided that the way to control their irksome young intellectual priests, those who wouldn't toe the current Curial line, was to banish them to Assumption, a frontier college of disheartening wartime prefab frame huts and one old brick Hall clustered beneath the Ambassador Bridge, a College that couldn't grant its own degrees, a backwater, known only because it had a great basketball team.

I found that I was being taught by five or six men — Father Fehr, Father Crowley (one of my English professors, and not my high school coach), Father Drouiard — who were tolerant and eager for every fresh idea in the world. Only ignorance and needless constraint galled them, and — discovering that they had all been closeted together "as if by divine accident" — they relished their freedom, teaching with a wondering enthusiasm.

I felt released. I wrote love letters to several women, full of arcane poetry . . . Catullus, Sappho. I began to read Kerouac, Camus, *The Evergreen Review,* Salinger, Kenneth Patchen, Joyce, *New Directions,* Beckett. Father Hartman, the Master of the Residence, took me aside. "I've heard about you," he said. "Life's simple here. I don't care what you do downtown or in Detroit. Just don't bring it back here. Leave it in Detroit."

I nodded.

"And I don't suppose we'll ever see you at morning mass," he said.

"Probably not," I said.

"Okay."

A gentle-hearted student named Murphy came into my room late one afternoon. He had a box of twelve bottles of whiskey. He was looped and entangled in the whimsies and joys of his dream world. He stretched out on my roommate's bed. He wasn't going anywhere. Drinking was forbidden in the residence. I smelled trouble for me. I decided to get as far away as I could, and went to Detroit. In the evening, when I came home, Father Hartman was waiting.

"We realize it wasn't your fault. Murphy says you didn't invite him in, but your roommate insists on being put in another room."

The gentle Murphy, drunk, had insulted my roommate and punched out a priest, breaking his nose, and then he had explained: "All the dream whiskey is in Callaghan's room." Father Hartman confiscated the twelve bottles and with a wry smile, left me to the room, alone. Two weeks later, he knocked on the door, the same wry smile on his face. Beside him stood a six-foot-one Chinese student.

"Fine with me, I got no racial stuff going on," I said, and Hartman said, "That's not why I'm smiling. Not at all. He doesn't speak English, not a word. Name's Lo Hing Yang. From Canton. He'll keep you fine company, talkative fellow like yourself."

He kept me fine company, being bright, sensitive, full of curiosity and incredibly brave. In the Liberal Arts program, he was forced to study English literature, Greek philosophy, German, Business Administration, and Chemistry, his field. He had nights of wrenching despair, but before the final exams I worked him through English and Philosophy and two other ballplayers drilled him in German and Business. He passed. When I saw him, feeling goofy with pleasure for him, instead of calling, "Hi Lo!" I yelled, "Lo hi! — Lo hi!" He looked around wildly and said, "Don't say. Don't say. It mean, *Let us fuck* in Cantonese, in street talk."

Just before Easter, Father Hartman called me into his office. He offered me a drink of whiskey.

"It's the last of the Murphy cache, I thought you should have a drop."

I did. Have a drop.

5

And then there was basketball.

I went out to the gym. It was clear who the established Varsity players were: they moved with measured aplomb, they knew the floor, the glass, the pace of the court. They had crew cuts. The slightly paunchy coach had a crew cut. My hair was long. "How are you doing, Elvis?" the coach said to me. He didn't laugh. His name was Hank Biasetti. I was told that he was a real pro, that he had played baseball with the Philadelphia Whiz Kids in the World Series. First base. Then I remembered him. He had played first base for Jack Kent

Cooke's Maple Leaf ball team in Triple A in Toronto. I liked that. I liked anybody who had been close to Cooke, who believed in grabbing hold of the sky. I did what I did best. I showed Biasetti my stuff, loops and double-pumps, switch-hand shunts off the glass. A player from Rochester wearing a rubber sweat suit said, "Shit, we got a guy who plays nigger ball." I had never heard of "nigger ball."

The coach lined us up. He counted off twelve for the Senior Varsity team, he counted off twelve for the Junior Varsity team — the team I was eligible to play for. I was left standing with a clutch of gangly, lead-footed jugheads. The coach thanked us — the jugheads — and told us to close off the day playing a pick-up game among ourselves and he turned away to his chosen teams. I was astonished, furious. I was cut. I had never been cut. I was a shooter, a star. For twenty minutes, I slashed toward the basket. I didn't know whether I wanted to cry or kill . . . so I threw in another hook shot. The coach suddenly came over and said, "Do you think maybe you can get your hair cut, you can play for us. Yeah, okay, you can play for us."

I played, I practiced, I played a game or two every week, and practiced and traveled the intercollegiate circuit from city to city, as far as Montreal. When we played in Toronto I stayed with the team in the King Edward Hotel. I liked being on the road. I liked being on the edge. I remember the first time I read Robert Lowell's line — "free-lancing along the razor's edge," I said very quietly to myself, "Yeah."

But — after a practice at Assumption or after a game on our home court — Detroit became my nighttime honky-tonk town. I have no idea what Detroit looked like during the day. I only went across the Ambassador Bridge at night. I don't know how but I found the West End Hotel and the Flame Showbar. I met Pepper Adams, the young baritone saxophonist, and Yusef Lateef, the very hip flautist, and little Joe Carroll, who had sung with Dizzy Gillespie, and we became friends, especially after Joe got a job at a bar in Windsor. I went there, too, and learned all his songs and one night he stood on the bar and I knelt on the bar so that we were about the same height and we sang:

School days, school days,

Good old golden rule days,

Readin' and writin' and 'rithmatic,

Taught to the tune of a hickory stick . . .

Rise Charlie rise, wipe your dirty eyes,

Turn to the east, turn to the west,

Turn to the one you love the best . . .

Go in and out the window,

Go in and out the window . . .

(It was one of two times I have sung on stage: the other, years later, was with Jimmy Witherspoon, and we sang "Time's Getting Tougher than Tough.") In Detroit I also met a "jiggler" — a tall beautiful black woman who shimmied her whole body to the beat of a honking rhythm and blues band while standing still. She shimmied till her skin had a sheen of sweat, glistening in a single spotlight.

Sometimes I would stay in Detroit in her flat. A very grim man with one arm — he had apparently lost the other arm in Korea — sat inside the door of her house that had often been broken into. There were ten or twelve tiny flats in the house. He sat at the foot of the stairs in a rocking chair, all night. She told me he had a gun and looked after the house. He used to charge me two dollars to come in with her and two dollars to let me leave in the morning. He called it his "white poll tax." She thought that was very funny. But after three weeks he stopped asking me for money, saying, "You either got shit for brains or more nerve than Dick Tracy."

She sang in a church choir every Sunday, and three times I went to gospel service with her to a small church that had fake stone siding on the outside front wall. I forget the name of the church, except it had Ebeneezer in it. Apparently, many of the congregation were not happy about my being there. She heard harsh whispers but was indifferent and said she liked seeing me sitting at the back of the church. "You look so lonely." The one-armed man by the stairs told me it would be a good thing if I stopped going to the Ebeneezer church, and he warned me that my jiggler's old-time boyfriend was coming home on leave from the army in Alaska. "And he *will* kill you," he said.

One morning after a night in Detroit, I came back on to the campus very early in the morning, crossing the front lawn, and I encountered the Assistant Athletic Director, who said, "Barry, up and at 'em early, eh, and I didn't think you went to church and here I find you going to mass."

"I'm not going to mass," I said, "I'm going to bed."

The Assistant Athletic Director seldom spoke to me again. I didn't care. I was having a good time with Father Fehr (who talked to me about Jung, the existentialists, the coming controversy over birth control, the role of the Church in the death camps, and the sometime comedy of sin in the confessional — telling me that he'd cautioned a woman who insisted that she was a great sinner, that what she liked to call "perversions" others called "positions"), and my English professor, Father Crowley — a tall, pie-faced man who indulged himself by wearing a sweeping floor-length black cape, a man who read widely and loved to intone all the contemporary poets — and I was not only reading novels and poetry but I was writing.

During the Christmas holidays, I had met a tall blonde at a night-spot in Toronto called Chez Paree on Bloor Street. I had gone there with my brother for a pre-Christmas drink. Some older men — friends of Morley's that I knew, including Harry Boyle (my godfather) — men who worked in broadcasting — came in and sat down. We joined them. They ordered food. The announcer for Harry's radio show fell face-first into his oyster soup, drunk, and waiters carried him out through the kitchen. The blonde, aloof but smiling, walked — with a stately, very erect, long-legged narrow-hipped stride — through the crowded room carrying a glistening frozen turkey on her shoulder. She sat at our table, the turkey still on her shoulder, an obvious independent gaiety about her. She said her name was Nina and that she had won the turkey at a bowling tournament (held for the staff and friends of CKEY, Jack Kent Cooke's old radio station), "which is pretty crazy since I've hardly ever bowled." She said she loved reading Steinbeck and I had been reading all of Steinbeck. She said her parents

had come from Russia and that she understood the turtle in *The Grapes of Wrath,*
crossing the highway, indefatigable, moving on, truckers trying to run it down,
a seed tucked under its shell . . . carrying a seed from one side of the road to the
other, the movement of life that would never be broken. I asked her if she read
Joyce and she said the moocow had just fallen head-first into his soup. I liked
that. I liked her. She told me to come out into the night and she would put down
her turkey and teach me how to play chess. She let me win. I asked her if she
ever played strip-poker.

Winter turned to spring. When my first year at Assumption was over —
I had paid my bills, passed my exams, and (despite the fact that I hadn't cut
my hair) was high scorer and leading rebounder for the Junior Varsity team.
I had also learned what real "nigger ball" was: we had played an all-black
team from Detroit. I had never seen anything like them. Gazelles. Free-flow-
ing. Full of panache, full of themselves. They walloped us. They went bounding by, shooting down instead of up. I knew that my dreams of being Bob
Couzy were done, but still, I had been high scorer on our team and I waited
for Hank Biasetti to say something. He didn't.

A long poem of mine in seven parts had also appeared in the college
magazine. It was called "The Outhouse." It was not what was expected. Part
of it read—

> . . . *gold, silver*
> *Copper, lead,*
> *This is the ulcer of man's mind, the quickest way to the dead.*

Several students said, "How'd you write that, you're a jock?" And my
other professor of English, Father Pappert, stopped me and said, "That was a
very interesting poem . . . how much of it did your father write?" I said, "You
goddamn mother . . . " We never spoke to each other again. As a ballplayer, I
wasn't used to taking anything from anyone. I wasn't going to take that from
him. I shudder to think how it might have been for me as a young writer if I
had not been Sweetwater, a high scorer, "a star" in my own mind, beating a

barrel with the handle of a broom,
with a silk umbrella and the handle of a broom.
Boomlay, boomlay, boomlay, BOOM.

The next September, as I was about to return to Windsor, Bisi Ajala was arrested, appeared in court, and was convicted on charges of false pretenses (I had bumped into him that August: he had been wearing brogues, socks to his knees, plus-fours and a tweed jacket, and two expensive cameras were hanging from his neck: he had laughed about his yellow convertible and the hooker and my refusal to "hand over" Rose of Sharon; he said his wife had left him and then he said, No, she had not left him, she was sick; he had been evasive about what he was doing — but after his conviction his "story" was reported in the scum-sheet, FLASH, and it is worth quoting, not just to get the details, but also to get the racist tone of the times). He was about to be deported:

SEND ME BACK HOME BEGS AFRICA FOTOG
AFTER MAGIC FAILS

Blaming his dark deeds on difficulty in adjusting himself to the Canadian way of life, a jet-black West African imploringly rolled the whites of his eyes at a Toronto court last week and pleaded to be deported to his native Nigeria, where the climate, he said, was more to his liking than in the Don Jail.

He was self-styled "dark-room artist" Olabisi Ajala, 25, convicted on 17 charges of false pretenses resulting from a few magic checks issued during a photographic safari among clients of the King Edward and the Royal York Hotels.

The "magic" of the vouchers consisted of the fact that while they weren't rubber, they still bounced.

Dressed in the latest fashion, Ajala was as loud as his clothes from the start of the proceedings. The court clerk and the Crown had a hard time cutting through his voluble protestations of innocence.

Police evidence, however, was that the African had tried to settle a $55 car repair bill by handing Allen

Motors, of Wellesley St. East, a check which showed a tendency to bounce from here to Timbuktu.

Then, police continued, Ajala had decided to try his hand at photography — of the practical and paying kind, by snapping happy couples in hotel cocktail lounges.

This was a highly profitable business, for he would collect $3 in advance, and forget the rest. Not much overhead there!

But police in time heard about this walking dark-room from which no pictures issued, and Ajala was nabbed while lining up more happy-to-pose suckers in the Royal York.

'What were you doing in this country, anyway?' asked Crown Attorney Henry Bull.

The Nigerian answered he had worked 'at least five months for the Highway Department at No. 6 Malton Division.'

He said his wife had become ill in December and needed hospitalization. Financially, this had become too much for him, he added.

'And now you want to go back home?' the Crown demanded. Ajala was jumping up and down in the prisoner's box in his haste to get going.

Magistrate Thoburn, however, decided to adjourn sentence for a few days, to see what immigration authorities would have to say about footing the African's passage all the way back to Nigeria.

In Windsor, I came out to the Varsity practice confident and stronger because I'd begun to thicken through the shoulders and I could feel the "weight" of the power in my thighs. I didn't just cut, I drove to the basket. Biasetti took me aside. "You're not going to play the way you're used to playing on this team. We're going to change that. We play by a system. On this team, we play a system." When I told this to a friend on the team, he laughed and said, "Haw, you don't get it. He doesn't like all that flash and slash shit."

Day after day I tried. Head down and dogged. I wanted to play. I had come to love the surety of each double pump, scoop and hook shot, each feint, each finger touch as I laid the ball to the glass. But I stopped all that. I put aside finesse. I tried to play into the system. I aborted any slashing drive to the basket so that I could pass-off into a staged mechanical weave, the pattern of perimeter play, the pattern of Biasetti's mind. The weave! I thought that was for slow learners in a basket-weaving class. That was for Hoosiers. I'd never been to Indiana but I knew that there were Hoosiers everywhere. Men who wore crew-cuts. Men whose eyes were too close together. Men who thought American college football was exciting: single-wing left, single-wing right, two bucks up the middle . . . I shook my head. I bounced the ball. I began to stumble, to lose anticipation, to dribble into my feet, fumble the ball . . . practice became a sorrow, an embarrassment, with other players wondering silently how I had become so hapless as Biasetti looked on. For years on the hardwood court I had felt totally secure. Now, I was confused, doing injury to myself, injury to whatever gift I had and injury to who I was, deep, deep . . . I couldn't comprehend why he would want to throttle what was natural and spontaneous in me, but I kept on trying, trying to please, trying to conform. I even went to one of Biasetti's prayer gatherings before the exhibition game that launched the season:

> Glory be to the Father,
> the Son, and the Holy Ghost,
> and may that Glory
> fall upon our team
> and keep us free from injury
> and humble in victory . . .

Nina came to Windsor to watch me play. I did not start the game. At half-time, still sitting on the bench, I was enraged. He was not playing me. By the middle of the second half I had sunk into sullen fury and humiliation. I had tried to do it his way and now I was on the bench. With one minute to play (and we were losing), he suddenly called, "Callaghan, go in." I thought of refusing. But I went in. Thirty seconds later the whistle blew. He took me out. I was dumbfounded. I couldn't understand why he would want to humiliate me at the end of a game.

Later, at her hotel, I found Nina's response bewildering. Her sympathy for me was half-hearted, thwarting my need for consolation, my need to steep in self-pity. Then, at breakfast, I thought, Wait a minute, she doesn't really know anything about me as a ballplayer. She only knows what I have told her. What she knows is what she's been through with me this past summer, that's what she cares about. And in a way, suddenly, that was what I cared about, too, because in the summer I had become a reporter, a writer.

I had come home from Windsor and entered into a whole new world, Canadian Press, the news wire service, working on the rim as a re-write man — and after I had been there for two months, they had let me sit in for Milt McPhail, the *Broadcast News* sports columnist . . . writing a column every day for ten days that went out on the wire . . . it was incredible, an incredible stroke of luck . . . it was exhilarating to know that those columns were being read by announcers on radio stations across the country.

Some columns were straightforward polemic. Others were almost stories. I had read those stories to Nina, and other prose pieces I was working on, and that's what she wanted to talk about at breakfast — the stories, particularly one I had called "The Muscle" which I didn't know how to end. She had typed a clean copy of it in the summer and we had sent it to *The New Yorker*. They had sent it back saying it wasn't quite right but they would like to see anything else I was writing . . .

Morley had been excited. "Do you know what it means to have a story plucked out of the slush pile? Fix the ending."

"I don't know how."

"Figure it out. I could fix it in five minutes."

"So, show me."

"No. Figure it out yourself."

"I might learn something."

"No."

That had been in August. Nina had been angry at Morley for not showing me how to fix the ending. Now it was September in a hotel in Windsor.

Nina ordered more coffee.

"And what are you writing?" she wanted to know.

"I'm working on a thing about Saul."

"You're not making fun of him?"

"No. Hell no."

"I was talking to John Harasti. He says he can get you a job next summer in television news."

"At the CBC?"

"Yes."

"That'd be great!"

"What's the Saul story about?"

"I'm trying to figure out how to make all those people, not just Saul, but Billie and Carrie and Poodles sympathetic. How to make you like them."

"I like them."

"I mean on the page, in a story."

As she got on the afternoon train, I said, "I don't know how I'm going to eat. If I quit basketball, I can't go to the team training table anymore."

"Don't worry. I'll send you care packages."

That night, a Sunday, I called Father Fehr and asked him to use his keys to open up the gym for me. He did. I got dressed in my uniform. We turned on a bank of lights. He stood and watched without saying a word as I played alone in the shadow-light for forty-five minutes, cutting, driving, looping in long hook shots, pushing as hard as I could, finally bending over, drenched in sweat, exhausted.

"It's okay," I said, as we walked to the dressing room. "I'll just shower and go home."

He went back to the gym, turned out the lights, and locked up.

The next afternoon before practice I said to Biasetti, "You're trying to kill what I love best in me, what I do best." There were tears in my eyes. "I've got to quit," I said, "you're not going to do that to me." It was clear that he didn't know what I was talking about, clear that he was one of those men who clipped the wings of birds and then said, "What d'you mean something's wrong . . . the birds are walking aren't they?"

I looked up his baseball stats. The man had played in 21 games, he'd had 24 at bats and 2 hits, batting .083 in the majors. I couldn't believe it. I couldn't believe that I had nearly betrayed my love of what I did best to such a man, that — in trying to please him, in trying to conform — I had nearly made the same mistake that I had made the last summer I played baseball for St. Peter's in Christie Pits, back when I was a kid pitching and playing center field.

Back then, in the Pits, we played several games against the St. Columbus Boys' Club team. Their coach was Carmen Bush, a roly-pudgy street-wise man with round, soft brown eyes. He was kindly but quick as a whippet.

In our first game I hit a home run. I hit the home run with a bat that was stained a dark mulberry. It became my special bat, my "signifying" bat, my home run "stroker" — and Carmen began to ride me from their bench about my peculiar colored bat, what he called my "left-hand" bat, cupping his hands around his mouth as he yelled, "You're on the wrong side of the plate, you don't know where you are!"

I decided I would show him. I could hit wherever I had to hit. In practice, I switched from the right to the left side. I discovered I had a sweet fluid swing from the left side of the plate, a straight stride into the ball, and I seemed to see the ball better.

The next game, as I came to the plate, Carmen called out, "You carrying that same old 'left-hand' bat?" Standing to the left, believing I was beating him at his own game, I stroked a clean single over second base. I went four-for-four in the game, four singles. I tipped my hat to Carmen. He smiled. Their center fielder hit a home run in the ninth inning and they won.

In game after game I hit singles. I became a "spray" hitter, hitting singles all over the field. But I had no power from the left side of the plate. I had a home run stroker in my hand that didn't stroke. Father McMahon, feeling a little betrayed because I had let Carmen heckle me into changing my style, suggested that if I could learn how to bunt I could bat second in the line-up. "The hell with this," I said angrily, and switched back to the right side of the plate, left-hand bat or not. I was a clean-up hitter, I hit home runs.

But I couldn't get my home run stroke back. I developed a hitch in my swing, I started stepping "into the bucket," my front foot falling away toward the foul line. And I wasn't seeing the ball clearly. I began to strike out. At last I hit a home run, but I struck out and struck out. I was still pitching well, but one day Father McMahon said, "Callaghan, I think we'll let Billy Daniels play center field today." I was benched. I got rid of the mulberry-stained bat, but I had lost my stroke. In a rage, I broke a new bat against the steel pipe at the corner of the dugout fencing. The drunks in center field were frolicking and falling down without me. I knew that I had made a terrible mistake. Even as I went on to pitch winning games, I nursed a grim disappointment, a sense of having betrayed myself. I swore I would never betray myself again — a joy-less decision because even when we won, I didn't feel the old elation.

After my words with Biasetti, I sat in my room for two days, bewil-dered, listening over and over to Bill Dogget's "Slow Walk." Then I walked to the phone and spoke to my father. "I've got news for you," I said. "I've quit playing basketball." He hung up on me, saying I must be drunk. I phoned back. "It's true," I said. There was a long pause. He didn't know what to say. He laughed. It wasn't a mocking or knowing laugh. It was a good, open, embracing laugh. The contention between us still hung in the air, but not the animosity. That had subsided. It had subsided over the summer as I had worked at Broadcast News. I laughed. I still didn't like the way he did things, but at that moment, what else was there to do but laugh. "Well, the great trick," he said, "is to make sure in your own heart that this is what your heart wants to do."

It was strange to hear him talk that way about the heart to me. Usually, he warned me against wearing my "heart on my sleeve." Being too open, too vulnerable. Now he was telling me to trust my heart.

That's what his Kip Caley had done. I had read another of his novels, *More Joy in Heaven,* about Kip Caley, a criminal, a bank robber, and I had been intrigued by it, remembering that Aunt Anna had said that the original hold-up man was a distant cousin of our Chicago Ryans. But if I liked the sensual intelligence and mysterious ambiguity that was in his stories, why wasn't I drawn to this intelligence and ambiguity in his life? Perhaps because, for all the love he had in him — and there was never any question that his love for his sons was unconditional — he kept to the freedom he allowed us which was also a curious detachment. He stood back, and perhaps he stood back because he knew what happened to the Kip Caleys of this world who openly trusted their hearts. They got betrayed and shot down in the streets. They left themselves open to the schemes and ambitions of meaner, smaller men. So what was he telling me? To trust my heart but not wear it on my sleeve? To trust my heart but keep my feelings close to my vest? To be Kip but keep my heart still?

As I sat brooding in my room in Windsor, I got a note from him. He had, I discovered, been to Michigan, to a town close by called Lansing. It was dated from the week before,

Thurs, no, Friday.

Dear son,

I got on the train and when we were composed I said, "How long do we stop in Windsor. I'm sure I'll be receiving a delegation of one. If the delegation doesn't show up I want to phone him" and I was told to my surprise that we were on the Chicago train which didn't pass through Windsor, but through Sarnia. When we got to Lansing a professor was waiting who took us for a drink and dinner and an evening afterwards; then there was a lunch next day, then drinks, then the dinner with the president, then the speeches and a party, and next day, after lunch we were on the way home, and I had to do my sports piece. You may not have been my wandering boy but I was your wandering father. There was no use you coming over there unless you just wanted to be there for the speeches which was why I didn't phone you. I was sorry to have got side-railed from my little boy.

We are going to Montreal this afternoon.

Love
Dad

Composed. A delegation of one! What a curious tone. That wasn't the way he talked. Anyway, I couldn't have gone to meet him. I had no idea he was planning to pass through Windsor. I laughed. This seemed so detached, so close to the vest, as to be comic.

When I told this to him on the phone he was angry with me and got off the phone and gave my mother a setting out, blaming her for having raised a totally self-absorbed boy.

My mother phoned and asked if I had any idea what it was like trying to act as go-between for two totally self-absorbed men.

I said, "I'm not self-absorbed the way he's self- absorbed."

She said, "And he's not self-absorbed the way you're self-absorbed."

"Right."

"Wrong."

"What d'you mean 'wrong'?"

"I give up. You're both ridiculous."

"I've never thrown a poached egg on the floor."

"You threw your life on the floor."

Three weeks later, Father Boland called me. He was my history professor. He was known as Pinky. He asked me how I was. I said I was hung over. Hmm, he said, and wanted to know if I would go to Montreal, there was a Model United Nations being held at McGill. He wasn't quite sure how Assumption College had come to be invited, he said, because the other schools were Yale and Dartmouth, Princeton, Queen's, University of Toronto, Cornell and so on.

He was sure it was a mistake but he had accepted anyway and he had been looking for me for three days and would I go? I had to leave that night. I said yes, I loved Montreal. I had been there to play basketball. He said, "Good. You're Sweden."

I phoned Morley and said he should meet me at Union Station in Toronto for half an hour between trains. "Think about Sweden," I said, and just before midnight Morley and I stood toe to toe in the marble halls of Union Station for twenty minutes, trying to get a handle on the essential shape of Swedish foreign policy.

"So long," I said.

"So long," he said. "Your grandmother Minn would be proud."

Our invitation had been a mistake. They weren't expecting me. There was no hotel room for me, only a couch in a frat house gaming room. I was no longer a ballplayer but I still knew how to behave like a star. I threw a first-class snit that got the secretary's attention. She was a sweet young woman with lovely breasts. She got me a room. After the first day's debate, she told me that there was an award for the Best Delegation. The professors and politicians from New York and Ottawa, she said, were talking about Sweden. After the second debate she said everybody was really talking about Sweden. A fellow from Yale, button-down collar and ovipositor mouth, had brushed me off as the "altogether too intense boy from the boondocks." I stayed up all night writing my speech, typing, retyping. The final debate was held in the afternoon. At the concluding supper in the evening, a professor and someone from the Department of External Affairs in Ottawa announced that the debates had been extraordinary, but someone had to win, so the trophy for Best Delegation went to Sweden. There was moaning at the Yale and Dartmouth tables. I let out a *Whoop!* Goddamn. Praise Satchel Paige. *Whoop!* The secretary had brought a mickey of whiskey to the table in her purse. We drank it. Feeling wondrously expansive, I offered to sleep with her in the hotel room she had found for me. She declined. Just after midnight, I called Assumption College and told the grumpy priest who answered the residence phone to shake Father Boland out of bed.

"Pinky," I cried, "Pinky, we won!"

"Who's this?"

"Callaghan, it's Callaghan."

"Where are you?"

"Where you sent me — Montreal."

"What d'you mean we won? Won what?"

"Best Delegation, Pinky . . . sorry, but tonight I got to call you Pinky. We're it. The best. We beat the ass off Yale and Dartmouth, all those dorks."

"You mean it. You . . . oh!!!!"

"What's the matter?"

"The bottoms of my pajamas just fell down."

"Whoop, whoop, whoop," I cried and hung up and called Morley — who was terrifically pleased — and then I went to the Esquire Show Bar behind the Windsor Hotel, where Arthur and Red Prysock were playing rhythm and blues. It was a snowy night. At one o'clock, as I stepped up to the front door, two men blocked my way. "That'll be two bucks, to get in," one said. I paid. I drank exultantly by myself at the bar as one of the Prysocks sang *Mercy Mister Percy, Mister Percy have mercy on me* . . . and after about two hours I left to the honking of a sax but at the door I was stopped by the same two bully men who said, "And it's two bucks to get out." They were surprised when I wasn't angry but laughed. "Gotcha," I said, "the white poll tax." It was snowing very heavily. I walked up toward the mountain, "that great jagged hedge surmounted by a gleaming cross" — as Morley had described it — but then I looked back at my steps in the deep, fresh snow, dark holes, and I had the sudden feeling that if I stood still those black holes, my steps, would catch up to me, overtake me and pass on over me, so I kept moving toward the mountain, quickening my stride, full of confidence in the night silence.

Book Three

1

*I*t was a bright July afternoon. I was about to become a reporter. On television. I was standing in a small field that I had played softball on as a child, a field at the foot of Casa Loma that had been used by Acme Farmers' Dairy to walk their wagon horses. The dairy had converted to trucks and the field was now disused, but I was standing there beside a horse. I was reporting for CBC news. It was in 1958. Premier Khrushchev had just appeared on television at the United Nations in New York, banging his shoe on the Soviet desk. I had been sent out to interview the horse. It was a talking horse. One *whinny* meant No. Two *whinnies* meant Yes.

"Did you see Mr. Khrushchev on television as he banged his shoe?"
"*Whinny.*"
"Do you approve of what he did?"
"*Whinny.*"
"Do you think the Soviet Union should be censured?"
"*Whinny, whinny.*"

The interview with the horse ran as the second item on the six o'clock news, after a feed from the United Nations.

"Great," my boss said, "and too bad about the kid."

Before meeting with the horse in the field I had spent the morning with a mother distraught by sorrow and desperation who was trying to raise money so that she could take her dying child to the evangelist Oral Roberts, hoping for a miraculous healing, a cure of cancer. The child — sitting in her lap — had screamed in pain and terror all through the conversation. The film editors had refused to edit the film for air.

"Without the screaming," my boss said, "it would have been great."

John Harasti, a young writer and actor, was a reporter at the CBC. I had met him at Canadian Press and he had found the job at the CBC for me. It was a wonderful place to be a young reporter. Those were the first days of television news. Nobody knew what they were doing, which meant almost anything could be done. As each show went live to air, anything could happen and so it was a forgiving newsroom. It had to be. Too many mistakes were made.

The executive editor took me aside. "You've got a weakness," he said. "You're trying to do too much, to do everything. You've got to learn to spread the mistakes around. Watch Harasti."

Harasti had a certain brilliance and charm, but had taken to drink. He had a bed at what became the Bohemian Embassy, a second floor coffee house above shops on Yonge Street where writers like young Gwendolyn MacEwen and Margaret Atwood read their poems. He drank all day, coming in at six o'clock to put his feet up on a desk and watch the news. He always gave the show a warm round of applause. Our exasperated boss ordered him to interview a local alderman live in studio. Harasti, half-soused, sat beside the alderman. The rather snooty floor director counted down. Harasti didn't see the count. "Just relax," the home audience heard Harasti say to the alderman. "They'll signal us when to start." The floor director ignored the two men who sat side by side in "live" silence for a full minute. The floor director then threw Harasti another signal. He turned, looked at the alderman, and said, "What the fuck is your name anyway?" He stood up and walked off the set. The boss went berserk. I collapsed in a heap of laughter. The assignment editor said in Harasti's defense, "I can't remember his name either." Harasti was not fired. He was given a month off with pay and told to dry out, which he did. At the end of the summer, he came back and replaced the assignment editor (who was on holidays) and told me to work up a three-part series on crime on the waterfront. "But there's no crime on the waterfront," I said. "There's always crime on the waterfront," he said. "Don't you go to the movies?"

I decided to ask one of the older reporters what he knew about crime down at the docks. I dropped by his small spare flat on Cumberland Street, next door to the The House of Hambourg. "Come in," he said. He had a copy of Gorki's *Creatures that Once Were Men* in his hand. He whacked me on the shoulder with the book. I took it as a sign of affection between men who liked books. It was a bed-sitting room: one chair, a bed, a desk, and a big heavy dresser. The walls were painted gold. He said the room had been previously rented by a high-priced call-girl. He called the room his Winter Palace. To my utter astonishment, I found the newsroom's dwarf copy-boy sitting happily in the top drawer of the dresser, listening as the older reporter lectured him on Soviet Socialist Realism. He gave me a warm beer. We talked briefly about Sholokov and *Quiet Flows the Don*. It was a Soviet classic, he said. The dwarf said he liked to listen to the Soviet Army Chorus. He began to sing *Kalinka, Kalinka . . .*

Several days later, I found a ship down around the Cherry Street docks that was unloading guns destined for Hercules War Surplus on Yonge Street. Thousands of old 303s. The Danish captain couldn't understand why I wanted to film the unloading of boxes of old guns but he not only let me film, he gave me two guns. An hour later, Harasti and I stood in the newsroom happily slamming the action bolts in and out of the unloaded guns. He was wonderfully pleased.

"Now what do we know about Hercules Sales?" he asked.

"I knew a graduate student last year who was so upset at failing his exams that he hid in Hercules and came bursting out through the window at midnight wearing camouflage gear and a gun in each hand."

"No kidding."

"Ran right into the arms of two cops."

"Too bad we don't have that on film."

The item on the unloading of guns ran at six o'clock, headlined:

GUNS ARRIVE AT TORONTO PORT

The real news, of course, was always covered and nearly always covered well — there were some excellent men there, like the young Morley Safer, and the seasoned, sometimes marinated and often brilliant Norman Depoe — but a slight loopiness was always in the air, at all levels.

Sometimes it was slapstick: as when Depoe's dentures slipped out of his mouth onto his desk in mid-sentence, or when Stanley Burke, in Zaire, told the nation: "Don't give me any more goddamn cues." Sometimes it involved incompetence: as when the federal Conservatives, convinced that the Toronto newsroom was not a hotbed of rest but a hive of Liberal animosity, ordered that a Convocation Hall speech by Prime Minister John Diefenbaker be filmed from start to finish. A newsman of Conservative bent who had just bought a camera was dispatched. He came back with rolls of film for processing. It turned out to be all black leader. He had forgotten to take the lens cap off the camera.

Sometimes matters were more insidious: as with the prominent city councillor who regularly extended "loans" to one of our City Hall reporters every time the councillor was on the news, but no one said anything until the reporter was suspended for being drunk and then the councillor showed up in a huff saying, "If my man is no longer working the City Hall I want my money back." The solution was to stiff the none-too-bright councillor, who slowly came to understand the position he had put himself in, and to punish the reporter by posting him to a plush job in the Caribbean.

This rawness was a godsend. If the newsroom was open to any approach, so was the whole network, radio and television. At the end of every afternoon I went across the road with Nina, who worked in radio, to drink at the Everene Hotel (known affectionately as the Neverclean) or the Celebrity Club, a serious watering hole for actors, agents, writers, raconteurs, singers and vaudevillians of almost no celebrity. After a short word with Terrence Gibbs, a producer, I was asked to discuss books once a week on the national morning radio show. I said, "I'm still in school." He said, "So what?" So I started talking about Faulkner, Burroughs, Genet, Williams, Blais, Eustace Ross. Whatever interested me. Gibbs never once pretended to know what the audience wanted or wouldn't put up with. "That's for people who read chicken's guts," he said. I stepped out of a studio one day and there was Duke Ellington passing Kate Reid in the hall. Glenn Gould and Marshall McLuhan were in the cafeteria. Bob Weaver was buying fiction and poetry for broadcast on radio from writers all across the country, and serious dramas, classic dramas, were acted every week. The city — with the CBC at its core — seemed rampant with men and women doing things . . . and none of it was conventional. Everything seemed possible as we turned the corner into the sixties. Nothing was charted, nothing pre-ordained. Writing, good writing, the best writing, was important. Harasti, when he was sober, made me read *Watt* while listening to Mahler. "There doesn't have to be a reason why," he said. "Every cripple has to have his own walk." The sophistication of radio, a sophistication honed during the War, had spilled over into television to combine with a reckless enthusiasm that only amateurs could afford.

I worked in the television newsroom and on morning radio for several years while going to the University of Toronto. After Windsor, the "Oxford-like" university was staid, even stifling. There were professors who seriously believed T.S. Eliot was too *modern*, too *contemporary* to be studied. There was, of course, no such thing as Canadian literature. At St. Michael's College, a young woman told me, as we discussed ethics, that she had worn "a Blessed Virgin bra" since high school in Boston. I longed for my "jiggler" in Detroit. A fellow I had known for years confessed with sudden passion that he prayed for my soul every morning at mass. His passion seemed sexual to me. His roommate believed the fluoridization of the water was a Communist conspiracy and there were several priests and young men who still supported Senator Joe McCarthy. At Trinity College, young men and women leading faux Oxford lives in black gowns lunched in "The Buttery." Marshall McLuhan was at St. Michael's, and he was certainly a whirly-gig of ideas, but the amiable, welcoming center of the University for me — as it had been for my father — was Hart House, a stone and oak refuge for men — a hall of leather sofas and leather easy chairs. A place to educate yourself, as Morley liked to say. There were music rooms, debating rooms, a library, an art gallery, a theater, all presided over by a former Deputy Commissioner of Penitentiaries, Joe McCulley.

He was a big-boned, ambling, articulate, well-read and hard-drinking bachelor in his fifties whose apartment in the Tower House was a well-appointed place for late night drink and banter. "The best men, the best minds," he liked to say, almost quoting Matthew Arnold as he lunged after a young man who had struck his fancy. He was homosexual and a couple of times at three in the morning he suddenly came crashing through his coffee table, arms open, seeking a kiss, but I didn't mind. No one minded. That was Joe. Some men wanted to sing at three in the morning. He wanted to kiss.

If he became a bit overbearing in his happy affection for me and my family (Morley still attended Hart House debates at the warden's invitation), I just said my good-byes and walked out without regret or rancor, well liquored and amused, and within ten minutes I would be sitting at one coffee house or another with friends, particularly painters, many of whom were also musicians: the Village Corner (the first uptown coffee house, run by an English actor, John Morley, who launched Ian and Sylvia in Toronto as separate acts), the Purple Onion (where I first saw John Lee Hooker), the Mynah Bird (which featured the "first nude dancer in the city" — she was nude but not seen: she choked on the dry-ice smoke she swallowed as it engulfed her), the First Floor Club (Clarke Terry, Art Blakey), the Penny Farthing, the Riverboat (where Bill Cosby began his career), The Pilot (where young painters drank until midnight and then went to Jimmie Hill's after-hours bar), clubs where the house singers were Joni Mitchell, Gordon Lightfoot, Brownie McGhee and Sonny Terry, Neil Young, Phil Ochs . . .

> *Black night road,*
> *No moon or stars in sight,*
> *Don't you lead me way out there,*
> *My poor heart is full of fear . . .*

There was no fear in my heart, the black night road seemed a straight run toward the stars, and way out there was just around the corner.

The Penny Farthing, on Yorkville Avenue, was a place where summer run-aways, gawking day-trippers, hash peddlers (but not the speed freaks), and folkies hung out. It was slightly upscale, a coffee house of chocolachinos and fancy rye bread sandwiches. It also had a tiny swimming pool in the intimate yard-space behind the old brick row house. I knew the poolside: it was a nice place to sit at a table and read of a summer afternoon because the yard was usually always empty in the afternoon. But in the evening, a trim cluster of young Germans — fit and blond — had taken to sitting at the backside of the pool.

I often ran into Larry Zolf in the cafés. He was an extraordinary young man. So was his father, an ex-Czarist draft dodger and ex-infantryman in Alexander Kerensky's Revolutionary army — Yoshua Falk Zholf — who had drifted to Winnipeg and become a teacher of Jewish liberal-socialist values to Jewish children at the Isaac Loeb Peretz Folk School. Larry — youngest son of Yoshua — had been enrolled in that school and he had learned to read from a Dick and Jane — Max and Molly primer. He had first read *Huckleberry Finn, Rip Van Winkle* and *Moby Dick* in Yiddish. He had learned that Franklin Delano Roosevelt was God and Canada was a temporary penal colony for temporary undesirables in the Great Several States to the south. He was thrilled when Barney Ross boxed someone's brains in and Hank Greenberg beat the leather off a baseball. He drooled at the succulent beauty of Miss America 1946,

Bess Myerson. He and his father cradled each other and wept when Harry Truman gave Israel to the Jews. Yoshua Zholf then wept again when young Larry Zolf left home.

Larry went to Toronto. Having read Dickens and Dostoevsky in Yiddish he re-read them in English. He became obsessed with Canadian history and politics. He married a *zaftig* girl from Newfoundland, Patsy. She was *zaftig* but she was not Jewish. He had a little paunch, a big bush of kinky hair and a very big, even bulbous nose. There was a wart on his nose. He became a stand-up comedian in the manner of Mort Sahl, though he was more mordant and more cutting than Sahl, who after all was only a Jewish Will Rogers.

In many ways, Zolf was the best of what I saw my city becoming: a place of acerbic loners entrenched in the lore of the country and the local politics, men who were self-absorbed but only so that they could be more public spirited, men who were profoundly parochial but only so they could be entirely at ease in the world.

As my grandmother Minn would have said, "Zolf was forthright to a fault."

He believed we could be forthright and I believed we were astute enough to get away with it.

"Be careful," my father said, warning us.

"My father," Zolf said, "saw the American dream this way — to be Jewish and human was to be American. As I see the American Dream operating in Black America and Yellow Vietnam, I am forced to conclude that somehow to be really human is to be neither Jewish nor American. Today the Jewish community in America is indeed a participant and more than an equal in the power elite of White America. The Jews are close to the top in education, affluence, status. But to Black America the Jew is as much Whitey as anyone else. The American Jew lives in a white neighborhood, worships in a white, cavernous temple, eats white kosher Chinese food at white Chinese restaurants, has white directors for his white bar-mitzvah movies. He likes it that way and is sure everyone will understand.

"I must admit that my stomach feels queasy when I hear Nicholas Katzen-bach gloating over the Viet Cong kill toll, the damned dead of American-style democracy. I must admit to a similar type queasiness when I hear Jews gloating over Six Day War Arab losses, the damned dead of Zionist-style democracy . . . It saddens me to see how the American Dream and the melting pot has coars-ened and vulgarized my racial confreres. I prefer the schlemiel wisdom of Gimpel the Fool to the Sammy Glick-shtick of Norman Podhoretz."

There were Jews in Toronto who said Zolf was an anti-Semite. They were the same Jews who said Mordecai Richler and Philip Roth were anti-Semites.

One evening, I sat in the Penny Farthing as eight or nine young and beautiful Germans arrived for their usual aperitifs, the men all looking like my friend Dieter, from the tax assessment office. Then Zolf came through the narrow door to poolside. He waved hello. Behind him, his entourage. Wherever and whenever Zolf performed, he had his traveling entourage: one club foot (the painter, Gershon Iskowitz, who had survived Auschwitz), one dwarf (a comedienne), and two very fat women who never wore bras, letting their great breasts loll. The troupe trucked in and sat around a table at the end of the pool opposite the young Germans.

After coffees and chocolachinos, Zolf suddenly rose and in a high nasal drawl he intoned, at the top of his voice, "Auschwitz, Auschwitz, I know noth-ing of Auschwitz. I vork at Dachau."

It was as if the young Germans had been pole-axed.

No one moved.

No word was said.

Zolf sat down.

His entourage snickered quietly.

A moment passed, the Germans, trying not to glance over their shoul-ders, stumbled back into conversation.

Zolf rose.

They saw him rise.

They waited.

He intoned, "Vee Nazis and Jews must stick together."

There were gasps. The dwarf began to laugh hysterically. Half the Germans leapt to their feet and fled.

I thought, He's going to clean the joint out . . .

There was a long silence. Hardly anyone spoke at either end of the pool. Iskowitz stood up. He had a sad face, a mournful smile. Dragging his foot, he got to the edge of the pool. He looked like he was going to jump in, but he stood staring at the iridescent turquoise water. What was he thinking, this man who had been a child in the camps, staring into the stillness of water? I realized I had never seen anyone swim in that water. I had never seen a ripple on that water. It was just there. The Germans were there. Zolf was there. He rose. He intoned, "Be ze first one on your block to turn in Anne Frank . . . "

The Germans fled. Zolf's entourage laughed and giggled. In a little while, they left, too, but not before the owner chastised Zolf: "After all, they were too young to do what their fathers did."

I felt sad for the young Germans. I felt triumphant glee for Zolf and his entourage . . .

I laughed.

Iskowitz was the last to leave. As he turned to wave good-bye to me, he asked, "Hey! How's Bill?"

"Good," I said, "he's good."

2

Bill Ronald had grown up in the small town of Fergus, northwest of Toronto. It was Presbyterian country, Orange Lodge country. Squat square-cut stone houses. The people had a purse-mouthed way of talking. Bill didn't talk that way. His father did, but he didn't. He had listened to the radio and had practiced throwing his voice. He could talk loud and well and he told everybody that he wanted to be a painter. He came to Toronto, somehow persuaded the Home Furnishing Department of Simpsons' department store to hang his "abstracts" — and in 1954 helped to found Painters Eleven. Then he went on to New York to study with Hans Hofmann. Ronald was brash, he had brilliance, and he sold a work to a well-known collector, Countess Ingeborg de Beausac. She introduced him to the Kootz Gallery. Shortly after, the Guggenheim Museum bought a large painting, and then the Rockefellers. His signature — RONALD — was often almost as big as the central image on his canvases. RONALD. He liked that. He painted hard, he was under contract to produce 18 canvases a year and he did so for seven years. Then his nerves frayed. Kootz cancelled the contract. A doctor in Princeton put him on uppers and downers. Confused, he came home in the early sixties, but being by temperament a man apart — expansive and certain of a destiny, an abrasive innocent who was wise enough to be paranoid — he did not settle in the central part of the city but on Ward's Island out in the bay. He had a friend on the island, an Anglican parish priest, Father Hopkins. He rented a house close to the small island church. He rested for a while, contemplated the calming waters and then he went on television as the host of an arts program, "The Umbrella." He heard me talking about Eustace Ross on radio and he asked me if I would like to come in out of the local rain and do all the literary interviews for the show, and I said sure. So we stood together under a geodesic umbrella — the stage set — and some people said, It's not raining, but I said, The little you know. Those look like thunder clouds to me. BOOM . . .

Morley asked, "Why is it you go in for that boom and rain kinda stuff?"

"It's what I hear."

"The rain?"

"No. The clip-clop of the caisson, the horses hauling JFK's caisson. I hear it all the time, like rain on the roof, on top of my head."

Wearing silver cowboy boots and capes lined with satin, refusing to work with a prepared script, Ronald was a flamboyant presence on television in the staid Sunday afternoon time slot of old movies, hymn sings, and football. He was so honest he could be guileless, so intently serious he could indulge in slapstick, or, as he told me, "Warhol makes pop art: I *am* pop art." But at the CBC, some of the men with the pipes and English accents wrapped in ivy looked at him as if he were the backside of the moon: what he thought was pop art they thought was mooning — loopy conversations with Marcel Duchamp, pie-throwing with the hockey player, Eddie Shack, banter with the Goons, hob-nobbing with Henry Moore, and the strippers — all his life he loved "exotic" dancers, insisting that their "nakedness" was their costume, that they wore their bodies as he wore his suits. But the cultural comptrollers said he was awkward, gauche, self-indulgent, flippant, outspoken, crass, tongue-tied, carping, élitist, hysterical, unresponsive, skittish, scatter-brained . . . and perverse, because he insisted on painting his own set, surrounding *himself* with *himself*, a defiant reckless image of openness and vulnerability. As a still center of turbulence, "The Umbrella" not only had an audience but one Sunday afternoon it actually outdrew professional football.

And I said, "What do you know today, Bill?"

And he said, "Boston hates Muhammad Ali."

He was listening to radio stations. He loved boxing and he loved radio. As a boy, he carried a rolled-up copy of *Ring* magazine in his back pocket. He listened to the *Look Sharp Feel Sharp Be Sharp* Gillette Blue Blade Friday night fights from Madison Square Gardens. He sat listening to the radio for hours. He talked on the phone for hours, to cities all over the continent. He was tuned in, I was tuned in, it's what we talked about, the whole of America's hopscotch game that had turned helter-skelter . . . assassinations, riots, doobies and draft-dodgers, the sardonic laughter in the songs (*Oh God said to Abraham, Kill me a son . . . Abe says, Where do you want this killin' done? God says,*

Out on Highway 61) — Rapp Brown and Ronald Reagan, Mayor Daley and Jerry Rubin, Dick Nixon and Norman Podhoretz and Timothy Leary, Black Panthers and Mortimer Snerd and the Maharishi Yogi, Ken Kesey and his Merry Pranksters, Herbert Marcuse and Ayn Rand, all of them — all shopworn gurus lying about like rubber dummies waiting to be inflated by some publicist, and then, when they rose up, once they were ambulatory, they followed Tiny Tim, alias Julian Foxglove, alias Derry Dover, alias Herbert Khaury, alias Larry Love, to the altar where he married the perfect Virgin, Miss Vicky . . . married her *live* on the Johnny Carson show, a singer devoid of talent, fêted precisely because he had no talent, rescued from obscurity to sing the good old songs, all teeth and hook nose, burbling . . . all of them burbling as they were introduced by their Master of Ceremonies, Ed Sullivan, hugging himself as he stumbled through the language, Ed Sullivan, who had single-handedly rendered the word *wonderful* meaningless; an opera singer was *wonderful* and so were the flea-ridden chimpanzees who followed her *wonderful; wonderful* acts parading on and off for a fee. They were total theater. They were the revolution. They were the apocalypse. They were midnight skulkers. They were naked. They were banal. They were the Big public Show.

"I'm so tuned in," he said, "I tuned out McLuhan long ago."

I always found a tension in Bill between his love of discipline and his love for the ludicrous. Often, he seemed at odds with himself — sometimes ingrown, reticent, whining and selfish, and then wide open, gentle and courteous, with an extraordinary generous streak. He not only gave away his paintings and watercolors, but gave his time and compassion to people he knew would not only disappoint him but double-cross him. It was as if his generosity came out of a quiet despair: aware that there was so little generosity in the world, he proved its existence by giving . . . and expecting little or nothing in return; and — with a determined, self-indulgent guilelessness — he insisted on imposing his style on the world around him, affirming himself . . . so that he was able, with a straight face, to agonize over having no money while standing outfitted in a beautifully tailored brocade suit with lace cuffs.

He was contemptuous of know-nothing radicals and mind wreckers, not because he was conservative — no, he wanted them to be more dangerous, more expert, more disciplined in their destruction, so that he could respect them enough to really hate them and to arouse within himself a fuller sense of triumph at his own individuality. He extended himself in all directions, as if he had no center, yet tenaciously held on to his family, to his wife, his children, his women, as if it were possible to patiently organize not only his emotions, but the emotions of others. Outrageously public and always on stage, he was enormously private with only two or three close friends whom he seldom saw; and though he was sometimes preposterous and ludicrous in the way he left himself open to attack, he worried and fretted and was upset when anyone he knew strung himself out, even a little, in pain. But he himself lived in pain, arthritic pain, tendonitis, high blood pressure . . . always alive at the ends of his nerves . . . to ecstasy, work, rage . . . MAINTAIN A STANDARD OF CHAOS, he insisted, slashing at the air with one of his silver-handled canes, as he had the pleasure of calmly contemplating his own distress.

One day I took Morley to meet Ronald. Morley was wearing a jersey-knit shirt with two little burn holes beneath his breast-bone; tiny live cinders from his pipe had burned through the knit. His shoes, unpolished, needed new heels. Bill was wearing snakeskin boots, pantaloon trousers, and a flouncy silk shirt. Morley said he hadn't seen anything like Bill since he'd got drunk with Lily St. Cyr. Bill wanted to know if Morley got his clothes at Saint Vincent de Paul. They liked each other.

"What do you make of Muhammad Ali?" Morley asked.

"I hate the guys who call him Cassius Clay. Milt Dunnell calls him Cassius Clay"

"What about Chuvalo?"

"He's got a heavy punch," Bill said.

"I remember seeing Chuvalo," Morley said, "when he was only twenty. He fought Bob Baker and then Mederos after that, an over-eager, desperately determined young fighter, planted too solidly on his great legs, bewildered by the straight lefts and straight rights, his black hair plastered down over his forehead, his face pale, his eye bleeding — a born fighter, exhausting himself in fury . . . "

"That's terrific," Bill said.

"What?" Morley said.

"What you just said."

"Thanks," Morley said.

"And you always had to hope that Chuvalo would knock 'em out," I said.

"Chuvalo doesn't have a knockout punch," Bill said. "He just beats them down, wears them down . . . "

"You know what Ali did when he was sparring in Miami?"

"Naw."

"Said Chuvalo fought like a washerwoman so Chuvalo got dressed up like a little old lady with a bag full of Lifebuoy soap and dish detergent and got into the ring and chased Ali around so Ali didn't know what was going on . . . "

"Still didn't have a knockout punch," Bill said.

"Maybe he'll learn a knockout punch," I said.

"No," Morley said, "I talked once about this with Deacon Jack Allen, the promoter, and he said it never happens. No one ever learns a knockout punch. I asked him why a scared man couldn't knock you out? And he said, Because the scared guy in his heart is really running away, a rabbit can't hurt you. Then he told me what the knockout punch really depends on. Temperament."

"Temperament?"

"The gambler's temperament. The kid with the great punch just naturally shoots the works. That's it. He risks it all."

"When I'm painting," Bill said, "I take so many risks . . . I always set out to do something wrong in the painting, absolutely wrong, some sore spot, otherwise it's too perfect, too safe. It's only beautiful if there's something wrong . . . and what's wrong with this town is, it's a town that wants everything to be right."

"Yeah, but that can work for you," Morley said. "I wouldn't like to live in a city that didn't stir up any resentments in me, that didn't provide an opposition to the things of my own spirit. In such a town I would feel inert or dead. When I was traveling from city to city across the country, I was always encountering somebody who would snort — *Toronto* — as if this was the place that embodied all that they disliked in Canada — a greedy, grasping city, it was cold and unfriendly, it was bigoted, stuffy and intolerant and puritanical. But I came to see an irony in this belittlement of my city. From my boyhood on I always enjoyed my own antagonisms to the city. I was right in step with the rest of the country, but what did that mean? It means we all, even those of us who live in Toronto, use the place as a gray dragon, a dragon representing what we probably hate in ourselves. It's a laughable situation."

"I hate your shoes," Bill said.

"And those pantaloons are ridiculous," Morley said, and they both laughed uproariously and settled back in their chairs, taking it easy, enjoying the breeze off the lake, the calm.

It was on the island that Bill had found calm, and a deep comfort in his friendship with the priest. He had painted the chapel of St. Andrew-by-the-Lake, painted the entire chapel . . . the walls, the ceiling, the radiator, the mouldings, the fireplace, the altar. It was a joyous gesture in prime colors, over a hundred undulating feet of bravado that had the feel of utter innocence, the feel of rebirth and a resurrection that was alive in the landscape, in the sand and the water that could be seen through the broad windows. It was a place of prayer free of the clichés of maudlin piety, a painterly testament to refuge, meditation and friendship.

Then Father Hopkins died. The chapel had been leased by the church from the Metro parks department for one dollar, and the church let the lease expire. The parks department let the chapel fall into disrepair, using it as a summer hostel for outpatients from the Queen Street Mental Health Center. In the winter, pipes froze and burst, a four-by-eight hole was cut into a wall, white paint was slathered onto the wall. Ronald said the destruction of the mural was a desecration. The parks commissioner, Tommy Thompson, scoffed and said Ronald had had no right to paint the chapel in the first place and that his work wasn't worth dog shit anyway. Ronald moved inland, into the city, leaving the barrens to the Church and turds to the parks department.

Inland, Larry Zolf had been hired as a political correspondent on the public affairs television program, "This Hour Has Seven Days."

He was like William Ronald, he was not "off-the-rack" — a perfect 42, a perfect 44, trousers cuffed.

He brought verbal energy, arcane anecdotes, scholarship, laughter, the capacity not just to see but to observe, to his televised conversations and his reporting.

He caused consternation.

A cabinet minister, Pierre Sevigny, was seen on film beating him about the head with a cane. Because he had asked an honest question.

Zolf had a future.

But McLuhan told me over coffee in Hart House that television could have no future. "It can't have a future, not as we usually use the term. Because it has no past. Everything on television is instantly forgotten. It has no history. How can it have a future if everything that has happened is forgotten?" He also told me that he believed there were angels on the planets.

"Angels!"

"Why not? They've been around a while."

"I guess so."

"Now they've got a future."

When I saw him again Zolf said, "Future, future . . . I'll tell you about future. The fucking Israelis have killed my father's language, his whole culture, who I am . . . Yiddish. They're killing off Yiddish. To them Yiddish is out.

To them there's only Hebrew. That leaves me, my father nowhere . . . what future? What culture have they got in Hebrew, you tell me that . . . No culture. That's what they've got. No culture."

Zolf, a future?

"He'd better zipper his lip," Morley told me.

"Morley says you better zipper your lip."

"Morley says . . . "

"This Hour Has Seven Days" had no future. It was taken off the air. The President of the CBC fired Zolf.

We met at night at the Riverboat. Brownie McGhee and Sonny Terry were on stage. Brownie sang: *My Father, my father said these words, followed me down through the years.* Zolf was upset. He had wanted to publicly denounce the Ottawa mandarins who had scuttled the program. *Believe half you see an' nothing that you hear.* I'd told him I was sure that the "stars" of the show — Patrick Watson and Laurie Lapierre — would gladly hang him out to dry for their cause."Patsy's your wife's name but that's what they'll play you for. A patsy." Zolf talked it over inside his head with his own father, and then with my brother, and came to a grim conclusion. "This is one Jew who isn't offering anybody either cheek," he said.

"So what d'you want to say?"

"What I want to say is one thing, what I got to say is nothing."

Brownie and Sonny came down off the stage, a crippled man leading a blind man, singing *Walk on, walk on, got to keep on walking to make my way back home . . .*

There was a heavy downpour as we left the Riverboat. Larry went home. Lessons were beginning to sink in. Brownie and Sonny and I went to my brother's flat on College Street. It was a steady drumming rain that kept on all through the night. Then at five in the morning it cleared and in the milk-white hour, in a lean side alley under a folded steel fire escape, Sonny

Terry, his wide-brimmed, stained fedora plunked on his head, shuffled along the cement alley, rapping his blind man's cane against the brick wall. Several paces behind, riding up and down in a hobble-step, was Brownie McGhee.

Brownie scowled.

As a child, polio-stricken at four, he had been hauled around by his brothers in a wagon as he tried to hide his stunted leg, a cripple whose mother had bought herself "a train ticket as long as her right arm," whose share-cropper father, Huff, a fish fry guitar player, had told him, "You going to play guitar, you best learn to pick. Otherwise, you'll strum all your life."

Brownie had picked.

He had picked up and left Tennessee.

He had picked his words, picked his time, and he had picked his friends. For forty years, beginning in 1938, he and Sonny had sung together.

They had met in Burlington, North Carolina, working the textile mills, Sonny playing with Blind Boy Fuller, but Fuller had died, and Brownie and Sonny latched on to each other, moving to Harlem, with Brownie talking the talk and Sonny settling — wherever he was — into a hulking quietude. Brownie was suspicious and prickly and sometimes abrasive — with his magisterial head and a hobble he hated; keeping a journal of misspelt sayings and poems, aware of his own pain and hatred and how chameleon he was, and how he tormented those who loved him with a bewildering evilness of temper. He had a smile that could kill. He didn't trust anybody. Not on the road. But Sonny had to trust everybody. He was not only blind, he couldn't write and didn't know his numbers and carried an ink pad and a stamp: SONNY TERRY. He was all pockets — for his harps, his keys, his papers, his money. He tried to separate his money into pockets . . . ones, fives, tens . . . but people lied to him, took too much money from his open palm or short-changed him.

On this morning, both Brownie and Sonny were alert and laughing, though — sitting around in my brother's apartment upstairs — we had been quick on the bottles of Johnny Walker Red all night. Brownie held his guitar under his arm. He called out, "Walk on, Baby, walk on. Break clean, come out fighting," and he swung the guitar across his paunch, singing out as we came into the ordered emptiness of College Street on a Sunday morning:

I'm a stranger here,
Just blowed in your town
If I ask you for a favor
Please don't turn me down . . .

A streetcar clattered by, pale mass-bound faces in the windows staring sleepily at two black men, one burly and blind, the other crippled, singing their way out of the narrow dead-end alley, followed by me, a white man with his shades on, black sunglasses. Sonny suddenly hollered, "Man, you see me do a buck and wing? You see me do that? Hold my cane."

"Watch that drainpipe, man."

"You watch your worried mind."

Sonny Terry was thick through the shoulders and arms, his hands meaty, and he moved his feet heavily in a carefree shuffle, staring straight ahead, a white film in his eyes behind glasses. He had a boyish smile and spoke with a country slur so thick that not everyone could understand him, and there he was, doing a buck and wing, big feet slipping back and forth — like a sandman dancer — and up and down, snapping his heels, and then he leapt into the air, crossed his legs and smacked his heels with his hands. After he took his cane back he said, "Man, I could do that the whole time 'fore I got the gout. Can't do nothing with the gout. Got me pills from a doctor in Washington, they hardly do nothing."

Sonny, Brownie and I stood under the fluttering dying neon of the closed restaurant beneath my brother's apartment. It was too early for Brownie to go to his hotel, a shabby flop for rummies and roach peddlers, the Hotel California, where they padlocked and chained the doors at two in the morning — despite fire regulations — and didn't open again until seven, trapping anyone asleep inside, but, "Never mind, a man should have an official room to rest his head," Brownie said, "and I surely do." He often slept in his car. He thrust out his chin and turned his mouth down like a disapproving wry preacher, stepping back to say as he aimed his guitar at me, "Mother, when the great day comes . . . I may just save you."

Suddenly, my brother appeared in the alley, buck-naked, loping towards us. Michael waved gaily to people in a passing streetcar as he came out onto the sidewalk, smiling broadly. "I forgot to say good-bye," he cried.

"Nothing I can do will save that boy," Brownie said as my brother threw his arms around him, and they stood there, embracing in the morning light.

Sonny tapped his cane. "What's going on, man, what's going on?"

3

"I had a friend, a Russian Jew," Morley said, "who had a serious problem with his eyes. He wore glasses with very thick lenses. I asked him what had ruined his eyesight. He said that when he was a boy in Russia his parents had been very poor. He had had to work hard. His mother always got him to bed very early and turned out the light. But he would have a flashlight in bed, and pulling the covers over his head, he would read by the flashlight.

"He read the stories of Chekhov, then book after book of Tolstoy before his eyes finally went on him. Looking back on it, he couldn't regret the damage to his eyes, he said. In his little tent under the covers his beam of light had opened up new worlds, worlds he would walk in for the rest of his life; worlds that put him far beyond his home and made him aware of lives far different than his own."

In *A Passion in Rome* Morley wrote:

. . . he waited for his eyes to get used to the light, and heard the rustling of her paper bag as she opened it. At first he could only see the rim and the highest row of colosseum stone seats in the starlight, then gradually as it got lighter, he could make out the descending tiers. In the shadows they were like the pock-marked face of the moon.

Before him stretched the blackness of the field itself. In the ghostly gray and black still-ness there was no sound now, not even the rustling of the bag. She tossed out a piece of meat. Nothing moved; not a sound. Then in the darkness he saw glowing eyes. He felt a little chill on his neck. As she kept tossing out the pieces of meat, eyes shone in the darkness to the left and right of him. A cat snarled, and he jumped. The fierce spit-ting scratching anger of hungry cats fighting for meat made him shiver. A dark form went leaping across the aisle, then another one in pursuit, and then came the frantic fierce spitting and crying of cats making love . . .

Poignant, awkward, wise, obtuse, original, inept, mature, tedious, pow-erful.

All those adjectives were used to describe *A Passion in Rome*, his 1961 novel.

A.J.M. Smith, professor at Michigan State in East Lansing and poet from Montreal, an old friend, arrived at the house unannounced, full of affability and affection. He had something on his mind. After two drinks, he said he had come around to tell Morley that he disagreed with Edmund Wilson: "After all, talking about you and Chekhov and Turgenev in the same breath is ridiculous — we just aren't that good in this country." Morley said: "Speak for yourself." It was aston-ishing; Smith had come to the door, to Morley's living room, to set Morley and Wilson straight, assuring Morley that his work through the fifties — the two nov-els that Wilson so admired, *The Loved and The Lost* and *The Many Colored Coat* — were not good, not good at all, and he was being wonderfully good-natured about it, acting like an amiable uncle who had come to visit with treats in his pocket. I had never heard anything like it. I couldn't understand Morley's for-bearance. As for Smith's own work, he told Morley that he only wanted a little piece of perfection: "I want only to write one perfect, one good poem, and that is enough. That is sufficient for me to remember that I have one perfect work."

"But I never remember what I've done," Morley said. "If I've written one good book, I want to write another, a better one. I want always to do new things, new perfect things. Look at Michelangelo. He went on and on."

"But . . . he was a genius. You don't think of yourself along with Michel-angelo."

"Why not?" asked Morley.

"You're hopelessly romantic, I want only to do a perfect thing once. That is enough. I'm a classicist, you're a hopeless romantic. Be satisfied that *Such Is My Beloved* is a perfect book."

"But Wilson says it's not nearly as interesting as my later stuff."

"Wilson's wrong."

"Look Arthur, twenty years ago you were astonished when I told you I was as good, better even, than Hemingway. Now what do you think?"

"Maybe you're as good."

"Well, you were wrong then and you're wrong now. I'm a classic."

"No, you wrote three classic books in the thirties."

"That's three, and three more make six."

"Who says so?"

"The world says so."

"The world," he said sourly.

"Look, go in there . . . " and Morley pointed to the library, "go in there, you'll find all the books you're talking about, you'll find those books in Japanese, Italian, German, Russian, Swedish . . . "

"Cut it out. Cut it out," Smith said, throwing up his hands.

Morley asked me to pour Smith another drink.

"The world . . . " he said.

For the rest of the evening, Smith bounded from chair to chair, an unlit dollar cigar loose in his lips, laughing and joking, full of ease and availability. Then Morley began to tell him about a new novel he was working on. He had two possible endings. Smith listened. He grew engrossed, meditative.

"This could be great," he said to Morley.

"Yes," Morley said, "but it all depends on how you look at criminals, whether they're clowns or saints . . . "

After an hour, Smith left, and as he left Morley said, "Well, Arthur, you attend a lot of conferences, you get with it, you participate. Tonight, I've let you participate."

Smith, a little drunk, cheerily waved good-bye.

"Happy to help," he said.

"I can't believe it," I said, "you put up with that crap. In your own house."

"He's an old friend. You put up with this stuff. And then you out-write them."

Decades later, my friend Austin Clarke — the novelist from Barbados who lived in Toronto — invited me to his home for a night drink with the pugnacious Norman Mailer. I said I was delighted to come. But in my heart I resented Mailer. I had resented him for years, ever since he had written an unfair and self-serving review of Morley's *That Summer in Paris* in 1963 in the first issue of *The New York Review of Books*. The big memorable scene in that book was Morley bloodying Hemingway's mouth and knocking him down. Mailer's review hadn't been about the memoir, it had been about Mailer. He had talked as if he knew about fighting, as if he could duke it out. He had belittled a wise and generous book. As I walked to Austin's house I got angrier and angrier. And all my resentment of self-serving reviewers who had cold-cocked me, too, rose in my throat. I knocked on the door. I told myself that I'd like the son-of-a-bitch to say just one smart-ass thing and I would clock him. I wouldn't tell him why. I'd just whack him in the head.

We shook hands. He was a little old guy who only came up to my shoulder. He looked like a tubby little *schlepper* in a tweed jacket. Fat Saul, who couldn't beat a rug, would have had him for lunch. I felt ridiculous, ashamed. What in the world had I been thinking? Mailer was affable and courtly to everyone in the room. He couldn't have been more charming. I sat in a corner of the sofa, stuck. What was to be said? Nothing. It went against all my inclinations, but I knew I had nothing to say so I stood up and said good-bye to

Austin. He asked me what was the matter, why was I going so soon? I said, "Nothing, it's just that I've got nothing to say to Mailer."

Once I was out on the street, I thought, Shit, I should have whacked him in the mouth. Or given him a short shot to the ribs. Break a rib, I thought as I walked down the street, picking up my stride. Yeah, break a rib. A cat was running along in the shadows ahead of me. My mind began to play tricks, the cat drawing me into the darkness. I decided I wouldn't tell Morley that I had met Mailer. He would just get angry all over again, and after all, what could he say that he hadn't already said to me? What could he say? What could I say? Silence. I dropped my shoulder as if I were about to let go a left hook, and went on home alone.

The flashing eyes in the shadows, the snarling, then the glint of moonlight on the tiers of seats, made him draw back, and his mind played tricks on him. The whole arena seemed to come alive; it seemed to be there in a reddish glow as the fierce sun was strained through the giant colored awnings on the poles around the arena; and the wild animals, the leopards, the wolves, the cheetahs and the tigers were there, circling around crazily, blind with fright, sliding frantically along the barricade, crashing into it, lashing out with their tails; and now waiting with wild glowing eyes, watching him because he was standing over the underground cells where the prisoners, doomed to be tossed out as meat, waited. The fear and the terrible anxiety of the prisoners was like a smell seeping through the ground to him, and there before him, waiting with glowing eyes, half-starved, the great cats.

It was a sunlit morning. About to cross the street before the light changed to red, I felt a searing pain in my right knee, burning wire drawn through the needle's eye of the joint; I couldn't breathe for pain. As I lay in bed in Wellesley Hospital my knee was swollen with fluid. "I've got goiter of the knee," I said. The doctor looked at me, smiled, and said, "That'd be easy to fix. You've got arthritis." My ankles were swollen, too, and there was a clamp-like pain in the middle of my backbone. The doctor laid his palm on the taut skin around my knee. "Really warm" he said. "This'll hurt." The needle looked like a ball-point refill. He pressed hard, driving the needle through the skin into the membrane. Pale yellow fluid whooshed out. "Terrific pressure," he said. "We'll shoot it with cortisone but we'll probably have to do this every day."

"How come I got this?"

"At your age?"

"Yeah."

"Arthritis hits babies. No surprise it hit you. You're in your twenties."

"It's a surprise to me."

"Look, I'll tell you something," he said. "Doctors'll talk to you all day about arthritis, and you've got three different kinds so far as we can figure, but fundamentally we don't know anything about it because we don't know why, we don't know why it is what it is, so we don't know how to cure it. Treat it, yes. Cure it, no."

Nothing had been more natural for me than running. The quick dart, the deceptive loping stride. Run. Run. Run. Now I was lying still on my back. The weight of the sheet on my knee was painful. The least movement, the least flex of a muscle was painful. A burning, gnawing pain. Breathing was painful. I thought I was having a heart attack. My heart was in a grip. The doctor told me pain travels, picks a muscle and travels, and sometimes you don't know where it's come from but you know where it's been and where it is. The inflammation was in my back, the pain was around my heart.

I lay still, as still as could be. Staring at the walls. In stillness. Trying so hard to relax while in pain that I broke into a sweat. Then nurses and interns came with a razor, big bowls of water and plaster. They drained the knee, shot in cortisone, shaved my leg, and began to swathe the length of my leg, instep to inner thigh, in wet bandages. Encased, except for an oval window to the knee. So that I couldn't move the joint, so that the pain would lessen, so that I might sleep.

"Want us to do that too?" a nurse, her hands thick with plaster, asked as she drew the sheet up across my legs and belly. "Might save you some trouble." She laughed. It was a sad, friendly laugh.

My mother and father and Nina came to see me. My mother seemed stricken, to see her dancing boy so, and I was stricken that she should see me so.

Days passed.

Days upon nights upon days.

I practiced holding my breath. I don't know why. Maybe to see how long I could hold it. I would imagine the second-hand on King Whyte's pocket watch, the night grandfather Tom was supposed to die. When I wasn't breathing I could listen to my body.

Pain seemed to be creeping through the whole of my body. I was sure I could hear it, feinting, receding, but traveling until one night around midnight I couldn't move. I felt a total silence. I could move my head, but nothing else. It was like my arms had been vacated. I felt a tear on my cheek. I was surprised. I didn't want to feel self-pity. I was afraid, and felt sorrow but not self-pity.

A nurse came into the room.

I said, "I can't move. Nothing."

She sat down and held my hand. She didn't say anything. She held my hand in the dark.

The night-light was the only star in the dark.

At some early hour, in a half-sleep my arms lost their numbness.

In the morning, I was able to move my arms and left leg. My hips felt like the lynch-pins had been pulled, grinding, unable to bear weight. A young doctor came into the room and told me that I had to accept a couple of things: first, most people got a serious illness every ten years and I was lucky because mine was not cancer; second, I was going to be in bed for a long time, and being young, this would be hard on me, but more important — especially in years to come, I'd have to learn to absorb all pain, in fact, to forget, as much as possible, every day pain and go about life like life was normal.

"You mean from now on pain is so normal it's not there?"

"Yes. If you can do it."

He left me alone to think and then came back to tell me that many arthritics could not drink liquor, it further inflamed the joints. He handed me a glass of Scotch. "Drink this," he said, "we're going to see what happens."

In the afternoon, after it was happily clear that the drink had not damaged me, he told the head nurse that I was allowed liquor in my room and he advised me to tell Morley and Nina to come with a bottle before supper, "a kind of small cocktail hour. You may be here for months."

I was. For months.

I decided to drink anything too thin to eat.

And that's when I was surprised at how easily I shut down the outside world, how seldom I even looked at the window, let alone outside. I accommodated myself to the bed, my narrow white boat adrift in white, like Pym, who had sailed into a great white womb of ice, wintering without committing myself to the walls, taking in everything in the room, the sudden apparition of faces, their stillness, the stillness of eyes and mouths suspended in the play of light on the walls, still waters, I had never known such stillness. Such refusal. That's what it was. A refusal that let me be free of everything that might impinge on me except my pain. A refusal in which I was learning to forget pain.

Of course, I also got drunk. At least once a week I drank myself to sleep. An amber sleep. I believed I could feel the amber in my bones. A balm. That left me smiling. I thought I was smiling in the dark. In silence. That silence the other side of the coin to my mother, her rice blossom face howling in pain. A sudden screech, a fierce silence.

A young but balding priest from Our Lady of Lourdes Church came to see me one morning. He wanted me to go to confession. I said No. I thought I had been through a period of purity, almost absolute. Not sexual purity, not that stupidity. But in the marrow of my mind. In the ice womb. I told this to the young priest. He smiled and smiled, bewildered. I felt sorry that I had talked to him like that, bewildering him. As he went to the door he said, "You're sure now, no confession?"

"No," I said. "I'd take the white wafer, but no confession."

"You know you can't do that."

"I know. But I would."

The blood rose in his face. He was angry and left.

Just before Christmas they took off the cast. My leg looked like it had been under water for a month, sickly white.

The pain had eased. I encouraged several nurses to massage my legs.

The bedpans had been cleared from their cabinet. A selection of single malts stood in place.

Nina had a drink at five, my father at eight, and two interns took to dropping by just before midnight.

Between Christmas and New Year's one of the interns wheeled me upstairs to a lounge where we drank pure alcohol. White lightning. We got pleasantly drunk.

"You know man is going to the moon soon," the intern said. "He's going to walk on the moon."

"Yes. Maybe."

"No maybe about it. He's going to walk on the moon. We're still going to be trying to figure out how to get you walking while somebody's walking on the moon."

"I don't think about the moon too much. Stars, yeah. I like thinking about the stars, but the moon leaves me cold."

"Standing there the guy'll look down and see how really small we are."

"You think about that?" I asked.

"Yeah."

We drank more white lightning.

"You think doctors are dummies?" he said. "We don't think about these things? Cut and stitch, cut and stitch?"

"Naw, I just like to know you keep your mind on what you're doing."

"You ever think about Medusa?"

"No."

"When they cut her head off, they did something terrible. She worshipped men, her hair was all snakes and snakes were like penises to those people."

"You sure?"

"Men who hated themselves cut off her head. Mass castration."

"You're gonna be a surgeon," I said.

"Sure."

"Keep your eye on what you're cutting," I said.

He wheeled me back downstairs.

Within three weeks, after physiotherapy, my parents came to get me. Morley brought me Tom's hawthorn walking stick. I was learning to walk all over again on the one leg. I moved very slowly.

"Be careful," my mother said.

"This is how they'll walk on the moon," I said.

I didn't know if it was the stiff drink I'd had or whether I'd learned how to forget, but I felt no pain.

4

In 1963, arranging my marriage was not easy. I was a lapsed Catholic and Nina — the daughter of people from Russian border villages, immigrants who had no affection for the Church, either its teachings or its randy village priests — had not been baptized. I went to a well-liked, white-haired old Irish priest, Father Kerridan, a man of deceptive affability, and asked him to marry us (that's when I learned I had a great weakness for assuming that affability was a sign of tolerance and generosity of spirit). Standing in the shadow of St. Basil's steeple, he dismissed me angrily, saying that I was lapsed — in a state of sin — that I was less than a Catholic, and the woman I was going to marry was nothing. "Nothing, you see. Nothing. The Church is not a recreation hall."

I phoned Father Fehr in Windsor.

"I made a mistake in talking to Kerridan," I said.

"No, no. I think we'll find that the Church is a little bigger than Father Kerridan," he said. He told me to call a Father Noonan, the pastor of St. Basil's Church, which was close to my office in the graduate school. "He's a priest who really works in the parish, he's gentle, he worries a little too much for his parishioners. Last week he was tipsy and walked through a glass door. You'll like him."

I met Father Noonan in his office and he said, as I sat down, "Do you know who a Catholic is?"

"No," I said.

"Neither do I," he said. "When would you like to get married?"

"In a couple of months," I said. I stood up.

"I'll talk to Nina a while. Instruction. Two or three chats. That'll be that."

"Good."

"Father Fehr says to say hello."

"Hello."

"Hello," another priest whispered, "hello, down here."

It was three o'clock in the morning, a month before the marriage. I was working late, my office light was the only light on close to the church grounds, except for the flashlight of the watchman who checked doors and kept an eye peeled for Father Teskey. It was Father Teskey whispering to me as I set out for home. He often whispered "Hello" to me, while he crouched down among honeysuckles and dogwoods, a little drunk, hiding from the watchman.

Father Teskey had taught me first year Philosophy.

"Heraclitus and the boys," he'd said. "Up to their necks in the changing tides . . . does any one have a rope you could throw to him that'd be worth hanging on to?"

He didn't teach anymore.

"Down here, down here," he said. The grass had been freshly cut, a sweet wetness was in the air.

"Would you come down and kneel for a while and have a drink perhaps, just a sip, mind, I've little to spare."

He was in his fifties, with close-cropped gray hair. "I've been watching you," he said, from behind a bush. He had narrow shoulders. "I sit in here waiting for the watchman and when he trots by I watch him. He's been told to look out for me, even found me once over by the tennis courts. He's a Scot, a bad breed, all calculating and no dreams and when they die, their mouths are holes. That's it. Holes. In need of a cork."

He held out a silver flask.

"One pull is what you get."

I took a drink.

He looked around warily. "The Boss . . . he told them to keep an eye out for me, you know. What's a watchman for if he isn't watching, and I'm what's wrong. You know that?" He touched my hand. "They tell me I'm all wrong because I don't want forgiveness, none at all. Any time I think about it I end up . . . You know what St. Teresa said God said to her? 'If I hadn't created Heaven for Myself, I'd have to create it for you.'"

The priest rose to a crouch.

"He's coming. I've got to beat it . . . "

"Never mind," I said.

"What?"

"I'll take off . . . "

I crouched forward, head down and bolted out of the bushes, half loping, half crawling up the slope of the lawn, a shadow in the moonlight. The watchman, running, called out, "Hold on there, Father, hold on . . . " as I headed off between the trees, leading him away from the old priest hiding in the bushes.

On the day that we were married, Nina was driven to the church by Goffredo in his "Mayor of Motor City" black Cadillac and the car was daubed all over with white paper flowers made by his children. There were two priests on the altar in the stalls behind Father Noonan, Father Shook, the president of the Pontifical Institute of Medieval Studies, and Father Teskey. I was very touched to see Father Teskey there. I hadn't seen him in the daytime for years.

It was to be a simple mass, only the families and close friends, with two choirboys from the Cathedral Choir School. There was, however, a huge *corpus* in agony on the Cross on a side wall of the church. I worried a little about that. The first time Nina had seen it — at a Christmas midnight mass — she had begun to cry. "What's the matter?" I'd asked. We had both been drinking at a Celebrity Club party earlier on.

"He's in terrible pain. Someone should do something."

"What?"

"Take him down."

"You can't. He's God. He's got to be there."

"Take him down. Look at him. He's a man . . . "

"He's God, and He has to die. You don't understand the story."

"That's terrible. I can't believe you don't want to do anything."

On Saturday afternoon, as Nina came up the aisle, she paid no attention to her man on the cross. The prayers were said. The songs were sung. Just before the vows, as I was about to be asked if I took this woman for my wife, Father Teskey stood up, crouched forward and hurried from the altar. I remember thinking, That's odd. My best man handed me the ring and I put the ring on her finger.

Years later, I remembered Father Teskey. I remembered the watchman and my taking off in the night in Father Teskey's stead: had he, at the wedding, taken off in my place? Had it been a signal missed? And if — as a signal — it had been taken, what would I have done? Nothing. I loved Nina. Still, signals are signals and maybe I had missed Father Teskey's as I had missed a signal my father had given me a year earlier.

Morley, Nina and I had been talking in the living room about pain, my pain, and the meaning of pain . . . and Nina had said something about "mind over matter" and overcominig pain and suddenly Morley said, "Of all the

Greeks, the great old Greeks, who's the one who's most important to you, to society?'

"Sophocles," I said.

"Solon the Law Giver," Nina said.

"What!" I said.

"Why?" Morley asked.

"Because, if there is no law, everything falls apart. There's nothing without the law."

"You believe that?"

"Yes. I even wanted to be a cop once," she said.

Ever since my childhood jaunt to Woolworth's, I'd been uneasy about cops.

"But Sophocles," Morley said. "The artist is an anarchist."

"Sure," she said gaily, and gave Morley a kiss on the forehead.

A month before the wedding, Nina's father had asked me, "What do English people drink?" To him, anyone who spoke English was English. He drank vodka, the English drank . . . Scotch, or rye, or gin; who knew? Some of my aunts didn't know what to make of my marrying a woman who wasn't of Irish descent, but a mysterious Slav . . . a strange, unruly people. Paul Rabchuk was Russian, his wife Ukrainian. While still young, he had gone from his village at the Polish border to Vladivostok and then had come back through Siberia to join the Polish army, and after he was mustered out and had returned to his village, he picked up a Canadian handbill. "I read it," he told me, "and it said 'Go to Saskatchewan.' I didn't know where it was, so I went."

My people didn't know anything about Nina's people, didn't know anything about Siberia, just as her family didn't know anything about the coffin boats, so no one knew what to expect. (I did enjoy explaining to Morley that many of Mrs. Rabchuk's friends thought Nina was marrying "down" by marrying outside their community.) All the English-speaking people gathered after the wedding mass at Morley's house, drank whiskey and soda or rye and water and ate little white bread sandwiches. By six o'clock, when they set out in cars for the Russian reception in a big hall, they were all a little tipsy.

The Ukrainian band blared out the "Wedding March" as each guest arrived at the door. There were long rows of tables, seating for five hundred, a bottle of Scotch at every third place setting. My people had never confronted so much free drink. They carried my uncle Ambrose out before anyone sat down to eat. A dozen women came bustling from the kitchen, carrying trays heaped with food that my people had never seen: braised brisket, heavy with garlic (my father and brother hated garlic), roast chicken and potatoes, deep-fried meat on a stick, thick mushroom gravy, *kapusta, perohy, holupchy, zakusky* . . .

By the time the meal was done and the tables taken up for dancing, Nina's 450 people were standing back against the walls, agape. The small band of "English," though they didn't know how to polka, had taken over the floor, turning themselves loose, twirling, hopping, whirling, trying to bound into the air like members of the Red Army Chorus . . . and Morley watched in quiet awe as the long line-up of guests moved to toast the bride and groom, each person carrying an envelope stuffed with cash. Mr. Rabchuk warned me that I could not drink a shot-glass of whiskey with each guest. "You will kill yourself. Drink water, pretend it's vodka." I danced with Nina, danced with my mother and then Mrs. Rabchuk said, "Time to count the money." We went into a closet filled with mops and pails. After the counting, Nina said, "That'll take us through Europe." (The bridal shower with 300 guests would help with the buying of our furniture.) As the dancing wound down, as the band played a last tune, the subdued Russians and Ukrainians shook their heads in amusement as the "English" straggled happily and hopelessly drunk out into the night, some picking up whiskey bottles that hadn't been opened. "Obviously," I said, "the English will drink anything they can get their hands on." My friends and family, some singing at the tops of their voices, an unruly bunch at one o'clock in the morning, drove off in all directions, some going up on to lawns, around lampposts, totally delighted and dead drunk.

And that is how Nina and I crossed the cultural barriers and got to Dublin, London, Rome and Paris.

5

How much truth can a man stand,
   Sitting by the ocean,
   Perpetual motion,
Fingerpainting in the sand.

MOSE ALLISON

"There has to be a sore point in every painting," Bill said, "some part where you've lost control. Nothing's deader than perfection."

"Part of St. Anselm's proof for the existence of God," I said, "was God as the artist. Perfection."

"God, maybe," he said, "but not me. Only God dreams of perfection."

We were on the Cape at Wellfleet, where the dunes rolled and dipped down to the ocean, where the sand was rippled by the wind, creamy-white in the sun at noon. There were small clusters of pine trees and scrub grass and along one high ridge the pines were thick. Bill and I were on horseback and had to duck our heads to get through the trees. The horses were sweating in the heat. Bill used his crop to keep his horse going. He was wearing brown riding boots, tan jodhpurs, and a black, hard hat. He was very erect and big in the saddle. Most people didn't realize how big he was, over six feet and two hundred-and-forty pounds, barrel chested. He cared about how he rode his horse. It was a discipline he took pleasure in on the dunes, keeping his horse at the right pace in the soft sand, the reins taut enough, so that the horse's head was up into the salt-wind, and then we dropped down into a gully, a big bowl of sand around our heads, which we slowly climbed, to a long flat drift down to the water, brilliant blue, and the sun . . . sequins on the water. Before we broke into a gallop I looked back and saw our trail, how it hooked up the dune into the trees.

We walked the horses, talking about his image of himself. "You see," he said, "image is much more important than ego, the image you have of yourself, but it's not show business. It's a completely surrealistic pop art thing. When I perform on television it's more pop art than Andy Warhol because I really get out there and do the thing and come out of that box into your living room, for real, except I'm not for real, I'm Ronald all dressed up as Ronald, pure pop art. When I was with Duchamp he said, 'Pop art just popped up,' so, here I am, the theater of myself . . . "

"And people in Toronto don't get it."

"Yeah, but a lot of folks from Europe, they don't have that problem. Not French Canadians either. WASPs and people who have their heads in WASP space, that's the sore spot."

"They see you showboating . . . Showboat, they're embarrassed for you . . . "

"Which is why there's no Canadian Fellini. Eddie Shack threw a pie in my face and the dog on the set began to eat the pie off my face because the stupid buggers had made a real pie and my eyes ended up stuck closed. When I painted the set live on the air, they threw it away. Just threw it away. They throw everything away. Their archives are empty." He was filled with scorn, and a sadness because other men didn't see it his way. "If Fellini had watched me he would have probably committed suicide and never made another film, because it wouldn't be necessary."

He let out a loud self-deprecating laugh. "I never said I was perfect," he said, and we got back up on the horses. We sat for a moment in the saddles staring out at the water. There were three or four gulls screeching, and the sound of the waves breaking.

"Did I ever tell you," he said, "this is the dune where Valentino made his film? Somewhere along here, *The Sheik.*"

Not far from the dunes, Marie-Claire Blais lived in the woods in a tiny frame cottage, a few miles from Wellfleet.

Bill stood on the stoop of his Long Pond Road cottage and scowled. There had been a coastal thunderstorm all morning and the sandy ground was soggy and the sky bleak. He had wanted to fly his kites in Cahoun's Hollow. But the winds were whipping and it looked like there was going to be more rain.

"I don't like thunderstorms, I wantta fly my kite."

He was wearing tan trousers, an emerald green shirt and ivory snake-skin boots.

"Come on," I said.

He went into his room for ten minutes and emerged all in white, except for his boots, which were silver. He stood out on the stoop again, felt the heavy dampness in the air, said, "No, I can't get in tune with myself to meet her, I'm not going anywhere. I'm going to listen to the radio."

I drove up the Provincetown Road and then into pine woods, the branches heavy with water. Blais came out of the cottage, striding forward, wearing a long black skirt and heavy black sweaters, her smile eager but fleeting.

She was small and attractive, round-faced, with a high forehead and a narrowing chin, a pallor that was white but not pasty . . . There was a bluish porcelain tinge to her skin. Her hands and feet were small, her breasts full. Her direct look had the innocence of sincerity, but a sincerity full of ardor. Black eyebrows. Bangs. The coastal wind blew her hair back.

We sat under an apple tree, the apples unpicked, hanging like little blackening bells or fallen into the long grass, and we talked. All her gestures were graceful, not childlike, but with a modesty that invited protection, a modesty that was seductive as she told me, "After all, each man is born to pain, to sorrow. Each child has something consumptive in his soul." Silly though it was, I felt I should be protecting her from her sorrows but of course, what I had to protect her from was the intrusion of the film camera-eye coming at her from over my shoulder and my need to put an overbearing, comforting arm around her. "It does not mean that the child does not laugh," she said, " but it is a loneliness . . . " She laughed. She had a good open laugh. Aware of the dampness seeping into our bones, we stood up, our shoes clogged in rotted fruit, and walked through the woods. She seemed like such a little girl, her black hair blowing freely in the wind, murmuring quietly when the wet branches wiped across her face. We separated to go around a dwarf pine, and she said:

"This place is good for me. It is very lonely and peaceful. I like the loneliness . . . My time is for walking and reading and thinking."

We circled around a line of white birch trees — white against the black sky. I could hardly see her pallid face for hair. The line of white in the sky widened. We were heading back toward the cottage, but then decided to drive down to the ocean, to one of the high hollows in the dunes. Going through the scrub-grass and along the top of the dune we could hear the waves, the surge, and then there they were, the waves, split ends of white on cold gray crests, collapsing, sprawling , thinning on the sand. We looked down the dune. "We are born evil, yes, and with fears, and you feel dependent upon your fears, you cannot escape, particularly in childhood. It is a kind of sickness, the dependence upon your fears." She touched my arm and said, "You have your tragic view of life. I can always see that in your face." I was about to laugh and let her know that a Mayan woman had told me the fish in my fingertips had teeth and needed to feed on tenderness, but I realized I had been assimilated into her view of things, her sense of *angoisse* which she accepted so cheerfully that she smiled, entirely at ease. She pulled her coat around her throat, the bright scarf at her throat the only sign of color on her body.

We ran down the dune toward the ocean, holding hands, half-loping, half-falling forward, and then we walked slowly along the line of spent waves, side-stepping in the sand when a wave rolled close to our feet. "Always it comes, the ocean, with such power, such determination, and then it comes to nothing," she said. Seagulls were criss-crossing, the sky was the milk-white that's more usual just before dawn, and then suddenly the sky began to close, to lower, darkening.

We took a winding path back up to the top and turned and looked out over the water. "You know," I said, "I hate to tell you this, but there are moments when what you are writing makes me feel . . . like the worst sin is to be born."

"It is a part of my feeling for life, though I feel the good part too. Besides, I think my poems are young and gay. I feel they are. Maybe they are not for you. But when I write them, there is a gaiety."

Later, at her cottage:

"You seem completely isolated. In this weather, it seems desolate." I was worried, which was a twist on how it usually is with her; she's always fretting about whether I have been drinking too much, eating enough, gambling too heavily, or whether I am frayed by the conflicts of love . . . she, who eats less than a bird, drinks straight gin, gambles on anything with number combinations or legs, and succumbs to love with joy . . .

"Yes, desolate . . . but I am not completely by myself," she said. "I have friends close by, this place is good for me. It is very lonely and peaceful. I think I will live in this country. I feel free and that is good. I am more objective, more than I would be in the city. I would not like to go back there, because I have found this freedom here in the country. But then . . . that is how it is now . . . it will not be possible all my life. I will go to Québec again I think, eventually . . . But now, when I return from time to time I am sad and not very hopeful. They are involved and very serious about their problems. They are passionate and there are some who like violence, who need it, but I try to understand though I do not approve of violence. There is confusion, they are not happy, they feel humiliated. Perhaps they sometimes fight against themselves. Anyway, emotions always change and give you the energy to love again . . . but still, we are born with fears, we cannot escape, particularly in childhood."

"Escape?"

"From fear . . . *la peur* . . . it is not rational at all. It is a kind of sickness . . . the dependence upon your fears. Mind you, children have very peaceful moments, a sweet and completely peaceful state. Life can be very fresh as well as frightening. I never deny that there is beauty in life. Other writers will speak often about it and I will speak more about it when I want. But up to now in my novels I have been interested in the problems . . . *le problème du mal* . . . good and evil."

Mary Meigs appeared. She was a painter, a lean, handsome woman who had a natural elegance but it was a naturalness so undercut by shyness that she seemed at a loss, embarrassed. She ducked her head. There was something resolute about her, in the firmness of her mouth, but also something wary, vulnerable. We shook hands, and she gave us two glasses of cranberry juice, which we drank, and then Meigs disappeared. Blais seemed thoughtful, as if she wanted to explain more of herself:

"I always change. I feel that I am always being born again, destroyed again. It is never all positive or negative. I like to live, I like to feel new and fresh. This sadness is not always there."

"When'll you write about people who did not destroy each other?"

"I make progress," she answered with a laugh. "There is a difference these days, a difference. I am not so tragic. Now there is a sense of humor . . . it is a difference that will come . . . soon . . . "

The novel that Marie-Claire Blais said would come, the novel with "a sense of humor," was published in France, where it was awarded the Prix Medici. It then appeared in English as *A Season in the Life of Emmanuel*. It was reviewed in *The Times* in New York by Robertson Davies. It was a sneering review. "Mlle. Blais is a genius — that is to say, a writer with an extraordinary capacity for imaginative creation, subject to laws of her own, and not amenable to discipline . . . [*A Season in the Life of Emmanuel*] uncomfortably suggests that large group of novels that Stella Gibbons knocked on the head in 1932 with *Cold Comfort Farm*. Nobody in those books was a homosexual, so far as I can recall, and nobody actually got to the point of masturbating or ravishing a hunchback, but the flavor was the same; nature was morose, and man was vile. The revival of this sort of novel in our post-Gibbons era is dangerous even to a talent so strong as that of Mlle. Blais, and we hope she will think better of it when next she publishes."

6

In the spring of 1966, Bob Blackburn, the television critic for John Bassett's *Toronto Telegram* — a wildly exuberant, slightly raunchy paper, the third largest in the country, that for a period was known as *The Pink Tely* because the front page was actually pink — asked me at the upstairs bar of the Celebrity Club what I thought of his newspaper's book review pages. "Absolute shit," I said.

"What're you doing with your life?" he asked.

"I just started teaching at the University."

"Yeah. You got your Ph.D.?"

"Naw. That's next, a year or so, after I write the exams."

"I've heard you talk about books on the radio."

"Yeah."

"So why not run our book pages?"

"Why not."

For two weeks, an agreeable man named Jeremy Brown courted me at the restaurant by the pool at The Four Seasons motor hotel on Jarvis Street, just south of the Celebrity Club. I had never been taken to lunch, never been courted at poolside. I was charmed. I showed Brown the only critical piece I had published, an essay admiring the fiction of Margaret Laurence. It had appeared in the *Tamarack Review*. I then wrote a piece for his paper about Eustace (W.W.E.) Ross, and the English theater and Arnold Wesker. The editors were full of praise. I met Tom Hedley, the associate entertainment editor, a nimble young man who had a fey brashness. I could see that even when he didn't know what he was doing he was going to do it with style and sureness, and it would probably turn out right. I liked him. It was May and Hedley asked me to start in July. I couldn't start until September because I was going to France and England with Bill Ronald for "The Umbrella," but Hedley — knowing I shared his distaste for the hothouse cultural nationalism that was in the air — asked me to write a long piece on Edmund Wilson for the September issue, a piece that would let the town know what the *Telegram* weekend book pages were going to be like, what they were going to represent. I was married, I had a child, I was teaching, I was on radio, I was on television, and now I was going to be writing weekly for the third largest newspaper in the country. I was twenty-nine.

"Come to my place for Sunday brunch," Tom said. "Coddled eggs and champagne."

7

At Tom's suggestion, at the noon hour in the Closerie, I had a bowl of *moules* in a white wine sauce and a glass of *death in the afternoon* . . . champagne and pernod, and then drove all afternoon from Paris to Tours. I met Bill Ronald in the early evening and we went to have supper with Alexander Calder and his wife at the Metropole Hotel. Calder was in his seventies, big, hunched forward, his arms hanging: he hardly moved his body or his head, making others revolve around him, the lumbering center of his world. He had white hair and he was wearing an expensive red flannel shirt and a green flannel tie; his hands were shaking; he mumbled little bursts of words down into his chest, self-indulgent thrown-away words, lost in his own chortling.

The hotel concierge treated him like a film star. Bill walked with him into the dining room. The maître d' bowed, treating him like a star, too. Calder paid no attention. I followed with Mrs. Calder, a handsome woman with very fine features. I told her that she and her husband, the way they moved, reminded me of Edmund and Elena Wilson. She said she had met them once at Harvard, hadn't known who they were, but had had an energetic, pleasant conversation with Elena. All she remembered about Edmund was that he was a bit drunk. Calder, sitting at the head of the table, said, "I don't remember him at all." He was more aware of what was being said than he let on.

"Well, Ronald," he said, "where've you been?"

"Paris. We'll go to Chartres on the way back. A few days ago we were at Much Haddem with Henry Moore."

"How'd you find him?"

"Okay. Very indifferent, English. He told me his father was a miner."

"And he's a minor sculptor."

We laughed but Calder didn't. He smirked. He drank more Bordeaux, having his own self-contained, gruff good time. Ronald, always surprised at anyone else's indulgent carrying-on, was trying to suppress a kind of small boy's glee at the old man who was so much his own man, his own character, and when Calder mumbled something again, Ronald said eagerly, "I can't understand you," and his wife said, "Don't worry, I haven't understood a word he's said for thirty years." Calder shrugged, as if he were dealing with incompetents, drank another glass of wine, looked out from under his brow, and smiled. He was having a good time.

The waiter brought dessert. It was a thin pancake folded into a ball filled with rich cream. As the waiter poured a thick chocolate sauce over it, Calder said, dead-pan, "That looks like a grandmother's fart."

Ronald collapsed in laughter. He could not eat the dessert. Calder spooned up the chocolate sauce, smacking his lips. I thought I was going to start giggling. Calder, eyeing Ronald, had let a little chocolate drool out of the corner of his mouth. We were saved by the hotel manager who appeared with an elaborately bound book and he asked if Calder wouldn't sign it. Calder cleared away the cups and plates and set the book on the table and his hand stopped shaking. He drew, very deliberately, a stabile which he had planned for Expo 67 in Montreal.

He then handed the book to Bill, who, with modesty, printed his name at the top of the blank page. Calder harrumphed and took the book back and did another drawing, all lines leading to Bill's name at the apex. It was a touching exchange.

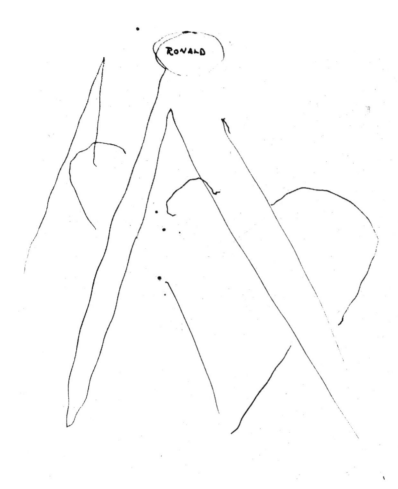

"Well, poet," he said, "what're you going to write?"

For some split-second-reason I decided to draw a caricature of Calder. Bill looked incredulous and said, "You've got the guts of a grave robber," but the caricature looked enough like Calder for the old man to applaud and call for cognac.

"Well, seeing as we're drawing maps," he said, "this is how you get to my place tomorrow."

As he made little arrows and road signs on note paper, Bill said, "Moore's secretary sends out printed instructions."

"That's no good," Calder said. "Dull. How can he send people he doesn't like in the wrong direction?" He eyed us and smiled, leaving us wondering what we'd discover on the road the next day.

His wife took him home, complaining he had drunk too much. He muttered, "Don't get personal," and took her hand.

Later that night Bill and I were walking along the empty boulevard in Tours. The dwarf trees set apart at twenty paces seemed artificial, plastic, in the yellow street-lamp light. Bill was overcome with a curious sense of something close to relief at having found Calder to be the way he was, as if he had seen something of himself in the old man, or maybe the way he'd like to be when his hair was white. The words flowed out of him: "He's completely beautiful, like a combination of W.C. Fields and Santa Claus. He's completely American and I am attracted to the American people in a way, but aside from that, it's a beautiful openness and childlike . . . he's very childlike, Christ almighty, he's very direct and honest . . . he's as famous as a goddamn Moore, and yet his whole being . . . Moore was like a dried-up professor by comparison, but Calder also, if you noticed, he's embraced the French people, too, and his lack of reverence, for all the sacred cows, you can tell that . . . the kind of thing you expect from a guy who's gone dancing every Saturday night of his life for years . . . "

Calder's map worked in the late morning. We were in the Loire Valley in his four-hundred-year-old stone house. Two walls of the house had been cut out of the side of a hill. At the end of the house were caves and in the caves, hundreds of bottles of wine. Calder met us in the courtyard and Bill said, "I hope you didn't find last night's supper too trying." Calder muttered, "What were you trying to do?" He snorted and led us into the house.

The main floor was one room, the length and full breadth of the house. On the work table to the left of the door, there were notes and letters in Calder's shaky handwriting, and in the middle of the room, a long pine table, rough-cut, that carried the eye to a kind of partition and behind that, a sink built into the stone wall. Calder, shuffling like an old fighter, went to the wine cellars and came back with his arms full of bottles. We sat down to a lunch of cold meats and tomatoes and cheese.

During conversation, Calder said little, except for some acid asides, like, "You, poet, you eating that Gruyère plain? That's a sissy cheese. Put some pepper on it." He seemed tired but after lunch he took us through the house; everything was color, old pieces of cloth hung here and there along with Miros and Légers, and from the ceilings, small mobiles turning slowly in the slightest wind from the open windows, and a beautiful wire head (of his wife?) and a wonderful wire hand with an extended forefinger on which sat a roll of toilet paper. After a while he drove us about two miles, at high speed, to his studio.

It was set on a hill, a big airport hangar designed by Calder. There was little sign of his doing much work there; it seemed more a museum for his current sculptures. Out back, looking over the valley, there was a long terrace, on which sat four or five stabiles — one of them, *The Falcon*, a huge black bird-like structure that seemed on the verge of taking off over the edge of the terrace, off into the vineyards in the valley below. Bill was walking from piece to piece, running his hands over the surfaces, and he said, standing beside *The Falcon*, "I'd like to get on and fly away."

"Are you a witch?"

"I'll find a broom."

"When you do, sweep up before you bugger off." He stuck out his tongue. "And what do you do, poet?"

"I think."

"I think you should buzz off." He stuck out his tongue again.

He went over to the side of the hill and sat down. "Look around as long as you want." He put his elbows on his knees and his chin in his hands and he deliberately dozed off. He did indeed go to sleep and when we were through looking around, he seemed for the first time to be an old man, hard to wake up, a little uncertain of where he was, and why. But he bunched up and shook his head and said, "I been everywhere, I can keep up with you guys."

It was late afternoon and Calder was tired but he took us up to his little block-house painting studio across the road from his home. "I'm going to do you guys a gouache." He stood over the sheet of paper, poised, the brush held straight up in his hand as if he were a Chinese scribe. Then he drew thick black lines, a face, round — with the tongue stuck out — and filling half the page, with zebra lines, and then a big hand, open, waving good-bye. Finished, he barked, "Okay whatchyur name," pointing at Ronald, "you and the poet on your way. Time to hit the rails."

He stood in the center of the road as we drove away and he watched until we neared a turn. I expected him to wave. He just shuffled off toward his house. Bill said, "He already waved, in his gouache, just like on television."

In the night, as we went through Chartres and then on to Paris, Bill said, "Don't you get the feeling, I mean in his work, the variety of it all . . . his whole personality, that's in touch with the whole world around him, even at his age he still sees life as a circus? I keep saying it over, but Jesus Christ, you can't create out of a void. At least I can't. Now Pinkham Ryder did. You know who Pinkham Ryder was? Pinkham Ryder was a very good painter of the nineteenth century and he painted little wee pictures of ships, you'd recognize them if you saw them, little brown pictures of ships sailing on the sea, and you've heard of Lydia Pinkham's Pink Pills, well, that's the Pinkham. Well, they sent Mr. Pinkham off to Paris. He used to live in Brooklyn in a small room all by himself, in this bloody room and painted these pictures, so his father thought, Maybe if we send him to Paris he'll stop painting these bloody pictures, and they sent him to Paris and he came back, he didn't stop painting those ships, and lived in his one room in Brooklyn. Now, he created out of a void. A void. I guess he had something going on inside his head, endless little brown ships . . . Now, why did I say all that?"

"He still sees life as a circus . . . "

"That's right. That's right. Calder's got the whole goddamn crazy world inside his head. Like a white-haired old child."

As we drove, I realized we were actually on the old pilgrimage route, the rue St. Jacques, that runs through the country from Paris to the Pyrenees and from there on to Santiago de Compostella. *Compostella*: A field of stars. And the *rue St. Jacques*, which is what the French call the Milky Way. Old roads in the great expanse of dark sky.

When I was a child my mother gave me a book in which all the stars (like dots in a kindergarten book) were to be linked by lines into their shapes, the Little Dipper, Orion, the Big Dipper, the Centaur, the Phoenix, ancient signs, the ancient stories . . . I traced the lines, one star to another, until I was sure I understood the night sky, a darkness full of tales, and maybe even then, like an old child, I was trying to hold the whole crazy world inside my own head.

In the summer at the cottage, my mother always let me lie on my back late at night on the boathouse deck; I drew the shapes in the air with my finger the same way I fingerpainted in the sand. Then in the winter when it was too cold to sit out at night, my father read the stories in the stars to me from *Bulfinch's Mythology*: a woman whose hair was snakes, a man who had the body of a horse, a woman who embraced a swan. As we drove through the night, following our headlights into unknown country, I told Bill about the pilgrimage road and how medieval pilgrimage had helped to draw villages out of the night of Dark Age isolation, and the stars, always the stars drawing travelers on. It seemed to me that ancient peoples had made up all those stories around the stars so that they could make sense out of the great emptiness that the sky is, empty except for a thousand helter-skelter glints of light. And they shaped those glints of light into little stories that were really about themselves, and it must have given them consolation to know that there were not only great magic figures and magic gods out there, but the figures and gods lived lives exactly like their own, lives in full emotional flight, as they maintained a standard of chaos, full of the desperate yearning for love, full of duplicity, aberration, disappointment.

"I like flying kites," Bill said. "You can't fly kites at night."

"The thing is," I said, "it's kind of the way I feel when I run into a guy like Calder, and anybody else, you know, like Marie-Claire or Brownie and Sonny . . . they're like glints of light. Each one of them is a little story, light extricated from the darkness, and when we hit the road, going from one to the other, we're linking them all together, making a bigger story, a kind of map of the mind of the times, a hotel register of the heart, otherwise there'd just be a great big emptiness . . . "

"Space . . . " Bill said.

"But it's those moments, those presences, maybe, that tie us into a kind of consolation."

"Negative space."

"Because they're there."

"It's what I do all the time."

"What?"

"Space. Every time I start a painting I'm in empty space, so powerful because it's empty. Except I'm more powerful, because I fill it."

"But you can't fly a kite at night."

"Me paint. So I make it through the night. That's what my little daughter said. 'Me paint, Pop.' And I told her Paint's a horse. And she stuck out her tongue at me and laughed at me."

"That's what Calder did, he stuck out his tongue."

Book Four

1

Often on those summer nights when I stood on the lawn facing my father as he sat in his work chair in the box of amber light, wisps of gray hair over his ears, eyes hooded, I wondered what he had been like as a child. He never talked about himself as a child. I only got a glimpse of his childhood when I ran into an old woman who said, "I knew your father when we were children, grade five or six, and he wanted to kiss me" — an old woman happily alive in her child's eye view of herself and Morley. But it was impossible for me to find in her face — in her shriveled smiling mouth — the child who was my father, so I gave that up and stared into his shriveling face, and stared hard and I found a good-looking, self-possessed boy with curly black hair sitting under an elm tree with three girls behind him. He was hugging his knees. At fifteen, he knew who he was and he liked himself. Would I have hugged him or liked him? Probably not (he had the look in his eyes of a Momma's boy, and I knew something about Momma's boys because I was my mother's boy).

Would I have liked my mother as a girl? Perhaps. She had a sultry, mischievous laughter in her dark eyes and I have been in love with women who reminded me of her. But I have also been in love with women who had nothing in common with her at all, women who made her bite her lip. Still, she was a sensual woman, shaken even in the year that she died by her sexual yearning. Even when she was a hobbled wreck I could feel her sensuality. As a young man, I might well have tried to get on her dance card.

Morley was not sensual. Mavis Gallant told me once in Rome that he was the least sensual man she had ever met. She didn't say so with malice. She had great affection for him. Maybe it was because I was hugging her outside a restaurant, saying good night after an amiable meal, and maybe she was trying to bolster me, a son standing in the light of her memory of his father. I don't know, but I do know he never kissed me. I never saw him kiss my brother. I cannot imagine the night I was conceived, I cannot imagine my father making love to my mother, not because I ever resented the idea or wanted to make love to her myself, but as a boy — seeing her naked — I thought she was beautiful, I thought she had beautiful breasts (Morley, with his gift for bizarre sexual images described such breasts as fitting perfectly into two champagne glasses) and I was sure she not only liked her own nakedness but would want a man to like her nakedness, too. It was hard to think of Morley naked. It was hard to think of Morley reckless with longing (to turn a phrase by St. Augustine, he was

> burning
>> burning
>>> burning

a burning intellect). But no matter what I thought, he loved her, he loved Loretto deeply, profoundly, and for life. And she loved him, only him.

So what was the nakedness I wanted to see in either of them? What was I looking for, and at what risk? Whatever it was, it demanded a curious eye, a cold eye. Not ruthless, but a lens eye unmoved by the impediment of emotion. The kind of eye Morley had. He could look at me that way, and often did. And at my mother. That, of course, was the distance I always felt in him. The distance that allowed him to take our intimate private moments and put them on the public page for his own purposes. He looked at himself that way. Unflinching. By temperament.

There is an astonishing scene in *A Passion in Rome*, astonishing to any-one who knew my mother, a scene in which the lovers are in a rented flat over a shop and they have been through a night of sexual ecstasy, a night of cries and moans — followed by fierce wrangling and loud recrimination. In the morning, to mollify the old landlady, the man tells his lover what to write in a note: "We are sure you were alarmed by the cry of pain you must have heard last night . . . I have a neuralgia of the face, an old disease. Perhaps you have heard of it. It is called *tic douloureux*. It strikes me suddenly. The pain, as doctors know, is unbearable. I am ashamed that I cry out . . ."

What did my mother think of that?

The camera-lens eye could steal your thoughts, your shames, your soul.

After I returned home from my honeymoon I had a casual conversation with my father in which I told him about the first little fights I had had on the road with Nina. Later, in *A Fine And Private Place*, I read:

He had her arm and felt her shoulder go up stiffly. Then he knew that she felt neglected and he trembled with resentment. Rome was the loveliest of all the cities, and here she was, wanting to be treated as the only really lovely thing in Rome. From then on, he was aware of other surprising little oppositions. He liked wandering at loose ends: unexpected ruins, restaurants, boutiques, tie shops and churches — they all delighted him. Then, if he suddenly wanted to cross the road, she argued: It wasn't where they had planned to cross. In Christ's name, what does it matter? And he was harsh with her, for there seemed to be a map in her head which only she knew and he couldn't know; if they didn't follow the secret map, everything would go to pieces.

I remember thinking, What a remarkable memory, what a remarkable piece of reporting, but at the same time, he knew and I knew — and perhaps Nina knew, too — that a private moment in my marriage had been seen through that lens of his and then laid bare, set naked.

Yet I never said a word.

It is dangerous to look upon your father, even through a window, but even more so to finally go into his tent and see him naked.

I did.

I looked at him with my own curious lens-eye, and at the worst of moments — when we both thought he was about to be told he had cancer — unmoved by the impediment of emotion.

Morley sat down one day and read in my novel, *The Way the Angel Spreads Her Wings*, about the actual afternoon we went together to Wellesley Hospital:

He was sick and worried though there was no quaver in his voice, not that Adam could hear, 'but the blood, you wouldn't believe the blood, it's like a great big yellow and red stain spreading all over my stomach and abdomen and it's like a stain in the wallpaper pushing through, all around my side.' Adam went for him in a taxi, suddenly afraid that if his father died, his blood, his tap root, everything would drain out of his life and he alone would be left, the root but of what? and who were you when your father died? a remnant, a repository, someone at last set free, especially after fending for him, for years yielding to the waywardness that comes from his life's long habit of doing what he wants, so a son ends up being the coddling forgiving father to a lifetime's acquired childishness *and as his father undressed in the cubicle in the hospital's emergency room he thought* I don't want to see him stripped down, defenseless: years ago I wanted him dead but now I don't want him defenseless. *His father stood barefoot on the gray marble floor, naked, talking about baseball as if nothing were the matter, as if they were in neutral space, all emotion neutered, and neither spoke of a silent unseen tumor, somehow spawned, nor said the dreaded word, cancer, the big C, but only stared at the yellow, purple, pink, sepia blood in rippled layers, a relief map under the translucent skin,* all the places he's been, the altitudes. *But the doctor, a young man wearing steel-rimmed glasses, shrugged and smiled as Web sat upon the brown rubber sheet of the examining table, his slightly bowed legs dangling* and his penis is so small, *remembering when he was a child in the bathroom, his father standing over the toilet, his penis between two fingers, thick, so big, so heavy, and now it looked like his memory of his own childhood penis, small, hooded,* shriveled by fear, his only sign of fear, and why am I looking at his penis? when it is actually his bony feet, the long bony yellow toes and toenails that appal me, the hard yellow nails and the thin shins and crinkled blue veins and the flesh hanging loose under his arms like a woman's, the little womanly tits with tufts of hair around the small nipples (why do men have nipples? what taunting sign of ineffectuality, lost powers, sign of the lost rib, surrendered out of loneliness) *and laughing lightly, Adam said, 'Goddamn, you sure look like the resurrection of the dead to me.' The doctor laughed too and said, 'Don't be so dramatic. You can thank your lucky stars, it's only a rup- tured artery. Like everything that's easy it looks terrible. What's always terrible is what you never see.'*

Morley never said a word.

He never said a word, except to say that the prose of the novel was very sensual, that it was not the way he wrote. No, not at all . . . he wanted to be glass. To not be there, to be seen through. The arrogance of such humility.

Yet we ended up yielding, in complete and silent trust, our private mom- ents to each other's story-telling devices and public scrutiny.

Perhaps that was a nakedness beyond a kiss, beyond sensuality. Beyond even trust, since it was neither asked for nor given.

Perhaps that is love.

2

"I know what the wilderness is like," Morley said, "what it is when a man finally comes to realize that he has let his imagination wither and die and has grown old in the heart. He knows he is half dead. I saw it one night in a man I knew who was with me at a big party, actually a party for Wyndham Lewis.

"He was a very successful executive and only 55. He was having trou- ble with his wife. Sitting on the stairs he called, 'Morley, sit with me. I want to tell you something.' Holding my arm tight, he said desperately, 'When I get ready for bed at night I'm tired. I have a drink, I pick up *Time*. I read three pages and fall asleep . . . '

"He had started to cry. Tears were running down his cheeks. 'I know I'm a little drunk,' he said, 'but I used to read all the time. When I was at college

I was crazy about Katherine Mansfield and Virginia Woolf. I read Sherwood Anderson, I read . . . what happened to me? I want to go home, I want to go home and find out what happened to me.'"

Morley often talked about going home, talked about the night in New York that he and Loretto decided they had to leave the city. It was late December, but the weather was good and they had three days. So they drove home for Christmas.

Somewhere upstate in the hills beyond Elmira it began to snow heavily. In the night the car skidded down a hill, crashed through a guardrail and went down a steep slope, knocking over bushes and a tree. Stunned but unhurt, they waited and soon they heard voices shouting at them from up on the road. Within an hour the car was towed to a village garage where the garageman promised to work on it all night.

Late the next morning they started out again, going fast on icy roads, and 150 miles from the border the car, out of control, skidded again, went off the road and clipped off a service station pump. They were held in the local bank manager's office until Max Perkins in New York convinced the bank manager that he would pay for the pump. Again they drove on. It was dark when they got to the border. The snow was falling so heavily just beyond Niagara that the windshield wipers stopped working, and while he cursed and drove on, Loretto — reaching from inside her open window — tried to work them manually. Her hands froze. She began to cry. They turned into a roadside farmhouse near Port Dalhousie and asked for shelter through the night.

Lying awake in the dark in a strange house, listening to the wind sweep snow against the window, Morley wondered at his maniacal need to get home. As he would say in later years, no beckoning star had appeared in the sky, leading them on. By hurrying home, was he reaching back desperately for his boyhood? The magic of unexpected gifts? The mystery of the security of family relationships? Then he decided that he had got a true sense of the way things were at the beginning, two thousand years ago. The birth of a child had been a most intimate family love affair. If a man could touch memories of the love and intimacy of a family home, then he was a man who had a secret fortress — a secret place of security that might sustain him during his most dreadful panic-stricken times.

By morning it had stopped snowing. They drove on, finally coming into the gray cold streets of Toronto, and soon they were home among their own people, our family, at the one right time of the year.

Year after year, against different obstacles, Morley repeated this journey. I have repeated it. My brother has repeated it. But what, year after year, were the obstacles? Not snow and long roads and windshield wipers that wouldn't work. It was something deeper than that.

Morley brought us up to be suspicious of all expansive public talkers, the Bishop Fulton Sheens, the Malcom Muggeridges. The big communicators, he called them derisively, public consolers like Harry Golden or Maya Angelou. He wanted none of that. He wanted to whisper to the loneliness in his wife and sons, or to the loneliness of any man or a woman, and since men and women felt most alone at Christmas, he asked us at that time to be intimate and personal and close and open and honest in a way no big public communicator could ever dare to be.

We hunkered down as Christmas came and tried to get through the electronic wash of phony public sentimentality. We grew purse-mouthed and pouty as the snows. One December, three large grown boys rapped on Morley's door and as soon as he opened it and they started singing a carol in horrible flat off-key voices, he said grimly, "Okay. So you want a quarter from me. Here. No, don't finish that song. Beat it."

Instead of watching television programs that told stories of oily benevolence and lugubrious sanctity, we hunted up gangster movies. I read Morley's old paperback copies of Mickey Spillaine. One evening, my mother, musing aloud, wondered, "Whatever happened to Jack Webb?" For days, we said to each other, "Just gimme the facts, ma'am, just the facts." Killing ourselves with toneless laughter. We called each other at two in the morning: "There's a terrific cop show on 4 . . . Clint Eastwood on 2." I urged my favorite restaurant to put filet of reindeer on the menu. "Call it 'The Rudolph Special.'" I avoided all streets where hired groups sang cheerful carols on the corners.

Yet there was one crack in our wall of reserve. We liked shopping for gifts. Morley — in the last weeks, as he became another grim shopper in a faceless crowd — assured us that the old magi must have had to shop around, too, picking up a little gold here, frankincense and myrrh there. "Think of the hustlers they had to deal with." We tried but before long, we lost our wry humor and began to feel pushed around and cynical.

One day a big, tired woman, red-faced and stern, who had a seven-year-old boy holding on to her dress, came crashing into Morley with all her bundles as he tried to get out of an elevator. She kept pushing Morley back from the door. Out of patience, angry, he lunged against her, knocking her aside. They glared at each other with hatred. Then, the hurt astonishment in the little boy's eyes shocked Morley.

"I'm sorry, son," he muttered, "I'm sorry. Have a good Christmas."

Then it was Christmas Eve. Michael and I were jovial. The decorated tree was in place in the big hall. It was quiet outside. There was snow on the ground. Around two a.m., after a few drinks while watching midnight mass from Rome on television, we got up to leave Morley and Loretto alone. We watched them start up the stairs, then turn to quicken with that intimation of a sweetness that would come on the morrow when the door would open and smiling faces would appear; their sons, grandsons, our wives, aunts and uncles; and in this quickening expectation, I knew they heard family voices, the living and the dead, in all the vigor of intimate relationships. They knew, we knew, that once again we had made it — we had all made it — to the private and secret place we called home.

3

There was a terrible snowstorm. Under three feet of snow, the city streets were closed, but on a Sunday afternoon a television producer, R. J. Paddy Sampson, asked if I would come to his house within the hour. I trudged through snow up to my knees.

He was an inch short of my shoulder, with steady socketed eyes, a blade nose, ruddy cheeks. Born in Belfast, he'd been a merchant seaman in the War, a stagehand at the Old Vic in London, a floor director and now he was a director at the CBC. He spoke his own lingo: dockside argot, flourishes of courtly rhetoric, an autodidact's pedantry (he was a ferocious reader of Second World War histories), and jive talk. He wore a cap. He wore it while directing, he wore it during supper at George's Spaghetti House (a jazz joint where I had first met him) and some said he wore it to bed with June, his wife, a full-breasted beautiful showgirl who was taller than he by a head.

I shook off the snow and sat down. He offered me Gentleman's Relish and champagne. He said, "You might as well know, I don't particularly like you, but you are the only guy to do the job." He wanted to gather great old black blues singers together, put them in a studio, let them play, and talk "hanging out talk," nothing formal, all natural. "I know you know a lot of these guys already, so you know how to do the talking with them," Sampson said.

"Okay," I said.

"Have another champagne. I drank all the Chivas last night."

"Champagne'll do."

All those old blues singers came together for that show in 1966 — Willie Dixon, Muddy Waters and his band, Lonecat Jesse Fuller, Brownie McGhee and Sonny Terry. Booker T. Washington White, Sunnyland Slim, James Cotton, Maybel Hillery, Big Joe Williams, and Otis Spann. During the three days' taping of music and conversation, Willie Dixon said, "You know, the blues is a universal feeling that's been here since Adam, cause as you remember, God made Adam and Adam was alone and Adam asked God for a woman and God gave him a woman and Eve gave him the blues all over again."

"That's a true saying," Muddy said, "but the blues is really about going up the road. When things get tough I sing about going up the road cause that defends. The blues is a defense. This whole show's gonna be a defense. There's never been a blues meeting like this here one. We know this is gonna be a document, man."

The program, *The Blues*, went to air. At first it was broadcast as an hour and then, extraordinarily enough, it was expanded and repeated at ninety minutes without commercials. It was authentic. It had a rare intimacy, conveyed by the camera work and the conversation. As film, directed and edited by Sampson, it was almost flawless. It became a bootlegged legend. Years later I ran into people in Copenhagen and Berlin who had seen it. Sampson went on to direct many fine shows — Ellington, Lena Horne, serious dramas, and the week of programming that capped his career — after he was levered out of the CBC — the Calgary winter Olympics — but *The Blues* stood through the decades as singular. No program like it was ever done again in North America. Every one of the players, but for James Cotton, is now dead.

Then, in 1996, men with the intentions of pimps brought the material out of the archives. They cut out all of the conversations and implanted a second-rate white blues singer, Colin James, to do musical bridges between the songs and to digitally fake a duet with Willie Dixon. The show, contrived for cable and airline sales, was a travesty. Everything authentic in the original was lost. But the show was indicative of what had happened to the CBC over thirty years — betrayed not by a peanut munching crowd of politicians in Ottawa, but scuppered from within by the network's managerial custodians.

My mother had a sudden severe attack. The tic. They cut into her brain. Severed more nerves. She came home and slept almost continuously for a week. And then she woke up.

I sat with her and she looked at me a long time and then she began to laugh.

"What're you laughing at?" I asked, amazed, because I wanted to cry at the sight of her swollen face.

"I was thinking of you in your diapers. No matter what we tried, they wouldn't stay on. As soon as you took a step you dropped your diapers."

"Oh yeah."

She laughed again, so I laughed with her. "We should have known," she said, "we should have known."

"This is not nice, Mom."

"Isn't it strange, you'll probably end up sleeping in this bed, my father and mother's bed."

"I suppose so," I said.

"Someone should write a novel about all the trips that are taken in a bed, never mind boats. All those boat novels in America, they're all about men, but a bed . . . a family bed, keeping it afloat . . . "

(In fact, after Mother died, and then Morley, and after I had inherited the house in my middle years and moved back into it, I slept in that bed, made it mine . . . the tooled mahogany bed her father had made on his lathe, the bed in which my mother had been conceived, the bed in which Morley had slept his last sleep . . . I made it mine to sleep in, facing the set of dresser drawers and the mirror standing on the dresser that my grandfather had also made . . . and after they were dead I felt no ghosts, no braiding of dust in the air . . . But one day I found one of my old baby shoes in a box, white and scuffed. I set it atop the mirror, the toe facing north. When I woke in the morning, it was facing west, the toe pointed at me. This happened during my sleep every night for a month until, slightly unnerved, I took the shoe down . . . I have never tried to figure out what this turning of a child's shoe in the night toward me could mean.)

"I hate making my bed," I said.

"And I'm bed-ridden."

"Get outa here."

"And Morley doesn't quite know what to make of what you're doing . . . "

"What am I doing?"

"You could write about what you're doing. It would be a bit like the old conversations, the Saturday nights."

"Naw."

"A bit," she said.

"Michael blames me for breaking up the Saturday nights, I guess I did."

"They weren't yours to begin with."

"But on end, after Eustace died, the people who were dropping around, they didn't care what we were arguing about, we were like a sideshow after the hockey game . . . "

"You're too harsh."

"Got to be what I do."

"No you don't."

"How about, I am what I see?"

At Gerdy's Folk City in New York's Village, Brownie and Sonny shouldered their way through the swinging kitchen doors, side-stepped the straddlers on the barstools with surprising deftness — Sonny following with his hand on the small of Brownie's back — and when they were on stage, Brownie, laughing, assuming the expository tones of a country corn-pone barrister, thrust his jaw into the spotlight, the tendons in his neck and forearms catching that light, and there was a slight curl at the corner of his lip, a clawtrack of anger under his high tone haughty air, and he turned to Sonny — sitting on his stool, arms limp, staring unperturbed into the glare of the spotlight, and Brownie asked, "What you doing, Sonny?" Sonny replied, "Just relaxin' my mind, man, just relaxin' my mind."

"How you relax your mind?"

"Fattening frogs for snakes."

A very small white girl with cropped hair had followed Brownie and Sonny out of the kitchen. She was standing back in the shadows at the end of the bar, with four colored felt pens and a wire-ring pad in her hand. As Brownie and Sonny sang, she sketched. Her name was Laura. She was so small and she worked with so little flair that no one noticed her. She sang along as she sketched. She worked very fast. I held her little books for her. She tore drawings out of the books and gave them to people. 'It's a gift of a gift," she said. "I got a gift and now you got a gift. Me to you, man."

After the set, when Brownie and Sonny were closeted again in the cramped dressing room downstairs below the kitchen, she appeared with a stringy black boy of about nineteen. He had a straggly beard and wore a patterned skull cap. She said, "Meet a friend, Sonny. He be from Chicago." Sonny jabbed his heavy hand into the blind man's nowhere space in the center of the room and the boy grasped it. She added, "He also be a artist." Sonny shook his hand again. After awkward, broken banter about Chicago, the boy departed. She said, "He be coming apart, bad . . . he be like me, man, messed up, man."

This girl, Laura Brown, had come alone to the dressing room one night. Since then she had looked after Sonny whenever he was playing in the club. Sitting with her in a corner of the tiny room, sharing bar Scotch in a paper Dixie cup, she told me that at sixteen she had received a Guggenheim fellowship and had gone to study in Paris. Returning to New York, she "was sickened — man. Really, I be so sickened of this town where the people be more like the roaches they trying to kill. It be a sewer town, man. Happy time in rat town." She married, continued to paint, made no effort to sell her work, and each evening moved nimbly after Sonny, guiding him up narrow stairways, taking him home to his old and dying wife, sometimes helping Sonny's wife sew Sonny's clothes. Her sketch books were filled with portraits, in brown, black, red and yellow, of Sonny.

I went around in the early evening to have supper at Sonny's. He had just moved to 85th Street, west of Central Park, a brownstone full of boosters and bootleggers. He had lived with his wife Roxanne for more than twenty years in a two-room, Harlem flat; but after the Harlem rent riots and all the junkie killings, no one — not even Brownie — would go into Harlem for a drink and supper with Sonny. Harlem, certainly Sonny's old streets, reeked of decay and dying and rats played hopscotch in the gutters. Stores, particularly the Jewish delicatessens, were boarded up, the broken glass of the looted windows catching the pale sun of the early winter days.

The afternoon that Sonny left Harlem, four young boys from a nearby building were struggling along the sidewalk with a mattress, trying to carry it home without it flopping over, but then, out of exasperation, they just dropped it and left it on the sidewalk, the vermin inside scurrying for cover in the torn quilting. The music Sonny could hear as he stood in the street not far from the mattress, the music from inside the Pabst Blue Ribbon bars and the open piss-smelling doorways, the music was grinding electric blues, electric, exactly the way he said he felt sometimes. "E-lectric, in my brain."

Street singers like himself had left Harlem years ago. In the old days, in the forties and early fifties, they had come straggling up out of the south where — he said — "the water tastes like cherry wine," and he had moved from corner to corner singing for nickels and dimes and there had been laughter and shared whiskey, but none of those singers was ever out on the street anymore — "Now, the water tastes like turpentine" — and some strung out dude could cut you with a razor, not only for your nickels and dimes, but for your guitar, rings, anything that might fetch a few dollars at the pawn shops, a few dollars down for a doobie.

So, Sonny had moved to West 85th Street, into big rooms down a dimly lit long hall that stank of pork fat and cabbage, the bleak light at the top of the stairs a small bare bulb in the ceiling. Sonny had brought a young man and wife out of Harlem. They had an agreement. The rent would be free for them and Sonny would teach the young man to play the mouth harp if the girl cooked, swept up, and helped Sonny's wife around the house while Sonny was singing on the road.

The girl, dark and shy and delicately boned, seemed to enjoy deep frying the chicken and rice and collard greens for our supper. It was Sunday, and Sonny was full of the expansiveness of a man comfortable in his home. He sent the boy downstairs to bang on the door of the house bootlegger to get more Scotch. After supper, blind Sonny stomped his feet on the hardwood and flapped his hands across his harp as he sang, *I got my eye on you, woman, there ain't nothing in the world you can do.* He reached out, his eyes wide open, unseeing, his big hand beckoning.

His wife, Roxanne, emaciated, her skin looking as if it had been brushed with wood ash, deep lines around her mouth — dying of cancer — began to hum, watching to see if Sonny would encourage her, and Sonny said, "Yeah," and then he told me that she had been churched as a child and had once sung church songs at Town Hall. Uncertain of the words, she started, "Didn't it rain children" — but lost the rhythm, and Sonny spoke gruffly to her. He stomped out the rhythm, making sure she got it, and she swung in, her aged voice deep and husky with sickness but sensual as she threw her head back and tried to roar — *See them coming in, two by two* . . . her thin arms, the flesh hanging loose under her arms, lifted and she was pet-patting with her feet — her felt slippers flapping against the floor, but her memory failed, she lost the words so we clapped and Sonny let out a fox-call whoop and spoke about the night she had sung at Town Hall, while Laura Brown took Sonny's bony and rangy wife by the elbow and helped her to her sick bed, a narrow cot under a window, under burglar bars in the window.

4

The next day, I was talking to Philip Roth for the *Tely.* He spoke in the tapered tone of a man who wanted to convey a casual intelligence and amiability, a man deft with an idea. Slender, a little balding, wearing a pullover V-neck sweater and a shirt open at the neck, he paced back and forth on the burgundy plank floors in his flat, and then sat at his writing desk — heavy oak, somewhat awkward to sit at — a gray metal elbow lamp clamped to the desk top, jutting into the air, it angled back over his typewriter.

"The American writer in the middle of the 20th century," he had written, and I was reading this aloud to him, "has his hands full in trying to understand, and then describe, and then make credible, much of the American reality. It stupefies. It sickens, it infuriates, and finally it is even a kind of embarrassment to one's own meager imagination. The actuality is continuously outdoing our talents . . . Who, for example, could have invented Charles Van Doren . . . or Sherman Adams . . . Dwight D. Eisenhower . . . ? The daily newspapers fill one with wonder and awe: is it possible? is it happening? And, of course, with sickness and despair. The fixes, the scandals, the insanities, the treacheries, the idiocies, the lies, the pieties, the noise . . . When Edmund Wilson says that after reading *Life* magazine he feels that he does not belong to the country depicted there, that he does not live in that country, I think I understand what he means."

Roth laughed, threw up his hands and said, "I've slightly changed my mind about that. The point I intended to make was not that the great subjects were missing. They're always there. But the problem was to find what attitude to take to a reality so bizarre as to stymie the writer. I myself felt baffled. It was hard to think of a writer who could imagine Richard Nixon or the Nixon-Kennedy debates. That was a brilliant Evelyn Waugh invention. But it happened. What novelist would have the guts, the wit to have made Marina — Oswald's wife — a Russian girl. The heavy hand . . . the archness . . . it would have seemed arbitrary."

I knew that the only way to be what I do, like I had told my mother — so that I could say "I am what I see" — was to get out there and actually engage the country depicted in *Life* magazine . . . to be among the dilapidated tenements, to watch women clothes-peg their wash to wire lines under yellow smoke, and then to walk east along the main street in the Newark Central Ward, Springfield Avenue — to pass by all the low-rent shops, package stores, the steel meshwork of designer burglar bars across shop-front windows, the fluttering light on half-dead neon signs, furniture bargain houses (cheap plush and arborite), check-cashing joints, laundromats — the way-stations for daytime hookers and hop-heads — and dives — *Jefferson Cut-Rate Liquors* and *Pabst Blue Ribbon at Popular Prices* . . . "Death be just around the corner," a man told me, "and he grinning."

Newark had erupted like so many other American cities. Eruptions of fire. The promise of the fire next time. During the four days of looting and killing, LeRoi Jones had entered the spree and been arrested by National Guardsmen. LeRoi Jones. A writer. Hauled from a Volkswagen Beetle and carrying two loaded .32 calibre pistols in his pockets, he was taken to jail and beaten up; he needed seven stitches to close the club wounds on his scalp.

What the devil was a writer doing packing two .32s on the streets of his home town? In a Beetle?

Though slight of build, thin, and hunched at the shoulder, though he spoke softly and walked with a small boy's bounce in his tan desert boots, Jones was gritty — he had a bad mouth, he intended to go upside the head of any white man: "The Black Artist's role in America is to aid in the destruction of America as he knows it."

LeRoi Jones, son of a postman, was a bleak poet, prose writer and dramatist — his talent real if somewhat derivative (Celine was in his prose line, he kept Oswald Spengler underneath his thinking cap). In his *The System of Danté's Hell,*

> *Dark cold water slapping long wooden logs jammed 10 yards down in the weird slime, 6 or 12 of them hold up a pier. Water, wherever we'd rest. And the first sun we see each other in. Long shadows down off the top where we were. Down thru gray morning shrubs and low cries of waked up animals . . . Chipped stone stairs in the silence. Vegetables rotting in the neighbors' minds. Dogs wetting on the buildings in absolute content. Seeing the pitied. The minds of darkness.*

Jones said, looking me straight in the eye: "I ain't got no time to truck or trade, I ain't got no time for offay liberals." All liberals did, he said, his voice soft, seducing, was encourage black integration — and liberals, he assured me, were eager for integration only because they craved black accomplices to their crimes.

"What the liberal white man wants is for the black man somehow to be 'elevated' Martin Luther King style so that he might be able to enter this society with some kind of general prosperity and join the white man in a truly democratic defense of this cancer, which would make the black man equally culpable for the evil done to the rest of the world. The liberal white man wants the black man to learn to love this America as much as he does, so that the black man will want to murder the world's peoples . . . But these are the Last Days Of The American Empire. Understand that Lyndon Johnson is a war criminal of the not-so-distant future. Understand that the power structure that controls this country and the world — the power structure has grown desperate. There are wars of national liberation going on all over the world. There is a war of liberation going on now in America . . . that will sweep — by the increase of its power — right over this failing power structure and push these sadists and perverts into the sea."

We were talking in a small bar on University Place, the Cedar Bar, famous among painters, and the white bartender called out, "Hey LeRoi, where you been? I miss seeing you." I was surprised at how small Jones was, how delicate his bones, how soft his eyes, and surprised at how his heavy rust-colored corduroys and the bulk-knit sweater he was wearing made him seem, though still a young man at the time — born in 1934 — stooped and fragile. In a whisper, he dreamed apocalypse, "If it was summer here all year round, there'd be civil war. The winter cools the blood."

We walked to the Eighth Street bookstore. There, too, they seemed glad to see him, as if he were an old friend who hadn't been there in the store for a long, long time. We puttered through the shelves making hesitant but friendly small talk, and he was helpful and then we agreed to meet the next afternoon at the Cherry Lane Theater.

To begin. There. Where it all ends. Neon hotels, rotten black collars. To begin, aside from aesthetes, homosexuals, smart boys from Maryland.

The light fades, the last earthly blue, to night. Tonight. Dead in a chair in Newark. Black under irrelevant low stars.

At the Cherry Lane Theater, we hoisted ourselves up onto the apron of the small stage, and he said, with no warning, "You know, white society is not just sterile. I say more than that. They are evil. America, in its official image, is a country that goes around killing people. They do it and they justify it by other things.

"The one cure," and he leaned back, spreading the palms of his hands on the stage, staring up at the ceiling, "would be to have white America altered, you know, like you do to dogs when you want them to function in a different way. You just alter them. That's what would have to happen to America. I've thought sometimes about leaving. I used to think that all those Jews that stayed in Germany after a certain time were fools, but now I see that I don't really want to leave. I want to see what happens, even though it might mean that I get killed or somebody else I love gets killed."

I spoke about his play, *The Slave:*

"It's about murder and rage and violence and hate and loathing and contempt and insanity, and you've said that if Charlie Parker had walked down the street and killed the first ten white men he'd met, he'd never have had to play the blues, so what is that all about? That's barbarism . . . "

"No," Jones said, "it's just artistic compensation. If you become an artist you somehow compensate, even if you feel you should kill the first ten white people. I feel every day like doing it. Well, maybe every other day . . . every three days . . . "

I said: "I hope you're practicing your fast draw . . . "

Lovely Dante at night under his flame taking heaven. A place, a system, where all is dealt with . . . as is proper . . . .Waved the cleaver . . . 'I'm gonna kill somebody' . . . Now the blood turned & he licked his lips seeing their faces suffering. 'Kill anybody,' his axe slid thru the place throwing people on their stomachs . . .

We left the theater and went around the corner to a long dark narrow bar, to have a beer. Sitting side by side on stools I was struck by Jones's attitude. Though reserved, making no gesture that would encourage any kind of personal relationship, he seemed at the same time to be asking that I understand what he had been saying, that I understand he spoke with a genuine concern for the sacredness of life, a concern that had to be filtered through death, filtered through the criminality of white men, my criminality. We talked of the riots in the sixties.

"Most blacks would never follow Martin Luther King because most blacks are not college graduates nor are they middle-class. Most blacks are, like . . . poor."

"Well, who is going to lead the poor blacks?"

"The first really intelligent man to actually preach a holy war."

"We're due for a holy war?"

"Oh, absolutely. You need it."

"Come on, Christianity's worst years were when men dragged little children across Europe, fighting for God."

"Well, we've had it — my people have had it for three hundred years. I know that there is nothing that will stop white America from killing people except force. I'm saying that this country is going to be ravaged by force, by racial violence."

"Do you think the blacks will win such a battle?"

"Look, this is weird . . . because the classical revolution, what the West has known, has been a minority oppressing a majority and then the majority rises. In America we have the reverse. It's a majority, the white middle-class, oppressing a minority. So other things have to happen. I don't know exactly what it will be, but I know that this society can't last a great deal longer. It'll happen as America becomes more and more repressive and begins to take on the exact characteristics of the kind of police state that Germany was. People will find it necessary to fight back to preserve any connection with human dignity."

"You see no alternative, finally a head-on clash."

"It's difficult to say. The black, the American black, represents energies within white society which would destroy it, just as there are energies outside the society which want to destroy it. Those two energies are coming together as a pincer movement. The blacks are not alone in wanting to see this society fall. You whites are gonna make it difficult for the rest of the world for some years to come, but look, the majority of the people in the world — now get that — the majority of the people in the world want to see this society fall — and it will fall — absolutely."

5

Back in Toronto, I was completing my final courses in the Graduate School and I had also been hired as a teaching assistant, conducting tutorials with undergraduates. This allowed me to have free coffee and biscuits every afternoon in the Faculty lounge, where I sat talking with Marshall McLuhan, Don Theall and several theologians from the Pontifical Institute of Medieval Studies.

Larry Zolf called me at my office on campus. "Be prepared," he said, "you're going to get a call from the CBC. Don't laugh."

When the call came, I didn't laugh. It was hard but I didn't laugh. One of those CBC managers with the long cigarette holders had got in touch with Zolf and had asked him if he would chair a half-hour discussion dealing with the Pope's encyclical on birth control. Zolf had cried, "What are you, crazy? I'm Jewish." They had asked him who he thought could do the job.

They were talking to me.

We did the show.

It was a success, a discussion among those priests I knew at PIMS, a discussion where we sat down and talked with a lightness that was not glib, a seriousness that was not sackcloth. We laughed. Our laughter was serious. "St. Anselm said the flesh was a dunghill," I said. "In that respect," a priest answered, "he was sick. But then, Luther spent a lot of time on the toilet, too." The CBC executive in charge, an Irish ex-school teacher from Winnipeg, John Kerr, decided the discussion was so successful the program should be one hour long, but then in the cafeteria he took me aside, one Catholic to another, and asked, "Before we do this, do you think we're giving scandal to the Church?"

"You mean, should we cancel?"

"Yes."

I was taken aback, and then appalled.

Sonny and Brownie were in town, playing at the Riverboat. While Sonny was changing shirts in his dressing room, shirts that had little slot pockets sewn across the chest to hold his harmonicas, he said, "Man, you remember that white girl what painted — Laura? Well, she's dead, man. It was at Christmas and I call her home and her husband answers and he says, 'Sonny — she killed herself. She took her life. She killed herself,' and I had to hang up on that crying man."

Sonny was putting harmonicas back into his leather carrying case and he said, "And that kid, you know — the one I was helping out — that mother what was in my home? He stole everything I had, man, stole it, and he busted his wife in the face so's she wouldn't tell, but she tole anyways."

Brownie, running chords as a counter to Sonny's anger, said, "I come over from Brooklyn and I open the door and Sonny's sitting there with a gun, waiting for the little mother to show."

"People," Sonny went on, "didn't believe I could see a man to shoot at, but when I was coming up street singing — in the thirties — a great big guy, he didn't pay what he was owing to me and I asked the man for my pay and he say go away boy, so I went to where I was living — with a Jewish drummer and his wife — and I got the drummer's gun and went on back round to that place and said, 'Gimme my money,' and that man punched me over a table and his woman was up on me, cutting me with her shoe heel, and I come up with the gun — and I could see where he was at 'cause I can make out black and white outta one eye and he was wearing white pants — and I shot him, man, in those white pants."

"You kill him?"

"Naw. He live. But the woman, she's screaming 'Get me outta here, this blind man's gonna kill us all. He's gonna kill ever' body.'"

"Everybody," Brownie said, wryly tapping his fingers on his guitar neck, "wants to go to heaven but nobody wants to die."

"Hell, no, man. I don't want to die."

"You'd a shot that boy?" I asked.

"The one in my home?"

"Yes."

"Yeah, I shoot him."

"You'd have gone to jail, maybe die."

"Yeah, I would have gone."

An executive producer, Richard Nielsen, asked me if I could find and film a speed freak in Toronto. I did. She lived at Rochdale, a "residence" close to Trinity College, a druggie, free-love home for flakes protected by motorcycle honchos.

She was guileless, about twenty-two. She sat in my room talking. She forgot about the camera. She talked about herself, her paranoias, her lover, her drugs. Amidst our talk, gentle and felicitous and anxious with concern, she said, "Look, do you mind, I have to shoot up," and she took out her rubber tube and needle and syringe and tied the tube below her bicep, and without stopping her honest talk she eased the needle into her arm, sighing with relief and release, and kept on talking.

When the film editor screened the film, he said, "That's the most authentic fucking thing I've ever seen."

I am what I see, I'd told my mother.

Nielsen, enthusiastic, scheduled it for his program. Then he was told it could not be shown on his program that led into the nightly news. It could only be shown after the national eleven o'clock news, and not only that, when the needle went into the girl's arm, the picture had to go "out of focus." The viewer had to be protected. I was told by Nielsen that that's what Knowlton Nash, the executive in charge, had said. It was his decision.

I was flummoxed.

To falsify . . . I had never run into that! The vacuous pretentiousness of presuming to protect people by running the show late at night was bad enough. But to take the needle out of focus . . . I had been brought up by Morley to believe that the job of the writer, the job of any reporter, was to see the thing for what it was in itself . . . to state it as such, and to move away from that principle was to slip toward fascism . . . toward what Orwell had so succinctly warned against in his essays in the thirties . . . the deliberate and determined falsification of reality. Knowlton Nash, or whomever it was, had not only decided on reality's time zone, he had decided to take reality out of focus . . .

You wantta know where the Vietnam war is, man, don't ask me because I was there and that don't count. You wantta understand the war, it's on television. McLuhan's right. If the war wasn't on television every night no one would give a shit. The war ain't real. It's television, man, the war is television.

"I saw then," Morley said, "that watching television and reading are two entirely different experiences. You can get so drugged by television that you can't take the time to read anything. Reading becomes an effort. Television is a spectator sport.

"But reading — this vastly different experience — requires work from me. My inner eye comes to life. If it's a story I'm reading, the figures come to life on the screen of my own imagination.

"Language, just words, is making the miracle. The greatest wonder of humankind is probably the development of language, and the second wonder, growing out of the first one, is learning to read; letting another man or woman who is maybe dead, or maybe 10,000 miles away, reach into one's imagination and create a vivid, moving world.

"A man sits alone with a book, the whole world around him grows silent, a voice so secret it can't be heard, just felt, is whispering to him and leading him deep into the world of the greatest wonder and power — his own imagination.

"To this day I remember the first long story I ever read. It was called 'The Fall of the House of Garth.' I was nine years old. The book was a cheap, pulp-horror story. I forget who gave it to me. But I'll never forget my rapt attention or how the figures were dancing around so wildly in my imagination.

"I had discovered reading and what it could do for the free, fresh imagination and how it could enlarge the whole world of wonders, and as time passed and I grew much older, and though I read and read a thousand works, I think I was always looking for some writer, some book that would give back to me the fresh imagination of a child."

6

There I was, walking up the beach
looking for ash trays in their wild state . . .

I was preparing for my Ph.D. exams, exams covering anything from Anglo-Saxon riddles in the *Exeter Book* to *Finnegans Wake*. I had completed courses in seventeenth-century metaphysical poetry, Pope's prose and *The Dunciad*, the novels of Joseph Conrad and Ford Madox Ford, Modern Criticism and Theory, the American Nineteenth-Century Novel, Aesthetics, Eighteenth-Century Social and Political Thought, and — those Anglo-Saxon riddles, with French and Russian as minor languages.

On entering the program I had been fortunate. A man of intellectual range and curiosity had befriended me: Donald F. Theall, a scholar who shepherded me away from those professors who were nestled into their own mind-numbing routines or were just plain mean and cruel. It was a punitive scholastic program in which one or two marks could mean the difference between a First and a Second, and a career. It was a stern, uncompromising world. The exams entailed a reading list of some 1,000 books. Baggy-panted professors joked about Ph.D. psychosis and worn-out students falling out of their chairs in a faint. Father Shook, the President of the Pontifical Institute of Medieval Studies, on the night I introduced him to Nina, my wife, said to her, "Thank goodness you're not a scholar. We try to work women out of the MA program, we try to fail them out of the Ph.D. For their own good."

Fed up with two years of courses and a year of preparation for the six exams, I confronted the great Milton scholar, the Chairman of the Department, A.S.P. Woodhouse — a man who seemed to shed gray light wherever he walked — and said, "These exams are pointless. Pointless. They don't prove anything about intelligence."

He looked at me pityingly.

"But of course you *miss* the point, Mr. Callaghan. Of course they're not about intelligence. They are about moral stamina."

Ah yes, I thought, I should have known.

Milton.

The Protestant virtues.

Moral stamina.

I wrote six exams, got a First in each exam, and was told that I had stood first among 33 candidates.

And then there was my oral exam.

We met in the pleasant office of my thesis director, Peter Buitenhuis. Marshall McLuhan was there and an examiner from Trinity College who was not pleasant. He wanted to talk about manners and morals.

"How does one, after all, differentiate between manners and morals in modern fiction, Mr. Callaghan, when one finds that any moral position must perforce be expressed by a series of gestures, that is to say, manners?"

I had trouble concentrating on this man who kept tugging at the end of his tie. There were other voices in my head (. . . *to get this stuff now, man, you got to go all the way down to Florida, check into a beachfront hotel, open up the windows and wait for the hurricanes to blow the seeds in from Cuba . . .*).

McLuhan, feeling jaunty and looking strangely fresh for a man in a heavy tweed suit on a hot Indian summer day, took over.

"Let's talk," he said, "about Hart Crane's *The Bridge*." I was delighted. I saw eyes cross. The Trinity man had probably never read *The Bridge*.

McLuhan gave a 15- or 16-minute talk on McLuhan. He skittered through *The Bridge*, a daddy long-legs dancing on the water.

When he was through I gave a talk myself, on narcissism, homosexuality, seagulls and saints, and bridges.

McLuhan beamed.

Buitenhuis had settled back.

McLuhan did a shorter dance — some ten minutes — through his own aphorisms and antipodal intuitions.

I replied with gusto, misquoting several lines from *The Bridge* but nobody knew the difference.

McLuhan spoke of inside-out impulses. Twiggy, Liberace.

I intoned my favorite lines from Dryden: *And the midwife placed her hand on his thick skull with this prophetic blessing — Be thou dull.* I smacked myself on the head. McLuhan laughed. I had nothing left to say.

Buitenhuis said quietly but firmly, "Gentlemen . . . a display of erudition . . . I don't think we have to ask Mr. Callaghan to leave the room . . . we can say enough is enough, and Mr. Callaghan has passed with distinction, I'm sure you'll agree."

The Trinity man stared darkly at McLuhan who seemed unaware of the darkness or any other frayed feelings in the room. He was pleased. "The hula-hoop," he announced at the top of his voice, standing up, "the parents tried to get the kids to roll it with a stick, but they refused. They had to get inside. Inside," and he shook my hand. "Inside," he said again, as if we were conspirators, and we walked outside together. He held my arm until we were under the chestnut trees on St. Joseph Street. I was very touched, and as we parted I said:

> We'll go off together
> in this delightful weather,
> Prometheus calls us on . . .

quoting that wheezer of a great old poet with one lung I had met earlier on in London. To my astonishment, McLuhan — who often gave the impression of not listening to anything or anyone — said, "Patrick Kavanagh . . . yes . . .

> Sitting on a wooden gate
> Sitting on a wooden gate
> Sitting on a wooden gate he didn't care a damn."

Book Five

1

I admired Edmund Wilson, an intensely private man of letters who had a card saying what he would not do . . .

EDMUND WILSON REGRETS THAT IT IS IMPOSSIBLE FOR HIM TO:

READ MANUSCRIPTS,

WRITE ARTICLES OR BOOKS TO ORDER,

WRITE FOREWORDS OR INTRODUCTIONS,

MAKE STATEMENTS FOR PUBLICITY PURPOSES,

DO ANY KIND OF EDITORIAL WORK,

JUDGE LITERARY CONTESTS,

GIVE INTERVIEWS,

CONDUCT EDUCATIONAL COURSES,

DELIVER LECTURES,

GIVE TALKS OR MAKE SPEECHES,

BROADCAST OR APPEAR ON TELEVISION,

ANSWER QUESTIONNAIRES,

CONTRIBUTE TO OR TAKE PART IN SYMPOSIUMS OR "PANELS" OF ANY KIND,

CONTRIBUTE MANUSCRIPTS FOR SALES,

DONATE COPIES OF HIS BOOKS TO LIBRARIES,

AUTOGRAPH BOOKS FOR STRANGERS,

ALLOW HIS NAME TO BE USED ON LETTERHEADS,

SUPPLY PERSONAL INFORMATION ABOUT HIMSELF,

SUPPLY PHOTOGRAPHS OF HIMSELF,

SUPPLY OPINIONS ON LITERARY OR OTHER SUBJECTS,

TAKE PART IN WRITERS' CONGRESSES.

---

and then, as a writer, a public intellectual, he went out and did it. He engaged the public world. On his own terms. He called himself a journalist. He meant that he was in conversation with his country and that he got paid for what he said. He knew what he knew. And what he didn't know. He was more scholarly than scholars, and believed that the written word — no matter how complex the ideas — should be plainly understood, marked by ease and lucidity. He assumed a moral authority resided in lucidity. He saw society through the individual, he took style as a mirror of personality, and he had a nineteenth century interest in writers as characters, writers who could be glimpsed as small exemplary stories themselves. He believed that the ordinary reader could be brought to an interest in writers no matter how obscure those writers were. So, deeply parochial — secure in his locale and his own inner traditions — he went to anywhere in the world that his curiosity took him, or where an editor who understood how to trust him, sent him. He wrote it all down — what he saw, what he read — writing by hand on long yellow legal pads. He imposed books on life, he imposed life on books. By disturbing the intellectual peace he sought to demystify, to clarify, to translate. I believed this could be done in the classroom. I believed this could be talked about on radio and television. I believed this could be written about in newspapers.

At this time, with *A Passion in Rome* and *That Summer in Paris* well behind him, Morley had been working on a novel for nearly six years, a novel set at sea during the War. It was called *Thumbs Down on Julian Jones*. He couldn't get it right. He was still buying thick newsprint pads of paper, tearing the pages in half, feeding them into the old portable Underwood, the keys hitting the bone-hard roller *clack clack clack* so that the o's and p's and d's hammered through the paper, leaving little holes . . . and if the pages were held up to the lamplight they looked like templates for an ancient lace pattern. He was tenacious, re-writing and re-writing, but he couldn't get it right. Late at night, after my mother went to bed, after the Jack Paar show, and then — as time passed — the Johnny Carson

Show — he sat in silence at the desk by the window listening for what he could not hear, crazed angels. The novel was dead. It was thumbs down on an idea he had lived with for too long. He understood it too well. He was like a man on the pump, priming and priming and priming, and having a helluva time because he knew there was water down there: he had been to the well before and the water had been sweet. *Clack clack clack.* Wilson told him to stop. He said no, he didn't like quitting. On his desk the brass ashtray was full of butts and ash and there were empty cigarette packs on the windowsill and cups of stale Maxwell House instant coffee, the cream turned scummy.

I said, "Stop . . . for Christ sake stop."

And he said, "Stop what?"

I said, "Stop writing that damn book over and over."

He said, "Stop yourself."

"What?"

"Writing the way you're writing."

"Like what?"

"You can't write in a newspaper like it's not a newspaper."

"I can so."

"You can't. You've got an audience. The newspaper's got an audience."

"The fish and chippers . . ."

"Who?"

"The fish and chippers. That's who they tell me their readers are. The fish and chippers on Danforth Avenue."

"They know who their readers are."

"They know shit. There are no fish and chippers on Danforth Avenue. They were all gone to Guelph ten years ago. It's all Greek out there now . . ."

"It's their paper . . . "

"It's my book pages . . . "

"And you think they won't fire you?"

"Only if Jack has his way. You know what Jack McClelland told me? Mr. Publisher? He told me my book pages were the worst book pages in the country.

Worse than *The St. Catharines Standard*. You know why? You know what he said? 'Canadian books . . . they're so fragile, so few and far between, they should be treated as news. They shouldn't be criticized.' Can you believe that? You know what an insult that is to his writers? If I was one of his writers I'd kill him."

I was summoned to J.D. Macfarlane's office at *The Telegram*. It was a Monday morning. He was furious. He had the Saturday book pages spread open on his desk. "A whole page," he yelled. "A whole page on what, a poet!" I had written a full folio page on John Montague — the Irish poet.

"Yes," I said.

"Yes. That's all you can say? Yes?"

"Well, no. He's a great poet."

"This is a newspaper . . . this is not news . . . a whole page that is not news."

"What if it was T.S. Eliot. Supposing that was T.S. Eliot. You'd look back and say that was terrific, we did a whole thing on T.S. Eliot before anyone knew who he was . . ."

"I don't look back. I don't care about T.S. Eliot. I know that tomorrow our readers wrap their fish in today."

"The fish and chippers."

"Don't get smart with me." He was flushed with anger. "Don't."

"Sorry. Look, I really think people read this stuff, people stop me all over the place and say they read my stuff . . . "

"You know that from the beginning I thought you were all wrong for this paper," he said, becoming wearily exasperated just as I was beginning to like him. "You know that?"

"Yeah."

"You're all wrong but Mr. Bassett thinks you're right. He's the publisher, so you're right. But there are others who think we should get rid of you, book people just like you . . . "

"Good old McClelland."

"He's an advertiser. He doesn't advertise."

"I can't help it."

"You can't help it. I can't help it that Mr. Bassett wants to keep you. It's ridiculous," and he stood up and began to laugh. "Ridiculous," he said, "a whole page on some unknown poet."

I had the feeling he was beginning to like me.

"If it's any consolation," I said, "my father agrees with you. And my brother, too."

2

I went to stay with Edmund Wilson in upstate New York. I had my son with me. It was early in the morning and going to rain. After a good sleep I stood barefoot on the staircase landing of Wilson's stone house in Talcottville, stood by a window with panes of glass that had been put in place by the Talcotts, the old panes marbled, and through them the trees were bent and twisted. Poems had been cut out with a diamond point in some of the panes:

> *What is peculiar is never to forget*
> *The essential delight of the blood*
> *Drawn from the ageless springs*
> *Breaking through rocks*
> *In worlds before our earth*

How peculiar it was to look through the windows of Wilson's house and see the world fade and come clear and fade through words as clouds mottled the early morning light.

The solid, wide center-hall door was decorated by a brass knocker and stood ajar. Flanking the door were leaded circles and diamonds of glass. A white porch and balcony ran the length of the stone house and at the rim of the porch were ferns and high raspberry bushes and stone hitching posts cut from the nearby Sugar River quarry. The lawn, scorched from the August sun, dropped down to a broad-shouldered two-lane highway from Boonville, and across the road, a large farm stretched to the Sugar River.

Wilson had come into the hall from his study. He was in white pajamas, a ragged black paisley dressing gown and slippers, and he held a broad-brimmed gray felt fedora in his right hand. "G-G-Good morning," he called out as he saw me on the stairs. He put on the fedora and wrapped the dressing gown around his stout stomach. "Did you sleep well? Come outside," and with a short rolling stride, staring straight ahead, arms hanging like a stubby-legged club fighter, he elbowed the screen door open, announcing, "I was just thinking of your dear old family . . . you know, your father is . . . quite different from mine, who was kind of . . . a tyrant."

There was something mildly wacky about the way Wilson often blurted out what he was thinking (a habit I think he inherited from his deaf mother — on whom he doted — a woman who had bawled out whatever it was that crossed her mind). So formidable in photographs and in his senatorial stance, he could suddenly be guilelessly foolish. (I had found him late one night with my father — when I'd gone to fetch Morley from Wilson's room in the Park Plaza hotel — and he had come out into the corridor of the high-toned hotel in his old pajamas, his fly open, in order to say good-bye to us at the elevator, as if the corridor were his hallway. He'd been so enjoying what he had to say that he got into the elevator — ignoring the couple already there — continuing to explain his point, his pink pecker quite there, too, and it wasn't until the doors opened onto the lobby that he sensed the light of another world than his own and people standing in it, so he said good-night heartily, his hand in the air as the doors closed.) "Yes . . . I miss talking to your father, and your father respects what his sons have to say. My father seldom did," he said as he shuffled in his slippers along the planks of the porch and sat in a weathered rocking chair. The mail truck, he assured me, would be by in a moment and I could set my watch by the truck. I said I didn't wear a watch. He shrugged. The truck, he said, passed every morning at nine o'clock. "Nine o'clock. Would you like a drink?"

The air was heavy, humid. The sky, in layers of pewter, glistened gray, and in an eastern corner, there was a sour smear of sunlight. A Buick convertible with night-lights on sped by, and after the roar of dual exhausts, the silence marked the isolation of Wilson's stone house, fortresslike off the side of the road, a curious relic, a memorial to the failed ambitions of his ancestors, the pioneer Talcotts: the house they had built with stone walls a foot-and-a-half thick, foundation beams secured by enormous hand-made nails, a house that had once been hostelry, town hall, post office and social center (the house as fortress was something he and Morley shared: my brother and I had been told as young men that the only reason Morley continued to live in a house of so many solid brick rooms was simple — if a boss ever said, "You work for me, I know you've got a mortgage, so you do what I tell you to do or else" — we were to quit the job and move into the family fortress).

Wilson hunched forward, his elbows on his knees, his hands soft and fleshy, and he let them hang between his spread legs, the tips of his fingers pressed together in an upside-down steeple. A general store with a gas pump had been built some years ago on the lot along the highway to the south, a store run by a bulky woman with a long curling black hair growing from her chin, and Wilson searched past the store and on down the road for the mail truck. Though he had recently been in Israel for several weeks and then at his summer home on Cape Cod, his face was white, almost pasty. There were blotches of pink in his cheeks; he was suffering from attacks of angina and the lines at the corners of his mouth were deep. He settled back in the rocking chair and said, "The truck is orange and has a flashing light on the top which gives it the appearance of an insect. It is an orange bug," and with his feet set squarely before him, his hat on his head, he faced the fields that were to have been the town of Talcottville.

"You've got two beauties up in Canada in Marshall McLuhan and Northrop Frye," he said, chortling. "That fellow Frye is very powerful in the universities, and McLuhan, as far as I can determine, is a fake. Thank goodness I avoided meeting them when I was up there." He spoke in short declarative sentences or in paragraphs, the flow broken only by stuttering. With him, even gossip was a deliberate exchange of information. He prodded anyone he met for opinions and facts and listened and then, if necessary, straightened them out ("No, no, Thornton Wilder's *The Eighth Day* is much the best thing he has done. I have reservations, but it is much the best thing he has done . . . No, no, Podhoretz, his book, it's ridiculous . . . "). He eased forward in the chair, amused by himself, looking for the mail truck.

Several years earlier, Wilson had come as a guest to our house in Toronto. He had come feeling terribly distressed; Internal Revenue agents were hounding him (he had, after all, neglected to pay taxes for years) but they had also humiliated him, had put him under surveillance, bullied him and threatened to seize his Talcottville house and leave him indigent. Almost every afternoon, he sat in a high-backed wing chair by our living room bay window, talking with gaiety and enthusiasm, and then, without warning, a bafflement would sap the color from his cheeks. In his own country, he was being sneered at, belittled, treated as if he were a criminal. He was shocked.

Every evening, however, he appeared unperturbed at the door with an armful of flowers and we sat around the dinner table for hours and he was always at ease as if he were at home, talking, talking. Could anyone ever interrupt such an authoritative talker? Well, yes. We did. At our supper table, anything went. That is how we discovered that he had the humility of a great listener. He would listen to anything in his passion for information, but just as we decided that he was the most wonderfully objective of men, that he had sustained himself in his life by his remarkable objectivity, he would suddenly utter an opinion rooted in raw condescension.

Yet the mystery of the man was that in spite of his overwhelming and sometimes overbearing seriousness and his unyielding and sometimes narrow judgements of people and things, he conveyed a very great sense of breadth and openness and warmth, even a playfulness that drew us to him and made us like him. He would show up with his gay bouquet for my mother (in his courtliness there was always an edge of sexuality), and then he'd step out to the kitchen after supper to congratulate her on her fine bone china. He was always patrician, a gentleman, not studied about it but easily so, and no matter what subject came up, no matter what rebuke he was offering, he was never quarrelsome. He never raised his voice. He told me I was wrong. He told Morley that he was wrong. He told my brother that he was wrong. Not triumphantly or maliciously but as a matter of fact, as if he were handing us a piece of information that was readily available if only we had cared to look.

His judgments, of course, were rooted in what he thought the "firmest ground in the world — the real excellence of the good and the real vileness of evil." He was determined to impose his opinions by force of eloquence on impostors and careerists, literary and political. Sitting on our back porch, Morley asked him, "When you look back . . . have you ever been wrong about a writer?" He threw his arms straight out, laughed and said, "No. Never been wrong." But then, as he got up and stood under the crab-apple tree that sheltered the porch, he said, "Never mind that. I only write because I want men to act, I want to be useful."

It was a touching, almost vulnerable little admission. Morley, of course, had no desire to be useful. To shed a spasm of light on the world through his imagination, Yes. To be useful, No. "Men with wheelbarrows are useful," Morley said, startling Wilson. But he laughed because we began to sing *Molly Malone who wheeled her wheelbarrow through streets broad and narrow, crying cockles and mussels alive alive-O* as if Molly and Wilson were on the road together, just trying to get the day's work done. It was a warm moment as we stood swaying to the singing of the song, and before going to sleep that night I lay in bed and re-read what he'd written about his sense of isolation only a few years earlier: "Am I, I wonder, stranded? Am I, too, an exceptional case? When, for example, I look through *Life* magazine, I feel that I do not belong to the country depicted there, that I did not even live in that country. Am I, then, in a pocket of the past? I do not necessarily believe it. I may find myself here at the center of things — since the center can be only in one's head — and my feelings and thoughts may be shared by many."

One afternoon, Morley, authoritative in his own easy-mannered way and equally certain that the center could only be in one's head, took Wilson out on a tour of the city in our family car. Morley seldom drove the car, and then only on Saturday nights when he and my mother went out to visit Mary and Eustace, or Hallie and J.K. in their homes.

Like Wilson, he knew what he knew; he knew the same few streets that he'd driven for years, but he did not know how the downtown streets had changed around him. At the end of the day, at the end of the drive, Wilson — who could not drive a car at all — told me that he had never seen such traffic, nothing like it in the world. "Terrible," he said, "but your father explained it to me. Chicken, they play chicken here, trying to see who'll stop before they collide head-on. One car drove straight at us," he said. I didn't have the heart to tell them that my father had driven south on Yonge Street — our busiest road, our action alley — not knowing that as a City Hall experiment, traffic had been made one-way on Yonge Street, going north. I can only imagine the havoc they caused, driving determinedly into the four-lane on-coming rush with Morley casually pointing out places he thought would be interesting while Wilson — his gray felt fedora pushed down on his head — peered out the window, half-scared to death and convinced that the whole world had gone suicidally lunatic, especially in Toronto.

3

"I will take you out into the city," I said. At that time, Wilson was learning Hungarian. His plays had been translated in Budapest, and the young woman who was his driver in the Adirondack hills was Hungarian. I had a girlfriend in the chorus line at the Barclay Hotel who was from Budapest, a brunette named Paula who had come to Canada with her husband and father during the Budapest uprising of '56. She liked her husband but did not love him; he had their two children with him in Montreal. Her father had been a ballet master in a small city but he was now a night watchman in an orthopedic shoe factory, also in Montreal.

On stage, as part of the opening kick-line for a belly dancer from Crete, she would lift her long, thick black hair off the nape of her neck and stare wide-eyed into the lights, strutting on her very long legs. She complained that she had always lived a cloistered life; she had always been afraid for herself, and uncertain with men, but now she wanted to learn something from every man she met. There was nothing to lose, she said, in her new world so she was going to trust life, see what happened. She had grace and good carriage, and an air of thoughtful concern, as if anyone could see that she belonged somewhere else, and certainly not in a chorus line; she was a beautiful woman and she had a well-bred tone but she also had too little talent and so she was, in fact, an elegant hoofer. We often sat together between shows talking about her childhood when she was a little girl, a girl who had loved her tights in ballet school, before she had become too big, too tall, too slow-moving.

I took Wilson to the Barclay because he said he wanted to practice his Hungarian and he liked to drink and, besides, "Good-looking women lifted the gloom." I warned Paula that Wilson was a man of letters, a great man, and he'd probably grill her because he had a passion for information. I told my old pal Goffredo the maître d' about Wilson and gave him one of Wilson's books, and Goffredo was excited and he said it was going to give him a good feeling to make sure that everything went well. When Wilson came up the stairs to the second floor club he was entirely at his own ease but he looked out of place; his suit was rumpled and he was wearing his old gray fedora. Goffredo, standing beside the big-bosomed hostess, looked startled, as if this were not how a great man should appear. Still, he took the hat and forgetting to say, "Follow me," stepped smartly ahead. Wilson went off in his own direction, and when Goffredo, alert and at attention, turned around to seat us, Wilson was gone, many tables away, sitting himself down. Goffredo, looking bewildered and hurt, bowed from across the empty tables, holding the hat.

We watched the show. The chorus line was wearing sequined shorts, halters and bolero hats. The belly dancer, a woman of lush sensuality, swiveled her hips, quivered, shook her breasts, and Wilson, enjoying himself, hunched forward in the low lamplight on the table. His head had a heavy, white, fleshy weight, like soft sculpture; his shoulders seemed too small. In the lamplight, one side of his face was soft and round, the other lined and stern. He stuttered as he tried to sing along with the comedian as the comedian sang our national anthem in a falsetto. The comedian then told a slew of coarse jokes, danced, stole drinks from ring-side tables, did pratfalls, and finally fell off the stage into the wings. Paula came to our table. She was wearing a black dress with a gold cross that hung between her breasts. Wilson put out his pudgy hand. Then, he sat down and leaned back, one elbow on the table and the other on the back of his chair, expansive, and then he blew his nose and told her a story about Broadway and his friend Mike Nichols, blurted out two or three sentences in Hungarian, and sat silently, staring at the empty stage. I was astonished. He had turned shy and he didn't know what to say. She told him about her family, her father, how she hated the Stalinists. He spoke to her about Russia, how he thought massive centralized bureaucracies were leading to the rise of national groups, like the Hungarians, the Québécois. Then he began to ham it up, telling her he was a magician. He palmed a coin, toyed with a handkerchief trick, a white mouse emerging out of his fist in a sly, wagging, sexual way. He said something more in Hungarian and she looked bewildered and disappointed. There'd been no real talk about books, the ballet or Budapest. He didn't seem to want any particular information from her at all. He wasn't ignoring her. He just didn't seem to know how to make small talk with that beautiful woman. He said, suddenly, that he'd been walking on Yonge Street that afternoon and had gone into a gallery and seen an interesting painter, and did we know his work, someone called Kurelek. "Very interesting. I almost wanted to buy one, a relief from those abstract fakes." Paula stood up and bowed and went backstage. When she came out, high-stepping again in the spotlight, he said to me, "You must be careful with Hungarian women."

"Careful?"

"Unpredictable, you can't count on them."

"Was it useful to meet her?"

"She's beautiful. My Hungarian's no good," he said.

He spread his arms that were like stubby wings and said, "No good," as if disappointed with himself.

The show was on, all the room lights were down, but he got up and so we got up and walked back through the tables and at the door Goffredo appeared out of the darkness and bowed from the waist. He had a lonely eager look on his face that I'd never seen before, as if he wanted to be touched. Wilson put up his hand, a small salute, and strode through the door, and as we went down the stairs into the lobby, he asked, "Can you afford that woman? These places are very expensive." I looked back. Goffredo, holding the hostess's hand, was standing at the top of the stairs. He smiled and waved a red flower. I said, "That woman, the flower girl, she got the job because she came third in a Miss Canada contest, but she's from one of the richest families in the country." Wilson, his fedora firmly on his head, led us into the street, away from the hotel. "Women do strange things," he said. "Especially if they're rich. I've had some experience."

4

On that wet gray day in his Talcottville hills, he was sitting on the porch, running his fingers around the brim of his fedora, muttering, "I don't know what's gone wrong with that truck." It was long overdue, but just then the truck moved through the haze on the highway from Boonville. It stopped at a roadside mailbox, the yellow panic light on the roof of the orange machine snapping wildly in the emptiness of the gray road and fields. He rose and pushed the fedora further down his forehead, but the parked truck did not rise off the shoulder of the road. The light whirled, propelling flashes of yellow into the sky. "Awfully late this morning," he said.

Then the truck rolled slowly toward the house and Wilson, tugging the lapels of his paisley gown around his throat, went to the side of the road. As he waited the breeze caught his white pajamas at the cuffs. He was standing peculiarly at attention, eyes straight ahead, like a soldier on review. The truck pulled up and it was just an ordinary jeep painted violent orange, and an amiable local fellow sorted through stacks of mail piled in the back seat.

As I sat there waiting, trying to see Wilson for who he was, trying to understand why he meant so much to me and wondering how my father's friend had become my friend, I recalled that he had written with deep feeling, even with a sense of comradeship, about his father's final years. "To have got through with honor that period from 1880 to 1920! — even at the expense of the felt muted door, the lack of first-class companionship, the retreats into sanitariums. I have never been obliged to do anything so difficult. Yet . . . we, too, have had our casualties. Too many of my friends are dead or Roman Catholic converts — I myself had an unexpected breakdown when I was in my middle thirties. It was pointed out to me then that I had reached exactly the age at which my father had first passed into the shadow. I must have inherited from him some strain of his neurotic distemper, and it may be that I was influenced by unconscious fear lest I might be doomed to a similar fate. I did not recover wholly for years . . . But now that I am farther along, I find I want to keep on living . . . after all, when we have seen how many entrants drop out, we must honor any entrant who finishes."

The truck shifted into gear and Wilson, hugging letters and papers against his body, came up the walk, not speaking as he passed into his study. He slumped down into an easy chair and ripped open the mail. The light from a reading lamp cast shadows on his face. Essentially, he had his mother's features, square-jawed and plump in the jowls, and eyes with crescent lids. But his eyes were curiously at odds with each other. The layers of lid on the right eye were delicate and there was a slightly bemused look in that eye. From that side, the rigid line of his lips seemed almost prissy. But the lid of the left eye lay heavier and the look was determined, even sinister. From that side, his mouth was grim and turned at the corners in contempt.

While he dealt his morning mail into separate stacks, I poked about the front rooms. They were perfectly proportioned, the windows large and letting in a lot of light. Creaks and noises and voices carried along the walls, and where they came from you were never quite sure, but I had the eerie sense of being in touch with empty chambers, with the hollows under the eaves, the halls and the back kitchen. Which was the door, I wondered, that Wilson's father had covered with green felt to cut himself off from his family, a demoralized man seeking solitude, those eyes of his so fixed in their direct stare in photographs taken in later life, the eyes of a morose man startled, suddenly aroused from deep gloom.

He flipped the temples of his spectacles from behind his ears and said, "Breakfast will be ready soon, and then I've got to go to Utica. Mopping up some material for my book on Lewis County." He moved to his reading chair and sat down. "You know," he said, "I'm not going to stay in this house. It's too tough up here in the winters. Wellfleet is becoming my base of operations now." Then he laughed and pushed some papers aside. "I'm going to send your father a card. Yesterday, I was in a town called Sodom, and I'm going to write and remind him of the sins of the people." He riffled through a stack of postcards and snapped one out.

After breakfast, he hailed me from the hall. His driver, the young local Hungarian woman, Mary Pcolar, was waiting at the end of the walk. We stood on the porch, my son Michael between us, and Wilson suddenly dumped his gray fedora on the boy's head. The hat settled down around Michael's ears and for a moment Wilson stood erectly beside him, like a sergeant-major on parade, and then he took his hat back. "Let that be a lesson to you," he said, and we had no idea what he meant. Perhaps he was trying to be useful.

Going down the walk, he gave us a jabbing wave, then got into the car. While waiting for the car to pull away, I saw that some teenagers were in front of the general store, drinking from cans and flicking cigarette butts high in the air. Then a white convertible swerved off the highway. There were yells and the driver, a straight-haired kid in black swimming trunks, socks halfway up his calves and wearing heavy black boots, got out and went through a round of hearty shoulder punching. His girl, her hair high in a ridiculous beehive, beamed in the front seat. Then he jumped back into the convertible, honking, and he tore off at high speed, stopped about four hundred yards down the road and returned, and sat revving up in front of the store. His friends grinned. They had passed the previous afternoon in the same fashion; aimless, putty-faced kids with nothing to do, with no purpose, stranded out in the foothills. Wilson was sitting very stiffly in his car, looking distressed at these aimless country boys and louts and presumably he was giving Mary Pcolar instructions. Then the car pulled away and passed the kids and Edmund, who meant so much to me and to my father, did not look back.

Book Six

1

I was five years old, wearing short pants. There was a boy up the street who was ten. One day, he saw me dressed in my choirboy's clothes: a red soutane that covered my short pants down to my ankles, a white lace surplice, a white celluloid collar, and a silk bow at the collar. He called me a sissy. I said, "You're just jealous because you can't sing." Two days later, without warning, he clouted me in the eye. I came home crying. My mother, furious, cried too. At the end of the week the big boy hauled me up the street in a headlock to the back of his house, pushed me under a small stoop, and locked the little lattice door. I was trapped in a tiny dirty-floor cell.

There were bugs and spiders. The bugs were gray and didn't seem to have eyes and looked like pieces of moving stone. I tried not to cry, but after about an hour alone I began to whimper. Then I began to cry, and howl. The big boy suddenly was on his hands and knees staring in at me. I put my face up against the lattice. He said, "Let's hear you sing." He spat in my face and went away.

I cried, whimpered, and cried.

Late in the afternoon, just before his parents came home from work, he let me out. I ran to my house, where I wept and shook in my father's arms.

"Go and punch that boy's father in the head," my mother told him.

The next morning, my father went out shopping. He came home and made me put on boxing gloves in our living room. He was on his knees. He bobbed, he jabbed, he talked to me about hooks and taking punches on the arms and then he snapped off a light left hook, catching me on the cheek. Rocking back, I was too astonished to cry, and then before I could cry he said, "See, it doesn't hurt nearly as much as you thought it would to get hit."

He was right. I wasn't hurt.

"Why don't you hit me?" he said.

"You're my dad."

"I just hit you."

I punched him as hard as I could. His head snapped back. He closed his eyes and then he said, "How'd you like that?"

"Good," I said.

"Tomorrow you're going to beat up that bully," he said.

At lunch hour the next day I stood shaking at our front door, waiting for the bully to come down the street. I was terrified of him, and terrified of my father who stood behind me, hands on my shoulders, ready to send me out. The bully appeared. With a great howl I ran straight out the door, then slowed down and loped across the street, slow enough for me to see the bewildered look in his eyes as I came head down at him and slammed my little fist into his face. He tumbled on to the grass, screaming, and then he bounded to his feet and ran home, crying, "I'm gonna tell my dad."

I felt cleansed, cleansed of fear, and wished I hadn't run so hard, run with my head down, so that I could have remembered how I had hit him. I wanted to see myself hit him in my mind's eye. I looked at my fist.

That night, the bully and the bully's father came to our door, a stocky, laboring man, well-muscled. He spoke roughly to my father. "I'm Al Atkinson. I ought to punch you on the nose," he said.

"I wouldn't try that if I were you," my father said.

They were grimly silent, Mr. Atkinson surprised by my father's refusal to be intimidated. I stepped from behind my father and Mr. Atkinson looked at me.

"That there's the kid?" Mr. Atkinson cried at his son. "That little kid beat you up? You got me down here because of that little kid?" He back-handed his son across the side of the head, sending him sprawling down the concrete stairs. The bully ran up the street and his father hurried home after him.

"It's time we got you some long pants," my father said.

2

On south Seventh Avenue in New York, in a narrow dusty second-hand shop, used books were stacked in double rows up the walls and windows, the gray musty binding of books long out of print; first editions of Saul Bellow and Ford Madox Ford, a rare copy of *The Evergreen Review Number One*, and seven novels by the Chicago writer, James T. Farrell. It was 1968. Some said Farrell was dead. Those who knew he was alive said he was crazy. As I stepped out of the shop carrying Farrell's books I heard singing and the clatter of steel wheels on cement. A legless man, riding his board, was driving his heavily gloved fists down on the sidewalk, propelling himself forward, a singing mouth down among the legs — then he was gone, leaving behind the sound of his laughing voice: "If you were the only girl in the world and I was the only boy . . . "

I had written about Farrell's novel, *New Year's Eve, 1929*, in *The Telegram*. I said: "The American critic, Philip Rahv, introducing a collection of Bernard Malamud's fiction, says that a specifically Jewish trait in Malamud's work 'is his feeling for human suffering on the one hand and for a life of value, order, and dignity on the other.' Mr. Rahv goes on to argue that non-Jewish writers have succumbed in recent decades to the temptations of nihilism and, as a result, they are not humanists, they are not sympathetic to suffering and moral values. Such postures, of course, such moral superiority, will pass and be forgotten. But (Malamud's genius aside) while this fashionable enthusiasm for Jewish writing goes on, while third-rate Jewish writers are boosted in New

York, many writers of talent and integrity are ignored. Such is the case with James T. Farrell. He has a world reputation and he continues to write novels at a prodigious pace. But, no matter what Farrell does, those who deal in the current cut of the literary cloth shunt Farrell aside. They know all about him: he is a 'naturalist' from the thirties (the author of *Studs Lonigan*) elucidating ideas that are no longer dramatic, fighting, as one critic recently put it, 'on a ground that was deserted long ago, after the issue had been decided.' This is grossly unfair to James T. Farrell."

At the time, one of the senior *Telegram* editors was a rabbi, Reuben Slonim. Because of his maverick concern for the plight of the Palestinians, he was thought to be something of a liberal in a conservative and unabashedly pro-Zionist newspaper. He surprised my editor, Ron Evans, by showing up with the Farrell piece in hand, angry at the opening paragraphs. "This man, Callaghan," he said, "is an obvious anti-Semite. He should be fired and you should fire him." Evans refused.

James T. Farrell lived alone in New York in the Tudor City apartments in one room with a cubby-hole kitchen (a hot plate on top of a mini-refrigerator, a bare bulb in the wall over a sink) and a thin mattress on a bed-box behind a desk, a chair and another chair. There was wall-to-wall carpeting on the floor, but no yield to the carpet. It had a strange metallic sheen. He was in his bare feet. He was abrupt in a friendly manner, with sane, alert eyes enlarged by his glasses, eager and decisive, and derisive. "Dead, my foot. I'm not dead. Call me Jimmie. Tell me about your father, I never really knew your father though we should have known each other."

He wore loose-fitting cobalt blue pajamas, the sleeves short for his long arms. He was raw-boned, beak-nosed, agile, a sinewy strength in his stride as he loped from wall to wall, talking, talking, chin thrust out, wagging his big hand in the air (the fingers stained blue-black from his several leaking fountain pens), suddenly stopping by the small sink to drink an "instant breakfast" in a glass.

It was 8:30 in the evening, his sense of time dislocated. "An hour is an hour is an hour." He told me he was working on three or four novels at once, in separate scribblers, writing in a broad hand, switching scribblers as the voices faltered. I saw as I sat on the edge of his bed that he often spoke aloud the conversations he heard in his head, cupping the spoken words in the air with his hands, as Morley did when he sat in his nighttime chair . . . Jimmie forgetting I was there, forgetting that we had been talking . . .

He was trying to write all his voices down, only sleeping, he said, when he was tired, waking whenever he woke, flattening his mussed hair with his long hands, scribbling down the rattle of words he heard in his half-sleep, saying, "We must go to a ballgame together. I love baseball," picking up another pen, pacing around the room, his bare feet paining with each step, stopping to open a packet of epsom salts, filling a basin with water and salts, setting the basin in front of his chair under the desk, easing his feet into the warm water, his feet chafed and bleeding because, he explained, the carpeting was harsh outdoor carpeting that had been given to him by a friend.

He sighed with relief as he sat for a few minutes with his feet in the water, opening another scribbler and writing a paragraph in his loose scrawl, the big open letters slanted backwards. He looked up and said, "What time is it?" and I said, "Two in the morning . . . Why not go for a walk along the river." He thought that was a fine idea. A little shy, he got out of his pajamas, put on socks and shoes, washed his face, and got dressed in slacks, a suit jacket, a top coat and a beret, the beret pulled down straight to his ears.

We took the elevator to the dimly lit lobby — overhanging iron chandeliers, each tiny bulb shaded, stone flooring and stone walls, a worn rug and red chairs against stone pillars — and I asked him why people thought he was dead.

"I don't know. I'm not dead. I write every day and all night. There are few days in over forty years on which I have not written. I developed a life plan of work. Years ago, I said I was going to see everything I could see and write twenty-five books, including novels, novellas, stories, plays. I was laughed at, needless to say," he said, as we passed *Tarkington's: Where Merrymakers Meet and*

Drink — The Super Smorgasbord, all you can eat: $2. It was closed, wrought-iron burglar bars drawn across the doors. Someone had broken a bottle against the bars, leaving broken glass scattered in the entranceway. "But I'm not about to go down. America is not about to go down. The problem is people in this country frighten easily. I'm not frightened now, I wasn't frightened by Senator McCarthy back then. He just managed to mess up a lot of things . . . "

"That's a generous view of McCarthy."

"No it isn't. I made the first speech against McCarthy. If he had wanted to call me I was ready, I would have taken him on. But he picked his people carefully. There was a Communist issue and he defined it wrongly. The issue was the attempt to infiltrate, to wreck American foreign policy. That was a real issue. I didn't take McCarthy seriously. I mean, in the frame of history, did McCarthy ruin lives in the same way that Stalin ruined lives? Historically speaking, McCarthy will go down as a pitiful clown. So too will Wallace. Wallace, and men like Wallace, represent a kind of fourth-rate Hitlerism. We have to have some measure of evaluation. Beyond ignorance. Mind you, human ignorance is so abysmal that you sometimes have to respect it. And beyond conformity. H.L. Mencken said conformity is living a life of received opinion. Shared platitudes. That's the country now. Polarized platitudes. But you know what else he said? I'll tell you, it is an opinion that is not received." He intoned, " James T. Farrell *is* James T. Farrell."

As we turned back toward his apartment, he was holding himself in his arms, hands to his elbows, looking fierce in his aloneness, indomitable. His stride was steady and firm, as if he felt no pain at all from the soles of his feet that he had bathed only an hour before, leaving the basin water tinged pink with blood.

When we entered the apartment house lobby it was three-thirty in the morning. The dimmed-down chandeliers shed little light. He took off his beret and then put it back on. He looked at himself in an ornate, old mottled mirror, his staring eyes — enlarged by his glasses — appearing enormous as he stood close to the mirror. He wagged his head. He didn't seem tired.

"What are you going to do now?" I asked.

"This is great," he said. "It's been great."

"It sure has."

"I'm going to write." He swung his long arm around my shoulder.

"I'm grateful," he said.

"Cut it out," I said.

"I don't talk to anybody. I've got an unlisted number."

The night clerk, in a gray shirt and gray slacks, his skin and hair gray, came out from behind the mail counter.

Jimmie shook his hand and wished him good night and waved to me from inside the elevator. The door closed.

The night clerk said to me, "You know who that is, eh bud?"

"Sure."

"Yeah well, a guy stood right here beside me the other night and pointed right at him and said, 'That's James T. Farrell, he's dead.' Pointing right at him."

3

The gutters and sidewalks on the East Side were piled high with garbage. Grease seeped from bags and boxes, a rat burrowed into the rinds and husks stacked around a lamp post on Avenue A, four fires glowing in the night, the stench of charred slops on the air as I went walking with Jimmie. In places, there was only a narrow walkway between plastic garbage bags piled against the buildings and garbage in mounds at the curbs. Someone started another fire, there were sirens and the fire trucks pulled up and firemen blasted the bags and boxes to pieces with a force of water and left the street swamped by blackened crud.

A black man standing in the doorway of Slug's said to no one, "Mother-fucker, I been used to rats running in the nighttime, but when they out to their heart de-light in the daytime, man, you knows darktown in some trouble."

I gave him a little chorus of

> *. . . grits and groceries*
> *eggs and poultries,*
> *Mona Lisa was a man!*

Jimmie looked at me quizzically. The black man said, "Yeah, Little Willie John . . . Little Willie . . . "

Inside Slug's there were mostly black men and women, some wearing dashikis and African tribal hats. Two white waitresses carried bottles of domestic cheaply priced domestic champagne. A girl lit an incense stick, sweet cloying smoke. Musicians shuffled along a red-brick wall toward the tiny stage. There were only women seated along the wall. The saxophonist, wearing large square steel-rimmed glasses, his hair conked and combed down over his forehead, looked like a young monkish intellectual. He was thin and as he hunched around his instrument his shoulder blades jutted out, stunted wings.

Jimmie said, "What the hell did you bring me here for? Dead. The place reeks of death."

"The horn player, he told me last night that Otis Spann would be here, he's the best blues pianist alive, you'd like his left hand."

The horn player sat down with us. He was a lousy player but he liked to talk. "I got a mouth that won't quit," he said, and then he told us that his woman's name was Mary Gail, a white woman with a very white name. "No black woman," he said, "would be called Mary Gail." He laughed heartily. "That white bootie, man, it keeps me awake at night, like ghosts in the night. You fuck a ghost, it's like robbing graveyards."

Jimmie said, "Let's get out of here."

A black man, his hair processed in long thin curls that stood straight out from his head, said, "Come on back y'all for our all-star show. This is where it's happening. Today. Man, it be an all-star show."

Out on the street I said, "Sorry, Jimmie."

There was a truck parked by the curb. It had been there for days. Garbage was jammed against the wheels and the sides of the truck. It was a Sanitation wagon, abandoned the day the garbage strike started. Someone had broken a huge bag of slop and scraps over the motor. There was a note under the windshield wiper: Battery Dead.

Jimmie was a nightwalker, his stride long but not quick, a swinging lope. He was nimble on the sidewalks, at ease, talking about baseball and the new-found power of the Mets, and Lena Horne — how he knew Morley had known Lena Horne and Bill Saroyan in New York, and how wonderfully out-of-whack it would be to hear Lena Horne sing "Oklahoma" — and then how he and Morley had known about each other for decades but had never met, except briefly at a cocktail party for Sherwood Anderson, and now that they did know each other — by writing letters — how remarkable it was, he said, that Morley never mentioned a review Jimmie had written back in the thirties, a review of Morley's novel *They Shall Inherit the Earth*, published in the Marxist sheet, *The New Masses*, "A review kind of like wet cardboard," Jimmie said, "written for people like Lillian Hellman, all those closet Stalinists. I don't know how I got mixed up with them. I should've been smarter, but then, Edmund Wilson took just as long to catch on, too. And he was supposed to be pretty smart. A writer's got to be careful. His hatred of what is done to defenseless people can lead him into doing things that are indefensible."

In the shadow light, we saw two young black men and a black woman on the street corner. They were yelling. *Muthafucka muthafucka muthafucka mutha-fucka.* A heavy-set man was shoulder-bopping and wagging his head, full of loud accusation. *Bitch*, he kept yelling, *bitch bitch muthafucka bitch.* The woman let out a keening screech. As we came near, the other black man, lanky and big-boned, suddenly threw a looping punch and struck the woman in the face, knocking her down. She stopped screeching, gaped, and Jimmie wheeled and cried, "Don't you dare do that, don't you dare hit a woman."

The two black men, astonished, glared at him, and then the lanky fellow lunged. Jimmie was planted, his very long arms hanging loose, and he hunched his shoulders and hooked with his left and crossed with his right, two beautiful clean shots to the head, and the lunging man went down, pole-axed. From Jimmie's blind side, the heavy-set man came lumbering at him. I caught him with a right as he was going by. He went down. The woman took off her high heels and fled. "Jesus Christ," Jimmie said, "let's get out of here. Maybe they've got guns," he said, leading me away from the two men on the walk.

"Don't tell anyone about this, don't tell your father."

"We could've got killed," I said.

"We still could," he said.

We sat in the red chairs under the iron chandeliers in the lobby of the Tudor City apartments.

"What're you doing tomorrow?" he asked.

"I'm going to see Muhammad Ali," I said.

"You are? Where?"

"In his hotel," I said.

"I hear he's a song and dance man now."

"He can't sing," I said, " and he ain't Bo Jangles, either."

4

"What's your story?" Ali said at the hotel room door, "man, 'cause I got mine."

"I got no story," I said.

"Too bad for you," he said.

Ali was wary and as usual, mildly abrasive, his shoulders drawn back, a sly arrogance to the cock of his head, to the pout of his lower lip, and there was a self-deprecating mockery in his brown eyes, a mockery that betrayed the pain and anger he obviously felt at having had his title taken away, at having been belittled by the political mugs of the sportswriting world who supported the Vietnam war. "They want to whup me the only way they can." He still couldn't understand why everyone did not see clearly that he was *clean* ("It is in the light of my consciousness as a Muslim minister and my own personal convictions that I take my stand in rejecting the call to be inducted into the armed services"), *clean* of meanness, avarice, calumny, vengeance . . . in the words of Drew (Bundini) Brown, his cohort in bop talk, he still *do float like a butterfly, sting like a bee an' America is where he want to be.* ("To me the U.S. is still the best country in the world. You may have a hard time to get something to eat, but anyhow I ain't fightin' alligators and livin' in a mud hut.")

He pawed the air . . . *jab jab* . . . *pitty-pat pitty-pat* . . . his lip running loose: *I'll say it again, I ain't got no quarrel with those Viet Congs* . . .

Then "Hello" — he said after I was already in the room — his girl-child hanging on to his pant leg. Clutching. *Think of all the hangers-on who have clutched at this man,* Bundini had said, draping an arm around his shoulders. Ali turned to the mirror on the wall of his small suite in the hotel, feinted *a jab and hook and bam bam combinations to the body.* He told the child to go to her mother in the bedroom, saying to me, "How you doing?" staring at me out of the mirror as I stood staring at him in the mirror . . . pretty-boy man solid through the shoulders, sleek, almost slender in his tight jeans . . . plain white shirt and tie, his eyes peeled for the least hint of animosity, so I said, "What's happening, man? What you been doing?"

"Since when?"

"Since whenever. When we talked."

"Singing my songs," he said, doing a little half-hearted pimp-walking strut and then lapsing into a weary moaning tone, weary with *the ticky-tac talk* he'd been forced to talk since 1963 when he had failed a pre-induction army mental exam and had been classified 1-Y, leading up to 1966 when, without re-examination, without any given reason, he had been re-classified as 1-A. That's when he'd said: "I ain't got no quarrel with those Viet Congs." Veterans had come out of the patriotic woodwork to pounce on him, calling *Cassius, Cassius, Cassius Clay,* (which he derided as his parody name, his *descended-from-a-long-line-of-slaves* name — not knowing that he in fact carried the name of a great Abolitionist journalist, Cassius Marcellus Clay).

In 1967, three months after his ninth successful title defense against Zora Folley in New York, two months after he had refused induction, and one month after he had been denounced by Jackie Robinson and Joe Lewis — the boxing commissions took a high moral tone and stripped him of his title — and he was found guilty in court and sentenced to five years in prison and a $10,000 fine. He said: "Some men complain because they got no shoes. Some men complain because they got no feet." Sportswriters chanted: *Cassius, Cassius, Cassius Clay.* In Toronto, the taunt was led by Milt Dunnell of the *Star.*

Ali — the man who had already redefined boxing — he "shut his mouf" about the ring and put his lawyers to work. They kept him out of jail. He divorced his first wife, Sonji Ro, saying she wore short skirts. His second wife was a Muslim sister, Belinda. She wore long skirts. They had a daughter. He "open up his mouf" about everything else. That's what Bundini said: *He open up his mouf,* laughing hard. He appeared on campuses across the country. He could hardly read or write but he made up poems, he scat-talked about morality, he mocked, he strutted, he said, "I ain't dead" but at the end of each day he found he was scuffling for dollars just to stay alive, so he agreed to star in a Broadway play, *Buck White.*

I had cringed watching him on stage because — as the most fluid of men on his feet in the ring — he looked like he was *walking* by numbers . . . giving a performance that diminished everything beautiful about him. He knew, despite his charming bravado, that he had agreed — out of necessity — to do something demeaning. He, who had been so authentic, was reduced to pretending he could sing and dance, draped out in a long blue robe, wearing a goofy little Afro wig-hat on his head, speaking and singing from a podium . . . a campy Father Divine, singing *We'll fill the street with dancing feet beneath big black balloons* . . . Coming down the stage, he gave off the seductive scent of shame (shameless men smell of death).

"Belinda," he called.

Bundini, wearing a camel's hair coat, whispered in Ali's ear. Ali nodded.

"Belinda. Try and not have no noise in there, babe."

"Bring the child back in," I said.

The toddling child came into the room and stood facing the television. The picture was on, the sound off. The child peered into the screen. Bundini looked into the silent tube, and so Ali watched the silent moving shadows, too, until Bundini, without a word, went into the bedroom and the child turned to Ali, who was sitting on a sofa, and climbed up on Ali's knees and into his lap and stared straight at me.

"She play-acting," he said. "Everybody in this family is play-acting now."

"I know it doesn't matter, I mean my saying so," I said, "but you made a mistake being in that play."

"I'll tell you about that play," Ali said. "This was really a black play. Each character represented the typical black man in all walks of life, you know, one militant, one a pimp, a hustler, one a dope peddler, one talks like a militant leader, you know, and the songs and the beat, the rhythm . . . "

He was playing *patty-cake* on his daughter's knees, the jive-talking beat behind all his patter . . .

"No black man, no black woman who's watched that play has said they didn't like it. They just laughed, they jumped, they wanted to see it again." He stopped patting his hands. He recited the trite rhyming words to a song, his voice flat, a schoolboy's recitation, no laughter, no verve. His plump-cheeked daughter looked up and began to rock in his lap as he sang *It's all over now, Mighty Whitey, it's all over now* . . .

He went on telling the story, suddenly excited, cutting loose from the text, wagging his free hand as he held his little girl, *You niggers don't talk like this in Georgia . . .* the whites of his eyes glistening, a glimpse of cunning in the whites, undercut by a brief boyish smirk.

"Take this white fellah, he was standing next to this black fellah in Georgia at the airport and he said, 'Are you a Blackstone Ranger?' The black fellah said, 'No.' He said, 'Are you Rapp Brown?' The black fellah said, 'No.' He said, 'You follow Stokely Carmichael?' The black fellah said, 'No.' He said, 'Do you believe in the Black Panthers?' The black fellah said, 'No.' He said, 'Do you believe in the Black Bosuns?' The fellah said, 'No.' 'But you like the late Malcolm X?' The fellah said, 'No.' He said, 'Well, nigger, get offa my damn toe.'"

Bundini, leaning into the room, collapsed in laughter.

"See, if he'd said, I'm a Black Panther, or a follower of Rapp Brown or Stokely Carmichael, he'd have got more respect."

The child, who'd slid down between his knees, reached up and began to squeal. He lifted her to his lap. He put the nipple in her mouth. "Here's your bottle. Come on, come on, get your milk, gotta keep her quiet, she loves the bottle, there you go. There you go, woman." She sucked and then she offered him her bottle. He took the nipple, slurped, said *Ahhh*, she slurped, said *Ahhh* . . . she slurped and smiled . . . *Ahhh* . . . *Ahhh* . . . .

"*A* man's woman, don't you see, is the field which produces his nation. And if he don't protect his woman he loses his nation. A farmer will protect his fields, but how much more important is a man's woman than his cabbage, his corn? In America a black woman is allowed to walk the streets, any strange man can come and carry her to the motels and use her, because men are not men, because if men be men they'll fend and take care of their own women. We must care and protect our women. How can we invite anyone to respect us if we don't even protect our women? The woman is the one long step to freedom, we got to control and protect our women, because from this little girl comes our future generation, and if she's nothing, then the nation will be nothing."

"I'm wondering how, when all this is over," I asked, "you're gonna come out of all this, you're going to find yourself?"

"I don't know. I might be in jail, with no bail. I don't worry about it. I'm just doing what my heart tells me to do."

"You don't calculate . . . "

"I plan, I may go to jail, but I don't care."

"You don't feel any bitterness?"

"Everybody pay great prices for stands. The Jews were put in the ovens for what they believe, the Christians were fed to the lions for refusing to deny their faith back in the olden days . . . I'm just paying for my stand. I'm not mad at nobody."

"Maybe you're already a martyr in the minds of black people."

"I don't know. I'm just trying to do what I'm trying to do."

"Don't you see, sometimes, that you set out to become a boxer, and you're already a legend. And you're not even through fighting yet, and the next fight is part of the legend."

"I don't really know what a legend is. I'm just myself, honest in my beliefs. Some people may wantta die for me, some wantta shoot me. I'm just an ordinary person doing my best. I don't know what I am."

He stood up, caught sight of himself in the mirror behind me, went *jab jab bip bam bam*, as he walked me to the door.

"By the way," I said, "Chuvalo says to say hello to you."

"The washerwoman," Ali said with a nod of affection. "He gave me a fight and he fought me a fight. I give him that."

"How come you call him the 'washerwoman?'"

"Because of the way he moved his shoulders. He fought me a hard fight, but he moves his shoulders like he's scrubbing floors."

Jab jab bip bam.

"Not me. I don't scrub no floors."

5

After a late supper at the Derby Steakhouse on McDougal Street in the Village, Jimmie and I took a taxi to Tudor City. There was drizzle in the air. The driver had a bent nose, perhaps an ex-pug. And a moustache. I was with him in the front seat. Farrell, his blue beret on his head at a jaunty angle, had wanted to stretch out after a heavy steak supper and he was in the back seat. But as it turned out, there was a bullet-proof barrier between the seats. It was insane. We were friends in a hired car forced to talk through a small square opening. After Jimmie told me about a lady who had made her husband's nurse her lover, I asked, "God, what in the world would you do with a woman like that?" The driver slipped a black and white canister from his pocket and said, "I'd know what to do with her." He asked, "You know what this is?" I said, "Looks like MACE to me." He wagged his head in approval, and blurted out: "I'm an arsenal." He had a seven-inch knife, and in a snug shoulder holster, he had a snub-nosed gun.

"I only drive cab on the side to pay for my daughter's wedding. I got the gun, 'cause you see, I'm actually a federal narcotics investigator."

"Really?"

"Yeah . . . I been everywhere with them goddamn hippies in the streets. I listen to you and the gentleman when you get in and I can tell you're the right kind of common sense people, so you appreciate what I'm talking about. They're pigs, those kids. They're swine."

"You were in Chicago? The Convention?"

"From the first days, and you better believe that Daley's right. You should believe that 'cause I tell you; he was right. I was there."

Farrell asked through the bullet-proof shield, "What was it like in the streets?"

"Sir, they should be in prison, all of them. Them hippies. They're ugly, filthy people. Do you know they expose themselves and the girls don't wear brassieres, and do you know they threw offal in the faces of the police and bags, sir, of urine."

At Tudor City, the driver didn't tell me the fare. He sat like an overgrown wounded child, staring through the cranking of the windshield wipers, and when I paid him he muttered: "Thanks." He was clutching his canister of MACE.

We got out of the taxi and walked into the lobby and I said, "Jesus. That guy'll kill somebody."

"Maybe. Maybe not. Didn't sound like a killer to me. More like what we used to call a blowhard. All in his head. I've known some killers. And some men who got killed."

We stepped into the elevator.

"You knew Trotsky?"

"I knew Leon Trotsky, yes, I once bought him a typewriter."

"When he was in Mexico?"

"Yes, he was a great man. He was one of eight men I have known who was the victim of a political murder. And, of course, he was a great writer, too."

"So what d'you make of what's going on now?"

"There are too many mouthpieces."

"Lawyers?"

"No, in the literary world, all mouth, what I call chandelier aviators. It used to be that in New York you could see Henry Mencken or Teddy Dreiser or John Dewey or Edmund Wilson. But now, you might see David Suskind or Norman Podhoretz, Tom Wolfe or some young guy hoping he's Scott Fitzgerald. Some guy hoping he's young enough to be brilliant. This cult of youth is most damaging to youth. I think a writer doesn't reach his peak until he's fifty but we have this example of a third-rate writer, F. Scott Fitzgerald, who substantiates the silly notion that you write your best book first."

"Fitzgerald's third-rate?"

"Read his books. Notice particularly his style. He always relies on adjectives. I was struck, re-reading *This Side of Paradise*, he wants to describe a girl, the character does, and he says he liked her for her 'gorgeous clarity of mind.'"

Jimmy shook with laughter.

"That's Fitzgerald. He was a Founding Father for advertising writers. He didn't advance the flag of literature to the North Pole or the South Pole."

"You don't think *The Great Gatsby* is a remarkable book?"

"No, I think it's an empty book, well put together, but Gatsby is an adolescent who retained his adolescence and became a gangster. He made money in some vague way. Then he created a dreamlike place, singing a song of love to the girl he loved."

"That's true for a great number of men, though."

"Well, I know, but . . . "

"Therefore, true of life . . . maybe of our time."

"But men can grow up. *The Great Gatsby* is the best book by an adolescent in America. But Theodore Dreiser grew up at twenty-eight. Balzac grew up, and Ring Lardner was mature. Henry James grew up. Your father grew up. It is theoretically possible to grow up and wear long pants."

As I was getting ready to leave, Jimmie was wearing his cobalt-blue pajamas and he was in his bare feet. He was picking through fountain pens, trying to find one that didn't leak.

They all leaked.

He opened his scribblers.

"Do I look like I'm dead to you?"

He laughed before I could answer.

A while later, I crossed through Cooper Union, I had to step around boys and girls stretched out on the sidewalk, tattered children. Someone held up a sign: *Love is Redemption*. There were whispers and low laughter. A girl wearing a nun's cowl looked up and said, "I'll do yuh, man, for five bucks." The bare-foot boys and girls lying on the concrete had tied long strings to their toes, and there, floating high in the air in the night, were white balloons attached to the strings — distress signals or gestures of contempt, or both?

I wondered if Morley, sitting in his window box of amber light, was seeing distress signals in the night.

6

Morley asked me, "Who killed Harry Houdini?" I said I didn't know. He said it was a Canadian who killed Harry Houdini, just stepped up out of nowhere in a crowd and punched him in the stomach and killed him.

"But why would a Canadian want to kill the magic?"

"Well," he said, "it's a complicated story."

He never did tell me the story. He just told me who had killed the magic, and I was trying to tell this to George Barker, the English poet, as we sat down at a literary luncheon in a big Montreal hotel dining room, one of those silver-plate hotel eating halls with huge acorn-shaped chandeliers, heavy white tablecloths and clumsy cutlery, the knives and forks you used to find in the dining cars of trains when trains had dining cars. Barker, wearing dark glasses, was disgruntled. "Now we get the rubber chicken," he said. We got rubber beef instead but that didn't cheer him up. He mumbled a lot and seemed not to hear anything I said. He didn't even nod when I said Houdini had been killed by a Canadian. Then he realized that he was still wearing his "Sleep Well" earplugs. He took them out and complained about the noisy clashing of cutlery and plates. He was a hard man to please, but he did say, "Not terribly easy, trying to have a conversation with me." As he jabbed his spoon into a frozen-froth dessert, there was the clinking of a knife against a glass, and Barker, out of the corner of his eye, saw that someone had risen to speak. He poured cognac over his froth and kept on eating. But then he stopped and turned to listen. A trim, sinewy man, hair cropped to his skull, was talking in an off-the-cuff fashion about writing and art. He had a natural grace that finishing schools cannot teach. After listening for five minutes, Barker asked, "Does he write good verse?"

Realizing he thought the speaker was a poet chosen to welcome the literary luncheon guests to Montreal, I said, "Poetry . . . I have no idea. He's the Minister of Justice."

"You mean he's a bloody politician?"

"Yes."

"Uncanny. The man knows what words are."

A year later, in 1968, Pierre Trudeau entered the federal election as Liberal candidate for Prime Minister.

Fascinated by him, I asked a senior political writer at the *Tely*, John D. Harbron, to arrange to get me on the campaign plane, to ask if I could have private conversations with Trudeau. Harbron did that.

One of Trudeau's young advisors, Eddie Rubin, a lawyer from Montreal, said to me, "We're doing this for us, too, you know. He gets irritated. He's got no one he really wants to talk to."

The Cadillac eased to a stop down a Chinatown alley in Vancouver. Pierre Trudeau, the Minister of Justice — running for Prime Minister — went in the back door of the Blue Eagle Café. White wash had been slapped on the rough-cast walls but the back rooms were still dingy, little rat tails of old paint hanging from the ceiling, and against one wall, an old chenille stenciled chesterfield, the stuffing leaking out.

Chinese men and their wives shuffled into a receiving line, the men in Tip Top Tailor blue and brown business suits, the women in glossy satin dresses, red, cream, green. Trudeau shook their hands solicitously. After the airport hoopla, the motorcycle sirens, the roses wrapped in crinkly cellophane, the clatter of firecrackers in the alley, Trudeau moved with a silent, elegant, contained energy through the shabby rooms, nodding with a slight tuck of his chin under the glare of tubular fluorescent lights. The Chinese were soft-spoken. At the end of the receiving line, Trudeau paused, as if something had skidded across his mind, as if there were more he might say to these people, but he was propelled by aides out the front door of the café, the overhead bell on the door tinkling as he went, propelled onto Pender Street.

The block between Abbot and Main streets was short but thousands were heaving forward and peeling apart for a procession of drummers, and firecrackers went off like distant guns in dry air. A policeman said: "Jesus you could shoot him in a minute." An old woman crawled on her knees under a flat-bed trailer, around the big wheels, and bobbed up on the other side, yelling with her hand out, "I'm eighty-five, Pierre, eighty-five goddamn years." She grinned, her black gums glowing.

Trudeau appeared entirely at ease, but behind his back he was stripping the petals from a rose. When only the stem and torn head were left, he snapped the stem in two and dropped the pieces. Scuffling and shoving broke out and Trudeau, with a smirk, teased the hecklers, "Cut out that rough stuff or I'll get in there myself . . . "

Years ago the Montreal poet, Abraham Moses Klein, described the conventional Québec politician:

> Worshipped and loved, their favorite visitor,
> a country uncle with sunflower seeds in his pockets,
> full of wonderful moods, tricks, imitative talk,
> he is their idol: like themselves not handsome,
> not snobbish, not of the Grande Allée! Un homme!
> Intimate, informal, he makes bear's compliments
> to the ladies; is gallant; and grins;
> goes for the balloon, his opposition, with pins;
> jokes also on himself, speaks of himself
> in the third person, slings slang, and winks with folklore;
> and he knows that he has them, kith and kin.

Trudeau darted into the crowd, letting himself be caressed, not just by girls, but by women and men. He had the passive manner that only a man of self-confidence could afford; smiling coyly, he appeared limp before the pummeling, "like a dumb leper who had lost his bell, wandering the world, meaning no harm."

He had no sunflower seeds in his pockets.

He had his style, the feel about him — the high cheekbones, the narrowed eyes, the sensuous but slightly cruel turn to his lips — his disciplined, tempered body, his taste for delights. He had let it be known that he was bold and authoritarian, widely traveled and amiably engaged in political philosophy. Because of a willingness to mix pragmatic wheeling and dealing with a diffident worldliness, his stern rigidity was seldom noted, but his response, when he had been left no room to manoeuvre, seemed tailored to Tyndall's description of the Jesuit: Accuse him of murdering your mother, father, brothers and sisters, uncles and aunts, and the family dog . . . he would triumphantly produce the dog alive. As each day on the road ended, he had the look of an innocent who had come through unscathed. Or, to put it more colloquially, in the admiring complaint of his campaign bodyguards: "Go-Go Trudeau Dodo" — he was always on the go yet he always slept in the bed of an innocent (*dodo* being French for a child's cot or crib).

I had a conversation with him over supper in his airplane cabin. Chinese food. He was miffed because he had no chopsticks, but also he was amused at his own displeasure, a man acutely aware of himself. He had no trouble shifting a sweet-and-sour rib from his left to right jaw to make a clear, articulate point.

I suggested that by presenting himself as a decisive man ready to take control he was offering the people an illusion; that, as French historian Jacques Ellul had argued, a third *aparachnik* class independent of both the public and politicians now constituted the real political power. Public involvement with the Prime Minister was only a game —

There was no question about that, he said: the technicians, the civil service, had long since been developing political policy quite independently of politicians. But it was just this fact that necessitated the best men getting into government, to cope with complex subjects, and more importantly, to take control and give policy direction to the *aparachniks*.

"What'll you do if the *aparachniks* get you?"

"I'll probably be the last to know."

What was one to make of his admiration for the historian, Lord Acton?

"I suppose my knowledge of Acton is out of one or two books. His essay on *Freedom and Power*, and another, the title of which I don't remember . . . I don't claim to know Acton in great depth. Though he's a rather conservative Catholic historian, I especially like his humanist approach. I find he is always trying to explain things. He's trying to look for the mainsprings in society. I just can't read history which is a description of events . . . "

"You mean stories?"

A natty steward appeared with a set of ivory chop sticks, apologizing because he had found only one set. Trudeau held them like twin batons as he repeated, "Description . . . "

"Stories."

"Have it your way," he said, rapping the batons on the edge of his plate.

"There's an opposition in you — just like there is a contradiction in Acton — between the rational and emotional; it's in your essays, and perhaps it's even an irrational fear of emotion. A faith in your own powers, the rational. I wonder if you're not drawn to Acton the absolutist."

"You are too hard on me," he said, deftly slipping the sticks into pincer position, "I think you are wrong."

"Absolutely?"

He laughed, and plucked a morsel of chicken in lobster sauce from his plate.

"Absolutely."

Beyond the front line of Trudeau-mania teeny-boppers and housewives wielding Kresge autograph books, staid citizens stood becalmed, their hands on their hips or their arms folded, guarding their emotions. They lived in Irving Layton country:

> *A dull people, without charm*
> *or ideas,*
> *settling into the clean empty look*
> *of a Mountie or a dairy farmer*
> *as into a legacy.*

Trudeau's speech to them was plain-spoken, sweetened by empty, trite phrases: "We are realizing in a basic way that this is a fabulous country." Watching Trudeau, I had to think of Mackenzie King, another bachelor Prime Minister, runty and bland, droning on, convincing the country that behind his pudding face there was a jack-hammer will. Trudeau, of course, was neither pudding-faced nor bland, but when he wasn't speaking off-the-cuff — and he could be brilliantly concise in conversation — there was something flat in his prepared speeches, something dull; the words were bare, the images barren. Yet, it was this very tone, with anecdotes of muscle and learning, that so impressed audiences. When talking of economic disparity, he retold a story by Saint-Exupery, a bold gesture. It was a good story — The Assassination of Mozart — about seeing a starving boy whose face was that of the child genius, but the nar-rator realizes with distress that the Mozart in the street urchin will have to die for want of food. An excellent device, except that Trudeau told the tale badly. He was right. He had no real interest in stories, the description of events. But it was this failure that worked in his favor. He didn't seem to be so much the intellec-tual. It allowed him to conclude solemnly, lamely, eliciting no laughter from the crowd, "We are our brother's keeper in the whole of Canada."

Trudeau hurried back through the Café rooms where several Chinese women were still sitting on the old chenille chesterfield. He went out into the alley where a small group of men milled about his car. "What about the Vietnam war?" someone shouted. Trudeau muttered, "*Quand je parlerai aux*

Chinoises, je parlerai en français." What did he mean? Had he misunderstood? Was he answering the man or was he carrying on some intense conversation with himself? I suddenly wanted to ask whether he knew he had been tearing that flower to pieces while jibing with the crowd. The Cadillac raised cinders in the air as it sped away.

7

Nina urged the book on me, *Steps.* And after I wrote about Jerzy Kosinski's stories in the *Tely,* he sent me a note from New York and then called to say that he was coming to Toronto. He wanted to use what I had written as a preface to the French edition of *Steps.* I brought him around to the house to meet Morley.

They bantered about Hemingway but Morley, puffing on his old pipe, a hole chewed in the stem, said he was bored talking about the old days. He said he liked *Steps* but he hedged on *The Painted Bird.* Jerzy became frenetic, stepping quickly around the room, hunching his shoulders, craning forward, his furrowed brow sloping to his small chin, darting, stabbing. I liked Jerzy, and felt a mischievous kinship with him. We wheeled on Morley, telling him that the actual turbulence of the streets was beyond him — the mindless eruptions of rage in the American cities, the bombs, the palpable lusting for death in Québec — and Jerzy said, pityingly, that Morley wanted to be a rational man. "You want to give form, through your storytelling, to the chaos of daily living, and not only that, you want to do it with the old ironic detachment."

Going closer to Morley, as if half-embarrassed, half-sorrowing, he suddenly said that a man trying to make sense of what was going on was truly a man trapped. "Forget it," he said, "no artist is in control." Then, sitting down in the nest of shawls where my mother usually sat (she was in bed with a head cold, not the *tic*), Jerzy said, "No one is in control now."

"No one's wearing Homburg hats," I said.

"Tell that to your pal Trudeau," Morley replied.

He did not like being told he didn't understand the temper of his time.

"My pal Trudeau," I said, "would have a nervous breakdown if he didn't think he was in control."

"He should save himself a lot of trouble and have a nervous breakdown," Jerzy said.

"The irrational, the violent," Morley said, "when was the world otherwise?"

"The trouble with you, you're still a Flaubertian. And always will be."

"And what is the matter with Flaubert?"

"Flaubert's in complete control," Jerzy said. "In *Madame Bovary* every word is in the right place. Emma's in Flaubert's complete control, every little event in her life. But look around, everything's out of control."

Morley lowered his head and looked at us over his glasses. "You make Flaubert sound like a fascist." He thought we were crazy.

I slumped down into my chair. I wanted a drink.

"It may be," Morley said, as Jerzy — for some reason — picked up Loretto's big ceramic ashtray full of ashes and butts and leaned forward to listen, "it may be that men grow tired of the completely rational, tired of all the things that can be measured, and . . . "

"I'm not making my point," Jerzy said.

"No, no, I'm not making mine," Morley said. "The point is, I get no delight out of reading a prose work or a poem in which the author is being deliberately irrational. Don't you understand, when a writer is creating absurdity, determinedly presenting the irrational, he's still in complete control, just as much control as Flaubert or Chekhov ever were?"

"What I'm telling you," Jerzy said, proferring the ashtray, as if someone, a waiter, an altar boy, were to take it from him, "is that things, methods wear out. Telling a story through dialogue, the controlled flow of the dialogue . . . Life is not like that now."

"All my life," Morley said, easing to the edge of his chair, "the world has seemed just as crazy to me as it does now to you. When I was at college, reading

H.L. Mencken, I discovered he said that there's only one way to look at a politician — down — and I rejoiced, as did all the young men of the time, and as for violence, the idiocy of war has been celebrated in a hundred novels."

Jerzy stood up. "It's different now," he said. "What you don't know is I was nearly killed a few weeks ago." He said he had been in a bar in New York. He'd been alone. People in bars talk to each other. Perhaps it was something he had said. A man of forty pushed him. Jerzy had laughed, made a derogatory remark, and then the man had suddenly come at him. The other men at the bar had intervened. But it was a terrible moment. "That man wanted to kill me," Jerzy said. "It was in his eyes, his voice," he said firmly. "I got out of that bar. I couldn't sleep. It was all irrational. He wanted to kill me. It had no meaning. No story, just suddenly wanting to kill me."

Morley smiled. He was unsympathetic. "There you go, " he said, "that's not new either. When you go into strange bars alone you make sure you know where you are," and Morley laughed and said Jerzy should meet James T. Farrell. "He still goes into bars alone and still gets into fights."

"You don't understand," Jerzy said. "In your world, in Farrell's world, it's a fight. You want to fight it out, it's a contest. That's why you fight, to win. But that man, he suddenly had the will to kill. Crazy. Irrational. But that's it. This will to kill is everywhere."

We paused. We caught our breath and eased into banter, light laughter. None of us had intended to be so intense, so argumentative at first meeting. *It is not without hope that we suffer and we mourn,* Morley sighed. We said goodbye and Jerzy and I stepped out onto the veranda — but I went back to see if Morley was offended. I felt that in a way I had betrayed him, set him up. He was standing in the hall beside the black marble fireplace. Unperturbed. "Jerzy's got a view," he said, "but look, isn't what he's talking about simply a new romanticism?"

"I don't know," I said. "I'll think about it." He was silent. I felt I owed him a gesture. "How about I bring you and Mom some dessert tonight. Okay?" He smiled. I walked out to join Jerzy.

We went along the street to the old footbridge. I pointed to the big house up on the knoll. "Jesuits live up there, and the ghost of a guy in a pink dress. Used to have these real good talks with him, like nothing at all was wrong, unless he'd broken a heel."

"You ever talk about his dress?"

"No."

"Tell your father, control or no control, all conversation is mad."

The sun was down; it was the summer solstice of 1968, the evening of the annual St. Jean Baptiste parade in Montreal, one day before the federal election. *Separatistes* in Montreal had warned Trudeau not to come to the parade. He was coming. I parked on rue Beaudry beside the Bibliotheque de la Ville. Chairs had been placed on a reviewing deck, the stand draped in blue and white bunting.

Five hundred *separatistes* had entered the crowded Parc Lafontaine from Cherrier and Amherst Streets, inching toward rue Beaudry, chanting: *"Trudeau aux poteaux"* (to the gallows). Hard-hatted cops with billies charged, punching and swinging. With a roar, cycle cops with sidecars swung into the park, leaving behind Chief Griffin in his dark blue suit and hat with gold braid, the man in control, his right arm jerking back and forth, directing officers who were no longer there.

Legs were wish-boned and bent back. Cops staggered, their helmets torn off by thrown bottles. A cop half ran, half fell out of the crowd, a giant firecracker — a cherry bomb — had exploded in his face. Tearing at his eyes, he was led to an ambulance; lime had also been ground into his face. This was it, *la pomme coupée à l'equateur*, a riot.

Four palominos and one chestnut, huge rib cages and pumping legs, struck terror in kids who ran blindly, banging head-first into trees, the horses plowing through cowering women, spurred on by the club-wielding cops who scattered the rioters north toward the lagoon and east to a steel mesh fence. It was 9:34: Trudeau had arrived, Archbishop Gregoire and Mayor Drapeau were already seated in their chairs. Trudeau appeared unperturbed, the others were shaken and white-faced. Paint bombs and pop bottles were hurled from the western knolls by the lagoon. Night sticks were shattered, some cops wielded broken tree branches.

Ten o'clock: Many police had suffered gashed faces; a pregnant woman, terrified by the horses, was on her knees screaming and pleading with the police to stop; a long-haired boy, stripped to the waist, was dragged along a walkway, suffering lacerations to his back, dragged through broken glass littering the ground, his screams lost in the uproar. An unconscious cop, whose horse had been levelled by a crow bar, had both legs broken. Most cops were running kids by choke-holds up to the Marias and heaving them through the door. Up the west side of the knoll, a huge fire had been built. Horses flashed through the flames.

With one leg crossed over the other, hands linked around his knees, Trudeau looked relaxed. The Bishop's hands were fluttering in abortive blessings. As bathing beauties rolled by on a float, Trudeau blew them a kiss. Motorcycles and ambulances were weaving in and out of the floats and bugle bands. Trudeau acted as though he were at a country fair. This was *Le Balcon*.

Suddenly a bottle was up in the lights. An arc. A sliver of the moon. It crashed behind Trudeau. It could have been a bomb, a Molotov cocktail. An RCMP guard tried to cocoon Trudeau's crouched body. The Official Party fled their chairs. The Premier's face was drained. He was not so much walking as being carried by his men.

Trudeau bounded to his feet, flushed with rage, pivoted, shook his fist, laughed, standing alone in the middle of a row of empty chairs, and then he sat down, spreading his elbows on the railing, holding his chin between his hands. Grimly, he watched, making it clear that he was in control of his space, his place. Another bottle crashed. The police beat back the bottle-throwers. Trudeau smiled. As Premier Johnson returned he was already a forgotten, ridiculed man, though not a word had been spoken. The Bishop returned, fluttering. Trudeau's steadfastness had been seen across the country on television. His election was certain. A police car was burning. The tires burst with a screech of boiling air.

It was two o'clock in the morning. Someone said a cop's throat had been slit. The Police Chief was holding a press conference. No writers I knew went. I heard the sound of a motorcycle far away. The tinkling of church bells. St. Catherine Street was empty. On the corner, there were two high fashion queens in lace pantaloons, tweaking each other. The bulge behind my eyes broke; there were tears. Those screams, the fires on the knolls and the children crumpled under a horse's hooves. The park turned into Desolation Row, the will to kill on the air. How would the allotment be made? *L'heure prend place.*

I thought of that old woman with her black gums scrambling under the trailer . . . and Trudeau stripping the rose . . . Was there a story there? I had almost forgotten the rose. What would Trudeau make of my telling that story? What else had I forgotten, trying desperately to remember? That for a moment, the magic had been killed? That for a tiny moment as Trudeau shook his fist into the howling mob I saw a look of execration in his eyes and I was swollen with grief and pride?

Book Seven

1

*I*felt ocean currents freshening the air, smelled bayberry and sweet tufts of lemon grass, and cleansing salt on the air, too.

I wanted the cleansing salt. The world had come to look like the act of an aged whore. The wild animals, the leopards, the wolves, the cheetahs and the tigers were out there, circling around crazily, blind with fright . . .

And that was just in the Chelsea Hotel in New York . . .

I turned off the Cape road to Provincetown and left into Edmund Wilson's summer house, back behind a clump of tall spreading trees and a rise of sand and field daisies. Though the front yellow room was darkened by overhanging branches, the rest of the rooms in the house were washed in light, rooms in which the light picked up soft colors, especially pale blues, rooms of wood and warm paint, not Talcottville's stone and cold plaster.

"Take a chair," he said, "take . . . take a chair."

He sat alone in the middle of a sofa, a quilt covering the wall behind him; checks of white and washed-out Wedgwood blue. Hung in the center of the quilt was a painting — I think it was an old *New Yorker* cover that Elena, his fourth wife, liked — and it was of a doorway opening out to the sand dunes. There was a coffee table in front of him and on it, an ice bucket and bottles. While carrying on conversation, he carefully laid out cards on the table, playing a complex double solitaire.

In her black bathing suit, Elena was slender and striking for her middle years. She was from the Mumm Champagne family. Wilson was telling with relish how he and Elena had visited a painter in Paris, Leonor Fini. This woman and her lover, he said, owned a pair of exquisite antique candlesticks. They told Jean Genet, who they knew was a thief, that he was to come and visit their apartment. He warned them that he was liable to steal anything. They laughed and told him to come for his visit anyway. He stole the candlesticks. Wilson laughed heartily, saying, "I like Leonor." Elena said over and over, "She's sick, quite sick, what!" and insisted that Leonor Fini was the only person in Paris she would not allow her daughter, Helen, to visit. "Sick, quite sick, what!" She said that the Fini apartment was done entirely in black velvet and everything had been covered in black cat's hair and Fini had been wearing knee-high black leather boots. "Leather, leather, what."

Wilson, his chin jutting out, said simply, "I like her. Now, what about this new man, Trudeau?"

My four-year-old boy, Michael, banged a chrome corkscrew on Wilson's whiskey bottles. Huffing through his nose, charmed as he always was by children, Wilson asked him if he'd like to see a little magic and fetched a coin from his pocket, palmed it, and then held it between his left thumb and forefinger. He drew the coin back and forth, Michael watching suspiciously. He tucked the coin into his other hand and waved his closed fists in front of the boy. (I thought if Wilson ever came to Toronto again, I'd have to put him together with Fat Saul for a little three-card monte.) Michael punched the left hand and got his penny. Wilson tried once more, and then again, losing each time. Defeat didn't bother him. He wasn't interested in winning. He was teaching the boy. In slow motion, he went through the coin manoeuvres, showing him how to hide the penny. Rocking back and forth on the sofa with laughter, Wilson was happily alive in the child's world, in his own love of magic, fairy tales, slight of hand, puppets and fantasy, while Michael — now holding the coin — prodded

Wilson's stomach, saying, "Guess again, guess again." Wilson pointed with his pudgy finger at Michael's closed fists and growled.

"These riots," he said, "nothing can come of them. These eruptions all over the continent, they are boils, eruptions. Whenever these eruptions are attached to politics, they burst and become the vengeance of the brutally stupid, the super patriots."

"Outside of Québec," I said, "it's hard to find a super patriot in Canada." And this, I added — trying to get him to laugh — was because no one could define what being a Canadian was — a House Committee of un-Canadian activities would reduce the nation to floor-slapping laughter — and so, free from patriots, I said smugly, "I can dissent against anything."

"American universities are full of dissent," he said, "men are saying what they want all over the place and besides," he scoffed, "even with Québec, there's nothing really at stake up there."

I tucked my chin into my chest, angered. As a smug Canadian I didn't find anything amusing about a smug American.

He had just returned from Jerusalem and he had told me about his commitment to Israel, his support for their pre-emptive military strikes. "I find it pretty funny," I said, "the way you've lined up with the Israeli army."

"Why?" he asked, pouring me a drink.

In an essay called "Confession of a Non-Fighter", he had written that he could not imagine killing men he did not know in cold blood, and so I answered, "Because you're a pacifist."

He rose, color in his cheeks, and he said loudly, "I've never been a pacifist."

He shuffled away from the sofa, from me, and there was anger and disappointment in his tone: "I disagreed with what those wars were all about, what was at stake in the Great Wars. But I've always believed in fighting for what you believe in. I've always been a fighter." He snorted, handed me my glass, and went off to the toilet.

2

Early one morning Morley thought he heard a noise in the library and came downstairs in his dressing gown and pajamas to find a well-dressed man in the house. The man said he was a tax collector and offered a card to prove it.

"My advice to the world is this," Morley later told the police. "Learn to make the distinction between your friendly neighborhood burglar and a real pro. And if a stranger in your house offers you a card, under no circumstances take your eyes off his eyes to look at it."

He chuckled, ruefully. "I moved to a window to get better light to see the card and he stepped in behind me like a ballet dancer and clubbed me on the head with a leather billy.

"I should have gone down — I don't know why I didn't. He kept coming. His workman-like quality was the most frightening — just like a butcher, just like a man beating a dog. My common sense told me I should yell but all I made was the strangest noises. I was angered and absolutely stunned."

He didn't panic. "I kept backing and he kept slashing with the billy. He seemed to be aiming at my temple but I guess I was bobbing my head — my right shoulder and arm ended up a mass of blue bruises. I took a couple on my left hand, too."

At 171 pounds and in his middle sixties, he was fairly fit because he walked every day, but he was nonetheless fending off a young, lean man — in his late thirties — who was armed with a billy.

"He kept coming, looking just like an executioner, and I was surprised that my head hadn't fallen off . . .

"I don't know how I got to the end of the dining-room table, but I did and — I don't know why — my head cleared. He ran around the other side to head me off and I grabbed this very heavy oak chair.

"If I'd been planning, I couldn't have picked a more perfect weapon. All I had to do was hold it between us and ram him and he couldn't hit me.

"Like a fool, I lifted it to crash it down on his head. I was trying to kill him by this time, like he was trying to kill me."

Blood was pouring over Morley's face, pajamas and dressing gown, "but I didn't know it until later. The guy still looked cold-blooded and vicious. But he saw I'd recovered and he was cool enough to know I had the one weapon that could help me. He saw I was trying to kill him and called me an old fucking shit and turned and ran.

"Loretto had been sound asleep upstairs and she woke up and heard moaning. She thought I was having a nightmare somewhere and came running down. I shouted to call the police.

"It was a nightmare," he said. "But after I took a beating for the first forty seconds, I really got mad. I got damn mad. You have no idea how abject it makes you feel to stand there helpless and be beaten like a dog."

3

I drove Wilson along a narrow paved road to a beach on the calm bay side. We went between small hump-like dunes, past wild plum trees and the pine cones of last fall lying like charred knuckles in the sand. We sat down near clumps of grass, Wilson in a white shirt and shorts, white beach shoes and hat, slowly tracing figures in the sand with a walking stick that he had inherited from his Kimball grandfather, a priest.

He leveled his stick at the water and said, "Yes, it is true." For the first time in his life he had taken sides in a war . . .

I told him to watch out . . . pointing his stick at the sea . . . he was liable to part the waters. "Yes," he said, ignoring my little joke, "the Israelis were producing a people who were scholars and men of action, handsome and beautiful, a new breed." They were not like the Jewish bourgeois from all over the world he said he saw tromping into the King David Hotel, Jews who were "pale and fat and amorphous — all bulges and bay windows and thick ankles and necks — and, though evidently prosperous, too dowdily dressed."

As we sat on the mound of sand, he said, "Nasser has probably done more for his people than any other Arab in centuries." But he found the Arabs hopeless, slovenly, irresponsible, and unable to organize themselves. He wondered if this were not due to the family structure; men who would father children and then move on.

I said, "I didn't know that Arabs did that."

He looked at me, his eyebrows lifted.

"No?"

"No."

The sun was on the nape of our necks, there were biting flies, and there was no breeze, so Wilson took a short stroll along the beach, poking at sea shells with his priestly stick, staring out over the water. I wondered what would happen if he looked back, would he turn like magic into a pillar of salt (we'd been talking earlier about Pasternak who had suggested that Lot's wife had looked back because she was the only one who had compassion for the dying). But he wasn't in a mood for looking back. When he sat down again I said, "Did you meet any Yemenite Jews in Jerusalem?"

"No, no . . ."

"I've an Israeli friend, one of your new breed . . ."

"Yes."

"He calls them blacks."

Wilson whacked the small rise of sand with his walking stick but said nothing.

4

I had the feeling as I got home to Toronto that I was at a meeting place of edges. I remember reading Robert Lowell's poem, "To Speak of the Woe that

Is in Marriage," the line, *free-lancing along the razor's edge,* and saying quietly, with conviction: "Yes." I didn't know how to explain this, the anticipation of woe. Or how to explain the increase of occluding light, a fascination with my own gloom.

As a child, it is true, I had loved to sing *Dem bones, dem bones, dem dry bones,* the shin attached to the knee bone attached to the thigh to the hip to the back bone, dancing bones, *clickety clack,* luminescent bones painted on vaude-ville leggings . . .

I didn't think this was lugubrious.

It was dance.

It was vaudeville.

On the edges.

Morley had begun to write regularly for my book pages at the *Telegram,* and so had Mordecai Richler and Irving Layton, Marian Engel, Susan Swan — as well as John Fowles, Arthur Koestler, James T. Farrell — and whether or not the pages were right for the old pink *Tely* legacy, we were printing poetry: Atwood, Avison, Voznesensky, Barker, Montague . . . We even printed fiction by Marie-Claire Blais.

The newspaper, full of wild contradictions and a boisterous rigor (the image of owner John Bassett), sent me out as a political and cultural reporter to the edge of everything that was going on. And so, too, with television, where I was working on a current affairs program, "The Public Eye," with Peter Jennings, Jeanne Sauvé — who would become Governor General — Larry Zolf and Norman Depoe . . .

At the university, where I was encouraged to design my own courses in contemporary literature, I had many brilliant students, mostly women, with incisive minds, voracious readers . . .

> *You are not here to verify,*
> *Instruct yourself, or inform curiosity*
> > *Or carry report. You are here to kneel*
> > *Where prayer has been valid.*

I was promoted.

I bought more cognac and good wine.

I decided that I had always read John Berryman's *Dream Songs* wrong, that Henry's syntactical idiosyncracies and breath breaks were the sprung inversions and air-locks of an alcoholic, that the way to read him aloud for all his pathos and laughter was to pretend you were the comedian Foster Brooks:

> *Deprived of his enemy, shrugged to a standstill*
> *horrible Henry, foaming. Fan their way*
> *toward him who will*
> *in the high wood: the officers, their rest,*
> *with p.a. echoing: his girl comes, say,*
> *conned in to test*
> *if he's still human, see; she love him, see,*
> *therefore she get on the Sheriff's mike & howl*
> *'Come down, come down.'*

I paid off the mortgage on my house and watched my four-year-old son turn the dining-room table into his easel, crawling over it, lathering paint onto paper and canvas, announcing, "I'm not Mister Bill, I'll be better than Bill Ronald . . . "

But in my ear, a *clickety clack*.

The *clickety clack* of dancing horses.

Ten cents a dance . . . There I was in the high wood, filled with exuberance but dangling in the breeze of dreadful thought, listening to the JFK *clickety clack* and then to RFK's funeral train rolling through the countryside, the officers, their rest, with p.a. echoing, the crowds at the train-crossings moaning . . . *a-moldering moldering in the grave, glory, glory* . . . hearing one *clickety* go *clack* on the *clack* of the other *clickety* . . . brothers shot dead, blown away, and then Martin Luther King, gone down, down in a silence that would need to be broken like bread.

After reading a short novel about seal hunters on the arctic edge, and writing about them, I ended the review:

> *In this*
> *land of eelgrass*
> *and ice drifts and snow, how does a*
> *man live through an endless winter of endless*
> *nights, and how does he stay sane while sitting*
> *squat hour after hour by a seal hole in the ice,*
> *waiting for the snout of the seal, for the one heave*
> *of the harpoon that he can make into the dark*
> *water, and then groping in the water under the ice,*
> *feeling for the dead bulk of the seal body, hauling*
> *it home, the moment of triumph as brief as the*
> *arctic summer in which the sun shines*
> *all night, exhausting itself in a last*
> *lunge against the dark*
> *and then the cleft*
> *of light*
> *closes*

"So much darkness," my mother asked, "and cold? Why do you feel it?"

"It's just like any old blues song," I said. *The sun gonna shine in my back door one day.*

But maybe I was seeking darkness, seeking an inner gloom in the way some men — the old seaboard witchers like Cotton Mather — had sought the devil: if they could prove he existed, then God had to exist; if I could find a darkness inside as ripe as roadkill, then maybe the abandonment of love — *like a lighthouse out to sea* — maybe abandonment could exist.

Maybe that's what Arthur Gordon Pym was after when he sailed into the great white womb of ice . . .

Late one afternoon, I was in my office at the *Telegram*. Otis Spann was singing the blues on my small portable record player, a half-written page on Isaac Babel was in the roll of the big old Underwood typewriter, and a tiny birdlike young woman — a beak-nose and dark raisin eyes ringed by mascara — sat down and said she had wanted to meet me for months. She was, she said, a novelist "from another country" and she had read my articles regularly and she was, she wanted me to know, worried about me . . . "because of a tone between the lines" in what she read and she had come down to the paper to read my fortune in the tarot pack.

"I don't believe in that kinda stuff," I said.

"You don't believe in the future?"

I told her to put away the tarot pack.

"At least let me look at your palms, let me hold your hands," and she reached out and drew my hands toward her lap and looked down into them as if she were looking down into wells. She touched, she prodded, and traced with her forefinger a line around a pad of flesh. It was an unprepared for intimacy, I wondered if she would hear the fish swimming in my fingertips. Then she let out a little cry and stood up, gathering herself, blurting out, "No life line, you've got no life line on your left hand."

"Wait a minute," I cried, as she stumbled against a glass partition.

But she hurried out of the office.

I looked at my left hand. I was sure that a line hooking around the base of my thumb indicated a route to my life . . . but I was filled with foreboding. And a sense of the ludicrous. Maybe there was no great darkness. Just gray. A yellow gray. Like smoke. A half-baked color. The color of accommodation, compromise. A stand-pat color, the color of a nun's hands, sperm on bedsheets.

When I told Nina about my life line and the woman, she said, "You've got to be joking."

"If I was joking, I'd be laughing," I said.

Clickety clack.

I went away to a cottage in the north for a week to relax, and I lay awake all night listening to deer mice run through the walls.

Deprived of an enemy, I nonetheless knew he was out there. Stalking.

J.K. Thomas, so jovial and generous, sat down to die. He knew he was going to die and he sat down alone to do it.

I came home for the funeral.

Morley lost a staunch friend.

He was growing more alone, more aware of absence, the absence of those his own age.

Sitting in his box of amber light, he stared into the black window and saw himself.

His nose grew longer, more bulbous.

My nose was clean, clear for the scent of woe and melancholy.

But I was the one playing on the black notes.

I told an executive producer at the CBC that I had heard the morose *clickety clack* of sorrow in the most surprising place . . . in the writing out of Israel . . . a deep and abiding mournfulness, a moral confusion that belied all the Six Day War bravado. This was no new breed, I said, no light unto the world; the paratroopers were weeping, remorse was their refuge . . . "Dust, they're obsessed with dust."

"Go there," he said. "Talk to them, make a film, let's see what's what . . ."

5

By a wrought-iron window in a stone house on a rise called Yemin Moshe, I sat looking across a gully to Jaffa Gate in Jerusalem. Yehuda Amichai, the poet, sat hunched forward, fleshy and solid through the shoulders and throat, and his round face was red from the sun. He spoke in a whisper. "When you live in a house here," he said, "it's like living in the skins of all the men who've owned the house, maybe not friends, maybe enemies. It's very tiring to walk around naked in your own house wearing so many different skins."

There were clouds over Jaffa Gate, strips of sheer linen, frayed at the edges. Early summer winds passed over the gravel hills and sudden gullies, the twisted olive trees and thorn bushes. In the alleyways, crooked as ecclesiastical sheets, there was no sound of water but, after several weeks of conversation with politicians and soldiers and writers throughout the country, I had heard the sound of water, heard it in a woman's laughter. Saya Lyran. Irving Layton, the poet, had given me her name. She was an actress who had studied in Minnesota and New York, and had known Kosinski. She had done her military service in the Navy. I liked that. Sister to Pym. She told me that the city, Jerusalem, was a stone boat overcrowded with prayers and hopes. "We could sink in such a boat," she said, laughing. She warned me that prophets and holy men had always got out of the sinking boat and escaped to the desert to be alone in the harsh light of their desert god. Instead of going into the desert I had sent the woman a note, a line in Hebrew . . . *snéynu beyéhad rehól ehád lehúd: The two of us together, each of us alone.*

An Amichai line.

Amichai and I sat in the cooling shadows of his house and talked of Yeats and Ted Hughes, Lowell and Agnon, and we ate dates. "Agnon," he said, "he's not so easy to get to see, not since he won the Nobel Prize." We were waiting for Saya, who was saying a final good-bye to her lover so that she could come to me.

"She's a story," I said.

"Stories, there are always stories," he said.

"I like this story."

"The place you are staying," he said, "Abu Tor, it means Father of the Ox . . . after an old man who lived there. Agnon has written a story about Abu Tor, but I forget it. There are too many stories here."

As a poet, he had been forced out of his attic mind into war several times, to lie on his belly and then limp back to his solitude, and then out into war again, and back, a man who thought with a limp. "In the beginning, God said — let there be light," he laughed. "But there was too much light. There is still too much light. We never get used to the hard light. We're forest people. We dream of the dark."

The previous day I had been on the Golan Heights, the *clack clack clack* of gunfire: cousin to the *clickety clack*, brittle sound of stones banging together, the sun strafing everything in sight.

"People can lose their minds here," Amichai said, "you better be careful."

I had seen the sea in the haunted faces of men on their way to the Wailing Wall, men who thought they were sailors.

"Yes, they think," Amichai said, "that Jerusalem is the Venice of God."

Herman Melville, the old pilgrim sailor, haunted by Ahab and the leprous white whale, had come to the Holy Sepulchre in 1857: "Ruined dome — confused and half-ruinous pile. Labyrinths and terraces of mouldy grottos, tombs, and shrines. Smells like a dead-house, dingy light. At the entrance, in a sort of grotto in the wall, a divan for Turkish policemen, where they sit cross-legged and smoking, scornfully observing the continuous troop of pilgrims entering and prostrating themselves before the anointing-stone of Christ, which with veined streaks of a mouldy red looks like a butcher's slab. Nearby is a blind stair of worn marble ascending to the reputed Calvary . . . and the hole in which the cross was fixed and through a narrow grating as over a coal-cellar, the rent in the rock!"

Haim Guri, the novelist, in Shemish Restaurant: "All you have to know about us is this, we are of the place, we live in the blood."

On July 15, 1099, Fulcher de Chartres, a Crusader, came clanking across a stone courtyard in Jerusalem wearing his iron suit, looking for the Holy Sepulchre, and he wrote: "With drawn swords, our people ran through the city; nor did they spare anyone, not even those pleading for mercy. The crowd was struck to the ground, just as rotten fruit falls from shaken branches, and across from a wind-blown oak . . . on top of Solomon's Temple, to which they had climbed in fleeing, many were shot to death with arrows and cast down headlong from the roof. Within the Temple about ten thousand were beheaded. If you had been there, your feet would have been stained up to the ankles with the blood of the slain . . . It was an extraordinary thing to see our squires and poorer people split the bellies of those dead Saracens, so that they might pick out the bezants from their intestines, which they had swallowed down their horrible gullets while alive. After several days they made a great heap of their bodies and burned them to ashes, and in those ashes they found the gold more easily . . . It was pleasing to God at that time, that a small piece of the Lord's Cross was found in a hidden place. From ancient times until now it had been concealed by religious men, and now, God willing, it was revealed by a certain Syrian. He, with his father as conspirator, had carefully concealed and guarded it there. This particle, reshaped in the style of the cross and artistically decorated with gold and silver, was carried to the Lord's Sepulchre and then to the Temple joyfully, with singing and giving thanks to God, who for so many days had preserved this treasure, His own and ours."

I was told I should talk to soldiers: I met a colonel in his middle fifties. He had mournful eyes, a soft fleshiness to his palms. He was responsible for operations in the Sinai. We talked about moral confusion in Israel, in the fiction and poetry, and the figure of the lone Palestinian in his *galibeyah* who looked more like father Abraham than any sabra, and suddenly his eyes welled up with tears, he whispered that all his life he had wanted to be a teacher, a writer . . . to write something . . . and then he yelled, "I was not born a Jew to become a killer . . . " and standing up, he slammed his fist into the wall, cracking the plaster. He stared at the crack in the white wall. With a wag of his hand he said, "It looks like an insane black thread lying on water . . . "

General Shlomo Gazit was General Moshe Dayan's protégé. He had large maps of layered colors on his wall. He had a pointer with a steel tip. He pointed to the Jordan River, he talked about "water as the central issue that *no one* talks about *because* . . . *it* is the central issue." As for the Palestinians, they were admittedly a problem but like all problems, it was there to be solved, and they would solve it . . . they were, he was, a twentieth-century problem-solver . . . studies, the best behavioral science studies had been done and soon "we will know, we will find out what the Palestinians want . . . you will see, they will be far more confused about themselves than we are."

She had the dark eyes of smoke at dusk, thick dark hair, a full red mouth, almost porcelain skin . . . and when she laughed I heard water run through a bed of ashes, the sound of ecstatic mournfulness. She was quick, she ran like a skipping child up stone stairs, she was agile in her ideas, able to make me laugh at nothing, and to sing:

Yelda scheli, Sayali.

And to write, to begin to break open that silence like bread—

Facing a courtyard of gray
and coral stone, her rooms: the long
narrow windows and wrought iron doors.
Two chairs, the round table, thick legs
of eucalyptus, the table-cloth, ivory-white,
embroidered with spears of long saw-tooth
grass. In the glass-doored case along the wall,
there were old play-scripts and one photograph of her,
chalk-faced in The Ghost Sonata *as* The Daughter
of the Caretaker's Wife and the Dead Man.
An oil lamp from Thessalonika hung between rooms.
In the drawer of her dresser her father's
violin, the bridge and strings broken. He loved

Wagner. Two novels on the bedside table: Light
in August, Death in Venice.
I had brought her an ivory comb and
oil for her arms and breasts.
She touched my eyes closed with her finger tips.
She was crying. Yesterday in the hills this side of Bethlehem
she was flying a blue and white kite.

"Yes, yes, of course, I've got to know what people like you are thinking,"
I said, invited to supper at the home of Ayala Zacks.

She was an established philanthropist and patron of the arts from Toronto
who lived in Tel Aviv, with David Ben Gurion as her neighbor.

We had met in the Galilee, and I had told her I was talking to Haim Guri,
novelist; Yehuda Amichai, poet; S. Yzar, novelist; Ephraim Kishon, journalist
and satirist; Ygal Allon, the deputy prime minister; Kosso Eloul, sculptor;
Muki Tsur, kibbutznik, and several architects who were restoring the old syn-
agogues in Jerusalem, and she said, "No, no, no, they will give you entirely
the wrong impression of the country . . . you will end up completely confused.
I will have a supper for you, so you will hear the truth, how things really are."

I was late, the guests had begun to eat. Ayala rose and said, "Ladies and
gentlemen, our guest of honor . . . " They murmured *shalom* and went on eating and talking, the woman to my right, in her early forties, a *Ma'ariv* columnist. "We are happy to have you," she said. The others were elderly, white-
haired, and with the exception of the man opposite me — a distinguished psychiatrist — they had come in sleeveless dresses, short-sleeved shirts. They had
numbers on their arms. No one was talking to me. I drank my glass of wine
and asked the serving woman for another.

Ayala looked distressed. Her guests were all speaking in Hebrew. She
clinked her glass with her fork. "Please, ladies and gentlemen, our guest of
honor speaks no Hebrew . . . "

"Aahh, aahh . . . "

"No Hebrew, no Yiddish either I'll bet . . . "

"What can one say . . . ?"

"What can one say? What can one think?"

I finished my glass of wine and said, "I think I'll have another drink."

"Another drink!"

The wife of the psychiatrist began to sing:

> Shick-er is a goy,
> Shick-er is a goy,

and they laughed and sang through several rollicking verses. No one seemed embarrassed. I was appalled and whispered to the columnist (having grown up among Jews, I knew what the words meant), "What's the song mean?"

She took out her pen. "I'll translate it for you . . . " I watched her write on a page from her reporter's notebook, "The non-jew is a drunk, the non-jew is a drunk . . . "

She gave it to me, beaming, glad to be helpful.

"Are you sure you'd translate *goy* as a non-jew," I asked. "Isn't it a little nastier than that . . . ?"

She put her notebook away, smiled, had a drink, and put her hand on my knee. Ayala looked bewildered. No one had said a word to me. I sang quietly to her, *If I had the wings of an angel, over these prison walls I would fly . . .* I thought I was in a madhouse as the psychiatrist's wife asked, "Angels, angels, who believes in angels except for the angel of death . . . ?" The psychiatrist smiled. A hand had firm hold of my thigh. Ayala announced we should all go into the sitting room for coffee. The columnist brought me a bottle of whiskey. I sat at the end of the room. They talked. They had a very good time. They ate cakes. They smoked cigarettes. It was time for the national radio news. They listened to the news. The columnist translated the news for me. When the news was over, they stood up, going home. The psychiatrist reached out toward me from the other end of the room, intoning — with the liquid *l*'s of a Slav — "Look at him, *l*ook, sitting there, so a*l*one, so *l*onely, a*l*l a*l*one . . . "

The columnist said quietly, "There is a free bedroom . . . "

Ayala, slouched on a sofa, seemed exhausted.

"So long," I said. *"Lehitrote."*

Ayala looked as if she couldn't remember why I was there and couldn't know why I was going.

Pinhas Sadeh, the novelist: "I personally was in the war and I have had to kill people. But I am a very little killer. I read in the Bible the other night — not for the first time, of course — about King David, the greatest of kings, at least in our nation. And also he was a poet, the poet of the Psalms, maybe the greatest man of our nation. He was, as I saw it, someone not absolutely different from Hitler. He did things . . . you can't call it otherwise, than genocide. Terrible crimes, over the wife of Obadiah, and so on."

It was 8:30 on a Thursday evening in the square that faces the Wall. The army was bulldozing Arab homes to open up more of the Wall. The Arabs were wailing. At the Wall the night before, I had watched — with Saya — a swearing-in ceremony for paratroopers, the stride of the troopers (very British), the abrasive nasal harangue of the company commander over the loudspeakers, and then the burning of their "insignia" — letters on fire in the dark night sky, unsettling to Saya as it was to me, as if we were looking through the lens-eye of Leni Riefenstahl. "Anyway," she said defensively, "they are giving the Arabs better homes than they've ever had before."

"Right."

"No, it's wrong, but sometimes you have to do something wrong so that you can do what's right."

Sons and fathers wrapped in fringed prayer shawls stood face to the Wall . . . that curious white-faced rocking of the men, a furtive pent-up sensuality in their bodies, pitching forward as if in pain, on the balls of their feet, tilting on their heels, like men trying to hold to the deck of a ship in a heavy sea.

I spoke of this rocking to Amichai.

"Rocking soothes a baby," he said, "but it's the circumcision of the baby that does it to us. Pain. We never forget the pain. We live with the memory of pain all our lives."

Haim Guri: "How do you have this feel for who we are as Jews? This sympathy for the melancholy, the moral confusion? This I do not understand."

I told him: "Irish blood. I live in blood, too. The Irish are the Yemenite Jews of the English empire . . . "

He laughed.

I told him about the eight hundred years of English occupation, the great famine, my great-grandmothers who were used as ballast in the coffin boats . . . "

He closed his eyes. I learned a lesson. Victims are interested in their own story. They are not interested in other victims.

"Anyway," I said, "the pain that you are going through here . . . "

He perked up.

S. Yzar, author of *The Days of Ziclag* — bedside novel for veterans of the 1948 war: "As a Jew I wrote about the hunting down of Palestinians. This was the first time that I saw, in reality, how you can exile people from their place. I couldn't stand it because the Palestinians became exiles . . . "

"That's the story where a character says . . . 'This is the *galut*?'"

"Yes."

"That the Jews are doing to the Arabs what was done to the Jews."

"We have to handle all the contradictions, we have to live with them. We don't know what to do, we can't escape. We close one eye, but we see everything with the other. It's like being operated on without anaesthetic."

The stones at the top of the wall were bleached white. Saya and I walked into the evening tent of shadow where there were faces stricken with yearning, and as we sat down among nettles at the foot of the wall that had been eaten by the morning sun she said, "Give me your mouth."

We didn't know who we would find in the tent of shadow. Elie Wiesel, the novelist, had written in *A Beggar in Jerusalem* of standing in the shadow of the Wall a long time, hearing the voice of a mad beggar talking to the murdered faces who haunted his mind. He ended up hurt and perplexed by the Six Day War paratroopers who told him that the murdered faces from the death camps were his dead, not theirs, and his dead had no right to be in Jerusalem, no right to stand up resurrected in his eyes.

Outside David's Tower, Amichai said, "My generation believed that through politics there was still a way out of this entrapment. Your generation believes this a little bit. But your son, you'll see that he has no interest in politics because he knows that there is no way out."

I went home. John Montague was waiting for me at my house, he embraced me, the touch of his lips on my neck, the prod of his fingers in my back, and no sooner were we alone than he said, "You're in love . . . I could tell by your letters, and you've been with her, which I can tell by your face . . . " He told me that he was on a reading tour across the continent, but only so that he could meet up in Chicago with a girl he had loved in Dublin, "And this involves my whole life, Madeleine, very hard. Very, very hard. Booker T. Washington White's in town. Why don't we go hear him. You're going back to Jerusalem?"

"Yes."

He stretched out on the sofa.

I asked after Hayter.

"Ah yes, Desirée's still with him. He's a great man," and then he said, "it is the strange power of women that the one you take to your breast becomes your destiny . . . "

He sighed.

He stretched out, silent, hands folded across his chest, needing to grasp a seed of light in the darkness, and then he said, ". . . and to change women is to change destinies."

Before dawn, before leaving to catch the plane to Chicago, Montague and I hugged good-bye. There was a tenacity about him, a strength in his grip of my arm, the tough pressure he put on my flesh, and then something yielding in the way he drew a circle of gentleness and mischievous laughter around himself, around love, and he gave me a poem he had written on a folded paper —

> *Love, a greeting*
> *in the night, a*
> *passing kindness,*
> *wet leaf smell*
> *of hair, skin*
>
> *or a lifetime's*
> *struggle to exchange*
> *with the strange*
> *thing inhabiting*
> *a woman —*
> *   face,*
> *breasts, buttocks,*
> *the honey sac*
> *of the cunt —*
>
> *luring us to forget,*
> *beget, a form of truth*

or (the last rhyme
tolls its half tone)
an answer to death.

When I told my father about Saya, he asked, "You haven't fallen for that new breed clap-trap that Edmund goes in for, have you?"

"No," I said, "I've fallen for a woman."

"Has she fallen for you?"

"Seems so."

"You are crazy," Morley said. "Absolutely crazy, that desert god of theirs, the desert is in their heart."

"The desert can be sensual."

"Rome is sensual. Go to Rome."

After the hour-long film of my Jerusalem conversations was broadcast, a woman from the Israeli consulate in Montreal came to Toronto and invited me to lunch at the Celebrity Club. She said, "I wanted to meet you face-to-face."

"Why?"

"To decide."

"What?"

"If you are an anti-Semite."

"Isn't that a little arrogant?"

"I'm going to warn you. You are in for big trouble. Everyone in the Consulate is convinced you are an anti-Semite, and they are saying so."

"How come I'm an anti-Semite? Whatever was said in the film was said by Israelis."

"It's not what you've said. They say that only an anti-Semite would want to ask the kinds of questions you ask, to get the answers you get . . . "

"You're kidding . . . ?"

"No."

She was not. Within some months, the revered moral theologian, Emil Fackenheim, had denounced me publicly as an anti-Semite. I was aghast. This charge was quoted on the front page of my own newspaper, the *Telegram*. Less morally sensitive men and women easily followed suit.

I went back to Jerusalem, to Saya, where a cat lay slumped in a roof gutter of the Hotel Moriah waiting for rain. Someone was playing an oboe. A beard of dry brown grass hung from a stone window ledge. In the long weeds at the heel of the city wall, near the ancient underground quarries, Saya held out her hand to me, a white hand. She drew her hand to her face, as if cupping water to her mouth. There was no water. A Hassid in his hot fur hat, wheeling an empty baby carriage down stone stairs, reached out to touch her with his long pale hand. She shuddered. I kissed her neck and tasted salt.

Close to the ninth station of the Cross, over a fruit store, a soldier on his haunches on a roof stared down at strolling pilgrims. Two black-hatted Jews — Neturei Karta Chassids — hurried white-faced along the alley, the wind flapping their long black surcoats. They did not look up at the soldier. They refused to recognize him and his citizen-soldier state. The Messiah, they said, had not come. The state, they said, was stillborn, and they spat when the state was mentioned, and outside the old wall, in Mea Shearim, they posted their signs: "The Nazis used our bodies for soap, the Israelis use our bodies for money."

"No wonder," I told Saya, "men flee to the desert sea. This place is crazy."

She poured a hot bath which we took together in her big old high-walled bathtub, water up to our necks. She let the water run to overflowing. It ran, flooding the tile floor, out into the hall, a cleansing, steaming luxury of water.

Driving from Jerusalem to Tel Aviv with Kosso Eloul — a sculptor born on the steppes who had a shock of black hair, dark horse-trader's eyes and deep lines down to his black moustache, an expansive man who — in his sculpture — sought minimalist effects (he had constructed a standing piece out of two stainless steel oblongs precariously balanced and called it KoBar . . . diminutive of our first names). We pulled off the road near Ramala and parked outside a small felafel stand.

"Spicy," Kosso said in Arabic to two slender young men.

As we ate, the men began to question Kosso, wanting to know if I was an athlete.

"He was a boxer?" they asked.

"No."

They were disappointed.

"He looks like a boxer," they said.

"He knows Muhammed Ali," Kosso said, trying to cheer them up.

"Ali," they cried, "Ali," and began to spar like little English schoolboys, elbows tucked, bouncing on the balls of their feet.

"He will learn you to box," Kosso said gravely. I rolled my eyes at him. Then, I tried to show the men the sensual power, the surge that comes off the swivel of the hip and they giggled like young men learning to dance. We shuffled and threw shadow punches until one of the young men asked if we would like to meet the Israeli heavyweight wrestling champion, a cousin, who lived with his wife in a house that was only five minutes walk away. They closed the stand. Kosso, astonished by this offering of intimacy, told me that I had to be careful. "If the man's wife is there, if she looks at you, do not look at her, do not let your eyes meet, it is a dangerous insult to her husband."

The wrestler, heavily muscled, had a somber, smiling benevolence. The young cousin told him about Ali and he clapped his hands. His wife served coffee and baklava, he listened to the young men describe our boxing lesson. His wife leaned forward, staring at me, unabashed, quizzical, until the beaming wrestler stood up and spoke to Kosso.

"He wants you to hit him," Kosso said, "and hit him hard, no faking, in the stomach."

"You're kidding."

"No, you are obliged."

I planted my feet and hooked him hard under the rib cage. He blinked, laughed, enfolded me in his huge arms, kissed me three times, and stepped back. "Ali," he cried. "Ali, Ali, Ali . . . "

Shmuel Yosef Agnon was the Agnon of Agnon Street, a small man with closely trimmed white hair, a black skull cap, thin lips, liver spots on his cheeks, bright eyes and delicately boned hands. He was open, friendly. His rooms were spare, austere. We sat at a small dining table. Amichai was delighted by his wit . . . "Oooh, what an insult, what an insult he made you, impossible to translate . . . " Saya served cups of ice cream. The old man hurried through his first cup and was spooning a second as he started telling stories, stories that seemed to be answers to questions no one had asked.

"And this happened in my town, a story that happened seventy years ago, a man who made nothing but trouble for the Jews. The whole town suffered. One day the commissar came to town and found that this man had defrauded the government. He was put in jail by the authorities.

"After a while, the man got out of jail, a very poor man. He came to my papa, who'd suffered at his hands, and asked for help. My papa took him into the house, gave him suitable clothing, trousers, a shirt, so forth.

"The townsfolk berated my papa. 'Rabbi Yedi, how could you do such a thing? He made life so hard for us.' My papa said he helped him because the man had once had power, but now he had no power and had come to him for help. 'Right now, I see only a poor man sanding in front of me.'

"That story is about Jewish morality," Agnon said, looking me straight in the eye. "You help the man who is helpless. Or kill him before he kills you."

He licked ice cream from his spoon and smiled wryly at Saya. She was flustered, trying to translate each phrase for me as Agnon spoke. She repeated, "kill him before he kills you . . . " but Agnon had begun telling another story.

"You know, in Jerusalem, when I came to this country, there was little water to drink during the summer. Well water was full of worms. Sometimes there were only worms and no water.

"Near the Street of Prophets, people would see a white and gray pole, and the pole was walking. You wondered, How can a pole walk? It was a Jew carrying his baby to a doctor, the baby swollen, the baby's eyes closed. And the reason, Arab women used to come to where we Jews lived. They brought flies with them. They were full of flies. It was horrible.

"But the Jews cured the city. So there was a clean meeting place for Jews and Arabs.

"But now, we are spending all our money on war, we are not disinfecting the meeting places, we are depriving our children of everything they were given on Mount Sinai.

"So I want to tell you something about Jewish morality, and the so-called good habits Jews have fallen into in the State of Israel. For nearly two thousand years, Jews stole and cheated and did what they had to do so they could make a living, but they never went in for killing and murder. Now, they murder the Arabs and they murder themselves."

The sun shone, bells rang, the crowds in the alleys were buoyant. Two Jewish soldiers were joshing a plain Swedish woman. She was trying to tell them they should care that Jesus, God, had risen for all men. "For our sins," she said.

"And what is sin?" one soldier asked.

"It is . . . " she started eagerly.

"No, no," he said. "If you think you can tell me so easily then you don't know."

He picked up his gun, walking toward the Holy Sepulchre. Theodor Herzl, father of Zionism, had written: "Earlier we had walked — rather quickly — through the Via Dolorosa, a route the Jews shun as something maleficent . . . I should have considered it cowardice not to go, and went along the street of the Holy Sepulchre. My friends restrained me from entering the Church itself. It is also forbidden to set foot in the Mosque of Omar and the Temple area, under pain of ex-communication by the rabbis — as Sir Moses Montefiore discovered to his cost. What superstition and fanaticism on every side?"

I took Saya into the Sepulchre, passing women shrouded in black — a face of burnt blossoms, a blind man's eyes bleached white, a coptic priest cowled in brown who hurled handfuls of rose water at us. In the deep shadows of jumbled scaffolding behind the Tomb, I put her against the wall and she lifted her legs, her bare legs in her short skirt. A tall Nubian priest strode by telling his beads. Seeing us pinned to the wall, he laughed, tossing his head back, as if we were — like winged insects — too ludicrous for his outrage.

There was a sudden early summer *khamsin*, a wind off the desert, heavy with grit, a wet grit that flayed the skin, and yet the wind pulsed with dry heat and people were warned to stay off the streets . . . to keep their dogs off the streets (in the vale of Kidron below Amichai's house there was an asylum for mad dogs), and to get out of the *khamsin* and into cooling darkness we stepped into the Church of Dominus Flevit (the Lord Wept) on Olivet Hill, a small church built in the shape of a tear —

> *We lay on a shelf*
> *of stone in the valley*
>
> *of Kidron. It was*
> *the dead of night.*

Our neighbors, scattered
among the weeds of

Olivet Hill, were common
headstones, their bones

the calligraphy of a final
hour. But we

were naked and
ignored the language

of moss along the bone,
and all grief, calumny,

rage, fell from my eyes
when she knelt and gave me

the gift of tongue. So too,
the moon swallowed

the sun. My cry named
her and in reply

we heard the muezzin
in his minaret,

that stone shaft into
the mouth of god.

That night in bed I felt exultant, sure that my own dead had stood up in
my eyes, resurrected, sure that a silence had been broken — and we began to

make love and a happiness long hidden in the rhyme of the everyday and the usual came unsprung in a white light that infected my whole body, bending it backwards in a suffusion of joy . . . an abandonment completed by a collapse into laughter.

(Years later, I told Morley about this "grace" moment, saying I knew then that I had heard a silent music in my body and between my own lines. He did not doubt this but was dubious about how such muse moments should be considered. "This light can be misleading. Look at what happened to you, and to Saya, to you and Nina."

"I got *The Hogg Poems*."

"You lost your marriage."

"Yes, there's always a wound in the light."

"A wound?"

"The lepers . . . "

"Ahhh . . . " he said.

"Ahhh," he had confessed to me ruefully in 1979 — he had confessed that my sojourn among the lepers in that year was the one moment as a writer that he had envied, a moment deep in the jungles of Gabon and the Cameroon . . .

I had gone in the middle seventies to be among lepers, the outcasts . . . men and women cordoned off, shunned, condemned to be alone with their living rot, as if they reminded men too terribly of the wound that no one ever wants to touch; I had gone there to be close to the possibility of death, a death so solitary that even the gods might shun you . . . and in that jungle a man had come toward me in the Village Lumière, his hooded eyes wide open and his hand out . . . the hand one man extends to another, the thumb, forefinger and little finger gone, the creamy white scar in the black flesh where his thumb had been, a stub hand, almost a club, and there in the still, hot silence of the afternoon there was no choice. He was inviting me to acknowledge, to share in, his manhood. To refuse was to recognize only his rot, his corruption, his death; better to cut and run than withdraw from the proffered hand. And yet as his two hard fingers went into the palm of my hand I felt a shudder of recognition. There was a bond with him, with myself; I had not turned away from him or my own fear and loathing. But also there was a welling up in me, an inevitability that was as pressing as those two fingers; the leper's kiss, death, deeply felt. I wanted to weep for myself, for him; but he was smiling, his eyes filled with laughter, some enormous satisfaction that seemed so simple, so open; a joyful embrace of life. "Who knows what I would have made of that hand shake," Morley said.)

I was about to leave Jerusalem. *Like a lighthouse out to sea,* I was no longer seeking darkness but was sending a pulsing light into the dark . . . happiness . . . eyes filled with laughter, full of an enormous satisfaction that was simple and open . . . a joyful embrace of life. Which meant that while I was clear-eyed, I was totally confused.

Sitting with Saya by the wrought-iron window in Amichai's house, I saw that he had his father's eyes, his mother's graying hair. In the middle of his life he had begun to return to them. To really go home. I, too, was going home. We were laughing about houses. His house was

a house that had belonged to an Arab
who bought it from an Englishman
who took it from a German
who hewed it from the stones
of Jerusalem . . .
I am constructed of spare parts
of decomposing materials
of disintegrating words . . .
I begin,
gradually, to return them,
for I wish to be a decent and orderly person
when I'm asked at the border,
"Have you anything to declare?"

6

Returning from Jerusalem, I drove south, south as planned with Nina and Michael, to the salt-box houses on Cape Cod, to Wilson, Blais and Bill Ronald: *Maintain a standard of chaos.*

Already, the Cape was another place in another life. Every day was like walking through rows of liquid mirrors, the light leaping on all sides but the landscape empty of feeling, of freshness. Despite the fact that Bill was with Helen his wife, Bill's new girlfriend (and her husband, a horn player), had come down to visit, and every time Bill and the woman — a former Miss Toronto — disappeared into the night, the horn player stood in the country road and blew his mournful horn, like a call to them in the dark. The night Nina and I agreed to our separation — standing on the beach facing the dark ocean — a man landed on the moon for the first time. We made love in the moonlight on the wet sand for the last time.

> *Rose of memory, rose of forgetfulness . . .*
> *Time the destroyer is time the preserver.*

Nina wrote my mother and father a long letter from the house on Long Pond Road.

Dear Morley and Loretto —

The situation here has been and is one such that not even John Updike would touch. In one half of the house are Barry, myself and Mischi and Bette. And you know what our situation is like! Next door Bill has been depressed and despondent since our arrival — partly because of his artistic career and partly because of the impending arrival of his mistress and her husband. Before they came, Barbara (Fefferman) arrived for a ten-day stay. At the same time Paddy Sampson and a female acquaintance drove down. Paddy's companion was a striking girl with a face which was edged in great sorrow most of the time. We discovered that she had to give up her 2-year child some four years ago to her ex-husband and now had visiting rights twice a month. It was sad to see her watch Mischi with such hungry eyes and at times reach out to caress his cheek (much to his annoyance & embarrassment). But Paddy was great fun and a source of much energy.

As for Barry & myself, it is very difficult to describe. For the first week here, he was very withdrawn and moody, but writing like mad. I would fluctuate between sorrow and some sense of relaxation. But as I came down here with no hopes of winning him back, I've been feeling quite lost, not knowing what I was supposed to be. There was a period where Bette did all the cooking and catering for him. Most of the time I can reconcile myself to our separation, but at night time, especially after a few drinks, I find the thought so unbearable and cruel that it's hard to keep myself under control.

I kept wanting to leave for home before the 20th of July because that's our sixth wedding anniversary and I felt that I would completely collapse on that day. But as Barry and I had been getting along quite easily for the previous days, we decided to go out on the 20th. It was a lovely evening, touched now and then with tearful memories. But it ended drastically as I tried to keep up my spirits with mixing the drinks. I have felt great sorrow for Barry in having to leave a woman who made him happy and felt that he must resent my being here instead of her. How could I fight to hold him after knowing about her, and his telling me that he can't live with me and must break off. I imagined that he knew what he wanted and how to go about getting it. I found out tho, that he is in as much pain as I about the separation but he has to do it. But oh how hard it is for me to give up 12 years — only the will says, go ahead.

Enough of my woes. Let me tell you about Barry, the son you seem to have misunderstood these past few years. Barry is almost the opposite of you, Morley, and Michael. Whereas you two are reasonable men, Barry is not. Witness his manoeuvrings of his careers at the Tely and University. Against yours and Michael's sane directions, Barry did what he had to do and won the positions he was after. What wounds me, and who knows how much greater is Barry's sorrow, is your complete rejection of Barry's writing this year in the paper. Instead of judging his pieces, you are more concerned with what the readers will think of them. But then you are a reasonable man. He has written some beautiful essays and

memories, which you, as an artist, have stubbornly refused to accept
and see. And your comment on the Montague work was most
deplorable. For heaven sakes, don't look at it in terms of a newspaper
article, but as your son's development into the kind of literary artist he
feels he is and must become. I know you are imprisoned with your
novel, but must you be so blind to Barry's sense of his achievements.
But Morley is a reasonable man. I remember what Kosso said about
you and Michael. "They have cultivated the appearance of outrageous-
ness, especially Michael. But Barry is the mad one." And as one who
is tormented and just surfacing over his black moods, he must be
looked on with different eyes. You might be interested in Barry's comment on your Julian Jones ending. He, like me, also believes some men
do see their fates, and it is these men who force a confrontation that is
exciting, he believes. They should be the ones you write about.
Otherwise Julian Jones will be a catholic novel with a unitarian ending. Absolutely believable, absolutely understandable, but it's hardly
Capt. Ahab or Raskolnikov.

I think you would be most surprised and pleased with Barry here.
He is just writing, writing and writing all the time.

I have waited many years for this onrush and am thankful to be
here at the onset. I am proud of him.

We haven't seen Wilson yet but hope to soon. Please excuse me
for berating you too much, but I can't stand by and watch your relationship with Barry dissolve because of lack of understanding.

Bette remains constant and content, Mischi demanding and
happy & things really aren't so bad. Write if you can.

Love, Nina.

7

Wilson, seated on the sofa, served me a tumbler of Scotch. The cards for double
solitaire were laid out but he was not playing. He was not feeling strong. I told
him that I had just returned from Jerusalem, and told him about the military

swearing-in ceremony for elite paratroopers staged in front of the Western Wall, the huge burning letters . . . words on fire in the night sky. He said he'd seen something of the same kind of thing in a stadium, that it was frightening — the images it conjured up — but he'd also found it exhilarating. We talked about the writers there, about Agnon, and I said that I had met Agnon, too, but Wilson agreed he didn't really know anything about the younger writers. I don't know why — perhaps because he started talking about his puppets — perhaps because I'd come to love his stuttering or huffing need to correct me — perhaps because I could never resist at least one moment's impudence — I said, "I think maybe you met all the wrong writers, they kept you away from all the good writers . . . "

"Like who?" he said.

"A guy named Amichai, he's a lovely guy, and good, and I heard about another guy, Yehoshua . . . "

"Well," he said with a sudden weariness that I'd never seen before, "you can get around, I can't get around any more. I see who I can manage to see." I felt ashamed for having pricked him, for having forgotten how old and ill he was — though in a way, what I'd said was a compliment, because I could not think of him being out of touch, could not think of him being anywhere but at the heart of his own interests. The cards lay on the table, untouched. He was pasty-faced. I kept silent. Then, he reached out into the silence for a book I was holding and he signed his name on a blank page, a little note for me. It was quick, it was deft. He might not have met all the new writers in Jerusalem, but he'd signed the note — a blessing — with his name, in Hebrew, the language of the place. I didn't know any Hebrew. Then he started to play double solitaire. It was the last time I saw him.

8

In Toronto, I moved into a first-floor furnished flat only six blocks from where I had been born. It was furnished because it belonged to the photographer Michel Lambeth, who had gone to live and work in the jungles of Yucatan.

Maybe, I told him, he would find my Mayan woman and he, too, would discover his fingertips.

Over the following months, Saya and I met on the wing, when we could. Amazed at our elation, candid in bed, we left our names, like empty shoes, in many hotels in many cities, Paris, New York, especially New York. She startled desk clerks by leaping into my arms in hotel lobbies. We felt that we were a prophecy come true. A pattern of timeless moments. Yet, after each moment of elation, each expansive gesture, we were left enervated, growing inward.

This free-lancing on the razor's edge of happiness only increased the intensity of my interests . . .

I was immersed in making films about Québec, the upheaval in the economy and the political culture.

People said, "If you're interested in the Québec *separatistes*, so interested, you must be anti-federalist . . . If you're interested in the Palestinians, so interested, you must be an anti-Semite."

"Why do you care so much?" Barbara Frum, the broadcaster asked me one day. "You're not Jewish, you're not Palestinian."

I told my father about this conversation and he said, "She's right. You care too much."

I had forgotten old Kavanagh:

> *Sitting on a wooden gate*
> *Sitting on a wooden gate*
> *Sitting on a wooden gate he didn't give a damn.*

The films on Québec were broadcast. No English-speaking Montrealers were asked to explain the Québécois. Jacques Parizeau, Robert Bourassa, Abbé Dion, Marie-Claire Blais, Michel Chartrand, Pierre Vadeboncoeur . . . these were the voices. An editor and columnist for the Montreal *Gazette*, Joan Irwin, wrote a scathing review, a review of such ill-will — suggesting that I had bullied these grown men into an alarmist view — that I was ordered by the President of the CBC in Ottawa to explain my on-air "misdemeanors." I did (all my public life I have thanked God for audio tapes and transcripts), but it took four days to complete the research and two thousand words to show that as a reporter, Irwin had entirely misrepresented what had been said. The President did not reply to my letter, the executive editor of the *Gazette* did not reply, Irwin did not reply.

"You win," Morley said, "and that's why they'll never send you again to Québec." He was right.

Sandbagged to a standstill.

I went to New York to see Saya.

It was our city.

Suddenly standing up and singing in the Palm Court. Eating hot dogs on the street. Going into Saks with mustard on our cheeks. Walking. Always walking hand-in-hand. And one afternoon, we were walking down Lexington Avenue to Washington Square. We were with Bud Freeman, the tenor saxophonist. Bud, with his natty moustache was wearing a bowler hat and a topcoat tailored to tuck-in at the waist. Unlike most musicians, his shoes were polished. In this case, shoes were the sign of the man: polished. He spoke the way he played: rapidly, each note clean, full, precise, combining a severe clarity with throaty earthiness. He'd come out of the gin mills, he'd played with all the junkies and hopheads, "But," he said, "I cannot stand the excusing, the forgiving of artists who are drunks, or on heroin or pot — the continual making of excuses — the assertion that such and such a man, if only he could get off the bottle, would be excellent. The bottle, drugs, they are the extension of what the artist knows about himself, about his own lack of confidence, his own lack of talent. The great artist's only dissipation is his art: that is where he destroys himself. And those critics who talk of the H-generation, the boozers and pot-head musicians, they are second-rate sociologists, or something, who know nothing about art." A man was lying on the sidewalk ahead. Bud started talking about Ezra Pound. It still saddened him, he said, that Pound — when he was arrested in Italy after the war — had been kept outdoors in an open cage. "Of course, it was even sadder that so intelligent a man, so great a man, could have been so stupid a traitor." He quoted my father's favorite lines from Pound:

> *Be in me as the eternal moods*
> *of the bleak wind, and not*
> *As transient things are —*
> *gaiety of flowers.*

He did not know that they were my father's favorite lines. "The elegance of those lines," he said, "that's what Pound had, a courtly elegance." The man on the sidewalk was dead. No one had come for the body. No one stopped. We stepped around the dead man. "The dead just fall down here," he said, "like tin soldiers," and then, "I wear a bowler hat, an English bowler hat, because then I can pretend that no matter what I see from under my hat I'm not here." Saya embraced him, kissed him, and said, "You are here."

"Here, we are here," that's what Saya and I would say every time we were together, as if *here* were magic, as if we knew — with terrible poignancy, and the perverse pleasure that such poignancy gives — that *here* was destined to be nowhere.

Later that evening I tried to explain to her how fitting it was that Bud should think of Pound as elegant; though he had come out of the gin mills of Chicago at about the years my mother was there, working not just as a tenor saxophonist but as a hoofer and a card-sharp, he was the most elegant player of his time . . . his recording, *The Eel,* was a piece of convoluted elegance worthy of the interwoven lines of monks in ancient Celtic books. She nodded. I lost her with *ancient Celtic books.* Her mind was elsewhere. I began to talk about the beauty of the *Book of Kells,* the sinuous Celtic line. She talked about the sinuousness of the desert hills on the road to the Dead Sea. I talked about mist, she talked about salt. More and more with each passing month, we did not have time enough together — time to waste — so that we could be silent. So we went to bed, talking too much, straying further from love. As Amichai wrote,

We multiplied the words,
Words and sentences so long and orderly . . .
"Let's be sensible" and similar curses . . .
We could have become a silence.

We met again in New York when the wind was slashing cold — we met *in frigid purgatorial fires.* A saleswoman in Bloomingdale's, shaking out a suit that had been too long on the rack, sneezing, said, "Such love, I see it in your eyes . . . have long life, be lucky." We took it as a sign that we were finished. Questions cropped up. Doubts, small betrayals, failures, like forgetting to comfort each other against the cold, these were pock marks on the moon. We shared a weakness for omens. For reading moon signs. *Who then devised this torment? Love.* We lay in single beds, holding hands in the dark across the space. She slept cocooned, arms around her knees. More and more she was going home in her head to her tribe. I slept with one leg out of the bed. Wondering, with one eye open. Desolate. We said good-bye in the morning in the revolving door of the hotel. Her limousine honked the horn. She faded on the blowing of the horn.

Michel Lambeth suddenly came home. He stood in the doorway and said, "I couldn't stand it there anymore than I can stand it here." I had nowhere to live. I borrowed a bed here, and a sofa there. Hitchhiking from house to house.

Kosso and the painter Rita Letendre, his Québécois wife, took me in.

Arthur Vaile — a canny, street-wise, acerbic and funny land developer who had been my advisor on the state of Québec's economy — took me in.

A woman I worked with in television, Claire Weissman Wilks, was an artist. She had a languid sensuality and race-horse legs. A lucid stillness. She was young but had four children. She had left them with their father. A week after she'd left, her widowed mother had moved into the house, taking her place — surrogate wife! I thought this was intriguingly ridiculous. More and more, things were taking a sardonic shape. Late one night, I asked to see her drawings. I had a toothbrush in my pocket. I asked if I could have a key. She said, No. I took an apartment across the hall. "Where are you living?" my father asked. "In my head," I said. "And I need a change of socks." Claire gave me a key.

Saya came to Toronto. Each time we turned on the car radio, B.B. King sang, *The thrill is gone.*

One day, Claire drove straight at us as we crossed the road.

Saya met my family and went home.

"She's better looking than I thought she'd be," Morley said.

"Well, I guess that settles that," I said.

Nina plunked a huge bundle of clothing at Claire's front door, saying, "If you're going to sleep with him, you'd just as well do his laundry."

My mother told me I was preposterous.

Claire whacked me in the head with a French stick.

"Think Sweden," I said to myself.

Saya wrote to say that she had fallen into a deep depression, so worrying that her father had come to sit with her. "I couldn't betray you," she told her father, "after you survived the death camps, to leave you and go and live with a non-Jew . . . "

"Do you really think," he said with disapproving sadness, "that I lived through the death camps so you would ever turn away from love?"

With every choice, a loss.

At the *Telegram*, I reviewed a book about bats, creatures hanging upside down by their tiny winged fingers in the caves of night. I began a series of drawings of men and women as bats.

"Bats," my mother said, staring at a large drawing, "why bats?"

I drew a bat lying on his back, the huge bare soles of his feet staring at the world. He was reaching up with winged hooks.

Imploring.

There was a feel on the bat-wing air. Like "breaking news . . . " the news that stays news . . . a flower, taking shape.

The phone began to ring late at night.

Sometimes it was one of Claire's old lovers. Or a new lover. Then, the calls came from Beirut.

"Kanafani . . . " a voice said.

I was planning to go to Beirut.

Living with Claire, my social life began to revolve around television. Producers, reporters. There were several who wanted to meet Morley. They came around to his house.

"What's going on," one of them asked me, "what's up with you?"

"I'm going to Beirut," I said. "Going to Cairo first and then Beirut."

"And what's up with you, Morley?"

"Nothing. Nothing. I sit here, forlorn, waiting for Barry to tell me what's going on. That's what Edmund Wilson said he envied about me, I had my two runners — Michael and Barry — out in the world, coming home with reports."

"What's the latest news?" one of the men asked, snickering.

"Carthage is burning," Morley said.

He was amused. He liked to be provoked. He puffed his pipe and smiled. Loretto sat in her corner of the chesterfield. Suddenly, one of the women, a chic television hostess, turned on her and said, "Mrs. Callaghan, you're not a liberated woman."

Loretto, startled, shook her head and then said, "Why?" A newspaper lay folded across her chest.

"You not only say almost nothing, but when you do you never say the words 'shit' or 'fuck.'"

There was an awkward silence. One of the men went to say something cautionary to the television hostess but then he saw that Morley was smiling so he kept quiet. Loretto, after a full pause, said, "Yes, that's true. But you see — I have done both."

9

Morley phoned. "They've just given me fifty thousand dollars. A bank, of all people."

"Do you think you know where your Homburg hat is?" I asked.

Pause.

"You remember the night Mordecai Richler came around to see me?" he asked.

"Sure."

"And you rode off with him in a taxi?"

"So?"

"So I spoke to him the next day and I said, 'How'd you get along with Barry' — that's the night you were wearing that beautiful Borsolino hat I'd brought you from Rome — and he said, 'I dunno, he didn't say much, but he loves his hat, he kept stroking that hat all the time we were in the taxi, like it was a cat he had on his head he was so proud of it, and then, just as he said good-bye to me he rolled it up in a ball and put it in his pocket, telling me — It's so soft, see, you can do that.'"

"Somebody stole that hat," I said. "Maybe it was Richler."

In the grand hotel with its high ceilings, he looked small, shrunken by age to five-foot-seven. He stepped, hatless, through the great doorway of the supper hall wearing "black tie" — a one-button roll evening jacket, with black braid piping on the lapel, a dress suit so old and far out of style it was chic. He liked that. His color was high. He looked fresh and impish for a writer who was being given the Royal Bank Award as a distinguished Canadian. The Mayor, drab Bill Dennison, who had the air of a remittance man, said his adieus to the head table after dessert and before the speech, hurrying off to greet a group of visiting Oddfellows. Morley stood up and said: "I don't know what to say. I was talking to my two sons, Michael and Barry, and I said,

'What do you say on such an occasion?' And they very quickly said, 'Just say thanks, and take the money and run.'

"But I can't do that. I've got to say something — I've got to tell you my little story. This is my hometown. I feel a little like the prodigal son, but here I am in my town among my own people. Hands come out to me warmly. The fatted calf has been killed. I feel that I was dead and now am alive.

"It may be that all of life is a longing for home. For me the satisfaction has been mainly in the longing. But the works of my imagination wouldn't stay at home. They never did. From the beginning, though I remained here in the flesh, my works, like prodigal sons, went off into strange countries. They had a life abroad, alone, before they were asked to come home. Over the years I've grown dubious about the great prodigal son story and how it worked out. What haunted me was this: What did the son do after the feasting was over? What am I to do now? Bask in the warmth, enjoy the great treasure heaped on me and feel at last that I am at home and at peace and at rest?

"When I started to write, it never occurred to me to be concerned with the national symbols of my time — the National Policy, Sir John A. Macdonald, the Mounted police, the CPR and the northern lights on arctic snows. I wrote about criminals, saints, priests and prostitutes, bankers and newspapermen, and always about the failure of love. These characters, in their desperate, intimate human relationships as I knew them, never talked about being a Canadian. I wrote about the people around me in the language spoken around me; the life around me strained through my own temperament.

"It only made me a stranger at home. But I was interested in the pursuit of excellence, in finding my own kind of excellence. My first stories, written while I was at college, were lifted right out of my Toronto life. I knew no other life.

"I had freed myself happily from what the politicians, the historians and the school teachers used to call 'our traditions.' When I was at college I used to wonder why people coming to these shores rarely came as lovers. They came with the old love for other places and other old familiar things deep in their hearts. Look around the old neighborhoods in this town. Duke Street!

Princess! Wellington! On and on; the country was to be a new England or a new Scotland, a new Berlin or a new Ireland.

"I used to say to myself that this was all wrong: this new land was like a wild, strange, new beautiful woman. Yet men came only to touch her, change her, put her in their own domestic pattern. They never wanted to see her as she was and love her for her own new wild beauty; they saw only the parts of her that reminded them of the woman they had left behind.

"What a terrible fate for a beautiful woman, to be loved only when she reminded the lover of someone else, only when he could dress her as the one he had left behind. And I used to think too — what would those colonial founding fathers with their sense of tradition know about Canada? For them there was just a vast blob on the map they called Canada. As a country, as a people, as a cultural pattern, it was all a conjecture! How could it be anything else? Canada — still a conjecture! Heraclitus' river! Always changing and becoming. And here's my point. I wrote of what I saw around me, not what should be around me or what we should pretend was around me. I wrote out of my love of my craft — I was paid eight dollars in French francs for my first story, and I wanted my conception of what was excellent to be as high as any writer's in any other country. I didn't want any protection.

"If my work has some place in letters in this country, and if as English critics and American critics have suggested, it has a quality or tone of its own, may it not be because it is Canadian?

"May I not, even as a very young man, have stumbled on the road to some kind of authenticity far superior to that of the strident new nationalists crying out for a card of identity in the police court of the world? I say only look upon my work. Is it something in itself? In the world of the artist you can't demand recognition of your singularity. They look upon your work. You have it , or you haven't.

"And when you really have it, people will come from afar out of interest and wonder. The new militant nationalists who seem to be mainly historians, politicians and economists, talk about culture, too. But it seems to me they don't understand the forces that shape a culture.

"Ownership in itself won't make you anything more than a landlord. You can own great museums, or you can buy great symphony orchestras and locate them here. Yet the compositions the orchestra plays, the stuff that stocks the museums, may be all products of the imagination of other cultures. Something to delight a rich man, an owner.

"A country may have great corporations, but if it has no literature it is a country that has no soul. It is a shop keeper's society. The new nationalists, it seems to me, are concerned only with who is minding the store. Yet I hear of busy men saying in the newspapers, 'I have no time for novels.' Or if they are critics of a certain sophistication they say, 'The story form is exhausted. Narrative is dead. It's a technological age. What we want is information. Useful information.'

"A long time ago Jesus of Nazareth told stories, baffling parables that go on haunting men. But I'm sure there was some business-like Pharisee in the listening crowd who muttered, 'Why doesn't he give us the facts? Why the mystery? Why doesn't he give us some real information?'

"Information! Instead of the knowledge, the intuitions of imagination! It is the bedeviling fantasy of our time. We are stuffed with information. It pours in on us from a thousand machines until life has no meaning at all. A time when there are no great new temples, no gods and no tombs because there is no sense of eternity.

"Just information. Just technology. Outer space and inner despair. Yet it is the artist in words, or in paint or sculpture or in music who has a sense of form; in the glory of form is a sense of eternity. In short, it is the artist alone in this wild babble of information who tries to give some meaning to life.

"I firmly believe that the young, more and more, will be driven out of dreadful necessity to the story teller, the mythmaker, to the world that belongs to the story teller alone. It is the private world, the domain of secret private relationships, the dead of night in a woman or man's heart.

"Technology may triumphantly take man to the moon, but the man takes all his despairing questions and his secret loneliness with him, no matter how far away he flies. Since all art has to do with the relationship of things, the great writer deals with man's relationships in his lonely inner world. A man must stand for something. I stand for the sanctity of this private world.

"I heard from Cardinal Léger who was given this great prize last year. A prince of the church off by himself in the outer dark of Africa's jungles, working with the lepers. When I am at work on a new book, I too am off by myself, hoping to get something down that wasn't seen or said before. We all go into the outer dark. I like to think I am being honored for the pilgrim soul that is in us. I like to think, too, that you are not saying now: 'Rest, the journey is over, enjoy the fatted calf.' You are saying, 'Tell us what it was like out there, in the outer dark, before you go off again.'"

10

Edmund Wilson died in the dark in the house in Talcottville. Two days before he died, a chipmunk got up on to his bed and sat beside him. No one knows if he took it as a sign. Mabel Hutchins, who turned the latch key every morning afraid that she would find him dead, found him dead and couldn't believe he was gone. I couldn't believe he was gone, either.

In his last years, he was sick with attacks of angina; he caught malaria in the Caribbean; there were colds and the gout, but he had worked with the same determination, never letting up his pace, full of ideas and curiosity. Still, the last time I saw him, on that August afternoon, he had looked terrible — white-faced and haggard and thinner (on a trip to New York he had fallen and hurt his back and I was told later that he couldn't get up from his sofa). But his wry sense of humor had been there: when we'd spoken about Jerusalem he said that he had been given the Jerusalem Prize, but when he'd made it clear that he was not well enough to travel to the ceremony in the Holy City, they had taken it back and given it to Borges. Wilson, who knew about the politics of prizes, was nonetheless wounded, and he had laughed and said, "I don't know what the devil Borges ever did for the Jews." Anyway, he'd said, there was another prize: he had just been given the Golden Eagle of Nice, which neither of us had ever heard of, but that didn't matter; it had a tag of five thousand dollars and the eagle came in a red box with little doors and brass hinges — like something from a bowling tournament. We had laughed. He'd liked showing me that red box. It was superior *kitsch*, the very best cornball. But he had been in bad shape, working hard finishing his melancholy memoir about his world passing away in Talcottville.

He died and was cremated and carried to the Cape. On a bright June afternoon, the young local priest had a Scotch-on-the-rocks in the family kitchen, and then several of us went in a small group to the Wellfleet cemetery, kitty-corner across the road from Eulalia's hotel with the second floor doorways into nowhere. The grave, a hole for the urn, was off and away from the other graves, alone under tall old pines.

It was strange that Wilson, so great a man, should have had so small a funeral. But then, he'd always been private. There were some literary people there — Arthur Schlesinger, Renata Adler, Morley and myself, Lillian Hellman, Jason Epstein and his wife. We stood in a loose circle on the soft sand and grass and pine needles. Rosalind, his eldest daughter, had planted his favorite flowers: a clump of ladyslippers. We waited. Then, one-by-one, couple-by-couple, the neighbors began to arrive: men with shocks of white hair drifting through the pine trees, and the priest waited, and when he was about to begin, another couple appeared, and slowly they composed an outer circle.

At last there were about thirty of us. The priest adjusted his glasses and began to read passages picked from the Knox translation of Ecclesiastes and the Psalms.

A man who had been a friend for years read a short tribute to Wilson, saying that Edmund was a religious man, that if religion meant anything, it meant his kind of spirit, his kind of devotion to the study of what was excellent in Christian and Jewish thought. With the sudden startling gesture of a medieval courtier, this elder gentleman drew away from the grave with a low bow and sweep of the arms, saying, "Shalom, Edmund." The priest went to this knees, taking the urn, and disappeared arms-first into the hole, like a bird diving for fish, his surplice falling around his shoulders, putting Wilson down into the earth. Most of us watched with that passivity that is a defense against awful melancholy.

The family, Elena, the son and two daughters, took turns at the shovel, slowly filling in the hole. There was some confusion, with no one sure of what to do, and from the children, the embarrassed little laughter you use in public to protect your private emotions.

With the sod at last set, the older neighbors, long attuned to funerals, drifted away — as unobtrusively as they had come. The family, the writers and editors, were left, and no one spoke very much. They splintered apart, yet refused to leave, as if Wilson were not a man given up easily. The priest sat by the edge of the road, staring into the long grass. I stood with Morley, farther along the road, singing quietly to him. And there was Renata Adler, walking by herself, head down, toward a patch of woods, going home alone; all of us alone, yet held together by Wilson's importance in our lives. What rare thing was it that we refused to give up? What beyond a man's life did we feel we were losing? We knew we were losing it.

Back at the house, there was a sea-bass cooked by the neighbors and some wine. Soon, we could feel the family drawing together into that protective knot for the hardest night, the first night when the body is down in the ground, and I wanted to flee, not from the memory of Wilson, or the pain of the family's loss, but from the loss itself, for I kept thinking of how Wilson had described himself in his memoir of Talcottville — disciplined, gracious, the very virtues of his old house, sitting watching the decay and demoralization of his countryside, the highway widened in front of his house to four lanes for no good reason, the old elm tree cut down to do it — the highway used only by the local young men on their motorcycles or in their cars as they sped up the road five miles and then back five miles, frenetic, making noise, showing off, frustrated and bewildered with nowhere to go, driving cars that soon would be repossessed.

That's how Wilson was for me: in a world of literary and political motor-cyclists — destructive and showboating, waiting to be re-possessed, he had been a man of integrity and faithfulness to himself — exactly what my father was — and that, after all, is the root of love, that kind of respect for oneself and others. Maybe that was what we had known was going out of our lives as we'd stood around the grave; maybe that was what the old neighbor had had in mind with his courtly bow — a rare kind of love for literature and life had gone from us and we weren't quite sure where we would find it again.

Just as we had stood alone after the burial, we would have to revive or find that integrity in ourselves. Wilson had found it in himself. Though we might have wanted to weep that he was dead, his triumph made us — made me, anyway — just a little ashamed at how little I had done; yet, at the same time, we all were encouraged by what he had achieved, encouraged to go on — *boomlay boomlay boomlay BOOM* — into the outer dark — to do more, to be true to our own best talents, obstinately, with as much grace as possible, with all energy.

Book Eight

1

*I*was in Beirut in September of 1970 to meet Ghasan Kanafani whose family had fled the town of Acre in Palestine during the 1948 war. Educated in Damascus, he had become a writer of short fiction, the editor of the Marxist newspaper *Al Hadaf,* and a strategist for the PFLP revolutionary movement. In Cairo, I had been told by President Nasser's people that Kanafani had set up the hijacking of a 747 passenger plane at Athens airport for Lella Khaled. The Lebanese army had been trying to kill Kanafani. There were armed men on the street, two bodyguards at his door. He spoke softly and was not big, not imposing. He carried an automatic jammed into his belt. We drank tea and talked about how his enemies had arms — airplanes and tanks, while he had guns.

That night, I went far up into the hills outside Beirut, passing crowded sheep pens, cowled women in dark windows, dogs fleaing themselves in the village of Door Schwein. I ate in an outdoor courtyard, knowing I had to make a radio broadcast at about two in the morning to the CBC, where Bill Ronald was the host of a network show, "As It Happens." I knew he was counting on me to give him news no one else had; he would want to know about the gun battles in Beirut and the hijacked planes in Jordan . . . three 747s had been grounded by the Palestinians and they were parked with their hostage passengers in the desert outside Amman at what the Palestinians called Revolution Airport. There was no airport. There was open desert. Hussein's Bedouin troops had tied brassieres to the long barrels of their tank guns as a sign of frustration at the King's refusal to fire on the Palestinians. I settled into a pleasant meal — *mezze* — a dozen dishes over two hours with bottles of arak (the best arak was in Lebanon because it was made by Christians), and then I was driven down into the after-midnight city to the hotel where I stretched out on my bed, the lean, louvered French doors open to the fresh night wind off the water, easefully drunk, surfeited, waiting for Bill's call, which came just before two in the morning, with Bill anxious for hard news.

"Bill," I said, "Bill, before that, let me tell you . . . you love food . . . wondrous, this city, it has all the courtesy and sensuality of the Arabs, all the élan of the French . . . "

"Barry, Barry . . . what's going to happen to those hijacked planes?"

". . . a dozen dishes, Bill . . . *baba ganouj* . . . it's a purée of broiled eggplant . . . *kofia* . . . . meat with crushed grains . . . and a beautiful *baádouni siyeh* . . . a parsley salad with sesame oil and lemon juice . . . "

"Barry, we're live, on air, they say there's going to be civil war?"

". . . brains boiled and spread on bread because the brains are so soft . . . "

"Barry — this has been awful. Good-bye."

Click.

I lay half-asleep, smiling, for a few minutes. Then I fell soundly asleep. Bill hardly spoke to me for a year.

Kanafani was in his office at the newspaper. He was slight but had presence, an intensity, not the intensity of a fanatic, but the feel of acuteness . . . a man on the edge of his nerves. He had a good nose, a moustache, and a little cleft in his chin. In fact, because of his good looks, the slightness of his build, his quick smile — he had the air of reasonableness about him. His hands were delicate, and he talked with his hands.

"If it is necessary to kill, of course we will have to kill."

"Without remorse?"

"Remorse is for when I write. Any man filled with remorse before he kills will get killed. Do you think the Israelis are filled with remorse?"

"I've met a few . . . "

"Ah yes. It is wonderful, how the Israelis can be so sorrowful for themselves over what they have done to us and not sorry for us at all."

"Well, I take your point . . . "

"But this kind of talk has nothing to do with the revolution . . . "

"Were you ever involved in killing?"

"Yes."

"Any regret?"

"Only that it was a partial success."

"Not enough died?"

"We are dying here. The Israelis are my enemy. The Lebanese are my allies. The Lebanese army is trying to kill me. Nothing is simple. It's not easy . . . "

"What?"

"Trying to be a thoughtful, reasonable man and fight for the revolution whose cause is just, not when I have to fear my friends . . . "

"So, a Palestinian . . . "

"Even among the Palestinians there are factions."

"There are guns everywhere."

"Those are guns. The Israelis have arms. Planes. But I can never be without hope. A man without hope is a dead man, walking but dead."

"You're alive."

"And walking. Come on, we'll go for a walk."

"With the bodyguards?"

"Well, it is necessary. But we cannot be afraid. Unless you are afraid."

"Of course I'm afraid."

"Quite right. You could get killed beside me. And for what? We'll stay here. Have some tea . . . "

We talked for an hour, about writers, journalists, television . . . I was puzzled, charmed, and yet wary of his detachment, his intellectual disinterestedness, his mild, even sly humor . . . as he sat discussing reporters and reporting. Was he guileless or clever, seeming to take me into his confidence?

Shatilla, one of the ugliest of the large ghetto camps in Beirut. Suddenly, we didn't know where we were, what factional lines we had crossed in the car, turning left *instead* of right. *Instead.* A dangerous word. Right. Commandos leapt up ahead of us, wagging their Kalashnikovs.

"Hit the gas," I yelled at the driver. He swerved, churning dust between donkeys and women and children, coming to a dead stop in front of four men who were about to open fire. "Mistake," I said. *Think of Sweden.* A dry laugh. With Kalashnikovs leveled, they waved us out of the car and walked me to a cinder-block jailhouse. The cell was a dank, square room behind floor-to-ceiling bars, and behind the bars, slack on the mud floor and hardly looking up, were three slumped men. Menace. I could feel menace in their eyes. The room reeked of urine and excrement in open pails. The Saqai commandos spoke no English. The prisoners spoke no English. They showed their teeth. I looked at them. They looked at me. These guys won't kill me, I thought, they'll bugger me and then kill me.

Al Saqai were the Syrian branch of the Palestinians, the least predictable of the fedayeen, the least literate, edgy, hair-triggered. After an hour, they drove me to their headquarters, an upstairs room where several men had gathered behind a table. I didn't know what to expect. I knew that there was a childlike charm to most commandos, a charm because they had been bred to extend social courtesies to each other and strangers, but also they were naïve and therefore dangerous when outraged. They believed they had been betrayed by everyone. Their sense of betrayal was matched by bravado. Amidst great lashings of language, you were safe. In a room becalmed, you were in trouble.

I was told that — along with my good friend and cameraman, Peter Davis — I was on trial as a spy. My Canadian passport aroused scorn. It was well known, they said, that Canadians were the dupes of Americans, who were Zionists, so Canadians were Zionists too. "Don't debate this with us as if we are fools. Without American money there is no Israel." For two hours I listened to four men seated at a table ask me questions in Arabic and argue among themselves in Arabic. I was charged and being tried, perhaps for my life, in a language I did not understand. I was no-man in the land of nowhere, among people who had been abandoned by all sides, people with no permanence of place — and because they had no passports — no freedom of movement themselves. Ironically, I counted on their fairness, on procedure and a recourse to reason. I kept my mouth shut. I could be shot and buried anywhere and never found, or cremated in a gasoline drum fire, ashes washed down the latrines and open drains. I stared out the one window and waited as the afternoon light turned to evening light. Silence. My silence was my best protection. Nothing offended these men more than mouthy North Americans. But I knew that if it got dark, if night fell, I might be in terrible trouble. They would feel compelled to do something decisive just to do something.

Then, one of the youngest got up and stood in front of me, staring directly into my face. He walked around me in a circle, once, and stood in front of me again. He spoke suddenly in a fine, clear English. "I was at Columbia University, yes. I've been watching you, watching your eyes watch us. You don't believe, do you, that we may kill you? Do you?"

I looked at him.

He circled me again.

"No," I said.

He circled me again.

"Why not?"

"Because my father is alive and I just realized a little while ago that I cannot imagine dying before my father dies."

"Haw," he said, and spoke to the other men. They laughed. I waited for him to speak to me again, looking to him for some opening, some line into what was going on. I decided the situation had become extreme, that they did not know what to do with me, and though there was always factional fighting, I asked them to call Kanafani. I offered them his private numbers. They stared at me. No one seemed to take note of what I had said. A boy appeared. He was carrying a tray. There was a Seven-Up bottle on the tray, opened. The lip of the bottle had a hardened orange grime around it. I was offered the drink. I took it and drank, knowing this was a test and a courtesy — to refuse the gesture because of the grime meant a refusal of the courtesy and also a refusal to share their everyday squalor. Within half an hour four men arrived, Al Saqai superiors! Intense talk went on for nearly an hour.

One of the four — who had a drooping eyelid — said to me with whispering urgency, "Our hosts would like to explain that they did not mean to frighten you, that foreigners who are friends are welcome." A man then spoke in Arabic to me. "Now," the man with the drooping eyelid said, "get up, thank them, move fast down the stairs ahead of us, we are from Kanafani and we are more scared than you are."

At the PFLP office Kanafani opened the door. He looked at me, smiled, and punched me hard in the chest, taking my breath away. "That," he said, "is for being so stupid, so reckless, that I have to send my men, risk their lives . . . "

He put out his hand. I shook it.

"I'm glad you are alive," he said.

"So am I," I said. "Though I don't know if they would have killed me. There was one guy, he spoke English . . . ?"

"Ah yes. My men have told me about him. He was the one who wanted to kill you . . . "

I spoke on the telephone to Toronto, to my executive producer, Dick Nielsen. He told me that my arrest had already been reported on national radio, that news must travel fast in Beirut. He also told me that the CBC's reporter for the national television news had refused to fly to Amman, saying the situation was too dangerous, there was going to be a civil war. (I had told

Nielsen in April that this — the civil war — was going to happen.) The reporter had been suspended. "Would you go?" he asked. "No. Are you crazy?" I hung up and went down the hall of the St. George Hotel, changed my mind, and spoke to the cameraman, Peter Davis. "Pack your bags, your stuff," I said. "There's a night plane to Amman." I sent a telegram to Nielsen.

ON MY WAY TO AMMAN STOP TAKE OUT INSURANCE ON US STOP NOT INSURED AGAINST WAR STOP TELL CLAIRE TO WIRE LANDAU IN ISRAEL I WILL ARRIVE ABOUT SEPT 19 STOP CHEERS SEND MONEY TO INTERCONTINENTAL AMMAN STOP BROKE

BARRY

After breakfast at the Amman Intercontinental Hotel, I went to the Popular Front headquarters on a street bent in behind the stone hillside ruins of the ancient Roman amphitheater. Bands of straggling men carried submachine guns up and down broken stairs between stone stumps and fluted pillars . . . loudspeakers blared martial music over the platform where Seneca and Sophocles had been staged . . . and where Medea had stalked and murdered her own children, commandos milled about . . . sullen but with a curious fey shyness, angry yet deferential. Caressing their guns.

The stores on South Street, toward the base of the cramped ruins of the amphitheater, were gaping dark holes over which a shutter was rolled down at night. The cafés were a jumble of arborite tables. The Philadelphia Hotel, by the amphitheater, was built like a barracks and was almost empty, the most recent group to perform there — a troupe of North Korean dancing girls. Children crowded along the curbs selling cartons of cigarettes, the women were thick and shapeless, their clothes drab. The only flashes of color in the street came from the commandos, green and yellow battle fatigues, red berets, flashing sports shirts (palm trees and gargantuan flowers), checkered *keffiyehs*, red-and-black, black-and-white.

They were tough and sometimes playfully dangerous men. One, as I went into the offices of the Front, wheeled me up against a wall with his Kalashnikov, the barrel under my chin, and he hoisted me onto my toes. Then he banged me on both sides of my rib cage with his barrel. He was small, wore a moustache, and had a wandering left eye: one black eye fixed on me as he banged, the other rolled loose. Trying to follow his eye, I thought I was hallucinating: his smile was ingratiating, he was hoping I would like him.

Like many commandos, he wore straight last shoes. Some wore cheap running shoes. A few were in army boots. Over three years, they had become the rag-tag cowboy cops of the streets of Amman, carrying submachine guns and grenade launchers, setting up their own roadblocks of iron sewer pipes and burning tires. Some cars and jeeps had their own "Palestinian" plates. In recent weeks particularly after the hijacking of the 747s — they had been holding the city by default, and why not, since Amman itself had become a city by default.

Before 1948, Amman had been a ramshackle town in the barren hills. Then, for more than twenty years, bedraggled bands of refugees — mostly farmers — had slumped away from the Jordan River to these slopes where they lived without work or dignity, hacking drains out of the harsh rubble, using open holes for toilets, hauling water for miles, broiling in their tents during the day, freezing in the wind and rain at night, raising up homes of cinder block, tin, canvas — spreading across the hills — slowly, and not by design, building the city.

Golda Meir said they did not exist. Not as a people. As a terrorist rabble, yes; as rootless spawn, yes; as cowards, yes. But she said they did not have the generations to be a people: the begat who begat who begat who begat . . . they were nobodies from nowhere . . . they did not go back by pronouncement in books to the misbegotten of Abram or the begotten of Moses who, for forty years had been on the march just around the corner from Amman in the Sinai . . . Moses, that was his story. But you can walk across the Sinai in two days, at most three. Forty years! What was he doing out there for forty years? Entering history. But why — in all the records of the greatest record-keepers of the time, the Egyptians — is there not one mention of Moses and his men and women? Didn't they exist? They did not. Not for the Egyptians, not as a people. Perhaps they, too, were invisible because they wore pointed shoes, camouflage pants and Hawaiian shirts. Who knows? Men who are good at counting the generations of families and angels on the heads of pins know. And theirs is an art not to be lightly dismissed. *One begat, two begat, three begat, four* . . . Men have died for miscounting the *begats*. And the potatoes. But whether the Palestinians are a "people" or not — in Golda Meir's nineteenth century use of "people" — there they were . . . forged by 1948, 1956, 1967 . . . begot by the Israelis, crowded into the amphitheater.

Kanafani said hello, wryly amused to see me. I was astonished to see him. His automatic was in his belt.

"Is it going to happen?"

"If you stay," he said, "you may get killed."

"So it's going to happen"

"For sure."

We drank glasses of tea.

2

Bassam, slender, compact, with black hair, soft black eyes (he would later lose an eye to a letter bomb sent to him by the Israelis, as the Israelis would eventually kill Kanafani, blowing him — and his niece — up in a car in Beirut), smoked a cigarette as we sat next door to Kanafani's office, a Kalashnikov between us on the table.

"Looking at the history of the Palestinians over the last twenty-two years, the position they find themselves in, disowned, forgotten by the West, disowned by most of the Arab governments, what you've developed here is a philosophy you associate with Marxism, but the real driving force is despair. That is, you have no place to go . . . "

"Well . . . "

"And even the skyjackings, these are desperate, desperate measures . . . "

"Well, I don't deny that this factor plays a role, but nevertheless the major point is exploitation. And this is the pivot of Marxism. We are fighting exploitation. Marxism is the philosophy of the exploited. Marxism is the philosophy of the . . . "

We paused. Looked. Startled, an incoming harsh rending of the outside air overhead, incredulous at the roar of a jet pressing down, pressing and crashing the calm. We fell to the floor — the plane leaving a drone and then a hiss of air escaping, as Bassam unruffled sat up and said, "The Israelis . . . No, he won't come back."

"Listen, I just had a thought," I said, picking up the Kalashnikov, "this is no damn good at all . . . " and we both laughed, "not against those things. Was he awfully low?"

"Yes, he was low. That was, you know, just a salute."

"A salute, eh?"

"Yes, we know you're there . . . okay."

"Okay."

"We're accustomed to that."

"Well, we were talking about the— "

"The exploited in this world . . . "

"And that Marxism," he said, "is really the philosophy of the exploited, everywhere."

We drove through the dark back alleys with a man known to me only as Ibrahim. Commando patrols crouched around small fires at road blocks. Our old Citröen, driven by Ibrahim, hardly gained the steep, stone-paved alleys of the hills. Ibrahim, always slow-moving and seemingly indolent, sped through the commando posts. Almost unknown outside the Party, he had directed the Front through the hijackings, the hostage negotiations and the conflicts with other Palestinian factions. Silent and impassive behind dark glasses, he went unnoticed by newsmen.

Inside a closely guarded courtyard, Bassam led us up narrow concrete stairs. As in all the refugee camps, the sour clinging smell of urine was in the air. At the head of the stairs there was a large frame on the wall with many photographs, like an assembly of graduating college students, lit by a kerosene lamp, the dead commandos from the camp (children in the camps spoke of the lives of the martyrs as I had spoken of the lives of the saints in grade school: those who had chosen the sweet light of death rather than the dark of compromise and betrayal).

Ibrahim, long delicate fingers, lean and olive-skinned with a razor moustache, sat in a wicker chair, and with weary lassitude his legs began to flap apart and together like the wings of an awkward somnolent bird, his right arm limp to the floor, his right hand working amber worry beads. He did not listen to me or Bassam. He leaned back, legs flapping, his dark head resting on the back of his chair, and he had a curious serenity about him, a sculpted calmness, the calm of a man seduced by inevitability aware of us only as shadows on the map in his mind of what was about to take place in Amman.

Bassam asked for tea. It came, served by an old woman cowled in black, and it was sweet. She also brought bread drizzled with olive oil and sprinkled with *za'tar*, a spice made from sesame, thyme and sumac. Bassam, married to Lela Khaled — the striking young woman who had hijacked a passenger plane at Athens airport — Columbia-educated and not unaware of the effectiveness of emblematic stories — explained: "It was the battle of Karameh that had such mythic importance for us. It was March of 1968 and they came with their armored brigade to wipe out the Karameh base, but the fedayeen, the men of sacrifice, did not run. Many tied explosives to their bodies and threw themselves into the Israeli tanks, and others carrying explosives lay down in the path of the tanks and blew them up. The Israelis like to strike fast and then clear out but our men had blown the bridges and the fedayeen stood and fought and killed themselves to kill the Israelis. We took heavy losses and the

Israelis destroyed the camp of Karameh, but for the first time they lost hundreds and the Israelis do not like to lose one man . . . Here it is the King's generals who have decided. It must be now. So, let it be. We can afford deaths. The King's men, like the Israelis, can afford very few. You will see. The masses will win."

He lifted his glass of tea in the liverish kerosene light.

The next day, in the early evening, Kanafani at the Front headquarters said, "It has begun. Get out. Get out. If you stay you will be killed. It begins any moment and you will be killed."

I didn't get out. I went to the hotel.

Dawn in the desert mountains, a dry wind hissing like a fuse through the twelve hills of Amman, no other sound except a howl and the barking of dogs, a long long long silence and then the arid rattle of automatic rifle fire and the rolling thud of artillery and in the after-silence cocks crowed. This was it. No looking back. No remorse. Across the road from the hotel, commandos, their heads wrapped in *keffiyehs*, passed like shadows into the stone and the concrete shell of a building and set up a gun site. For days commandos had ridden through the city in jeeps and panel trucks perched behind .50 calibre machine guns, defiant, abrasive. Day after day. A pulse. *Boom, Boom.* A child had stood on a downtown corner beating a bass drum. A pulse, *clickety clack,* and men with a strange languorous ease draped themselves over their guns, parading in the scorching sun in their camouflage suits, determined to be seen as invisible, ready to erupt to the boom boom beat of a Lion's Club drum.

The hills, rust-brown and maroon and an ivory rubble, were an echo chamber, shots caromed across the valley. Between bursts of fire, a distant, faint wailing sound, like hundreds of women keening — it was the hysterical screeching of the hens of Amman laying eggs. A muezzin in a minaret made his call to prayer.

Third day. There was a Palestinian spotter in one of the hotel rooms. Under dusk, four troop trucks of Bedouin infantry parked by a row of trees and a stone wall. Within two minutes mortars from Nazzal Hill blew out the yard beside them. The Bedouin heavy-gunner reeled and pumped jackhammer rounds into the hotel. They tore a four-foot-wide hole in the bathroom. I was pinned to the floor. (A Swede had been shot in the leg, a Russian reporter between the eyes.) If I had thought that death could only come in sanctioned ways, I was wrong. Insanely, lying on my belly, I remembered a sweet orange Amichai had given me and the Amichai poem I had read to Saya in New York as we parted: *They are all engineers. All of them. A pity. We were such a good and loving invention. An airplane . . . wings and everything. We hovered a little above the earth. We even flew a little,* flew the way I used to bend over, arms outspread, and run with my son on my back, flying with my son, Michael. Mischi. *Absalom, Absalom,* my son. No, no, that was my father calling to me . . . when he wrote letters he always called to me that way. I had written back: Call me Ismael. I knew Ismael couldn't die. He was in the outer dark. The desert. Condemned to it. That was history, too. And Morley was still alive. I could not die while Morley was alive. I waited for the night and hauled my mattress into the hallway.

If I'd called Pinky Boland, would his pajama bottoms have fallen down again?

But of course I couldn't call.

No electricity, no water. No candles in the rooms. The Bedouins and commandos would shoot to kill. I closed myself into a bathroom with a candle and a typewriter. Nearly choked on the smoke after an hour. Crept on my belly to the balcony, the red fires in the camps and on the hills, bleeding. Red tracers like red cinders streaked across the sky. A phosphorous shell exploded on the rooftop of a large house on Ashrafya Hill . . . searing light and then luminous smoke. Heavy machine guns scatter-blasted the walls, the house came alive, a tortured face, hollowed eyes, a gaping mouth; hollow laughter, gyring, that swallowed the incessant thudding of mortar fire.

Short-wave radios spluttered . . . lost connections ricocheting along the corridors of the hotel, this was now known as the Black September war, the Fatah radio, earnest, militant, playing Victorian martial music and they announced that the commandos in this war had destroyed twenty-one tanks on the Webda Road but I had seen the Webda Road. It was clear. The army radio proclaimed that the commandos had been driven into their camps. But the commandos were shelling the American embassy on Webda Hill and controlled the traffic circle south of the hotel. *Liar, liar, pants on fire.* Perhaps neither knew the truth. Voices crackled in the darkness, *pants on fire, pants on fire,* the echoing thud of mortar fire shaking the hotel, *shumpf shumpf* sound of giant footsteps trailing into the distance, BOOM, as the houseboy in the hotel sitting on his haunches whispered, "The time of the fedayeen is of the night."

The Bedouins were riding their machine guns like jockeys, the bullets clawing the stone houses, showering orange sparks into the air, wooden awnings raked to pieces. A pocket of silence. Machine guns in the distance, a steady *chug-chugging,* the pumping of death's plunger. The Bedouins mounted a mortar position beside the hotel, and a 105 Howitzer rocket rifle on a jeep truck, the Howitzer barrel long and obscene in its thin insect hardness, its recoils a concussion cast through all the surrounding houses and the hotel. Windows shattered. The army was shelling the five-story insane asylum on Webda Hill, one pounding eruption after another. Trees fell. A body spun like a rag doll from the roof. Or maybe it was a rag doll, a madman's toy, the insane trapped inside, huddled along the walls of their corridors, calm, unruffled, talking for the first time of the good old days that had been long forgotten, suddenly at ease with themselves, the thunder of the outside world matching the thunder inside their heads, knowing for sure what they had known all along, that they were sane. Hysterical hens, eggs, eggs, more eggs, commando bodies, embers, glowing beside their burial ornaments, brass shell casings, and Ibrahim, seated in a sculpted calm, finally went to sleep.

Churchill boasted that he had created the Emirate of Transjordan "one afternoon in Cairo." In 1920, Field Marshall Abdullah had set out for the desert town of Moab with two thousand Bedouin tribesmen. He'd told the British he intended to seize the area and to march on Damascus, the center of French influence. By March of 1921 he had occupied the whole of British Transjordan. Four months later, the British accepted his *fait accompli,* on condition that he recognize the British Mandate and renounce his intention of invading Syria. The shrewd Abdullah agreed. He wasn't crazy. He had never intended to invade Damascus. The British gave Abdullah Transjordan to keep him out of a country he could not have entered. Suddenly, Abdullah was Abdullah of Amman, there was a Hashemite throne. If the Arabs said Israel was an artificial nation, then what was Transjordan and what was the Hashemite throne? Churchill had another cigar. And when the Black September was over, Hussein the Hashemite King said: "As for the sea of blood, it was not of my making and not my wish . . . "

At the bottom of the hill, four floors beneath my bedroom window, a building erupted in flames, the roof caved in. The Bedouins said we had fifteen minutes to get out of the hotel . . . the commandos were attacking . . . an old bus would be at the shattered front door . . . we could stay and take our chances or they would try to drive the bus safely through the hills (held by Palestinian gunposts) to the airport, where a call had been made for a Red Cross plane . . .

We crowded into the "tin coffin on wheels" and white shirts were hung out open windows from either side . . . red crosses smeared on the cotton . . . and the old bus wheezed as we inched up an incline into the gap in the mountains . . .

utterly defenseless . . . and everyone was brave until someone began to say a prayer and then several men began to shake and mewl as we drove slowly through the pass to the airport, and at last to the runway. No one had fired, but there was no plane. There was no food. No water. We hunkered down for a sleepless night in the glass-walled airport, watching armored cars and tanks wheel past . . .

In the morning, a Red Cross cargo plane landed and took us to Beirut, to phone calls, to food too rich to eat, to a flight home.

3

I lay in Claire's bed dreaming of when I was a child when it snowed for three days. The schools were closed. I stayed at home. The snow was piled nine feet high along the roads. On the third day, I began to tunnel into the snow in front of the houses, carving out corridors, smoothing the walls of the corridors so that they had an icy crust. It kept snowing. My mother noticed a flashlight was missing. I told her it was dark in the snow. She was horrified.

"You've tunneled into all that," she said, standing at the opening, a little round dark mouth, "it could have collapsed on you, suffocated you."

In my dream, I told her I had been in God's mind in the cold corridors in the snow.

Wrapped in a bedsheet, in Claire's apartment in Rosedale, I broke into cold sweats, hearing the screeching of hens and remembering the hysterical houseboy who had tried to masturbate in the shadows after six sleepless nights and failed, too weak. My mother stood looking down at me. She tried to laugh. She sang *Went down to St. James Infirmary, saw my baby there, stretched out on a long white table* . . . The elevator door *thudded* down the hall. BOOM, I jumped as if a mortar had gone off. I stared out the window at the ravine slope and played a one-hour audio tape of non-stop gunfire over and over. I had my own *clickety clack*. The gunfire soothed me *quaquaquaqua* and I called it God's drum solo and whether he was on the 2-4 or the 1-3, he never lost the beat *boom boom boom boom Boomlay*.

I returned to lecturing at the university, manic, and without giving any warning to my class, I performed the whole of Act One of *Waiting for Godot*, chanting Lucky's speech: "Given the existence as uttered forth in the public works of Puncher and Wattmann of a personal God *quaquaquaqua* with white beard *quaquaquaqua* outside time without extension who from the heights of divine apathia . . . " and told Claire that every evening I heard the sound of chalk, a stub of chalk writing on the wall . . .

"Chalk is how they marked the medieval houses of the plague," I said.

"You need a drink," she said.

> *I drink to keep from worrying,*
> *And I smile just to keep from crying.*

Muddy Waters met me at the elevator door and took my hand and said: "These the shank hours, man, these are the shank of the morning," the lilt of the churched and once sanctified in his tone. He smiled, satisfied that he had pronounced a truth.

He had conked hair. Straight up. We went into the room where he sat apart from his sidemen, who were scrunched together on two soiled sofas in the Jarvis Street hotel. They were drinking bar booze. He was drinking Chivas. Brownie and Sonny, beside the window, were seated on low stools.

"You bad," Otis Spann said.

"I ain't bad as Jesse James," Pee Wee Madison, the guitarist, said.

"Lil Son Jackson," James Cotton said, "he carry a black cat bone in his pocket . . . "

"And he die too one day," Otis said.

"He die one night, seven stab wounds in his back," Muddy said, "a seventh son, he was a son-of-a-gun . . . "

Everybody laughed.

Brownie, his good foot hooked behind his cripple boot, said, "River, what you doing?"

Sonny sat hunched forward on his stool.

"River," Brownie called again — because he and Sonny had named each other River — and Sonny answered, "Yeah, what you want, River?"

"Rivers don't die," Brownie said, "they heal."

"I can't swim," Sonny said.

Muddy sat back, posed, like an old, pomaded church warden listening to the cryptic gospel of the cotton fields, sporting houses, jails and juke-joints. Cotton sang out:

> O they 'ccused me of murder and
> I haven't harmed a man.

He had a round freckled face. Cotton blew his harp.

Sonny listened, impassive. He sat running his hands over the eight pockets sewn across the front of his shirt, narrow slots for his Hohner harmonicas. Brownie, always alert — a cross-wiring of gaiety and defiance — jabbed the neck of his guitar straight up in the air and smacked the apron with the palm of his hand, saying, "The night JFK was shot and killed, I pulled into a gasoline station and the gasman leans his head in my window and he says, 'I don't serve no black gas' and ever since I wonder why people drinks their coffee black."

Sonny whipped his C harp from a pocket just below his chin, cupping the harp in his huge hands. He sent out a wailing sound, a country train-in-the-night cry, and then he let out a falsetto *whoop* . . .

Cotton blew hard. He was used to always having a microphone. He grinned impishly at Sonny, forgetting that Sonny couldn't see his grin, and he blew harder and harder, but suddenly Sonny said, "You playing in my face, man?"

"I'm doing my thing, Sonny."

Sonny let out a *whoop*. He didn't need a microphone.

He blew. He blew *fox chase*.

He made his harp sound like a mewling child and a lost hound and a fretting woman and a lonesome train, blowing so loud that Cotton put his harp down. "You going to blow my tree down, man."

Sonny shot his massive hand out, saying ". . . Seeing is believing, that what they say, man . . . "

He let out a loud Haw!

As we left, Sonny said to me in the hallway: "Man, I lost my wife. She died. I got back and they tried to put a derby hat on my head for the funeral, but I said that that derby hat was slavery times, and the undertaker, he had a plot for me, too, and I said, Fill it over man, 'cause I ain't about to die, and when I do you can toss me in the river. I don't care. I'm too busy living.'"

4

The 1970 October Crisis broke in Québec: a British Trade Commissioner had been kidnapped by *separatistes,* a small FLQ cell. National War Measures were declared . . . *to apprehend an insurrection.* There was no insurrection, there was absolutely no insurrection, *liar, liar, pants on fire* but all civil rights were suspended, *all,* and the police had prepared lists, lists, *We have lists,* the Montreal police chief said, and the knock on the door came in the night, arrests were made in the night. The portly, bluff premier of Ontario, Mr. Robarts, said that the nation was in a state of war. *War!* This was a kidnapping.

Pundits like Peter C. Newman said the country had lost its innocence.

Not at all. The politicians, the police and the pundits behaved like innocents.

War!

Trudeau went on television to justify the Act. He was persuasive. He didn't sound like himself: he sounded like Bishop Fulton J. Sheen. . . the old Jesuit in him had come through.

quaquaquaqua

Claire and I made love through the whole speech.

An admirer of my father's work, who had been awarded the *Croix de Guerre* as a tank commander, said, "Just give us half a chance, we'll go and blow those flatulent frogs to smithereens." He had a certain turn of phrase, being a master of Latin prosody.

After my short films on Egypt, the Palestinians, and the Black September war were broadcast, several rabbis asked for a private screening to "monitor the fairness." Barbara Frum stopped me on the street and said, "I just wanted you to know that I defended you before the rabbis, but I have to tell you, the weight was all wrong . . . "

"But this was the first time the network treated Egypt as Egypt and the Palestinians as Palestinians, not the Arab world . . . "

Looking wounded, she walked away, saying, "I just wanted you to know that I told them you had been fair."

"Why did you have to tell them anything?"

I started tunneling down corridors of silence, keeping my eye peeled for Houdini . . .

Morley compiled a list of writers who supported the knock on the door in the night, the War Measures Act. *F.R. Scott, Irving Layton, Hugh MacLennan* . . .

We intoned the names:

> *Hinge of silence, Scott,*
> > *Creak for us*
> *Rose of darkness, Layton,*
> > *Unfold for us*
> *Wood anemone, MacLennan,*
> > *Sway for us . . .*

A sardonic joke. We lost the list. Morley debated Mr. Justice Samuel Freedman on television — Freedman supported the Act. Morley said the government had no justifiable cause in law and had panicked and the next day he was attacked in Parliament as if he were a traitor.

I tried to talk to Knowlton Nash at a cocktail party in The Four Seasons about the Palestinians, how it was not a matter of pro or con . . . they were in the lynch-pin position, they had to be seen for who they were . . . a people in the process of becoming, multiplying in the night, and also . . . the Israelis were the only conquerors I knew of who continued to see themselves as conquered.

He looked weary. I suppose because he hadn't read anything on the wire services that matched what I was saying to him, so how could what I was saying be true?.

Perhaps a subscription to I.F. Stone's *Weekly* . . .

Or *Le Monde* . . .

But Golda Meir was coming to town.

I warned Dick Nielsen that an interview with her could be trouble. She allowed no rebuttal. I had recently watched her reduce the reporter Leslie Stahl to compliant silence in New York.

"You'll do great," Nielsen said.

I took his word for it.

I was about to go dockwalking.

5

"It's not the worst, I know."

"What?"

"To have thought."

"Obviously."

"But we could have done without it."
"Que voulez-vous?"
"I beg your pardon?"
"Que voulez-vous?"
"Ah! Que voulez-vous. Exactly."

SAMUEL BECKETT

We met on her turf, a temple in north Toronto. Her handlers milled about. They had asked for this encounter. To counter the program on the Palestinians. As I stood waiting in the darkness behind the lights, I kept thinking, This would be perfect for Bisi . . . dolled up in his knickers, taking everybody's picture . . . but no film. NO FILM. And everybody would go berserk because all that mattered was the film. But *of course* there was no film. This was being recorded, primed for instant editing in downtown control rooms.

Such is life, at least live to tape on television.

Meir wore black, a black suit, a collarless blouse of black, with a necklace of white beads. Her back-lit, frizzy iron-gray hair pulled into a bun, had a luminosity. When she talked, she wagged her left hand, her head moved, nothing else moved. She was solid. Her eyes were hard, evaluative — plainly, with a little pout to her mouth — she was sizing me up so that I could see she was sizing me up.

"I asked you last year in Jerusalem," I said, "whether or not you'd ever be prepared to negotiate with the leaders of the Palestinian commandos and you gave me a very firm No. Have you changed your position at all?"

"No. It doesn't make any difference what you call them, you call them commandos, or guerrillas, whatever you call them, they're terrorists and their aim is to kill every Jew just because he is a Jew, certainly every Jewish Israeli, but also any Jew anywhere else...If something happens in Jordan and Arafat is the head of the Jordanian state, and he wants to call that Palestine, as a head of state I will deal with him. As head of a terrorist group that is out to kill Israeli men, women, and children, I will not deal with him."

"But of course," I said, "they insist that they are not out to kill Israelis —"

"Pardon me . . . "

"— just as Israelis. That this is a war of liberation."

"Anyone that kills, it doesn't make a particle of difference to me what label he puts on it . . . "

"The fact is the Palestinians in Jordan, now, think of themselves as a people, think of themselves as a nation . . . "

"In Jordan? Wonderful . . . "

"And they now represent a military and political force, and a disruptive one, and it seems to me that what you're saying is that unless the Palestinians successfully take over power in Jordan they're simply going to be out there, on the loose . . . "

"They can do whatever they wish to do, except one thing, and that's what they want to do, to take Israel away to themselves, and drive us out. That they can't. We won't let them. If the people of Jordan will consent that Arafat is their head of state, as a head of state we will deal with him . . . "

"But what if his policy then is exactly the same as his policy now?"

"So, we won't deal with him. I mean, you're asking peculiar questions . . . "

"I don't know that they're so peculiar. You won't talk to him now but you will talk to him then, but if he states the same position you won't talk to him . . . "

"Israel is not accommodating, it is as simple as all that."

"You don't think there is any kind of manoeuvre, politically, that you could go through —"

"There can be no —"

"— to head off a final confrontation."

"Final confrontation! With Fatah . . . Nothing could be worse than '67. You think that Arafat is stronger than Nasser was in 1967? That he has a bigger army than Nasser had, more equipment than Nasser had?"

"I'm not thinking of the possibility of a Six Day War, I'm thinking of a war that might go on for twenty or even thirty years with those people . . . "

"You're a young man." She did not mean it as a compliment. "You'll be around in twenty or thirty years. I'm sure that in twenty years people will have forgotten there was anything like this . . . "

Pause.

"Well, let's turn to Egypt. Do you believe that the Egyptians want peace at this stage?"

"It's difficult to answer in the affirmative. The Egyptians do not work on their own. They have a big partnership. The question is, do the Soviets want peace?"

"Do you believe that the Soviets want peace."

"No."

"Do you believe the Egyptians can act independently of the Soviets?"

"With difficulty."

"Do you think they can though?"

"I don't know."

"If they find the moral strength?"

"If they find the moral strength they can do everything."

"There are Egyptians who tell me that they have the moral strength . . . "

Her eyebrows went up. "Are these Egyptians in power?"

"Some of them are. Yes."

"Then they're not intellectuals."

"Yes. They are."

"Oh . . . then they're both intellectuals *and* in power . . . !"

"Yes. Intellectuals and in power."

"Good."

"The same as in Israel," I said sarcastically.

She gave me a scoffing smile and said, "Exactly."

"Now, the position that some of those men have put to me is – and they want peace, for them, peace is a given — they want out of the war."

"I'm sure they do, many Egyptians want peace . . . But I will never negotiate with anybody who beforehand is somebody I cannot trust."

"If the Egyptians say to you that they now want to negotiate for peace, what is your position?"

"We won't negotiate for peace with anybody, or state, who has proven that it violates any agreement . . . Let me ask you something. Supposing in our negotiations we agree to step back from the Suez Canal. This is something tangible, isn't it?"

"That's right."

"We say to the Egyptians, look, we're going to step back as soon as we sign this agreement. You come in, we're out, the Egyptians have received something very tangible. What have we received instead?"

"Presumably peace."

"What do you mean peace? They've signed an agreement that there will be peace. Who is prepared to guarantee that this signature, that this agreement, that this promise, is going to be honored more than the promise we now have for cease-fire?"

"What you're saying to me is you never can trust the Egyptians in terms of any cease-fire."

"No, I didn't say that."

"That's the implication."

"No implications. Please. Just what I'm saying. I'm saying that the Egyptians in the first place have to live up to agreements that they make. If they make an agreement that there should be no missiles brought into that area, then they have to take those missiles out and we start afresh."

"But the Egyptian position, as it has been explained to me, is that they start afresh as complete losers, with no strength."

"Then," she said with finality, "they shouldn't agree."

"If anything goes wrong you can move right in and strike them."

"Then — they should not agree."

The conversation was over. Head lowered, she gave me a look, grim. I stared at her big black shoes. She leaned forward, "I've never had an interview like this in my life."

"You should have more of them," I snapped.

"Schmuck," she said and stood up among her handlers. One breathed into my face, "How do you like getting smacked in the mouth by an old lady?"

"I don't see any blood," I said.

But I was totally taken aback. I had never in my life been looked in the eye as if I were a fool *and* scum.

The bleeding had begun.

In the control room our conversation was edited to the above eight-and-a-half minutes and then it went on the air.

I went off the end of the dock.

But before I describe my night of the dark waters, there are matters of history to consider, and that is — the way what we had talked about actually worked out: the intellectuals of some power in Cairo in 1970 were Muhammed Heikal, the editor of *Al Ahram*, special advisor to Nasser, and then to Sadat; Clovis Maksud, who, under Sadat, became special ambassador of the Arab League to the United Nations; Tashin Bashir, who became advisor to Sadat and Ambassador to Canada. It was, in fact, Sadat who shed the Soviets and seized the moral initiative by going to Jerusalem, an initiative that ushered in a peace that has held. As for the Palestinians, after twenty-five years of a fruitless war of attrition, after years of *intifadah*, people have not "forgotten there was anything like this"; Arafat is still not head of a state, but Rabin and Peres finally came to understand that they had to deal with him, in Oslo and Washington, and Netanyahu — step-dancer in the shoes of Shamir and Begin — will have to deal, too.

The water at the end of the dock was cold, and it got darker.

As soon as the interview was broadcast, Eugene Hallman, the CBC's Toronto-based head of English-network TV, sent a telegram of apology to the ambassador of Israel in Ottawa (his action must be seen in context: Hallman, a few months earlier during the War Measures crisis, postponed a documentary called *The Legacy of Lenin* — presumably because he feared any broadcast reference to revolution — and ordered the removal of a song from our program "Weekend" by the Québécois singer, Pauline Julien, presumably because she was a *separatiste*. He also canceled a documentary that dealt with the Hollywood Ten, those writers who were black-listed during the anti-communist hysteria of the 1950s — deciding that the country should not be told about a campaign of indiscriminate smear while civil rights were being suspended across the country and arrests were being made in the Montreal night and reputations impugned. None of this was new to Hallman. He had shown who he was early on, having canceled an exclusive radio interview with Fidel Castro just before Castro captured Havana. Why? Because Batista's ambassador in Ottawa had complained).

Morley was enraged by Hallman's action. He sent telegrams to Pierre Trudeau and Paul Martin, saying it was an insult to all citizens that the nation's news gathering network should apologize to a foreign government for a conversational exchange over political policy.

He discovered that the President of the CBC had also apologized. He got no reply from Trudeau or Martin.

The public response, soon known to the CBC, was revealing. The mail and phone calls broke down clearly. There were expressions of outrage from the Jewish communities in Toronto and Montreal, but "a very high enjoyment index from across the rest of the country — a 90." Letters from Montreal and Toronto spoke of the "indecency of allowing that man to scream at a distinguished woman on television," but our voices had *never* risen above a low monotone of rectitude (again, I am thankful for recordings and transcripts). There had certainly been an intensity, but it was the intensity of a capped skepticism meeting controlled derision.

My phone rang.

Men and women I had thought of as friends — the art patrons, Jesse and Percy Waxer (brother to my bookie) — forbade me to enter their houses.

But Ruby Waxer continued to take my bets and share an ice cream with me at Diana Sweets.

Then Kosso, my sculptor-friend, astounded me: "Please," he said, "don't let what the Jews are doing to you turn you into an anti-Semite."

He stopped inviting me to his apartment for social occasions: as an Israeli, his clients were Jewish land developers.

A man walked up to me on the street and spat on my coat.

Claire lunched with a long-time friend who righteously dumped soup in her lap, condemning her for living with me.

Albert Franck, the painter, stepped out of his *vernisage* at Moos Gallery. "At last somebody called that old bully's bluff," he said.

"Haw," I said.

"I guess you won't be coming in," he said ruefully, turning back toward his patrons.

"I guess not."

I no longer had long conversations about programming with Nielsen on the telephone.

I continued to make short films, about J. Edgar Hoover, American prisoners in Hanoi, the massacre at My Lai and the use of 2-4-5-T in the Vietnam jungles.

Silences set in.

I was exploring the ethics of silence.

I was teaching a course in post-concentration-camp literature.

Auschwitz and the Gulag.

Given what was said in those eight-and-a-half minutes, the consequent anger, the virulence is astonishing. Fifteen years later, when I tried to describe what happened to me to Yehuda Amichai, he turned aside in disbelief, as if I had been out in the sun too long, hallucinating.

"This Golda . . . Golda," he said, "good riddance."

Haw! Easy for him to say.

I had begun my public life as a commentator on CBC morning radio, and I had appeared regularly for eight years. I was cancelled. I have never appeared as a political commentator again.

At the *Telegram* I suddenly came up lame in the water. As the Books editor, I had written for the pages for more than five years. John Bassett, the publisher — an avowed Zionist — had never said a critical word to me; in fact, he had only offered me encouragement. But his editors were another matter. Trying to get me out, an entertainment editor accused me of embezzlement. After going through the financial books, J.D. Macfarlane told me I had three choices: he could post a bill in the newsroom saying I was not an embezzler; I could punch the editor in the head; I could let it pass. "I told you at the beginning," he said, "you're the right talent in the wrong place."

"That's what Morley told me way back when."

"Let it pass," he said.

I did.

Then the managing editor, Doug Creighton, sent me a memo: he said my salary and the cost of the book reviews each week were too much for the paper to bear. He proposed that my salary — $10,000 — be used to pay reviewers, that the pages be taken over editorially by a staffer, and that I be paid $75 for a weekly column. It was an offer I could only refuse.

I went to see J.D. Macfarlane in his office. I had developed great respect for him, even a perverse kind of affection. I showed him the memo. "You know about this?" I asked.

"No," he said.

"Didn't think you did," I said. "Not your style."

I wrote my letter of resignation.

With the exception of one article commissioned by *Saturday Night* magazine in 1972, I was not asked to write for a magazine again until 1976, and never again asked to write as a commentator or columnist for a newspaper.

I argued with Nielsen, argued about his repeated use of Malcolm Muggeridge and his use of Doug Collins, a west coast columnist whose politics were far right of a sting ray. Nielsen was not the man I'd gone to work for; I was not the man he'd hoped to work with.

6

As these months passed, Morley began to work on a novel about an older writer who had been praised abroad but demeaned at home. He was going to have some serious fun: he was going to run himself and a few reputations up the flagpole in what was going to be a *memoir*, not of his actual life, but his imaginative presence, its shapes, its form. "I've looked," he told me, "into the inner darknesses, I've even tried to look into the eye of the light. There is only one truth. Form. Everything has its form. Why a butterfly is a butterfly and a bee a bee I don't know, but they can't be anything other than what they are. We get born and become who we are. Call it temperament. It's as if we had maps in our brain cells, and some of us are map readers and some of us just wake up one morning to discover where we've been. But the map is the map. Some are more obvious maps than others. That's what they'd say in the movies in the forties, you know, looking at some ugly killer's face — 'You got an ugly map.'"

In this *roman à clef,* as in all his novels, it would be the criminals and saints who would be the stiltwalkers, the men and women who always held his sympathy — striding through crowds of timorous men and women sticking their wet fingers up in the wind to see which way the wind was blowing. His heart, he liked to say, lay with "such people, who are a little outside the circle of approval on this earth . . . people who can't be approved of but who have somehow a quality of warmth in them that almost shocks us . . . A prostitute may be the servant of God in her own strange fashion, just like Anatole France's story of the Juggler of Notre Dame . . . he didn't know how to pray to Our Lady but he knew how to juggle little balls so he got out in front of the altar and juggled . . . "

I couldn't juggle worth a damn.

I began to wonder how deep the water was at the end of the dock.

Did I have my water-wings?

I heard a splash.

My brother was in beside me.

The CBC had hired John Crawford, a "head hunter," to find the right man for the times to take over public relations for the English-language television network. The "head hunter" — after reviewing dozens of candidates, presented the CBC with his choice — my brother, Michael — impressed by the fact that Michael was not only a man of acute perceptions, but he was producing, as they spoke, short television documentaries of quality. He had gone into television after a superb stint as Assistant to the President of MacLaren Advertising, the largest company in the country. Michael met with the committee, which was in the hands of Eugene Hallman and an assistant, Peter Herrndorf. After about fifteen minutes of energetic discussion about television, its role, its possibilities, Hallman blurted out, "Mr. Callaghan, I'd like to know from a public relations point of view how you would have handled the response of the Canadian Jewish Congress to your brother's interview with Golda Meir?"

Michael, taken aback for a moment, said, "I think I would have been less precipitous, I would have waited a day to see what the rest of the country seemed to feel."

The meeting ended.

Michael did not get the job.

My mother and father seethed with rage. But they kept their silence. "Should I wait thirty years?" I asked my mother. It was the only time she glowered at me. "Think Fackenheim," I said.

But the bottom was yet to come.

There was the blow.

I can only think of it as the blow.

I had been teaching full time at Atkinson College, York University, since the September that I had started writing my weekly column at the *Telegram*. I loved Atkinson. It was modeled on London, England's Birckbeck College, founded in 1823, serving adult students with a full time faculty.

I got a phone call from a philosophy professor, Howard Adelman. He was Associate Dean and, he told me, he was Chairman of the initiating Tenure and Promotion Committee in my college. Would I come in at nine in the morning to defend myself?

"Against what?"

"You've been put forward for tenure and before being turned down one of our members insisted that you be interviewed."

"I didn't ask to go forward."

"You were put forward."

I phoned a man I hardly knew, the Dean, Harry Crowe. He said he didn't understand what was going on, and he'd meet me at the committee room in the morning. "Howard's a good friend of mine, he'll understand," the Dean said.

"Beware good friends who understand," my father said.

In the morning, the Dean went into the room and sat down. Adelman looked surprised. "Harry," he said, "you have no standing on this committee. No vote."

"I know," the Dean said, "but I just wanted you all to understand where I'd vote if I had standing and I'd vote for Callaghan's tenure."

He left.

Silence.

One of the committee members began to eat an apple.

He ate it down to the core. In silence. Except for his chomping.

I listened to Adelman belittle and demean everything I had written over six years, dismissing it as "mere journalism" and "intellectual entertainment." Though I was supposed to be a good teacher, my classes, he said, "were in disarray, sidetracked by politics . . . and one class, according to a teaching assistant, Levine, was in open revolt."

"That's a lie," I said.

"Let's find out if it's a lie," John Unrau said. He was the man who had insisted on the interview.

I learned later that a man in our small department had played a key role in the move against me. This was the blow. I couldn't believe it.

"His wife's a fierce Zionist," I was told.

Then Unrau let me know that he had been instructed at an early meeting of the committee by two members, Kater and Carter, that although Adelman was going to be out of town, he had made it clear that I was to be denied tenure.

The department tore itself open, as only family can.

Matthew Ahern, professor, was the keeper of six German shepherds. (The mother and father were called Cathy and Heathcliffe, and the growing pups were named after characters in Jacobean revenge tragedies: Bassanes, Crotolon, Castruccio, Cariola.) Ahern had a rack of ten guns on his farm and threatened to feed the kidneys of several men to his dogs.

I was charmed: he was not your everyday academic. (An American, he had taken a year's leave of absence without pay in 1968 to go home to the States to run in primaries as an Independent against "that Nazi" Nixon: it was "a matter of principle, no matter how absurd it looks to wise guys.")

But I grew more and more silent.

The initiating committee voted by a majority of one in favor of my tenure. Such a vote was the kiss of death. The initiating committee vote had to be unanimous.

Harry Crowe said, "Be prepared, that's all, prepared to become very sad."
I was sad.

He told me that Adelman had threatened — "as a self-respecting scholar" — to resign rather than remain on the faculty with someone like me. Harry smiled. "You have to understand, Howard gets excited, he'll never resign."

A tenure file, organized by Unrau and thick with letters of support from political scientists and poets and literary theoreticians, went forward.

The College Committee met and was guided by the initiating committee: 4-3 in favor of tenure. A second death kiss.

One afternoon, Harry — an extraordinarily complex man who was becoming more and more of a friend — told me that he, himself, was an ardent Zionist, "One of those failed Protestants, you know, who finds something that satisfies his heart in the Jews. And as for Meir, so what, no one I know over there votes for her . . . "

"That's what Amichai told me. He doesn't vote for her, what's the big deal?"

"And as for Nielsen," he said, "I know all about him . . . "

The Senate refused my tenure.

This meant that I had to resign from the university in one year. My life as a teacher was over, a done turkey.

Harry said, "We'll see."

He went to visit the President and came back two hours later. "Well, that's it," he said, "the President overturned the Senate, you've got tenure."

"How'd you do that?"

"I told him I'd make his life hell," he said and smiled.

A Jewish professor in my department drafted a report identifying "the members of a Jewish conspiracy in the college" to deny me tenure. Don Fine and Stanley Fefferman, the two men I'd known longest in the department, had stood by me with a sternness of intelligence that matched Ahern's fierceness of rage. I said I would not cooperate with such a report. I did not believe in conspiracies. But I did believe in what Margaret Atwood has called "the witch-word," the sloppy, self-serving, mean-spirited, ill-thought-out, glib, malevolent, cynical, paranoid, opportunistic use of the witch word, which, once it is laid on anyone, sticks: *anti-Semite.*

Among the first to congratulate me on my tenure was Professor Adelman. He shook my hand. I thought, Don't they teach shame in philosophy? But I kept my mouth shut. The hoods and grifters at the Barclay would have been proud of me. I kept my mouth shut.

At the same time, I became engaged in three film projects: an hour-long California documentary; a two-part series on the Knapp police commission in New York — the investigation of corruption that became the basis for the movie, *Serpico*; and a highly charged political interview: Angela Davis.

Called from Philadelphia, I was told that sources in the international "revolutionary movement" — whatever that was — had put me forward as a writer/journalist who could be "trusted to come without bias." Would I be interested in an exclusive interview with Angela Davis, the Black Power militant who was being held in prison in California under a charge of murder, the interview to take place in the prison?

At that time, Angela Davis and Che Guevera shared poster celebrity across the western world.

I put the proposal to Nielsen, he agreed to terms, and I flew to San Francisco. When I arrived at the Sheraton Palace Hotel there was a telegram waiting for me: "CBC policy decision has forbidden us to do Angela Davis interview . . . CBC may not do interview with her under any circumstances."

I felt the hand of Eugene Hallman. I argued on the phone with Knowlton Nash for nearly an hour. To no avail. I argued with John Kerr. "Barry, Barry," he said, "it *is* politics. It *is*. Face it, it *is*."

I was told to come home. I said I could not, that I had given my word and I intended to live up to my word. Nash told me my obligation was to the Corporation. I said my father had long ago explained to me that my obligation was to myself.

I drove to the small jail. For a woman under a murder charge, she was composed. She articulated her distress, her ideological view of America, her sense of herself as a black intellectual, a black woman. I left the jail, flew home and gave the raw footage to Nielsen.

I edited the processed film to twenty-eight minutes. Nielsen said it was good but to take out three minutes.

I took out three minutes.

Nielsen asked for more.

Days passed.

I took out two more minutes.

He told me, and Claire — as researcher for the show, she was there, too — that he hesitated to put Angela Davis on the air . . . she was too attractive, too persuasive. He told me to take out two more minutes.

The film did not go to air.

On a Saturday, a California judge announced that Angela Davis was innocent, she was not a murderer. She was free to go.

The CBC ran the interview — on Sunday.

Accuse him of murdering your mother, father, brothers, sisters, several cousins and the family dog and he will triumphantly produce the dog alive.

In a cutting room where I was working on a film about Leda the Witch and others from Los Angeles, Nielsen said he was going to fire me. He wanted me to understand the sorrow this caused him. I said I was sure he felt distress, we had done good work together. "What I can't understand," I said, "is why you'd say the things you said about me in last weekend's *Montreal Gazette*." He had mightily slanged me. And Zolf (who would soon disappear from network television himself). "Oh," Nielsen said. "I hoped you wouldn't see that." I heard a line from out of nowhere in my head: *The abrasive lie, the perturbed loving look in the eye.*

I was fired.

I came up out of the dark water and sat with Claire in the apartment at the bottom of the Rosedale ravine. "Docks," I said, "I know nothing of docks. I work in dark waters." Because of the very specific research done for my tenure papers, I knew that in eight years I had spoken on radio about writing and politics 110 times; in four-and-a-half years I had written 127 pieces for the *Telegram*, and in six years I had made three hour-long films, and 53 shorter films.

I did not make a film for CBC television again.

I had my friend, the cameraman, Peter Davis, but he lived and worked in the States, in the Catskills.

I chose not to go to the States.

I began to listen to silences.

To the grinding of bones in my back.

To the music between notes.

Since I had nothing to do at lunch hour, I saw my grade-school son for lunch, picking him up in my car. I thought he had a fine intuitive sense of things, a natural sardonic awareness of the world. We bought box-lunches at a hamburger joint and drove to the cemetery and sat contentedly in the Mount Pleasant Crematorium chapel, eating burgers and listening to Mendelssohn. On winter days, after heavy snows, there were always two or three long-distance skiers poling their way between the tombstones. This seemed very funny to us.

7

I woke one morning with pain in my back, a small iron bolt driven deep between the shoulder blades. I sat cross-legged on the bed. I told Claire I would be all right, I'd been through this before. "Don't worry," I said, hardly able to breathe.

She came back to the apartment for an early lunch and found me sitting in the same spot, still cross-legged, but sopping wet, the sheets wet, too. I could only whisper two words through clenched teeth. "Don't worry," I said.

I had no idea how long I had been sitting there.

I didn't believe that I was in pain.

I got to the car. Claire drove me to the hospital, to Dr. Urowitz's office. He was busy. I sat patiently, sure that I would eventually find a tranquility inside my bones if I just took it easy in my head . . . Dr. Urowitz looked down and said, "You are in a state of shock." As they wheeled me down the hall on a stretcher, he said he was going to Jerusalem that very night for the first time and I said, "Oh, you'll love it, but look, don't stay in a big hotel, certainly not the King David . . . see if you can find a house or apartment to sublet in Yemin Moshe, see if . . . "

"Of course he's making total sense," I heard Urowitz say, "but just the same, he's hallucinating. We'll knock it out of him."

They gave me Darvon (opium), morphine, valium, 222s (aspirin and codeine). I went into a world of eerie ice-locked silence where stones were seeds that sprouted wings. Claire brought me drawing paper, 11 x 6 sheets, and I churned out drawings during fits of wakefulness over three days, filling the bedtable drawer . . .

Hogg and his drawings, stone seeds . . .

A child's white hands cut at the wrists . . . a child's white feet cut at the ankles, separated by a body of green water. "Meet my son," I said to Claire. "Or maybe it's all that's left of my own childhood."

After a week, I was walking. I was okay, just a little bit too light on my feet . . .

Everyday, Claire brought crêpes and white wine for lunch from Le Provençal.

As it happened, during the Black September war, a rash had broken out under my foreskin . . . it had kept recurring. "It's like you got an incubator on there," a doctor said, "a foreskin's an incubator. Cut if off."

"Yes, while you're here, cut if off," my doctor said.

"As an artist," Claire said, "the foreskin is ugly, it hides the shape." She brought me a loose-fitting elegant black and white dashiki.

"Okay," I said, "cut it off, just don't cut into my brain."

They wheeled me into the operating room. I lay on the table bantering with the nurses. "Nothing can hurt me after this," I said. They began to handle me.

"You going to get an erection?"

"No."

"Good." The nurse produced a razor and began to shave me. "You can stay awake a while longer," she said, wielding the blade. "Look into my eyes."

When I woke up, I wore a crown of thorns on my cock. Stitches. I thought that was very funny.

"You see what all this has come to," I said to Claire.

"God," she said, "it looks like barbed wire."

The arthritis specialists asked if I would stay in the hospital another ten days. They wanted to conduct more extensive tests. I said, "Sure, I've got nothing to do." They probed and prodded and administered pills, seeking the sources of pain. "You want to know where the pain comes from?" I asked, incredulous. I continued to stroll the halls in my dashiki. "You see," I told Claire, "they want to know why the white cells attack their own joints. That's what arthritis is. The white cells gang up and attack. You might as well ask why Cain killed Abel." Finally, they had no more probes, no more pills to give me, and the crown of thorns was removed.

"You have three kinds of arthritis. There's one that can surprise you, in the future, it attacks the membranes. Wrighters, it's called. It seems to be in your eyes, too."

"My eyes?"

"Yes."

I packed all my drawings. I had begun to write poems and sequences of images all over the drawings. I went home eagerly with Claire.

My scarred warrior had need to be with her.

8

Saul phoned me. "Mr. Ellison here," he said. He only used his last name, affecting a butler's accent, when he was in trouble with the bookies. He told me jokes. He complained about his boss. He complained that on his day off, Wednesday, he and his wife, living in her father's house, had to spend two hours sitting in the family car in the driveway listening to the radio because the old man . . . "eighty-one, for Chrissake, is busy banging his old lady girlfriend and he has to be alone." He admired the old man in the same way that he admired the tough old city hall politician who had had his testicles removed and said boldly, when he was being measured for trousers, "I got no politics, you can't hang me to the right or the left."

"So how much, Saul?"

"Three hundred."

I told him I would pick him up for lunch in two days. To amuse him but also to cheer myself up, I took him to the Courtyard Café in the Windsor Arms Hotel, the chi-chi café where the movie and television shakers ex-changed expense accounts. I asked Helen Hutchinson — Kosinski's friend, who was host of the CTV national morning television show, a star — to be his date. He was shy, but therefore more expansive, telling her stories about all the grifters and gamblers on Yonge Street, which she delighted in because her father had been a famous west coast gambler. She kissed him on the forehead when she left, saying, "I dunno Saul, maybe you and me, twenty years ago . . . " He knew she was kidding and so he was free to love it. He loved to kid around.

"Barry, I got to ask you," he said, suddenly serious.

"Sure."

"They're telling me you're an anti-Semite. My friends are telling me that, this rabbi, he tells me . . . "

"What d'you know, Saul?"

"What d'you mean?"

"In your heart."

"What I got is into a big fight with this rabbi, he tells me I'm stupid, that what I tell him I know for sure, that you're my friend, is stupid . . . He tells me, Jew to Jew . . . "

"Aw, Saul . . . "

He began to cry. There was no shudder to his body, this man in his fifties, just tears on his round soft cheeks, his big sorrowful eyes looking straight at me.

It was the only time through those months that I felt a physical rage. I wanted to hammer the Fackenheims, the Slonims.

"Forget it," I said. "Come on, take the afternoon off, we'll go and watch girls take their clothes off, there's a great new joint . . . "

"Naw. I can't, my boss'll fire me. It's not the way it used to be. Nothing's the way it used to be."

Brownie McGhee and Sonny Terry were playing at a club in Montreal. Sonny had married again, and I had met his wife, a cautious, caring woman. He had stopped drinking and had become "a sober citizen." Sonny's sobriety, his restored health, his incurious businesslike approach to each show — playing the same old songs over and over again — nettled Brownie, who had come to like singing the sardonic songs of Randy Newman. Brownie felt that as an artist he had been sealed in the amber of country blues. He sometimes called Sonny the "Wabash cannonball around my neck."

I bought a bottle of whiskey and tucked it under my arm. They were ending their set when I got to the club, coming off stage singing "Walk On" . . . *I got to keep on walking to make my way back home* . . . but Brownie got too far ahead of Sonny and Sonny stumbled and almost fell. They split apart and ended up at tables in opposite corners of the bar. I sat down in front of Sonny.

"Who, who sitting there?"

"Man, it's me."

"Who me?"

"Barry."

He gave a *whoop* and put out his big heavy hands. I shifted the bottle in the brown bag under my arm and took his hands in mine. He heard the rustle of the paper. "What you got there?"

"Bottle of whiskey."

"Give it here."

"You drinking again?"

"Naw. Give it here," and he reached toward me.

"I got it for Brownie."

"Fuck 'im."

I was astonished. He found the bottle and yanked, setting it down by his shoe.

"How come you here and not in Toronto?"

"You gonna drink that?"

"Naw, and neither's he."

"But I want to give it to him."

"You gave it to me."

I had never heard such hardness from Sonny.

"You talking to Brownie?"

"Naw, we don't talk 'cause we got nothing to say, he wants it that way, so so do I."

Other patrons wanted to talk to Sonny. I stood apart as he basked in compliments, but then I leaned down to his ear and said, "I'm going over to see Brownie."

"He don't want to play with me," he growled, "but he got to play with me otherwise he don't play at all. You ask him that."

Brownie, when he saw me, cried, "Break clean and come out fighting," and he laughed and opened his arms, but then he closed them, smiling but shutting me out.

"How's your brother, man?" he asked.

"Doing what brothers do."

"Shit. Say hello."

"So what's with you and Sonny?"

"The man's a fool. Can't get around a fool."

"Come on."

We tried to talk small talk. The tendons in his forearms, in his neck, were hopping. There was something vengeful in his eyes. There was an old man I had seen in my dreams, an old man with one tooth in his mouth like a nail, laughing.

I thought, That old man is sitting in Brownie's head. And then I thought, Vengeance like jealousy is second-rate emotion. That's why you took your vengeance in thirty years; you couldn't remember what you wanted to avenge. My mother had taught me that.

On stage again, Brownie and Sonny sat ten feet apart. While Sonny played, Brownie rested. While Brownie played, Sonny doodled and drummed on his knee.

They went through their sullen paces of dissonance and disregard.

The enthusiastic crowd applauded. Couldn't they hear, couldn't they see that those two great men were betraying each other's gift, sullying themselves? I left without saying a word, and did not ever see them again, disheartened by such a display of disdain by men who had once been a joy.

At supper with Irving Layton in his Montreal apartment, we talked about fathers and sons, how my father had got his name, Morley, how his father's name was Moses, a man of prayer harried by angels nibbling at his ears. "They talked to him," Irving said, "all the prophets talked to him, but he didn't talk much to me." His own child, David, was standing beside him and he gently brushed back the small boy's hair, saying, "I'm worried. He should be talking. I talk to him all the time and he says nothing."

We stared at the boy who was about four years old, and he stood and smiled at us and then left the room. "Since we're talking about prophets," I said, "I'll tell you who my favorite saint is, Simeon Stylites, an old Syrian in the days when the Church was in the desert, and he built himself a sixty-foot pillar and shimmied up and mounted it and lived and preached from that pillar for thirty years. Prophet to some, but for me, he was the world's first flagpole sitter, perched up there on top of the image of his own ego."

"It was the image of his sex."

"By the way," I said, "what does a man do with his shit for thirty years up on top of a pillar?"

"He sits in it. Any writer, any poet who's any good has to have sat in his own shit."

The little boy wandered back into the room and Irving took him in his arms and spoke softly to his silent face. He held the boy's hand in his and said, "My mother held me up by the heels. There I was, the first Jew, she said, since Moses to be born circumcised. To her, I was the Messiah. I could do no wrong. She gave me freedom. Of course, she was backward, ignorant, but a woman of power and feeling."

"Now I get it," I said, feeling for my poor crowned cock, "all that mad saint of the mountain stuff of yours, all your arrogance and strutting, it's as simple as that. Your mother told you you were the Messiah. My mother told me I was a sweet little angel."

"Haw," he laughed, "some angel."

"Some Messiah."

It was of course not that simple, but he had — to my relish and satisfaction — always carried the peculiar vituperative fever of the prophet with him, slanging other poets, dismissing them as liars and poor toadies and trained seals; he had always been the avenging angel, a little ridiculous, wrong-headed, striding out of his Judean hills; always in the stance of the lover, trusting no one, standing as erect as he could be (Morley had found his ridiculousness to be just that: ridiculous . . . whereas I had found it endearing), and there he was at his supper table with his child beside him, holding the little boy's hand, trying to nurse a word out of him.

The boy refused to speak so he said to me, "What's the best thing that's happened to you lately?"

"I was out in the Townships," I said, "visiting Marie-Claire Blais and Mary Meigs, and Mary's got this dog, a hound that likes to howl, and it lies on the grass and howls. So I got down on the grass, too, and howled along, and the hound had four notes and finally we got so good, with Mary killing herself laughing, that we would lie face to face and chord together, and they had a time getting me off the grass because we were a chorus and it was a little miracle. But finally the dog was half-hysterical and all worn out, so I had to quit, but it was something primal and beautiful, the kind of miracle with an animal you dream about when you're a boy."

When he was a boy, Irving had heard primal howls: he had lived with his family in a tenement room under a semi-brothel, and he had been wakened each night by the screams and shouts of roistering drunks. His mother had begged her small son to get the broomstick, to thump its handle into the ceiling, the pole always making a dull wooden sound in the darkness. It was then, he said, that his miracle took place.

"The loud cursings and clatterings would stop suddenly, and silence like some mysterious night flower would blossom from the tip of my broomstick. It was uncanny, and in my child's imagination I saw myself as a boy Moses parting the filthy noise-filled blackness so that the long-suffering Israelites might pass safely into a region of peace and slumber . . . Each time the mysterious flower of silence opened its invisible blossoms over my head I felt the same thrill of power, of exulting joy . . . "

Layton, since his childhood, had been the oracle of God — nothing sniveling and sneaky about him — he had been Moses among the whores, the peddlers, the blacks of St. Antoine Street, Moses to his ineffectual visionary father who actually was named Moses . . . all the noise and pain of his childhood had presented a huge possibility to him: a flower of silence, but a silence that required weapons.

Layton's world had always been a battle. Broompoles. "You broke someone's skull, made a profound philosophical dent in it, or they broke yours. As a boy I looked forward to the nightly battles with the youthful Jew-hating Christians who descended on the tiny Maccabean band waiting for them with stones, bottles and bricks or anything else." When he was writing pieces for me at the *Telegram*, he wrote a letter from Tel Aviv, saying

The up-to-date poet
besides laboring at this craft
should be a dead shot . . .

That's the new poetry
minted June 1967
in Tel Aviv and Sinai

That was lousy poetry. He also wrote to me defending the war in Vietnam, defending Johnson, sneering at the men and boys and girls who were protesting in the streets. I thought back to Simeon Stylites and Irving saying, "Any poet that's any good has to have sat in his own shit."

I admired the way he could boldly sit in his own shit and still shout and hurl imprecations. He could give it. He could take it. There was little or no malice in him. Invective was a sign of his energy. He would have had a grand time at the house on Saturday nights. BOOM. But whatever his beating on a big bass drum, I knew he knew

Redemption comes,
but never
in the form
we think it will

And we are broken
on no wheel
of our own choosing

I wasn't exactly sitting in my own shit. But what could he say to me that he hadn't already said about being sand-bagged:

Idiot!
The one human I'd trust
is a deaf mute paraplegic
behind bars

The cry of a man of contradictions who had trusted too much. I loved his contradictions: decorous as a scourge and sour in the sweetness of his love: in the night he studied his Talmud — in the light of day he shot from the hip . . . and oftentimes, as with Vietnam and the War Measures Act, he got it all wrong, but then, he also got it right . . . condemning the joy-haters, whose only great skill was compromise, and only concern was money, money, money . . . the jingle-jangle in a businessman's pockets. To move among such men, Irving had turned himself into one of Morley's deranged stiltwalkers, a buffoon, a quiet madman . . . and I loved him for it, loved him for being a sensualist "naked with mystery," loved him for being a BOOMLAY boy.

"I've got to thank you. Irving."

"For what?"

"Introducing me to Saya. Giving me her phone number. You forget?"

"Forget, why should I forget. Those black eyes, those beautiful eyes. And you were with her?"

"For a while."

"Serious?"

"Serious enough. Sometimes I think we ended up marooned in a lost movie."

"So what's come out of it?"

"Poems."

"Really!"

The little boy, David, came back into the room looking for more dessert. Irving spoke heartily to him. The boy, tight-lipped, just stared. Irving shook his head. "Manner redeemeth everything," he whispered wryly and laughed, a laughter tinged by bewilderment. "How can a kid eat cake and say nothing?" he said, reaching for the child but the child side-stepped his grasp and ran from the room, leaving Irving marooned for a moment, stalled in a tranquility of acceptance . . . in a silence. To my surprise I found that the silence drew me closer to him. In his life, he had pumped out his vituperative poems, full of the ghosts of women he had impaled on a rumpled bed, fantastical, bawdy, and with his broompole in both fists he had urged the injection of ecstasy into our dry world, a tormented and wise and sorrowful flag-pole-sitting saint who had been dumb enough and holy enough to sit in his own shit for all the world to see . . .

But there he was, full of acceptance, in a silence.

A smile hung on his face as he said good-bye. He brushed back the hair of his son. "It is puzzling. He did say something to me the other day, it was raining and he told me, 'Look, the air is crying.'"

"I'll tell you something," I said. "Some people have double-crossed me, put the boots to me, but all I feel is this terrible sorrow, this acceptance, and silence, so maybe you and your son and I could have a lot to say just by sitting down for a while and saying nothing."

"Until . . . ?"

"Until one of us laughed."

9

I was lying in bed in the morning, reading John Berryman's *Dream Songs*, about ole Henry, *at odds wif de world & its god . . . Henry, how he lay in de netting, wild, while the brainfever bird did scales . . . an image of the dead on the fingernail of a newborn child.*

Later at an Atkinson College cocktail party, Harry Crowe, in a banker's double-breasted gray suit — ah, he had a portly sedate aplomb — sporting a lush young Budapest woman on his arm — his "social convener" in the college — said, "What're you going to do with all your free time." I do not know why I answered, "How would you like to have one of the two best literary quarterlies in the world at Atkinson?"

"How much'll it cost?"

I said, not knowing what I was talking about, "For a year, four issues, twenty thousand."

"I'll give you ten this semester, ten the next."

"OK."

I heard on the radio that Kanafani had been killed. Blown up. A bomb. In his car in Beirut. With his young niece. The Israelis had got him. A ruthless man taken down ruthlessly. I did not blame or bemoan, but I owed him, I was in debt to the moment of the sweetness of his concern . . .

Six months later: in June of 1972, at another college cocktail party, Volume One: Number One of *Exile* was launched (I had no idea that Ezra Pound's 1928 journal published out of Rapallo — the quarterly that had printed Morley's first stories *Ancient Lineage* and *A Predicament* and Yeats' *Sailing to Byzantium* — had been called *The Exile*), featuring fiction and poetry by writers who had been important to me at the *Telegram*: Marie-Claire Blais, John Montague, Yehuda Amichai, Jerzy Kosinski.

In the only editorial to appear in the journal, I said we believed — in a time when so many others were relying on everyone else's information, everyone else's critical view — that the writer was in a kind of exile. "There are many excellent reviews in which the writer of imaginative prose and poetry seems to become merely fodder for the dancing scholarly horse. The writer of the critique becomes more important than the writer of the poem, especially if the critic offers a new fund of useful scholarly information. But useful for what? It is the day of the information deluge. Who sorts it all out? The imaginative writer, who can rely only on his own eyes, his own heart and sensibility for his information, is, in a sense, in exile now. There ought to be a small haven somewhere for such exiles. In these pages the imaginative writer will not be led in by a scholarly praetorian guard. He will be on his own."

Morley thought it was an arrogance on our part to publish the first three chapters of his *roman à clef* — *A Fine and Private Place* — in *Exile*.

"People will not cozy up to this," he said.

"Look, I'll tell you something," I said. "The first job I was ever up for in television, remember . . . I was twenty-two, in college, an educational program, *Let's Speak English,* and the writer of the show had to threaten to resign because a woman on the CBC board of directors, Charity Grant, remember her, one of the goddamn Massey family, friends of yours, George Grant the great philosopher and all those folks, she said, "Really, gentlemen, don't you think one Callaghan on the air is more than enough . . . ?"

"Charity . . . ?"

"Charity. And you can't mollify those folks, ever."

"Oh, those people have always been around here," he said. "I always knew they were here but that didn't stop me from feeling that this is my town. I'm perfectly at home. Charity Grant was just a comic figure . . . "

"Look, you're the one who was worried . . . "

"I'm worried about you."

Within the decade, Harry Crowe, who had a bad heart, died. His heart exploded. His secretary told me that my name was on his desk pad the day he died: "Call Barry . . . " Through all the years as I have entered the College I have called his name and sometimes tears come to my eyes. I gave Kosso's big, standing stainless steel sculpture, *KoBar*, to the university in his memory: it seemed — in its exploration of precarious balance — appropriate. It is in the courtyard of a student housing complex that bears Harry Crowe's name.

10

I went north. Into another silence. Not deeper, but different. I discovered that there is an hour so poised that light and dark cast no shadow, an hour toward the end of the afternoon, just before dusk on Georgian Bay. The wind drops, the water stills, and as far as the eye can see across open water, stone islands levitate. They lift off the horizon line and sit suspended in the sky. There is a tinsel line of light under the island, the water and air separate, ease apart, opening up a place — so it seems — beyond words . . .

Just before dusk one day, I eased into the water off my stone island that lies close to Spider Bay, dragging shore slime and weed fronds, moving out into the clear water. The air was warm but the water cold. Morley and Loretto were sitting half-asleep in canvas chairs on a shelf of stone above me. When they were young they had camped in bush country north of Lake Superior, but this was the only time they'd been on my island in the Bay, sheltered by tall pines rooted in rock crevices and moss. I lay in the water watching the far-away islands float. Then, quite close, there was a break in the water, and I kept still, adrift alongside a snake. I could see its length on a slant in the water. There was no sound. We hung in the water. For some reason, Morley roused. Very slowly, quietly, he came down the slope of stone from the shelf, smoking his pipe, watching me and the snake, saying nothing. His eyes told me nothing. I could smell the smoke from his pipe: scent of vanilla. In his shorts, he had the legs of an aging man, thick veins, blue pale skin. The snake hung in the water. I was afraid Morley would say a word but he said nothing. Not a sign. He had the snake fixed in his eye, in a silence. My mother was watching Morley watch me. I was getting tired, chilled, hanging in the water, astonished at the snake's complicity in the stillness. Then the wind rose, chopping the water. The sky closed down, the tinsel light went out, islands came to rest, and the snake swam away into the reeds and shallows.

Sitting on the cement stoop to the cottage, Morley said, "You know, years ago I was with your mother, even farther north than this, up in the Algoma hills, and I remember we were wondering whether *Anna Christie* was Eugene O'Neill's best play, and we were alone, high up in the deep silence, in snake country, where it was like watching the night come on for the first time in a new world . . . "

"Snake country . . . ?"

"The intense clarity . . . of what you could see, the stars, it was so clear."

"That was a fox snake, I've seen him twice before."

"In the water?"

"No."

"I was dozing, didn't see it at first," Morley said.

"Looked like a stick, a water-logged stick."

"I remember back then a small purplish bird sitting perched on our windowsill, and I saw quite clearly one of its wings in the sunlight and I just stared at the bird's wing the way we stared at that snake just now, and I suddenly looked for a long time at my own hand as if I'd never seen it before and then I thought that maybe the ecstasy, the only real ecstasy, would be getting right up close to your hand, to everything for the first time, maybe a kind of snake's eye view . . . "

I had taken the snake's appearance beside me as a silent word. An omen. But to Morley, it was no omen: the trick was to see it as a snake: it was hard enough, he thought, to see it as a snake without turning it into a metaphor. Morley didn't trust omens. He was suspicious of men who attached omens to themselves — "They're seeking a significance that's not there . . . " It was the job of the writer, he thought, to see the omens, the signifiers, in a man's life. That was revelation. But to believe you could see the signs of your own life along the road, to live your life as if a pattern had been revealed to you . . . as if your life could be a lived poem, No! — "No sir, that's delusion." Still, the snake had come down into the water, holding me in his eye as I'd held him in mine. There was some kind of sign in that. Maybe that's why I had been so moved by Jerusalem: a city of parched stones so full of signs of water.

That night I wrote:

He should have known. Each morning the old women came with baskets of beheaded fish. The eyes are best for soup, one said. The beautiful hand-sewn skirts they wore were winding sheets.

One of Morley's back-country Blue Mountain uncles — born just south of the island — had been a clock maker. Springs. Springs and cog-wheels. *Clickety clock clickety clock.* Apparently he was a man in a hurry. His motto — *There's No Time for the Present.* This was uncle D.P. (Pudge) Dewan, who told

Morley — while whittling a stick in front of the Salvation Army headquarters in Collingwood — that Alice Dewan, grandmother to Morley, had been a nervous young woman, and at Cork, just before the coffin boat on which she, her children and husband had booked passage had sailed out of the harbor, she had got off and gone home to her mother, and her husband hadn't missed her until the boat was a day out at sea from Cork city. Compelled to sail on, he had settled and raised his children alone by the Blue Mountains, reading poetry to his daughter, Minn, in his crofter's stone cottage. This was not, however, Minn's story. She said she had a mother who was all too alive, a rangy woman who was a diviner — who had the gift for finding water with a willow or an apple branch — and early on she got lost in the woods and when they found her she was crazy from blackfly bites — the blackflies so ferocious in May that they could drive deer mad. Minn did not say how her mother died. But she said that when her father was a white-haired old man with piercing almost translucent eyes, he sometimes said that he saw his wife's face in the forest light and his wife was holding out a branch to him.

My mother doubted both these stories, but I think there must be some truth to them as I, too, have the diviner's gift — I, too, go witching for water, and the pull is so strong I can follow the veins of water on land or track the plumbing pipes in a house.

Morley's other uncle, Eugene (known as Gene "the douce" — not because he was a card player who liked to play poker with the deuces wild but because he was so soft-eyed and soft-spoken), was a Great Lakes captain — captain of a steamer, *The City of Buffalo.* He was notorious in our family, or my mother's memory of Morley's family, as a ladies' man and a frequenter of Detroit and Chicago dice houses and trotting tracks — pooch-faced, a malleable-seeming man — lacking his sister Minn's height and wide firm mouth, her set jaw and shoulders — he was a man who polished the brass buttons on his captain's blazer (I have a photograph of him on the bridge of his ship), and he was last seen on a radial car in Cleveland, boasting that he could "pilot" his way through the city's gambling dens. He was never heard from again, but it was rumored that he had fallen in love with a woman of "a darker hue, a negress, a courtesan in a colored sporting house." I was told this not only by my mother but by Minn.

Minn did not often tell stories.

Sometimes she was about to, but then she would stop, like the way she absent-mindedly opened the middle button of her blouse and then quickly, with a little blush, buttoned it back.

The only Dewan I have actually been able to find to talk to is a cousin, a Dominican priest, Larry Dewan, now in his sixties. I had met him in passing on the street once before when I was a young undergraduate and he was beginning his serious work as a metaphysician. He must have been a brilliant student. He studied with Etienne Gilson at the Pontifical Institute of Medieval Studies, was Marshall McLuhan's first special assistant, went to Paris where he worked with Gabriel Marcel, Claude Lévi-Strauss and Maurice Merleau-Ponty. He returned to Toronto, and at a late age for ordination, became a priest at 44 (though he says the priesthood had always been his intention). He is a socially able, sweet-tempered, insightful man, and a jazz afficionado. He travels a great deal and recently was made a Master of Sacred Theology. Though he obviously knows a good deal about God, he could tell me very little about the family.

"It's the fate of the Irish," Father Larry said, "the roots disappear. It was the famine did it, I suppose." He remembered that as a child of eight coming down from North Bay, in which his side of the family had settled, he had been brought to the Wolfrey Avenue house and he'd sat on Tom's knee and Tom had talked to him seriously about politics. Two or three years later, on another visit, Minn had shown him Morley's political speeches from his collegiate trip to Pittsburgh with Paul Martin. He had no clear picture of Burke and remembered only that around the same time as Burke died, a priest from another part of the family had died, and the rumor was that he had committed suicide. "But of course, no one knew for sure."

Father Larry had an old photograph of his grandfather, who was Minn's brother, or — he also had a recollection that maybe this grandfather was a half-brother to Minn (if so, this lends credibility to the "story" that there were somehow two "mothers" to the first family Dewan in Collingwood). He also thought the ship captain had been called Phil, not Eugene, but he agreed that the gambling man had disappeared and he had never come back.

The brother or half-brother to Minn had worked for the CPR as a freight conductor and he'd gotten into trouble because his train one day cut another train in two at a crossing. His son (Father Larry's father) also worked for the CPR as a ticket agent, and Father Larry's brother to this day works in travel related to railroading. It's a family with the *clickety-clack of the railroad track* in its bones. As Father Larry said to me, as if life were a railroad yard, "Most of my life I've shunted back and forth from Toronto to Ottawa." He lives in Ottawa in a Dominican house.

Though Father Larry had little information, I was more than pleased to meet him, to know that he is "family." He struck me as the very best kind of priest. The conversations that he has had about God (or with God?) are reflected in his generous ease as he talks to men and women.

I sat on a stone ledge on my island and stared at the dark, deep, blue water and twisted pines. There were few stories down there in the water, and no one was interred in that Cambrian stone. No voice was heard. Water spiders rehearsed their dance. The wind came up, it went down. There were birds nesting in the tall pines. A snake curled around an empty nest on a branch, waiting. It was the fox snake. A fox snake was good. It looked like a rattler and killed rattlers.

In that landscape, so stark, so utterly empty of human shape, the snake uncoiled, it was the ancient emblem of the flute, the flowering stem, the hooded priest's backbone.

At dusk, the sun flared over the islands, red in the scattered clouds. I took that as a sign, too. Iscariot means red. I had begun to write about Judas . . . over and over I heard the line that had come to me when Nielsen had told me I was gone: "The most abrasive lie was the perturbed loving look in his eye . . . " — betrayal. I was fascinated that in the early Egyptian church Judas had been venerated as a saint . . . I had come to see that without Judas there could have been no "story"— and maybe Judas alone — along with Christ — understood this . . . understood as He looked down the long supper table that a betrayal had to take place before the beautiful could begin . . . That the kiss was the ancient invitation to the abyss and that the abyss without the kiss was a story without meaning . . .

"Not exactly your kind of saint," I said to Morley.

"Oh, I don't know, I've been thinking about Judas for years."

We fixed each other with a playful, tart, accusing eye, wagging a finger as we began to toss the hairball of betrayal back and forth in our lives, wondering why the story of *the traitor betrayed* seemed to be bred in the bones of the Irish; how betrayal might ignite not only passion but renew love, if the love were deep enough; how the law, the rules — from every day discipline to dietary laws — that a patriarch imposed on his family or his tribe could become a betrayal of all that was spontaneous in the heart . . . "And what such a father creates," Morley said, "is a captivity, with the rules all written down, and of course, in such a captivity of the heart they all quarrel fiercely over the rules, among themselves . . . "

"Like our Saturday nights?"

"Unruly discussions."

"Sounded like quarrels."

"Nonsense."

"You didn't find Eustace quarrelsome?"

"Often he was hilarious. He was the Old Flag . . . betraying everything his whole upbringing stood for."

The mysterious time on the water was at night. In the moonlight, I could read the trees along the shore and canoe in the dead of night, following channel markers in the map of my mind. I could go a long way, the water dark and the whole sky moth-eaten by light, stars.

Some nights, the depths of the sky had an astonishing clarity and seemed close; infinity became intimate. One still night, I heard the sound of wings and then from far, far away, the laughter of a woman, laughter carrying across the water, again an intimacy with the unknown; it was like laughter at laughter itself.

After supper, we were talking about the snake, how it shed its skin in the grass, how it could shed its past, come out clean — not diminished but more powerful, more sleek . . .

Then Mother spoke about the men at the CBC and at the university — the ones she thought tried to ruin me. And forgiveness.

"I don't know who I forgive," I said. "I don't forget . . . "

"I won't forget . . . "

"You know what you told me?"

"What?"

"He who takes his revenge within thirty years has acted in haste."

She blushed and laughed.

"That was a long time ago," she said.

"Not so long."

"Long enough."

"What I remember best about back then is Dad throwing his egg on the floor," I said.

"I did not," he said. "I've never done such a thing. Your mother made that up."

"You did so," she said.

They were both sputtering with laughter.

"Never," he cried.

"Poached," she said.

"It bounced," he said, triumphantly.

Morley, trying to contain his laughter, got a stitch in his side. He bent over to breathe.

"You ever read Beckett on laughter?" I asked.

"No."

"You want to?"

"No."

"I'm going to read it to you anyway."

It was a passage in *Watt*, a novel I had always read aloud in bits and pieces to my students:

The laugh that now is mirthless once was hollow, the laugh that once was hollow once was bitter. And the laugh that once was bitter? Eyewater . . . the bitter, the hollow and — Haw! Haw! — the mirthless. The bitter laugh laughs at that which is not good, it is the ethical laugh. The hollow laugh laughs at that which is not true, it is the intellectual laugh! Not good! Not true! Well, well. But the mirthless laugh is the dianoetic laugh, down the snout — Haw! — so. It is the laugh of laughs, the risus purus, the laugh laughing at the laugh, the beholding, the saluting of the highest joke, in a word the laugh that laughs — silence please — at that which is unhappy.

"I think my mother," Morley said, "would have understood that. I remember coming home one day as a boy and finding her sitting by the front window, her face in the folds of the lace curtain, and she was laughing, not at anything out on the street, but she was just sitting there, laughing, her face wrapped in lace, laughing."

When the morning sun was strong, I often canoed across an open stretch of water, paddling into what appeared to be a blind of stone wall and trees. But there was a gap, a passage wide enough for the canoe to slide through. It opened on to an enclosed small lake, shut out from the world and surrounded by high, stone hills. It was oval, windless, the water heavy with water lilies and floating pollen. There were water-logged trunks, wrecked drifting trees, and hovering dragonflies. The water — clogged with braided roots — had the feel of ointment. Islands of distress levitated, calm was palpable.

On the last morning with my parents on the island, I took my mother in the cedar-strip canoe into the enclosed lake. It was hot and the stillness had a physical presence. A weight. Skittering bugs left silver veins under the surface of the water.

"I've finished a long poem," I said.

"Yes?"

"This is the craziest place for it . . . "

My voice caromed across the water:

> . . . *that's why old Stuck*
> *has come undone,*
> *free, and telling you the essence of all*
> *be not mendacity*
> *but complicity, for if Judas and Jesus are One,*
> *if by betrayal*
> *the beautiful is begun, then not only Judas*
> *be in you,*
> *but Jesus, too. You wear His face no matter*
> *your disgrace.*

11

Back in Toronto I felt compelled to be alone. I took a flat across from the Cathedral, down among the pawn shops. Claire was forgiving, she tried to understand. She had the grit, I had the gloom. Having left Nina and Mischi with our house (so that they would always have a bastion, a place where no one could touch them), I needed money. I bet on baseball games with my bookie. I lay in the dark late at night listening to scores roll in from the coast on radio, hearing old Kavanagh lines in my head:

Child, do not go
into the dark places
of the soul.
There the gray
wolves whine,
the lean gray wolves.

I ate every night with Claire at her place in the ravine.

I was still teaching.

A beautiful lady I knew from one of my classes sent me a long-stemmed rose in a slender vase, and week after week a rose came in a long thin white box. I stacked the unopened boxes against a wall, building a cardboard cemetery of roses.

O rose thou art sick,
the invisible worm
that flies in the night . . .

My cleaning woman was a cripple. Small, in her forties, she had deformed feet. She came to the flat on Thursday mornings, short of breath from the pain in her feet. On cold days she often showed up with tears in her eyes. One morning she was in such pain she asked me to rub her feet. She said it eased her, and so every Thursday before she started work, she sat in a chair beside the rose boxes and I massaged her misshapen feet. Then she began to take the boxes home.

I didn't ask what she did with the boxes of dried out roses. She didn't stop asking me to massage her feet. She just sat down in the chair, took off her shoes and waited. She was obviously pleased, but there was a strange mordant air of mockery to her pleasure.

"This," I said to Claire, "is what happens to old TV stars."

One morning she fell asleep in the chair. Her clubbed feet were in my lap. I wondered: Am I doing this as a penance? If so, for what?

But then I saw a smile at the corner of her mouth as she slept.

That little twist of contentment reminded me of another older woman's smile when I was a boy, a woman who had showed me how to caress her, fondle her, toy with her . . . so that I became a nimble boy able to move over her body . . . fascinated by her wide-eyed, almost glazed inward look . . . sorrow . . . perhaps a dispelling of sorrow.

That smile on a woman's face has always given me more pleasure than my own pleasure, but then, sitting there holding the cleaning woman's twisted feet, I realized that Claire — two or three times a week, after she had taken an evening bath and soothed herself with body creams — would rub my feet with those same creams, easing me. Had I become a cripple haunting her nights with my own disappointments?

Was my man Hogg the voice of this cripple?

Hogg, in his poems, came up for air and along with him, *Exile.*

I was a publisher. How did that happen? It was Harry Crowe's doing . . .

Many volumes appeared, with works by Kosinski, Montague, Seamus Heaney, Amichai, a slew of French poets, Susan Musgrave, Yehia Haaki (of Egypt), Jacques Ferron and Réjean Ducharme, Yannis Ritsos and Joe Rosenblatt, Roch Carrier and Marie-Claire Blais, and many young, unknown writers.

And Morley.

He published chapters of another new novel in *Exile.*

This meant we now read his texts together in an especially acute and intimate way.

"How could you say that?"

"Easy."

"If it's so easy . . . "

"That's what style should be, easy."

One night I surprised him. I said that he should re-write *A Passion in Rome*, the style was too slack.

"There you go again. The style's absolutely natural," he snapped.

"You can be naturally slack," I said. "It's like you're wearing loose shoes. Too many words flap flap."

"That's your honest view of it?"

"Yeah."

"It's possible to be honestly stupid."

It was a playful shot. Neither of us blinked.

"I once knew a guy who thought Dreiser's *Sister Carrie* would be a better book if someone just re-wrote it, cleaned up the style . . . "

"You've got a point," I said.

Then I put a strain on Montague. I gave him the early Hogg poems.

"I can't tell you the dread," he wrote in a note, "and the relief. So many friendships go down when a friend asks a poet to read what he's been writing and it's not poetry and you have to tell him it's not poetry when he hopes it is poetry. But, thank god for the good of our friendship, these are real poems. They are a real contribution."

A short while later, after the same poems appeared in *Exile*, I got a note from a writer I did not know, Joyce Carol Oates.

31 December 1974

To put it mildly, I am impressed with your new issue (of *Exile*) . . . it's remarkable, a remarkable grouping of imaginations . . . and your own contribution is brilliant. I had been studying the drawings before reading the magazine, thinking "Hogg" was an extremely talented and disturbing artist, and then it was revealed to me that you did the drawings . . . It's an incredible achievement, really.

Joyce.

I showed her letter to Morley.

"This is great," he said, "it reminds me of when I first heard from Ford Madox Ford and Hemingway. A writer's got to have someone he doesn't know whose judgment he can trust."

"You mean I shouldn't trust you?"

"Well, she doesn't know you, she just knows the work. Montague knows you, knows what's going on, he'll *want* to like the work. So you should probably trust her judgment."

12

"I don't know what's going on," my mother said, putting down the evening newspaper. "It's all too crazy. Sometimes I want to laugh, but I know I shouldn't laugh. Look at this," and she held up the front page. There was a big picture of Anita Bryant, the former singer who had peddled Florida orange juice on television. She was in town as an evangelist, telling anyone who would listen that the real Vitamin C was Jesus, and outside the hall where she was preaching, her enemies, five hundred homosexuals, had gathered to parade in the biting cold. "And look," my mother said, running her finger down the page to where there were revelations of illegal break-ins by the police "they're like the old woman who lived in a shoe. The police have committed so many crimes they don't know what to do."

She was sitting in her nest of mohair shawls in the corner of our living-room chesterfield. She was chain-smoking. Though several days had passed, she was still bristling about the Super Bowl football game. She had placed a bet with my bookie, Ruby, and had lost. "That wasn't a game," she said, "it was a religious service. You hear that, Morley? In that cathedral the Super-dome . . . all the players were born-again Christians tackling each other for Jesus."

I saw her point. The quarterback, who had had a terrible day and was the game's goat, kept repeating afterwards that he was blessed, blessed, he was really blessed by the Lord as he had been blessed all year, although he had just set a record for having been intercepted four times and finally he had been taken out of the game.

"Maybe," she said, "it only makes sense if you see that those cops and the religious football players and the orange juice evangelists and the cops and politicians who say they've got to break the law in order to save the law are all clowns clowning around," and she laughed until there were tears in her eyes. I didn't often see her laugh so whole-heartedly. Usually the tears in her eyes were caused by excruciating pain.

13

September 6th, 1974

Dear Montague:

These fits of my rage (lying in the dark, ankles crossed, hands linked, listening to my blood — debilitating explosions of gloom, black light, swamp water on the brain, furious . . .) and then to read Montaigne: "To accuse others for one's own misfortunes is a sign of want of education; to accuse oneself shows that one's education has begun; to accuse neither oneself nor others shows that one's education is complete . . . "

14

Uncle Ambrose, my mother's brother, was a gentle-spoken house painter. Tall and broad-shouldered, he had been a corporal during the first World War but had not gone overseas. He had driven a motorcycle with a sidecar. After the war, he had driven a motorcycle, then a modish car, a coupe de ville. In photographs he seems to have had style, a confident thrust to his body, a confident look in his eye. But he was shy. There were very few women — other than his sisters — in his life. He was also devout, in a straightforward way, without flair, going to mass every Sunday, and sometimes during the week with one of his sisters, most likely Anna, the oldest, who didn't have a job in an office but looked after the family (both the Dee mother and father were dead by the time my mother was ten), and she ran the big house on Roxton Road. Ambrose ran with the men, though he was not much for the drink, and ran with the horses. His father had loved the trotting horses (keeping Scribbler books closely written with results and times from all the little tracks around Toronto), and Ambrose loved them, too. It was his only vice.

And from about the age of thirty-five, Marie had been his only woman, a gay good-looking woman with good long legs. She never seemed unhappy. She was always smiling. She seemed as subdued in her social needs as Ambrose — satisfied with church dances, summer dances on the boats to Crystal Beach and Port Dalhousie, motor trips to visit the Ryans in Chicago, the trotting races and baseball games played in Fred Hamilton Park, which was just behind the house on Roxton Road.

As he was about to turn fifty, Ambrose announced he was going to remain a bachelor until he died. Marie went to their parish priest, the Church of St. Francis (where Morley and Loretto had been married), complaining that she had given all of her youth to Ambrose. She asked the priest to tell Ambrose to marry her, that he had an obligation. The priest told that to Ambrose and Ambrose did what he was told. In his fiftieth year, he married Marie.

At first, they seemed happily enough married. Ambrose had saved money and he bought a house. He had not, however, counted on Marie's two bachelor brothers, Rae and Wilfred. Rae, timid, with an eerie fascination for the wounds of Christ, lived with them as a boarder. "He never talks about anything except suffering," Ambrose said to me. Rae had had terrible acne as a boy, and there were healed red craters on his neck and throat, with black bristly hair in the craters that he couldn't trim. He wore light mauve scarves in the house, even in the summer. Wilfred, however, was outgoing. He lived alone in a room or with them in the house, depending on whether or not he had a job. Most often, he clerked at one of the government liquor stores. He was full of political opinions (all of them angry and abusive, in a hapless way), he had a pencil moustache, wore black vests — sometimes of silk — and he loved the trotting horses. He kept Ambrose company at the track, and he had one slightly mad indulgence whenever he won a lot of money. He bought shoes. He bought the most up-to-date stylish shoes he could find. He would wear these shoes for two weeks, three weeks, and then he would tire of them and give them away.

Wilfred and I had the same size feet. Three or four times a year, wearing my everyday baggy gray trousers and a tired blue school blazer, I would show up — to the amazement of my fellow students — shod in two-tone suede, or "Spectator" black-and-white brogues, or leather inlaid with patent leather, or twin-tassel loafers . . . Wilfred said to me, "Waste not, want not and since I want nothing, nothing goes to waste." Though he was always angry at the government, I never heard him say an angry word to anyone. Wilfred died of a heart attack, and not long after, Ambrose had a heart attack, too.

Marie, though she was in her early fifties, wanted children. She was, as she said, "only recently married." Her search for a child became a cruel affair, for everyone. She went to the Catholic adoption agencies. They thought Marie and Ambrose would be perfect adoptive parents, so, one after another — over a period of three years — young boys entered their house hoping to be wanted, to be liked, to be loved, to be given a home. Ambrose was fairly easy, but Marie always became dissatisfied: not one of the boys could ever conform to her idea of how perfect he should be. She was a good woman, determined, yet at the same time, docile, wishing no one any harm. She just didn't have any felt understanding of children. She sent them all back. This was heart breaking and led to my only angry words with her, because she had asked me to meet one of the boys, and his yearning to please was terrifying to me . . . his knowing after two months with them that he was losing what he wanted to win with all his heart. When, smiling, she sent him back, too, I told her I thought she was brutal and ruthless, and when she turned to Ambrose for a defense, for the only time I ever saw, he put his head down and said with firmness, "That's it. No more. It's over." It was over. No more children came to the house.

She got into the habit, after each of the children, of soothing herself by buying a piece of furniture . . . a side-table, a pot-stand, a bedroom chair . . . all of which she did not need, and most of which, after a while, she gave away. She continued to be very gay, dressing always in very bright colors — favoring cashmere and angora sweaters — keeping her very good legs. Even after Ambrose had a very serious heart attack and was confined to bed, she kept her gaiety. And then he was taken to hospital, and after two weeks, he died.

At the funeral home, Marie's smile for everyone (shades of aunt Alice) seemed to be what perhaps it had always been: hysteria. She took me by the hand and led me to kneel beside the body of Ambrose in the casket.

"He looks better now than he ever did," she said.

"I suppose he does."

"A fine looking man," she said.

"Yes."

"And a good man."

"Yes."

"It was a blessing that he went at last when he did."

"It was?"

"Yes. It was a problem of circulation."

"It was?"

"Yes. His feet were rotting."

"The rot."

"Yes. Black, they were black."

"Were they?"

"Yes."

"Well, I guess it was a blessing he went."

"Yes."

"And he looks very good."

"Yes he does, and he was a good man."

"Yes."

"Would you pray?" she asked.

"No, I would not," I said.

"No?"

"No. I've no need for it."

"Oh, that's terrible," she said, breaking into a broad smile.

"I know but there's nothing I can do."

"You could pray."

"I can't."

"Can't you try a prayer for him?" and she took my hand.

"Yes I will."

"To God," she said, and she was laughing.

"No, just a prayer," I said.

Later that week, after the burial, Marie went to see my mother and father. She had with her one of the pieces of furniture she had bought after sending a boy back to the orphanage. It was a chair.

That same night I came to the house. I looked at the chair and said nothing. It was in the hall, near the white paneled wall, in front of the black marble mantel. It was a chair unlike any chair of theirs: a chair done in burnt pumpkin quilted velvet with a high back that was cut straight across at the top, and the sides of the back sloped into the seat, so that the chair had no real arms.

Finally Morley said, "How do you like the new chair?"

I hesitated, smiled politely, but said nothing.

"Oh, come on," he said. "How do you like it?"

"Where did you get it?" I asked.

"Well, I didn't buy it," he said.

"I hope not," I said.

"It would have been too expensive," he said. "Marie gave it to us as a present."

"So you have to use it."

"No, we like it," he said.

"I think it's awful. And you were never crazy about Marie."

"And why is it awful?"

"It's right out of Miami. Or maybe Las Vegas. You're sure, you're going to keep it around?"

"I'm going to leave it just where it is."

I was disgruntled. We both knew that little things like this come between people. He had his view — I had mine. It was an eyesore to be tolerated. I tried to maintain a patient silence.

Then, one night he said, "Look, I know how you feel about that chair and its place in the world, but here's how it is in itself. It is a very ancient style, and I like very much the burnt orange velvet. And what do I care if a hotel manager in Miami has picked on something I like for himself. I'll never meet him or his customers. The relationship is between me and that chair. That's all. If I write a story, and such a hotel manager likes my story, I'm delighted. That's all."

I tried to hold back my hostility. I knew, or believed, he was trying to tell me something about myself, about our relationship.

The chair remained where it was. It didn't look burnt orange to me. It looked pumpkin.

We didn't speak about it.

A few weeks later, he said, "Look, I like my chair. Here it is. And here I am. Incidentally, a very attractive woman who's lived in many cities, but who's never been to Miami, came by the other night and she said, 'Oh, that chair looks lovely there.'"

He knew that in telling me this story he wasn't drawing me any closer to him. He knew I was disappointed in him and resented his refusal to remove that chair. In a small way, the chair had come to stand between us.

Maybe he was telling me that no matter how much we trusted each other there always had to be something that stood between us.

Then Marie died of breast cancer.

I would come around to the house and find him as I often had — standing in the hall, lost in thought, standing in the petalled light from the stained glass window at the staircase landing, standing beside the chair. But until the day he died I never saw him sit in that chair.

Book Nine

1

My friend Peter Davis, the cameraman, called from his home in the Catskills.

He wanted to know how I was and I said, "Claire and I are living together again."

"Good. I've got a story for you. I want you to go to Africa with me."

It was 1976. Five years without a phone call. At last I was going to make another film.

As a boy, sitting in my father's library, I hauled a dark leather-bound book down from the shelves . . . the leather spongy and crumbling at the edges. Inside, amidst the double columns of text, there were several dozen engravings . . . it was *The Last Journal of David Livingstone in Central Africa.*

Since childhood, I had been fascinated by explorers, Magellan and Vasco da Gama, and Ponce de Leon . . . Ponce clanking across the sea in his iron suit in search of the Fountain of Youth . . . and Livingstone, in search of the five fountains at the source of the Nile, the five springs that would "cleanse the five wounds of Christ." I read the journal and repeated names slowly — Lake Nyassa, the Loangwa, Lualaba, Ujiji, Lake Bangweolo, Unyamyembe, Lulimala, Ilala . . . chanting the names, watching Livingstone in my mind's eye as he crossed the Zambesi River, dazed with fever, wearing a pair of too tight French patent leather shoes, weakened by dysentery and dreadful ulcers . . . a walking "ruckle of bones" . . . baffled by his baggage bearers and struck dumb-mouthed "by the impression that he was in hell" as slavers shot down hundreds of helpless women in a market. He was cheered for the moment by the arrival of "Mr. H.M. Stanley, the richly-laden almoner of Mr. Gordon Bennett of the *New York Herald*," only to end up, after Stanley was gone, being carried on a litter through spongy jungle to the banks of the Molilamo where he died on his knees.

I had dreamed as a child of getting to the wide Zambesi River and following it to the great Victoria Falls, that long deep chasm, a seam that had split open. I had always wanted to go there, to look down . . .

2

I have photographs of Claire when she was seventeen. Beautiful, lithesome . . . a child-woman in art school . . . struck by tuberculosis. Two and a half years confined to bed in a sanitorium. Her back cut open, a rib taken out, the diseased part of the lung removed.

She was courted in her hospital room and she married shortly after. Her husband built a grand home for her. Cautioned about the wisdom of bearing children, told she could never nurse, she had two sons and two daughters. In her early thirties, secure, pampered, she began to draw again, and took a small studio close to other artists on Markham Street. She had a passing affair, discovered her phone had been tapped by her husband and came home one night to find her clothes on the lawn. Conciliatory conversations led to apologies, promises of fidelity, and *one* demand: she was told by her husband that she could return to her home and children on condition that she *never* draw again.

She left.

She had her car, her wardrobe, twelve hundred dollars, and no business skills.

When she tried to rent a very modest apartment, the landlady dismissed her, saying, "I know a high-class call girl when I see one."

She got a job as a saleswoman in an upscale gift and trinket shop. She was an outcast among her neighbors. They became her customers. They came to see her to treat her with contempt, and a certain awe. In those days, women did not leave their homes and children. Certainly not Jewish women.

Her own mother — a Sumberg — portly, sharp-tongued, divorced and then widowed, moved into the family house to take her daughter's place and she remained there till the children were grown (the Sumbergs were interesting: born in Lithuania, schooled in Berlin, one of Claire's uncles became professor of German Drama at NYU; the other, Harold, was leader of the second violins with the Toronto Symphony Orchestra; and her aunt Esther, rehearsal pianist for the National Ballet, married Milton Cronenberg, a writer, philatelist, and collector of books . . . and their son — Claire's cousin — is David Cronenberg, the film director).

Claire then got a job as a switchboard girl in CBC television's aggressive current affairs department.

Within two years — hired by the legendary producer, Ross Maclean — she was in charge of all visual research for the network's flagship show. Within five years, she was *the* authority in her field, and by the end of of her career, she shared in a dozen national awards, five Emmys, and an Oscar.

Through these television years she continued — always working from models — to draw.

In early 1976, I had decided to gather the drawings she had sold to collectors over the years — going back to her first exhibition at the Pollock Gallery in 1967 — so that I could bring them together in a hardcover book, a gift for her birthday. As this book was being completed, the master printer — Ernie Herzig — told me the book should name a publishing house on the title page. Thinking of the literary quarterly, I said, "Sure, call it Exile Editions."

We had supper at home. She assumed I had forgotten it was her birthday. The book drove her to her bed. For hours she examined her work as if she had never seen it before.

Strange fruit!

Claire went on to have one-woman shows in Stockholm, Venice, Rome, Jerusalem, Bologna, Zagreb and New York.

Exile Editions, a birthday whim, is now a publishing house with 180 titles in print.

3

After a year of negotiations, the Afrikaners agreed to let me and Peter Davis into South Africa.

It was to be a film about the white tribe — not the Bantu, not the colored, not the English whites — but the Afrikaners, the *laager* people, self-enclosed outcasts, who had all the power, their own police state.

But first, hired by the other national network, John Bassett's CTV (the CBC under Herrndorf did not answer any of my inquiries as to interest in the project), we flew to Salisbury, to the civil war in Rhodesia . . . to sundowners at the Meikles hotel, BOOM, ice skating at a rickety rink, mid-town lawn bowling among old geezers, white mercenaries brawling over black hookers. BOOM, bombs went off every night in the suburbs. Outside the suburbs, particularly in areas controlled by the Ndbele (minority Zulus as distinct from the majority Shona), it was dangerous to travel through farming country towards the borders.

But the tobacco farmers, the backbone of the country, boasted that the guerrillas were on the run. They said this while sitting on their country porches, their homes surrounded by twenty-foot-high electrified fences, the gates closed, the juice turned on at eight o'clock every evening and kept on till six in the morning. Unable to understand that they weren't shutting the guerrillas out, they were shutting themselves in.

They were a Looking Glass people.

I traveled north through police check points and wrote to Claire from Victoria Falls:

> Stood this morning on the edge in the long grass across from the Zambesi as it narrows and powers toward the falls I dreamed of as a child, and there is something relentless about the plunge, the pulsing roar of water's roaring fall into the great cleft . . . the plumes of mist driven upwards, drenching the growth, the rough grass "greased" with a film of water so that when I lay down on the edge I began to slide . . . the slide seemed inexorable and I felt the land "tip" — the "fall" of the water drawing me down — a promise of comfort, bliss, as I panicked and clutched at the grass trying to hold on . . . ridiculous because the "tipping" was all inside my head, and then on the other side, riding on the lip of the falls in what looked like a giant pneumatic tube, and seated in the center of the tube wearing his captain's hat — better not tell matter-of-fact Morley about this — was David Livingstone trying to talk, his jaw clacking but there was no sound no word, only the roar only the sound of perpetual plunge and I closed my eyes and held on digging into the roots of the grass certain the roots would give way in the mud and that what was best was to let go of the roots to surrender to disappear into the mist . . .

I went back to Salisbury, to the lawn bowlers, and the Prime Minister, Ian Smith.

Smith, sitting on his front lawn, told me the civil strife was completely under control, and confined to the borders.

When I showed him a map I had made of explosions in Salisbury over ten days, a ring of bombings closing in on the city, I knew I had entered into Houdini land when he said that it was all news to him and he handed the map to an aide, asking, "This make any sense to you?"

Peter and I flew to Johannesburg, to Afrikaner country.
Within a short span the Smith regime surrendered.

4

South Africa is the homeland of exile.

BREYTEN BREYTENBACH

Jo-burg, 1976: the Boer country that nearly caused the lynching of my grandfather Tom. Poor Tom, and what would he have made of the place I found myself in, a bar on Twist Street, clean and quiet, dimly lit, dispiriting. The barstools were chained to the floor. The chains were heavy. The plank floor was polyeurethaned, it was a hard mirror. I was with a pretty young woman who worked for the government, and the police, too. She was demure and reticent, tight-lipped. When I told her I knew that she worked for the police she stared at me, unblinking. She saw that I had been reading the work of a poet who was in prison. "That poet," she said softly, "is a traitor." He was the Afrikaner, Breyten Breytenbach: *Looking into South Africa is like looking into the mirror at midnight when you have pulled a face and a train blew its whistle and your image stayed there, fixed for all eternity. A horrible face, but your own.*

"What about my work permit?"

"You mustn't worry about your work permit," she said.

"Why not?"

"Because it is in our hands. There has only been a delay, that's all."

"If you say so."

"No no, it's not what I say, it's what you will say that must be so."

David Goldblatt was an amiable man, modest and wary. He lived in a comfortable house in Johannesburg. As a photographer, he had a lean eye.

This was a fat land for the eye, fat for the freakish, for caricature. He laughed as he shuffled a stack of contact sheets and prints on his worktable. His work was remarkable: whether among blacks or whites, he seemed to have come upon a face or a room and those in it by accident and yet you felt the accident had its own authentic logic, as if it could have been no other way. He had intruded without being intrusive (when you see a black couple holding a chrome car bumper with the license plate — TJ199-491 — still attached, you are sure that it was their idea to pick it up and turn it into some kind of icon or talisman, not his). It seemed that people trusted him and believed that he would not steal their dignity, their souls. And so they appeared as who they were — as if they were looking into a mirror without guile — and this had been devastating for the Afrikaners he had photographed — they were forthright, so incapable of irony or dissembling. "Half of those Afrikaners look demented," I said. He smiled wryly and said Nadine Gordimer liked his work, too. "You must meet her."

Then, leaning across his worktable, touching my hand like an old friend, he said, "There are a couple of things you've got to watch out for here."

"Like what?"

"The secret police will be watching you all the time."

"Sure."

"And don't trust anybody, particularly someone who offers to be helpful, to be your friend."

"Right."

"You just made your first mistake."

A private road. Old Potch Road. The sign was at a tilt. It was illegal for me to be there; it was a chance taken, to see Soweto for myself. Private meant black, no whites allowed without a permit, chained space, blacks in cement blockhouses, rows and rows of blockhouses, ribbons of corrugated asbestos roofs (from a distance, from a far hill, it seemed a mad monster-child had laid down track after track of abandoned tank treads on the gently rolling hills). There were utility poles along the road, and overhead wiring and street lamps, and for a while you were fooled, you thought there had to be light, but there were almost no lines into the houses, there was no wiring in the rooms, no lights at night, no electric kettles, toasters, stoves, brooms, clocks, heaters, none of the equipment of domestic comfort, only cold-tap plumbing, few ceilings, little plastering, many mud floors, no pavements, one movie house, no hotels, no bars, hapless garbage collection, only outhouse shacks set over holes in the backyard dust, the mushroom brown soot, soot from the coal stoves, the sour smell of smoke. Soot and nicotine-stained smoke clouding the sun, clouding the brain. An old man, a coal merchant, was dismembering a horse that had dropped dead, lying in its own blood, the blood smoored by soot. Women lined up to buy the meat-cuts. A one-armed black man was rolling a cigarette with his one hand and under the same arm he carried a loaf of bread and a small carpet for sleeping.

"Oll the time I tink mebbe they get free from us, maar mos white mens they tink how to be baas inne blek land but make sure the bleks be nobuddy. They plenny of police and they part of us here and white mens dere. The wishbone don break for nobuddy, we bleks en white mens locked hold like toads. Toads thet are fucking en canno let go, sometimes die that way, so Soweto like a toad locked on white mens for death, mebbe. You go see the blek toad inne Soweto, maar you need a permit to go inne Soweto."

"I've been."

"The police mens know?"

"No."

"You tink they don know, maar you mos fool, they know."

One million black men, women and children eighteen miles from Jo-burg — half of them officially unknown, officially elsewhere, or nowhere — sometimes sixteen to a blockhouse, sucking in coal smoke. Soweto, a name that

wasn't a name, only a euphonious abbreviation for South Western Townships
— something somebody thought of in 1963 to describe these 85 square kilo-
meters, fifth largest city south of the Sahara, a brutal bunkhouse for black
Johannesburg workers (it is the nature of this mining city that everything is
abbreviated — Soweto, Jo-burg, a life in a pocket passbook, childhood and
marriages dwarfed and broken). If you were black you had, on the average,
40 years, 40 bleary years of a little desperate Jesus joy on Sunday in one of the
hundreds of holyroller churches, or at soccer games (the scoreboard sponsor,
a cigarette company, says LIFE IS GREAT) cheering for the big teams, or
maybe — with tribal scars freshened on your cheek — you sat for half an hour
outside on a kitchen chair and hosed down the mud, the hose like a lariat
around your feet, and then went and got drunk on laurentina in a shebeen,
more afraid of the night-prowling tokoloshe than the cops with their shot-
guns, and then, maybe you did a deal with a skollie for a finger of zol and
ended up with a shebeen queen — her makapulan tight around her hips —
which your wife wouldn't say anything about because she was scared of
divorce because divorced women had almost no rights and could easily be
sent off into nowhere, into one of the reserves, unless of course she had an
inside track to a sangoma, a witch doctor, who might have made a potion and
made nowhere bloom inside your head . . . and you might have gone crazy:

> *if i pour petrol on a white child's face*
> *and give flames the taste of his flesh*
> *it won't be a new thing*
> *i wonder how i will feel when his eyes pop*
> *and when my nostrils sip the smell of his flesh*
> *and his scream touches my heart*
> *i wonder if i will be able to sleep . . .*

in the dreary digital monotony of the blockhouses . . . where, no matter the
bustle in the streets and the dust rousted up . . . there was a feeling of stagnancy . . . stagnancy at the heart of the violence . . . Three murders a day in
Soweto (South Africa averages 5,700 killings each year and through the past

two decades 220,000 men have borne approximately 1,220,000 strokes of the lash; over five years in the sixties, 508 persons were executed, almost half the world's reported total of 1,033).

"They plenny zims, you watch out for zims . . . "

The police station was surrounded by an eight-foot steel fence, capped by razor wire. Every day a quarter of a million people traveled in and out of Soweto to work in Jo-burg, by car, taxi, bicycle, but most of them were sardined into the long brown trains that left every two-and-a-half minutes at peak periods. The travelers were terrorized every payday by tsotsis, the young thugs who stabbed in the back, robbed, and left the dead jammed upright in the crowded train cars, or attacked out of the dark on the street with long sharpened bicycle spokes, hitting directly into the heart or above the coccyx; instant paralysis, and behind the police barracks, there was a billboard with letters in day-glo colors: The Whole World's Sold On Benson & Hedges Gold . . . and parked under it a pick-up truck with Old English lettering: Rapid Rubble Co. As the sun went down, the sky was a pale blue piece of airmail writing paper whose bottom end had been dipped in mud, and the sun hung there in the mud, bleached, a dead moon . . .

At the root of all this was violence, the violence of apartheid, apartness, men and women with no tenure, and it was the women who were worst off: the houses were allocated under the Bantu (Urban Areas) Consolidation Act to men who qualified under Section 10 (1), (a) or (b), that is, those born in Jo-burg, those who had lived in Soweto for fifteen years or had been employed by one baas for ten years. If a husband was arrested and lost his qualification, the woman left home with him. If a husband died and a widow was left with minor children, and qualified for the allotted house, she still had to find a man to marry her who also qualified under Section 10 (1), (a) or (b). If not, she and her children were out, removed, or gone into hiding, scavenging for a corner to lie down in.

A zim is a Xhosa cannibal creature from the Transkei. He is born with one bitter leg and one sweet leg. At birth, the parents pounce on the child and eat the infant's sweet leg. Nonetheless, the grown zim moves with great speed, a cannibal running on one bitter leg.

In a sprawling city dump, children picked through high sloping garbage mounds, on a tilt on their haunches, so that they looked short-legged and long-armed, like hyenas. There were also huge hills of slag, the built up waste from the gold mines, hills with an almost luminous, sometimes honey-cyanide sheen in the sunlight, the slag crusted and polished by the wind and rain, polished into smooth steep slopes — perfect angles, perfect curves — and children ran up and down the slag hills that overlooked rutted broken fields in the suburbs . . . and there were cannibalized cars all over the fields or in the yards, stripped clean, like eruptions of shaped steel out of the earth. Nothing went to waste and everything was waste, this is the endgame logic of apartheid, Vulture Culture: Breytenbach said, "Apartheid is the White man's night, the darkness which blurs his consciousness and his conscience. What one doesn't see doesn't exist. White is the Black man's burden and what he wishes for most, probably, is for the man to get off his bloody back and stand on his own two feet. Obviously, this instrument of repression is also used, structurally, on White society itself. In the name of the State — the State is the daughter of apartheid — all dissidence is suppressed. White workers too are told to sacrifice their legitimate claims on behalf of apartheid. It is fascist. It is totalitarian. Apartheid is alienation. It is schizophrenic — a mental disease marked by disconnection between thoughts, feelings and actions. It is paranoiac. Apartheid is White culture. The culture of the Whites is Saint Albino — this state of whiteness, the prison of laws and taboos — negates all political consciousness. Apartheid justifies itself in the name of Western civilization, in the name of the Afrikaans culture."

Lord come to our help Yourself, send not your Son, for this is not the time for children.

FIELD MARSHAL JAN CHRISTIAAN SMUTS

Every night, while half-asleep on the fifth floor of a Jo-burg hotel, I thought I heard whistling outside the bedroom window. A man's sharp whistle, in the high mid-air.

The cleaning maid told me not to be troubled, it was the night birds who whistled.

"What kind of birds are those?" I asked her.

"The soul birds of the dead," she said. "They crowd around."

I opened my door at five one morning because I thought I could feel someone breathing on the other side of the door, and there was a man staring at me, as if he'd been standing staring all night at the door and now he was staring at me.

He wheeled around and hurried out the Emergency Exit and ran down the flights of stairs to the street.

I watched for him in the street.

He didn't appear.

I heard a loud keening, a woman in the empty street, a hurt animal's cry. At the intersection, she lurched from corner to corner, a Hillbrow woman, a poor white holding her high-heel pumps in her hands.

No one was molesting her, or even talking to her.

But she was keening.

Blacks, huddled against the walls with their wool hats pulled down over their faces, made no move, as if she were not there, as if she had never happened, though she was fleeing from curb to curb, on her own cat's-cradle path in the dawn light, crying out — *Wat soek julle in die straat die tyd?* — crying out to a small old black man who sat up straight on his coal wagon, a wagon with heavy rubber wheels, noiseless, the wagon drawn by a clopping bony horse.

He drove past her. He was wearing a kind of jacket cut from an old khaki canvas duffel bag; armholes had been sliced into the sides, and he had split the bag up the front so that the clear plastic handle of the duffel bag sat on his back between his shoulder blades.

He was sitting straight. He didn't look as if he was expecting to be picked up by the handle.

But he was ready.

Ready, ready to be hauled up by the handle, somehow I was sure he could tell, could smell it in his children's clothes, he was ready to rise up.

Early that morning, I talked to David Goldblatt. He gave me Nadine Gordimer's phone number. Her husband, a man named Casirer — apparently wealthy, in the jewel business — invited me for cocktails. It was a comfortable house, the rooms smaller than I had expected, or perhaps they seemed smaller because there were many people in the house, guests at a late afternoon cocktail party. Casirer, shrewd-eyed, was gracious, Gordimer perfunctory, taken up with encouraging an avuncular frumpy old man, a family friend or favorite uncle who was given to telling stories about himself which the guests found very funny, stories that were pointless and boring to an outsider, and so I sat alone, drinking Scotch, trying to listen to the bluff old man until finally, with a sudden sigh, he stood up and left behind a room that radiated affection for him. Almost all the other guests were gone, too.

"What are you doing here, my husband says you're making a film?" Gordimer asked.

"I'm a friend of Goldblatt's. I think he's a wonderful photographer," I said.

"He's good. I wrote an introduction for his book on the mines."

"Yes."

"And you're making a film about Afrikaners."

"Yes," I said.

"You're making a film about the Afrikaners, I don't understand that. You've just come over from Canada and you're making a film?"

"And it's going to be something," I said.

"In what way?"

"Well, I've got them talking, quite openly."

She scoffed. She seemed full of anger and suspicion. I wished I had said nothing. But instead of keeping quiet, I said, "Yes, they're singing like canaries . . . explaining who they are. Almost guileless. "

"Do you know the BBC has been trying for two years to get into the country to make a film about me, and the government won't let them in?"

"Maybe so. It took me a long time to get in, too."

"The BBC . . . they can't get in to film me, and you're here, and they're telling you exactly who they are . . ."

"Yes."

"They don't tell anybody who they are. They say what they want you to hear, and they listen. They're probably listening to us, now, in this house . . ."

"Maybe."

"If they're making a film with you, you're either one of them, or you're a dupe."

There was silence in the room. I was sitting, she was standing. I wished there was ice in my Scotch. I wanted to chew on ice.

"I hardly think," I said, "Goldblatt is dumb enough to send around a dupe to meet you."

She remained silent, refusing the offering of a way out of the awkwardness, the insult.

No one said anything.

"I'm no dupe," I said, "and I'm not stupid either. Time for me to go."

Casirer held out a conciliatory hand.

A young man (her son?) offered to drive me to my hotel.

It was a silent drive, not a word spoken.

Umtata was a sullen scrub town in the Transkei, with low-slung houses, a few flickering neon tubes in the night and a drive-in short-order grill at the cross-roads gas station: on a dimly lit street a drunken black soldier in a flapping great-coat and one sole slapping loose on his boot, whistled and hooted after passing cars. At the Savoy — a four-floor hotel, there were two white women at the desk, and one wore her hair in a bun; it held four yellow pencils. Both were brusque: "Coffee in the morning, 6:30 . . . room service quits at 6:45, you're on your own after that . . . No, no calls, we close down the phones at evening, getting lines out of Umtata's too much trouble. Don't know about trains neither; it'd take maybe two days to the Cape, can't say, it's years since I traveled . . . "

There was a semi-spiral staircase to the musty second floor; battleship brown walls, doors ajar with single men sitting back-to-the-wall, staring out; the numbers made no sense . . . 209, 222, 290, 201, 216 . . . my room had a steel frame single bed with wire springs and a thin mattress, threadbare rugs, a broken wooden seat on the toilet bowl.

I propped two pillows, got between the sheets, and began to read André Brink's banned novel, *Looking on Darkness*: " . . . . sometimes of an evening I take off my clothes and stand with my back pressed against the wall of my cell, or lie down on the narrow bunk, studying and touching this body, strange and familiar as that of a beloved. Even when I know they are watching me through the peephole in the door it doesn't upset me . . . " I heard foot-steps in the hall, a whisper, then a knock in the night!

"Who's that?"

"The police, come to the door."

Naked, I opened the door. Two men offered no identification. They were in their thirties, casually dressed. The one with a moustache and a belly hung back, as if his presence were a mistake. The other, self-assured, taut, wearing a mustard-green pullover, dust-pink jeans, loafers and tinted glasses, spoke as if his jaw were locked at the latch. He made no accusations or explanations, he only wanted my passport and said, "We'll be back." I got into bed, yield-ing to a dread that had been with me all day, yet suddenly too tired to worry

— thinking with a kind of mordant amusement, If it ain't one tribe it's another ... why the fuck do I do this to myself? — and when they knocked again and came in and the cop in the pink jeans said sardonically, "Did you have a little sleep?" I sat cross-legged, naked, on the bed and smiled, a wan smile, but a smile, waiting.

"You're under arrest."

"You're kidding." I got up, staring at them in the dingy sixty-watt light, certain for some reason that by not covering myself I would make them shy away. "I did have a little sleep," I lied, feeling the pit of my stomach go hollow.

"Get dressed, put your clothes on, get your bags together."

"What for?"

"I just told you. Put your clothes on."

"You mean I'm going to jail?"

"Yes."

"Why not leave the bags here?"

"Jail's in East London."

"What?"

"Get dressed."

"But I just came from there, that's three hours, it's midnight for god's sake ... "

At the front desk, the woman with the yellow pencils in her hair had the bill prepared (she had obviously known what was going to happen).

"I don't care if you just arrived, you've got to pay full-rate, and it's none of my doing, remember that, none of my doing."

Liar liar pants on fire.

The bags were put in a Land Rover. I got up into the cab with the cop in the pink jeans who told me he was a Captain.

He said, "If you have to fart open the window."

"Thank you," I said.

We drove for almost two hours in silence. Peter was in another car with another cop. I had heard that under South African law, they didn't have to tell anyone they had me for 180 days; and then, once admitting they had me, they didn't have to charge me for another 180 days. Driving deeper into the dark I thought that maybe I was about to disappear for a year, and then . . .

As we came to the heart of the Kei valley, a dipping mountain road in the dark down to the Kei river, with the Southern Cross at our back, the Captain asked, "Do you need to piss?"

Yes," I said.

He parked by the shoulder of the road and we walked through the wet long grass to the river bank. We stood side-by-side on the bank, holding our pricks, pissing into the night — a curious, even comic moment of vulnerable shared relief, a bonding.

"You're a professor?" he said.

"Yes."

"I know a lot about you."

"Yes."

"A hell of a lot."

"Yes."

"I thought you'd like to know, I studied criminology by correspondence course."

"Really," I said, but then couldn't help myself and broke into laughter, still pissing. I was laughing alone. He wheeled in the dark and punched me hard in the chest, on the breast bone. He'd hammered my breath away. I couldn't breathe. I couldn't cry out. I thought I was going to die, everything collapsed inward, my lungs felt broken. He stood and waited for me, hunched over, to get my breath, staring at me, saying nothing, very patient, but grim, and my breath came back and we walked back to the truck.

"We are," he said, turning the ignition key, "a peace loving people."

"What am I charged with?"

"They'll tell you."

At the crowded police station in East London, crowded at four in the morning, he said to the desk Sergeant, "Do what you want with him." After a quick pat-pat search, the desk Sergeant said to Peter, "You've got all that cash, two thousand, you take it into the cell, we're not risking responsibility for that . . . " and they led us into a dank, damp yard, a high plastered brick wall with long doors like open coffins upended in the flood-lit wall. We went through a mesh door and a solid steel double door into a cell's courtyard, thirty-foot walls of concrete. There was a second set of mesh and steel doors into the cell itself. The six-by-eight cell had two windows, one to the courtyard, the other facing onto a blank wall. The damp coldness clung to the skin, like a fungus; I had the strange feeling that I was about to lie down where mushrooms grew; the cell was, in effect, an open room, the windows creating a wind current, the concrete holding the coldness. I felt strength ebbing out of me, a kind of surrender by my body, a weeping by my bones . . . the white cells beginning to attack the joints. I knew that the long night drive, this cold cell . . . it was all intended to exhaust me as quickly as possible, to break down my morale; demoralization, standard procedure.

"They plenny zims, you watch out for zims."

The mattress on the cement floor was three inches of foam rubber covered by a zip-on soiled bed sheet. There was a charcoal-gray blanket made of fine mesh (impossible to rip in strips, to use in a suicide). The walls were painted black, to gloom me down even more. Lying on my side, knees tucked up into my armpits to cradle my own body warmth, I smelled sweat in the stiff bed sheet, the sour sweat and puke of frightened men, and shit on the wind from the open filthy toilet. Sour shit, piss, puke, black walls . . . the overhead light, a bare bulb, always on, the freezing floor, my body aching with exhaustion, yet aware of everything at the tips of the nerves . . . except for moments when my mind reeled off into blackness, a dislocation from the self, almost like drifting under water, eyes closed, lost in the peace of unknowingness, and then BO-AM BO-AM . . . Every half-hour there was a cell check; the double steel doors opened and slammed, BO-AM, sleep was impossible. Rest was impossible. I had a taunting awareness; no matter how smart I was, I could not defend myself because I had no idea why I was held, why this was being done to me (for a moment I wondered if the secret police had been listening to the conversation at Gordimer's house, if the house was tapped, the police had heard me call the men I'd met canaries). I cursed my ineptitude, incompetence, amateurishness and then tried to laugh. Laughter echoed. Laughter hurt the ears, the joints. I meant to sleep for ten minutes, remembering the calm I had kept in Amman, imperviousness to panic . . . but then, like a trickle of water into the joints, the arthritic pain . . . where was Claire with her bottle of Pouilly Fuissé and lunch from Le Provençal? "Peter," I said. He was in another cell. At 6:30 a young cop with a line of little pimples along his left jaw came to the cell door and called out, "Graze time . . . " and I asked, "What's that?" and he said, shoving me toward the door, "You know, like animals, you graze . . . " He had put a tin plate of stale brown bread, and a tin cup of thin coffee, and a tin cup of fish bones and a fish head in a rancid gruel on the open courtyard floor.

"Kneel and eat," he said.

"When will I see the Colonel?" I asked.

"The Colonel isn't here."

"I was told by the Sergeant I could see the Colonel."

"He's not here."

"Why was I arrested?"

"Kneel and eat."

"Why?"

"Someone'll tell you. They'll tell you. You're not eating."

He seemed angry, personally insulted, because I had not got down on my knees to slurp up the fish gruel. He was narrow through the shoulders, he had a slouching animosity, his uniform didn't fit, he looked like he wanted to hit me . . . a litany ran through my mind: The Criminal Procedure Act, The Immorality Act, The Abolition of Passes Act, The Sabotage Act, The Terrorism Act, The Suppression of Communism Act . . . BO-AM BO-AM . . . black walls, nubbly cement black walls, boasts of love cut with . . . what? . . . into the paint: HE SCREWED ME GOOD, drawn bombs exploding, dream-drawings of long nipples, huge

erections . . . TELL THEM THE TRUTH, THEY'LL FIND OUT ANYWAY —
AFTER ALL BLACK COCK IS BEST — had they put me into a woman's cell? Or,
perhaps the police had cut the messages into the paint CONFESS. I'd crawled
beyond sleep into small fevers of interrogation, the pain now dull because it was
everywhere as I knelt down and tasted the gruel and wanted to vomit, a surge of
nausea . . . "Tastes like someone pissed in it," I said. The cop laughed. He left me
alone, kept laughing in the outer courtyard as I knelt, like a child at my first confession, yes — my first, how hilarious it had been because — desperate to have
something serious to confess — I'd looked up the inside of a girl's thighs, I'd
looked up her dress and thought — that's what fucking is, so I'd told the priest
in my six-year-old voice, "Father, I F-U-C-K-E-D," spelling it out because I didn't
dare say the word to a priest, the magic word, and he had burst into laughter, giggling laughter and I had wanted to punch him just like the cop in the pink jeans
had punched me down by the riverside but the priest said, "Don't worry, sin'll
come along soon enough," and he had rolled the little door shut over the wire
mesh, a small BO-AM, leaving me in the dark, resentful and wishing I knew
about sin, wondering how long it would take before I would learn, learn to know
— like the Shadow — what evil lurks in the hearts of women — it took only
three years before that older woman, nodding acquaintance to my mother on
our street, found and took me into the nooks and crannies of her body, playfully
teaching me how to pleasure her . . . so that all the later admonitions against sex
by my priests, the warnings of perdition, the promise of hell for the spilling of a
little semen, seemed ludicrous to me. I'd come to love the memory of spelling
out the magic word, and that first priest's laughter . . . Whenever I was confronted by real crimes, those deep inner sanctum mysteries, my own, or anyone
else's, I said to myself, "Bless me Father, I F-U-C-K-E-D," I fucked up, came up
out of silence and laughed, and so I got up in the courtyard and leaned on the
walls and laughed and circled and stood in the courtyard for three hours, aching
to lie down, to sleep, waiting to see the sun, waiting for it to slide down the wall
and touch me, but because of its angle and the height of the walls, it was never
going to slide down into the corner to dry me out, warm my bones, the throb in

the joints, pain traveling the muscles, enervating pain . . . that burns, sears the nerves until pain becomes like a cold fire beneath the skin, a chilling heat that obliterates . . . until pain turns the nerves inside out and becomes a comfort, a pure coal of concentration . . . a clarity you begin to cherish because it shuts everything, including fear, out . . . you cannot fake pain but you can fake fear, desire, guilt . . .

I thought wryly — as I had once called on Kanafani when I was in trouble — maybe I should call on Gordimer. Haw!

At noon, they took me for interrogation; we went out of the courtyard into the brilliant sun, the polished hoods of police cars, the chrome exploding like flash-bulbs, magnesium, blinding . . . already the sun had become alien . . . dizzying . . . and then to their offices, passing up a caged staircase, wire mesh with floor-to-ceiling bars on the landing, and another cage that enclosed an inner office. There were two men; one old, about sixty-five, pasty skin, compassionate eyes, a bemused smile; the other, the Colonel, was wearing smoked glasses, and had fine even teeth, olive skin tight on the bone, skin like a polished gourd. "I am the Colonel," he said, "and Professor Callaghan, you have the right to say nothing; but if you speak, your words will be written down by my associate."

"Okay."

"And no need to be afraid — my associate, too, has been in prison."

The old man smiled.

"What would you like to know?" I asked.

"Tell us why you are here."

The old man, a clipboard on his knee, began writing, nodded, and then stopped as I told them about Esther from the Ministry of Information and my meetings with Judge Marais of the Supreme Court, van Jaarsveld, the great historian, my visit to Pelindaba, the nuclear plant . . . and how Esther had always been with me — except when I met the novelist André Brink . . . as for the Captain in the pink pants who had arrested me . . . "All unnecessary," I said. "They knew I was in the country to talk to Afrikaners . . . they arranged the meetings." The Colonel was flustered, he apologized. He looked for help to the old man. I realized that the questioning, this talk with the Colonel was taking place because he had no idea why he had me in his prison; no one in Pretoria had given him an explanation; he was interrogating me because he wanted me to tell him why I had been arrested.

"Will you have tea?" asked the old man.

It was all unreal, murderously unreal . . . Livingstone in his patent leather shoes, Ian Smith staring at the map of explosions all around his town, asking, "What do you make of this?"

"Have some tea," the old man said again.

"And," said the Colonel, "after I make calls . . . you say you and your partner, Mr. Davis, were going to the Cape . . . You want to fly, we'll book you on the late afternoon flight." The Colonel extended his hand and I laughed, and the old man, wagging his head as if arrest and police work were all a mystery to him, led me into a sitting room, served tea and biscuits, and looked mournful, his hands blotchy with liver spots. I told him I was hoping to meet J.M. Coetzee, the novelist, and Fugard, the playwright, in the Cape. We talked about South African brandy, and he explained that he had been in prison during the War, first in Italy, then in Nazi Germany.

"I'm not Jewish," he said, "but I was in one of their work camps — Bad Tolz — and then one of their concentration camps."

Peter joined us.

The old man stood up and went out of the room to see if anyone was getting the airline tickets. I wondered if I dared ask to see the old man's concentration camp number. Verification. He left the room. I riffled through files in an In-box on the desk, security reports: "Joseph Poni appears to have no political interests or involvements. We will therefore continue to keep him under surveillance." Somewhere, Solzhenitsyn had said that governments are never moralists: they never imprison people for what they've done; they imprison them *to keep* them from doing something.

"I speak six languages, you know," the old man said, coming back into the room.

"No kidding."

"It is I think because I never knew my father. Never had one. Not that I ever saw. I was I think looking for a language I could trust."

"And Afrikanse is your mother tongue?"

"No. My mother spoke Portuguese."

"And your father?"

"I have no idea. My mother refused to speak of him. Maltese. He was Maltese, so she said."

"Well, it's hard to know what to say about your father."

"You're close to your father?"

"Pretty close."

"I could tell. I can always tell. I'm a translator, an interpreter . . . The right word in the wrong place can do a man a lot of damage."

"And the wrong word?"

"That, too. Make no mistake."

He smiled.

"And there's no one in your family who doesn't know his father?"

"No, not that I know of," I said.

"Hmmh . . ."

"Should there be? You know something I don't."

"You'd be hard-pressed to know what I know," he said, standing up. But he didn't leave the room. He faced the door and then sat down and stared at me, unblinking, and said in a curiously flat tone: *"Ich will mit dem herrn Kommandanten sprechen . . ."* I felt a little chill and then was sure that he wanted me to feel that I had been unfair to him, not forthcoming enough, now that my arrest had been resolved and he had given me tea.

"You know," I said, figuring I would mollify him with a story, "there was a cousin in my family, he was called Johnnie Clock because he was born with one arm shorter than the other and he got a touch of polio too in his arms, making the one short arm bent across himself so that when he stood straight he was standing at twenty to six, and some people said that that was the hour to the minute that his father left home. But then, he knew who his father was and you don't so that doesn't count, I guess."

He didn't seem to find the story amusing.

It was clear that something had gone wrong. Two hours had passed. The Colonel had locked the cage doors to his office. He had locked himself in and would not come out. The tea in the pot was cold. I looked at the clock on the wall. Peter looked at the clock on the wall. The plane for the Cape was taking off. A tall thin man came into the office. His skin was mottled, as if dappled with peroxide. Apparently he had flown from Pretoria, he had papers. The old man stood up and put on his tie and suit-jacket. He stood aside, at attention. "Please sign this paper," the mottled man said.

"What is it?"

"Sign please."

"Can I read it?"

"No."

"Can I read it after I sign?"

"Yes," he said, a tired man with scuffed shoes, his face and body all pouches, carrying a pouch of papers: *Under Section 8 (2) of the Aliens Act No.1 of 1937 and in terms of Section 5 (1) of the said Act, you are required to leave the country within twenty-four hours, otherwise you will be liable to prosecution under the said Act.*

"But what did I do?"

"That's a matter for them to explain . . . "

"Who's them?"

("*. . . interrogator Mironenko said to the condemned Babitch: If it is necessary to shoot you then you will be shot even if you are altogether innocent. If it is necessary to acquit you then no matter how guilty you are you will be acquitted . . . "*

— Solzhenitsyn).

"What time is it?" I asked.

"Five."

"When's the plane to Jo-burg?"

"Six. That's when the twenty-four hours starts. There's a plane out of Jo-burg tomorrow at six, for London. You'd best be on it."

The old man walked us down the caged staircase, past the sullen, grumbling policeman, toward a car parked in the lot on the other side of the police station. "At least soon you'll be home," he said. As we approached the corner of the brick station house, he said, "Pay attention." Then, as we were at the corner his hand touched mine. "This is the only place we cannot be seen. I've just given you a piece of paper, it has a private number . . . phone that man, that number. This is all wrong, he will do something." I thanked him. We drove to the East London airport, where I read the note. It was a phone number, Connie Mulder's home number, the Minister of Information who was also the Minister of the Interior, and the old man obviously thought Mulder would rectify the situation. But it was almost certain that Mulder had ordered my arrest. The man who had let me into the country, the man who had arranged for me to meet everyone I'd met, except for Brink and Beyers Naudè, was the man who had had me arrested. And now he was removing me from the country, and the old man, who wanted me to think of him as wise and sensitive and helpful, thought Mulder was the man to help me.

"Hello Houdini."

I saw the mottled man appear. For a moment I thought he was going to re-arrest us, but he was very polite and said quietly, almost pleadingly, as I picked up my bag to board the plane, "You have to understand, the laws have to be followed, they made an oversight perhaps . . . but you have to understand, too, the old man, his wife's sick you know, a good man . . . he's a good man. Problems, you know . . . they . . . "

"But what did I do?"

"That's a matter for them to explain. But don't blame the old man."

"Ah, he's probably painting his windows white . . ."

"What?"

The plane was almost empty, except for two men I'd seen talking in a corner in the police station. They were sitting in front of me. I was carrying a sweater over my arm, the stink of the prison cell in it. The steward delivered a brown paper bag. The plane rolled down the runway. My name was written on the bag, ball-point pen. Inside was a bottle, South African brandy, reserve stock.

A gift from a white beetle.

Book Ten

1

I had lain low for several years.

Then I'd been swarmed by white beetles.

But Hogg was coming out to play.

He had been

> *thunder-*
> *clapped with a two-by-four, roped up*
> *by the arms between two trees and this inscription*
> *had been nailed to his jaw bone latch:*
> *HERE HANGS THE KING OF THE HATCHING DEAD.*

He had climbed down, believing there had to be a place where the word was Holy Holy Holy. He had gone to Jerusalem, fallen in love, fallen out of love, entered a silence beyond words, come home, and done his underground stations. Then, he had heard from Joyce Carol Oates again.

May 13, 1977

. . . Hogg is a remarkable achievement. It's really powerful: with the apparent artlessness of genuine craft. (Craftiness as well.) The supple lines, the sounds which are almost gentle at times, make most of the poetry we come across sound merely labored and contrived — self-conscious language. But it frightens me to say anything about it.

Joyce

This frightened me too: I had never intended to be Hogg.

And I didn't want to frighten anyone, let alone Oates. I'd never met her.

Then I got a note from *Punch* in London.

Mr. Callaghan, I've seen your story. "The Muscle." It's wonderful, worthy of Chekhov. I have to print it. I'm going to print it.

Yours,
Allen Coren

I didn't know who Coren was, I had never read *Punch*.

And again, Oates:

November 28, 1977

You have . . . an uncanny intuitive *feel*. There are of course others (I admire Margaret Atwood immensely) who write good poetry, who know how to create images and drive home 'themes' and that sort of text book thing. But, like Montague — like Berryman — like Thomas — and Philip Levine (do you know his work?) and much of Merwin – you have got the inner grasp of what poetry is: a sort of muscular 'music' as an incantation that always means more than it says.

Joyce

My mother said: "You should include the drawings in the book. Hogg's drawings."

"Really?" Morley asked.

"Of course," she said.

John Montague sent a note, quoting Henry Miller—

> *As I ruminated, it began to grow clear*
> *To me, the mystery of this pilgrimage, the flight*

Which the poet makes over the face of the
Earth, and then, as if he had been ordained
To reenact a lost drama, the heroic descent
To the very bowels of the earth, the dark and
Fearsome sojourn in the belly of the whale,
The bloody struggle to liberate himself,
To emerge clean of the past a bright gory
Sun-god cast up . . .

While Morley puzzled over the idea of the Hogg drawings, he too was toying with the sun.

His new novel, *Close to the Sun Again*, was published in the fall of 1977. It was a final version of the novel I had told him to quit, that Wilson had told him to quit. He was no quitter.

It was a wartime story suggested by a man he had met out on the Atlantic — a naval commander, "Ribbons" Simmons. I had met Simmons as a boy: he had come to Toronto after the war, and to amuse Morley he had umpired a baseball game I was pitching in at Christie Pits (the regular umpire, impressed by his bearing, his air of authority, had agreed to step aside). I remember the way he called strikes: his arm wheeled straight up in the air and down, as if his shoulder socket was a hub, an arm like a railroad crossing wig-wag.

In the novel, he has much the same air. He is Ira Groome, the Commander: "And in civilian life, he still carried with him all the marks of a superior officer . . . that relaxed assurance of the naval man, and just as a captain on a ship can't afford to get personally involved with any member of his crew and has to be utterly impersonal, he had no personal involvements with anyone who worked for him. This meant he could be utterly ruthless with his underlings, and yet fair, because he had no close personal relationship with any of them."

By the end of the novel, the man doesn't just betray himself, he "commits high treason against himself."

Obviously, he had never hit a home run with a left-handed bat or been coached by Hank Biasetti.

Then, my old friend Tom Hedley came back to Toronto. He had left *Esquire* (his finest moment of editorial flair had been getting Jean Genet, Terry Southern and William Burroughs to write about the 1968 Chicago Democratic convention) and he said he was going to make films, but in the meantime, he had been asked to take over *Toronto Life* magazine, to give it depth and verve.

He asked me to write a column. Never a wilting flower himself, never self-effacing, he called it *Callaghan*. He said, "Write about the city, you can just report, or you can tell stories, fiction, the more fiction the better. We won't tell anyone which is which. Let them figure it out."

Hedley had turned me loose as a critic, now he turned me loose as a story teller.

I began writing short stories.

The city was ripe. It had begun to take on an edge. Half the pilgrims on the way to work every morning on the subways were "high yaller," tan, brown or blue-black. The police force was an increasingly surreal enclave for pale and pink Ulster Irish and Scots. Hash and designer drugs were in the schools and H was in the parking lots. I knew a guy who kept vials of amyl nitrate instead of bullets in a revolver. He owned a strip bar. Homosexual and transvestite dance bars had opened up, too. Long white limos moved from bar to bar.

Editorial meetings with Tom were held in one such bar, at the corner of Lombard and Victoria streets, Gimlets.

There was a dancer he particularly admired at Gimlets. "She gets it, uses her nakedness so perfectly you can never get a glimpse of who she really is. And who wants to know anyway. How boring, to actually know who she is."

Hedley had little interest in knowing who Hogg was either. "Poets are coddled," he said, "as if they have some special gift other writers don't have. It's not true. A coddled egg is an egg. The only thing the creative writing schools have given us is the cult of tiny perfect sentences. Page after page of tiny perfect sentences, all of them dead." The only gift Tom ever gave me was an egg coddler.

And he sent me to Germany. He said: "You're looking melancholy, I'm gonna send you somewhere." He had a wry sense of humor. I had never wanted to go to Germany, though for several years I had taught a course in post-concentration-camp literature (in which a ludicrous but sad situation once arose: on the same day, two students insisted on seeing Dean Harry Crowe — they said they were going to resign from my class, one insisting that I was an anti-Semite, the other insisting that I was anti-German, and Crowe offered to send them to supper so they could talk to each other but they declined and quit the course).

I traveled southern Germany not once but twice and wrote about the Bavarians at length. *Toronto Life* had become a writer's magazine but the owners let Hedley go, he was too rich for their blood. A few years later, he wrote *Flashdance*, the film's aesthetic shaped by those afternoons in Gimlets and at last — after the film's huge commercial success — Hedley had enough money to afford his style.

And at last Hogg had his second hatching. This hatching, the publication of *The Hogg Poems and Drawings*, took place at the Isaacs Gallery in 1978. The drawings were on exhibition in the back gallery, and the Downchild Blues Band played in the front gallery. The book, splendidly produced by Nelson Doucet of General Publishing, was in three parts: poems in Jerusalem, the drawings of silence, and poems in Toronto. Downchild, a powerhouse rhythm and blues band, was led by Donnie Walsh on harmonica, his beautiful wife — dying of leukemia —on piano. His brother, The Hock, sang. The launching was a celebration cast up on the sedate literary shores of Toronto, Hogtown. The wine was Bordeaux, the stretcher-tables sagged under the weight of rumps of roast beef, the band blew "Rocket-88," and the academic poet, Miriam Waddington, came up to me and complained, "I can't hear myself talk." Everyone else was dancing.

Irving Layton wrote:

. . . Though many apostles of Ez Pound and followers of Bill Williams have tried to make prose read and sound like poetry, you're the only one I know — certainly in this benighted country — to have pulled it off successfully. You've done it with your customary verve, panache, wit and because someone put a large Jewish ache in your heart. I do honestly believe it's the last-named that worked the alchemy. It's that — forgive my chauvinism — that makes the difference between THE HOGG POEMS and bp Nichols dead piece of shit. Forgive me too for mentioning your book together with The Martyrology. The mere thought of his volume gives me a violent cramp and I have to relieve myself. THAT'S poetry???? Barry, you big wonderful sod of a man, I wish I had written at least six of the lyrics in your book. I won't name them all lest I turn green with envy at the final one and can't ever regain my original hue. *The Gift of Tongue*: why hadn't I written it? And *Seed-bed*. Both are Layton poems, no offense meant, only compliments. But I have to protect MY turf, right? But the Irish in you makes *Southbound Hogg Meets Woman Northbound* an authentic BC poem. And nobody but Barry Callaghan could have written *Judas Priest,* juggling so expertly the tones of humour, wit, exasperation, humility and compassion. Yup, that's got the whole Hogg in it. Congrats, a warm handshake, and once more many thanks. Peace and Joy,

Irving

I was satisfied. The only other Canadian poet I would have liked to have heard from at the time was Margaret Avison.

A short time later a prominent anthologist and editor took me aside at a cocktail party and said: "I wouldn't put any of those poems in an Anthology of Canadian poetry. They're not Canadian."

I thought I was dealing with a fool. After all, Hogg had just appeared as *Les Livres de Hogg* in Québec, translated by the great French poet from France, Robert Marteau.

A local critic tried to explain this to Morley: "Don't you see, they are so Catholic."

I went to live in Munich, and then to Paris, 22, rue de la Chaise. Claire came to stay with me, and my son, too. I met Con Levanthal. Then Beckett. I wrote short stories, studied engraving at Hayter's, and translated poems. The last story I wrote in Paris was "The Cohen in Cowan," published by Coren in

the Christmas issue of *Punch*. He liked the story so much he "killed" a story
he had already in type. Then, at home, it was published in *Toronto Life*. I heard
the witch-word. I was stunned. I told Coren — a Jew. He was flabbergasted.

The Toronto editor, Don Obe, told me that a well-known television actor
and his wife, and a critic on the magazine itself, had castigated him for publishing the story. They insisted it was anti-Semitic. I was enraged. I said I was
going to call Utica. "I'll break their fucking kneecaps," I told Claire. "Enough
is enough."

But in reality, what could I do?

Nothing.

I found myself seated beside the critic at the magazine's annual party.
He gave me a cheerful Hello. He did not know that I knew what he had said.
A loathing welled up — I wanted to drive a hook to his body, to drive his nose
back into his skull. Instead, I began to sing out loud to myself, nasally, like
Little Willie John or Jackie Shane . . . *got a toothpick in my hand, dig in ten foot
ditch* . . . knowing that my singing, my refusal to talk, would drive him away.

Years later, when I did get to know Joyce Carol Oates, we talked about
left hooks to the body, about fighting. "As a matter of fact," I said to her,
"someone asked me the other day what were the two or three things I shared
with my father that I had then passed on to my son, and I said, 'Well, my
father told me never to lie, which I had told my son,' and then I have to say
that my father had never hit me, ever in my life, and I had never hit my son,
but my father had taught me how to fight, how to box, and I had taught my
son how to box, and one of the first things I did with him about the age of six
or seven when I gave him boxing gloves was hit him hard, so he would know
what it was like to take a punch."

"Well, boxing . . . there's so much to say about it," she said. "It is the art of
self-defense and it is an art. I approach it as a woman, of course, very excluded
from its world and just kind of looking at how men express themselves in terms
of this art. It's very stylized and very arcane, almost. It's very unnatural. When
a boxer meets a fighter, when a man is trying to hit another man and doesn't

have any training he's fighting naturally. He's doing all sorts of wrong things but the boxer is doing things that are not natural and he is the one who is going to win. It's a sort of symbol maybe of the artistic element, you know, against nature, against learning . . . That's not natural fighting. That's not unleashing aggression but really cultivating a strength and a cunning — so boxing is all these things; it really appeals to me on many, many levels."

"And the absorption of pain?"

"The absorption of pain is very, very important, and I am wondering, since I have never boxed and you obviously have, I would guess that you don't even feel the pain in the role of boxer . . . you know, if you got hit suddenly right now, not defending yourself, the pain would be probably extreme, but in boxing, you might not even feel it. You just absorb it."

"It also applies to all violent sports but do you think that boxing really is a sport?"

"I would have to think about that. I would. I have never really thought of — "

"Or is it really a tabu world that — "

"You play tennis, you play baseball but nobody plays boxing. It's just a misnomer . . . "

"And what boxers share," I said, "the winner and the loser, if they have really exchanged pain in a fight, is that boxers love each other."

"Well, they do because one has given the other the fight. They made the fight possible."

"There's real compassion there."

"Right, right, and when I have worked on something that has been very frustrating to me and caused a good deal of emotional distress, when I am all done with it, I feel a sense of elation and gratitude . . . so it is when a fight is all over, then one looks back on it with a good deal of gratitude that some tremendous challenge was given to us."

"So you can look at yourself as a writer and your struggle with yourself and your struggle with your individual works as a kind of boxing match?"

"Each novel is. The hardest novel I wrote in recent years is called *What I Lived For,* and in that I was in a man's psyche. For quite a long time — that novel is about six hundred pages long — an Irish-American with a drinking problem and problems with women, but his name is not Barry Callaghan."

"Ah, you're smooth."

In amiable gossip over lunch, I saw — having talked to Oates about boxing — I had intuitively understood all along that the only response to the *witch-word* was silence, that to fight with any of those slandering fools, at any level, would have implied a bond, compassion, love.

The Black Queen Stories appeared in 1982.

The reviews left my publisher, Lester & Orpen Dennys, ecstatic.

Morley was ecstatic, too. (This ecstasy was not instant: as I wrote the stories over two years, my brother was of the opinion that they were too constant in their melancholy, and Morley took up this tack, which led me to moments of doubt, but then one afternoon — when I was telling Morley and Loretto how much the little story, "The Black Queen," was admired by the editor who had published it in *Punch*, he waved it aside, saying, "It's too easy, cheap effects, homosexuals are always the easy butt of attitude." I was totally taken aback. The story is about two men who happen to be homosexual who are growing old; it is about aging. But Morley was full of dismissive scorn. Then my mother spoke as I had never heard her speak before. "Morley," she said, "you are absolutely wrong. That's a beautiful story, and as a matter of fact his stories are not too sad. They're often quite funny." Morley blinked, and said no more. Thanks to my my mother I ceased to doubt. I went back to work, untrammeled in my heart. That story is now in a dozen anthologies.) We went to Cowan's Bottom Line, to the table reserved for us on Thursdays, to have supper.

He had the book with him, he put it on the table between us, he wanted to say something.

"These stories," he said, "there are three I could not have done . . . 'Crow Jane,' 'Silent Music,' 'The Cohen In Cowan' . . . These are all the real thing." I had never before seen tears in his eyes. "If I had read these when I was young, when I was seeing Hemingway, I'd have thought, boy, these are real, the real thing."

This was a remarkable moment for me, not just because he was my father, but because he was a master, he had written stories as good as Hemingway, as good as Sherwood Anderson. I felt a curious shy humility and yet exultant, and I said, "You know what, you can throw your egg on the floor any time you want."

Bob Cowan, the owner, the boyishly amiable ex-football player, sat down and said, "Morley, who's going to win the World Series?"

"The Yankees," he said.

"How many games?"

"In six."

"Mookie at the bar is laying 3-1 on Los Angeles."

"Yankees," Morley said. "Make no mistake."

"Put a hundred for us," I said.

"Don't," Morley said.

"Two," I said. "Make it two."

Morley bit down hard on his pipe, glowered, and said nothing.

2

Gambling was in my marrow. It was not in my father's, but my father's uncle, the Great Lakes captain, punted at trotting tracks through the midwest, and finally disappeared among the doxies and roly fat guys of Ohio and Illinois. And my mother's father — who looked like a parson but knew how to sport a black coat with a claw-hammer tail — kept stacks of Scribbler books in a sailor's pine box at the foot of his bed, the pages broken into columns of Ontario track times, distances, conditions, all noted in a cramped careful hand.

As a boy I carried my marble-bag of royal purple with a gold draw string — Seagram's Crown Royal — to school and I knelt at the chalk line with my heavily veined shooter snared between trigger knuckle and shooter finger, aiming at coins propped against a curb. Then, as a young man, I learned about "real money" and side-bets and bookies and knew more about dice and back rooms than horses. I didn't favor horses, I liked the men, the players, their acid wit, their self-serving or self-deprecating stories about themselves, and in my early thirties I cherished my "gentleman" bookmaker, Ruby Waxer, who conducted all his weekend NFL "phone work" at a wall payphone on the fourth floor of a Jewish old folks home.

"The whole floor's nothing but old people with concentration camp numbers on their arms. No cop'd dare go up there looking for a guy, asking about numbers."

He drove a dark green Mercedes, lived in a mock-Georgian house across the road from Harry Crowe — my Dean — and insisted that we meet to pay each other off in the revolving door of Simpsons' department store and then we always walked up to the prim, blue-rinse restaurant on Yonge Street, Diana Sweets. "I started making book in the thirties when there were no jobs. I operated out of a cave on the old Kingston Road. Now it's plush for me. Even the cops are plush, the top cops all wear Italian suits." With Nina I had played cards — cribbage and Chicago gin — and both of us played with guys — actors, agents, show business lawyers — who were prone to pencil moustaches in the gaming room of the Celebrity Club, but I was only competent at cards, and in fact, I was lousy at poker. I had no face for it.

Through my marriage years and long after, I followed my stars south to the islands in the winter — particularly Puerto Rico — going to the casinos to shoot craps. My old childhood pal Ponce de Léon was standing in his iron suit on the city square in San Juan, one hand on his hip, the other pointing off into the hills of his illusions. My illusions, the craps tables in the casinos, were lush valleys between those hills, a seductive sinister sheen to the green baize, overseen by acolytes, croupiers in matching maroon suits, the stick man and pit bosses in black, and behind and above them all — The Eye in the Sky — the authority beyond appeal — all of them acting with an air of well-groomed disdain . . . efficient, bemused, and mildly indulgent of the lunging fast-talking bettors who were waiting for the touch, the gift, the hot dice as the croupier cried *Saliendo*, the dice caroming around the curve of the table. "Snake eyes. Crap."

I had been through mystical moments at the tables, alive with electrical intuitions as the numbers tumbled up — "Winner. Pay the good shooter, good shooter coming out" — a lust for luck seizing a table as listless players realized someone was suddenly on a streak, blessed by a grace descending — with racks of chips stacked and broken so fast on the table that it sounded like the clatter of small gunfire in distant hills — while The Big Dick From Boston Took Out His Balls And Washed Them. "*Ten*, the point is *ten, Saliendo*" — all of this watched by the Dead Hand man, who I first saw years ago at Paradise Island.

He was the carrion bird, the bone-picker, who talked to no one, sidestepping through the crowds, always looking for the cold table and the sour faces of shooters who were losers. His left hand, encased in taut, shining black leather, was like a little black sack for his roll of $5 reds. He wore a darkbrown double-breasted leather jacket and a gray shirt with a brown leather tie; his face was lined like soap left a long time under water; he had closecropped hair and perfect half-moons in the nails of his good hand.

He only played the Don't Come Line, 10, 20, sometimes doubling to 50, but always betting against the shooter, always hoping for craps. And when the croupier cried, "*Saliendo*" and the dice fell of the curve of the table, he waited for the cry, "Se-ven . . . Crap," and the shooter's muttered, "Shit," so he could reach down to the Don't Come, a winner. I always looked for the Dead Hand man. I tried to keep an eye on him.

At the El Convento Hotel, which was an old converted Carmelite nunnery of carved wooden spindles in the windows, wood-beamed ceilings, balustrades, white plaster walls, tapestries, and a courtyard, I sat under the trees at a table and drank chilled white wine with my old friend and former student, George Gardos.

He was short, stocky, in his late thirties, the son of what he called a "skimmer" — his father had drifted out of Hungary lying on the bottom of a skiff and he now moved from city to city in Canada with six or seven "hot" watches on his arms, hustling them on the street. Gardos was no hustler. He had a conceptual mind, he saw patterns, and was trying to route his real life into those patterns. He was after the light. When he became a father, he named his son Paris. "What goes around comes around," he said, "and I was perfect when I was born and I'm going to be perfect at the end." He had a round face, a moustache, quick hands, and his head bobbed while talking, like a fighter slipping punches. "Right," he always said, "right," even when he knew he was wrong. He was a plunger who also happened to be a school teacher. He read novels, played the ponies every day, and went to the Saratoga thoroughbred meet in the summer so that he could sit on the porch of the Rip Van Dam Hotel and read the Racing Form. He liked to play pick-up basketball, playing an aggressive game (his only frustrated dream: he had not been born as Doctor J.), even though he hated being touched by other players.

Above the noise in the casino, I heard Gardos calling, chanting, "Here come the hand, here come the hand . . . "

A woman in a chiffon dress was carrying a silver ice bucket and Gardos was beside her, resplendent in his pale blue suit, his hair a little ruffled, his right hand wrapped in a large white napkin, and he was holding his hand down in the bucket, and before the startled croupiers could stop him he was at the table laughing, and when the table boss said sternly, "Sir," a bosomy good-looking woman in her forties, her neck strung with jewels, called across the table with a cow-puncher's drawl, "Leave that boy be, he's my man, he's gonna make the rooster crow, you just hold on an' roll them bones boy." Gardos, drawing himself up, feigning an arch dignity, waited for the dice. When the stickman whipped them in front of him with his looped stick, Gardos unwrapped his hand with mock formality, all eyes on him, curious, perplexed, amused, and he said to me, "You go with me and make all the bets, I'll roll, you bet," and then he yelled, "roll over Beethoven, the big bird's gonna fly, we're gonna knock these suckers dead," alive with that sudden clarity a gambler gets, an inner lightness heavy with conviction, in which he knows, he can see, despite all previous fluctuation, faltering, and hesitation, that he is going to win; he is seized by doubt and all risks are not only possible but reasonable, because an inner note is totally in tune with an outside music. Gardos picked up the dice and threw them backhanded, an 11, and came right back with a seven, crying, "The hand is here . . . "

There was a crush around the table, bets from all sides, and back-up bets, all the numbers covered, and then there was that curious moment of faith a shooter faces when he knows he's on a run . . . the waiting as the croupiers get all bets down, the waiting that looms up longer and heavier than any boredom after every winning roll, time for doubt to weasel in on you, wonder, worry, caution, and that is it, the first crack in the will comes with precaution, the decision to cut back on your bet, put something aside, a few dollars for the old cookie jar, and not play under the reckless head of steam . . . it is a breaking of the faith, the faith in yourself.

But Gardos stood slowly wrapping and unwrapping his hand in the wet towel, sternly oblivious . . . and suddenly I realized it was because he didn't have to handle the money, he was flying, playing to himself, touched by no one, and he picked up the dice to roll for his fifth straight pass, the Dead Hand man beside me, heavy-browed and with little black hairs on his cheeks, suddenly smacked a stack of chips down on the Don't Come Line, saying loudly into the pocket of silence before the roll, "He's wrong." Gardos, startled, hesitated . . . the declaration, the money stack and the cry had its own potency, but instinctively I doubled my bet and yelled, "Gardos, goddamn, you are right," and he let out a whoop and rolled a four and a three, seven, yelling, "The Hand is upon you . . . be-ware, be-ware." That strange generosity of the greedy was loose around the table, men making bets on behalf of the croupiers, on behalf of the glum losers standing idly by, or good-looking girls . . . wanting at any cost to keep the favor of fortune alive.

A southern woman in a scoop-neck dress leaned toward Gardos, "Touch me boy, touch my tits for luck, you got it all," and Gardos, suddenly taken outside of himself, his single-minded sense of himself, looked flattered, bemused, and then brazen, he drew his forefinger down between her breasts, deep into the cleavage, and picked up the dice and rolled boxcars. It was over.

Gardos sat head down at the bar, disappointed with himself, yet suffering a surcharge of exhilaration so strong, an inner glee so light, that he was drained, exhausted. He was a big winner. The woman in the chiffon dress, when he stood up, a little dazed in the saloon's semidarkness, and drifted down along the bar, yelled, "Hey!" He turned, said, "Oh yeah . . . yeah," but kept on going. "Son of a bitch, and the ice bucket was my idea, too," she said.

When I caught up to him he said, "This is good, right, but it ain't the best. Saratoga, you got to go to Saratoga, right. It's the longest stretch run, it's where all the favorites die in the stretch. The horses, right, horses . . . "

My fascination with horses came later and began in the South China Sea, in Macao.

I had been approached by another old student of mine — George Yemec — an entrepreneur who had found a loop-hole in Canadian mail-order law that not only let him buy, sell and store gold on behalf of American citizens, but those Americans were able to avoid paying all taxes on the gold. This business success allowed Yemec to travel short distances in long limousines, and publish *Millions* — a magazine devoted to money, art acquisitions and gambling. He wanted me to go to Macao to interview the casino king pin of the Far East, Stanley Ho, for the magazine, and so I went to the Macao casino as the guest of Ho, who also owned the hotel, the trotting track, the jai alai, and all the jetfoils that crossed the South China Sea.

I ended up shoulder to shoulder in a casino with men and women who stood sleepless for hours waiting for someone to surrender a chair at the 21 or roulette tables and then they would hold onto that chair with squatter's right for ten hours, a day, two, some men and women carrying plastic containers to piss in, all of them counting on stamina and a burst of luck from the clattering steel ball in the wheel, the hours slipping away, all sense of time and the sense of self lost, until bored by the ache in my shoulders, by a profound sense of absence — *dans l'Orient désert quel devint mon ennui!* — I quit and went out to where only a few feet from the door the ocean slapped against the breakwall and there in the dim filtered light I walked along the ocean road, calmed by the curious milk-gel to the air before dawn, everything fresh, cleansed, but there were no birds flying or crying along the shore, and the few black birds that were clustered together on a slope of sand looked like coals abandoned by fire.

I took that as an omen and went to a temple and had tea with an old monk under a huge tree that was three trees twined together. He tossed the fortune sticks:

Que dis-je? En ce moment mon coeur, hors de lui-même,
S'oublie, et se souvient seulement qu'il vous aime.

I said a prayer. I knew George Yemec was in Hong Kong. I went there on a jetfoil, passing between islands that were stone humps in the sea, arriving at the Peninsula Hotel, a palace of grace that catered to illusions in the hills, and I sat in the spacious lobby surrounded by the scurrilous and reputable, by film producers and perhaps a gunrunner, by exquisite women and the odd counter-culture warphead. I strode between Silver Clouds and the white stone lions at the door and little boys in white suits wearing white pill-box hats and found Yemec — lean, aloof, and graying at the temples — and he said, "Hello, can you get up at four in the morning? You should come with me and see the horses."

In the cold hours overcast with no stars in the sky I found myself hunched against the wind beside a racetrack and there were great amber floodlights high in the morning mist, suspended flowers, but I couldn't see anything, not around the turn in the rail, but I heard the muffled sound of hoofs and suddenly a huge horse broke into the half-light, lunging past.

"Aw, she's a might slow this morning," said the small Cork trainer, clocking the horse and staring into the gloom, waiting. Other horses, appearing out of the dark, disappeared.

After half an hour, I shuffled down the slope, shivering, to sit alone in a steel shed that cut the wind, but I was so cold I crouched down and thought, Jesus, goddamned horses in the gloom. What am I doing?

As the sun rose and the sky cleared, I went with Yemec to eat at a local market of sprawling stalls and narrow walkways covered with corrugated tin sheeting or corrugated colored plastic, and the tables were piled high with fresh meats, fish, squid, eels, crabs, lobsters, melons, rice, fruits — and the gutters ran with water and blood. In the centre of this flesh and pulp, this hacking and chopping and slicing, women were sitting beside steaming chrome tanks sipping tea, eating delicacies. We sat down, warmed by steam from the tanks and tea, but in a near corner an old man huddled beside a large wicker basket, lifting live quail out of the basket, and with his long thumbnail he slit the breast and belly, peeling the skin off the still live bird.

"Yemec," I said, "the omens are all wrong."

"Omens mean nothing," he said.

"You believe that? You and my father."

"Omens are for when you're confused."

"I don't know what I'm doing here," I said. "I don't know anything about horses."

"I don't know anything about women."

"You mean I'll end up dreaming about horses?"

"I do all the time, wonderful dreams. I wish women were horses."

We were at Sha Tin racetrack north of the Kowloon foothills, a racecourse on land reclaimed from the sea. We had our own air-conditioned box with a balcony, a small kitchen, a chef and serving boys. The two of us were welcomed on the trinitron electronic billboard. There were 35,000 people in the stands betting on geldings and a few odd mares (there are no pastures in Hong Kong, and therefore no breeding), and throughout the city another 500,000 people were crowded into off-track betting shops, wagering more than $26-million a day (the daily average at the Woodbine track in Toronto was $15-million), and while seemingly soothed by escargots in pastry shells and white wine, I sensed something sensual in Yemec, a rush of energy, covert under his diffident graceful air, a channeling of all his attention while still making small talk. I grew fascinated watching him read the *Form*, constructing out of circled fractions and underlined times a conviction about the upcoming race. Even when surrounded by backslappers, he had a strange capacity for silence, sealing himself off so that he could concentrate, and when we went down to the paddock to look at the horses he disappeared, melted into anonymity, so that I was left looking around, wondering where he was — and then he appeared again out of the crowd, casually elegant in his Armani jacket, saying quietly, "I'd box the 2-4-7," striding off to the windows as if we were all grown men who knew exactly what to do. We began to win a lot of money, betting three-horse boxes, key-wheeling, back-wheeling, catching exactas. It was all magical — and when the day was over, we had won several thousand dollars. It was like that for three days and I said, "Those exactas are terrific, the payoffs . . . "

"You should try the triactors back home."

"What's that?"

"It's the last race, and you pick the first three horses, in order. I once hit for $23,000 with a $2 bet."

On the last night, we celebrated at Gaddi's, the finest European restaurant east of Suez, eating quail breast and pigeon with truffles. We drank Chassagne Montrachet and a Chateau Pichon-Longueville, Comtesse de Lalande, sitting in the shadow of a Ch'ing Dynasty Coromandel screen that depicted gay summer scenes with the emperor.

Back home, the weather was cold, the gray tail of winter, suspended time, the ice melting down to stubble on the ground. In the morning I considered what I was going to teach that day . . . Camus' *The Plague*, Primo Levi's stories, Tom Kinsella's *Notes from the Land of the Dead* . . . and then on some mornings I looked at the race results, fascinated by the triactor — $350 one day, $4,000 the next — and then one night I had a dream. There were three birds in white wicker cages, the cages like cubes or dice. The next night I had the same dream, except the birds suddenly became numbers: 2, 3, 9. In the morning I phoned Yemec and told him to book a table at the track. It became a long meal. We lost race after race and I was almost tapped out, weary and saddened, but I held on until the ninth and made the bet: it won, 2, 3, 9, and paid $1,400. That was my first triactor.

It was a curious summer, casual and yet intense. Each morning I took an espresso while sitting at Claire's living-room window that looked onto the ravine slope of ferns and tiger lilies, and I sifted through drawings that she had worked on the night before — men and women and women and women in the tremors of love, faces stricken with joy, hands eagerly open to pain, and I wrote poems of dread about men I had met the year before — I had been in Moscow and Leningrad — who had stainless steel teeth, who smiled as ink fell on a blotter and a name disappeared, and I learned from a woman I'd met along the ice-locked canals that

> *we know what love is*
> *when it's over,*
> *the trail of two people*
> *bending into the echo of their own laughter*
> *across a lake fresh with snow.*
> *'And this, this,' you cried, looking back,*
> *'is the whiteness of God's mind.*
> *Without us he is nothing.'*

At about ten, I drove to the university, to the rose garden campus, and talked for two hours to students seated on the lawn under a weeping willow tree about Robert Lowell and Hart Crane and John Berryman, about "freelancing out along the razor's edge," and then I took a light lunch at Cowan's Bottom Line, across the road from a firehall, the firemen regularly running their extension ladders into the air, practicing, climbing higher and higher into nowhere. Sometimes Morley joined me for lunch to watch the run of the ladders, and we talked about gambling.

"You're a gambler" he said, "in the way I'm not a gambler. You're a real gambler, I'd tell little children to keep away from you. But I gamble on my life. I've taken a risk on my life, my work."

"Always with little back bets, though."

"Yes."

"In case it didn't work out."

"Yes, but I think *you* can have runs of luck. There are days at a big crap table when a guy can get on a roll, you want to touch him, to get a piece of his luck. I believe you can get on such a roll. I don't know why this is. I've no idea. You can get on a roll as a writer, too. You remember how I thought Hemingway — when I was just starting out — was showing my stories around, and then I found out it was Fitzgerald who'd showed them to Max Perkins. A little later I got a letter from Hemingway and he said, 'I never spoke to Scribner's about you, your work, because,' he said, 'things were going great for you. You were producing and I knew you were producing and I know it's very dangerous to interrupt a writer when he's going so good.' He meant I was on a roll. That's luck, he meant that I was lucky, as if I was fulfilling a destiny that he didn't dare interrupt."

Toward two in the afternoon, I began to feel an almost sensual arousal, and eased by the sun and the talk with Morley, I drove to the track for a late-afternoon outing, carrying with me a small notebook of poems — the Miodrag Pavlović poems that I was translating from Serbian — a little work for between races.

There were several men I saw every day: my friend Yemec; the Bajan Shoebox Victor in his blue suit and bow tie, a clipped moustache and pockets stuffed with sweet pink candies and computer print-outs — soil conditions and speed ratings, quarter-fractions and breeding, all visioned in his mind along the arc of quantum mathematics; Patrick Donohoe, a gentle-spoken Wexford man, whose love was the horse, quoting not fractions but a whimsical line from Yeats or Robert Service; Fat Saul, Gardos, and sometimes Michael Magee, astute horseman, and afficionado of military brass bands, pipe bands, drum corps, an unforgiving acerbic satirist who had written a good-selling book, *The Golden Age of BS*. Behind us, the benign silent presence of the old great hockey player King Clancy, a man who seemed to know how to bide his time when there was so little time left to bide. It was always fine there in the afternoon, casual and yet intense — making a small bet or two, sitting in the open stands with sea gulls far inland circling and swooping overhead looking "for crusts of bread and such" until horses broke from the gate, striding beautifully, six or seven sprinters turning for home, to the wire, all of us together on our feet at the finish, yet each of us alone, the best at ease with aloneness, and the worst filling every space with complaint, chatter, confusion. Myself, I was waiting, translating a line or two

> *A curtain of smoke*
> *descends:*
> *an angel falling*

waiting for the last race, waiting until it was time to concentrate on the triactor, or as it was known, the Tri.

So: what had I learned since Sha Tin, what did I know?

Among other things, the track — like the literary life — was a hive of opinions. Free advice, tips, tip sheets, doubts, touts, they were all about, beating like mad butterflies on your brain. The horses constituted enough confusion without all that clatter and clutter. So, the secret was to stand alone in the whirlpool, singing silently to yourself. *Silently.* In that spirit — I never listened to losers. Losers cheered each other up by beating each other down. And if you lost, forget the loss immediately. Celebrate when you won and celebrate when you lost. Never let losing become a habit of mind. The more experience you had with losing, the more ways you'd find to lose.

There was one exception to this rule. If I was lucky enough (for punting purposes) to have a friend who lost all the time, then I sought out his top choice and immediately stroked it out, even if it was the odds-on-favorite. This required real strength, being the betrayal of a friend's best judgment, and such betrayal became a bond.

I avoided the advice of players who never looked at the horses and only read the *Form*. They were like poets who never read poetry — or theologians who reduced God to checkpoints on a chalk board (I once had a professor at the Pontifical Institute of Medieval Studies, a humorless man, who drew the operation of God's "intellect" as a series of little doors opening and closing, at the gate, so to speak).

So, I had to look at the horses as they saddled and paraded. But look for what?

The smell of liniment, iodine stains on the fetlocks, fatness, a horse "washing out" (over-sweating), a tail boltout from the backside (the horse was hurting), front bandages, etc.

Haw: once I'd seen what I thought I saw — then what?

Well, anything was possible, but unless a horse had a proven record of winning with front bandages, I never bet on it.

A horse dripping wet was usually washed out. But not always.

Fat was fat. But not always.

You had to use your own judgment. Anything was possible. Anything. I have never forgotten a schoolboy equation:

$$\text{If } x = y = 1$$
$$\text{then } x^2 - y^2 = x2 - xy$$
$$(x-y)(x+y) = x(x-y)$$
$$x + y = x$$
$$x + y = 1$$
$$2 = 1$$

And so I said to myself: if only I knew someone in the backstretch — the vet, the trainer.

Well, in a way, I did. As soon as the odds for the last race went up on the tote board, I checked the "win pool" — the amount of money already wagered, the "barn money." I often found that long shots heavily bet by men who thought they knew something was a factor.

And then there was that "gift" — the thing that fascinated me about Yemec at Sha Tin: the ability to "see" that a horse was ready. There was no way to explain this, but I acquired it. The trap, however, was that you "tried" to see, and then you believed you saw what was in fact not there.

The same was true of hunches. You had to trust your hunches (intuitions) but not seek them. The sought intuition was a sign of confusion. The true hunch came to you clean, like grace. And like grace, it was preposterous.

So: what else did I pay attention to?

The *Racing Form:* but I never gave too much attention to speed ratings. Track conditions and situations were too variable. This was as bad as relying on statistics.

The opening mutuel odds (or "morning line") of *each* horse in the program. This was the result, after all, of a considered judgement.

The horses carrying the five top jockeys: good jockeys tended to get good horses, or the sleeper that was ready. I won Tri after Tri because a top jockey had nosed out, for third place, an inferior rider on a superior horse.

The percentage jockeys: the leading riders were not always the top jockeys in terms of percentage finishes in the first three positions, and this was a crucial triactor consideration.

A marked low weight advantage.

The top trainers.

And the three-minute money move: the movement of the horses in relation to the morning line, from seventh position to fourth, for example, as a betting favorite. This calculation had to be done at the very last moment and factored into all the other information, judgments, intuitions, considerations.

All of this took place in some 25 minutes, and most of it in the seven minutes before post time. And even as I stood alone, I was confronted by all my confusions and calculations. Obviously, concentration was the key: concentration while surrounded by shuffling, mumbling crowds, concentration while standing in line at the wickets, concentration while friends interrupted to say hello, ask advice, give advice, all of this as time, relentless time, clicked away. The secret was to lock your will, to focus on what you knew, seeking the conviction that had the most clarity. When the moment came — that still moment of lucidity — indecision ceased and you heard the sound of a piercing, almost pure moment of perception. The immediate temptation was to suspect such clarity. The solution, I thought, could not be so simple, so I was tempted to go with the last hunch or a word whispered in the ear. This was unavoidable, and panic set in, because even clarity of choice was not enough. I had to know how to bet my choice.

I had a simple procedure: if in a field of 14, my top choices were 3, 5, 8, 11, 12, I would bet a five-horse box as a security (in a box, the three horses can finish in any order).

Then I constructed a series of bets that "pressed" those choices, so that when I went to the window I had a card that looked like this:

3 5 8 11 12
5-horse $1 box, cost $60

4 8 11 12
4-horse $1 box, cost $24

8 11 12 6
4-horse box with long shot possible, $1 box, cost $24

8 11 12
3-horse $2 box, cost $12

11 12/12 11
2-horse bet on top, with the whole field for third, $1, cost $12 each; total $24

11- 3 5 6 8 12
key wheel, in which the 11 must win and the others finish in any combination, $1, cost $20

Total: $164

This was a minimum bet, and any individual move could be increased, but if — in the above series — the first three horses had finished 11, 12, 8, I would have had the Tri six times. If the payoff had been $1,000 for a $2 bet, I would have won $3,500.

This was not a system, this was a method that only an amateur could create, and only an amateur could afford. This was not the world of the pro. As Patrick Donohoe said, "Like the story of *The Song of Bernadette*, for those who believe, no explanation is necessary; for those who do not, no explanation is possible," but by the end of the first week in August, I had won the tri-actor 66 times, and on two or three occasions, five days in a row. Now I was able to afford to take Morley out to supper every Thursday night at Cowan's Bottom Line. It amused him that I now paid the bills, so he could chastise me for my profligate ways. I put a $40,000 down payment on a house for Claire on Sullivan Street. Morley began to read the race results in the morning newspaper. He told me he had written a story about a horse player years ago but he didn't know where it was and didn't know why it wasn't in his collected stories. I told him I was going to Saratoga and he should come, it was — I told him, quoting Gardos — the loveliest race course in America, the Graveyard of Champions, a town of healing waters and a track with a long stretch run that sapped frontrunners and broke the hearts of bettors who put their money on favorites. "How many times can you break my heart?" he asked.

"Try me," I said.

"No, and who'll look after your mother, and Nikki?"

Nikki was the dog, a giant standardbred poodle, brought into the house after the burglar had tried to beat Morley.

The rhythm of the town of Saratoga revolved around the track: the *Racing Form* arrived the night before the race and Bronx plungers and balletic puffs sat side by side on the balcony of the Rip Van Dam Hotel or in the lobby of the Adelphi Hotel, hard at work in the half-light; there were afternoon cocktail and *petit-four* parties on the lawns of graceful mansions, the very rich idling in town for the four-week meeting; lunch at Mrs. London's Bake Shop or Hattie's Chicken Shack was over by one o'clock, and the woman behind the desk at the Adelphi told the hour to customers in terms of how long 'til post time; after lunch, people hurried along the streets and through the central park past the duck pond, where orthodox Jews who were in town only for the waters took the sun; prayerful men wrapped in their black coats, like black birds: *"Prophet still, if bird or devil!/whether Tempter sent, or whether tempest tossed thee here ashore,/ . . . is there balm in Gilead? — tell me — tell me, I implore."/Quoth the Raven, "Nevermore."* And the track — set among homes so that it seemed nestled in the neighborhood — was groomed beautifully: a grassy saddling area under tall maple and plane trees with the horses within arm's length, a small jug and string band and step dancers and two fiddlers among the crowd and restaurants that were open to the race course serving lobster, crab, and tender veal. It was a place of intimacy, grace, style, first-rate horses, first-rate jockeys, first-rate trainers, first-rate stewards.

For nine days, despite lovely sunlight and the close feel of the horses, I went into the graveyard. And when you're down in the hole "there's nothing to do but dig." I hardly held on through the daily card and nine times in succession my tri-actor picks placed 1, 2, 4. This was perverse and punishing. It was like what Joyce Carol Oates described as the fight with a work that you can't get right. It kept me awake at night because it was hard to sleep when the devil had his porch light on. Too many good horses kept sneaking in from nowhere. I couldn't get a rhythm. Logic faltered, concentration slipped away. Losers began to talk to me under the maple trees. I expected the Dead Hand man to appear. I told Gardos to stay away. I began to smell loss between my sheets, the loss of a sense of self: because after all, betting was, among other things, a confirmation of the self. To fail is to fail yourself. Still, I tried to start each afternoon with a freshness: I looked for a sign, an opening, a move. To surrender was to suck wind: the tailing wind of the Holy Ghost.

On the day of the Travers, the big stakes race of the meet, I found myself in disarray, caught between anger and dismay. I'd fallen into the slough of the bettor's despond, second-guessing myself, making my choice and then betting against myself. So, I decided to just back off and wait, wait and see if that still moment of perception would show up. The moment of *the right word*. I would let the rhythm find me since I couldn't find it.

The Travers promised to be an extraordinary race, with the three winners of the Triple Crown — *Conquistador Cielo, Gato del Sol* and *Aloma's Ruler* — running against one another. *Runaway Groom*, a Canadian-bred gray, was also entered, a horse I'd bet on once at Woodbine. It had finished second in the Queen's Plate, and now I looked at it sentimentally but not seriously, until I saw that Jeffrey Fell was the jockey, an excellent rider who sat ramrod straight in the saddle, just the kind of rider to go into the Valley of the 600. The odds were 19 to 1 (*Conquistador Cielo* was 2 to 5) but then I thought, those are not long enough odds for an unknown horse: someone had to have put money on the gray. For days I had been alone with the loneliness of the loser. Suddenly I felt a quickening and pressed close to the parade rail to look at the horses. I was astonished. *Conquistador Cielo* was wearing front bandages. I knew the horse had never worn bandages, and I thought, No horse bandaged for the first time should be going off at 2 to 5. I hurried to the windows, noting the odds had gone down another point, put $40 to win on *Runaway Groom* and, suddenly seized by conviction, by the belief that I was right, doubled the win bet and wheeled him for the late double (that is, bet him with every horse in the field in the next race). When, a few minutes later, the *Groom* turned into that graveyard stretch, coming from 20 lengths off the pace, surging, his long neck straining, the crowd roared in disbelief as the *Groom* ran down *Conquistador Cielo* and *Aloma's Ruler* and won at the wire. I felt as if I'd come back from the dead, blessed by my own best judgment, and that gray, running from nowhere, appearing as if he'd come out of the dark morning mist at Sha Tin, had suddenly put out the devil's porch light. Suspicion and second-guessing, gloom and disarray, disappeared. *Runaway Groom* had come to Hogg like a gift of grace, and when I left Saratoga ten days later, I had not only taken the healing waters but had both feet out of the grave. I had beaten the track. Down the killing stretch of the last days of the meet, clear judgment had clicked in, still moments of clarity had come to me. It was like the first time I ever wrote a short story flat-out. *The Black Queen*, no block, no meditation, no wondering how to "end" the story. No, the clarity of every detail and gesture had fallen into place, leaving me with a rush, the gambler's sure sense of the harmony of all things.

As I left town on a bright morning, I saw two old men in their black coats, the coats billowing in the wind as they hurried away from me, birds of night, and somehow I knew that the strange fascination begun in the dark of that cold, steel shed at Sha Tin had reached a fruition. I had come back from the dead, I had been given a gift. Having won the triactor 101 times by the evening of December 7, the end of the year's racing, Morley called for a late night supper at Cowan's Bottom Line. Jan the chef had spent the whole day in the freezer carving a huge horse's head in ice. It was sitting in the center of the table, surrounded by Claire, Yemec, Shoebox Victor, Yolande (the woman in the wickets who always got my late bets down, no matter the crowd), Gardos, Morley and me. We drank champagne. "Celebrate, Morley," I said, "We got to celebrate more often."

"The horse is melting," he said wryly.

"Yeah, but he looks even more beautiful in the light."

Then I dedicated the book of Pavlović translations, *Singing at the Whirlpool*, to the boys of my summer:

> *for*
>> *George Yemec*
>> *Patrick Donohoe, Michael Magee/*
>> *Fred Dobbs,*
>> *Shoebox Victor, Statistician Steve,*
>> *Nelson the Bat,*
>> *Gardos,*
>> *King Clancy*
>> *and*
>> *the dream numbers*
>> *2 3 9*

Book Eleven

1

One day the printer, Ernie Herzig, told me he had been trying to assemble work from across the country for a limited edition of erotic drawings. "But," he said, "no erotica. Can you imagine. It's a country with no erotica."

"It shouldn't surprise you," I said.

"Well, it does . . . "

"The national painters . . . the Group of Seven . . . the painters everybody loves, there's no one there, never mind naked people. No one. Nobody. Nowhere. Just rocks and stones and pine trees. It's a crazy fucking country . . . "

He looked sad. He was an immigrant. I think he wondered why he had come to such a country.

Claire and I talked about this.

She was still working from models. Single models. Erotic in their frankness. But single, alone.

I wondered whether she could produce a series of erotic drawings of couples in embrace if she continued to work from models.

Within two weeks, an intelligent, athletic and beautiful young woman who worked in current affairs television was posing with me in our living room.

She had to be athletic. For Claire to "see" the "tension" in the bodies — an arched back had to be severely arched, severely turned. A session might last an hour, even two, lying still, tensed, twisted in pain.

Those several dozen drawings had a sculpted stillness, the real weight of flesh.

Then Claire discovered an infidelity of mine, a short intense affair with a woman she had seen once but did not know.

She was stricken with rage. There was something ice-cold in her fury.

She broke loose. Four, five, six small drawings a day — visionings of lovers. There was an urgency. Tremors. The models were in her mind. I was stunned by the drawings, the sureness of line, unforced . . . a painful ache inherent in every moment of pleasure, each gesture of longing containing a seed of contempt, all lust undercut by lethargy, and love aroused only to become lax. Her intimacy with these figures was extraordinary.

As Marie-Claire Blais said:

> *all artists have a predilection*
> *for debauchery.*

Charles Pachter, painter and entrepreneur, offered Claire his gallery on Queen Street West. The opening was a celebration: thirty large drawings titled *The Two of Us Together, Each of Us Alone* — and sixty small works, the *Tremors* series . . .

Racks of wine and racks of lamb.

The Rainbow Garden Orchestra.

We wondered about the thought police, but the only cop who came by said, "Looks like life to me."

Over six weeks, three thousand people signed the guest books.

Bill Ronald marched around the gallery in his silver cowboy boots and said: "This is not the city for you . . . the critics are still holding up their pants with safety pins." He then wrote: "She is one of the few artists of this or any other time whose output has been forcefully involved with these most intimate and natural moments . . . timeless faces that stare into the blinding space of the moment, faces that are a mixture of pain and awe, pleasure and disbelief: emotions that no single word can sum . . . tight, incestuous, tangled relationships which, because of their aloneness, take on their own life with their own laws, their own morality . . . "

Morley read Ronald.

He sat down and lit his pipe.

"Not bad," he said, "but I could write a better piece. The thing is, you see, drawing the body well is one thing and the great trick is in the eyes, and even harder, the hands . . . to get life in them, but even harder is to get a relationship between the look in the eyes and the gesture of the hands. That's the mystery in her drawings, not the sex . . . the contradictory emotions, the relationship, that's her story . . . "

He never wrote the piece.

2

On a drizzly night in 1984, Pierre Trudeau was in town for an exhibition of paintings by Bill Ronald at the Ontario Gallery of Art. It was a daring idea, abstract expressionist portraits of all the prime ministers. Board chairmen and sensibly dressed Junior League women clustered around the Gallery's inner courtyard, wanting to be close to Trudeau, who arrived and approached the crowd with that curious deferential shyness that always made him seem aloof and self-possessed. A local politician, a conservative councillor, said snidely, "The man's a mere ghost of his self."

I had to smile, I had once been Trudeau's ghost.

During the election of 1979, as he had crossed the country, he seemed to be flat-footed and distracted: his beautiful young wife, Margaret, was frolicking with the Stones in Toronto's King Edward Hotel and his aides said he looked weary every morning because she was on the phone taunting him every night. The word was — he had clouted her in the eye in the back seat of his limousine. He was also being humped in the polls by an opposition leader known derisively as "Joe Who?" Trudeau's advisors at the MacLaren Advertising Agency in Toronto decided that unless he gave a "heartfelt" speech — "a speech in which he is not aloof and half-dead on his feet" to launch the last week of the campaign, a speech that would be televised to the nation from Maple Leaf Gardens, "the fat lady can uncross her legs, it's over. Fucked, we are!"

I was asked to write the speech. I had one week. I decided to turn his private disappointment with Margaret into a metaphor for the public's disappointment with him. Discreet but direct, I took up every major social and political question — particularly Québec — as if each were a sorrow he had to share with his family, his neighbors, the electorate. At the end of the week I read the speech to an agency executive, Jerry Goodis. When I was through he was crying.

As the days passed, Senator Keith Davey, the *éminence* in Ottawa, could not say whether Trudeau was going to read the speech. The Toronto boys started pushing their noses into their hands.

On the night of the speech, we sat at the south end of the Gardens: among us, a senator who had recently come out of the closet, several local MPs hoping to ride Trudeau's coat-tails, Claire, Morley and Jerry Goodis. The Ottawa word had come. He was going to read the speech. Sixteen thousand people were on their feet roaring as he stepped to the podium, opening his arms to the crowd. "Tonight," he said, "I want to speak to you very personally . . . " Goodis clutched my hand. " . . . personally, so that I can touch the private . . . " He paused. " . . . the private places in the heart . . . the private places of the heart in this great land, that is strong . . . " Goodis moaned. "The land is strong . . . " Trudeau went on to deliver his usual speech about the land, bereft of sentiment, timing, twist of phrase or turn of thought, the speech of a man trying to please. Goodis looked at me, ill with disappointment. "The check will be in the mail," he said.

Trudeau, eager and spry, embraced Bill Ronald in the Gallery courtyard. Bill was leaning on his silver-handled cane, as barrel-chested as Chuvalo, with a great mane of black hair, wearing dark glasses and a hand-stitched white silk suit, and a white cape lined with pink satin. There were jade and coral rings on all his fingers. Earlier in the year, Trudeau had spent hours several afternoons with him at his Mowatt Street studio. He admired Bill's spirit. He'd invited Bill to Ottawa to pass an afternoon in the prime minister's office. Bill had done so. "When I told Trudeau that when I was young I was so pissed off with the morose resentfulness at anything excellent in this country that I'd become an American citizen, he didn't believe me. He refused to believe me."

They shook hands and embraced.

The paintings — *The Prime Ministers Series* — were expressionist "portraits" of sixteen leaders, all of them strange men: one, who had dressed up in a bearskin and hop-danced and played the concertina, another who had boiled to death in his bathtub, another who kept a mistress and chewed tobacco while quoting Latin, one who had built a temple garden to himself as he tried to convert hookers to Christ, or Trudeau, who had told striking cab drivers to eat shit, who had dated Barbra Streisand and given the finger to the people while pirouetting behind a Queen.

When he stood beside Bill in the courtyard to speak, Trudeau said it was the sense of wonder in the paintings that fascinated him, the astonishment at life itself.

"There is a difference," he said, resting his elbows on a podium, speaking off-the-cuff, as if he were sharing a private thought, "between the craftsman on his trapeze and the artist who expresses life as he sees it. An artist must always be wary of trying to please, and in that, he is like some politicians. He must never seek to please." The crowd clapped and Trudeau smiled. "The bad politician," he said, "like the bad artist, seeks to please."

"Well," a local critic known for his acerbic opinions and dark depressions whispered, "I do not intend to be lectured on the nature of art by a politician." He took three busy steps to the right.

"The artist who sees for himself," Trudeau went on, "opens up the treasure of innerness, the pleasures of wonderment, and such a man is basically a loner, but although he's a loner, if he has genius, he creates something universal; out of his aloneness, he can reach out and become and remain universal . . . "

Ronald lifted his arms, opening up the cape of pink satin. Trudeau's security men in steel-gray single-breasted suits cleared a path as Trudeau shook hands, talking, often touched on the arm by women, his head bobbing back, always wondering — so he had confided to me years before — wondering at the way grown women girlishly crowded around him.

"That," my father said, "may be the most remarkable little spontaneous speech ever given by a politician in this country." The critic, seeing that the security men had changed direction, leapt nimbly around a pillar, trying to place himself in the prime minister's path, a tight ingratiating smile on his lips. I found myself wondering: what would have happened if Trudeau — instead of trying to play it safe and please his Ottawa handlers — had spoken openly and genuinely about the private places in his heart that night in the Gardens?

3

"Politicians are of a breed in a democracy," Morley said, "and as a breed they are all the same. I believe in democracy. It's my favorite form of government. But to live happily and intelligently in a democracy you must be continually on the alert, your job as a citizen is to watch the politician with a cold eye because the whole system leads to corruption. It is natural, because the politician is the courtier of democracy and he must go out and he must get elected. There's nothing as dead as a politician who can't get elected and everyone of them knows this. So he'll do anything to get elected."

The Liberal Convention, 1984: The Ottawa Coliseum. I was there because *Toronto Life* had a new editor . . . a former Moscow correspondent for the *Telegram,* a subtle and complex man . . . born of one of the founding Afrikaner families, his father a Senator of independent integrity who traced their ancestors back to the seventeenth century . . . and this editor, well-traveled and alert in several languages, was Marq de Villiers, who offered me every opening he could in his pages, publishing my political writing, my poetry and fiction (looking back, I can see that as a journalist — and that's what Edmund Wilson called himself — a journalist, a writer who gets paid for his writing, I would have had no presence, no public output in my country if it had not been for Tom Hedley — and Ron Evans after him at the *Tely* — and Marq de Villiers. A writer is only as public as his editors will encourage him to be and pay him to be).

Thursday night at the Coliseum: Trudeau, stepping down from power, sat between his sons and his sister as the crowd celebrated his years in office. It was a time for nostalgia and praise, film clips in the huge hall: moments of incredible grace, quick contempt, a man so measured and so mercurial, so much a star and so star-struck, a man of inexplicable contradictions. As the crowd chanted *Trudeau, Trudeau,* I remembered the night in 1968, the night of the LaFontaine Park riot, when snarling people chanted *Trudeau aux poteaux,* and the bottle throwers who'd broken through the barricades, and while other politicians fled, Trudeau — brushing his bodyguards aside —had shaken his fist, standing alone . . .

Rich Little, the comedian and impersonator, the perfect man for his times, a man with everyone's voice but his own, reminded the crowd of what a cuckoo's nest the Diefenbaker-Pearson parliament had been in the early sixties.

The Honorable Marc Lalonde — looking like a slightly oily maître d' in his white dinner jacket — ushered Trudeau on stage to a huge, happy ovation. Trudeau had no notes, no prop other than the rose in his lapel.

"I relived tonight," he said, "in a certain sense, my youth . . . " As he often did, he offered a halting handshake to the empty air (I remembered a moment in Sai Woo, a chinatown restaurant, when Morley had reached across a big bowl of hot and sour soup for that halting Trudeau hand and missed and a waiter had laughed so hard that he'd dropped a dish of crystal shrimps at Trudeau's feet), and he quoted lines of poetry:

I went out under the sky and stared,

And oh, I dreamed of such splendid love . . .

"Yes, we have dreamed of splendid love," he said, "for ourselves, for our country. We rebuilt this country, the country we carry within ourselves . . . Oh la la such splendid loves I dreamed of . . . our hopes are high, our faith in the people is great, our courage is strong, our dreams for the beautiful country will never die."

There was applause from those who loved him, those who admired him, and those glad to be rid of him. He suddenly called out a line from the *Marseillaise*, calling for his children: "*Allons enfants de la patrie* . . . come on kids." Trudeau, with his kids, waved and went off-stage, and then came back for one moment of whimsical childishness, mocking his own emotion, pirouetting for the last time, as he had done behind the back of a Queen.

"The great struggle in a democracy among politicians is for power," Morley said, "to stay in power. The great weakness of our time is that our politicians stand for nothing as individuals. A politician today will not stand up and make his own speech. He will have the three best speech writers he can hire working on his speech. That is true of every one of them. It used to be considered a disgrace for a politician to stand up in the House of Commons and read a speech, but the politician today, reading speeches that someone else has written for him, doesn't know what disgrace is. Such a man does not stand for anything."

Friday night: John Turner said of himself: "What you see is what you get." Well, perhaps not — because his open face contained a coldness that gave an edge to all his well-groomed ease; as a man of the broad corporate world he kept to narrow, rigid rituals; industrious and dominating, he seemed insecure and not to have done enough; on display at Table 23 at Winston's in Toronto, he had no anecdotal life; a private man, he had no secret life; a devout man, he seemed to have no spiritual concerns. His tone was corporate decisiveness. That was it: that is what he meant: he was decisive. "He bites all his words," a woman said to me. "How could I be comfortable with a man who told me to take off my clothes and butter my toast in exactly the same tone?"

Turner, standing beside his wife in the tunnel under the stands, flicked his tongue, flicked it again, jabbed it around the inside of his upper lip. Instead of jogging at the starting blocks, he was giving his mouth a workout, a nervous loosening up. Peabody, an ebullient black photographer, called out, "Hey Mr. T . . . Keep the faith." Turner broke toward him, stumbling, wide-eyed, a false start. One of his floor-men screamed into a walkie-talkie, "Wait, wait . . . wait as long as we can, let them wonder when he's coming."

Turner smiled.

A cop said, "What a set of clackers."

Then he strode across the cement floor to the platform. "He's got to be great," one of his advisors said to me. "We're stalled, if it goes to three ballots we could lose. He hasn't made the connection, he hasn't hit the right chord." Turner, with that abrupt clipping of words that would be abrasive if he weren't smiling, mounted the stage and looked at Trudeau, and despite his animosity to the man he told the crowd, "I have said on several occasions, but never face-to-face to him, that he has surely been the most remarkable Canadian of his generation." Slumped in his chair, Trudeau nodded. "Holy Christ, if he can say that he can say anything," a Chrétien supporter said. "I can't believe it." Then Turner, despite his declared determination to cut the deficit, spoke like a reformer, saying economic recovery would never be at the expense of the aged, the sick, the poor or the unemployed. A tall, bony woman with peculiar fat hands, as if her fingers were swollen with water, said: "Now that's a prime minister."

Jean Chrétien mounted the stage, looking drawn, dour, gray-faced, a raw man who wore his heart on his sleeve. "*Il est un dure qui ne ferait pas mal à une mouche,"* one man said. But he hurt himself: *le petit tough,* trying to be prime ministerial, read from a prepared speech, tying himself to the rhythms of calculated incantation. It was a mistake: his emotion ended truncated, trussed. He pounded the air with his fist and mocked Brian Mulroney and mocked Turner, but every time he rose on a reverberation from the crowd, he returned to his text. At last, he cried, *"Vive le Canada,"* and strode across the stage, punching the air to the roar of affection. He was asking to be leader, but it was a rousing farewell.

As the hall cleared, the woman with the swollen hands sat in the shadows of the tunnel under the stands, little beads of sweat on her upper lip. "Oh, I think Turner's got it," she said, "I think we've got it."

"Are you going downtown to the tents?"

"Oh no," she said. "No, I've got delegates to talk to." She stood up and licked her lip. "My goodness, I'm sweating," she said, and took a small linen handkerchief from the breast pocket of her blouse. We walked up the stairs, and there was Peter Newman, the journalist, talking to Jerry Grafstein, the Senator, and Jim Coutts the pale *éminence grise* talking to Peter Stollery the Senator. "You know what?" she said, looking at them, half askance, half admiringly, "you know what I like? This is power. It's clean, you never have to worry about sex."

Liberalism is essentially revolutionary. Facts must yield to ideas. Peaceably and patiently if possible. Violently if not.

LORD ACTON

Chrétien and Turner talked a business talk bereft of ideas. Turner, for all his tactical energy, had no strategy other than wanting to win. That was the Word. *Winning.* Winning was the game, the convention had the feel of a television game show. But a winner of what, other than the power game? The rich, political power-player, Hal Jackman, had put the matter perfectly: born a Tory, he could not imagine being anything else, but it was not a matter, he said, of embracing a set of ideals — "I don't have an ideology. I could have been a Liberal. But if you play the game you have to be on one of the teams." It was a team exercise, such as the war games Jackman played with his famous collection of toy soldiers. Turner, too, was a wealthy man good at games. He knew how to play, and in terms of his tactical positions, he might just as easily have been a Conservative. And lurking behind Turner was the son of Morley's old debating pal at school, Paul Martin . . . Paul Martin, Junior, a rich man, a Liberal, who approached all economic and political problems not as one of Lord Acton's revolutionaries — with facts yielding to ideas — but as a plumber in a blue serge suit . . . for him, it seemed successful politics was akin to a corporation turning a profit.

"I keep thinking of when I was a little boy," Morley said. *"My mother and father used to talk about Sir Wilfrid Laurier and John A. Macdonald, and we went to Massey Hall to hear the great orators, and in those days the Liberal Party was the reform party, and my father as a voter used to make a special study of the issues, like the tariff laws. The liberals were reformers. None of that matters now. None of it. So people should be more cynical. In a democracy the more cynical you are the better government you will get. A successful democracy requires an intelligent electorate, a cynical electorate. No politician today will have a thought without consulting an expert. He won't go to the washroom without consulting his washroom consultant. You never know what the man thinks. He is so neutralized that he has become — in terms of self-respect — a kind of eunuch."*

Saturday afternoon: As voting began, there was a rush around the former minister, Allan MacEachen. The old bachelor, self-enclosed, shrewd, moved across the floor and up the stairs to Turner's seat. *"Maintenant,"* a man wearing a Chrétien scarf knotted at his throat said, *"tous les poissons sont dans le filet. Le problème avec les filets c'est qu'ils ramassent aussi les vieux pneus et les capotes usagées."* (To get the thrust of this insult, one should know that the full slang phrase for "safe" — as in prophylactic — is *"capote anglaise."*) MacEachen was embraced by Turner. The Turner supporters were ecstatic. Jerry Goodis had told me the Turner vote would be 1,600: it was announced at 1,593. It was all over.

Iona Campagnolo, on the heels of her own career, asked Trudeau and the candidates to come on stage. She was candid, introducing Chrétien as "the man who fought so hard and came second — but first in our hearts." Turner blinked, someone handed him a maroon folder. If ever a moment in a man's life called for spontaneity, this was it, but he had a prepared speech. The moment of triumph took on the tone of an after-dinner talk. The speech was wrong, full of old planks and tactical bric-a-brac. He was running for election when he had just been elected . . . pitching to the people who had just given him their hopes. He bit his words, he looked firm, decisive, but what he was saying, unless you were an election junkie, was irrelevant. Women shuffled, exchanged buttons, whispered, talked out loud.

Watching a winner, the question is, What will the winner do, what will he become after he wins? It is the same question Morley asked about the prodigal son: what would he become after the feasting? John Turner was a winner. He had the power to match his big cigar. But would he always seem to be a man of energetic zeal who left a question: zeal about what? Would he ever learn that a speech to a crowd could be like a private word to a person, something singular, and it is the singularity that touches the heart? Would he discover an outlaw country inside himself or would he always seem to be a man seeking only to please?

As he stood there, at the fullest moment of his political career, life drained out of the crowd. The man was conjecture: maybe his friends didn't know where he would go, what he would do? Maybe he didn't know? It would all be a discovery. The music blared. There were huge clear sacks tied to the ceiling, filled with colored balloons, signals of buoyancy and dreams. Two men pulled the strings but the strings broke. Someone cheered. Chrétien punched the air, Turner clapped a man on the shoulder. The sacks shuddered. People stood and stared, waiting for the air to fill with balloons, but the balloons would not come down to join the party.

4

Morley's editor at Macmillan was Douglas Gibson. He called me on the phone to say that he thought his publishing house — since Morley's 80th birthday was coming up — should host a little party for him, something for a few people in the late afternoon, drinks and snacks, perhaps in one of the nice rooms in the Park Plaza Hotel.

I said I would think about it. I didn't think about it. I talked to myself about it. I was enraged. I drove out to the track, told Yemec about the conversation, and he was appalled. "Drinks, drinks and biscuits!" Together, we fumed and said snide things and did badly with the horses, which I blamed on my fuming, so I fumed some more as I drove back into town.

By the time I got to Cowan's Bottom Line for early evening drinks, I had turned grim, seething, speechless. Yemec spoke to Cowan. Cowan came up behind me and said with an open boyish earnestness, "But Morley's a great man. They can't do that to him. I will throw the party. You pay for the music and I'll put on the supper party."

A week later, when Cowan assured me that the arrangements with Jan Serozynski the chef had been made, I told Morley about the plans and then said, "Enough is enough, we gotta get you a new publisher."

"I've been with them all my life," he said.

"That's how they treat you," I said.

"There's no need . . . "

But he didn't finish the sentence.

In February, Morley and Loretto arrived at Bob Cowan's in a white limousine. My mother showed her incredible resilience; a little aged since most had last seen her, her face was aglow with gaiety, no trace at all of pain in her eyes.The Rainbow Gardens Orchestra played. Ninety-one guests sat down.

Before supper was served I took the microphone and said, "I'm sure as you look around, you've thought to yourself . . . I recognize that guy, but what's he got to do with Morley? I'm going to tell you, tell each of you and everyone else, why you're here." Very quickly I explained that Morley and Paul Martin had been on the same debating team, that George Chuvalo was an old family friend going back to my school days, Gordon Sinclair, the broadcaster, had been with Morley at the *Star,* David Staines had hosted a symposium on his work, Claude Bissell, the President of the University of Toronto had awarded Morley an honorary degree, especially for his novel *The Loved and The Lost* (a degree that had been vetoed by the former President who found the heroine morally objectionable), Harold Towne the painter, Bill Ronald, Jim Coutts the *éminence grise* in the Prime Minister's office, Irving Layton, Bob Weaver of the CBC, and on and on . . .

This actually took very little time, and then everyone, loosened up by lashings of Dom Perignon, was served a tomato consommé with gin, baked oysters in a bouchée with spinach, bacon and goat's cheese, an endive and watercress salad, lime sherbet, lemon sole in a champagne and grapefruit sauce, and tournedos topped with goat's cheese and artichoke hearts. It was splendid, but as supper began my heart sank. The champagne had upset Morley's stomach. He'd gone downstairs and suffered an enormous diverticulitis attack. Loretto signalled to my brother. He went downstairs. There was blood all over the washroom, and Michael thought he was going to have to call an ambulance but Morley said, "No, no." In ten or twelve minutes Morley was back at his table, white-faced but refusing to acknowledge that anything had really gone wrong. He asked for a poached egg.

As the novelist and editor, Gary Ross, wrote in *Saturday Night:*

The wine took hold, the decibel level rose, and people began to move about. Graeme Gibson, the novelist, changed tables and removed his pipe long enough to ask Mordecai Richler, "How old are you?"

"Fifty-two," Richler replied through a vapor of cognac.

"Won't be long now," Gibson joked, and stuck his pipe back in his mouth.

Richler has a way to go yet. He wasn't even born when Scribner's published *Strange Fugitive,* Callaghan's first novel. His name is now grouped with Callaghan's in course descriptions of "The Modern Canadian Novel," but the modern Canadian novel is largely Callaghan's invention. As for the short story, of which Alice Munro is so splendid a practitioner these days, Callaghan mastered the form before the Depression. There was something mythic in the image of Richler, Munro, Margaret Atwood and Margaret Laurence sharing a table in a Yorkville restaurant — one tainted bottle of wine could have wiped out the best part of a literary generation — but there's something even more mythic in the image of the youthful Callaghan with Fitzgerald, Joyce, and Hemingway in a Montparnasse café.

Now, half a century later, a writer who'd been internationally celebrated before the invention of television was squinting at a portable set showing street scenes of Paris while Barbara Frum informed viewers of *The Journal* that the country's most venerable writer was turning eighty. When a clip was broadcast of Callaghan's arrival at the restaurant a couple of hours earlier, the twelve-inch screen commanded the room's attention in a way that the flesh-and-blood entrance had not. Twenty feet from the old man, Atwood sipped red wine and watched footage of Margaret Atwood shaking Morley Callaghan's hand. Irving Layton beamed at the sight of himself and then scribbled something — a poem?

Having facilitated this titillating bit of electronic voyeurism, the television set was removed and dinner resumed. There were chocolate truffles and glasses of Hennessy, and Barry Callaghan read telegrams to his father from absent well-wishers. Al Purdy contributed an interminable poem, Pierre Trudeau wired his regards, Jack Kent Cooke offered his good wishes, and someone sent a message that prompted Barry, at the finish, to ask his father, "Who do you think this is from?"

"Sounds like Farley Mowat," someone called out.

Barry read the signature: "G. Emmett Cardinal Carter."

At last the old man himself was prevailed upon to take the microphone. "I don't like birthdays," he began, and explained that he had agreed to all this hoopla only because he had a new book (his twentieth) coming out in the fall (and books nowadays, he had no need of reminding this group, rely on hoopla in a way they didn't used to). There was a twinkle in his eye as he recalled being offered a seat on a bus by a young woman he'd more or less been ogling — a charming tale about an aged man's difficulty in seeing himself as aged. There was no twinkle, though, when he described old age as a jungle full of dark fears and potential danger, or when he firmly told the ninety people who'd gathered to honor him: "You don't want to be eighty."

"*I* want to be eighty," a woman called out.

Morley Callaghan cocked his bald head and peered at her through his spectacles. "You want to *live* to be eighty," he corrected her. "You don't want to be eighty."

As Morley sat down, I introduced the surprise guest, Harry O'Grady, our choirmaster from St. Peter's Church . . . my brother had sung for him, I'd sung for him . . . tears came to my mother's eyes, and then I reminded Morley of one of the cherished moments of his life. Harry and I broke into *Clancy lowered the boom . . . Oh that Clancy, Oh that Clancy, whenever they got his Irish up, Clancy lowered the boom boom boom boom . . .* I'd forgotten the words as a child and couldn't remember them that night, so amidst laughter and catcalls we sat down and the Orchestra began to play for dancing, and Morley and Loretto stayed till almost two in the morning, when nearly all the guests were gone. The last man on the dance floor was George Chuvalo, huge, but light on his feet.

Morley muttered to me, shaking his head, "Blood . . . blood . . . "

Bob Cowan said, as Morley and Loretto left, "It was terrible, that's the toughest most gracious old man I've ever seen."

5

Mother died in the late afternoon. I didn't see her die, I didn't know she was dying. I had talked to her on the phone about Rome, about a woman I had met who was just like Morley's Carla in *A Passion in Rome,* a woman who wasn't Italian who thought she was — whose whole being came alive in the language, in the dialect, so that Romans believed her when she said she had been born in Trastevere, that she was a woman of ancient Rome, who cried *Mama*

Mia in the night in her bed, and I said, "It's crazy, it's like I ran into Morley's dream made flesh . . . the only difference is, Morley's man, Sam in the book, he wanted to free her from her fantasy, he thought then she could be herself and be free, but I thought this woman was never more free than when she was alive in her fantasy."

"You can never be free inside a fantasy," Morley said, having come on to the downstairs phone.

"Nonsense," I said. "You yourself, you're never more free, you've never been freer than when you're totally alive inside whatever story you're writing, when you're really rolling. You should have seen yourself the way I saw you when I used to watch you through the window at night . . . "

"Ah, the life of a Peeping Tom," Morley said.

"There were moments, talking to yourself, you looked absolutely ecstatic . . . "

"They put people who talk too much to themselves in padded cells," mother said, laughing.

"Certainly one of us should have been locked up long ago," Morley said.

"Can I have the key?" she asked.

Over a decade, she had thought she was going to die three times, and we had whispered slyly to each other those three times, her head sideways on the pillow, her hair dark, matted, a forgiving little smile on her face, urging me to follow my heart. "As a child you used to play even with the dust in the air in the sunlight coming through the window."

"We used to dance too," I'd said.

"True," she'd said, and held out her puffy brown-spotted hand, and I'd taken it in mine so that we could pretend to dance for a moment, her voice skipping from note to note as she tried a song, as her infectious smile, that was always there for her sons . . . mischievous and conspiratorial . . . made her seem buoyant.

But I was not there as the ambulance men wheeled her out . . . the *tic* attacking again, her heart stuttering. Morley — with his own ache in his neckbones, in the nerves all through his shoulders — told me he turned and turned in the hallway, confused, churning in his mind, the years of emotion spent on pain, all piling in on him . . . and then learning from the ambulance men that she had pushed the oxygen away, and pushed it away again, saying, "Enough, enough . . . "

Her last words.

She didn't have to die, so it seemed, but it was, she thought, time to die. "Enough."

I remembered two years before her death, the Sunday morning Morley called. Could I come to the house? He couldn't find her. He was distraught . . . after all, how could he lose his wife in his own house.

She had been up with him until three in the morning, sitting in her shawls and small blankets, watching the late night television talk shows, musing on how hard it was to be a survivor — alone without Wilson and the others who were gone. He had no one of his own age to talk to, and then he had spoken sharply to her, he couldn't remember why. She had gone up to bed weepy and distraught. He had wakened early in the morning and while lying in his bed he realized that he was listening for her breathing in her bedroom and could not hear her. Rushing into her room, he had found the bed empty and had hurried through the house, calling her. And then he had called me, and I had come over and hurried through the house, too, unable to find her. Then, we went out into the backyard and looked along the fences and beneath the big mock orange bushes. We walked briskly down the street to the Jesuit house and the foot bridge. He went onto the bridge and stared down into the trees, down into the underbrush of the slopes, Morley white-faced, exhausted. All the years, all the love that radiated out of every line he had ever written about her, every word he had ever spoken about her — his devotion, and the drain of his devotion — was there in his face, stricken by the thought that maybe she had gone over the side of the bridge . . . stricken . . . yet for a second

I was sure I saw a flicker of relief in his eyes . . . that this might be it. Gone, the burden of being a broken old man looking after a busted old lady, gone. He looked terribly tired, and hunkered forward as if he wanted to lie down on the bridge, thinking perhaps that for a moment he had betrayed her. He could have thought that, but I didn't, even though I'd seen the relief flicker in his eyes. I said, "Don't worry, we'll find her, she'd never do that."

"No, you bet your life, she'd never do that."

"At least put your pecker in your pants," I said. He had come out onto the street in a raincoat and his drawstring pajamas. The draw was open.

"Who's to see me around here?" he said. "They don't open their drapes till five o'clock in the afternoon." He did not close his pajamas. He was exhausted, worn. He walked up the center of the street. I thought: — you and Edmund Wilson could have formed your own pajamas marching band. Maybe you were your own marching band. That's why I'd had a girlfriend who was a champion baton twirler. She was supposed to lead the band. The Dale Avenue Pecker Society and Marching Band . . . me in my white suit and *keffiyeh* at my throat and dark glasses — the drum major and Morley in his raincoat and open pajamas . . . where was the guy in the pink dress when we needed him?

We went into the house, entered the stillness. I sat in the pumpkin-colored chair in the hall, leaning forward, listening. I didn't know for what. He didn't know for what. Some sign, some direction,

Like the sound of a great Amen . . .

"Wait a minute," I said, and went upstairs. Attached to my schoolboy bedroom, there was a summer sunroom . . . closed off by a summer door. I hadn't looked in the sunroom. I opened the door and there she was, curled up on a cot under blankets, peacefully asleep.

"I couldn't sleep, I was so restless," she said when she woke. " I didn't want to wake Morley, walking around in the hall, so I came out here, and I thought it would be wonderful, I could sit here and watch the sun come up all around me and it was wonderful. It was so bright. The morning light. The dawn."

She had a strange smile, sitting on the edge of the cot, looking upward . . . nearly all the way home to death, half-taken, half-accepting. Still, as a woman, restless in the dead of night, a restless woman walking the halls (like the frustrated priests in my school days who were said to walk the halls), and I remembered her telling Claire one night after Claire had washed her hair that Morley had been angry with her. He had come up to bed at three in the morning and found her walking around and said, "What are you doing up?" and she had said, "Oh, I just couldn't sleep." Then she'd leaned close to Claire and said, "It would never have occurred to him that I might want a young man." They had laughed quietly, two gentle, unadmonishing women, gravely sharing what women know . . . "It is like a question without words," Claire said, "it is always there, the sexual yearning, it never ends for a woman until it all ends."

Morley was behind me, out of breath, almost goofily happy.

"How about I make you a fried egg, on toast," he said, and he hurried downstairs.

"Was he upset?" she asked.

"He was worried sick."

"The old floors . . . if you walk on the old floors late at night they creak so loud and I was so restless . . . "

Like everyone in our family, when she died she was laid out in Rosars Funeral Home on Sherbourne Street. It was early evening. A big oak box, the lid open, at the end of a long room. We walked to the coffin — the three men in her life — and Morley said, "It doesn't look like her, I don't know who that is, it's not her."

That made it easy: we didn't have to deal with the body in the box again. We didn't go back to the coffin.

(Some time later, Morley explained: "I've been to many a graveside and I see them sinking the casket into the good earth but I don't feel that this person I loved has anything to do with that casket. If the person was close to me the person seems to live in my mind and live in my imagination all the time as a person. I don't have the slightest interest in the withered away corpse.")

We sat at the other end of the room.

We told stories, old jokes, greeted writers and publishers, and neighbors and friends like Hallie Thomas, who sat down and kept us company. I found myself remembering those Saturdays when the family would gather — mother and dad, Michael and his girlfriend, me and mine — to watch Toronto Argonaut football games with a passionate concern that was broken only by half-time when mother made hot dogs and we ate them as if we were in the stands at the game. And during the World Series we did the same thing . . . These family reveries were disrupted as a number of Michael's schoolboy chums — men he hadn't seen in twenty years — came by. It was very touching. There was something about the death of a boy's mother that other boys who'd known her felt, and there they were, balding, a little stooped.

The young local priest stopped in. He seemed thrown a little by our laughter, the gallows wit. I was doing an imitation of a down-and-dirty blues saxophone by humming into a piece of paper folded over a comb . . ."Night Train" . . . and my brother sang *Champagne, champagne, mellow mellow wine* . . . Then Hallie said, "Who's that?" An older, balding, portly man was standing in the doorway, and a woman with thinning floss-colored hair wearing bright red plastic boots stood beside him, looking lost.

"My God," Morley said, "that's Fat Saul!"

"You're right," I said.

"Saul," and Morley went to him, to his wife, Morley with his hand out, "Saul, Saul, how extraordinary of you to come . . . "

"How'd you get here?" I said.

"Streetcar. We saw it in the newspaper and took the bus and the street-car." I saw that his wife was looking to the end of the room, to the coffin.

"That's my mother," I said.

"It is?"

"You keep the box open?" Saul said.

"Yeah. So you can say a last word to the living if you want."

"She's dead," Saul's wife said.

"Why don't you go and have a word with her Saul," Morley said, "You and your wife."

"What'll we say?"

"Nothing. A prayer."

They walked to the open coffin, stood looking down, and then came back.

"I don't remember her looking like that," Saul said. "I only saw her once at your wedding, but not looking like that. I'd remember."

"Naw, you're right," I said.

"I think — no disrespect — you should close the box. Jews close the box. You go from life, you're gone, you know?"

The priest said he had to go.

We told him that the readings during the funeral mass were to be from the *Song of Songs*. "The only place in the Bible I know," Morley said, "where approving talk about the flesh is not followed by an admonition to cut it out."

The next morning at a mass in Our Lady of Lourdes Church, attended only by family and a few friends, the priest read:

> *My love has come down to his garden,*
> > *to the beds of spice,*
> *To browse in the garden*
> > *and to gather lilies.*
> *My lover belongs to me and I to him,*
> > *he browses among the lilies.*
>
> *How beautiful you are, how pleasing,*
> > *my love, my delight!*
> *Your very figure is like a palm tree,*
> > *your breasts are like clusters.*
> *I said: I will climb the palm tree,*

I will take hold of its branches.
Now let your breasts be like clusters of the vine
and the fragrance of your breath like apples,
And your mouth like an excellent wine —
that flows smoothly for my lover,
spreading over the lips and the teeth.
I belong to my lover

On the way to the graveyard, I told the priest that Morley had written a novel called *Such Is My Beloved*, and it was about a young priest who ended up mad in a resthouse trying to reconcile *The Song of Songs* to the religious life. "The priest felt closer to a couple of prostitutes than he did to his own bishop," I said.

"Really," he said, getting into step beside Morley, a lean, tall, earnest young man, and Morley looked up at him, realizing he was suddenly in step with a priest, and he smiled. He had always been fascinated by young priests. "There have been young priests in the world for 4,000 years," he had said. "They stand on the threshold of a spiritual voyage, and I guess I feel touched, wondering if they're going to make it. Ultimately, they have to learn to accept life."

Michael and I took the front end of the coffin and six of us — the pall bearers — walked the box to the family plot where she was to be buried on top of Burke, leaving one spot open. "Now I know why I go to the Y," Michael said, "the older I get the more coffins I carry." I laughed out loud. The men from the funeral home looked alarmed. They weren't used to jokes, to laughter. When the priest had finished his prayers, when the cross had been pried off the coffin lid and given to mother's sister, Anna, and when a silver shovelful of soil had been cast into the hole, I stood singing to myself:

Squeeze me mama,
Squeeze me till my cheeks turn cherry red.
Chee-ery red.

6

It was just after Christmas and we were standing in the dining room. Morley said that back in the 1950s he had probably left two or three stories out of his big *Morley Callaghan's Stories*, which included 57 stories. "I got bored I guess . . . I just said, 'That's enough,' and let it go at that."

"Where do you think they are?"

"Over there, I think. With the bills."

He was pointing at a small mound of brown and blue envelopes — unopened telephone and gas bills. Months went by and Morley never paid his bills. I don't know how he got away with it. They didn't cut off his phone or his gas. They didn't even prod him, and he just went on stacking his little mounds, and then after six months or so, those got swept — along with letters and notes — into big manila envelopes or old used padded Jiffy bags, and it all got put away somewhere. It was his comfortable clutter in the big house.

I looked for the three stories and they were there, with one — "Fugitive" — in the onionskin manuscript my mother had typed years ago.

"What else do you think you've got hidden away?"

"I don't know."

"You want to look?"

We went up to the old linen closet, closed for years off the back stairs. The cupboards, with their little iron button-latches on the doors, were piled with broken Christmas decorations, an old pair of boy's hockey shoulder pads, frayed curtains and cardboard boxes. The boxes hadn't been touched in thirty years. The flaps and the papers on top were heavy with dark dust and, inside, the papers and magazines were jammed and rolled and bunched in no order at all.

As I rummaged through them, with Morley standing behind me chuffing on his pipe, muttering that he was sure there was nothing anybody would care about in the boxes, I found a letter from Sinclair Lewis, and then the proofs of a piece Edmund Wilson had written about his work — with Wilson's corrections in the margins — and the complete manuscript of *More Joy in Heaven*.

"Why, I thought I'd lost that years ago."

"And what's this?"

"Oh, that's *John O'London's Weekly*, an English magazine. They used to print a lot of my work."

"Well," I said, lifting the brittle brown newsprint into the air, "it says here you wrote a story called, 'The Fiddler on Twenty-Third Street.'"

"I never wrote any such story. Not with that title."

"You sure did."

"I wonder if it's any good?"

After an afternoon of sifting, shuffling, and thumbing through dirt, crumbling book reviews, and old, worthless gold penny mining stocks, I found a letter from his friends in Paris, the manuscripts of all his 1930s novels, the manuscript of an abandoned novel from the forties that he'd forgotten all about, photographs of himself with mother in Montreal, with Madame Thérèse Casgrain, and Slitkin and Slotkin, and some twenty short stories.

He seldom remembered the titles and couldn't remember most of the stories. "You see," he said, "in those days I was living only off the stories I wrote and sold. I had to get the money to keep us. I was the only guy I knew of in America somehow selling my non-commercial stories in the great commercial market and staying alive."

But the stories brought back forgotten memories — a memory of Max Perkins came back to him as I held up an old orange *Scribner's* magazine, or of George Grosz, as I brushed off a floppy *Esquire* dated 1937 and found that a story of his had been illustrated by Grosz. "Yes, I was supposed to go and meet Grosz one night with my old pal Norman Matson, but we got talking and never got there."

Soon, the old magazines — the staid *Yale Review* and *Harper's Bazaar* with line drawings of lean elegant women on slick heavy paper, and *The Saturday Evening Post* with a water color of a fanged dog frightening a boy, *Cosmopolitan* and a pristine page of print from *The New Yorker*, *The North American Review* and *Weekend* with garish pulp drawings of wide open faces full of wonder at the possibilities of life — were all there, big magazines that were meant to be spread open just as families and life were meant to be big and open back then in hard mean secretive times. His stories had been printed everywhere all through the thirties, forties and fifties, stories that told with such deceptive ease about the little moments that are so big in everyone's life.

"Well, there they are," I said.

"I suppose so," he said.

"How come a kid with a flute keeps coming up in the stories?"

"Ah, the guy who plays the flute, he strikes a blow against the world. It has to do with the lightness and airiness of the human spirit. If I'd heard that when Richard Nixon found out that he was going to be defeated, if I'd heard that he had withdrawn into a room and played the flute, I'd have revised my estimation of him entirely."

Week after week I kept coming back, finding another story and then another in a box in another room, and then one night, just as he'd finished tinkering with a few of the stories — and while I was upstairs trying to find a George Grosz drawing he was sure he'd put somewhere — I came across a manuscript that had never been published, "A Couple of Million Dollars."

"You should stop," he said, as he sat down and read the story.

"I should say so," I said, wiping the dust off my hands.

"But they're all pretty darn good," he said.

"Yes."

The next night, as we went on looking for the Grosz drawing, he reached for some small colored sheets of children's scribbler paper that were sticking out between two books on a bottom shelf. They were the titles to another twenty-five stores. "Where are they?" I cried. He didn't know. He couldn't remember the stories. He didn't know where the list had come from.

"Cut it out," I said. "This has got to stop."

"Perhaps it will," he said, as he sat in the lamplight, his elbow on the desk beside a mound of old telephone and gas bills I'd never seen before.

Saul Ellison's daughter telephoned to tell me that he had died. She said I was the last person he asked for. I broke into tears.

Who can figure who and why we love?

When I told Nina that Saul was dead, she started to sing *School days, school days, good old golden rule days*, reminding me of those mornings with Saul in the store on Yonge Street . . .

Morley offered his found stories to his editor, Douglas Gibson. He offered them for immediate publication in the fall. His editor said No, he wouldn't do that, it was too late, and besides, they had fiction by Mavis Gallant in the fall. Gibson said he didn't want conflict, and so he proposed February . . . and not only February — a dead zone as far as Morley was concerned — but Morley's birthday, the 22nd. Morley reminded me with disdainful anger that was almost a snarl, "I hate birthdays."

"This means," I said, "he's broken the contract."

"Right," he said. And then to my astonishment, "Do what you want."

Back at the time of his 80th birthday, when I had been so angry that I had said to him, "Enough is enough, we've got to get you a new publisher . . . " I had wondered how that could ever happen. Now the opportunity was simply there.

I took the stories to Lester & Orpen Dennys, where Louise Dennys, tall and beautiful, generous and intelligent — exactly the editor Morley needed at that time in his life — had established an International Fiction List of distinction. With a courtly energy, she quickly published the book, gave Morley more money than he'd got at Macmillan, and placed *The Lost and Found Stories of Morley Callaghan* where he should have been, alongside writers from around the world — Josef Skvorecky, Marie-Claire Blais, Joan Didion, Graham Greene, Joy Kogawa, Aharon Appelfeld, D.M. Thomas, Italo Calvino, Thomas Keneally . . .

7

In the lobby of a waterfront hotel, late one autumn afternoon, two men dressed in drab double-breasted suits — men from behind the Iron Curtain — walked by me as I waited for the director of the International Authors' Festival, Greg Gatenby, saying, "And there is this house on street call Sullivan where writer is welcome . . . "

I was taken aback.

69 Sullivan was our house . . .

Claire and I had not thought of our house as a way station for writers, but I suppose what they said had become true through the 1980s. Montague stayed in the house two or three times a year, and Amichai passed through, and Voznesensky and Yevtuschenko, Joyce Carol Oates, Kosinski, Charles Tomlinson and Richard Ford, Salmon Rushdie and Michel Beaulieu, Robert Marteau, and Gwendolyn MacEwen all spent time there, and D.M. Thomas, and Patrick Lane and Joe Rosenblatt and Seamus Heaney, Alexandre Tishma from Slovenia, Schadlich and Delius from Berlin, Vasko Popa and Pavlović from Beograd. Sometimes the darkness of ethnic hatred shook us: Anton Pavić, when asked what the Serbs would do if Zagreb were suddenly vulnerable, licked his small red lips and wagged his pipe at Milivoj Slavicek and Slavko Mihalic from Croatia and with a chillingly forceful whisper, said, "Tanks . . . "

But usually these were evenings of wines and grappas, easeful hours, revels without rancor. Celebrations. And that was surprising: after all, these men and women were volatile, self-absorbed people. Sometimes I wondered if this celebratory air in our house was not a defiant gesture, a defiant dance on the bones of an incurious town, an act of celebration as rife with despair as Bill Ronald's determined generosity.

Early one evening, several writers — Austin Clarke, Seán Virgo, Paul William Roberts — had stopped by, but the man I was to meet was the great Kiev poet, Ivan Drache. Several intense Ukrainian nationalists living in Canada had come to meet him, too. Small, he had a domed balding head with longish hair hanging straight down over his ears, big owlish glasses, and a sensual mouth. He was the leader and founder of the national movement for democracy in Ukraine, a movement waiting — as a consequence of Gorbachev and the fall of the Berlin wall — waiting to separate from Moscow. He began to read aloud to a small group standing by the piano. It sounded too flat for poetry, yet a woman began to weep. I was told that he had in hand the final draft of the new Ukrainian Constitution. He was reading it publicly for the first time outside of Kiev.

"Do you realize how astonishing, what an honor — in your house — is read for the first time a Constitution — *the* Constitution of a new post-Stalin free state?" The Ukrainian man who said this was pounding the air with his fist, wrought up with joy.

"No, I didn't realize," I said.

"A Constitution."

I sat brooding about writers like Drache — tough, resilient, for whom the word was sacred, the word was all . . .

Miodrag Pavlović, poet, who had sent his wife and two daughters to live out of the country so that he could hold to his line, free from threat to them, in that fribulating hall of police state mirrors, Beograd.

Robert Marteau in Paris, poet, pursuing his lonely vision, asking for nothing, expecting nothing, writing a sonnet a day . . . transforming the world in his mind's eye, like light passing through a stained-glassed window, forms suddenly visible as if he had revealed what was in the whiteness of God's mind . . .

Such friends left me incredulous. Not a craven bone in their bodies. They knew the price of nothing and the value of everything.

I remembered an evening when Montague had me drive him into the hills of Vermont where I met the American poet, Hayden Carruth. He had an effect on me like a blow; not his pursuit of poetry in a state of near penury, but his obvious integrity, his generosity of spirit despite his own suicidal demons, his love of good whiskey and jazz, his way of talking about music as a felt thought . . . his air of guilelessness as he stood on the lip of some private abyss, wanting only to write.

I looked up and there was Seán. Story writer, poet, novelist. He seemed to have no rooted place, to have come into my life all of a piece from several parts of the world, yet he was more *of* the earth than any writer I knew, his *current* grounded in the soil, unsullied by cheap ambition . . . trying to stay close to the ground, to write a story, another, a novel . . . each true to its own form, kowtowing to no fashion, a confidante who knew how to keep his mouth shut, to subsist in silence . . .

Drache knew silence, and Pavlović, too.

Integrity has its silence.

Carruth *is* this silence.

To quote Marteau, it is the sound of the word when

> *the unmoved mover is moved.*

I suddenly suffered such joy I almost wept: I had this utter conviction that my son, Morley's grandson — whatever the depths of his talents — was incapable, not of doing wrong or even breaking laws, but of betraying himself.

He had that silence.

He had his own Constitution, still in draft form, but a Constitution.

Late that night, long after Drache had departed, Bill Ronald came through the door with a young, dark-haired, dark-eyed, not beautiful but attractive woman of great sensuality. Bill wheezed with the pain of tendonitis, he laughed, he whispered, he was entranced with this woman, Alana. It was three in the morning. I poured a bath in our huge upstairs tub, filled it with scented oils, lit two candles and put a bottle of cold champagne and chilled glasses on the ledge and said, "Claire and I are going to bed, there's a bath that'll soothe you, then sleep upstairs in Claire's studio." A good deal of long distance swimming took place in the tub over the next hour but Claire and I dozed off, only wakened by body thrashing upstairs on the studio floor and loud cries. "Goddamn," I said, "he's got himself a screamer."

Claire said, "If I'm going to have to listen to this, I'm going to get something out of it." She went upstairs in her nightdress, said "Never mind me," and over the next hour did two splendid large drawings of the lovers in each other's arms. Bill said, "Holy Cow, I have to have those so no one sees them," and I said, "Suddenly you're shy! Besides, only Harry Caray of the Cubs can get away with saying Holy Cow."

A new standard of chaos had entered Bill's life. He moved with Alana to Montreal and though awkward in French, he quickly developed Québécois friends and a clientele. As in Toronto, he disdained dealers — selling directly from his studio . . . "off the rack, off the easel" he used to say, laughing . . . some 30 or 40 paintings a year . . . supporting his Toronto family and his every day flamboyance. Some nights he phoned, with strange amazed mutterings about the police being called, threats of suicide, "not mine, stupid, hers." Then he divorced Helen, taking Alana to his hometown, Fergus, in a white stretch limousine to marry her. He booked a room at the Bluebird Motel for himself, a room for her, and an empty room between them: this was partly pre-wedding propriety and partly intuitive wisdom — any time they were together they risked eruption. The driver slept in the limousine in the snow-bound parking lot. The ceremony was held in town on stage in the Grand Theatre, a disused and under-repair movie house (the right-hand aisle was almost impassible because of stacked lengths of drainage pipes) where he had spent Saturday afternoons as a child at the movies. Peter Appleyard, the fine jazz musician, his old friend (who had begun his career in Toronto playing for Calvin Jackson at the Plaza), had flown in with his trio from a performance at Albert Hall in London. They were set up — vibraphone, bass, guitar and drums — toward the back of the stage, in the semi-gloom. A minister, who didn't know the bride and groom and who had been told to say as little as possible, waited. Bill announced to the small gathering that I was to be "the Master of Ceremonies, not the Best

Man." He retired to a tiny dressing room as if he were an old-time vaudevillian. There were a few friends sitting staggered through the rows of seats — painters his age — and two or three staunch collectors and his adopted Ojibwa daughter, and Alana's Jewish family — perplexed and bemused by Bill's rituals — and George Chuvalo with one of his sons. The bride wore a beaded sheath dress and Bill wore a double-breasted white suit with satin lapels, a dust rose satin shirt, and dark glasses. To open the ceremony, I cobbled a few words about love and how wonders never cease, Appleyard played an artful tune, the minister spoke blandly, Bill *harrumphed*, the minister pronounced them married — and Bill invited everyone to the Bluebird on the outskirts of town — the motel where he and Alana had rented the roadside restaurant bar for a reception.

A horse-shoe table (for luck?) had been set up in front of a platform stage. Bill explained that we had two hours to eat, talk and celebrate before the Saturday night male strippers arrived at six o'clock, in need of the stage. Glitter-letters had been scissored out of paper and strung overhead: CON-GRATULATIONS. The buffet was roadside diner oriental, prepared by the Pakistani owners. Bill seated everyone and then got on the payphone behind the bar. He couldn't live without the phone, he was on it all the time. Drinks were drunk, words said. I told the story of how their marriage had begun with champagne in my bathtub. I shot a game of eight-ball with George Chuvalo on the small snooker table that faced the wedding party, hugged Chuvalo's shoulder, and hugged Bill, who said, "I'll be okay, if I can just control her. She's fantastic."

He called me from the Bluebird in the afternoon. "The food's terrible," he said on the phone, "and the showtime entertainment is male strippers and all the local frumps go crazy. I thought I saw Barbara Frumpf in the front row. Alana's wild." They drove to the Royal York in Toronto. I got a late-night call: something incoherent about her calling the house police and their having to leave the hotel.

Helen says he spent at least two nights of "his honeymoon" at her house, and as far as she knows, Alana went to Montreal alone by train.

It was the holiday season. *Boom.*

He spent Christmas Eve in a Québec village slammer, charged with assault. He said she had called the police but I'm not sure how he got there. "Can you imagine," he said to me from the jail, "assault, and the only fight I've ever been in, Senator Peter Stollery hit me with my own cane?" He got out of jail and went to his studio in Montreal. He loved her and he painted furiously.

More phone calls about how erratic she was, how sensual, how intuitive, how perverse — "She's a Jew who trusts the police. Can you believe it?" More talk about suicide. He said he liked it in Montreal. "I don't run into any of that language crap. They see I'm their kinda guy." He said that he had been talking to Trudeau on the phone. "You gave us a Constitution," I told him, "but I am my own country, my own Constitution."

It all, apparently, came apart at the seams. I got a completely confused call about "color field painting" — how it was all a form of paperhanging, except he had real respect for guys who knew how to hang real wallpaper, and he was thinking about this because he was thinking about hanging himself, which he knew he would never do, but what else could he say, exasperated being the way he felt. She had disappeared. "For fuck's sake, I'm in Toronto pretending I'm a fucking bloodhound. She either calls the cops on me or tells me she's going to kill herself."

He went to divorce court. Stressed out, broken-hearted, he suffered two heart attacks. He had a quadruple bypass, and moved back to Toronto, to the third floor of the Brunswick house, where Helen still lived. She cooked for him, and sometimes tried to make his girlfriends feel at ease. He phoned. He was upset. I said, "Bill, I'm feeling morose, life's a crock, this has been a hard hard week . . . "

He said: "It's terrible, Barry . . . "

"Bill, I got all the terrible I can handle."

"Incredible, she not only went off and got herself pregnant but today the baby was born dead . . . "

"Aw Bill, that's terrible."

"That's nothing. I was sitting here in my chair, and my dog, my beautiful bulldog, he just keels over at my feet, dead."

"Bill . . . ! Terrible."

Pause.

"It is. But that's not the worst of it. I just found out, I just got a call, my father died. He died two fucking days ago, and it took them two days to tell me. Can you believe that?"

"It's terrible. You're right. Holy Jesus."

"I don't know whether I'm going to go crazy or not. There's no point going crazy. The world's already crazy. And I've been painting fantastic paintings, I'm painting faster than a speeding bullet, I'm afraid I'm going blind, but they're an embarrassment, an embarrassment of joy, and here I get all this death and dying dumped on me. All I can do is keep painting. I feel so sorry for the bitch. And my dog. I loved my dog. And my father. If I were a normal guy, any normal guy would go crazy . . . "

I started to laugh.

"I can't help it, Bill . . . "

"What?"

"It's too fucking funny for words . . . "

"Right. Right. You're right. It's so goddamn awful it's funny. I can't stand it . . . It's right out of the Kuchar brothers, you remember New York, the Kuchar brothers . . . ?"

"Sure."

"One of their movies, their movies were all about their own lives. Their lives were a movie . . . I wish this was a movie."

"You're okay?"

"No. No. I'm not okay. Two days it took them to tell me about my father. I'll never forgive them for that."

He moved to a big four-thousand-foot foot studio in a former Bell Telephone building in the town of Barrie.

"They've taken all the wiring out but I'm in touch with the whole world anyway. I got my own wiring."

Local businessmen said they would rename the three-story-red-brick site: *The William Ronald Building.*

He seemed to be thinning down. Not his spirit but his body, the flesh on the bones. His color was waning. Still, he was a man of the flesh. He was always with extraordinary young women, but he was going deaf and I would hear him cry, "What? What?" when a woman whispered a kindness to him. He was white-faced, drawn, his beautiful suits hanging on his shoulders, wagging his cane like old Morley wagged his blackthorn, but his paintings grew more and more celebratory . . .

All the enthusiasm I had ever felt for life I felt in those new paintings. Morley used to tell me — the great trick was to outlive the bastards, to outwrite the bastards. Bill had outlived them, he'd outpainted them all. He'd worked hard, and harder. He believed the harder you worked the luckier you got, but there was no sense of hard work in the paintings at all. They had the fluidity, the spontaneity of a man totally in touch with his talent, his "voice" . . . they were so confidently done, so fresh, I'd have sworn that a nineteen-year-old genius, who had the luck to know nothing of failures, had done them. These were not the paintings of a 71-year-old man but perhaps only a completely confident old man could have appeared to be so young, so full of light while standing with one foot in the darkness, and I thought exactly that at the time — not just to embellish a point, but because in his last years he had started his paintings by coming out of the dark, not by covering his canvases with a white gesso but by painting the canvas entirely black and then creating images that seemed to have their seeds of light in that darkness, in that void, because he understood that all the colors contained in pure white are also contained in absolute black. Those paintings exploded with light coming out of the black, out of the pure night, out of pure terror, pure absence, the pure abyss. Those paintings were a dance, anyone could see that, but they were a dance of death, full of delight, full of his private rituals and signs, his bravery . . . a tap dance done on all the powers of darkness.

He bought a used Rolls-Royce, metallic sand with dark green leather upholstery. Two ladies of the stage, one of whom "had the most beautiful nipples in the country," drove him around as he sat in the back seat, all in white, wearing dark glasses, looking to all the world like Father Divine. "I can't remember a day without pain," he said, "I'm a great fighter, a great painter." He was preparing an exhibition for Berlin. "Life is a bitch but I'm going to show Berliners how beautiful the toothless old bitch can be. Do you know how hard it is to actually paint beauty?"

Then, on New Year's Eve he came to our house. He looked surprisingly pink-faced, healthy. He was with one of the pretty dancers. Her black dress was right out of *Gunsmoke*. He was with Miss Kitty. They had come from Bill's studio in Barrie to change at Helen's. Seeing the dress, Helen had applauded and sent them off to celebrate. He was celebrating. He talked to everyone. He left his cane in a corner. He said to Claire: "These parties, I look forward to them, they're like family, everyone's like family. I love it. I love it all. I love everything about it all more than anyone can know. I'm a lover."

A few weeks later, his heart blew up. Three attacks, he told me on the phone: "I died. I know I died. It was very calm. I was very confident. I said, OK, here I go, but I'll be back. I'm coming back." And he went.

And he came back. To talk. To laugh on the phone.

"Here I am talking to you."

Then, two hours later, he died.

The funeral was without pretension — as his life had been (he, of course, saw the constraints of respectability, all those Jackman lead soldiers in rows, as pure pretension) and therefore every gesture at the funeral went against the grain of expectation, defiant in its singularity and simplicity. Helen, his longest love, his two children, and their children, his young lawyer, Claire and I, were asked to accompany the casket into the Fergus country graveyard. Family who had shied clear of him in life — who had taken two days to tell him of his father's death — stood out on the road. A lone piper also stood on the road and played one lament. There was no minister. No formal prayer was said. No one at the graveside was allowed to wear black: only colors . . . vibrant colors, to match the patterned cloth that covered the coffin. Like figures in a child's coloring book, we held colored balloons. The lawyer, in harlequin clothes, spoke of his love for Bill. I spoke of his generosity, of enduring friendship, my oldest friend, so curious about everything, born among so incurious a people, so abrasive with fools, so full of a fool's wisdom. The balloons were let go, slowly gathering upwards in a wind spiral, into a cluster . . . disappearing over the tall trees. Gone: a cluster of colored balloons to perplex birds, to bedazzle a child far away. I sang to myself, *Is that all there is, is that all there is my friend, then let's keep on dancing, let's break out the booze*, and I wanted to tell him that I was singing for him just like Peggy Lee so that I could hear him laugh and tell me I was no Peggy Lee . . . I knew he would hear my voice and laugh along with me . . . because his children had cut his phone from his studio wall, it was buried with him in his coffin, within easy reach, and I had to tell him that Trudeau had called, yes, he didn't know that . . . Trudeau had called to say good-bye to Bill. Trudeau didn't know his number there in the coffin. But he had called to say good-bye. Bill would like that.

Book Twelve

1

*I*arrived in Paris two days early to arrange where we were going to live. I had to be sure that Morley — with the deteriorated disc in his neck that caused searing pain in the muscle-lining of his hips and lower back — would be comfortable, that his energy would hold. At that time, the U.S. dollar had slumped and tourism in Paris was sluggish. I met with the manager of the Lutétia, the posh art deco hotel on the left bank that faced the Sèvres-Babylon Metro and a small enclosed park for nannies and children and the bustling department store, the Bon Marché. I negotiated a lower rate for a very large bedroom for me and Claire, and a comfortable room with two single beds for Morley (we were hoping Montague would come by train from Florence and join us). Two days later, Morley and Claire arrived at old Orly airport. It took great courage on his part to come, and some on mine to have him. He was going to show me his Paris, I was going to show him mine.

He slept through the afternoon in his high-ceilinged room, and Claire slept in her suite. I drank in the quiet hotel bar where, in the summer of 1979, after Claire and my son Michael had returned to Toronto, after I had gone to Deauville for the racing with Con Levanthal and met Samuel Beckett, I sat and corrected the proofs to my short stories as they appeared for many weeks in succession in *Punch* — and I remembered Alan Coren (I had learned how brilliant a wit and satirist he was), asking me to come to London, to be his guest at "a Punch lunch" — and I had gone and liked him immediately when we met in his office. Liked his drive, directness. We sat to lunch at the old long oak table, some twelve of us, Coren presiding: Heath, the cartoonist, the actor Robert Morley full of bloated Public School good will and Melvyn Bragg and Simon Hoggart. There was something 'Bak to Skool' about the house editors and artists at the table — a lot of elbow-nudging, toilet jokes, several snickering mentions of snot, and finally a rapid-fire exchange of bread-ball bullets over dessert. The man beside me, an editor — ignoring the brittle jokes and pellets — said, "Your stories, I know why Alan so admires them. I know they're set in Toronto, but they could be anywhere, you know, anywhere, though they're set in Toronto, they could even be my street . . . " An elderly woman was seated to his right, a regular contributor for years. He said, "Excuse me," and turned to her. She looked a wreck: rat tails of hair under a soiled cap, cheesecloth skin, little sags cresting on little sags on her loose cheeks, and a gob . . . I finally understood what a *gob* was. He talked to her for two minutes, let out a burbling laugh, and came back to me. "Sometimes," he said with a sigh, "at these lunches, I feel like I'm guesting on the Muppet Show." I laughed, and for the sin of loud laughter I was hit on the forehead by a bread ball. The hurler beamed. "Friends," he cried. "Romans," I cried, trying to get in the spirit. "No, friends will do quite well, thank you," he sniffed and tucked Robert Morley with a delicate finger under one of his chins. Morley snarled. "Little shit," he said. As the lunch ended, I hugged Alan Coren, genuinely thankful for his printing my stories and for inviting me to such a lunch. "Not quite your style," he said, knowingly, and smiled. "No, but the bread was good," I said.

When he awoke, Morley was cranky, worried about his diet. He wanted his poached egg and bran flakes for breakfast. I went to the Bon Marché and bought him a bowl, a spoon and a box of flakes to put in his mini-bar. To set

Morley at ease, and to let him see how luckily at ease in Paris I had been over the years, we went to the Hayters' for supper. Bill, older but more agile than Morley, was in spry form as we sat for drinks and hors d'oeuvres on the balcony sofas that overlooked his studio, surrounded by the intense colors of his engravings and paintings, and the Miros, the sofa blankets . . . and Bill's energy was a goad to Morley's memory, as they exchanged small tales of those they'd known in the twenties in Paris though they'd not known each other . . . and Desirée, still so beautiful — along with a lovely Turkish woman who was sleeping in the bed under the stairs — gave off a happy sensuality that helped Morley to quickly see the deep affection and regard between me and Bill though he was Morley's generation and shared Morley's acquaintances. He then — as if he wanted to make sure that Morley knew — explained how fine Claire's drawings were. "This is drawing I seldom see, and I'm sure you see little of it in Toronto." Morley was up for the sport and said, "I'm pretty sure little of it is seen in Paris either." We told old tales of when I'd first met them . . . the boxing match, the cemetery . . . It was all a way of giving the present a quick root for Morley, and so Morley told Bill several stories about Miro and how the great painter had sometimes dressed in an undertaker's suit to carry Hemingway's boxing bag to the gym. We drank far more wine than Morley was used to. Then, as we said good-night, Morley was taken aback when Bill embraced him, so that he dropped his cane — trying to embrace him back. (Some years earlier, Morley had said to me: "I don't get it, all this sudden hugging and kissing among men who hardly know each other. I can count the people I want to kiss on one hand.") Astonishingly, given the hour and Morley's health, we walked all the way home, past the Closerie, along Blvd Montparnasse, past Coupole, Rodin's Balzac, Le Select, and along Blvd Raspail . . . Morley's old stomping streets . . . arguing about kissing, one kiss on the cheek, two, or three, and the embrace, deft, or heart-felt, the meaning of the pressure of fingers on the back or the little bow and embrace, and then the implications of deeper kissing, and, as we turned into the hotel lobby, he said, "And as for that novel you're working on, people crazy for cunnilingus, I never went in much for that stuff . . . "

In the morning, after breakfast, we walked around the corner from the hotel to rue de la Chaise, 22, ground floor. We were talking about Robert McAlmon, an editor in the twenties, and how McAlmon had showed Morley's first stories to Ford Madox Ford and Ezra Pound, and I said, "Here it is, Pops, where I lived when I wrote most of *The Black Queen Stories* . . . I came here from Munich, the overnight train, and waiting for me in the mailbox was a letter from *Punch*, and Alan Coren had taken my story "Crow Jane's Blues" and I remember going across the road to sit in that little park, thinking . . . Not only was that a great little story right out of the years I hung around Spadina Avenue — remember Bisi Ajala? — but it was totally my own . . . you could never have written it, not if you'd had to, and I felt I had really become who I was, and I was sitting here in Paris with nothing to do that summer but write stories and in a strange way, I suddenly felt terrifically close to you . . . 'cause I knew I didn't owe you anything in that story."

He stood leaning on his cane, hands crossed on the knob. Though hunched forward he suddenly looked very light on his feet, and he said, "That's great, that's great, that's the way it should be," and as we walked over to the park he said to Claire, "Do you remember that little story of mine, 'The Snob?' It's a simple story, about a boy and his girl in a bookshop, and the boy happened to look up and there, two or three counters away, was his father and his father was reading a book and his father looked a little shabby, and the thing is, the guy's girl was rather high-toned, and though he knew that his father had caught his eye he didn't say anything, he pretended he wasn't aware of his father, that his father wasn't there. Anyway, when they got outside, ashamed because for the first time he'd ignored his father, treated him as if he weren't there, he began to quarrel with his girl. Now that's a story," he said, turning to me but taking Claire by the arm, "that's been printed all over the world, even in Chinese, because there's something true in it, and I just want to make sure that before this trip is over you don't end up quarreling with Claire."

Morley spluttered with laughter at his own joke, still holding Claire by the arm, and then he turned to her. "All young men should have a chance to go to Paris," he said, "and they should be able to go with a beautiful woman."

We walked to the hotel and were standing happily in the sunlight when long arms wrapped around Morley from behind. It was Montague, just off the train from Florence.

That night, with Montague and Marion Leigh, we went to supper at La Coupole, rested and eager for the clamorous feel of conversation that always animated that big well-lighted dining room where Loretto had danced on a table, and Claire had drawn a portrait of Hayter's head on table paper, where Montague and I, over the years, had raised a toast to our losses and small victories with bottles of Chambertin.

Morley, ordering oysters, white asparagus and filet, exactly what he had had the last time he had ever gone there, said when he'd first arrived in Paris as a young man it was like he had finally come home, come to his intellectual home, and now that he was here again it was like coming home again. "Which, as we all know, you aren't supposed to be able to do." He began telling us about a woman he had known in those years, not at the Coupole but across the road, at the Select . . . a tall slim American girl with a beautiful white and pink complexion . . . "And she was from Kansas City or someplace like that and she had taken a few vocal lessons, and with her wild bawdy style she got a job singing at Zelli's, which was famous then, but she drank too much and her voice began to go, and quite suddenly it cracked and she couldn't sing and couldn't get any work. Robert McAlmon my old friend had become her lover, this effeminate guy, and one night just across the street, at the Rotonde, crowded with French people, she stood up on a chair and began to sing the *Marseillaise* and when they applauded she shouted, *'Merde, merde.'* The Frenchmen rushed at her and the Americans formed a circle around her and she was taken into the café and down the cellar stairs and she escaped through the cellar window."

"Whatever happened to her?" Claire asked.

"For a while the two boys, John Glassco . . . you remember . . . and his little pal, they took her up . . . for some reason they thought her friendship would give them prestige in the Quarter, but it just made them seem funnier than they were, and Madame Select, she would often give her a meal at midnight, but it got so she had no income and only had one dress, green, with stains on it, but she had all the audacity of a woman who's always been given things, a woman who's got used to it. The end, I suppose, came at Bricktop's . . . Bricktop was a famous black singer who had her own club . . . and the girl took a New York newsman to Bricktop's on condition he pay for all the drinks and she got up on stage and began to sing along with Bricktop but Bricktop just got off the stage and left her alone in the spotlight and the newsman left her, too, standing in the spotlight and that was devastating, but what I heard through Madame Select was that she soon after ran into a very wealthy woman, also from the midwest, a lesbian, a stern woman who bought her new clothes and fed her and all her audacity now lay in boasting that she'd always known she'd find a way to get home, and I guess most people were relieved that it had worked out so she could get home with some dignity, even if everybody knew she wasn't a lesbian at all but was just bedding down for the free boatride home, and she was even open and friendly with the two boys, Buffy and Graeme, except now that she was with a lesbian and was going home our two little pals snooted her, wouldn't have anything to do with her at all."

A ritual began: in the sumptuousness of our bedroom — vases of freshly cut flowers every morning, the sheen of fantail satinwood art deco headboards, alabaster floor lamps in each corner, and several easy chairs — we ate breakfast, from two wagons . . . Morley having his poached eggs. It was jocular, with Montague nettling Morley, telling him that his generation was all pugnacity . . . it was all about "poking people on the nose" — "You're the old counterpuncher," Montague said, "waiting for the bigger man to make a mistake, waiting . . . waiting for New York to come to you, waiting for Barry to come to you . . . all that self-sustaining insularity of yours, as, with some men who are very shy, it's a weapon, a curious form of aggression . . . "

Morley sat with a sweater around his neck, holding his cane across his knees. He looked at Claire, who was cross-legged on the bed, drawing with conté crayon in a big black book.

"You're preposterous, John," Morley said, amused as usual by needling banter. "Particularly as you know nothing about boxing. You talk about fighting the same way you talk about politics, the politics among writers. It's clear, looking at your own career, that you don't know anything about politics either . . . "

"Two guys by the side of the road," I said, "who don't know nothing."

"Two tramps," Montague said.

"A couple of bums," Morley said.

"A couple of Beckett's bums," I said.

"He's out of town," Montague said.

"I was thinking about him," Morley said, "he's extraordinary, but you know, in a way, his appearance as a stoic, with his tramps, the hopelessness of his tramps by the side of the road, he has turned romanticism inside out, raised their hopelessness to a new romanticism, a new pathos, the apocalypse of the downtrodden whose heroism is that they know they have nowhere to go before they've begun . . . "

"That's why it's so strange to meet Beckett, he's so dapper. He's almost natty."

"You've gotta be careful. A lot of what he says is not what it seems. His work is very funny. It may be apocalyptic, but it's the explosion of laughter."

"He's always got something up his sleeve."

"Or a hat, a hat behind his back."

"Wouldn't that be something . . . "

"What?"

"Beckett in a Homburg hat."

We walked to the small fine arts gallery on rue de Seine where Robert Marteau worked at "keeping watch" three days a week, seated at a desk, working through his journals or translating — he was completing my book, *As Close as We Came* (poems set in Leningrad), and several of John's poems for his *Selected* in French (Gallimard had decided to publish Seamus Heaney so Beckett had stepped forward to arrange that Editions Minuit, his publisher, bring out the John Montague *Selected*). Morley was gracious, Robert was gracious, but neither was quite sure what to say to the other (Morley had read very little of Robert, Robert had read almost none of Morley . . . and all intimacies with the world of the Hayters, Montague, the Levanthals and brushes with Beckett aside . . . my writer friends in Paris were French poets: Michel Deguy, Robert Marteau, Guillevic . . . and their cousins from Québec, Gaston Miron, Pierre Morency, Fernand Ouellette, Jacques Brault and Marie-Claire Blais. It was a divide between Morley's Paris and mine . . . so that I entered very gingerly into his nostalgia, a world that was largely American expatriates, and he came quietly into my world which was largely Irish and French. Robert, with a courtliness, said to Morley, "This is your son," as if he were offering him a gift:

> *L'amour, nous le fînes face à face,*
> *sans crainte de l'obscurité,*
> *et nous vîmes au matin*
> *un insecte*
> *qui se déplaçait*
> *sur la vitre*
> *et suçait*
> *la lumière.*
> *Une telle intimité venait*
> *parfaire le silence.*

For a moment there was almost a tear in Morley's eye. Then he surprised us all, saying, "Absalom, Oh my Baudelaire . . . "

A little later, as we walked through Saint Sulpice Cathedral Square, Morley was in high spirits, pleased to have met Marteau, to have felt that he "was the genuine thing," and pleased to see a dog running in gleeful circles around the water-filled basin beneath the fountain, and he said, "One night when I was sitting eye to eye in the living room with our dog (it was a giant standardbred white poodle whose grandsire had been owned by François Sagan), I kept calling him Baudelaire Baudelaire and your mother finally wanted to know why, and I told her to remember that he was French, and anyway, he seemed to like the name, Baudelaire, Baudelaire . . .

"But then I found myself thinking of my old days in the thirties,"he said, "when these two young Jews who were converts to Catholicism had come to the Pontifical Institute of Medieval Studies to work under Etienne Gilson."

We left the square, walking slowly up the rue Ferou incline toward the Luxembourg Gardens.

"These two spiritual comrades had lived here in Paris and they'd grown intoxicated on Peguy, Max Jacob, Cocteau and Maritain, and I had grown very fond of one of them, Chapman, a guy from Chicago. He had a rough time at the Institute, being outspoken, wearing his heart on his sleeve, he was easily hurt. His aesthetic superiority, his French friends, his special bond with Maritain, exasperated most of his colleagues. The thing was though, he and the other Jewish convert had each other. Maybe I tended to separate them. Chapman alone was my friend. Then, one night after Christmas vacation when Chapman, returning from Chicago, came straight to see me, we got into my car to go and pick up his friend returning from Paris. After embracing each other, they got into the back seat of the car where they sat in silence. As we drove along, I heard Chapman say softly, *"Notre Baudelaire."* His friend repeated just as softly, *"Notre Baudelaire,"* and in the silence that followed I felt entirely left out, a stranger to them, even to Chapman, who had become my close friend."

We stopped midway up the short narrow street.

"Here," Morley said.

"Here what?"

"This is where Hemingway lived, this is where he wanted me to put on the gloves with him in his front living room, and we squared off with this

Miro painting of a fish on the wall and a big Spanish chair between us in the room, it was ludicrous, but he had to get in a couple of swings before he could be happy . . . "

It was 6 rue Ferou.

I had gone past the door fifty times over the years. I remembered Montague's exasperation with me when we'd first met, when I'd shown no interest in going into the American Club to see where the famous boxing match between Morley and Hemingway happened, but standing there with Morley, it suddenly seemed like just any other recollection . . . an idle afternoon when Hemingway and Fitzgerald had picked him up at his flat over the grocery store by the prison and they had taken a taxi to the American Club where Hemingway appointed Fitzgerald as timekeeper.

"Right at the beginning of that round," Morley wrote, "Ernest got careless; he came in too fast, his left down, and he got smacked on the mouth. His lip began to bleed. It had often happened. It should have meant nothing to him. Hadn't he joked with Jimmy the bartender about always having me for a friend while I could make his lip bleed? Out of the corner of his eye he may have seen the shocked expression on Scott's face. Or the taste of blood in his mouth may have made him want to fight more savagely. He came lunging in, swinging more recklessly. As I circled around him, I kept jabbing at his bleeding mouth. I had to forget all about Scott, for Ernest had become rougher, his punching a little wilder than usual. His heavy punches, if they had landed, would have stunned me. I had to punch faster and harder myself to keep away from him. It bothered me that he was taking the punches on the face like a man telling himself he only needed to land one big punch.

"Out of the corner of my eye, as I bobbed and weaved, I could see one of the young fellows who had been playing billiards come to the door and stand there, watching. He was in his shirt sleeves, but he was wearing a vest. He held his cue in his hand like a staff. I could see Scott on a bench. I was wondering why I was tiring, for I hadn't been hit solidly. Then Ernest, wiping the blood from his mouth with his glove, and probably made careless with exasperation and embarrassment from having Scott there, came leaping in at me. Stepping in, I beat him to the punch. The timing must have been just right. I caught him on the jaw; spinning around he went down, sprawled out on his back.

"If Ernest and I had been there alone I would have laughed. I was sure of my boxing friendship with him; in a sense I was sure of him, too. Ridiculous things had happened in that room. Hadn't he spat blood in my face? And I felt no surprise seeing him flat on his back. Shaking his head a little to clear it, he rested a moment on his back. As he rose slowly, I expected him to curse, then laugh.

"'Oh, my God!' Scott cried suddenly. When I looked at him, alarmed, he was shaking his head helplessly. 'I let the round go four minutes,' he said.

"'Christ!' Ernest yelled. He got up. He was silent for a few seconds. Scott, staring at this watch, was mute and wondering. I wished I were miles away. 'All right, Scott,' Ernest said savagely. 'If you want to see me getting the shit knocked out of me, just say so. Only don't say you made a mistake,' and he stomped off to the shower room to wipe the blood from his mouth."

That was the fight that passed into legend. The three friends were never reconciled. Morley never saw Hemingway or Fitzgerald after that summer in Paris.

We drank a lot that night, starting at the Falstaff, off Montparnasse, an oak-paneled English bar where Morley and Hemingway had gone for beers after their boxing matches, a bar presided over back then by Jimmy, a former pro lightweight fighter who had leaned across the bar and told Morley that Lady Duff, the Lady Brett of *The Sun Also Rises* "was one of those horsey English girls with her hair cut short and the English manner. Hemingway thought she had class. I could never see what he saw in her."

And then we had more drinks on "the terrace" as Morley called it . . . the corner of La Rotonde, Le Select, La Coupole . . . the terrace that was my terrace that was John's terrace that was our terrace because little had changed since Morley had written that "a whole life went on there, a life in the open, the talented and the useless, living in each other's pockets, living on each

other's dreams, and living in comical backbiting rather than love." We turned
from our comical nattering and our drinks in the light of dusk and had supper and two bottles of Chambertin at La Coupole and then late-night drinks
by the piano at the Closerie: *My heart is sad and lonely, For you I yearn, For you
dear only, I'm all for you, Body and soul . . .*

"Oh, how your mother loved that song."

In the cool early morning hours, Morley and John walked slowly ahead
of me and Claire on Blvd Raspail, arm-in-arm, two teetering tramps ahead of
us in the shadow light, one tall, the other small, one lean, the other portly, one
drunk, the other tipsy, and because — as they entered the hotel lobby — they
were talking about Saul Bellow, whom John admired, Morley said, "John,
John, of course you have this sympathetic approval of Bellow. And why not?
He's an academic, and you're an academic these days, a professor at Cork.
You've got to hang together. You recognize that the whole academic world is
at work in Bellow."

After a moment's silence, Montague shrugged. "Well, yes, I'm an academic and so is Bellow. But let's face it. These days, we're all in the academic
world. Yes, you too."

"Well, professor?"

"Yes, professor."

"Who was that woman I saw you with last night?"

And they laughed like two vaudeville comics.

They rode the elevator upstairs and went to bed half-undressed and fell
asleep. But two hours later (Morley told me bleary-eyed in the morning), he
woke up with his heart beating heavily, as if he had been in a hopeless struggle.

"Still half in a dream," Morley said, "I could see I was in a large bare,
brightly lit classroom, and all around me were figures who talked gravely to
each other. At the blacked-out windows stood several hooded prefects. Others
also guarded the doors so no one could get out, or in. Only faint sounds came
from the outside world. No one listened or showed any curiosity about these
sounds, these cries from the street, because the prefects were watching alertly

and suspiciously. And I, staring at the blacked-out windows, my heart beating heavily, was crying out within myself. What goes on out there? Will we ever know? Will we ever know again?"

And then Morley came to, fully awake and upright in his bed. Montague was stretched out in the other bed beside him snoring, a deep droning, half-gagging, hauling-for-air snore. Morley tried to shut out the drone and go back to sleep, but all his senses were alive. His nervous system was coming apart at the seams. The pain in his neck, his lower back, made him clench his teeth. He didn't want to wake Montague but he had to get away from the snoring. He pulled the blankets off his bed, tucked a pillow under his arm, hobbled into the bathroom, and closed the heavy oak door. He made a pallet of blankets in the bathtub, dropped in the pillow, and then climbed the high side wall of the bathtub, lay down, and as soon as he began to drift off to sleep, Montague stopped snoring.

After lunch, and led by Claire, we went to the Rodin Museum, to be greeted by the Burghers of Calais . . . six nobles, bareheaded, clad only in long shirts, and each with a noose around his neck, carrying the keys to the town . . . the moment caught, always exhilarating for Claire every time she came to see the doomed six . . . the weight of their gesture, the possible redemption of their town, there in their huge feet, huge hands; it is Claire's strength, too, in her drawings — those rooted hands and feet, her love of great rooted trees, the light rising up out of the darkness of roots into the limbs, the leaves, like arms, wrists, the vulnerable parts . . . with always the earth implied in the roots, implied renewal.

Her excitement, her caressing and stroking of the bronze flesh, got Morley talking — not in his usual well-wrought way of story telling — but just blurting out observations, as when he stood in front of a lush Renoir and said, "After Renoir there never again could be sins of the flesh: the flesh was now too beautiful." And out on the lawn — trespassing on the lawn — as he confronted the great bronze of Balzac: "See. Rodin broke the nose of classicism . . . the broken, chiseled surfaces catch all the light, so there never can be any of the dust of decay." He eyed Balzac, who leans back, folded inside his cloak, inside himself, staring . . . the socketed dark eyes of he who has seen the ghost in us all . . . and Morley wagged his cane . . . his "baton" . . . at the old brooder and then sat at his feet, undaunted by the big man or the sign that said *Keep Off The Grass*, and Claire sat beside him in a gay dress of Miro-like colors as he gazed, looking lost in thought but then he said he'd had a glimpse of Loretto, just a brief glimpse, and he sat holding his cane like a small shepherd's crook, a hedge of white roses behind him, a patch of white clover at his feet, the dome of Napoleon's tomb in the gray watersilk sky behind, content, until a hysterical guard came running, astonished at such audacity, and ordered them off the grass and away.

After lunch, in the quiet of the little park on Ile St. Louis where men play at *boules* in the afternoon, Morley said, "Look, this ought to be a time of sadness, of nostalgia, nostalgic sadness, because remember that my constant companion, my confidant, my love, my friend, Loretto isn't with me this time, you see. I'm following in the footsteps that we made and I got a sudden glimpse of her in those other times but oddly enough I haven't felt sad at all. That was not the high point of my life. That was the beginning of my life as a writer. What the hell, I had books to write, I knew I had books to write. I knew I had to go on and write and write and write and by the grace of God, with a happy, happy, happy beginning here in Paris, I've been able to go on writing. I paused from time to time for station identification sometimes for a few years but I've come out with another book, and I'll come out with another book, and I'll come out with another book after we've made this visit to Paris."

We met for supper at the Café Voltaire, a restaurant facing the Seine, around the corner from rue de Beaune, where Marteau lived with Neige.

Morley sat beside me, the two of us cornering the long table, with Claire opposite Morley, Marteau beside her, and cornering the other end, Gaston

Miron, his wife, John Montague, and beside him, Michel Deguy. It was a supper to introduce Morley to the poets in Paris who were my friends, along with Gaston Miron, the *parrain* of Québec writing, who set a lighthearted tone by playing a tune on his tiny three-note harmonica.

We ordered from Madame. Morley disliked most soups but he had always loved French onion soup, so he ordered it and it came, crusted with cheese, a gooey gruyère. He ate happily. Miron, from the other end of the table, asked me if I thought Marteau had been either a priest or a "bull-leaper" in another life. "Like in ancient Crete," he said. I was about to say "both" — a bull-leaping priest in ancient stone amphitheaters — when I heard Morley moan, a sudden stricken look in his eyes. He whispered: "The cheese . . . it's all caught in my teeth, I can't get it loose." Morley's teeth, his dentures were always a problem. I could see that they were partly clamped together, he was having trouble breathing. "This is awful," I said, trying to smile at Miron.

I closed my eyes. "Open your mouth," I said as Marteau asked me a question, but before I could answer, Miron said, "No, no that's not the question, the question is . . ."as I made a hook with my forefinger and without looking at Morley reached into his mouth, feeling between the teeth, hooking my finger around the main lump of cheese . . . saying to Miron, "It's true, Peter the Great used to keep dwarfs, he was almost seven feet tall, and they would dance around him like puppy dogs . . ." slowly drawing the cheese out of Morley's mouth, feeling strands snap away from the molars as he stared straight ahead, and then I curled the cheese into my palm, passing it into a napkin as Morley took a drink of wine, showing no flush of shame or fluster, and I said, "The whole city of Leningrad is crazy that way, particularly in the winter, because Peter's architects were all Italian so you have these yellow ochre and carmine and lime green elegant palladian houses all along the ice-locked canals . . . " and no one who had watched me with my finger in my father's mouth — in that moment of completely vulnerable intimate trust — had said a word, or faltered or blinked with embarrassment or even surprise. As a moment of social courtesy it was consummate in its grace. I was so moved by Morley's tranquil acceptance and my friends' refusal to admit that anything awkward had happened that I wanted to cry and leap up and kiss them all, but then Miron — encouraged I think by Montague — played another three-note tune on his harmonica in time for the second course as it was carried out of the kitchen. Morley was having filet of *sole meunière.*

July 5, my 49th birthday followed an afternoon with the paintings of Monet at the Marmottan Musée, a grand old mansion near the Bois de Boulogne . . . almost no one is ever there . . . so we were able to sit amidst rooms of Monets. All ideas of a tentative, half-blind, squinting old man padding through his rose garden painting his pondscape of lily pads dispelled . . . Nonsense! The strokes are bold, the colors discordant: a palette closer to Munch than Seurat . . . and it was interesting, the closer, the more personal I got with the texture of the paintings, the paint, the farther I was from the "thing" — the roses, the house, the trees — that is, the closer I got, the more impersonal the effect, but as I stepped back, stepped away into a distance, the more removed I was, then those paintings captured the intimate concreteness of the "thing."

Desirée Hayter had laid out a table of several patés and a salmon pasta, grilled aubergine, saucissons, cheeses. Our little party slowly assembled: Miron, who had the curious capacity of seeming to shyly retreat as he came forward to embrace you; Marteau — with a hand-written sonnet on rag paper as a gift, confessing that he had two hundred unpublished sonnets among his papers; Guillevic, as rotund as a corrupt monk, with the lean eye of an ex-Stalinist; Montague, Morley, several ladies from the Pompidou center, a Turkish poet, Russell Brown of the *Herald Tribune,* Bill, Marion Leigh, and the television producer, Terrence McCartney Filgate . . . It was a casual, rollicking party.

At the appointed hour, after enough drink, Montague made a preposterous stentorian toast, convoluted and combustive in its stuttering delight, deeply felt but comic. Something about his performance — his seizing of the floor — nettled Morley; he seemed to resent it and clammed up, refusing to say a word, as if somehow he had been upstaged. He seemed to resent all the open affection. Something had wounded him.

"It's Barry's Paris birthday," Desirée said. "Say something."

Morley was adamant. He refused to speak.

I hadn't seen this petulance in him for a long time.

Years earlier I would not have let it pass.

I would have picked and picked to find the wound and open it. I would have been wounded myself.

I had a drink.

Marion, wonderfully drunk, complained of drunken poets.

The hours passed and guests passed into the evening.

We went happily home.

At two in the morning in the Lutétia, we sat in the big bedroom with wine and coffee laughing and giggling as we rehashed and restructured the evening.

"A fine gaggle of French poets turning up for a poor benighted Canadian," Montague said, "and no one can miss how powerfully Marteau loves you. Very impressive. Would never have thought it."

He gave me a hug. Morley got up to go to their room.

"Darling," Montague said, as playful and mischievous as ever.

"I dread the snoring," Morley said. "He'll snore me awake all night and tell me it's love in the morning."

After breakfast, with Claire cross-legged and drawing (she completed some fifty works over the two weeks, which became the basis for her exhibition in Venice the following year), we sat in a silence that was not morose but moody: John was going home to Ireland, and Morley still seemed to be brooding.

"Silence," Montague said.

"It's an endangered species," Morley said.

"Silence."

"I think someone is trying to say something, about silence," Claire said.

"I'll tell you a story about silence," Morley said, lighting his pipe, forgetting that this irritated Claire in the bedroom in the morning, "the power of silence. It was back when we were living in New York and Thomas Wolfe used to drop into our apartment often. When Wolfe wrote, he poured words onto paper. He talked the same way; the words just spilled out of him. Around noon one day, Wolfe was in our apartment. We had been given tickets to a new Clifford Odets play and we were getting ready to catch the two o'clock show. Wolfe made himself at home and started talking. He talked and talked, and was still talking as two o'clock drew near. We didn't want to miss the show because the person who had given us the tickets might feel offended. On the other hand, we didn't want to offend Wolfe by walking out on him. Wolfe talked on. And on. Finally, Loretto slipped out. I stayed behind. To listen. It was well after six o'clock when Loretto returned and Wolfe was still holding forth. I was groggy but still listening.

"Wolfe was a giant of a man. Wherever he went people noticed, and people he met for the first time invariably said something about his size. He had got used to it, he'd come to expect it.

"As he kept on talking, Michael — he was about two at the time — came into the room. He didn't say anything; he just looked solemnly up at the towering Wolfe. Wolfe kept talking, but I noticed that every so often he would glance around at Michael. He was expecting the question that never came. Michael kept still. Michael didn't say a word. He just kept looking up at Wolfe.

"Suddenly, Wolfe swung around and scooped Michael up and held him against the ceiling — and it was a high ceiling, too. 'I'll bet you never thought you would be up this high in the air did you? I'm a big man, aren't I?' Wolfe demanded, but little Michael looked soberly down at Wolfe, and said nothing. Nothing. And Wolfe was speechless."

Mavis Gallant invited us to supper at Place des Vaux, a lovely quiet restaurant under the arcade on the square. She was, as always, elegantly dressed in a white suit and a red blouse with white dots. She was bright-eyed, very happy to be seeing us, especially her old friend from Montreal days, Morley. He had been fidgety and keyed-up in the hotel as he dressed, putting on his double-breasted suit, what they used to call, when he was a boy, "the good, blue serge suit with the belt in the back."

This was the first time that she had been with the two of us together and, after pleasantries, Morley and I fell into our usual playful, needling banter. "You talk to him like that?" she suddenly blurted out, looking startled.

Like my mother, she had been convent-schooled. She had a sense of decorum, and a certain shyness. She had learned as a young woman reporter in the man's world of Montreal in the forties to be forthright and forthcoming, to walk up to people and say, "Hello, I'm Mavis Gallant," but there was a deep-seated shyness in her.

A shy person can confuse you. Just as shyness is often the secret weapon of the aggressive (as Montague had said to Morley), so the acerbic is often the public weapon of the shy. The word on Mavis, particularly among like the fellow who told her, "My girlfriend is doing a paper on you and she thinks you're a bitch," is that she can be acerbic. This is true, but only when she feels she must defend herself from the uninformed or the unmannerly.

At the root of every shy or pointed thing she says is her extraordinary sense of discretion — her refusal to violate anyone's privacy or to allow her own privacy to be impinged upon. Once she is certain of who she is dealing with she is open, even gregarious, and may arrive strolling at a measured pace bearing flowers.

A friend, toying with one of those flowers, knows that all the personal things she has to say over supper are intended to be kept private.

It is the bond.

It is also the vulnerability felt by a writer who lives only by her writing.

We stayed talking and laughing till past midnight, and in a way Morley seemed happier than at any other time during this Paris stay: he truly liked her, admired her work, and was pleased to be with someone who was his friend, not mine. I was reminded that he had only two or three of *his* friends left alive. No matter how much I surrounded him with things to do, places to go, people to see, he carried a deepening aloneness.

At last we parted, taking separate cabs — Mavis to her home, and we to the Coupole, where Montague might be waiting for us. We had grown accustomed to closing that place.

A last lunch alone with Montague at the Coupole.

"You know, after all these years," I said, "we never have gone to Baudelaire's real grave . . . "

"I'm waiting for your son . . . "

"What for?"

"To come to Paris. I'll show him the real grave."

"He's already been, when I was writing *The Black Queen Stories*, in '79. He stayed with me on rue de la Chaise, a great time."

"Where was I?"

"I dunno. Cork?"

"Cork. I suppose."

"So Paris is in him. He's got his own Paris to step into whenever he wants to come back."

"Does he know his Baudelaire?"

"I think he wants to be a painter. He reads but he doesn't read Morley, he doesn't read me . . . He feels very close to my mother, in a way he still talks to her, so he says . . . " (as a child, he had discovered — he says — a deep sense of the "presence" of those he loved entering him, and once that "presence" was in him, their deaths were neither frightening nor disheartening; they were "alive" in him. As a child, every Sunday he and Loretto went through family photograph albums . . . each face, each person, he says, entering him, and when Loretto died her "presence" and all those faces became a family album that spoke out loud to him visually. "I hear what's in their eyes.")

We made a toast to our children.

I went with him to Gare du Nord, and then, on the Rossy rail out to Charles de Gaulle airport . . . bantering, shaking our heads sympathetically at each other's sweetest sorrows, each other's rancors in need of healing, such a good friend, who — with no envy or reserve — had always wished me everything my talent might bring. We embraced good-bye on the train

my
smaller hand in yours
trustful

and I went back to Paris.

As I paid the hotel bill, Morley stood a judicious ten paces to the side, leaning forward with his hands folded over the head of his cane. I paid with cash and four separate credit cards. Morley did not ask what the cost of the rooms and room service was. "Well, you handled that, did you?" is all he said.

We walked out to the little park across the road. He was going home in the afternoon, and Claire and I were leaving for Munich.

We sat in the sun. He seemed satisfied, as if he had done something he had never counted on doing and it had been better than he could have hoped for, yet he looked pale and hunched and shriveled. Small children kicked up dust around him, one child tripping over his cane. "Pardon, pardon," he said to the child.

I could see that Paris had been a pause for him: like he had said, over the last ten years he had paused for station identification a couple of times, but he had written three novels and he was going home to write another. That was what he did, that's who he was. A writer.

He had published *The Enchanted Pimp* (and we'd had great fun giving the hero — a club-footed thug — a name . . . "Let's call him after Wilson . . .

Edmund . . . Edmund from nowhere . . . Dubuque . . . every vaudeville act that died a forgotten death died in Dubuque . . . Edmund J. Dubuque"). Then *Lady of the Snows,* followed by a tour de force, *A Time for Judas* — his "found manuscript by Philo of Crete" — the story of Judas the betrayer . . . all those late-night conversations we'd had about Judas, the arcane little details . . . and he had taken himself back to stand in the skin of an eyewitness, a scribe to Pontius Pilate. Audacious, the way he'd set out, as Margaret Atwood wrote, to provide "an engrossing set of answers to questions that must have puzzled more people than Callaghan. Why did Jesus have to be betrayed at all? He'd taught openly in the Temple, and had just paraded through Jerusalem; many must have known what he looked like and even where he was. Why did Judas do it? Thirty pieces of silver seemed hardly adequate. If Jesus was supposed to know so much, why did he pick Judas to be an Apostle in the first place? And when the sop of bread was handed to Judas at the Last Supper with a clear explanation from Jesus of what it meant, why did everyone just sit there? Why didn't anyone stop Judas from going off to do the evil deed? Through Judas's confession to Philo, we learn all.

"Not only that, we get a new version of Mary Magdalene, and, for a hair-raising climax (and it really is), we get the truth about what happened to the body of Jesus after the Crucifixion . . .

"It's all pretty daring, ingenious, and even convincing; and when you get over the initial shock, you realize that this particular subject is right down Callaghan's alley. His interest in betrayals of various kinds and in scapegoats, innocents who are misunderstood and / or suffer for the good of all, has ample scope here. Then there are the conflicts between the letter and the spirit, between self-righteous respectability and *caritas*, between carnal and spiritual love . . . Realism — psychological or otherwise — it isn't, nor is it intended to be. The story has the same sort of ritualized reality, the brightly colored enclosed clearness, of Mexican crèches. This too is part of Callaghan's point, both about the story of Judas and about the nature of story itself. In a story, one is a human being, yes, but one is also a role."

He banged the end of his cane in the dust, BOOM, raising a little cloud. He looked at me and shrugged.

"Time to get this act on the road," I said.

"Yep," he said, standing up, stumbling, a *king with feet unstable, Boomlay Boomlay Boomlay Boom* . . .

Book Thirteen

1

M orley fell down. He had just crossed the bridge, coming home from the Dominion store, wheeling his wire mesh hamper cart, a pound of ground beef, a bottle of orange juice, a half-dozen bran muffins, a pumpkin pie, and his cane in the cart. He didn't eat many pies: he'd bought it on a whim. The bran in the muffins was for his diverticulitis, the internal bleeding in the bowel. He came across the bridge feeling good.

That week we'd had our usual Thursday night supper at Cowan's Bottom Line. We'd had a rollicking time: Senator Molson had been there, and Johnny F. — the ex-owner of the Toronto Rifles football team — and Mo Deegan, a big lug who wore Lou Myles suits but said he was "a demolitions guy" for the motorcycle gang that blew out Arviv's, the bar on Bloor Street — a silk-sleaze and cocaine bar. "You see how it went, Mawley, clean, better than a whistle, the side walls didn't even shudder, the insides . . . poof BOOM." He kept calling Morley Mawley, as if he were from the Bronx, when he was from Sudbury.

"I knew a Hollywood producer who used to call me Mawley," Morley said, amused by Deegan's insistence on his BOOM BOOM skill. "Eddie Blatt, little Eddie Blatt. That's the way he talked. 'Mawley, we're gonna make a million . . .'"

"I like that," Deegan said, "Blatt. Things that go BOOM in the night. Like Arviv's . . . " and he slapped the table, rattling the cutlery.

When he left, Morley noted that he had pocketed an ashtray. There were men who just had to steal something, anything, he said.

A little later, over dessert — a chocolate soufflé that the chef Jan always made for him — he said to me, "Tell me about about Petra, the desert."

"Petra? Why Petra?"

"It's one of the last things I've got to get right in my new novel, my man Monk goes off to Petra . . . "

I told him about the drive from Amman . . . the Bedouins, their black pointed shoes — the kind of shoes poolroom sharks wore when I was a boy — Bedouins wearing straightlast shoes up on their donkeys, riding through the desert that was more gravel and grit than sand, and then in the jutting rocks, a great cleft, the Siq, a passage that opened onto a womb of light, cliffs 200 meters high, and apartments carved into the rosy cliffs . . . a hundred empty sockets . . . and King Aretas of the Nabateans who was said to have fathered 700 children in that womb of light . . .

Two days later he showed me the chapter. It was astonishing. He had brooded on those few details, absorbed them, and then he had written as if his man Monk were getting it all down freshly, with the authenticity of first-time sight. Morley had taken my little bit of reporting and he had let his imagination make it his own, make it into something entirely his, as if he had been there, and because his eye was the reader's eye, the reader was there, too.

A week later his novel, *A Wild Old Man on the Road*, was finished and he was buoyant. Some were surprised. He wasn't surprised. He was sure he could imagine anything. A young woman had asked him if he could ever think of going to China, with her, and he was thinking about it.

"China," he said, "imagine seeing China. Do you know what Napoleon said about China . . . ?"

He came off the bridge, and as he crossed in front of the Jesuit house, he fell down, the cart skittered away, the cane sliding out of the cart. He tried to get up and couldn't. He was astonished and angered. He pushed against the cement walk, the pain through his shoulders from the deteriorated disc in his neck was excruciating, but he couldn't get up. A woman stopped her car and offered to drive him home. He refused. A young fellow helped him up and got him his cane and the cart.

He walked home, humiliated. He had been helpless lying there on the road. Furious, furious at his body, the wild old man closed the door to our house behind him.

2

It was a long ride for Morley, seven hours. In the early evening we turned off a foothills road into Saratoga, heading for the rambling, spacious Queen Anne house of Zachary Solov, who had become a friend over the racing seasons.

Born in Philadelphia in the twenties, he was the son of Russian Jews who were deaf and signed to each other to communicate. He never knew what village or town his parents came from: neither his mother nor father could pronounce the name. His father was a clothing sponger, foreman in a factory who kept his family fed in a nine-foot-wide row brick house in Philadelphia, on a brick street that had three gas lamps. In this house of silence and signing, Zach talked a streak but because his parents couldn't hear him, he had to jump up and down on the furniture, bounding from wall to wall to get attention, and soon he bounded out the door to busk and dance in the streets for pennies and dimes. He would work at anything and asked for work all over town, and one day, when he was six or seven, his aunt Mary, who was holidaying in Atlantic City, came across him as he sat on a board-walk stoop, resting because he had been working all day as a towel boy in a bath house.

By sixteen, he was on his toes in New York. He had gone to the Manhat-tan offices of the great Balanchine and brazenly announced that he was the best male ballet dancer in Philadelphia. He was ushered into class. At the end of the afternoon, he was told to get his mother and father's permission so that he could join the American Ballet Caravan as it set sail for South America. Zach went with the company. Coming home, he continued to dance with Balanchine but he also had a tap dance role in a Broadway show, toured several small cities, and danced with Carmen Miranda, four shows a day at the Roxy. He discovered there was a dispute among the Rockettes, because Miranda always was seen wearing a turban, so many of the dancers said she must be bald. Zach, who had a gift for boldness, went to Miranda and told her what the dancers were saying. He wanted to know the truth. Was she bald? She told him to tell the dancers to wait for the curtain of the last show. "Everybody had made bets. She stood there and then undid the turban and mounds of black hair unrolled and rolled and fell and fell all the way down to her ankles." To Zach, this was a sign of how his own life, his own secret dreams, might yet open up. His father signed to him: "Why don't you change your name and become a big success, like Jerome Robbins, he was Rabinowitz, or Michael Kidd, he was Greenwald, then your mother and I could walk down Broadway with a white poodle and your mother wearing diamond earrings."

Zach kept his name and his father never did get a white poodle, but Zach became a great dancer, working in India, China and Burma during the war, and then later in London, New York and all across the North American continent. He traveled with everyone from Frank Sinatra (who appreciated his work so much that "he insisted on writing my name on his shirtcuff so that at the end of the show he could read it out to the audience so I could take a bow in the spotlight"), to Elaine Stritch, the Meadows Sisters (Jayne and Audrey), and Anna Maria Alberghetti. At the age of forty, he took off his dancing shoes.

The phone rang. It was 1951 and it was Mr. Rudolph Byng of the Metropolitan Opera on the line. He asked Zach to choreograph a dance sequence for *Die Fledermaus*. Immediately after the performance, he was hired as the first American-born Ballet Master and Chief Choreographer at the Metropolitan.

Over two decades he choreographed at least seventy works, among them *Orpheus and Eurydice, Samson and Delilah, Aida* and *La Giaconda.* During this time he choreographed the first opera played at Toronto's new O'Keefe Centre, the National Ballet's *Aida.*

In the late 1970s, having been given the first Cappezio award, he retired to a mansion that faced the playing fields of Skidmore College in Saratoga, N.Y., a good place for retirement because Zach could teach small classes at Skidmore during the winter, and in the summer the town became the center for ballet society and the wealthy racing set. In July, the Philadelphia Orchestra and the New York City Ballet set up shop and studio, and in August the finest racing in North America took place at the old horse track.

Claire and I had met Zach in a bar favored by horsemen.

We pulled into his driveway. Standing on the stairs to the wide veranda that wrapped around the house, he greeted us, wearing a cherry-red double-breasted suit and white shoes, and he cried, "I've booked us at Sam's for eight o'clock. Hello, Morley, I'm Zach. Look at him, isn't he wonderful," he said, pointing at Morley.

Sam of Sam's Diner was Anselmo Zolio, a meaty man, broad, round-faced with a graying black beard, who conveyed a consoling, slow-moving sweetness that was undercut by a distinct air of menace. He loved Zach. He seemed to like me. He very much liked Claire and hung her big lithographs on his restaurant walls. He could talk aesthetics or talk about how to crunch money. As a man, I would never cross him but I suspected women often and easily played him "wrong" — I sensed a real loneliness in him, a vulnerability. But I didn't know. It was said that he couldn't go into New York, but no one said why. I would never ask. That would have been an intrusion and he was a private man.

What mattered to me was that Sam was a chef, a natural cook, the great-est cook of Italian food in America I've come across, and the August racing folk knew it, too, as they crowded into his small diner with its bar and stools in front, the two rooms in the back. The greeter in black tie at the door — who was not in the fight game but had the feel of the fight rackets about him, the plant of his feet, the slope of his shoulders — made it clear, as he led people to their tables, that he took tips. The tall, boyish waiters from the Bronx wore white shirts and wide, red suspenders, and one of them whispered to me that he wanted to leave his newly-wed wife but was terrified that his *capo* father-in-law would kill him.

At the height of the supper hour, if the heat and the crush got too much, Sam, who was willful, was liable to quit cooking, as he did while I was waiting there with Morley, George Yemec and Anita Rapp at the front counter for a table. An irate customer, who had been there ahead of me for an hour, strode into the kitchen. He came running out, and Sam was behind him, wielding a foot-long knife. "No one comes in my kitchen." The police were called. Sam had a word with them. I had an ameliorating word, too. The police said that they understood a kitchen is a cloistered place. The diner fell silent, customers went home, and when the place was empty, Sam said, "You and your friends, I'll cook supper." Zach said, "And this is Barry's father, a great writer."

"Oh yeah," Sam said, shaking his head, "I thought Barry was the writer. I'll get a marker, you'll write your name on the wall, this is where you sat, write it on the wall. What's your first name?"

"Morley."

"Mawley."

"Yeah."

"Mawley, for you, what do you want, lobster diablo . . . ?"

Zach made Morley feel at home in his big house, fretting over him, acting out show business stories of life on the road with Balanchine, Melissa Hayden, Sinatra, Patrice Munsel, Maria Tallchief and Zero Mostel, and he opened up his home so that we staged small, slightly camp cultural evenings in the front sittingroom . . . after six different kinds of caviar (Claire had just returned from an exhibition of her sculpture in Stockholm, the work introduced by the great poet, Tomas Tranströmer). Morley read manuscript pages from his *A Wild Old Man on the Road*, Zach performed a dance routine with hats and a shawl, a young Russian pianist played Chopin, I read "Sisyphus the Crack King," and a young woman, Patricia Sonego, sang Schubert, Strauss and Puccini:

Oh! Mio Babbino Caro . . .

Zach got to know my *babbino caro*, my father, and after a week of Morley in the house he spoke to him gravely at breakfast and said, "Morley, you know how it is with artists. I have to charge you room and board, three dollars."

Morley's head went back slightly. He said, quietly, "No."

I fell out of my chair laughing.

Later, Morley — knowing that he had been had — asked me, "If I give him the three dollars, do you think he'll take it?"

"Sure, he'll bite. It takes one to know one."

But he never did offer the three dollars.

When we were not in the big house we drove all over the countryside to suppers, at the Adelphi Hotel where Teddy Wilson from the old Lionel Hampton Trio was playing the piano while bats careened through the dimly lit dining room, or to the grand old Saguenay hotel on Lake George, or to a cocktail party in a great mansion where an aging Rudolph Nureyev was the guest — severe weather in his eyes. On special evenings we went among the socialites, the chief convener being Mary Lou Whitney, whose husband had made millions as an investor in *Gone with the Wind*.

We men dressed in black tie, and the women — as in days of yore — having traveled with extra suitcases, wore elaborate and elegant gowns. Zach took particular care in helping Morley, who was always in pain, to dress and tie his four-in-hand. Friends came to Saratoga to stay at Zach's house and join us at these parties — my publisher Louise Dennys, her film-producer husband Ric Young, Hallie, Seán Virgo, my son Michael, and Claire's son Eric. They came to watch Mrs. Whitney, vivacious for her age, descend from on high in a hot-air balloon and she came to rest in the town's central park in exactly the spot where friends of George Gardos — some years later when he died of cancer — would spread his ashes, as he had requested.

Mrs. Whitney, once out of her balloon, joined a parade of horse-drawn carriages that was on the road from all over the eastern seaboard. The carriages were carrying *Bellefleur* ladies and gents to an enormous tent where two hundred guests were to sit down around gleaming circles of white linen and silver wine buckets. We were among the guests.

As we learned, after going to several such parties, the rich have their own society orchestras and Mrs. Whitney's preferred band was Lester Lannin, a faux swing band that played "King Porter's Stomp" or "Rock Around the Clock" or "Greensleeves" with the same irrepressible, bouncy cheerfulness that was optimistic and seductive only if you were sufficiently empty.

"Nice band," Morley said, going *bump bump bump* on an empty chair with his cane, and then he sat down. Someone had given him a pair of dark glasses with fluorescent purple rims and he put them on. "Nice glasses," I said, and tapped him on the shoulder with my finger *bump bump bump*. He poured himself a glass of champagne.

Claire was asked by a man of about sixty to dance. He was from a nearby table of another man and two women, also in their middle years. As he took Claire's hand, he said to me, "I just want you to know how beautiful I think she is." They danced, and as I watched them I thought: it was true, she was enormously attractive, and she had great style — sometimes a panache — but something deeper emanated from her, something that caught the eye not only of men but also of women when she entered a room . . . something akin to the mystery that was in her drawings, the pain at the heart of pleasure, the pleasure at the core of pain, and not only an achieved awareness of such tensions and the contusions they could cause, but a gaiety, a resilient gaiety of flowers whatever the bleak winds. She stopped dancing and went with the man to the other table, and sat and chatted.

"They're from Washington," Claire said, when she came back to our table. "He told me he'd been to Toronto once, he was there to teach synchronized swimming."

"This is good . . . "

We were eating shrimp.

"They come every year — the women are upset, they've had to wear the same ball gowns the last three years."

Morley took off his dark glasses, looked over at the table, put the glasses on again and cut into his bacon-wrapped filet of beef.

"I mean, the men are homosexual."

Despite big overhead fans, it was very hot in the tent. Zach had knotted a handkerchief around his neck to catch sweat pouring down his cheeks. Morley was unperturbed. He was eating. I looked directly into his dark glasses. "Hi," I said. He kept on eating.

"The thing is," Claire said, "they're priests, and the women are nuns."

Morley ordered a double dish of ice cream and a green crème de menthe. "I lie down in green pastures,"he said, chortling at his own joke.

Mrs. Whitney was dancing. She was beaming. Except for Morley, we all got up to dance. Men and women were doing a herky-jerky waltz step or the twist: they were shaking their shoulders, not their hips. "Kinda makes you ashamed to be a white person," I said, but the dancers were having a determined good time, smiling relentlessly. A young man came by and said, "Do you mind if I steal your ice bucket?" He stole it. My dress shirt was soaked from sweat as I whirled Claire around the dance floor. The old priest, the synchronized swimming coach, tapped me on the shoulder. "May I?" he asked. I was glad to see him. He spun away with Claire in his arms.

I walked back to the table. A young woman was sitting beside Morley. I didn't know who she was. How does he do it, I wondered. He was spooning the last of his ice cream and crème de menthe. He looked up, saw me and smiled, still wearing dark glasses with purple fluorescent rims. I started to laugh, he looked so at home and happy at wherever he was in his head.

Every morning after such evenings we sat in the lush garden behind Zach's house, drank good strong coffee and read the *Racing Form*. Then we went to the track.

Grooms usually began to saddle their horses shortly after noon under tall plane trees, and then they led the horses into the walking ring. The air was heavy with humidity. Some horses, dripping wet, looked washed out, with no alertness in the eyes. It was a sign but it was hard to know if a horse was sweating because of taut nerves or the heat, so I looked for the blind man.

As I walked along, I passed two men, regular bettors. One asked the other, "How'd you do yesterday?"

"Took a beating, man. Took a beating."

"You took a beating."

"Yeah. But I don't care, I really don't care about money," he said, jabbing a cigar at his friend. "It's why I'm a dangerous man to deal with, see?"

I stood against the rail along the shute from the walking ring at a crossing where the horses clopped by over hard clay. The blind man came every season on the arm of a moon-faced guy. And they always held to the rail as the horses crossed, the blind man listening to the sound the horses made. "3" he said at last, "the 3 horse." The horse was dripping wet from the belly but I went anyway to the window to bet on the blind man. The horse ran dead last. Back at the rail, the moon-faced guy complained, "That horse looked so old they've got to dunk his hay. He ran like he was tied to a post." The blind man said sternly, "I can't close my eyes to what I see." Still, the horses he heard often ran very well. One day he called four winners in a row. I couldn't afford to leave him out of my bets. He was as good as Jimmy the Greek, the well-known Vegas gambler, if not better.

One afternoon I was standing in line at the 50-dollar window and I realized that Jimmy the Greek, a big beefy man, was in line beside me. He made his bet, and as he turned from the wicket, our eyes met and the Greek nodded as if he knew me, and I nodded as if I knew the Greek. From that day on whenever we crossed paths in the area in front of the long row of betting wickets, or if he stepped out of the Clubhouse elevator and our eyes met, we nodded like serious men intent on the same mission.

On Morley's last day in Saratoga, after eating a light lunch, he asked me to show him the workings of the track, where the betting was done. I said, "Okay, but you have to make a bet."

"Two dollars," he said, never a gambling man.

"On the 2 horse," I said.

We walked into the crowded area of the betting wickets, going slowly. He was wearing a camelhair jacket, a canary yellow shirt and a maroon tie. He looked like a man of bold style but he had, in fact, a catch-as-catch-can way of dressing, wearing whatever came to hand. In those clothes, with his quick, pale blue eyes, he seemed to be a man who had to know exactly what he was doing as he went forward, prodding the air with his cane.

Jimmy the Greek ambled toward us. Morley recognized him from television, and then he saw that the Greek had nodded to me and I had nodded to the Greek. We had never spoken, but when I saw the Greek look at Morley as if Morley were someone he should know, I said, "Jimmy, Jimmy, this is Morley."

"Mawley, how are you?"

"Fine," Morley said, startled, but tugging at his nose as if having a serious thought.

"Who you like?" Jimmy asked Morley.

"The 2 horse," Morley said, tamping his cane on the cement for emphasis.

"Right," Jimmy said, and continued on his way to the 50 dollar wicket.

Just like Morley, I thought, trying not to laugh out loud, now it's Jimmy and Mawley, old pals, and Jimmy doesn't even know my name.

3

The supper to launch *A Wild Old Man on the Road* — a story about two writers, a meditation on the nature of celebrity, youth and age, fathers and sons, betrayal and love — was given at George Guernon's Le Bistingo by General Publishing, his new house headed by my old friend and first publisher, Nelson Doucet. There were some seventy people there . . . the one writer in the country that Morley truly admired and felt affection for — Alice Munro — and the premier, David Peterson, and Zachary flew in from Saratoga, and Peter Gzowski and Greg Gatenby, Robert Fulford and Northrop Frye all had a chair. In charge of chairs, I had mischievously put the actress Gale Garnett beside Frye on a banquette. The great scholar, whose public manner was often "shy reluctance" (masking an enthusiasm for the scatalogical), eyed her ample cleavage. People kept interrupting with "Good evening, Doctor Frye" and "Very pleased, Doctor Frye," until Gale —a forthright literate woman of gumption, beauty and wit, a trouper in the finest sense (schooled as a girl by John Huston, a star in *Hair*, a companion to Pierre Trudeau, a journalist for *The Village Voice*, novelist and a mature actress in fine movies, including *Mr. and Mrs. Bridge*), said, "Doesn't anyone ever talk to you like a human being?"

"Not often," Frye said.

"I've a cure for that," she said, taking two red sponge balls out of her purse. She squeezed one, it opened, and she clamped it on his nose. She clamped the other on her own nose and the two sat side-by-side beaming, clowns on a banquette.

A film producer from Amsterdam cried, "Nore, how are you?" Frye stood up and clasped his hands, saying, "Fine, fine." Gale handed out a half-dozen clown's noses and soon Greg Gatenby and Francesca Valente, director of the Istituto Italiano, and Premier Peterson were posing with Frye for snapshots, all clowning, happily wearing red noses.

Frye, sporting a red nose, was strange, but Frye partying among us was more than strange. In graduate school, I had avoided him: I'd thought I smelled the manse on him, the Presbyterian mange.

Then, in the early sixties, when Edmund Wilson wrote that many of Morley's "compatriots seemed incapable of believing that a writer whose work may be mentioned without absurdity in association with Chekhov's and Turgenev's can possibly be functioning in Toronto" — the last to come forward and affirm Wilson's judgment, as far as Morley was concerned, was Northrop Frye. In his *roman à clef, A Fine and Private Place,* he savaged Frye, in the figure of Dr. Morton Hyland.

A few years had passed and I published *The Hogg Poems.* To my astonishment, Frye wrote me enthusiastically about the work and when my second book of poems, *As Close as We Came,* appeared in 1982, he offered a fine prose response for use on the book jacket. When we met, he told me how much he admired *The Black Queen Stories* and then said, "How is Morley, he's been having quite a burst, fucking wonderful?" I nearly fell out of my tree. But when I told Morley that I had been with Frye, he surprised me, too, saying, "How's he holding up, his wife has Alzheimer's, it must be awfully hard on him, all the things he has to say, and no mind or memory in her to hear it. Awfully lonely."

On a Sunday at noon, Claire and I hosted a brunch at 69 Sullivan: Alberto Moravia, Northrop Frye, Morley, the French writer Alain Elkann, Greg Gatenby and Francesca Valente. This was the first time Morley and Frye had found themselves together since the publication of *A Fine and Private Place.* It was astonishing. Frye was shy but not in retreat, self-deprecating but only so that he could be in quiet command of his space. Morley — who could be feisty — as he talked, kept sweeping his arm toward Frye, like a courtier, as if he wanted to make sure that Moravia, a fellow novelist, would take the unassuming critic seriously, and when it came time to sit down, Morley actually drew Frye's chair back, gallantly, as if he were the host (of course, one has always to be suspicious of gallantry: is it an admission of superiority or a gesture of disdain, or the blend of both?). It was hilarious and touching and grew more so as the three great men began to quietly explain the world to each other, offering little insights, playful and provocative observations — three heavyweights flicking ideas like nimble featherweights, *tap tap, jab jab,* until Morley got around to Sophia Loren and — as Morley explained that the mystery of her beautiful face was that everything in it was wrong — Frye made a loud sensual *umming* sound. "The eyes are too far apart, the nose is too big, the mouth too big,"

Morley said, "yet she is beautiful, she is her own perfection," and Moravia, who had a perky light in his old eyes, said, "Si, Si, so much for Botticelli . . . ." and they laughed loudly as if they had just exchanged an insight on behalf of a beauty that was sensual in all its surprising irregularities, irregularities that had their own harmony . . . and Morley started in on one of his favorite notions: "I've been watching all those nature films on television, down deep in the Amazon, all that insect and animal stuff . . . and I've been fascinated to see the way a bug can't be anything other than the bug he was meant to be, living only to realize the beauty of its own form, the form — whatever it is — emerging out of itself, completing itself, whether it's a butterfly or Sophia Loren."

"And this is why," Moravia said, "Michelangelo's last *Pietà* is so great, it is like watching a butterfly emerge out of the stone," and Frye said, "But this is all I ever meant by archetypes. There are forms, they are in us, they emerge . . . we become who we are."

"And with all our everyday exercise of the will," Morley said, "we become who we were meant to be, freely."

"Of course," Frye said.

"Well, now . . . " and they paused for dessert.

Within a year, Frye's wife died.

On several occasions, Claire and I were invited to Branko Gorjup's and Francesca Valente's flat to have supper with the lonely old scholar. I picked him up at his house, the rooms all in darkness as he got into his coat or looked for an umbrella. It seemed he was going to live out his life as a solitary man. But then he astonished everyone. He got married, and was quoted in the papers as saying that he'd known Elizabeth since college days when they had dated, but then they had each married, and so it was not until both their spouses were dead that they could get together again, to marry. He had taken her to a hotel in the small town of St. Mary's where they had had their last college date and he had proposed.

When I saw him next I said, "You old coot."

He smiled shyly, tucking his head into his shoulder as he often did and said quietly, "Fucking right."

It was clear: as a wise-acre student I couldn't have been more wrong: my man from the manse had a quiet liking for four-letter words — and women.

Branko and Francesca held a small post-wedding supper for the couple. What, I wondered, could Claire and I give to elderly newlyweds. I asked Morley. "A truss," he said, and went off giggling into his kitchen. "Helpful," I cried, "always helpful, that's what I like about you."

He came back carrying a cup of watery instant coffee and said, "Give him what Jack McClelland gave me on my 80th birthday."

"What's that?"

"A year's subscription to *Playboy*."

"Jesus, you're kidding."

"How could I kid about that?"

In an antique store I found an inlaid and laminated wood kaleidoscope. "For the visionary critic," I said triumphantly, and then couldn't believe my good luck as I picked up a scale-model toy refrigerator from the fifties . . . the motor on the back being a roll of scotch tape, and inside, the eggs were tiny erasers, the steak filets were tiny red marking stickers . . .

Before supper, the gifts were opened. Frye allowed himself a cursory look through the kaleidoscope and reached for the refrigerator. He opened the little door. His face lit up as he spilled the contents into his lap. He took the motor off, put it back. He rubbed an egg-eraser on his wrist as Elizabeth peered through the kaleidoscope, crying, "Oh, look at this. Look."

"Haw," he said, pressing a little red sticker to the nail of his forefinger. "Looks like sirloin to me." We toasted the couple with champagne and Branko called us to table. Frye, on the sofa, did not move, engrossed in trying to get all the pieces back into the refrigerator. In the entrance to the dining room we stood watching him. He knew we were watching him, waiting. Francesca, in this gap of silence, said, "We should make another very important toast." She explained that the University of Bologna, the oldest university in Europe, about to celebrate nine hundred years, was going to mark that celebration in the spring by giving an honorary degree to Frye. "This is something very special," she said, lifting her glass. Frye lifted his head, smiled, and all the eraser eggs fell out of the refrigerator into his lap.

Frye went to Bologna with his new wife. I had coffee and biscuits with them there the day after he received his honorary degree. He and his bride were very happy and he chattered to her the whole time. They went off like honeymooners to Venice. Within the year, she, too, was stricken with Alzheimer's.

4

We were asked to rise for a toast at Le Bistingo — Frye and Gale were wearing the red noses again — and we raised a glass to Morley: "To the wild old man," Nelson Doucet, his new publisher, said, "who is still on the road." (When Morley had finished the manuscript for this novel, I found myself conducting a three-way bidding war for the book: Lester & Orpen Dennys, General Publishing and Macmillan, who were trying to buy him back. Morley signed for almost five times more advance money than he had received in Canada before, and I loved the idea that such bidding was rooted in a matter of drinks and biscuits in the Park Plaza Hotel.) Alice Munro took off a long silk scarf and looped it loosely around Morley's neck and kissed him firmly on the cheek. Commissioned by Doucet, my son Michael had painted the book-jacket's image of a wild old man on a pink sweatshirt. Morley gave the sweatshirt to Munro who put it on to applause. It was a playful folderol scene . . . Frye wearing his red clown's nose, Morley wreathed in a long ladies scarf, Munro, breast emblazoned by a wild old man going down the road, and Morley, holding his cane like a hockey player holds a stick when he's about to cross-check another skater into the boards, stood up as a young writer cried, "What do you make of all this, Morley?"

"Nothing."

"Come on, you never make nothing out of anything."

"There are many, many many eyes," he said, "like all the eyes on Egyptian tombs and many many people in this world and a thousand ways of looking at things, at life, and everyone should look at life and try and see it for themselves, as their own." He was about to sit down but then he kept on, liking what he had to say, and so did I because I'd heard him say it before: "A man who has no view, who sees no relationships or no value to relationships, that means he has no way of identifying the fact that he's ever been in this world. He didn't make anything out of it. What a terrible thing, to have been dumped on your rusty-dusty in this world for seventy or eighty years and then to come out of this world and somebody sitting outside the Pearly Gates says, 'My boy, what do you make of this, the world?' and you say, "'Nothing.'"

"So what do you make of this?"

"I told you, nothing."

To great laughter, he gestured toward Munro and recited like a schoolboy:

> *These wakeful eyes*
> *May weep, but never see,*
> *The night of memories and of sighs*
> *I consecrate to thee.*

His mother would have been proud.

At the evening's end, Frye — shuffling up to Morley's side at the front door of the bistro — holding his red nose in his left hand and smirking, slipped his arm under mine, saying, "Great girl that Gale."

5

For several years, at the end of February, we invited friends to celebrate two birthdays in the Sullivan Street house . . . this was announced by a hand-bill as the MORLEY-MONTAGUE BIRTHDAY PARTY. Montague — and Joe and Vera Gagen, and William and Dana Kennedy would drive up from Albany — and we would have a little orchestra or a trio play to the long narrow, turn-of-the-century working-class red-brick row house, two French marble fireplaces mounted over the old rough brick coal burners in a living room crowded with writers, race-track hounds, reporters, film directors and television producers, a gun runner to the Balkans — Zagreb — and one fugitive from the law. Morley's *A Wild Old Man on the Road* had been well received and he was working on a new novel, *In the Park*. Montague had been nominated for the Nobel Prize, Kennedy —with *Ironweed* on the screen — had published his novel, *Quinn*, and Claire had just shown her drawings in Venice. On the way back from Italy, we had gone to the Prix de l'Arc in Paris, spending days with Robert Marteau and Miodrag Pavlović Everyone in the house had disencumbered energy, a gaiety in their eyes.

C'est la fin, c'est la fenaison, Robert wrote.

"Can you know," Montague asked, sitting down beside Morley, "can you say you know that a woman you've only crossed eyes with is about to become the woman you love?"

"Ah," Morley said, "Pascal . . . Pascal said the heart has ways of knowing that the mind does not understand, something in the mind that works more quickly than logic. And then you watch the slow steps of reason catch up. And the eye, too, has this strange power of jumping ahead of the mind and recording a kind of knowledge. In a sudden glance. Nothing need be said. Like the first time you came around to the house with Barry and I laid eyes on you. Nothing had to be figured out. It was as if a hundred messages between you and me were transmitted and sorted out and I knew that I knew what I now know about you, John," and he smiled mischievously, not saying what those messages were. "Indeed, there may be, in the exchange of a glance, a recognition as profound as that old intense Greek recognition of a blood relationship or bondage. It's a kind of eye knowledge, it's a language, it has always fascinated me."

Montague caught my eye. "Your son is hopeless," he said, "he doesn't seem to be able to write a poem unless he believes he's fallen in love." He was being provocative, but Morley said, "'Oh, the young in one another's arms, the young in one another's arms.' That line, you know, it repeated itself in my head a couple of years ago, Yeats's great line . . . while I used to sit and listen to Malcolm Muggeridge explain to his television audience that copulation without procreation in mind is squalid and silly, and I hoped then that if I was to grow old — and I'm eighty-seven, John — I would not find myself wallowing in that pathetic falsification of life, that barnyard breeding view of a man and a woman in bed."

A young woman nestled against Morley for a moment. Morley kissed her neck.

"Oh Morley," she moaned and kissed him on the forehead.

"Oh Muggeridge," he cried, and holding her hand he said, "you know, I'll tell you a mysterious little something about the eyes, this business of the language of the eyes, it was years ago in Montreal. It was after midnight when I came out of the Ritz with a woman. Six inches of snow had fallen and it was still snowing. While we waited for a taxi she held her fur collar across her face, but I could still see her eyes, and I said, 'Satisfy my curiosity, will you?'

"'If I can,' she said.

"'Lying on the bed, I was sure you really wanted to . . . '

"'Yes, I think I did,' she said.

"'What happened?'

"'You didn't turn out the light.'

"So I nodded and said, 'Tell me something. Didn't you go to college?'

"'No,' she said. 'I was privately educated in France.'

"'My mistake,' I said. 'College girls always like to leave the light on.'

"'No kidding?' she said, and she shrugged and when the taxi came along we got in and she remained silent. Riding slowly in that silence through the snowbound Montreal streets, all my confidence with the woman came back to me."

Neither John nor the young woman said anything. It was as if they had been taken into a private moment in which no one had been compromised but something very intimate had been revealed and despite all the talk and music around them they were seeing that moment clearly with their own eyes, in their own silence, seeing it for what they thought it was, since it was their own.

Bill Kennedy was sitting close by Morley in a chair surrounded by several men and women. He was writing in a little notebook. An old newspaperman, Bill always had this notebook with him. He took it out of his pocket several times on any night or day. It all depended what he had heard. He knew how to have a good time — he played the banjo and sang, he played the horses at Saratoga, and he played pool with a passion on his home table — but he was always working, working. That's why he sometimes seemed frenetic. He didn't want to miss a thing, stocking up phrases, thoughts, quips for new novels.

I wondered if he had a drawer for these small notebooks, if he sat down and read through them, or did they just collect as some people collected matchbook covers?

I had not asked him. I still found something mysterious about Kennedy, and Joe Gagen, too, in a way neither would suspect.

I liked them enormously, and admired them — Gagen as a former journalist and currently a film producer, and Kennedy for his Albany trilogy, particularly *Billy Phelan's Greatest Game*. But the root of their mystery for me was that they were real Irish-American Catholics — they celebrated the St. Patrick's Day weekend, they marched in a St. Patrick's Day parade.

I knew nothing about such things.

Morley disdained Irishness of all kinds.

Clancy lowering the *boom* was a Tin-Pan Alley embarrassment to him. If you were going to sing those songs you might as well be totally confused and wear a sash and bowler hat and drink green beer.

But there was nothing confused or fraudulent about Bill and Joe. Being Americans who were Irish was bred in their bones.

Morley and I thought of ourselves as Canadians, plain.

When Bill and Joe invited me to come to Albany to march in a small parade through Bill's old Irish neighborhood, I accepted, knowing what a Jew must feel in Tel Aviv when he goes into a butcher store and asks for white meat, knowing he's going to get pork.

"Going to see Montague," I told Morley, "he's teaching in Albany."

The parade formed up outside the North Albany American Legion Hall, Post 1610.

Montague and I marched side by side.

Brought up in Ireland, Montague had never been in such a parade either.

We turned around and there was "Miss Limerick," a girl from Albany on a float, and behind her, The Middle Fort bagpipe band, policemen, a judge, two severe political figures dressed like undertakers (I hadn't seen a Homburg hat in years), and other local politicians wearing green. It was cold. There were snow flurries, so Joe Gagen's three little schnauzers were wearing green coats.

We marched through the neighborhood. It was now, however, largely black. Young black men stood on the sidewalk and stared at us. Montague and I, laughing light-heartedly, with a kind of foolish boyish pleasure, began to sing some Tin-Pan Alley ditty. Kennedy was beside us. He was not wearing green. He was looking patrician in a camelhair coat. Someone said, "There's Bill's house." We passed a house and a plaque on the house that said William Kennedy had lived there as a boy. This was serious. But I was totally confused. I wanted to hug Bill. His pride of place, pride of being, was genuine, palpable. Yet I felt I could easily see us marching in the street through the eyes of those black men. I said to myself, Look at them goddamn crazy offays.

As the parade approached its end, the Kennedy-Gagen group stepped into a matchbox café, Sweet Lorraine's, for whiskey, Guinness, and cabbage soup. It was crowded with locals from the remaining Irish families in the area. The owner, in his kilt, played several tunes on the pipes. A portly fellow, to make conversation, said to me, "And how many of the Seven Beatitudes do you remember?"

I said to myself, Grumpy, Sleepy, Dopey and Doc . . . ? I couldn't remember one Beatitude. What, I wondered, had happened to my catechized childhood? I found myself singing "Danny Boy." I could see Morley hanging his head but I felt goofily happy. Watching the regulars at the bar, I suddenly said, "Jeezus, this is daughter-fondling country, there's no more than two fingers of forehead on anybody here."

Before Bill could get out his notebook, I was writing that down in mine. I knew exactly where I was going to use it. This was good. This was real. As two old nuns dressed in gray sat down and said that I should pray for them, someone put a quarter in the juke-box. The music blared. I couldn't believe my ears. It was my old pal, Gale Garnett, singing her hit song from 1968, "We'll Sing in the Sunshine." Surely no place in America except Sweet Lorraine's still had that single on its juke-box rack. I thought of how much I had lived through since that song had been a corny optimistic anthem for a generation, and I'd come all the way to Sweet Lorraine's to feel this rush of nostalgia, and to be left with a burning question: What are the Seven Beatitudes? Montague wouldn't know, but surely Gagen and Kennedy would. I would have to ask . . .

Kennedy wrote a last word in his notebook and put it away. He said, "Morley . . . Morley," reaching toward him, but Morley stood up and headed for the stairs just as Claire brought a birthday cake into the living room.

Halfway up the stairs, he ordered Montague to blow out the candles. "Blow hard," he said mischievously and disappeared on his way to the bathroom. Montague blew. The little flames went out. Everyone clapped. The cake was cut.

I kept my eye on the stairs. Since his 80th birthday party I was nervous whenever he ate rich food. He wouldn't discuss his worsening diverticulitis. He'd look after himself, he said (it's a curse I've inherited: when sick, I cannot make myself call a doctor . . .). He re-appeared, putting one foot carefully in front of the other. Those in the living room began to clap, they began to sing in a great swelling of pent up affection that caught him by surprise, bringing him to a halt: "For he's a jolly good fellow . . . for he's a jolly good fellow . . . which nobody can deny." He let the singing and the applause end. He fixed the crowd with those eyes of his — a blue as pale as ice, mischievous off and on. He shook his cane. With a tone of stern bemusement he said, slowly, pointedly, "I have never been . . . a jolly good fellow."

That was true. But his last years did have a certain jolliness about them. He was as self-sustaining as any man could be and though no one could impinge upon the place in his heart for my mother, he enjoyed the company of good-looking, thoughtful women. (He revealed something of the singular unyielding capacity he had for love and loyalty when he told a friend that when his beloved dog, Nikki, came to die, he would never get a second dog. "It would be unfair to that dog," he said.) Hallie, of course, was always there for him, if a confidant of a family kind was needed, and she was a companion on many public occasions. But a much younger woman — tall, striking, devoted to his work, Dagmar Novak, a former student of mine (I liked to call her "Our Lady of the Single Roses") — gave him the kind of enthusiastic comfort that only the young can give to the old; she spoke with him several times a week, accompanied him as he walked Nikki, typed several of his final manuscripts, often was his date, and she has a shadow presence in at least two of his late novels.

They were a startling pair, an apparition that gave me great delight, as on the last New Year's Eve we spent together. It was a supper with George Yemec and Julie Bungaro, me and Claire, Morley and Dagmar at the Sutton Place Hotel. When we arrived at the supper club, five people from the "first sitting" were just getting up from our table — the elderly Cardinal Carter and his entourage. The maître d' suggested that a glass of champagne be shared by his distinguished guests — the Cardinal and Morley — in an anteroom. I cherish the image of those two older men facing each other, one tall, bony, and still imposing, though hobbled by bad feet and hollowed in the cheeks, a Prince of the Church, and Morley, carrying his cane, shrunken, but a wry, feisty smile on his face as he held the hand of a beautiful doting woman who was almost as tall as the priest. The light in Morley's eye was not the light in the priest's eye.

A few months later, his hip broke. He did not fall down and break his hip, his hip broke and he fell down, and he was taken to St. Michael's Hospital. But he was in good spirits. A big Jamaican woman came in to his room every morning and slathered him down with soap and water. She paid no heed to the shape or crook of his body. "As if I'm a horse in a stall," he said, laughing. He read novels and all the newspapers, received guests, and watched the Blue Jay baseball games on a tiny bedside TV. "I don't get it," he said. "I have never dreamed in words. I've always dreamed in pictures, Monet, Cezanne, Matisse, but last night I dreamed in words, words under my eye, like Joyce obviously dreamed in words, words that had to be the phantoms of his dreaming mind when he wrote *Anna was, Livia is, Plurabella's to be* — because you can sing those words, they sing themselves, they're the music of his dreams about the Liffy river, the Lethe, a music I'd never heard before, the music of Lethe."

The broken bone knitted, he healed very quickly, and after two weeks of convalescence in a nursing hospital he was home and walking, saying, "I suppose I should go down to the store. Get some groceries." He came to supper at Sullivan Street and insisted on eating some pickled beets, "Though they're bad for me, very bad for the bowel, but I haven't had pickled beets since I was a boy." We watched a Blue Jay baseball game and talked about going to Saratoga in August, wondering whether the three of us could drive down comfortably in a stretch limousine. "I could arrive like Frankie Sinatra," he said and went home. A week later he agreed to buy a new chair, one that would cradle his body, ease his neck pain. We talked on the phone. He said his nerves were rattling blackly. The next day, Claire's son, Eric, bought the chair, brought it around to the house, and found him lying helpless in his blood in the vestibule. Eric cleaned up the blood. My brother got the call to come over. It was the middle of an early July afternoon.

Waiting for Michael, Morley was sitting in his study in his rocking chair. In his notebook, Michael wrote: "He was in his stocking feet with a blanket pulled loosely around him. He had a sharp eye when he needed it. As I sat down he turned his head slightly away, raised his chin, and then sideways out of its corner he focused that eye on me.

"We were sitting in the same positions as we had one night, months earlier, when I walked in, sat down and told him, struggling to keep my voice steady, how extraordinary it had been to have him as a father, how he had filled my life with wonders.

"'I just need to tell you how much I have loved you, that's all.'

"I couldn't go further. He said nothing, just focused that eye on me for a moment. I don't know what he thought. We watched the TV news and I went home. Was that look quizzical — an assessment? A judgement?

"What can I say about that eye? He had been an outstanding pitcher in senior ball. He believed in fierce focus on a small spot in the general field of view. 'A good pitcher,' he said, 'can throw a ball sixty feet into a teacup.'

"That blue stiletto eye pinned on me. 'Call the ambulance,' he said. I did and told him, 'They'll be half-an-hour. Is there anything you'd like?'

"'Yes, one of those little Laura Secord rice puddings from the corner store. Is there time to get it?'

"'Sure, they'll wait.'

"And when I got back, they waited as he ate his pudding, and then they put him on the stretcher and he went through the door for the last time. As I pulled the door shut behind, that house was shut of me forever."

Michael made sure that Morley was admitted to the hospital.

By supper time I was standing beside Morley's bed. He was in talkative spirits but his nerves were frayed. His eye kept drifting inward, as if he were trying to step into himself, to get an accurate and objective view of how he was, of what lay ahead. The doctors said to me, "Your brother went to his club, better call him, decisions to be made."

Michael hurried over from the Press Club.

The bleeding was general throughout Morley's small intestine. The young doctor said the choice was between slim and none and Slim had gone home. Morley, too, he said, could go home and bleed slowly to death, or they were willing —if we were willing —to take a long shot by removing the entire small intestine.

We consulted.

We bantered. We gave him a good verbal setting out for not having a housekeeper in to cook proper meals, for not letting us know what was in his will, for not buying a chair years ago that would have eased the pain in his neck, for not . . .

We were laughing and slanging and the nurse looked alarmed.

Finally, I said, "Go for it."

"Give it a shot," Michael said, "one last fight."

"That's right," Morley said, "we've always been fighters. We were never quitters."

He was 87.

We told the doctors, "Go for it."

I heard Morley, as the nurse prepared him to be wheeled away, consoling her, "Don't get them wrong, they're laughing, they're picking on me because they can't stand what's happening." She looked dubious. They wheeled him out. I clutched his hand as he went by, that eye on me . . . that piercing eye, like it was swallowing me, absorbing Michael . . . full of sorrow, almost certain it was seeing us for the last time, taking me and Michael with him, a little accommodating smile on his face, his sons, fixed in his mind's eye as the doors swung closed behind the stretcher . . .

Michael came to believe that it was the worst decision our family ever made, that we shouldn't have gone along with the idea of the operation, "But, what could we do," as Michael said, "he was such a fighter. 'Mind over matter.' 'The will.' He even believed in the 'paranormal' and 'thought transference.' And certainly he believed in curing himself, the once-and-forever champion, the man who said, 'I gamble on myself because I win.'"

Maybe it was a terrible decision, but I think it was a decision we had to make, being who we were. How could we have done it differently? It wasn't in the nature of any one of us to go home and bleed to death, not if there was a chance, any kind of outside chance. So, we waited for them to take out almost all of his small intestine.

As Michael said, "He came out of the operation into a space station called the Intensive Care Unit, with his skin tight and sheened like a plastic balloon of a giant-squid waving tentacles, clutching at glowing boxes floating above him. His features were gone, lost in the water-bagged edema that puffed his whole body to look like grandpa Tom's ankles before he died, tight, yet soft and indentable. He stayed gigantically swollen in the ominous hush of that ICU for nearly two months."

Day after day we went to see him, to stand in silence beside his silence.

From time to time he seemed to surface.

But his head lay like a stone on the pillow, face impassive, locked into a stillness.

"Is he in there?" I asked a doctor.

"Yes, I'm sure he is."

"You're sure?"

"Yes."

As the days went by I had the feeling that Morley had turned into a tiny dwarf. At night, he was running in the dark forest of his body, trying to find a way out . . . trying to break through the opaque sheen of his bloated body . . .

"A brain can stammer," said Seán Virgo, who was keeping me company.

Michael was precise in every word he said. Calm, modulated. But his clothing grew strange: plaid shirts that clashed with check trousers, ties totally out-of-whack with the color of his shirt. A way to divulge silent terror in full color?

Day after day, there was no sound from Morley, no movement — only the *beep beep beep* of the machines . . .

"Mostly he's down deep inside his body," Michael said.

He hoped Morley had the time and power to hear, to listen.

I was sure he was *in there*. "He's in there," I said confidently to a doctor. But where was there?

I woke up dreaming of braided waterfalls, great falls of water sucking Morley down into gyring pools . . . and at the center, there was Edmund Wilson as a portly child, sitting naked, smiling, saying, "Morley, Morley, we are of the first water, the very first . . . " and in front of him, his cards, double solitaire, and Morley said, "I should have learned that game, I only bet on myself . . . "

But during the days, there was only a bloated stillness. Beached. He was beached. Like a great whale lost inland.

Be in me as eternal winds . . .

Gaiety of flowers . . .

I began in the mornings to write a novel, to write compulsively, going into the world of a country woman, *In a time when the light drops to an hour so still you can hear all the elms along a road crack in the cold, we were standing at a crossroads beside a snow-bound cemetery called Primrose, out on the shoulder of the highway hitching a ride home to the home farm* . . . writing in her voice, dark murderousness . . . as if she had taken hold of me, possessed me.

"When things get worst, how are you?" she asked.

"Mawley, Mawley," Eddie Blatt called, "how are you?"

And Dink, whispering Dink showed up, golf clubs in hand, saying, "He's not here, Morley's not here . . . you'll find him at the Ritz. He and Lily St. Cyr, they're having a snowball fight in the hall . . . "

Hallucinating.

Was Morley hallucinating, too?

Was he seeing everything I saw . . . Eddie Blatt, Dink . . . with the clarity implied in the stern composure of his body.

Clarity.

Sounded like a name for Slitkin's daughter.

Clarity Slitkin.

If I had the wings of an angel,
Over these prison walls I would fly . . .

"Wake up Mr. Prime Minister . . . "

Then the doctors said: "You must decide. As of last night, we're not sure anymore if he's in there. He may be gone. He may just be ticking inside an empty clock."

"We'll think about it," Michael and I said.

I sat thinking about it all night. I thought, if Tom or Minn had any smarts and any feeling for their son they'd show up and tell me what to do; or Eustace, what was the point of his mesmerism if he couldn't come back with a coded message from beyond . . . ?

If ice . . .

In the morning, I walked along Queen Street in the sunlight with Seán.

"I know what I'm going to do," I said. "Either he's in there or he's not, either he wants to come out to play or he doesn't, either this is it or it ain't."

I went into the ICU. I took his swollen hand.

"Now, goddammit," I said, "either you want to go on or you don't."

His eyes were sealed shut but could he see? Was he using his imagination? I raised my voice in the hush of the room. "You hear me, yes or no, because there's no way Michael or I can know what you want to do so you got to tell me. You want to go on, you squeeze my hand, not once, but twice. Twice, you hear me twice. No twice, and we're pulling the plug."

The nurse, who had come to stand beside me because I was yelling, looked very upset as I folded his bloated fingers around my hand and waited.

"Blessed Lord," she said, because the clutch came. A pause. And then another clutch.

"He's in there, he's fucking in there and he wants to come out," I cried.

Michael, when I told him, was dismayed. "This is awful," he said.

"Right," I said. "So what do you want to do?"

"I don't know."

"Neither do I."

"So we don't know what to do."

"No."

How sane can we get, I thought. We don't know what to do.

In three days, I was supposed to be in Germany, in Baden-Baden, to write about the running of the German Grand Prix, and then I was to go on to the Prix de l'Arc in Paris.

The doctor said, "You know, I really think he's turned the corner. I think he's made it. You should go. If you go, by the time you get back he'll be in his own room, we'll have him out of here. Go! He'll never be the same but he'll be here and himself."

We went.

Claire and I flew to Frankfurt and then took the train to Baden-Baden, checking into a swank hotel on the canal, facing the great gilded casino. As we fell into bed, exhausted, trying to quickly bridge the lag of hours, I said, "Dostoevsky lived just around the corner from here, when we get up I'll show you . . . where Dostoevsky lived when he wrote *The Gambler*."

The phone rang, waking us.

"Come home," Michael said, "he's dying. He's going to be dead. Hurry."

Only an hour earlier Michael had got the call: "Your father's dying, come quick."

He had run through the streets from his office and he had paced the empty hospital hall, waiting for the elevator, listening to the clicking of his heels on the terrazzo floor. "I tried to picture him at home," Michael said, "in his chair, in his socks, in his blanket as he might have been if we hadn't had him butchered, piercing me with the awl of an eye that strung the stories of my life together." The elevator came.

"A nurse sat with Morley, shy concern stamped in her eyes. 'He's dying,' she whispered to me. I bent over him. 'Morley, it's me, Michael, I'm here.' His eyes were wide open, racing in his sockets, flickering wildly. I grabbed his hugely swollen hand. I tried to follow the racing eyes. 'The cells have tipped,' I whispered. 'The fluids spilled.' I shook my head helplessly at the young nurse,

'His body's out of control.' She nodded. My stomach knotted. 'I'm sorry,' said the nurse, and turned from the room."

We were trapped for twelve hours in Baden-Baden. We had an early supper in the great dining room of the hotel, the two of us alone at that hour under the thirty-foot ceiling, the pendulous chandeliers swollen with crystal. We ordered paté of thrush and lobster bisque, white wine. As we lifted a fork, a spoon, we both looked up. There, high above us was a speck in the air, falling, falling . . . a spider hurtling down from a chandelier, spinning its own silk thread out of the light in descent . . . stopping, hovering over the center of our table, between us.

"Oh my God," Claire said, "Morley . . . Morley's gone . . . "

"No. He's not dead yet. Look at him, he's waiting. We'll get home first."

We flew into Toronto in the late afternoon and went to the hospital, to the space station.

Morley was wired but the circuits were closing down. I don't know if he had already died, but his heart was beeping . . . maybe they'd kept him alive, maybe he'd stayed alive . . . I whispered as strongly as I could into his impotent ear, "So long, Pops, so long . . . you dance where you're gonna dance and we'll dance where we're gonna dance."

The lights, the *beeps* went off.

He was dead.

The penny fell, then the hammer.

Gone.

"If only he had died at home."

Michael wrote in his notebook: "Perhaps Thornton Wilder was best, 'Good-bye to clocks ticking . . . and Mama's sunflowers. And food and coffee. And new-ironed dresses and hot baths . . . and sleeping and waking up. Oh, earth, you're too wonderful for anybody to realize you.'"

I thought, "OK, there's nothing to do but celebrate."

The body was taken to Rosars. On the first day, the coffin was open. He didn't look like himself at all. The bloat had settled into his face. I slammed the coffin shut. "Nail that fucking thing," I told the funeral director. We stood a photograph by John Reeves on an easel beside the coffin, and moved upstairs.

Many came to pay their formal respects, view the coffin, and sign the book. Some thought we had abandoned the box, for we were seldom there in the long sitting room.

Whiskey had been stocked in the second-floor cabinets.

Close friends were sent upstairs.

Tom Hedley flew in from Connecticut. Paul Martin, his old debating partner, flew from Ottawa, accompanied by his own priest. George Chuvalo — in broad braces and white shirt — embraced Bill Ronald, and Ronald pounded him on the back, saying, "Morley would've beaten you to the punch, he would've." After an hour, Ronald, using wine and bread sticks soaked in wine, began to draw on the tablecloth . . . he began to draw everyone who was there . . . Hallie, Morley's oldest pal, who loved him, yes, she did love him, though not in any way that interfered with the love she maintained for her man, J.K . . . and Paddy Sampson and Bette, and Stephen Williams . . . and dipping bread sticks into wine, Bill drew great broad strokes across the linen . . .

"Irish linen," the funeral director said, "so you make sure to take it home . . . "

We laughed and drank and sang, and wall-eyed Paul Martin stood up and said, "I have a speech to make on Morley's behalf," and sat down without saying a word, to "Bravo, bravo . . . "

He whispered, "We'll all go, Morley, we'll all go, but you won't die . . . "

I had been on the phone to the Monsignor and he'd agreed that the mass for Morley should be said in the Cathedral. I said, "There's a little wrinkle I'd like to bring off . . . there's this band . . . in recent years, whatever was going on with Morley . . . this band always played, and after the boy from the Choir

School sings during the mass, I want this band, the Rainbow Gardens Orchestra, to play . . . to be up in the choir stalls at the back, and to play when the mass is over . . . "

"Will it be liturgically sound?"

"What?"

"What they're playing? The music?"

"What'd you mean sound?"

"Liturgically?"

"Spirituals, they're gonna play spirituals."

"Do you know what they're going to play? The Bishop has to know what's going to be played in the cathedral."

"'Just A Closer Walk With Thee . . .'"

"What?"

"'Just A Closer Walk With Thee,' it's a spiritual."

"Don't think I know it."

"Everybody knows it."

"Could you hum it a little."

I found myself humming . . . *Um, uh, um . . . um, uh a um, um uh . . . um, uh, humahuhuh* . . . over the phone.

"Oh, that sounds good enough for me."

"It'll be, don't you worry."

"I read *Such Is Thy Beloved*, you know," the Monsignor blurted out.

"Yes . . . "

"Very interesting. Very. The two prostitutes . . . "

In the morning, the mass went forward with an open sense of space . . . no clutter, no unnecessary device . . . a chime, odor of incense . . . as the Choir School boy in white surplice and red soutane (the colors of resurrection) sang in a high sweet soprano, the sound of purity of intention . . . and Morley's grandsons, Michael, Brendan and Darcy, read . . .

> *May he endure as long as the sun,*
> > *and like the moon through all generations.*

He shall be like rain coming down on the meadow,
    like showers watering the earth.
Justice shall flower in his days,
    and profound peace, till the moon be no more.

I may speak in tongues of men or of angels, but if I have no love, I am a sounding gong or a clanging cymbal. I may have the gift of prophecy and the knowledge of every hidden truth; I may have faith enough to move mountains; but if I have no love, I am nothing.

I looked around astonished: the cathedral was crowded with writers, artists, television people, journalists and government officials (led by Lieutenant Governor Lincoln Alexander and the Mayor, Art Eggleton), but the Bishop was not there . . . Ambrosic wasn't there, and no one . . . not one priest or professor from St. Michael's University or the University of Toronto was there . . . their President, Claude Bissell, had pleaded with him for years and years to accept their honorary doctorate and finally he did and now, no one was there . . . "The greatest Canadian writer the country had yet seen, the greatest Catholic writer they would probably ever see" . . . that's what they said, and they weren't there. Those totally goddamn lace-curtain Irish. They treated McLuhan like shit when he died, I thought, and now Morley.

My reveries of rage were interrupted by the tinkling of bells: the consecration! Transubstantiation! People began to shuffle out of the pews, going up the aisles to communion. I remembered my gangster friends in upstate New York ("What's he done that's so bad he can't go to communion?"), and then I heard my brother, in the pew in front of me, say, "Aw shit . . . " as his sons went up to communion, and he bolted from his pew and followed them and I followed him. I, who had not been to confession since my scholastic conversations with Father Fehr under the shadow of the Ambassador Bridge. I stood and took the wafer on my tongue from the Monsignor, saying to myself, "For the sins I've done to others, whenever, wherever, I'm sorry . . . but this is for Morley, between me and the Word and Morley, and if it galls God's eye, let it gall."

I sat down in my pew.

The Monsignor, sprinkling holy water, moved toward the casket at the head of the center aisle. There had been a casual lightness, an easy unpretentious pace to the mass. People were choking back tears. As the coffin bearers turned to wheel the body down the aisle, at the back of the cathedral, the Rainbow Gardens Orchestra — outfitted in white, in the front row of the upstairs choir — broke into "Just A Closer Walk With Thee," the mournful raw blare of the trombone laying down tone.

People turned, astonished, to the back.

People wept.

A woman stuttered over the words and then began to sing loudly, *Truly walking close to Thee* . . .

The coffin was rolled by the pall bearers toward the back doors.

The band, without change of inflection, so that the Monsignor did not notice, slid into the "Saint James Infirmary Blues" . . . causing among those who were last to leave the cathedral a strut to their step. A lone priest . . . old fragile Father Mulcahey from the high school . . . who had taught my brother, me, and my son . . . stood in the empty church in the center aisle, and as the band closed on a bent note, he held out his hands and clapped, an old man's affirmation and blessing.

At the graveyard, at Mount Hope cemetery, the sky was cloudless, pale blue. Led by Ric Giorgi, blowing a bulbous bass saxophone —the band strode up the grassy slope between tall stones in single file, playing "Basin Street Blues," and then —with the small assembly of mourners clustered behind — "Didn't He Ramble." Short prayers were said at the lip of the grave, the tiny metal cross was pried off the coffin lid and Michael gave it to Hallie, dry reddish earth was cast from a silver trowel into the hole. The knoll with its pale stones seemed all in sunlight. Ray Ellenwood linked arms with Michael and me in front of the coffin and we sang with a baritone boisterousness —*Let 'im go, let 'im go, God bless him, wherever he may be . . . you may search this whole wide world over, but you'll never find another sweet man like Morley.* The boys in the

band straggled in loose step up the hill, six men in white —long distance skiers
— etched against the stainless sky, playing *Bye Bye Blackbird, Bye Bye . . .* until
they disappeared over the hill, still playing, high notes in the high trees.

Le Bistingo was bustling for the feast, the front French doors wide open
to the street . . . open to the clang of streetcars, to the brittle shrillness of Much
Music girls with their Brillo-pad hair-dos, a punk-haired kid on stilts handing
out balloons to children, and skinheads, pan-handlers, pimp-walking dudes,
video-cam newsboys . . . all of tattooed Queen Street went by the open doors,
on the sashay and hustle . . . and inside the bistro, the walls were posted with
John Reeves' last photographs of Morley, the scowl, the smiles, the howls, the
smirks, the nods, the pouts, the mourns . . . Morley, amiable to all, lover to the
happy few. A long pine table was layered and stacked with food and wine and
whiskey and champagne, and it was twelve noon, on the stroke of — as the
Rainbow Gardens men took off their white jackets, snapped their suspenders,
parked themselves by the front doors and began to play the sweet mournfulness of Morley and Loretto's music, jelly-roll piano and clarinet:

> *You see pretty browns in beautiful gowns,*
> *You see tailor-mades and hand-me-downs,*
> *You meet honest men and pickpockets skilled*
> *You'll find business never ends*
> *Till someone gets killed . .*
> *I'd rather be here than any place I know . . .*

music for men and women to strut their sorrow to in jeans or Bogart duds, to
strut against the wronging tide with no whingeing . . .

After talk and drink and eating, Zachary — who had flown in for the
funeral mass — slipped off his suit coat, knotted a handkerchief inside his
shirt collar, performed a cakewalk past the bar, and then . . . the Rainbow men
broke into "The Anniversary Waltz" and Zach — so close to infirm in recent
years — threw his head back, and with the sure flare of a great dancer, each

step a hieroglyph, he conjured between his hands — in the silence he held in that space — an absence, a wedding-night companion, a lover . . . until "Muskrat Ramble" sent Zachary prancing, taking sorrow by the heels and stepping it off into exuberance, joy . . . sweat pouring down his face till I worried he would hurt his heart, but he gave a low sweeping bow, the schooled courtier, calling for me and Claire to come on the floor behind him . . . and I wished that I had remembered to bring a Homburg hat, a good stiff-brimmed hat to twirl — and a cane, and what, I wondered, ever happened to the guy with the moustache in the pink dress — as Claire snapped a hip at dying, and I thanked God for my mother teaching me songs, dancing the blues with me, so that stepping through pain eight beats to the bar was as natural and cleansing as prayer, an affirmation of the flesh, and I could feel Morley and Loretto there, not Morley biting his lip in pain and dragging his grocery basket on wheels nor Loretto in her nest of shawls, but the two of them gliding in new "store-bought" shoes along a Paris embankment in the early morning freshness by the Seine, knowing with the gaiety of flowers in their hearts on their honeymoon that they had lives ahead of them richer than they had ever dreamed, Loretto wrapped in a fur-lined velvet coat given to her by Helena Rubenstein, holding a Serbian Count's rose — daughter of a house painter who knew how to paint towns red, and Morley, son of an indentured child servant, a sandlot player with a big sweeping curve ball, standing in a bowl of light on the 'Boul Miche, sporting a moustache, assured by Joyce, Pound and Hemingway that all he had to do was write, to tell stories . . . he was the real thing, and though the box of amber light would now be empty, though there were men and women out there in the dark who would never know he used to sit in the box and talk to his world, his people, that didn't matter, they had his stories in their hands . . . "The guy, you know, who wrote the story about Judas, the same guy as wrote the book about the priest and the two hookers — that guy."

As the afternoon closed down, people plucked photos of Morley from the walls. Soon the wall was bare, his face was gone. I asked the elderly

saxophonist to play "Body and Soul," their favorite song, and with a great formality that reminded me of Bud Freeman, moving back to stand against the
pale late afternoon light coming through the doors, he blew effortlessly, a
deep sonorous plea:

> *My heart is sad and lonely,*
>
> *For you I cry,*
>
> *For you dear only.*
>
> *Why can't you believe it,*
>
> *I'm all for you,*
>
> *Body and soul.*

In a moment's hush, heads bowed, the saxophonist stood hunched over
his horn, his head down, too. People on the street had paused to peer into the
bistro, the last throaty notes hovering. The kid on stilts with spiky lemon-tinted
hair, his balloons gone, all given away to children, leaned down into the open
doorway and asked, "What's that, what's that there?"

"We're celebrating Morley Callaghan."

"Oh yeah," the kid said, his eyes brightening. "Right, I can see him."

ACKNOWLEDGMENTS

Nina Callaghan, whose editorial intelligence, humor and devotion to this text has exceeded anything I have known; my brother Michael, Hayden Carruth, Austin Clarke, Gordon Sheppard, David Sobelman, and especially Seán Virgo for reading the text in various stages and always responding with wit and acuity; Branko Gorjup and Francesca Valente, who gave me the pleasure of their social and intellectual companionship; George Bigliardi restaurateur and his waiters, Ben and Manuel, who allowed me to turn their Champions off-track bar into my private scribbling room; Tim Hanna, Michael McShain, Dean Vincent, Priscila Uppal and George Murray for being helpful when a little help meant sanity preserved; Susan M. Young and dear Marilyn Di Florio for deciphering my scrawl in typing and retyping; my agent Bruce Westwood, who responded with such forceful enthusiasm when he read what turned out to be Book One; my publisher and loyal friend Kim McArthur, who was wise editorially and refused to blink at the spanner I threw into the publishing and business works with my delays, visions and revisions; my son Michael, who regarded me with wry amusement as he designed the book, which is to say he had the wry pleasure of shaping his father's life; my mother, who taught me to dance and sing and persevere, and finally Claire Weissman Wilks, who has had to live for too long a time with a man turned inward, and did so with the outward exuberance that only deep caring can muster.

FRONT ENDPAPERS:
A: Barry Callaghan, age 8, at St. Peter's Grade School
B: Morley Callaghan, age 15, 1918
C: Uncle Ambrose Dee and Aunt Marie, 1952
D: F. Scott Fitzgerald, in the twenties, from *The Romantic Egoists* edited by Matthew J. Bruccoli et al, Charles Scribner's Sons, 1974
E: Loretto Callaghan, 1941
F: Ezra Pound, Ford Madox Ford, John Quinn, James Joyce, from *Shakespeare & Company*, by Sylvia Beach, Harcourt Brace, 1959
G: Le Dôme, from *The Glamour Years – Paris 1919 – 1940*, by Tony Allan, Bison Books, 1977.
H: Samuel Beckett, in the late seventies, from *Damned to Fame: The life of Samuel Beckett* by James Knowlson, Simon & Schuster, 1996
I: Burke Callaghan, Morley's brother, in the late thirties
J: Saul Ellison and Barry at Greenwood Race Track, 1984
K: Ernest Hemingway, in the twenties, from *The Glamour Years – Paris 1919 – 1940*, by Tony Allan, Bison Books,
L: Assumption College Lancers, 1958 (Barry fourth from right)
M: Family portrait at the house: Morley, Michael, Barry, and Loretto, 1972
N: Nina Callaghan, 1957

BACK ENDPAPERS
1: Slotkin and Morley at Slitkin's and Slotkin's, Montreal, 1946
2: Barry, age 18, 1955
3: Saya Lyran, Jerusalem, 1969
4: Barry and William Ronald on the set of "The Umbrella," 1965
5: Barry's Press ID, 1960
6: Ghasan Kanafani and Barry in Kanafani's office, Beirut, 1970
7: James T. Farrell at his writing desk, New York, 1968
8: Barry, on the set of "Weekend". 1970
9: Edmund Wilson and Morley on a picnic, Talcottville, N.Y., 1963
10: Sonny Terry and Brownie McGhee, 1967
11: Cameraman Peter Davis and Barry, Port Said, Egypt, 1970
12: Barry in front of ancient pyramid, Sakarah, Egypt, 1970
13: Morley signs the Golden Book for Mayor Houde, Montreal City Hall, 3 AM, 1946
14: John Montague, Claire Weissman Wilks and Morley in La Coupole, Paris, 1986
15: A lunch at 69 Sullivan Street. From left: Northrop Frye, Alberto Moravia, Alain Elkann, Greg Gatenby, Branko Gorjup, Morley, Francesca Valente, Barry
16: William Hayter, Paris, 1986
17: Barry's son Michael in front of John Reeves' portrait of Morley, Morley's wake at Le Bistingo, 1990
18: Rainbow Gardens Orchestra at graveside, Mount Hope Cemetery, 1990
19: Rainbow Gardens Orchestra playing at the wake, Le Bistingo, 1990

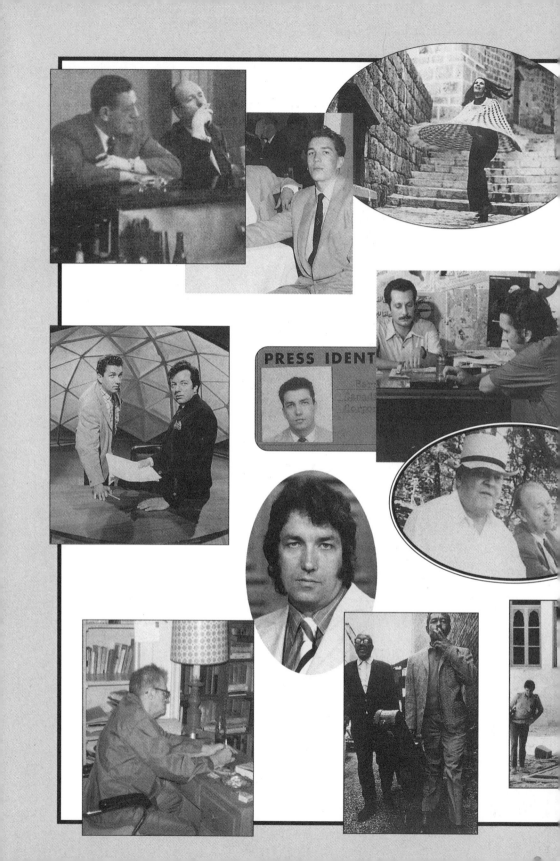

PRESS IDENT